Traditional Jewelry of India

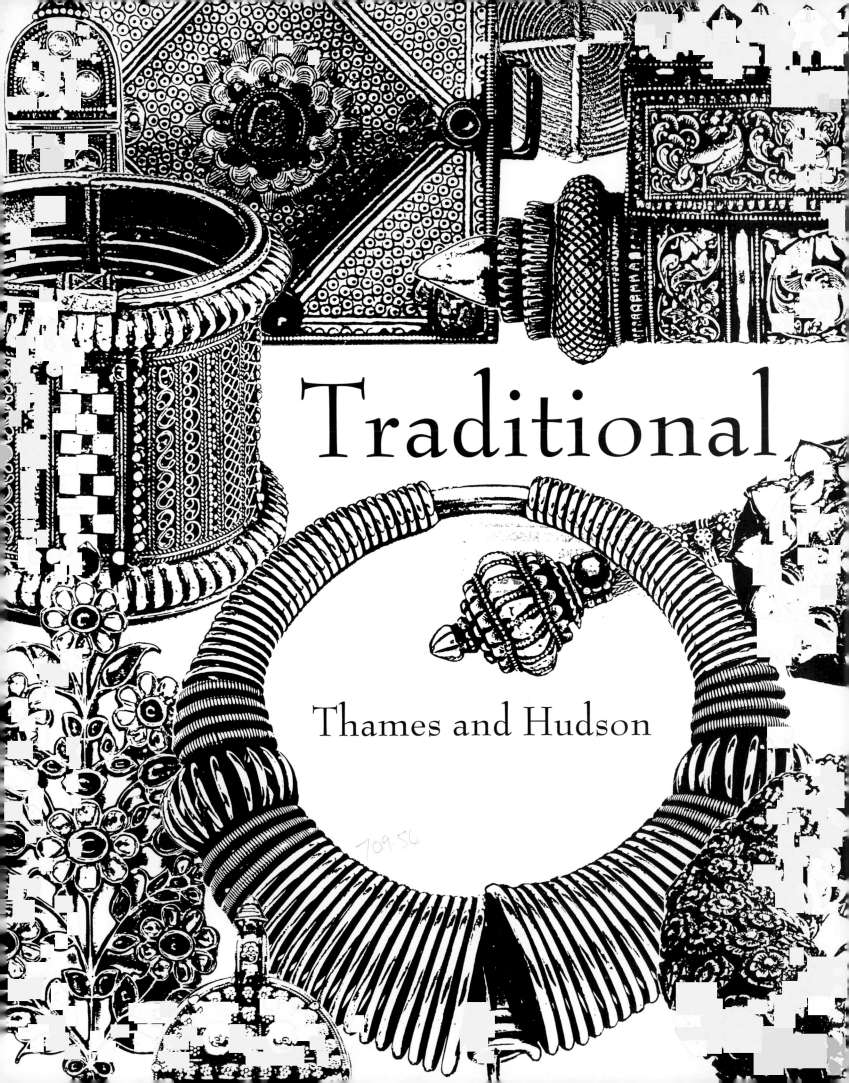

Traditional

Thames and Hudson

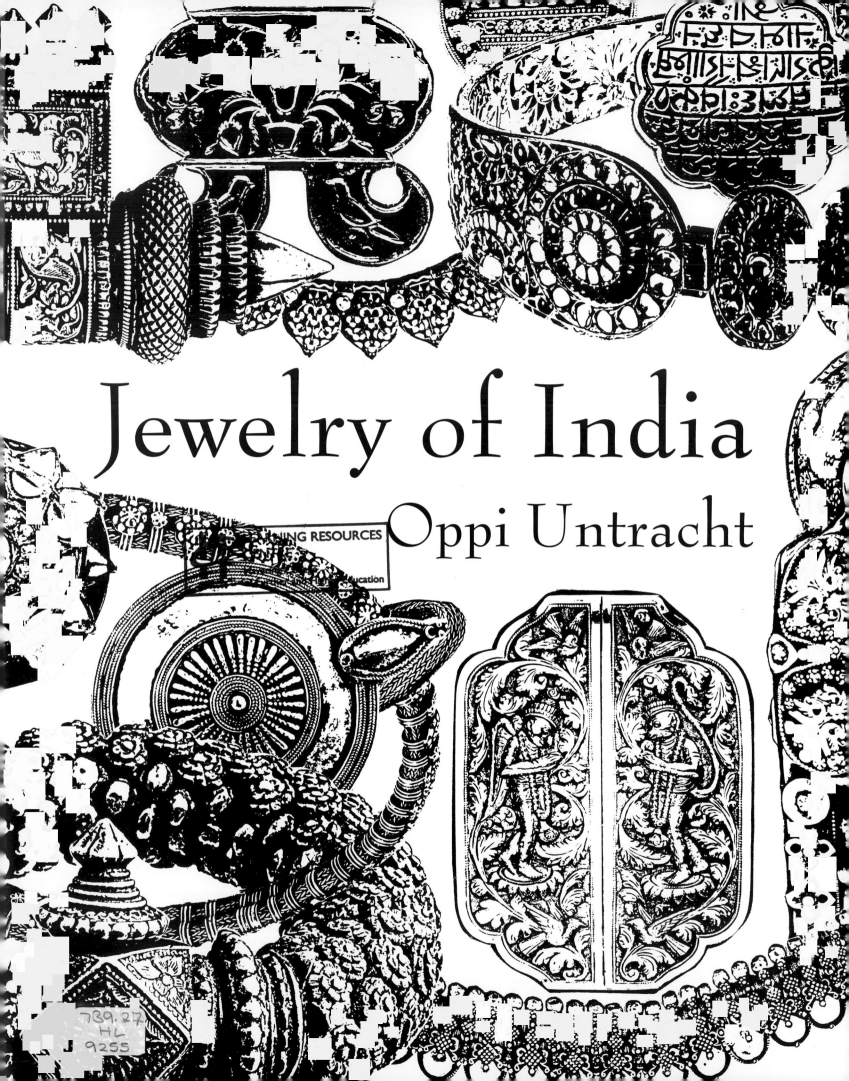

Jewelry of India

Oppi Untracht

Kamaladevi Chattopadhyaya   and   **Jasleen Dhamija**

This book is dedicated to:

In addition, I salute India's past and present goldsmiths,
specialists in related aspects of jewelry manufacture,
and merchants who made and continue to keep
traditional jewelry alive. Although the creators are for
the most part anonymous, their achievements speak with
silent eloquence of their outstanding skills and imagination.

Project Manager: **Marti Malovany**
Senior editor: **Harriet Whelchel**
Designer: **Maria Learmonth Miller**

First published in Great Britain in 1997
by Thames and Hudson Ltd, London

Published in 1997 by Harry N. Abrams, Incorporated, New York
Copyright © 1997 Oppi Untracht

British Library Cataloguing-in-Publication Data

A catalogue record for this book is available from the British Library

ISBN 0-500-01780-8

Printed and bound in Hong Kong

Page 1: **Southern India**
*Openwork gold turban ornament (sarpech) with elephant motifs, kundan set with diamonds,
rubies, sapphires, and an emerald; reverse unornamented.*
3¼ x 1¾ in. (8.2 x 4.3 cm)
Collection Bernadette van Gelder, s'Hertogenbosch, the Netherlands

Pages 2, 3: **Jaipur, Rajasthan.** *19th century*
*Gold pendant (latkan), obverse with Sanskrit Om subject in diamonds, on a ruby ground;
reverse with same motif in polychrome enamel*
Collection Ivory, New York

*An imperishable Hindu sacred root monosyllable, Om embodies the concepts of origination and
dissolution. Everything existent and nonexistent can be grasped by uttering, mentally or in a low
voice, the syllable Om at the beginning and end of a quest for knowledge. As Manu, in his Code
of Institutes of Manu (Manava Dharma-shastra ii.74), said, "Without Om before, [knowledge]
slips away; and without it after, it disappears. By uttering Om at the beginning and end of learning, acquired knowledge is retained, and its utterance counteracts errors."*

*The endpapers are a special Indian rose color called gulabi in Persian, from gulab, or "rose," the
paragon of Indian flowers. Traditionally, all Indian goldsmiths wrap jewelry purchases in tissue
paper of this color, which is said to augur good fortune, prosperity, and happiness.*

Contents

Preface

This survey of the traditional jewelry of India is the summation of more than thirty years of actual involvement with the subject. In tracing my initial interest in it, I must go even further back and return to childhood fantasies in the 1930s involving India's reputation as a place of fabulous wealth, rich traditions, and exotic artifacts—ideas I shared with many in the West. This was reinforced by American movies that took place in a cardboard India of romanticized, partly true, partly fanciful images.

Later, at the New York High School of Music and Art, my interest was furthered by an admired art teacher, Helen Ridgaway, and her enthusiastic description of her journey to India. In another class, I had my first experience with jewelry making. In the pursuit of cultural knowledge encouraged by that wonderful school, I visited many museums, and even now I can visualize the collection of Indian jewelry on view at The Metropolitan Museum of Art, to which I returned many times. One day the collection disappeared, and I learned that it had descended to an underworld storage room to make space for renovations. Now I am sure it was reclaimed by Nagas, those mythological Indian snakes who rule the nether regions and whose duty it is to protect gemstones.

In my adulthood, I was further inspired by the exhibition, *Textiles and Ornaments of India,* held in the spring and summer of 1955 at The Museum of Modern Art in New York. In this exciting, attractively installed exhibition devised by Alexander Girard could be seen beautiful hand-created products of Indian artisans, gathered from museums in America, Europe, and India, as well as private collections. It was organized with the cooperation of the Indian Government and offices such as the All India Handicrafts Board, whose chairman then was Kamaladevi Chattopadhyaya. She later became a friend and is one of the persons to whom this book is dedicated.

A slim but important exhibition catalogue, *Textiles and Ornaments of India,* includes texts by John Irwin and Pupul Jayakar, each of whom did so much good work respectively in the research and development of Indian textiles. Today this book is one of my treasures in what has become a considerable private library of volumes on Indian arts and crafts.

Particularly vivid in my memory of that installation is the display of traditional Indian jewelry, which crystallized my interest in the subject. Realizing that personal fieldwork is indispensable in the investigation of a culture not one's own, I became determined to go to India and witness jewelry being made and used. I applied for and was granted a Fulbright Scholarship that did just that, and, with a renewal, I carried out research there from 1957 to 1959. Overwhelmed by what I saw and experienced, India changed the course of my entire life and gave it direction.

My research in India was facilitated considerably by the two women to whom I dedicate this book. The aforementioned Kamaladevi Chattopadhyaya, now deceased, is known to all India as the guiding spirit behind the renaissance of still existing Indian crafts, and the revival of those on the verge of extinction. Kamaladevi (Sanskrit for "Lotus goddess") took a sympathetic interest in my projects, and gave the necessary orders to help them into realization. To her and her then assistant, Jasleen Dhamija, I owe my eternal thanks.

In her official capacity as Crafts Development Officer, Jasleen was an intrepid traveler, and she still is. Her energetic, unflagging interest in the handcrafts produced by her compatriots, who regard her as a pro-

1. Kishengarh, Rajasthan. *c.1780*
Raja Savant Singh and Bani Thani as Krishna and Radha
Tempera on cotton laid on board
40 x 36½ in. (101.5 x 92.7 cm)
Courtesy Spink and Son Ltd., London

Raja Savant Singh of Kishengarh (died 1764) and his enamorata, the poetess and singer Bani Thani, a name he gave her. The story of their spiritualized love was a popular subject of eighteenth-century Kishengarh miniature paintings (Kishengarh kalam); they were characterized by exaggerated profiles, large, elongated, gazelle-like eyes (mirg naeni) framed by arched eyebrows (dat ka bhaun), and serpentine locks (nagini zulf). Representing them as a youthful, beautiful royal couple alludes to a parallel with Krishna and his beloved Radha. Dressed in sartorial splendor, they are profusely ornamented with a carefully rendered traditional Mughal-Rajput–style ornaments. The Hindi term bani-thani (well decked out) became a north Indian colloquial expression.

2. New York, New York. *April 13–June 12, 1955*
Exhibition, Textiles and Ornaments of India, The Museum of Modern Art
In this exciting installation designed by Alexander Girard, Indian jewelry was displayed under an appliquéd wedding canopy from Pipli, Orissa. Edgar Kaufmann, Jr., assembled most of the objects with the assistance of Kamaladevi Chattopadhyaya, then chairman of the All India Handicrafts Board, and Pupul Jayakar, then special deputy to the All India Handicrafts Board. Seeing the exhibition crystallized the author's obsession with things Indian and confirmed his need to go there and "see for himself."

tecting angel concerned with their well being, puts her high on the short-list of Indians knowledgeable about nationwide indigenous crafts. With characteristic generosity, she freely shared her hard-earned knowledge and offered valuable advice. In advance of my tours of each of the then fifteen Indian states, Jasleen suggested itineraries and alerted state government officials with magic messages that galvanized them into action wherever I appeared.

This peripatetic life lasted nearly two years, during which I learned to live Indian-style, acquiring a new palate, which I came to love, along the way. Travel in India meant journeys by air, rail, bus, taxi, scooter, tonga, bullock cart, bicycle rickshaw, and foot. Each day ended with accommodations as diverse as grand hotels, circuit houses, *dak* (mail) bungalows, primitive village huts, second-class railway sleeping compartments, station retiring rooms and platforms, and other places difficult to name. The reward was a life of exciting adventure. Armed with cameras, lighting equipment, a large box of film, a bag of bananas, hard-boiled eggs, life-sustaining Britannia Biscuits, and a plastic bottle of boiled water, I could go anywhere.

Many of the more than 250 places visited would have been inaccessible without the help of unflappable government Department of Industry drivers assigned to me who gallantly charged their jeeps over land, sea, and—yes—air. We crossed trackless deserts in Kachchh, shallow rivers that suddenly filled with flash floods in Orissa, and high, swaying, gorge-spanning "bridges" that hung perilously in catenary curves and connected Himalayan cliff-edge trails in Himachal Pradesh. Some of these life-threatening journeys resulted in only *one good photograph*—say—a nose ring, as at Brahmor in Himachal Pradesh. There were also crowded fairs, markets, temple celebrations, and processions that resulted in thousands of others, several of which are visible here. After commendable service to the cause, three cameras gave up the ghost, literally worn out by the attack of insidious, powdery road dust and moisture-thriving monsoon mold, mildew, and fungus.

In such climatic conditions, it was vital to have film developed and prints made as quickly as possible. The miraculously reliable Indian Post never misplaced a package. Deep-felt thanks go to my good friends Madan Mahatta, a talented New Delhi photographer and a man with a luminous soul, and G. R. Nair of the Bombay Photo Stores in Calcutta. Their results are well represented here.

In 1960 I married Saara Hopea-Untracht, a well-known Finnish designer of glass and jewelry. Seeing the photographic results of my first Indian stay, she became as enthusiastic as I was about the subject and like myself wished to go there and continue the research.

In 1963, another Fulbright grant renewed until 1965 took us to Nepal to study the crafts of a culture related to India. Immediately following, I received a grant to India from the American Institute of Indian Studies. Saara's enthusiasm for the subject, related to her work as a jewelry designer in Finland, added her fuel to mine. Together we made an incandescent second, nearly two-year round of visits to craft centers in all of India, including many places I had not visited before. Through it all Saara displayed great adaptability, and a better partnership could not be imagined. She made excellent line drawings of jewelry to later identify their names and place of origin; took notes; maintained the growing collection of numbered contact prints and negatives; and even held back crowds that gathered wherever I took photographs in a jewelry bazaar. With her help and drive, we accomplished *more* than twice of what I would have been able to do alone. When this second stay ended in 1967, we settled in Finland, from where we made several private trips to India.

3. Bikaner, Rajasthan
Saara Hopea-Untracht wearing a gold necklace (Raj: aad or arya) with diamonds and pearls, the reverse polychrome-enameled, a traditional Bikaner form (see 772)

In 1972–73, I received a third grant to India, from the John D. Rockefeller III Fund. Obviously reluctant to divulge all at once, the culture/country constantly presented us with surprises. Our mutual interest in Indian jewelry continued until 1984, when after a short illness following a last stay in India, Saara passed away.

Altogether, we spent six years in India trying to formulate an overall picture of this intriguing and sometimes evasive subject. Research could continue for more than one lifetime, but, facing reality, I decided to gather my contribution of information in this book. It is my hope that it will awaken a greater interest in this too long neglected subject and, perhaps, inspire someone to continue the investigation. To that person, or persons, I say: The time and energy expended will be rewarded by more than enough satisfaction, even for a lifetime of effort, as it has been for me.

Acknowledgments

Acknowledging and thanking the many people and organizations I have encountered over the forty years of my involvement with Indian jewelry and crafts is a humbling, heartwarming experience. In retrospect, I fully realize that their major, and even minor, guidance and assistance in the self-appointed task of researching this fascinating subject, and trying to give some idea of the variety and meaning of traditional Indian jewelry to others, would not have been possible. Their names and/or organizations are given separately below.

First of all, thanks go to the organizations who provided fianancial grants to do indispensible fieldwork in India. Their names are mentioned in the Preface. But to this must be appended the Indian staffs of their offices who must share in these thanks. By their readiness to provide helpful, practical information, and by suggesting means of coping with an initially unfamiliar, exotic environment and way of life, they made an easy transition possible.

In the Preface I allude to three special persons whose help and moral support rose to an eminence above all others. They include Kamaladevi Chattopadhyaya, Jasleen Dhamija, and my wife, Saara. It is impossible for me to adequately offer my thanks to them in words.

To Indians with whom I had contact throughout this challenging, vast subcontinent, I am forever grateful. They facilitated this study in so many ways by generously sharing information, and providing access to sources of objects for examination and photography. This group includes many Indian individuals, several now sadly departed, private and government organizations, and persons connected with Indian museums.

Another group in India to whom warm thanks must go are persons in the Indian commercial jewelry world. Their cooperation over the years has resulted in several in this community becoming precious personal friends.

Outside India are others to whom I am equally indebted. Of particular importance are people who possess outstanding collections of traditional Indian jewelry because they sincerely admire the admirable Indian goldsmith's skills. Their highly selective, impeccable collections include pieces in many cases no longer found in India, or superior to those in museum collections anywhere. By allowing me access to their collections, and granting permission to select and photograph many objects for this book, they generously made it possible to share major and minor masterpieces in this field with a wide public.

In a very special category for thanks are those connected with the many American and European museums that have an Indian studies department, and their photography departments, which were ransacked for illustrative material.

Bountiful thanks also go to the several Indian and Western photographers who patiently and sensitively threw their best light on the objects they photographed for this book.

A special category of gratefulness goes to persons, in India and elsewhere, not directly involved in the field but good friends who offered a sympathetic ear to listen to an outpouring of whatever was new and exciting at moments of discovery and, not least, their hospitality, a share in their home environment for a weary, nomadic friend, and a good bed to sleep in and recharge energy sources. They include Naomi and Stanley Cohen, Michael Croft, Roberta and Leonard Gang, Eleanor Moty, and Lillian Samenfeld.

I thank those who assisted me in the preparation of the manuscript, illustrations, translations of inscriptions on jewelry, and an indirect entry into the world of computers.

Finally, to those in the production team at Harry N. Abrams, Inc., I offer my grateful thanks for their accomplishment of a daunting task, done with their usual finesse. Deserving special thanks is my editor, Harriet Whelchel, for her skill and patience in rendering tractable the Untracht voluminous manuscript. I am also grateful to designer Maria Miller, for her ability to cope with the complexities of the subject in visual terms.

Private Collections
Anonymous; Samuel and Laurel Beizer, New York; Allan Caplan, New York; Jacques Carcanagues, New York; H. B. Torbjörn and Judy Carlsson, Washington, D.C.; Ivory Friedus, New York; Jay and Jean Gang, New York; Jean-Pierre and Colette Ghysels, Brussels; Anne Jernandier de Vriese, Brussels; Nasser D. Khalili, London; Zaïra and Marcel Mis, Brussels; Harry Newfeld and Taila, Gwynned, Pennsylvania; Jerry and Genevieve Prillaman, Paris; Oppi Untracht, Porvoo; Thilo von Watzdorf, Brussels; Benjamin Zucker, New York

Individuals
Claus and Gertie Anschel (London); Susana Bacharach (London); Henning and Deitlind Bock (Berlin); Vivian and Irene Bose (Nagpur); Edward and Michele Chandless (East Hanover, New Jersey); Georgia Chrischilles (Brussels); Ruth Christensen (Copenhagen); Stanislav Ciosek (Helsinki); Bruce and Anne-Marie Clark (Paris); Derek Content (England); Geoffrey de Belaigue (London); Simon Digby (Jersey, Channel Islands); Diane Dubler (New York); Verrier Elwin (Shillong); Ratna Fabri (New Delhi); Cleveland and Manuela Fuller (New York); Jay and Jean Gang (Merrick, New York); Robert and Maniza Boga Grosskurth (New Delhi); Claire Ross Gupta (Calcutta); H. M. Queen Elizabeth II of Great Britain; Walter and Rosemary Hauser (Charlottesville); Irene Ketola (Porvoo); Momin Latif (New Delhi); Mimi Lipton (London); U. Maharathi (Patna); Jagdish and Kamala Mittal (Hyderabad); Pran Nath and Prema Mago (Delhi); Aspi and Kitty Moddie (Bombay); Ajit Mookerjee (Calcutta); Aman Nath (New Delhi); Manjula Padmanabhan (New Delhi); Linda Pastorino (New York); Michel Postel (Bombay); Emma Pressmar (Ulm/Donau); Shona Ray (New Delhi); Sue Rossiter (London); Ranjan Roy (Bombay); David G. Rubin (New York); Dr. Joseph Sataloff (Philadelphia); Bandana Sen (New Delhi); Homi and Nelly H. Sethna (Bombay); Shakunlata Seshadri (Madras); Haku Shah (Ahmedabad); Louise Ann Smith (Berkeley); Eleanor Smoler (Cliffside Park, New Jersey); Joseph Allan, Margaret, and Ethan Stein (New Delhi); Mahendra Singh and Swarn Singh Talwar (Jaipur); Tauno and Liisa Tarna (Porvoo); Romila Thapar (New Delhi); Herbert Tillander (Helsinki); Dora Untracht (Merrick, New York); Robert and Marcia Untracht (King's Point, New York); Jhaveri Vithalbhai (Bombay); Solveig Williams (New York); Solange Wohlhuter (Paris); Beatrice Wood (Ojai, California); Mark Zebrowski and Robert Alderman (London)

Individuals and Museums
Jean-Paul Barbier and Monique Barbier-Mueller, Musée Barbier-Mueller,

Geneva; Gilles Béguin, Conservateur des Musées Nationaux, Department des Arts Asiatiques, Musée Guimet, Paris; Shirley Bury, Formerly Deputy Keeper, now Keeper Emeritus, Department of Metalwork, Victoria and Albert Museum, London; Gwyneth Camping, Assistant Curator, Photographic Services, The Royal Collections, The Royal Library, Windsor Castle, Berkshire; Steve Czuma, Curator, South and Southeast Asian Art, The Cleveland Museum of Art, Cleveland; Brian Durran, The Museum of Mankind, The Ethnographic Collection of the British Museum, London; Joseph M. Dye III, Curator, Department of South Asian Art, Virginia Museum, Richmond; Fritz Falk, Director, Schmuckmuseum, Pforzheim; James Harle, Curator Emeritus, Department of Eastern Art, Ashmolean Museum, Oxford; Dr. Gerd Höpfner, Curator Südasien Kunst, Museums für Völkerkunde, Berlin; Marilyn Jenkins, Associate Curator, Department of Islamic Art, The Metropolitan Museum of Art, New York; Manuel Keene, Formerly Department of Islamic Art, The Metropolitan Museum of Art, New York; Steven M. Kossak, Assistant Curator, South and Southeast Asian Art, The Metropolitan Museum of Art, New York; Dr. Stella Kramrisch, Curator Emeritus, Department of Asian Art, The Philadelphia Musuem of Art, Philadelphia; Martha Longenecker, Director, Mingei International Museum of World Folk Art, La Jolla, California; Dr. Marina Lopato, Curator, Decorative Arts, State Hermitage Museum, St. Petersburg; Cornelia Mallebrein, Rautenstrauch-Joest Museum für Volkerkunde, Köln; Stephen M. Markel, Assistant Curator, Indian and Southeast Asian Art, Los Angeles County Museum of Art, Los Angeles; Laurence Mattet, Musée Barbier-Mueller, Geneva; Dr. Gabriel Moriah, Director, L. A. Mayer Memorial Institute for Islamic Art, Jerusalem; Graham Parlett, Indian Section, Victoria and Albert Museum, London; Gira Sarabhai, Calico Museum of Textiles, Ahmedabad; Pauline Lunsingh Scheurleer, Afdeling Aziatische Kunst, Rijksmuseum, Amsterdam; Robert Skelton, Keeper Emeritus, Indian Section, Victoria and Albert Museum, London; Susan Stronge, Assistant Curator, Indian Section, Victoria and Albert Museum, London; Deborah Swallow, Curator, Indian and South-East Asian Collection, Victoria and Albert Museum, London; O. P. Tandon, Director, Bharat Kala Bhavan, Varanasi Hindu University, Varanasi; Marianne Yaldiz, Director, Museum für Indische Kunst, Staatliche Museen Preussischer Kulturbesitz, Berlin; Wladimir Zwalf, Department of Oriental Antiquities, British Museum, London

Individuals and Organizations
In India

Rajesh, Anil, and Ravi Ajmera and Eklavya Swami, The Studio, New Delhi; Archaeological Survey of India, Government of India, New Delhi; Assam Government Directorate of Information, and Press Information Bureau, Shillong, Meghalaya; Bahadur Singh and Srimati Premlata Backliwal, and sons Ashok and Anil Backliwal, La Boutique, New Delhi; Chhote L. Bharany and son Ramji Bharany, New Delhi; Bihar Tribal Research Institute, Ranchi, Bihar; Pesi F. Choksey, Surat Diamond Industries Ltd., Bombay; R. K. Dulabji, Gem and Jewelery Promotion Council, Jaipur, Rajasthan; P. Eswaramoorthy, New Lakshmi Jewelery, Tiruchchirapalli, Tamil Nadu; Gem Palace, Jaipur, Rajasthan; Mukesh Jain, The Jewel Mine, New Delhi; Natana Kasinathan, Director, Department of Archeology, Madras, Tamil Nadu; P. R. Mahenderatta, American Institute of Indian Studies, New Delhi; J. K. Mehra, Ellora, New Delhi; G. R. Nair, Bombay Photo Stores Pvt. Ltd., Calcutta; Anand Nowlakha, New Delhi; C. L. Nowlakha, Sundaram, Calcutta; Photo Section, North East Frontier Agency, Shillong, Meghalaya; Press Information Bureau, Ministry of Information and Broadcasting, Government of India, New Delhi; Publications Division, Ministry of Information and Broadcasting, Government of India, New Delhi; Public Relations Department, Government of Rajasthan, Jaipur, Rajasthan; Rajasthan Press Information Bureau, Government of Rajasthan, Jaipur, Rajasthan; Registrar General, Census of India, Government of India, New Delhi; Bhagwan and Vijay Roopchand, Roopchand Jewelers, New Delhi; Sangeet Natak Akademi, New Delhi; Ritu Singh, Public Relations, Air India, Bombay; Bhuramal Rajmal Surana, Jewelers, Jaipur, Rajasthan; Kushalchand and Prakashchand Surana, Jewelers, Jaipur, Rajasthan; Tribal Research Institute, Chhindwara, Madhya Pradesh; Tribhuvandas Bhimji Zaveri, Jewelers, New Delhi

Outside India

Catherine Arminjon, Conservateur en Chef du Patrimoine, Direction du Patrimoine, Paris; Artemis Fine Arts (U.K. Ltd.), London; Henry Brownrigg, London; François Canavy, Van Cleef and Arpels, Paris; Allan Caplan, New York; H. B. Torbjörn and Judy Carlsson, Art Expo, Washington, D.C.; Heleyne Chaumet, Chaumet S.A., Paris; Christies, New York, London, Geneva; De Beers Consolidated Mines Ltd., London; Beatrice de Plinval, Chaumet S.A., Paris; Maharukh Desai, London; Namkha and Pemba Tsering Dorjee, Bodhicitta, London; Ralph O. Esmerian, New York; Ulla Tillander Godenhelm, Tillander Oy, Helsinki; Linda Golden, Berkeley, California; Harry Halén, Department of Asian and African Studies, University of Helsinki, Helsinki; Her Majesty's Stationery Office, London; Betty Jay, Archives Cartier, Cartier S.A., Paris; Joan Jones, Liberty Retail Ltd., London; Laurence S. Krashes, Harry Winston, Inc., New York; L. C. Hutton Archives, London; Lehtikuva Oy, Helsinki; Fred Leighton, New York; Jackie Little, Costa Mesa, California; Brendan Lynch, Islamic Art, Sotheby's, London; Elizabeth Markevitch, Sotheby's, London; Arthur Millner, Indian and South East Asian Art, Sotheby's, London; Geoffrey Munn, Wartski Jewelers Ltd., London; Alby Nall-Cain, Frontiers, London; Professor Asko Parpola, Department of Asian and African Studies, University of Helsinki, Helsinki; Prudence Cumming Associates Ltd., London; Anja Rannström, Copy, Porvoo; Carlton C. Rochell Jr., Indian, Himalayan, and South East Asian Works of Art, Sotheby's, New York; Royal Anthropological Institute of Great Britain and Ireland, London; Ambaji V. Schinde, Harry Winston, Inc., New York; Sotheby's, New York, London, Geneva; Michael Spink, Spink and Son Ltd., London; Stillab Center Oy, Helsinki; Unicorn Oriental Gallery, Scottsdale, Arizona; Dr. Géza von Habsburg, Habsburg, Feldman S.A., Onex, Switzerland; Benjamin Zucker, Precious Stones Co., New York

Indian Government Officials

These government-employed people were met on tours in every Indian state. They were all helpful in various ways in facilitating my study of Indian jewelry and crafts. Their names are too numerous to be given here, and only their titles are mentioned. My heartfelt thanks go to them all.

All India Handicrafts Board, Directors, Craft Development Officers, Research Officers; Arts and Crafts Institutes, Directors, Personnel; Chauffeurs of jeeps used on state tour surveys; Collectors, State, City; Cooperative Societies; Cottage Industry Development Officers; Craft Development Officers; Craft Survey Officers; Department of Industries and Commerce, Directors, Joint Directors, and Additional Directors; Design Centers, Regional, Directors, Personnel; Export Promotion Officers; Handicraft Development Officers, Field Officers; Handicraft Emporiums, State, City, Directors, Personnel; Handicraft Museums, Regional; Inspectors of Handicrafts, Regional; Inspectors of Industries, Regional; Inspectors of Weights and Measures; Jewelry Promotion Councils; Marketing Officers; Museums, National, Regional, Directors, Curators, Superintendents, and Personnel; Public Relations Officers; Refugee Craft Centers; Tribal Craft Museums, Regional, Curators; Tribal Research Officers; Schools of Art, Superintendents, Directors; Small Scale Industries Officers

Assistants

Petteri Koskikallio, Helsinki (computer work); Jaana Lahtinen, Helsinki (computer work); Salme Martikainen, Helsinki (translations); Bengt Mattson, Helsinki (line drawings); Asko Parpola, Helsinki (translations); Jukka Uusitalo, Helsinki (computer work)

Book-Production Team

Marti Malovany; Harriet Whelchel; Maria Miller; Eve Sinaiko; Margaret Braver; Christine Edwards; Nanice Lund; Jennifer Davenport.

Introducing Traditional Indian Jewelry

(Numerical references given in parentheses throughout the text correspond to illustration numbers, unless otherwise indicated.)

India, like no other country on our planet, can rightfully boast of an unbroken heritage of jewelry design that spans at least five thousand years and extends back into antiquity. Its people have expended limitless energy and creativity in the invention of ornaments that celebrate the human body and in developing opportunities for their use. By adorning the visible, material body, they also seek to satisfy a universal longing for the embellishment of its intangible counterpart: the human spirit.

Indian jewelry comprises a vast and complex assortment of marvels. Traditional ornaments—having a distinct cultural identity—play a significant and fascinating role in characterizing Indian civilization. Presenting this complicated subject in a single volume, however, imposes physical limits on exposition and images. The challenge became how best to organize primary aspects of the subject into a logical sequence. One possibility would be a combined geographical/chronological approach. Complicating this direction is that, throughout its unrecorded and historic eras, the immense Indian subcontinent has always been divided into a multiplicity of dynastic kingdoms and tribal areas, generally grouped into northern and southern. These divisions in turn were fragmented into yet smaller principalities whose political history interacted with, or that were threatened by, their neighbors. No single dominion ever gained political or cultural hegemony over the entire subcontinent, which might have resulted in a broader cultural uniformity, although the Mughal dynasty of northern India came closest to this achievement.

Another problem with such an approach is that with very few exceptions extant examples of jewelry from the past, with a clearly attributable provenance, are meager until sometime in the eighteenth century. For evidence before that we must rely almost totally upon secondary sources such as sculpture, painting, and literature. Although these mediums present us with interesting information, they are one step removed from the actual objects, with the result that much of the developmental picture is unclear.

Instead of using geography and political chronology as exclusive organizational parameters, therefore, I chose a more organic arrangement following the general pattern of human cultural evolution and incorporating religion, economics, politics, and regional customs and resources.

It would be difficult to locate a single country with a richer natural diversity at its disposal than India. Its varied climatic zones, from tropical to temperate to frigid, provide a bounteous offering of vegetable, mineral, and animal resources, which have, from earliest prehistoric times, long been tapped for use in body decoration. When the first sedentary tribal societies who held primitive religious beliefs such as animism formed rudimentary social systems in protohistoric, Stone Age India, their technology did not include metals but used natural materials manipulated into ornaments suited to their inherent character.

Formally structured social and religious systems developed concurrently with the growth of urbanization as early as 2000 B.C. As social hierarchies evolved, jewelry made in particular forms, especially in the much valued metals, became a means of differentiating the social status of individuals. The new metal technology of the Bronze Age, which included the use of gold, led to a greater degree of specialization—and interdependence—among craftsmen, ultimately resulting in a more refined product.

The consolidation of political power in urban societies fostered an imperial era during which states with considerable military forces directed their energy toward the conquest and domination of areas possessing desirable resources. Conquering leaders concentrated the wealth they gained in the form of precious materials. Their ability to control these resources and costly materials symbolized their power over the people of the conquered territories, and precious metals and gemstones fashioned into luxurious objects visibly expressed this power. Under the patronage of a new ruling class, such as the Mughals of the thirteenth to nineteenth century, artisans (who were essentially slaves) developed virtuosic technical skills, and their work in all mediums reached an unprecedentedly high level of achievement.

Due to the relative physical isolation of some of its tribal peoples, India today is an ethnographic museum without walls that spans all levels of cultural development. The most elementally primitive culture of indigenous aboriginal tribal people still living in remote enclaves coexists with the achievements of the highly evolved urban civilization that represents Hindu society today. The survival of tribal cultures such as that of the Nagas provides a unique opportunity to trace the general evolution of personal adornment to present times in this great living cultural complex.

Rarely is an Indian traditional ornament simply decorative and devoid of inherent meaning or symbolic value. The ability to create and use symbols is a uniquely human characteristic. Symbols found in traditional Indian jewelry act as a metaphorical language communicated from the wearer to the viewer. Perhaps the most extensive use of symbols in Indian jewelry occurs among the rural people of Indian society, who constitute about 70 percent of its total population, now rapidly approaching one billion. (This fact often comes as a surprise to those who have witnessed the crowds of its many great cities.)

The highly evolved semiotic symbolism of traditional Indian jewelry may relate either to popular magic or theological metaphysics, both of which involve the general concepts, concerns, aspirations, and fears shared by the entire populace. For example, the cosmologically inspired circle, with its reference to sun, moon, and the harmonious cosmos, represents the cyclical pattern of movement in the universe. Divided, it also incorporates the cyclical dualism of alternating light and darkness that delineates time. The square is frequently used to symbolize direction in space; and the triangle, a central, cosmic world mountain orienting the individual in relation to the universe. Vegetable, mineral, and animal forms from nature are used symbolically in jewelry design. The seed symbolizes potential growth; the ammonite, an aniconic deity; and the tiger claw, bravery. The earliest jewelry functioned as amulets, which worked because they incorporated accepted symbolic forms believed to offer the wearer protection. Jewelry bearing fertility symbolism, such as the prolific fish, is intended to assist in reproduction and, in so doing, assure the regeneration and continuity of the clan and race, a subject of paramount consequence. From this infinite reserve of symbolically sig-

New Dehli ⊕ National Capital

Bombay ■ State Capital

Raipur • City

— · — International Boundary

——— State/Territory Boundary

PUNJAB State Name

Anadaman & Nicobar Islands, Chandigarh,
Dadra & Nagar Haveli, Daman & Diu, Dehli,
Lakshadweep, and Pondicherry are union territories.

Parts of Kashmir are claimed by Pakistan and China.

300 km

0   300 Miles

AFGHANISTAN

CHINA

Kabul

Islamabad

JAMMU &
KASHMIR

Leh   Hemis
Srinagar   LADAKH
Chamba   Rewalsar
Nurpur LAHUL-SPITI
Jammu   Gosha Palampur
Sialkot Dharamshala Kullu
Kotli Loharam Kangra Jogindar Nagar
Lahore Amritsar Mandi
Hoshiarpur   HIMACHAL
PUNJAB   PRADESH
Multan   Zira   Shimla
Patiala   Chandigarh
Kurukshetra   Tehri
HARYANA   Hardwar

PAKISTAN

Gandhara

Bikaner

New Delhi ⊕ DELHI
Gurgaon   UTTAR
Vrindavan   PRADESH
Mathura
Jaipur   Agra Firozabad
RAJASTHAN
Jaisalmer

Pushkar Kishangarh
Jodhpur Ajmer
Sawai Madhopur
Pali   Gwalior
Shivpuri
Nathdwara Bhilwara
Udaipur Shahpura
Kotra   Rajghat
Partabgarh

KACHCHH   GUJARAT
Bhuj
Kandla Gandhinagar
Gulf of Ahmadabad
Kachchh Chhota Udepur
Rajkot Khambhat
Porbandar Bhavnagar
Junagadh SAURASHTRA
Veraval   Vadodara
Diu Gulf of Cambay Dabhoi
DAMAN & DIU Daman
DADRA & NAGAR HAVELI Silvassa
Nashik

Bombay

Banswara
Bhopal Nimkhera
Sanchi
Indore Jabalpur
MADHYA PRADESH
Chhindwara
Nagpur

MAHARASHTRA

Ahmadnagar
Pune
Adilabad
Karimnagar
Bidar
Golconda Hyderabad
Kolhapur
ANDHRA PRADESH
Panaji
GOA KARNATAKA
Narasaraopet
Amaravati
Guntakal
Honava Gudimallam
Shimoga

ARABIAN SEA

Mangalore
Somnathpur Bangalore
Madikeri Mysore Pudukkottai
Calicut
Palghat Udagamandalam
KERALA Coimbatore
Cheruthuruthy TAMIL NADU
Irinjalakuda Trichur Madurai
Ernakulam Ambasamudram
Cochin
Aleppy Tirunelveli
Trivandrum Gulf of
Manaar
SRI
LANKA
Colombo

LAKSHADWEEP
Kavaratti

NEPAL

Bahraich
Lucknow Barabanki
Kanpur Faizabad
Sitamarhi
Allahabad
Varanasi
Khajuraho
BIHAR
Shahpura
Chotanagpur
Ranchi
Jamshedpur
Raipur
Bastar
Jagdalpur

Kathmandu Bodinath
Patan
Darjiling

TIBET
Lhasa

SIKKIM BHUTAN
Gangtok Thimphu

ARUNACHAL
PRADESH
Ziro
Itanagar Sibsagar
Jorhat
Dispur ASSAM
KHASI HILLS NAGALAND
MEGHALAYA Kohima
Shillong
MANIPUR
BANGLADESH Imphal

Murshidabad Agartala
Dhaka TRIPURA Aizawl
Navadwip Dumbur MIZORAM
WEST BENGAL LUSHAI HILLS
Vishnupur Calcutta
Tamluk

Dumka
Santhal Pargana
Asansol

Sambalpur
Bargarh
ORISSA
Tarbha Kantilo
Baligurha Vidyadharpur
Russelkonda Cuttack
Belugunta Bhubaneswar
Parlakimidi Puri

Vishakhapatnam

Papanaidupetta

Nellore

Madras

Vellore

PONDICHERRY
Puduchcheri
Cuddalore
Thanjavur
Tiruchchirapalli

Bay of Bengal

MYANMAR
(BURMA)

Yangon

ANDAMAN &
NICOBAR ISLANDS
Port Blair

ANDAMAN SEA

Great Channel

Palk Strait

INDIAN OCEAN

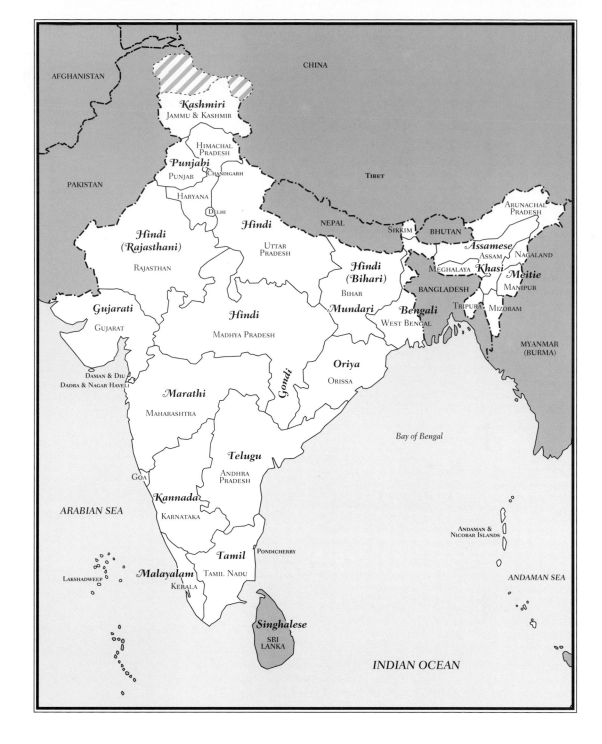

Maps of India showing all contemporary states, their capitals, and the major cities cited in the text (opposite) and representing primary language areas (right)

Language Abbreviations

A: Arabic
Ben: Bengali
Ch: Chinese
Fr: French
Ger: German
Guj: Gujarati
H: Hindi
Kan: Kanarese
L: Latin
Lad: Ladakhi
Mar: Marathi
Mal: Malayalam
Or: Oriya
P: Persian
Raj: Rajasthani
S: Sanskrit
Sing: Singhalese
Tam: Tamil
Tel: Telugu
Tib: Tibetan
Tur: Turkish
U: Urdu

nificant forms and images, some obvious, some subtle, others whose meaning is forgotten, traditional jewelry is created.

Religion, the all-pervading element of Indian culture, is practiced there in every possible manifestation, from primitive animism to highly intellectualized and organized religious systems, including Hinduism, Jainism, Buddhism, and Mohammedanism, to mention only those with the most numerous adherents. Religion remains the major motivation for wearing ornament, whether it be a simple amulet used by the poor and uneducated to propitiate an animist spirit, or an elaborate precious-metal, gem-studded crown honoring a Hindu deity.

Marriage and religion are inseparable in Indian culture and together provide another major motivation for the use of traditional ornaments. By custom, almost every bride is provided with a dowry whose composition and value depend upon economic circumstances and are previously agreed upon by the families concerned. In many communities, requirements are so precise as to particularize obligatory ornaments, a custom that perpetuates specific traditional jewelry forms.

Unlike in the West, where the marriage ring is a universal symbol, in India marriage ornaments are generally worn on the nose or neck and take on a variety of forms according to region. Other ornaments placed on different body parts may also have a connection to marriage. All proclaim the religious, social, and economic status; group identity; and geographic origin of the wearer.

In India, all parts of the body—head, torso, limbs, and between and appended parts—have consistently been used to support ornaments, often in ingenious ways. The book thus presents what might be called a positional and structural typology of Indian jewelry, an innovation not previously attempted. This structural analysis allows the organization of a vast array of ornaments and illustrates the wide variety of regional methods of their fabrication and decoration in each case.

Many of the ornaments shown in this section belong to what might be termed the "rural ornament tradition," which for economic reasons uses mainly the base metals and silver. Because of the active life-style of the people who wear it, and the custom, for security reasons, of its constant presence on the body, construction and decoration are robust and express the concept of suitability of design and decoration to the material and use.

When one realizes that all these objects have been handmade with elementary tools, one cannot help but be amazed by the ingenuity and skill of the traditional jeweler, who generally is anonymous. In India, no universal hallmarking system such as that used elsewhere was ever adopted to identify the maker and place of origin of precious metal objects. Only in a very few instances, as compared to the magnitude of the volume, are jewelers' or lapidaries' names mentioned in documents or are any identifying marks found in jewelry that make it possible to know its maker.

Part of the explanation for goldsmith anonymity can be attributed to the Hindu caste system, in which the jeweler, surprisingly, held a relatively low position. Despite the fact that his works were in wide use by the entire upper-caste echelon, as well as the religious community, even master jewelers were considered unworthy of personal acclaim as far as records are concerned. Another factor was the long-dominant Hindu philosophy, eroding today, that a person's occupation is preordained from birth. One's work is one's destiny and ethical *dharma,* or moral and religious temporal duty, a fact to which one willingly submitted. Formulated within the framework of a sacerdotally dominated social order, the jewelers' creations were made for the glory of the Divine. Any desire to express personal ego through one's work was an alien concept. The aim was simply to perform one's occupation to the best of one's ability and serve the needs of the community of earthly clients and celestial divinities.

This state of anonymity was furthered by the organization of related, interdependent occupations within a trade, a concept that originated as elsewhere with medieval Indian guilds. Creating a single ornament might involve the combined efforts of the designer, goldsmith or silversmith, engraver, enamelist, polisher, lapidary, and stone setter—all distinctly individual occupations involving long training in specialist skills. Which of these deserved the credit for the creation of that ornament is a moot question.

Technology does, however, provide a bridge to the anonymous maker's mind. By understanding the basic systems by which an object is made, we are able to reconstruct the fabricator's thinking during the creative process. In the world of the anonymous Indian traditional jeweler, this connection is as close as anyone can get to a meaningful contact with that mind. Even a limited knowledge of what is involved in creating an object stretches the dimensions of understanding and appreciation of the jeweler's achievements.

In the evolution of jewelry technology in India, metal decorative processes developed that were practiced throughout the country, in one area, or only by a particular clan or family. Even in cases where similar techniques may have been practiced outside India, the result as interpreted by the Indian creative mentality retains an unmistakable Indian identity and contributes to the rich resource of the Indian jeweler's repertoire.

The masterful Mughal jewelry tradition, a unique style, generated a body of related work that appeared all over the Indian subcontinent, side by side with the local tradition. Unlike the Mughals themselves, Mughal jewelry concepts penetrated as far south as the independent Dravidian territory. For many outside India, the Mughal style in ornaments represents the quintessential image of Indian jewelry. To balance this picture, recognition is given here to several other styles of work also distinctly "Indian" in character, such as tribal and rural jewelry. Another is the South Indian jewelry tradition, a Dravidian style until now not widely recognized. Examples of all these styles shown here will perhaps correct misconceptions fostered to a great extent by scholars' neglect of some of these areas.

Unfortunately, because of the high intrinsic value of the precious metals and gemstones used, the greater part of this class of jewelry in India has been melted down to make new creations, a process that parallels the Hindu concept of the eternal cycle of creation, preservation, and destruction through which everything passes. Enough examples survive, however, from the eighteenth to nineteenth century and are includ-

4. Madurai, Tamil Nadu. *18th century*
Ivory panel
5 x 3½ in. (12.6 x 9 cm)
Victoria and Albert Museum, London (IM 137-1926)

An amorous Nayaka couple (S: mithuna, according to Indian tradition an auspicious symbol of energy) is seen embracing on a raised couch within an arched pavilion, observed by a parrot and a deer, both symbols of love. Though nude, both wear all the ornaments consistent with their high social status; their presence heightens the couple's erotic pleasure (kama), pursued in the fulfillment of worldly satisfaction (bhoga).

ed here to give an idea of what those missing masterpieces, in all styles, must have been like.

Gemstones constitute an exciting aspect of Indian jewelry. Since antiquity, India has been famous for its diamond deposits. Until 1729, when diamonds were discovered in Brazil, India was the world's sole source of that magnificent gemstone. Jewelers in India also had access to the other four of the "five great gemstones" (S: *maharatnani*): rubies, sapphires, emeralds, and pearls.

Traditional Indian ornaments have become established symbols of ethnic unity and identity, which is why, in India, from generation to generation, all women within a rural community aspire to own the same traditional objects. In a country such as India, where the geographic origin and caste of an individual is often a question of great curiosity, traditional, symbolic jewelry often helps to enlighten.

Jewelry as an erotic enhancer is commonly expressed in Indian art, where woman's role as procreator of the race is far less celebrated than her function as an object to stimulate and gratify man's erotic sensibilities. In Hindu temple sculpture, which was designed and created by men, secular women are depicted at the peak of their maturity, engaged in various acts of personal feminine toilette, for instance, gazing with obvious approval into a mirror while adorning themselves with garlands and jewelry.

In later Mughal, Rajput, Kangra, and other schools of miniature painting, and in artistic creations in other mediums, popular subjects were beautiful women being prepared by handmaidens who bathe, scent, and adorn them with jewelry in anticipation of the visit of a celestial or earthly lover. Ready to receive him, some languidly stand in a flowering glen. Finally he arrives, and the pair are shown engaged in pleasurable acts, some in a state of nudity, but *never* without their jewelry. Less fortunate is the woman who, after a long wait, finally realizes that her lover will not materialize and, in irritation and frustration, throws her now-useless ornaments to the ground.

Jewelry is part of the iconography of physical appeal. Worn by men, jewelry symbolizes power and wealth, with the attendant attraction they convey. Women in Indian art and in life pursue adornment as a form of devotion to men, and with a fervency that parallels religious conviction. Only when they can no longer perform this role, as in widowhood or old age, do women abandon jewelry by custom. While youth, fertility, and men exist, women in India follow a terrestrial theology in which jewelry plays a significant role in achieving male and female union.

It has long been recognized that no culture exists in a vacuum. Thus, this organized journey through India's jewelry world concludes with a look at the cross-cultural exchange between Indian jewelry concepts and those of the West, a process that continues today. The fabled maharajas who possessed impressive accumulations of ancestral traditional jewelry were well aware of the highly refined level of design and technical skill that Western jewelers could offer them. During the nineteenth and early twentieth centuries, they commissioned the *grands joailliers* of Europe to produce elaborate ornaments for them. At the same time, jewelers of the Western world fed upon the creative design concepts of Indian jewelry and invented a synthetic Indo-Western style by adopting several of its characteristic elements. Once these entered the lexicon of Western design resources, their Indian origin was often unacknowledged or overlooked.

Copies, Fakes, and Pastiches

When in the late 1950s I and, in the 1960s, my wife, Saara, began to collect traditional Indian ornaments, we followed the practice of going to the jewelry bazaar of the cities and towns we visited and asking permission to be allowed to search through the metal boxes all shops had in which they stored jewelry they purchased from sellers. Periodically this gathered jumble was delivered to the local precious metal refiner to be melted and converted into raw metal, then recycled into new ornaments.

Most of this material was ordinary, but from the tangled mass, a few silver pieces always emerged of more than pedestrian interest in design or workmanship. Reprieved from their death sentence, several of them appear in this book.

Since that time interest in traditional Indian jewelry has grown to such an extent that without exaggeration it can be said that a small army of people, at first only foreigners, and now also Indians, are on the march, collecting. Sellers were quick to learn that these sought-after objects, whose value as works of art they formerly ignored, should be saved, if for no other reason than that their sale brought a better return than simply recovering their value as precious metal. Collecting Indian traditional jewelry has become a worldwide phenomenon, and today people with sufficient economic resources readily pay high prices for good examples.

It often seems that the artistic resources of India are infinite, if one is to judge by the regularity with which objects from India appear on the world art markets. Although pieces of traditional Indian jewelry continue to materialize, in recent times one hears the phrase "not like before." As the demand and the number of purchasers continue to grow, dealers must work harder to find them. Following an ancient pattern, Indian people still sell their precious metal jewelry to assure their survival when the need arises, a practice that has always been one of their important functions as readily convertible wealth. Nevertheless, the supply available to satisfy the collector's demand is diminishing.

As a result, in perhaps the last twenty years, an entirely new industry has evolved in the manufacture of new copies of some forms of traditional jewelry judged to be suited to foreign use or desirable to collectors. Another development is a completely new range of nontraditional-style ornaments, especially earrings, manufactured by Indians familiar with the taste and requirements of Westerners.

The field of reproductions intended for export can be divided into two main categories. One is the curio market, which supplies the tourist and foreign trade with a variety of relatively inexpensive silver, white metal, or other metal objects that *may* resemble objects in actual Indian use. Related to this group are the objects made to supply the highly popular Western fashion jewelry market in which used and new metal elements such as reproductions of traditional Indian metal bead forms and amulets are combined with not necessarily Indian metal, stone, and glass beads. This market has evolved a Western style of costume jewelry that relies heavily on the mystique associated with ethnic ornament. The Indian jewelry makers who produce new components for this trade do so by traditional work methods, which impart a certain air of authenticity to the results, especially in the case of sheet metal amulets that were and still are made with stamping dies, often using old, discarded ones that are readily available.

Another dark and unfathomable category of objects in the Indian world of jewelry is "fakes," meaning contemporary jewelry manufactured in gold or silver in a traditional style and often marketed as antique, or jewelry of totally new, nontraditional designs that employ traditional fabrication and decorative techniques. The intention of such pieces is deliberately to deceive an unwary purchaser, usually a foreigner, as to their authenticity and age. In the case of authentic traditional designs, the originals are either quickly becoming obsolete because they are no longer affordable to the Indians who used them, and so go out of fashion, or, like an extinct species, they have already disappeared completely. Unscrupulous merchants employ goldsmiths and silversmiths to recreate or create such objects, and in many cases they are sold as "antiques."

Looking at these works objectively, it must be admitted that they usually are admirable achievements in goldsmithing, and as such prove the continuity of traditional goldsmith skills. While most of these results closely follow traditional prototypes and are accurate in detail, others incorporate changes such as rearranged elements of ornamentation. In some cases traditional designs are made on commission in unprecedented sizes following the principle that bigger is better, and entirely new forms are created whose "authenticity" is suggested by their inclusion of known traditional formal elements and decorative techniques.

Learning to judge whether a piece in a seemingly traditional style is authentic depends on several factors. Primary among them is knowledge of traditional jewelry design styles produced in the Indian subcontinent. This is a formidable and challenging task, considering the vastness of the subject, the great variety of regional types, and the enormous size of the physical area to be covered. A substitute for personal knowledge is dependence upon the experience and expertise acquired by others who have seriously pursued an attempt to become informed. In India this group of people includes a few dealers and a surprisingly limited number of professional and amateur scholars. In the West there are some dealers with widespread, direct Indian experience, as well as auction-house experts, museum-staff specialists, researchers, and—yes—some writers on the subject. I hasten to say, however, that on occasion, any and all of these can be innocently misled to an incorrect judgment.

Probably the first observation to be made in judging the authenticity of a traditional piece of Indian jewelry is its stylistic correctness for the claimed provenance. Next, attention must be paid to its physical condition. With experience, it becomes possible to judge whether an object shows the normal, expected patina that results from use and could be interpreted as an indication that it has been worn. Wear, however, is not necessarily an indication of great age, especially in the case of rural ornaments that are constantly worn and in a short time acquire an appearance of antiquity. Goldsmiths who produce deliberate fakes are sophisticated enough to know that patina can be an important means of convincing a buyer of age. To achieve this illusion they employ manual or mechanical abrasive methods on the finished work and are not above introducing an occasional dent that would normally also imply long use. At times their skill in patination is so accomplished as to delude an expert. Adding to the difficulty of making such a judgment is that it is quite possible to come across an authentic, even old object that shows no sign of wear from use because after its acquisition it may have been placed in storage, and for various reasons, never used.

In the detection of fakes in silver, another clue may help. Crude attempts are made to create an artificial patina of dark oxidation, which normally occurs in time with this metal, by the amateurish use of a black pigment or even soot paste. Unlike real oxidation, this can be washed away easily with plain soap and water. The appearance of Western-style (regularly faceted) gemstones, which were never used in traditional ornaments, indicates either a replacement, a fake, or a recently made object.

Techniques used in decoration are another indicator but are perhaps more difficult for the uninitiated to judge. For example, jewelry originally made with fine, greatly detailed repoussage and chasing, or pierced work, are characteristic of some South Indian jewelry. In new work from these places the decorative processes may appear coarsened due to an inability to match the high quality of workmanship common in old pieces. Conversely, some objects may be overrefined and too precise in execution in a manner atypical of the originals.

The *pastiche* is yet another form of fakery that may be less detectable to a person not oriented toward stylistic authenticity. In one type, disparate elements are combined either using forms that never belonged to the original design concepts or representing an incorrect arrangement. Old elements can be put together to make what in effect is a completely new design, for use on a part of the body different from the original. Units may be added to a simpler form in order to produce a more impressive-looking piece. Unfortunately, doubtful pieces of this type can be found in the collections of some major Western museums, and they are also encountered in auction catalogues. One has to be careful, however, as surprises do occur, and the mistake may be made of judging an object to be "wrong" simply because it is unfamiliar, when in fact it may be authentic.

The most offensive pastiches are obvious fragments cannibalized from a complex traditional ornament. These are often deliberately divided into parts to make them more salable and "wearable," a term that must be interpreted within a cultural context. It must be said here that in this category it is Indians who are guilty of accepting and even encouraging this cruel form of destruction and conversion since most foreign-ers, unlike Indians, do not know what the original form was like and simply accept what they see. In defense of cannibalism one frequently hears the remark in India that some of the old, traditional forms inherited by the present generation of a family cannot be used because they are too large, heavy, unwieldy, or ostentatious for modern times. This acquiescence is responsible for such practices as drastically shortening a long necklace and recycling the lopped-off parts, sometimes ingeniously, for example, as pendants worn on a simple, modern chain or as earrings. Objects that result from this form of sacrifice regularly appear in good shops in India.

The way to good judgment lies in the accumulation of experience. This requires interest and a desire to learn, and acute observation. Ultimately, such a concentration of motivation may lead to what can only be described as an intuitive sense of judgment in which all the visual clues act simultaneously to broadcast a message of authenticity which then, if necessary, can be confirmed by rationalization.

Perhaps it is naive and unrealistic to feel that traditional jewelry should be preserved, if for no other reason, as a family heirloom that represents a significant aspect of one's ancestral culture, of which one should rightfully be proud. Possibly this moral obligation can only be practiced by a museum; in India, unfortunately, museums are not generally in a position to do this due to a lack of funds or, more sadly, a lack of interest. It must therefore be pointed out here that a great deal of this preservation is actually taking place far from India, where foreign private collectors, and some city and university museums, for the last fifty years or so have slowly accumulated excellent collections of representative traditional Indian jewelry. These collections, from which many objects are represented in this book, in effect, will safeguard these wonderful works for the future enjoyment and edification of others, including Indians. We are grateful for those works that, despite the overwhelming weight of negative forces and the exigencies of life and commerce, have evaded destruction and can be seen and appreciated by all.

Note Regarding Indian Vernacular Terms

India is a huge country with many distinct languages, almost all originating from or influenced by Sanskrit. The Indian government has tried, unsuccessfully, to introduce Hindi, the primary language of northern India, as a universal language. People in other areas, for example the Tamils in southern India, strongly oppose this, preferring to retain their individuality, of which language is a strong element.

Many Indian vernacular terms are given throughout this book. The reasons for their presence are manifold. First is simply that the sound of a word often gives an aural cultural dimension to the visual object. Second, a connection frequently exists between the meaning of a word and the symbolic significance, actual appearance, and function of the object. References such as these help illuminate the pattern of thinking of the people who make and use these objects. Vernacular terms and definitions often uncover obscure or hidden aspects of the object that heighten the understanding of its significance.

Of the millions of vernacular terms surrounding Indian jewelry, only those that relate to specific jewelry types and/or terms that represent concepts intrinsic to them are given. Unless otherwise indicated, the language used is that of the culture being discussed. Most of these terms have been gathered from intensive personal fieldwork over many years.

Study of unfamiliar vernaculars involves persistent observation, careful interpretation of what you think you have heard and understood, and repeated verification, even when the assistance of a language interpreter is present, as they always were. Any errors here are strictly those of the author.

Transliteration of vernacular terms (with apologies to scholars) has been made without the diacritical marks that differentiate sounds in the languages. Pronunciation is therefore approximate. The spellings of place names are in accordance with those used by the Survey of India, as given in *An Atlas of India* (Delhi: Oxford University Press, 1990).

5–7. Orissa; Rajasthan; Kerala
Jewelry boxes are made in a variety of regional forms, often of cast brass (6, 7) or of painted wood with cast-brass fittings (5).
Collection the author, Porvoo

5

6

7

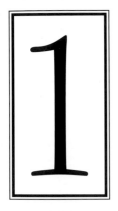

ORIGINS: EARLY ORNAMENT

Body Decoration and Marking

8. Andaman and Nicobar Islands. *1872*
Onge man
Musée de l'Homme, Paris

His body decorated with a paste made of olive-colored mud and pig fat, marked by fingers drawn through it while wet, the man's only material ornament is a cane belt (koie) of many turns. The Andamanese are Pygmies who live in a preagricultural, premetal culture. Of twelve distinct tribes, the Onge, in the majority, live in the southern islands of the archipelago.

Paleolithic Ornament: Andaman and Nicobar Islands

In the Bay of Bengal are a group of about six hundred islands off the coast of Burma, known collectively as the Union Territory of Andaman and Nicobar, a part of the Indian Union. Only forty of them are inhabited, by primitive tribes totaling about 200,000 people of Melanesian Negrito Pygmy stock. Until recently, almost all of the tribes lived in complete isolation, and some, like the Jarawas, still do. They inhabit remote forest areas, are rarely seen, and remain fiercely hostile to outsiders because of memories of former Arab slave raids in past centuries. Others, such as the Andamanese, Onges, and Shompens, are more amenable to outside visitors, although many still maintain the food gathering and hunting existence of an essentially Paleolithic Stone Age society.

It is because these people are practically frozen at such an early stage of cultural development that they are of special interest here. They illustrate concretely the importance that even people of very primitive, relatively undeveloped cultures have always given to body ornamentation. To satisfy this seemingly innate human need, they draw upon and exploit whatever suitable materials exist in their circumscribed island environment, and with them create uses and forms that give us an insight into their basic concerns, and the nature of their creative ability.

Thanks to the tropical climate, tribal islanders do not wear clothing (except for those who live today in urban administrative settlements where acculturation is rapid). A brushlike fiber apron (*haguiheghe*) has only recently been adopted by the women of the Onge who live on Little Andaman Island and have been most studied.

Of longer practice by the Onge is the almost daily custom of decorating their very dark-skinned bodies to avert illness and death. With fingers or a stick, they smear face and torso with a mixture of yellow ocher and fat, which they then inscribe in geometric patterns that strongly contrast this light pigment and dark skin color. Women work on their own

bodies while looking into a primitive mirror consisting of a giant *Tridacna* clamshell filled with water. After a feast it is customary for women to decorate their men and children, vying with each other in their invention of new decorative patterns, devoid of any specific symbolic meaning beyond their general purpose, which is to repel evil and sickness.

Like most primitive people, the Onge pay homage to their ancestors, whom they bury inside the grass-roofed structures in which they live in order to retain the ancestor spirits, which they believe assist them in their daily lives. Old bones are later disinterred, cleaned, painted with yellow or red ocher, and reburied. For the purpose of ancestral propitiation, women wear a necklace of several human jawbones (*ibidanghe*); a skull painted with yellow ocher; or a necklace of wrist bones, ankle bones, and parts of the ribs of relatives.

The most elaborate ornaments are worn during important festivals, such as those celebrating the harvest, which always include group dancing. Headdresses of fresh palm leaves, manipulated in waves and tufts so they resemble the wig of a British judge, are worn by both sexes. Garlands of flowers, leaves, and fruit are common. Necklaces (*chena datu*) are made by stringing tooth or dentalium shells on a twisted cord made of screw pine or pandanus leaf fiber; several are worn at a time. Young screw pine leaves are combined with many other kinds of fibrous material to make necklaces that are worn together.

Waist decorations for men and women include the rigid stem of a climbing palm, remarkable for its extraordinary length. This is wrapped around the body many times, or cut into sections that are joined by thread. Green and flexible when cut, it turns black when dry. The thread used for joining and tassel-hung decoration often comes from unraveling red cloth formerly dropped from airplanes by government agents as conciliatory gifts to gain access in a friendly future visit, or (today) given by official visitors. Other kinds of belts are made of pandanus leaf fiber, bark, and shells. Anklets and armlets made of fibrous materials in straplike constructions are tied on tightly with cord hung with shells, using fabrication techniques mainly derived from the arts of shelter construction and basketry.

Ash, Mud, and Pigment

If we define body decoration as any means used by humans to embellish, disguise, or transfigure the body, then we must include the most elemental of substances used for these purposes. Since prehistoric times in India, mud (H: *mitti*) and ashes (S: *bhasma*), the very substance of the earth to which all humanity returns, have always been significant to Hindus. Of special importance is the mud from sacred places such as the Ganges; the ashes of a sacrificial fire after the performance of a ritual involving a burnt offering; or ashes remaining from the cremation of the dead.

The ashes of burned and dried cow-dung patties and straw, commonly used to make a cooking fire, are often applied by Hindu mendicants or *sadhus* and Muslim *fakirs* to partially or completely cover their bodies, which are usually near nakedness because they have renounced all worldly possessions. These ashes are considered by Hindus to be sacred because of their association with Shiva, whose vehicle is the bull. After the daily bath, *sadhus* spend hours powdering their entire bodies with a carefully applied, uniform or patterned ash coating. A common Shaivite pattern consists of three horizontal lines placed on the forehead, chest, and upper arms to symbolize the Hindu triad—Brahma (the creator), Vishnu (the preserver), and Shiva (the destroyer)—or the trident of Shiva, one of his symbols. Here the body decoration is intended to trans-

form the user's natural appearance and project that person into a supranatural state of mind.

Of a more purely decorative nature is the application of mud or pigment to the face and body of rural, tribal, or professional dancers when celebrating a festival. While some of this body decoration has a semireligious purpose, beggars, magicians, street performers, and minor cult priests often decorate their bare bodies with temporary streaked, painted or printed patterns simply to attract attention.

Clay and dust are gathered by pilgrims from holy places, wrapped in cloth or paper, and placed within a charm box. Believed to be imbued with the spirit of the divinity of that place, their protective power is thereby imparted to the individual. Similarly, ashes from a sacred fire or burnt sacrifice offered to the gods are regarded as having a prophylactic effect and are also placed in container-type amulets.

Hindu Sectarian Forehead Marks

Various types of ashes, earths, powders, and pigments have been used for ages by Hindus in India to mark the body, particularly the forehead. Such marks are important among orthodox Hindus because, in caste- and religion-conscious India, forehead marks inform all who behold them of the religious sect to which the wearer belongs. Especially prevalent in south-

9. Port Blair, Andaman and Nicobar Islands. *1872*
Onge tribal chieftain and his wife. Albumen print 8⅔ x 7½ in. (21.9 x 19 cm)
Royal Anthropological Institute of Great Britain and Ireland, London

The chieftain's sole body ornament is a koie of cane at his waist. His wife wears many necklaces of cylindrical dentalun shells (chena datu) strung on pandanus-leaf fiber thread, a girdle of strung plant-stem sections, and a palm-leaf buttocks cover (partially visible).

10. Lomdak Village, Lower Subansiri District, Arunachal Pradesh
Miri woman fetching water in sections of hollowed bamboo culms. She wears a multitude of cane (Calamus) stems as a torso ornament as well as glass seed-bead necklaces and shell bangles.

◄ **11. Chhota Udepur, Vadodara (Baroda) District, Gujarat**
Rathva male folk dancers in Holi Festival dance costumes, bodies painted with stripes and spots. Three dance leaders wear headdresses of bamboo and paper. Suspended from their waists are dried, hollow gourds, phallic symbols of virility, containing pellets that rattle. The belts have cast-brass bells.

12. *Sectarian Forehead Marks*

Arranged by sect: 1–5, Brahma; 6–35, Vaishnavas; 36–69, Shaivas; 70, Shakti; 71–74, Buddhists and Jainas

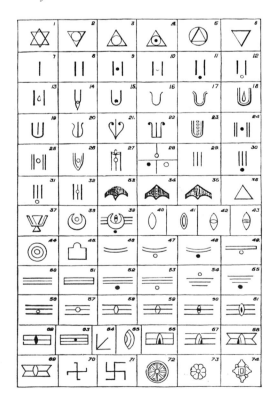

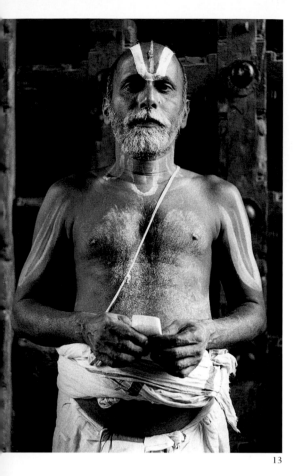

13

14

ern India, they are applied daily whenever possible. Sectarian marks of this kind are essential to Brahmans, those of the highest priestly caste in the Hindu hierarchy, as they cannot perform their daily prayers and sacrifices (*pujas*) without first putting the forehead mark in place. No person will approach a Brahman to ask his blessing unless he wears such a mark (*chhappa*) on his forehead.

Vaishnavites, or followers of Vishnu, use mainly vertical marks. In some cases only one vertical line is made on the forehead between the eyes, but more usually there are two pairs of parallel vertical lines with a black dot or open circle between or under them. The dot (*purma*) represents the deity because it is self-existing, contains nothing, and has neither length nor breadth. The circle (*brahm*) is a unit of perfection, without beginning or end.

Shaivites or followers of Shiva use mainly horizontal or upward-curving semicircular marks. Most common are three horizontal or semicircular lines, open or closed at the ends. Shaivites add to this a red dot over, under, or centered on the lines depending on the particular sect. Other Shaivite symbols include the triangle, an upward-pointing crescent moon with a dot above, or the trident (*trishula*), a symbol of Shiva's power over heaven, earth, and hell. Shaktis or followers of the dynamic female divine power use a yellow dot made with saffron, turmeric, and borax, or a yellow powdered pigment.

The red dot on the forehead (*bindu*) used by Hindu women has no religious function, but is simply a cosmetic beauty spot. In some places its use is confined to married women only.

Sectarian marks are made from alkaline ashes (H: *bhasma*) prepared from vegetable or mineral substances. Brahmans prepare the composition with ashes from cow-dung cakes burned in the sacrificial fire of an Agnihotra Brahman, and Shaivites similarly from a fire fueled by the same and offered as a sacrifice to Shiva. Both can be purchased ready for use in the bazaar. Brahmans mix the ashes with cow's milk, gum, and water, form it into a ball, and store it. When needed this is crushed and made into a paste with water, then applied. The same powder preparation is also used when cleaning metal ritual objects and pots, to make them sacrificially pure, and when cleaning precious metal ornaments.

Common magnesian clay is also used, as is pure white clay or kaolin, particularly that from Dwarka, Gujarat, because this is said to be taken from the earth of the pool in which the milkmaids (Gopis) drowned themselves upon hearing of Krishna's death. Yellow ocher brought from Hardwar at the source of the Ganges, and red ocher made by calcining or heating yellow ocher to cause its iron content to be raised to a higher state of oxidation, which changes it from yellow to red, are both used.

Red pigment is often used as a part of the forehead mark. Formerly this was red ocher or ground red sanders wood (*Pterocarpus santalinus*), but now powdered synthetic red pigment is available for purchase in any Indian bazaar.

16. Shri Rangam, Tiruchchirapalli, Tamil Nadu
Man wearing a Shaivite sectarian forehead mark, which consists of a broad, upward-curving, horizontal ash mark (tiryakpundra or vibhuti-pundaram), often of three stripes. A red-pigment dot (tilaka or pundra) symbolizing Shiva's third eye, placed at the center, is believed to have protective powers.

17. Southern India
Sadhu Hanuman Hari Das, follower of Rama, an incarnation of Vishnu, wears an elaborate personalized sectarian mark (namam) following the basic format of that used by a Vaishnavite: two vertical outer white stripes (gopichandanam) and a central red one (tiruchurnam), joined below. He also wears ten necklaces (tulasimanittavadam)—an allusion to Vishnu's ten incarnations—of beads made from the stem of the basil plant (Ocimum sanctum), sacred to Vishnu.

18. Maisur (Mysore), Karnataka
Madhava Brahman, follower of Vishnu, stamped with sandalwood or white kaolin-paste (gopi) applied with a chhapp daily after the morning bath, during the first worship (puja). Each stamp subject has a prescribed position on the body. Among related sects the stamp is also used for body branding when a devotee visits his or her guru, usually the head of a temple complex (mutt).

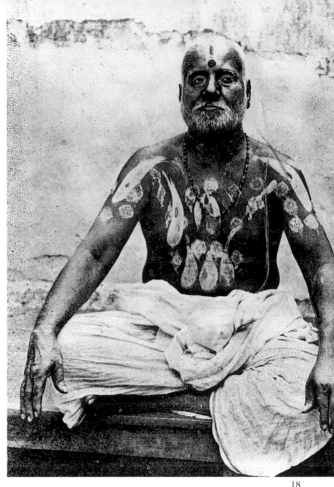

18

17

Sectarian Body Stamps

An important wood used for forehead marking is aromatic white sandalwood (*Santalum album*), also used for body stamping. It has long been a customary sign of devotion among some Hindu Vaishnavite, Shaivite, and other sects to stamp the body with a stamp or seal (*chhappa* or *mat chhap*) bearing a symbol, sometimes with script, related to the deity. The prime purpose of body stamps is to confirm and give visible proof of the wearer's devotion to the sect deity. The marks are believed to transfer the powerful beneficence of the deity to the wearer.

Stamps are applied after the devotee has undergone a purifying early morning bath. Then, in the course of worship, Vaishnavites prepare stamping paste by rubbing a piece of white sandalwood and water on a rough stone slab. Shaivites do the same, but instead use red sanders wood or a *rudraksha* drupe, the fruit of *Elaeocarpus ganitrus*. The resulting paste is gathered in a shallow container. Into this the flat stamp face is dipped, then applied directly to the body, on the forehead, cheeks, shoulders, torso, abdomen, flanks, and arms. The impressions remain for the day until they wear off.

The main Vaishnavite body-stamp symbols are the conventional weapons and symbols of the god: the lotus (*padma*), conch shell (*shankh*), quoit or weapon wheel, Vishnu's or Krishna's mace, the sun (*shamsa; suraj*), and the name of

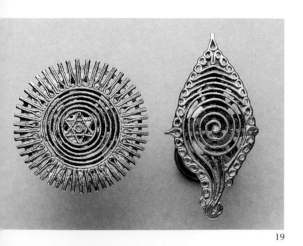

19. Navadwip, Nadia District, West Bengal
Cast-brass chhapps of Vishnu's primary symbols (lakshanas), (left) the disc (S: chakram); (right) the conch (S: shank), each held in the two upright of his four hands

20. Navadwip, Nadia District, West Bengal
Cast-brass sectarian body stamps (chhapp). In use by Vishnu devotees (gokul sampradaya) and others, they are dipped into a paste prepared of sandalwood, then pressed on the skin. They are purchased, often in sets of five different symbols held on one ring, from vendors near Vishnu temples and shrines. This stamp represents Vishnu's footprints above the U-shaped forehead mark (namam), and an inscription. It is applied with the hope that upon death the wearer will be carried to Vishnu's heaven (Vaikunth).

21. *Forms of Sectarian Body Stamps*

Top to bottom: yoni, *square, rectangle, circle, ogive, oval, octagon, footprints, crown with mukut, and heart*

the god. Footprints (*padaka*) of various deities are also used. Depending on the sect, they may be any of the following: God's footprints (*charanapadaka*); Vishnu's footprints (*Vishnupadaka*); or those of incarnations of Vishnu, such as Krishna (*Krishnapadaka*) and Shrinathji (*Shrinathjipadaka*). At times when it may be difficult for various reasons to apply all the necessary marks, a single one containing a compound composition of all the necessary symbols (*mudras*) is sufficient.

Traditional body stamps were manufactured at various places in both northern and southern India. One way of determining from which area they came is the language of the inscription, if present.

Productive north Indian stamp-making centers were at Nadia Navadwip District, West Bengal; another was Orissa. Both used the lost-wax process, which starts with the fabrication of an openwork wax wire model, from which the stamp was then cast in brass. At the back, opposite the face, a supporting, bracing structure was formed that terminated in a handle, pierced by a hole. This makes it possible to link together with a ring a set of several different stamps, the symbols on them chosen according to the sect preference. Today, single stamps, or sets of them, can be purchased by pilgrims in the bazaar near a temple or shrine.

Seal Branding

Most stamps can be likened to a temporary tattoo. In some places in the south, however, the stamp is heated before use and when applied burns the skin like a brand. Thurston, in *Castes and Tribes of Southern India*, describes the southern Sri Vaishnava and Madhva Brahman sect custom of branding the body with Vaishnavite symbol stamps as a form of devotion. Devotees are expected to submit to this at least once in a lifetime, when they visit the head of their sect. It is optional among other sects and castes who follow Vishnu.

After a purifying bath and worship, disciples are initiated with the brand of Vishnu's symbols of a wheel (*chakra*) on the right shoulder, and the conch shell (*chank*) on the left shoulder. The brand (also called *mudra*) is heated enough to singe the skin and leave a permanent deep black mark on adult males. It is less hot when used for women, young people, and babies, so it leaves a light mark that may ultimately disappear. Branding renders the person fit to participate in all Brahman ceremonies and is believed to remove all previous sins each time it is done.

Mehndi: A Festive Temporary "Tattoo"

Unlike a real tattoo, which is permanent, some decorative patterns created on the skin with stain or dye are not immediately removable but, depending on dye strength, can last for three or four weeks. *Mehndi*, the Hindi term for "henna," the dye used for this purpose, and the result, can therefore be designated a temporary tattoo.

Applying *mehndi* decoration to the palm of the hand and the feet is popular in Rajasthan, Gujarat, Haryana, Madhya Pradesh, and Kashmir, and less so in Uttar Pradesh, Bihar, West Bengal, and Orissa. As in the case of most ancient folk traditions in India, rural women are mainly responsible for its perpetuation and design invention. Urban women also practice this custom, but its function with them is mainly cosmetic. The practice also exists among Muslim women.

Mehndi is said to have been introduced to India by the Muslim Mughals, who used henna widely as a hand, foot, and hair dye. However, in Buddhist wall murals at the Ajanta caves in Maharashtra (second century B.C. to seventh century A.D.) a famous scene depicts a princess whose attendants are decorating her hands and feet, presumably with henna. The practice also occurred in Persia, but the extremely elaborate patterns found in India seem to constitute its contribution to this delicate folk art.

Rural women generally prepare the dye paste used for *mehndi* and apply it at home, the women of a family working on each other. The paste may also be purchased readymade in the bazaar. Friendly competition exists among the women to produce the most fashionable, inventive designs. Urban families are often scattered, so these women may hire a recommended professional *mehndi* applier, who will come to the home. Such professionals are also found in a city or town bazaar, where they often ply their trade on a particular day of the week.

Mehndi and Marriage

Mehndi is one element of a Hindu woman's "complete decoration," or *shringar*, of which there are sixteen (H: *solah shringar*). Sixteen, a significant number among Hindus, corresponds to the sixteen phases of the moon, which in turn is connected with a woman's menstrual cycle. A woman of sixteen (H: *sodasi*) is considered to be at the peak of physical perfection in her life and ready for marriage. Men agree that *mehndi* patterns on a woman evoke thrilling, erotic sensations, perhaps because they associate *mehndi* with a bride's initiation into mature womanhood.

The practice of applying elaborate *mehndi* patterns to the hands and feet of Hindu and Muslim brides is widespread (see 621). Among Hindus, the custom is a symbol of satisfaction (S: *bhog*) and happiness in marriage (H: *subhagya*). This belief derives partly from the dye's red color, universally considered to be auspicious; red is also the color of a bride's

22. Rajasthan
Mehndi decoration. The palms (H: hatheli) and feet (paya) of a woman can be so decorated at the time of private festive occasions, such as a wedding. Brides are commonly ornamented by their female relatives, who are also decorated. This temporary tattoo lasts for about one month and is considered to enhance a woman's erotic appeal to her husband.

dress. *Mehndi* is commonly applied to propitiate Ganesha, the Hindu elephant-headed god, son of Shiva, who overcomes obstacles and is always invoked to attend a Hindu marriage ceremony.

Mehndi is carried out on a bride's hands and feet (see 655) the night before the marriage celebration begins, called *mehndi rat*. A party of the bride's women relatives and in-laws spend several hours at this joyful task, during which they sing appropriate songs. For the bride, the process is therapeutic in calming and preparing her for the event.

Mehndi may also be applied to a groom's feet in a manner similar to that of the bride. When applied on a boy, as is sometimes done, the design is never elaborate but executed in broad dabs, and the boy's little finger may also be dyed red.

After marriage, *mehndi* may be applied to a woman on any auspicious occasion, such as the birth or naming of a child, or when a son is initiated into the family caste and given the sacred thread (see page 42). In some communities it is customary to so ornament a woman who has died and dress her in a marriage costume before cremation.

The *Mehndi* Process

Henna, the dye used in *mehndi*, is a product of the leaves of a tropical shrub or small tree, the Indian myrtle (*Lawsonia inermiss* or *Lawsonia alba*), widely cultivated in India as a hedge around a compound and so easily available. Henna is also used at festival times to dye fingernails and hair on both humans and animals, such as horses and bullocks. The white horse customarily ridden by a bridegroom may also be so decorated, and it is common to find horses so represented in Mughal and Rajput miniature paintings.

Rural women pluck fresh *mehndi* leaves and macerate them in water and unboiled milk in a bowl reserved especially for this purpose. The paste that results is strained through a muslin cloth and some lemon juice is mixed with it to act as a mordant, which intensifies its red color. Catechu, sugar candy, and a few drops of kerosene are added as an extender, and tamarind gum and water are introduced to increase its viscosity and smoothness, both aids in its application. The result is allowed to set for a few hours or overnight.

Depending on the complexity of the design, applying *mehndi* requires from three to five hours when decorating two hands, or six to eight hours if the feet are also done. This considerable length of time gives the process a ritualistic aspect.

The skin to which *mehndi* is applied must be clean and grease free. The viscous paste is applied freehand with the thin stick from a broom, a matchstick, or a wire. When manipulated evenly on the skin the paste will produce a desirable thin, even line. Borders in a design are applied first, and internal details follow. The completed application is allowed to dry slowly; the longer it is left undisturbed, the deeper is the color and longer-lasting the result. Finally, the dry paste residue is removed simply by rubbing the hands together, and the skin is then rubbed with sesame or mustard oil, washed with water, and oiled again to deepen the color effect.

Mehndi designs (H: *mehndi bhant*) are an aspect of folk art requiring a well-developed decorative sense. Old patterns are perpetuated by the community, but innovative designs may be introduced by an adept and thereafter emulated by others, thus entering the communal design repertoire.

Designs often vary regionally and within a particular group. Some designs are considered to be seasonal, corresponding to summer (*dhupkal*), the rainy or monsoon season (*barkhakal*), or winter (*sitkal*), the three main Indian annual periods. Others are used at important Hindu festivals: the winter solstice (Makara Sankranti) in January, spring saturnalia (Holi) in February–March, and the Gangour festival in April–May, when the spouse of Shiva is worshipped for good luck and wealth, and others. Designs consist of geometric and figural motifs, the latter including flowers and leaf and vine patterns, all with symbolic significance, as well as traditional Hindu religious symbols. Many are related to patterns used in ritual floor decoration (Ben: *alpana*).

Among Muslim women, *mehndi* patterns are geometric and are applied mainly during the Muslim festivals of 'Idu'l-azha, the feasts of sacrifice, and as part of the Makkan pilgrimage; Muharram, which commemorates the martyrdom of al-Husain, the second son of Fatimeh, the Prophet's daughter, by Ali; and Ramazan, the ninth month of the Muhammadan year, in which each day involves fasting from dawn to sunset.

Tattooing: A Permanent Body Symbol

Actual tattooing (H: *gudna*, to prick) has for millennia been common among Hindus in Rajasthan and Gujarat, and various tribal people in northern India including the Juang, Munda, Ho, Kol, and Oraon. (Its use by Muslims is forbidden.) In northeast India, the Abor tribals tattoo their faces (see 357, 358), and in the south, Sudra and Paraiyan women tattoo arms and torsos. In Telegu country in the south, professional tattooing women (*pariki-muggula*) travel around providing this service to rural women.

In early primitive societies, the tattoo served to identify the wearer's social rank and status. In general, however, in India the purpose of tattooing is mainly apotropaic: to it is credited an evil-averting, magical function. Especially in animist societies, the tattoo acts to repel the forces of evil believed to be constantly active and attempting to gain advantage over the unwary, unprotected individual, causing misfortune, illness, or even death. Tattoos cannot be eradicated without destroying skin tissue. Because the apotropaic tattoo is permanent and always present on the body, its action is unrelenting protection.

This protective function explains why tattooing is often performed during ritual acts initiating a youth into manhood or a girl into puberty, or formally inducting adults into group membership. Because belonging to the society is of great importance to the initiates' sense of well-being, they willingly undergo the pain experienced during the tattooing process. At the same time, their ability to endure pain becomes a rite of passage testing their maturity. Submission to the process therefore indicates acquiescence to and bonding with tribal custom and tradition. In such communities, therefore, tattooing is not meant to indicate deviation or protest—as it often does in the West—but quite to the contrary, it is a symbol indicating the acceptance of and compliance with the prevailing social norm.

All visible (and in some cases hidden) parts of the body can be tattooed, including forehead, temple, nose, chin, chest, breasts, arms, hands, legs, and feet. In the iconography of the Indian tattoo, common signs are made with dots, stars, and lines. Figural subjects usually of a religious nature are also found, as are group totem symbols and others of a purely decorative nature.

In a process unchanged for centuries, the usual tattooing technique involves pricking the skin with an instrument such as a sharply pointed needle or group of needles of wood, bamboo, bone, or metal set in a wooden handle. Before use, the needle is dipped into a pigment or dye, the most usual being ordinary black soot gathered after burning a vegetable substance such as a nut or feathers. Carbon black, or sometimes blue indigo dye, are most common; other colors are rarely used. The point or points are placed upon the skin and hit with a stick to puncture the skin and introduce the pigment through skin ruptures. After the wounds have healed, the tattoo is permanent.

23. Madhya Pradesh

A married Gondh tribal woman with tattoos (godna) on her arms. The tattooing of women in tribal India is often a prelude to marriage. The patterns used by particular tribal groups all have local symbolic significance. Here the sets of parallel lines represent steps (ghats) often found descending from riverbank shrines and temples. Between them are separate figures, some representing protective gods or goddesses.

Natural Materials

Pavitram: Ring of Sacred *Kusha* Grass

Grass must be high on the list of nature's most abundant creations. Even this common natural material was not overlooked in India as a source for the creation of ornaments. Today, in many places in India various grasses and cereal stalks are plaited, braided, and formed in other ways into a variety of decorative personal ornaments.

In a special category is *darbha* grass, the most sacred of all Indian grasses, in its religious use called *kusha* grass (*Demostachya bipinnata*). Hindus regard it as sacred because it is said to have been the first plant created by the gods. As a result its stalk was claimed to be sacrificially pure and able to purify anything it touches. From this belief came the concept of using it to make a sacrificial ring worn at every important Hindu ceremony by the officiating priest and participating attendants. The ring is called *pavitram* in Sanskrit, from the word *pavitra,* meaning "clean, holy, physically and morally pure."

The origin of the sanctity of this grass is found in Hindu mythology. For a good cause, Garuda, the bird-man vehicle of Vishnu, stole ambrosia (*amrita*) from the gods. In the process, a few drops spilled from its container and fell to Earth, landing on *kusha* grass, which rendered it eternally consecrated. Serpents observing its fall greedily licked up the ambrosia from its sharp-edged leaves, which cut their tongues (which is why serpents today have forked tongues) and, by its contact, the serpents became immortal.

For eons *kusha* grass has been used, either loose, or in the form of the *pavitram* ring, in all Hindu Brahmanic ceremonies and on auspicious occasions. Included among these are the *kamyartha* rites, or "deeds that lead to worldly happiness," such as the monthly purification and fertility rite performed at the completion of a woman's menstrual cycle; the ceremony of hair parting, done with three bound stalks of *kusha* grass on a woman six to eight months pregnant with her first child, to ensure a successful birth; the writing of the child's horoscope after birth, as well as the name-giving, weaning, and first-tonsure or head-shaving ceremonies of a child.

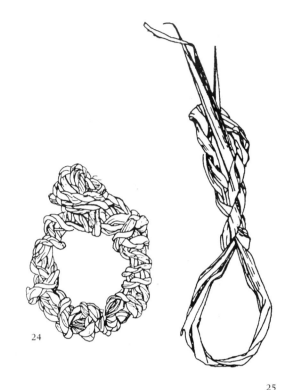

24. Maharashtra
*Ritual rings (pavitram) of darbha or kusha grass (Poa cynosuroides), worn by Hindus to dispel the intervention of malignant spirits during the performance of a ritual
Courtesy Dr. Emma Pressmar, from Indische Ringe, with permission*

25. Kotra, Udaipur District, Rajasthan
Straw ornaments (gajra) worn by Bhil and Garasia tribal women of Rajasthan and Gujarat. Grass chain is braided into the hair and the wheat-stalk tassels (choti jhumka) dangle. Flattened rice- stalk bracelets are braided in a four-square spiral.

24

25

26

27

26. Maharashtra and Karnataka
Silver pavitram ring with three garnets. The wire simulates the concept of the darbha-grass pavitram ring, here fabricated in an interworked and knotted form.
Collection the author, Porvoo

27. Maharashtra
Rings (pavitram) of gold or silver wire permanently fixed in place by soldering. It should not be confused with the wire puzzle ring (H: gorak-dhanda; Ben: gorakh dhaudari, an intricate affair), which the wire pavitram superficially resembles. A puzzle ring parts are made of 5 to 12 separate, interlocking units that, when together, appear to be a knot but are not. Top: Interlooped double knot of six round-sectioned wires. Center: Back view of the above ring, with a seven-dot rosette soldered to the shank to cover the wire junction. Bottom: Four strands of interlooped wires forming a symmetrical knot set with a red stone.
Courtesy Dr. Emma Pressmar, from Indische Ringe, with permission

Later in life, the sacred *kusha* grass ring is worn by the priest who performs the ritual Hindu Brahmanic ceremonies marking the various ideal stages of a Hindu's life and by the participant. After the age of seven, these stages comprise four subsequent periods called *ashramas*: that of religious education (seven to twenty-five); life as a married householder (twenty-five to forty); retirement to practice meditation before renouncing worldly possessions (forty to fifty); and renunciation of possessions and freedom from wordly duties (fifty to seventy-five). It is also used at funeral ceremonies (*sraddha*) privately performed to honor the deceased and facilitate their progress through future births.

The *pavitram* is also used by the officiating priest and the boy undergoing the initiation ceremony at which a boy is first invested with the sacred thread. It is made by twisting or plaiting together two, three, five, or seven stalks and knotting them to form a loop.

The Hindi version of the word, *pavitri,* today has been extended to include a special copper, silver, or gold ring worn during religious worship. In Bangalore, Karnataka, a *pavitram* ring is made of silver wire arranged in parallel series and formed into a symmetrical knot, often showing great ingenuity in construction. Some are mounted with a red-colored stone or stones. The Nambudri Brahmans of Kerala wear a gold *pavitram* ring formed like two V's joined at their tops. This form resembles a Tamil upper armlet (*vanki*), which may be its inspiration. It is worn on the third finger of the right hand, while performing or undergoing religious ceremonies. Any *pavitram* ring works as an amulet to frighten away evil spirits.

Flowers as Personal Decoration

Probably the oldest plant materials used in India for personal decoration or in rituals are fresh flowers, some found in the immediate environment, others cultivated for their beauty. From time immemorial in India, the sensual appeal of flowers has made them a most acceptable offering to both feared and revered ancestors (S: *pitr*), spirits (S: *preta*), and gods (S: *deva*) to appease them and enlist their supernatural sympathy.

Encouraging this usage was the idea that the flower is a generic symbol of creation and regeneration. Such concepts are also expressed by many Indian vernacular language idioms with flower references. To give but one example, the Sanskrit word *joban,* meaning "to blossom," can also mean "puberty," "the flower of youth," and "the prime of life."

Flower Garlands

Among the majority of Indian people, loose flower petals and destemmed flower heads are preferred to stemmed flowers in vases for important occasions, both religious and secular. When flowers are brought into a Hindu home for any purpose, they are first offered symbolically to the household deity, then put to use. Petals or flower heads used in worship are typically scattered over the object of veneration from cupped hands (*puspanjali*). Their symbolic ritual function lasts only as long as they do.

Since antiquity, people have strung flower heads to make head, neck, wrist, and other ornaments composed of flowers. Flower wreaths for the hair have always been popular, but the form in widest use is the garland, or flower necklace, generally called *mala* in the north, and *malai* in the south. By transference, *mala* has become a generic term used to designate almost any long necklace, which can also be of beads or metal. The term is usually modified by the material used, as in *motimala*, a bead or pearl necklace.

28. Prime Minister Shri Jawaharlal Nehru, with folk dancers from the Andaman and Nicobar Islands at the Republic Day celebrations in New Delhi, January 26, 1958. Nehru wears a presentation garland (jaimala) of marigolds and roses and a palm-fiber Andamanese headband.

Flower garlands, whether simple or elaborate works of art, are considered highly appropriate as an oblation to a temple deity. Both bride and groom wear them during the wedding ceremony as good-luck symbols. On secular occasions, a garland is used to indicate respect, as when welcoming a private guest or honoring a dignitary at a public event. Actors often wear garlands appropriate to the character they play. After a theatrical performance, appreciation to an actor, actress, dancer, or musician is normally expressed by the bestowal of a flower garland. The person honored, cupped hands held together in a respectful counter gesture (*anjalimudra*), bows to receive the garland placed over the head and around the neck. Wearing a flower garland is said to impart an intoxicating feeling or mood of contentment and pleasure in its wearer.

Making a flower garland simply requires a long, sharp pointed needle threaded with strong cotton string. Some flowers are held by a knot to the string; others are pierced through their densest part, the ovule. Garlands can be made of a single kind of flower, or a combination of several, alternating in type, color, and size. Many are imaginative and elaborate creations. Often at the front hangs a flower or tinsel tassel (H: *phundna; jhabba;* Tam: *kuchcham*), corresponding to the terminal bead of a rosary. Not all flowers are suited to garland making, and some are longer lasting than others. The most favored garland flowers today are the marigold, champak, and lotus, closely followed by jasmine and rose.

Fresh-flower garlands are always of prime importance in Indian ritual. As an expression of an ever-growing desire for novelty, however, garlands today are also made of a variety of natural and synthetic substances manipulated into flower or other forms. These alternate substances include *shola* pith, paper, sandalwood shavings, cloves, silk cocoons, tinsel, and metallic ribbon. A relatively new variation is a garland made for a groom from unused Indian rupee banknotes, folded and joined in decorative arrangements.

Flower garlands can be made by anyone who cares to take the trouble, but their professional creators have always been men and women of the Mali caste, the name derived from the Sanskrit word *mala*. Members of this important pan-Indian hereditary caste, low in the social hierarchy, traditionally occupy themselves in the cultivation of vegetable crops. The sub-caste called Phulmalis specialize in growing and selling flowers. This is the group that must be credited with the development of the specialized skill of making garlands, as well as many other forms of fresh-flower ornament and decoration.

Since antiquity, Malis have provided flowers for use in Hindu temple worship and have manufactured garlands for offerings to the gods. In every city or town of any size, and also often outside the wall of even an isolated tem-

29. Puri, Orissa
Fresco-secco folk painting of the Hindu goddess Kali on the wall of a shrine dedicated to her. She wears a long garland of severed human heads (mundmala), and other ornaments.

30. Dariba Bazaar, Delhi
Hindu groom wearing a wedding garland of two hundred rupees-worth of new one- and two-rupee Indian banknotes folded into floral forms and ornamented with gold tinsel and sequins.

31

31. Tamil Nadu

Tiruchendur Murugan, the Tamil name of Karttikeya or Skanda, whose main pilgrimage center is at
Palni, northwest of Madurai. He is represented in
a polychrome oleograph, a type commonly placed
in homes for worship. A popular south Indian god,
he wears the traditional ornaments of a south
Indian deity, including the temple necklace (linga
padakka muthu malai) with a rudrakshamalai suspending a lingam case (see 46), and a fresh flower
garland (pumalai) descending to his feet.

32. Calcutta, West Bengal
New Bazaar

32

33. Ramnagar, Uttar Pradesh
Young actor representing Rama in the annual nine-
night Ramlila festival held here at the palace-fort of
the Maharaja of Varanasi. In this enactment, the main
characters are always ornamented with fresh flower
garlands and wear crowns (mukut) decorated with
metallic wire and tinsel (zari, see 379).

33

ple or popular shrine, one or more Malis can be found making fresh flower garlands to sell to devotees or pilgrims entering the temple for worship. Today some of the larger, wealthier temples, where elaborate daily rituals are performed, employ Malis permanently to make the garlands needed for ceremonial use. In the flower bazaars of large cities are always numerous stalls where Malis display their cleverly manipulated and combined flower garlands in long series.

Flower garlands are favored as offerings to the Divine because Hindus and other religious groups in India consider flowers in any form to be ritually and sacrificially pure. This idea renders the flower garland suitable for adorning an image of a deity and for decorating a temple shrine during a religious ceremony. They are seen in ancient sculptures hung from venerated, sacred trees, or decorating the domes of stupas.

Hindus also believe that good spirits reside in garlands, in particular Vishnu's consort Shridevi, identified with Lakshmi, also a consort of Vishnu, and personifying beauty, prosperity, good fortune, and victory. Consequently, anyone who receives and wears a garland will automatically be graced by Shridevi's bounty.

Because they are in such high regard, flower offerings and garlands that have faded are preferably consigned to water, considered to be a sacred element. However, Hindus believe that the flower garlands worn by deities never wither, but remain eternally fresh. This indeed is one of several signs of an immortal god or goddess, should one be encountered.

Flowers as Erotic Stimulants

The association of flowers with the erotic impulse is manifestly evident in association with Kama or Kamadeva, the Hindu god of erotic love (equivalent to the Greek Eros and the Roman Cupid). He is married to Rati, a seductive celestial nymph (apsaras) who personifies desire, sensual delight, and affection, and his vehicle is the garrulous, gaudy parrot.

To excite lovers, Kama carries a pointed goad (kamakusha); he also shoots arrows at couples to provoke their mutual passion. Kama's bow is made of sugar cane, and its sugar-coated string is covered by vibrating honey bees whose sting also stimulates love. Each arrow in his arsenal is tipped with the bud of one of his five favorite flowers—gigantic swallow wort, jasmine, mango, cobra's saffron, and champa—all of which have a strong scent and are believed to have body- and blood-heating qualities.

Appropriately, each of these flowers is supposed to preside figuratively over one of the five senses, all of which are employed in love-making. From these symbolic implements come several of Kama's many epithets, including Kusumayudha (armed with flowers), Push-pa-sara (whose arrows are flowers), and Push-pa-dhanya (he with the flowery bow).

The famous Indian manual on the art of love, the Kamasutra (from the Sanskrit meaning "love's string of rules"), was written by Vatsyayana in A.D. 500. A guide in preventing disharmony between husband and wife through sexual adjustment, the book refers frequently to the use of flowers for personal adornment and to stimulate erotic arousal. According to Vatsyayana, included among the sixty-four arts practiced by a perfect wife as a means of holding a husband's affection and attention are: gardening and the care of plants; spreading and arranging a bed of flowers upon the floor; stringing rosaries, necklaces, garlands, and wreaths for decorating the body; making crests and topknots of flowers; a knowledge of jewelry and gemstones; arranging and matching jewelry and renovating old ornaments; making artificial flowers and tassels; and decorating horses, elephants, carts, and carriages with flowers. A wife is advised to wear her good ornaments when her husband is near, and simple ones when he is away. When he returns, she should show her pleasure by receiving him with a flower garland.

The Svayambara Marriage Garland

In a pre-marriage ceremony practiced in ancient Vedic times, a special kind of flower garland played a significant role. The ritual in which it is used is described in the Mahabharata, the most important of the Indian epic poems, completed between 200 B.C. and A.D. 200, which centers on events concerning the five Pandava brothers and their adversaries the Kauravas. Ordinarily, marriages were arranged by parents, as they mainly are today. In those times, however, a noble girl, if she wished, had the right to choose her husband in what was called a svayambara (S: svayam, one's own; bara, choice) marriage.

Her intentions were announced and a tournament, also called svayambara, was proclaimed to which eligible suitor-contenders gathered. Before their trials began, their names, lineage, and accomplishments were announced to the audience. At the contest's conclusion, the girl made her choice of husband, usually the best performing participant. Her preference was indicated to all present when she placed a white flower garland around that man's neck.

Flowers as Deity-Attribute Symbols

A single flower, for example the lotus, is often represented in jewelry, and symbolizes the unblemished beauty of ever-regenerating creation. It may be held in the hand or hands of multiarmed deities, including among others Chandra, Ganga, Indra, Kama, Lakshmi, Ruk-mini, Sarasvati, Surya, and Vishnu. Knowing in which hand the flower's placement is proper in conjunction with various symbolic objects held in other hands representing the god's or goddess's attributes, plus the hand gestures (mudras) the deity manifests, are all useful iconographic means of identifying the deity.

Therefore flower and other kinds of garlands since remote times became established as an element in the correct iconographic representation of deities in paintings cast in metal, or sculpted in stone. When depicted on an image, the presence of a specific kind of flower or type of garland is another means of assisting a layman to determine the identity of the image, which considering the multiplicity of Hindu deities might otherwise be uncertain.

Flower Forms in Jewelry

The two most distinctive stages in a flower's development are the bud and the full-blown blossom, and fresh flowers in both forms are commonly used in India for body decoration. As flowers are perishable, it is not surprising that, early in Indian culture, flower forms were also incorporated in jewelry made of more durable materials such as fibrous substances, bone, ivory, stone, and metal. The best example of the bud (S: kali) as a motif in Indian jewelry design is the ubiquitous champakali necklace, which consists of many identical hanging units representing strung buds of the champa flower. Produced by a tall evergreen tree (Michelia champaca), these sweetly scented flowers are used for loose oblation offerings to deities in shrines and temples. Their buds are also strung in close series into garlands, from which the idea of the champakali necklace derives. Another floral jewelry form is the nose stud, universal in the north, called laung (Hindi for "clove"), inspired by the nail-like form of the clove spice, which is actually the dried flower bud of the tree Eugenia aromatica.

Additionally, mature flower petals and flower sprays are often represented in jewelry by clusters of gemstones. A metal flower ornament is worn in the hair bun (H: sisphul, from sis, the head; phul, flower). From the idea of a single flower placed in an earlobe hole (S: avatansa, an ear ornamented with a flower) comes the Hindi term karanphul (ear flower), an important, universal, large, round metal flower-form earring with a central stud at the back equivalent to a flower stem, fixed in an earlobe hole. Related to this concept is the common small, circular, metal, stylized full-flower-formed ear or nose ornament (H: phulli). Flower sprays (H: buta, large spray; buti, small spray) are worn in head and turban ornaments, earrings, necklaces, and bracelets. These terms also refer to such flower motifs used in woven, printed, and embroidered textiles, as well as in floral carpet designs.

34

35

36

34. Madhya Pradesh. *12th century*
Carved-stone image of Shiva wearing a champakali har

35. Madhya Pradesh
*Silver necklace (champakali har). A classic pan-Indian
design, its units represent the fragrant flower buds
of the evergreen champa tree, given as an offering to
Shiva and other deities. It exemplifies the adoption of
auspicious flowers for jewelry design because they are
believed to possess the power of repelling evil spirits.*

36. Orissa
*Silver, two-part, hinged bracelet with central lotus-
flower motif
Outer diameter 2⅞ in. (7.1 cm); inner diameter 2½ in.
(6.4 cm); width 1⅜ in. (3.5 cm); weight 1,219 g
Collection Ghysels, Brussels*

37. Tamil Nadu (opposite page)
*Gold necklace (milligai arumbumalai) with eighty
stylized Arabian jasmine (Jasminium sambac) flower
buds, each set with a ruby, and central back clasp
in the form of a peacock
Total length 32½ in. (82.5 cm); unit length 2 in.
(5 cm); weight 348 g
Collection Barbier-Mueller Museum, Geneva (2504-104)*

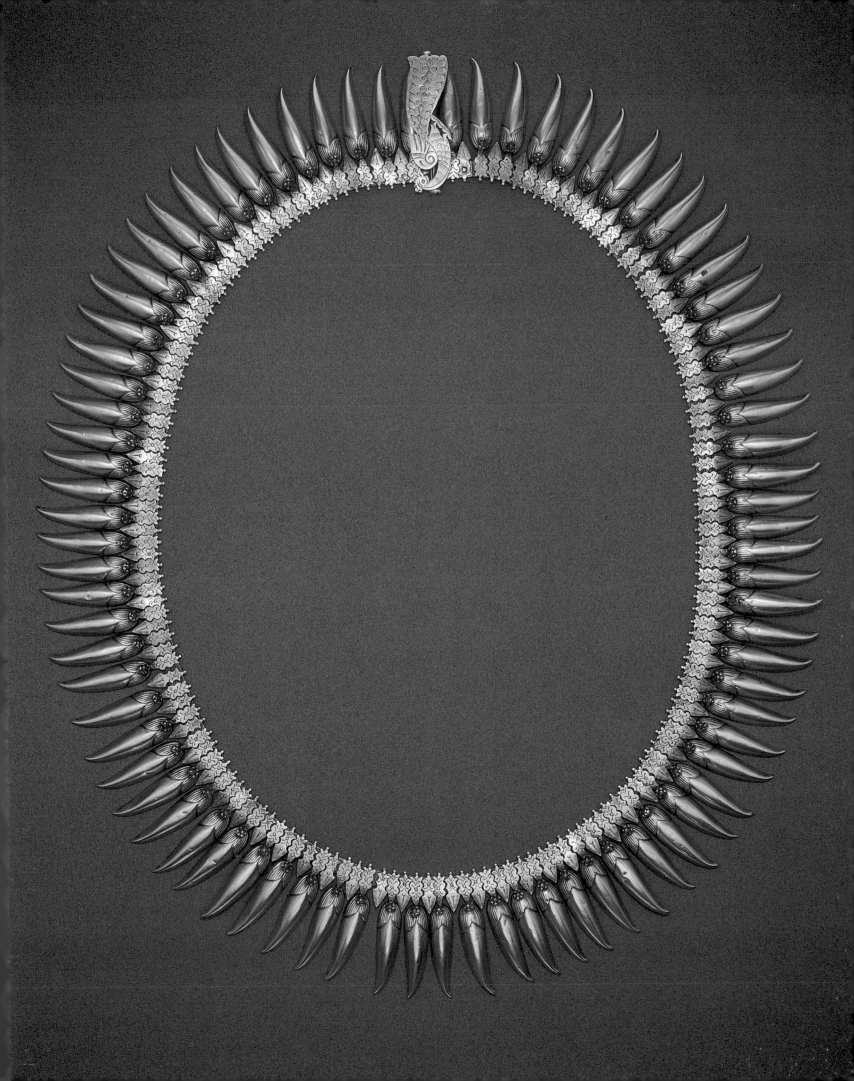

38

38. Leh, Ladakh, Jammu, and Kashmir. *c.1900*
Necklace of twenty strands of red coral beads, with turquoise and other gemstones set in gold units
Length 12¼ in. (31.1 cm)
Courtesy Sotheby's, London

The central, hanging, turquoise-set pendant is a mandala in the form of a stylized lotus (padma). In Tibetan Buddhism, the lotus is one of the eight good-luck symbols; it is also a symbol of divinity associated with Avalokiteshvara or Padmapani, the bodhisattva of compassionate mercy. A hovering butterfly connects the lotus to the suprapositioned symbolic Tibetan flaming, wish-granting jewel (Tib: norbu; Lad: yizhin norbu; S: chintamani), a motif repeated at the two gold terminals. The mother of gemstones and the bringer of prosperity, the magical flaming jewel is one of the seven gems (S: sapta ratna) that are the attributes of the universal monarch (S: chakravartin), who represents the highest worldly temporal power.

39

39. Vidyadharpur, Orissa. *19th century*
Silver two-part ankle bracelet (pancham) with upward-projecting flower-bud finials
Victoria and Albert Museum, London (IS 1909-1883)

40. Imphal, Manipur
Meithei woman representing Radha in the Vaishnavite Ras dance that honors Krishna and Radha. Its movements are based on the earlier, indigenous, annual Lai Haroba (rejoicing of the gods) ritual dance. Her costume includes gold necklaces created in the local jewelry-making center at Keisampat.

41. Imphal, Manipur
Gold-plated brass necklace (lik), in the form of strung flower buds and flower heads, worn by a Manipuri Meithei woman during the performance of the traditional Ras dance
Collection Viscount and Viscountess Scarsdale, Kedelston Hall, Derbyshire (31-347)

42. Delhi
Silver necklace (champakali har), each of whose fifty bud forms is set with a silver-foil-backed, tapered-glass, cabochon-cut "stone" and another round, red-foil-backed one. The fringe is made of a cluster of small stamped sheet-metal units.
Collection Claire Untracht, New York

43. Calcutta, West Bengal. *1787*
Francesco Renaldi (1755–c.1799)
Portrait of a Bengali Indian bibi, a woman kept by a foreigner. Signed and dated
36⅜ x 29¼ in. (92.7 x 74.3 cm)
Courtesy Christies', Manson & Woods Ltd., London

European painters in India during the eighteenth century, including Renaldi, Johann Zoffany, Robert Home, Tilly Kettle, George Willison, Thomas Hickey, and August Theodor Schöfft, are important to a study of Indian jewelry because they aimed for verisimilitude, not stylization, as was often the case in traditional Indian painting. The carefully executed representations of jewelry worn by their subjects, such as the champakali har necklace here, can be taken as accurate representations of contemporary traditional ornaments whose dating, because of design repetition over long periods of time, is always problematical. Paintings such as this help to narrow dates and allow us to follow design changes.

40

41

42

43

Seeds, Leaves, and Vines

In India, many plant forms in addition to flowers carry traditional cultural or religious associations among particular social or religious groups. Plant components such as seeds, leaves, and vines have also entered the Indian jewelry vocabulary.

Prolific, miraculous generators of life, seeds have always been looked upon by humanity as symbols of reproduction, and, since the advent of human self-adornment, seeds have served as a raw material for body decoration. From India's vast assortment of legume-rich vegetation, especially in tropical areas, seeds possessing special colors, shapes, surface patterns or textures, and hardness have been selected for use in ornament. What makes them attractive for this function is their relative durability in an unaltered state, natural high polish or the ability to be polished, and the ease with which they can be pierced for stringing or attachment to a substrate material. Their organization and arrangement can be counted among humanity's earliest essays in aesthetics. A single variety can be used alone, or several can be combined in irregular or regularly repeated sequences.

Seeds (S: *bija*) imply fertility because they possess the mysterious, potent energy to develop into complete plants. The Sanskrit word for seed, *bija,* is also used for a sound or word that has the energy to invoke a deity associated with it when uttered in prayer. For the same reason, those seeds associated with particular deities are commonly represented or actually used in ornaments such as necklaces, and in rosaries in order to propitiate a deity (see Rosaries of India, page 69).

The leaf (H: *patti,* small leaf; *patta,* large leaf) is nature's means of nourishing a plant, and in its multitudinous forms is another, much-used jewelry design source. As in the case of flowers and seeds, particular plant leaves for factual, anecdotal, mythic, or religious reasons became associated with specific personalities or deities. As their sacred symbols, they are also represented in jewelry designs, where they serve the purpose of being permanent oblations.

Vines or creepers (H: *bel; lata*), which constantly grow toward light and support, are forms that suggest the urgency of life vitality. In Hindu mythology, for example, the *kalpalata,* a fabulous creeper, is believed to link plants with gods, men, and animals, evoking the life force shared by all living things. Its spirit is said to grant the wish of anyone who reveres it, and for this reason, it is often represented in jewelry designs. Undulating or meandering creeper and vine patterns are commonly depicted on necklaces, bracelets, and other jewelry forms by the techniques of filigree work and flat linear chasing as well as other decorative processes.

44

45

46

47. *Detail of the necklace (46). The enshrined Shiva Nataraja performs the Tandava dance, representing the perpetual creation, maintenance, and destruction of the universe. He is flanked by male and female deities and mythic griffins (yalis). Below is the container for a lingam and sacred ashes. Both parts are ornamented with rubies.*

47

◄ 44. Lushai Hills, Mizoram

Mizo woman wearing a headdress of orchid stems ornamented with feathers, strings of white Job's tears seeds alternating with red crab's eye seeds, and pendants of the iridescent wing cases (elytra) of beetles of the class Buprestidae, first order Coleoptera. Characterized by their hard, brilliant, permanently colored metallic green or gold, shield-shaped dorsal wing cases, which protect the actual wings folded beneath them, these beetles are popularly used for decorative purposes among tribal people whose religious philosophy does not prevent them from taking the insect's life.

◄ 45. Madhya Pradesh

Copper belt worn by Gondh tribal women
Length of belt 27½ in. (70 cm); length of unit 3⅛ in. (8 cm); weight 770 g
Collection Mis, Brussels

Each sheet-metal, hollow unit is in the form of a seed pod, a fertility symbol.

46. Tamil Nadu. *19th century*

Gold necklace (rudrakshamalai, or linga padakka muthu malai)
Length overall 31½ in. (80 cm); height of pendant 6⅞ in. (17.5 cm); weight 315 g
Collection Mis, Brussels

Worn by men over the age of eighteen and by Shaivite priests, the pendant is suspended by strung rudraksham drupe seed-nuts alternating with gold spacer beads and held by a gold back clasp. The central unit depicts Shiva Nataraja (Lord of the Dance). The pendant is a container for a movable lingam and sacred ashes (vibhuti) from cremation grounds or a ritual fire, with which Shiva smears his body, a practice emulated by devotees, sadhus, and practitioners of yoga.

50. Gurgaon, Haryana
Handmade beads of water-buffalo horn, some inlaid with mother of pearl and brass wire; others lathe-turned of laminated varicolored tropical woods

51. Malabar, Kerala. *Late 16th century*
Carved polychrome-wood dancer's headpiece
41 x 34 x 4 in. (104.1 x 86.3 x 10.2 cm)
Los Angeles County Museum of Art.
Gift of Mr. and Mrs. Harry Lenart (M.77.60)

The headpiece is worn by a man representing Bhairava, a terrifying form of Shiva as the all-pervading ruler of death, during the Bhuthamkali Devil Dance performed by celebrants of the Nayadi tribe. Bhairava has protruding tusks, wears elephant-decorated ear ornaments (yanaikundalam), and a crown topped by two intertwined cobras. The aureole features twenty-four cobra heads and a central face of glory (kirtimukha), terminating below with two lions.

52. Kerala
Devil dancer wearing a polychromed, carved wood headdress, gold-leaf-covered wooden neck ornaments, armlets, bangles, and a waist ornament

48. Calcutta, West Bengal. *c.1789–1804*
"Company" drawing in watercolor by a Calcutta artist of a fisherman wearing a dye-colored, fiber-plaited, cylinder penis sheath
9 x 7¼ in. (23 x 18.5 cm)
Collection India Office Library and Records, London (48 xiii F. 92; Add. Or. 1189)

49. Dumka, Bihar
Santhal woman wearing a cylindrical ear plug made of a sectioned length of the bark-peeled, white inner stem of the shola pith plant (Aeschynomene aspera) to stretch the lobe opening. The plug is inserted dry, then made wet, when, like a sponge, it expands, stretching the hole size. White-cock tail feathers decorate the hair. (See also 291, 292, 295.)

49

48

50

51

52

Wood in Ornament

The wood of the trees that flourish in India exhibits a wonderful diversity of color and texture. Wood is used for the manufacture of ornaments that range from gigantic headdresses to armlets, bangles, beads, and buttons. It can be carved and inlaid with metal, mother of pearl, and other materials, which contributes to an infinite range of decorative treatments. Among the more popular ornamental woods, all generally close grained, are sandalwood, red sanders wood, sissoo, rosewood, and ebony.

The practice of tree worship (S: *vriksh puja*) is among the oldest of animist beliefs in India. Specific trees are believed to be inhabited by beneficent deieties, both major and minor, or evil spirits who must be propiated. Supplicants tie or hang votive offerings (S: *bali-danam*) from the branches of deity trees. Tree products—wood, leaves, flowers, fruits, and seeds—are considered suitable as sacrificial offerings to particular deity images as well as for manufacture of ritual imagery or seating for worshipers. Additionally, some trees are considered sacred to a particular Hindu deity, and such wood is therefore incorporated in ornaments used by devotees of that deity.

String Ornaments

The Sacred Thread and Caste

String, or thread, is perhaps the first hand-made artifact invented for the creation of ornaments. Thread (S: *sut;* H: *sutli*) symbolism adopted by Hindus (as in S: *sutra,* a religious manuscript, originally on palm leaf, held together by thread) originated in the concept of thread-making technology, which involves the ideas of connectiveness, continuity, and endlessness. When spinning thread, as long as fiber (matter) is added, thread can be created without a break. Ancient Hindus therefore chose thread as a symbol of sacredness embodied in a deeply significant religious and spiritual object: the sacred thread worn only by men deemed entitled to do so as an indication of the wearer's preferred status with the gods.

From the concepts of thread connection and endlessness comes an analogy between the sacred thread and the umbilical cord (S: *nabhi;* H: *naru*), literally the thread or cord of human existence by which humanity maintains its continuity with ancestors and, in India, assures the desirable purity of the birth line. The purpose of the sacred thread (S: *yagna-sutra* or *yagno-pavitam*) is to reaffirm a man's caste, that unalterable social status a Hindu automatically acquires at birth. The concept of caste originated in ancient Vedic times with light-skinned Aryan conquerors who invaded India and dominated the dark-skinned, indigenous Dravidians. Fostered by racial pride and skin-color prejudice, the Aryans' intention was to define social distinctions and create a ruling hierarchy with them at the apex. In Sanskrit, *varna* or "caste" means "color" or "external appearance," used to denote groups having different skin coloration.

Caste has been a jealously guarded institution throughout Indian history, especially by the high-born, who wished to maintain their privileges. Although legally void today, caste, particularly in rural India, still dominates Hindu society. It is perpetuated by caste rules that determine to a great extent whom an individual may marry and with whom one may attend religious, social, and political functions, or interdine.

Four main castes, each separate but functionally interdependent, form the structure of the Hindu social system. They are the Brahman, or sacerdotal caste; the Kshatriya or, traditionally, the military caste, which includes kings and soldiers; the Vaisyas, or mercantile community engaged in trade (which usually includes goldsmiths and gemstone merchants) and cultivators; and the Sudras, who comprise some artisans, mechanics, and laborers obliged to serve the three higher castes. A fifth group is the Chandalas, or outcastes, who are considered by others to be untouchables because they are either of mixed-caste origin or perform unskilled, menial work thought by the rest to be polluting. To this last group also belongs the majority of Indian aboriginal tribal people. The establishment of caste predetermined hereditary craft occupations, in which an individual's work was his *dharma* or moral and religious duty, resulted in the apprentice system by which fathers taught sons, thus assuring the transfer of skills and the perpetuation of a high standard of workmanship in all crafts.

Among the multiplicity of privileges accorded the four main castes was that Brahmans were permitted to wear ornaments of high quality gold and silver, Kshatriyas those of inferior quality precious metals, Vaisyas of brass, and the Sudras of iron. This distinction clearly recognizes the existence of a parallel between the hierarchy of social classes and the values given to metals. Of the five castes, only men in the first three have the sanctioned privilege of wearing the sacred thread. Exceptions exist, however, and in some places the right may also be extended to members of the Panchalas or five artisan subcastes: blacksmiths, carpenters, coppersmiths, stone cutters, and gold- and silversmiths (see 677).

The sacred thread actually starts with three threads, each ninety-six hands, or forty-eight yards, long. These are twisted together, then folded into three parts. The result is twisted again to form nine threads, and this is again folded into three, this time without twisting. Each end is fastened by a knot (S: *parwal*) and the three lengths joined. The three threads that result now also symbolize body, speech, and mind, and the knot their control. The thread is worn on the torso next to the skin, and passes over the left shoulder and under the right arm. Over time, the sacred thread was elaborated into many forms and could be of materials other than thread, such as pearls or gemstones strung on cord, as seen in representations of Hindu deities.

The sacred thread may be of cotton (Brahman), hemp (Kshatriya), or wool (Vaisya). All must be made by a Brahman priest. The investiture of the thread occurs in a solemn ceremony (*upanayana*), the most important in a Hindu boy's life. Performed by a Brahman priest, with the father in attendance on his son, initiation occurs at ages five to eight (Brahman), six to eleven (Kshatriya), and eight to twelve (Vaisya). During the ceremony, the boy is inaugurated by his teacher (*guru*) with his "chosen" or assigned tutelary deity (*ishta devata*) or personal god, who thereafter will assist him to attain his goals in life. With this ceremony, the youth acquires the right to study and become a pupil (*bramacharya*), the first of four stages in a Hindu man's life. The thread is renewed ceremonially by the various castes at different times of the year. This act gains the wearer remission of all sins committed during the past year. Old, worn threads are committed to water, considered to be ritually pure.

Because of the significance given to thread, it is used as a major element in other types of religious ornament, foremost among them, the rosary (see 101). Purely functional, it is used to string beads and metal units to compose an ornament (see 222, 235, 598–600).

The *Rakhi*

Knotted string or thread used as an ornament in India embodies the magical concept of having the power to create unity, to bind a deity, or to repel evil spirits once they are consecrated and worn on the body. Such an ornament is the *rakhi,* a string-type charm that symbolizes protection. The term *rakhi* is derived from the Sanskrit *raksh,* meaning "to guard." From this root comes the Hindi *rakhi,* a protector, guardian or watchman, and the term also designates the string charm itself.

The Rakhi Purnima Festival, also called Saluno, at which this cord amulet is used, is celebrated by public and private rituals on the full-moon day (*purnima,* an auspicious day of enormous significance for the performance of any Hindu ritual or sacrifice), of the Hindu calendar month of Sravana (July–August). Hence it is called *Rakhi Purnima* (Rakhi Full Moon). Fairs are held at ocean or river shores accompanied by ritual bathing and the worship of Varuna, a Vedic overlord of the primeval waters (*apah*).

On Rakhi Purnima day, celebrated in every Hindu household, as a form of sister-brother worship, sisters privately pay homage to their brothers, or if none such exist, to another man whom they wish to honor. In this veneration, as a mark of respect, the woman binds a cord (*rakhi*) in an act called *raksha bandha* (to tie the *rakhi*), on her brother's right wrist. By this sign of affection, each reminds the other of their mutual filial duties and responsibilities. On accepting the *rakhi,* the man becomes a *rakhi-bandh-bhai* (a *rakhi*-bound brother) to the woman who in turn receives a present from him, such as a new *sari,* or money.

As an amulet, the *rakhi* works in general to protect the wearer against evil spirits and bring good luck. However, should it ever be necessary that the woman needs the man's actual physical presence for assistance, should he not be nearby, custom decrees that she can send for him by forwarding to him by messenger one of her personal ornaments, such as a bracelet. With his acceptance of the bond, he is obliged to immediately come to her aid. The time of the *raksha-bandha* ceremony is also the occasion when a Brahman annually replaces the Brahmanical sacred cord (*yajno-pavita*) he has worn during the past year.

Formerly, the *rakhi* was simply a multi-strand length of cotton or silk threads, twisted or braided together, and dyed yellow with turmeric or saffron, or red with henna. These are still used, but most *rakhis* now are elaborated into far more complex ornaments. They are inspired perhaps by those of former times when, among the wealthy, the *rakhi* could be an expensive ornament of gold chains and gemstones, sent to the man wrapped in one of the woman's silk, satin, or gold brocade waist cloths (*kachhli*), which Tod terms "appropriate as an emblem of devotion." The man may never have seen the woman who sent it; nevertheless, he was bound by custom to protect her.

In Rajsathan and elsewhere, the contemporary simple cord *rakhi* is dominated by a centrally attached, large flower-like rosette often elaborate to an astonishing extent for an object intended for such short usage. Rosette materials include a fringe of gold or silver tinsel yarn, sequins, and at the center plastic ornaments, sometimes metalicized. The subject of these central ornaments can be religious, such as the image of a deity, or secular, such as representation of a currently popular movie star. Imitation pearls, beads, and cast-plastic faceted "gemstones" also enter the ornament repertoire. In effect, the *rakhi* rosette has become more important than the original cord, now reduced to the simple function of holding the rosette on the wrist.

The *Salgirah*

A cord ornament used in a Muslim rite has marked similarities with the *rakhi*. This is the *salgirah* (P: *sal,* year; *girah,* knot), a knotted amuletic cord that a parent ties around the wrist of a child on its first and each subsequent birthday as a sign of affection and protection.

53. Jodhpur, Rajasthan
In the raksha bandha or solana *ceremony, a sister ties a string and tinsel decoration* (raksha bandha) *on her brother's right wrist.*

54. Jodhpur, Rajasthan
Typical present-day rakhi wrist ornaments of tinsel, colored thread, flocked-velvet paper, fake pearls, and "gemstones"

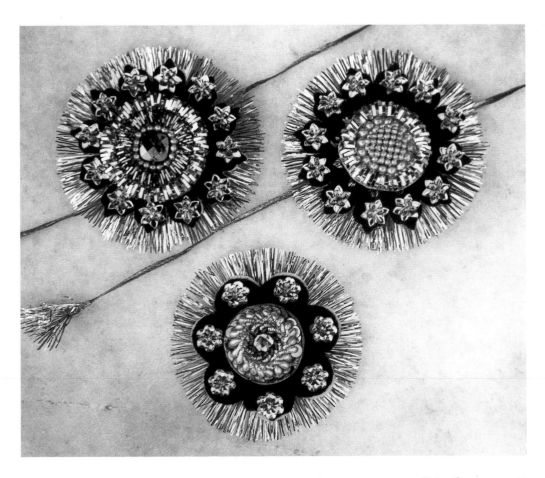

Animal Ornament: Materials and Subjects

Various animals and their products are widely believed to have amuletic powers. By their use, the idea prevails that the courage, strength, agility, and cleverness of the animal from which they came will be transferred to the wearer. In this category are the claws of the tiger, cheetah, leopard, lion, bear, and pangolin and animal horns and bones.

The teeth of many animals, especially those having sharply pointed incisors, are common amulets. Preferred are those of fierce animals such as lions, bears, and tigers (see page 91) who when attacked ferociously defend themselves. Probably the most widely used and popular animal tooth product is elephant ivory (see Ivory Bangles, page 177). The talons, feathers, and tongues of birds are also believed to possess amuletic value and are placed within amulet containers.

Feathers

The use of actual feathers, representations of stylized feathers (see 827), and bird images (see 421) in Indian jewelry and ornament is ancient, suggested perhaps by the inherent beauty of its many indigenous bird species. In India's diverse typography, different species inhabit the hot, sandy deserts of Rajasthan, the large, swampy area of the Rann of Kachchh in Gujarat, the humid evergreen forests of Assam and the southwestern Ghats, and the temperate, high-altitude valleys and cool mountain range of the Himalaya. The existence of about twelve hundred species representing twenty orders and seventy-five families of birds makes India one of the richest and most varied avifauna countries on the globe. From this vast assortment, the feathers of about seventy birds, considered attractive in color, form, or both, are used as ornament (see 74).

Indian bird feathers include all the colors of the spectrum. Their unfading color, ability to retain form, light weight, and the ease with which they can be manipulated account for the popularity of feathers for ornamental purposes. Among Hindus, the special appeal of feathers also relates to the association of particular birds with several important and lesser Hindu gods and goddesses. In Hindu mythology, each deity is assigned a vehicle (vahanam),

in some cases a bird who thus becomes sacred. Brahma, the creator, rides a goose or swan (see 625); Saraswati, his consort, the goddess of wisdom, patroness of the arts, music, and speech, a peacock; Vishnu, the preserver, rides Garuda, a mythic bird-man with the beak, wings, and talons of an eagle; Lakshmi, Vishnu's wife, goddess of feminine beauty and prosperity, in Bengal rides an owl; Karttikeya, god of war, also rides a peacock; Kamadeva, god of love, a parrot; and Bahucchara, a minor northern Indian goddess, a rooster.

In theory these associations should protect the birds, but in practice they do not. Despite the general Hindu injunction against taking life, and in particular birds, as expressed in early writings such as the *Ordinances of Manu* (*Manava-dharma shastra*), c. A.D. 500, where it is said, "Killing birds…produces defilement," birds are widely hunted for their feathers. Fowlers (H: *jalkar*) still ply this extensive trade and annually traverse the subcontinent in groups of five, especially in the months of September and October, when millions of migratory birds return to India. Bird skins and feathers are collected and sold to the feather merchant, who generally provides fowlers in advance with funds for their travel.

Until the end of the nineteenth century, a large trade in the export of Indian bird feathers to Europe existed, and even more went to Burma, Singapore, Malacca, and China. Realizing that the existence of widely hunted species was being threatened, as early as 1887 the British Indian Government instituted a law for the "Protection of Wild Birds and Game," which attempted to repress the unremitting slaughter of plumage birds in rural areas. In 1902, Lord Curzon, then Viceroy of India, issued a Notification to stop the export of feathers and skins, with the exception of bonafide specimens meant for ornithological study. Though feather export was checked, the internal feather trade continued, as did the capturing of birds to be reared in cages for the pleasure of people who admire their appearance, song, or their ability when trained to perform tricks and to speak.

The Indian feather trade encompasses entire bird skins, separate feathers, and quills—all of which find use for ornamental purposes. Feathers plucked from living birds,

which is sometimes done, or those freshly killed are usually brighter and more durable than when removed sometime after death or that have molted, although molted feathers are nevertheless commonly collected.

Feathers are made of keratin, a hornlike protein of which hair, horn, nails, and claws are also composed. They grow from the skin of a bird and constitute its outer cover or plumage. Complex in structure, flexible and strong, feathers, and the light, bony frame of a bird, are what provide power of flight. Feathers also protect the bird's body, retain body heat, and often camouflage it in its normal environment. In general, according to sexual dimorphism, male birds have brighter and more showy plumage, which they use to attract females during courtship and to chase away competing males. Birds, unlike most mammals, are not colorblind, and much to the detriment of birds with bright plumage, neither are humans. In most species, females tend to be nondescript in coloring, which helps them to camouflage themselves while hatching eggs and raising the young. For this reason, male birds are hunted more than females.

Several different types of feathers grow on a single bird, some more differentiated and decorative than others because of their color, length, or form. Some birds are killed for only a few special feathers they bear. Feathers most commonly sought after are the flight quills on wings and tail; the semiplumes that are downy, because their barbules lack the hooklike hamuli that hold a feather together; and the especially showy feathers grown by males during the mating season or incubation period, which are often molted afterward. The barrel, calamus, or quill—the feather's central, tapering, hollow shaft stripped of its other parts—is also used in India for decorative purposes, as in fan making.

Feather color is derived from the basic background pigment, when present, and the nature of the feather's reflecting surface. Unreflected light is absorbed, and reflected light is often interfered with and scattered, causing the attractive iridescent effect found in many feathers. In India feathers are generally used with their natural colors, though the feathers of ordinary domestic fowl (see 52) may be dyed and used as decoration.

Birds with Decorative Plumage

The feathers of numerous wild birds are used for body ornament, especially by tribal people all over India. Among these are bee-eaters, bitterns, bulbuls, drongos, great Indian bustard, grebes, hornbill, Indian darter or snakebird, Indian hoopoe, orioles, purple sunbird or honeysucker, red jungle fowl, shrikes, and storks. The most popular feathers for trade are given below.

Peacocks, family Phasianidae, are indigenous to India and southern Asia, and a peacock is the Indian national bird. In India they are found especially in Kachchh, Gujarat, Rajasthan, and parts of central India, although they are also found in all the drier areas and ascend to an altitude of about two thousand feet (610 m). The peacock, the male of its species, has the dubious distinction of being foremost among the birds that are hunted for their especially attractive and richly varied feathers. Head, neck, breast, and the very long upper tail-covert feathers that the peacock lifts and spreads to form a spectacular, vibrating

55. Adilabad District, Andhra Pradesh
Raj Gond tribal men dressed as Gusari dancers who perform in the festival when their Dandaro gods visit friendly neighboring villages during the Diwali festival (October). Dances and elaborate rituals are enacted to gain the favor of powerful, demonic beings who can influence one's fate. Their headdresses include many peacock feathers to give them an imposing height and accent movement. They also wear neck ornaments of beads, snail and cowrie shells, and seeds, and ankle bracelets of silver and brass.

fan—supported by the real tail feathers behind them—to attract peahens are all popular in body and object decoration. Best known are the tail-covert feathers with their terminal ocelli, whose centers are a peculiar bluish-green—designated peacock blue—encircled by an iridescent golden green. All its parts, including the loose barbules attached to the calamus, and the calamus itself stripped of barbules, are used for decoration. The form of the bird with its entire plumage is commonly represented in jewelry (see 575, 775).

Feathers as well as live peacocks were an item of commerce to countries of the Eastern Mediterranean long before the Christian era. Alexander the Great is known to have sent many back to Greece. Today peacock tail-covert feathers from India are found throughout the world. In recent times, farms have been established in Rajasthan for the purpose of rearing peafowl, whose molted feathers are collected for commerce.

Paroquets, family Psittacidae, or green parrots, so-called because their plumage is predominantly a bright green, are commonly seen in India, where they fly in large flocks. Because of the brilliant color of their plumage, they are extensively killed. Several varieties of paroquets exist, including the rose-ringed paroquet, the most common in India, with tail feathers about 10 inches (25.5 cm) long; the large Indian paroquet, with tail feathers more than 12 inches (30.5 cm) long; and the western blossom-headed paroquet, most common in southern India, with tail feathers more than 8 inches (20.3 cm) in length. Next to the peacock, the paroquet is second in the frequency of its representation in Indian folk art and jewelry (see 507, 572, 859).

Among the common birds in India, the piscivorous kingfisher, family Alcedinidae, lives wherever there is water containing fish, on which it feeds. A large group of birds, kingfishers are characterized generally by their long bills and short tails. It is the brilliant blue feathers that occur on its wings and body that have always attracted attention. Among the thirty-two species of Indian kingfishers, the most common are the Indian pied kingfisher, so-called because of its speckled black and white markings; the white-breasted kingfisher, whose tail and wings are a uniquely bright blue; and the great Indian kingfisher, whose back is bright pale blue and wings a greenish-blue. Until the early twentieth century, these bright blue feathers were shipped in quantity to China, where they were used as insets in silver and gold jewelry worn by court women and ornaments used by performers in Chinese opera.

The Indian roller, family Coraciidae, commonly called a blue jay, is another familiar Indian bird, sacred to Shiva. Most desirable to fowlers are its alternating bright- and dark-blue wing and tail feathers, not visible when the bird perches but readily seen when it is in flight (see 81).

Five species of egrets are found throughout India wherever marshlands or shallow lakes exist. All varieties of heron, family Ardeidae, generally are white and vary in size. The most common are the large egret, the small egret, and the cattle egret, which perches on the backs of cattle to feed on the insects the animal attracts and stirs up when grazing. Normally seen singly or in small groups, during the mating season they become gregarious and form rookeries in which they number in the thousands, allowing the fowler an opportunity to slaughter many. At this time egrets grow elongated, graceful, decomposed (barbs separated from each other) dorsal feathers on the lower back, which they erect in mating displays, then shed when this season has ended. It is these feathers, sometimes dyed black, that are the goal of fowlers (see 65, 395, 751).

The highly decorative feathers of most Indian pheasants, a numerous species of large, brilliantly colored, long-tailed gallinaceous birds of the family Phasianidae (to which peafowl also belong), have always been avidly collected for use in body ornament. Perhaps the most popular among them for this purpose are the feathers of the monal or Impeyan pheasant, who like all other true pheasants in India lives only at high altitudes throughout the Himalaya hills. The male's head crest of blue-green feathers, its gilded purple neck feathers, shining green and blue body and rufous feathers, and variegated red-yellow tail feathers are all used. The feathers of other pheasants, such as the horned pheasant, argus pheasant, Chir pheasant, Kalij pheasant, peacock pheasant, tragopan, and others are all popular.

Feather Ornaments

In times past, black heron feathers were worn to decorate battle helmets and turbans, as were egret feathers. Throughout Indian history, the greatest use of peacock feathers has been for fans (*pankhi*) and fly whisks (*morchal* or *chauri*). These were and are made of tight bunches of complete tail-covert feathers mounted in a silver handle. Formerly they were symbols of royalty and were used in Hindu religious ceremonies, as they still are today. One such brush is used in Jain temples to brush the floor as one advances toward an inner part of the temple in order to whisk aside and avoid trampling upon small insects, believed to be reincarnations.

It is common in India for certain craft specialties to be practiced only in particular places. For example in Mathura, Uttar Pradesh, a large handcraft industry exists in the manufacture of carefully made feather decorations used to ornament domestic and temple images of Hindu deities by fixing them to the head or crown (*mukut*) of the image. These decorations (*shringari*) in the form of miniature fans mainly employ the ocelli ends of peacock feathers (*mor phanki*) combined

56. Mathura, Uttar Pradesh
Peacock-feather ornaments (mor pankh shringar), ornamented with silver wire (zari), used to decorate small images of Hindu deities, especially those of Krishna
Length 2 to 5 in. (5 to 12 cm)

Each of the many forms produced here has a name: mor set, *kalanghira, resham kalangi, mor chanderka, etc. (Mor means "peacock"; kalangi, rising head ornament; resham, silk; chanderka, moon-shaped.) These were made by Ramchand Malpani and Seth Ganesh Das Kanhiya Lal Malpani, feather specialists in Bishram Bazaar, Mathura, and others there.*

57. Kullu, Himachal Pradesh
Male folk dancers perform during the famous Kullu Dussera festival (September–October), wearing their highly valued male monal-pheasant (Lophophorus impejanus), green- and blue-body and gilded-purple-neck feathers of this gorgeous bird, as hat ornaments (kalgi). Because the bird is now a protected species, old kalgi are valuable ancestral ornaments. This dancer also wears a woman's head ornament (daoni) on his hat.

58. Vrindavan, Uttar Pradesh. 19th century ➤
Cast-brass image of Balakrishna (Krishna as a child), holding a butterball (see 154)
Height 12⅝ in. (32 cm)
Collection the author, Porvoo

The kalangi-decorated cast-brass headdress separates from the head like a helmet. Here it is further ornamented with peacock feather ornaments from Mathura. The figure wears a miniature teen lara necklace of zari and fake pearls, also made in Mathura to decorate deity images. Such images are used in home shrines by Krishna devotees.

with colored silk (*resham*) and silver tinsel yarn (*zari*). For this reason they are also called *resham shringar*. Fabricated in a variety of forms and sizes, each has a special name based on its form, the materials used, or its placement in use (see 378).

Many amateur and professional dancers and actors use feathers placed on crowns or turbans as well as to decorate the body. In Mathura, several costume factories exist that produce ornaments and costumes for use by characters representing deities in the Ramlila, an annual nine-night festival celebrating the Hindu god Ram, whose life story is episodically reenacted each night. Accessories include crowns, ornaments, and garlands, all often richly decorated with feathers, tinsel yarn, false pearls, and glass beads (see 379). The costumes of the Kathakali dancers of Kerala make good use of feathers or feather parts. In rural tribal communities, festivities celebrated with dance are common, and participants have devised fantastic forms of body decoration, almost always including the use of feathers (see 52, 55).

Other feather uses can be mentioned. The whole wing of the Indian roller, the feathers spread out, are used by Nagas as ear ornaments. In Kullu, Himachal Pradesh, bunches of crest and neck feathers of the monal pheasant are highly esteemed on the cockades (*kalgi*) of men's hats (*bushari topi*), the feathers set in a silver holder. A single such ornament requires the feathers of ten birds.

Cowrie Shells: Marine Currency as Ornament

The cowrie shell (S: *kaparda*, H: *kauri*), a marine gastropod, belongs to the genus *Cyprea*, of which there are many species. The one of interest in Indian arts is *Cyprea moneta*, a small, oval, white species that lives in abundance in the waters of the Arabian Sea and the Indian Ocean, especially on the shores of the Indian-owned Laccadive and Maldive Islands, and elsewhere in East Africa, but not in the Atlantic Ocean.

What made this shell attractive and meaningful to Indians is its unique physiology, its hard, white, glossy surface, and its extreme durability. Like all cowries, its dorsal side is curved into a convex form, and the ventral side is divided lengthwise into two equal parts by a compressed opening, edged with serrations on one side, and depressed on the other. This form gave rise to important symbolic interpretations, discussed later. Because its convex surface form resembles the back of a pig Europeans called it *porcello* (from the Italian word for "pig"), from which in turn came the English word *porcelain*, suggested by the similarity of its shining white surface to Chinese porcelain. In fact, in the eighteenth and nineteenth centuries, cowries were brought to England

and calcined to produce powdered calcium carbonate, used as an ingredient in British porcelain manufacture.

For centuries, in India and other countries of Southeast Asia, as well as Africa, the prime importance of cowries was quite different: they were a form of low-value money (hence the subspecies designation *moneta*). Because of this value placed upon them, for more than two thousand years, up to the end of the nineteenth century, cowrie shells were an important item of trade between the Laccadives, Maldives, and continental India, especially with Bengal and Orissa, where they were in wide use as currency.

Cowrie shells washed up in quantity on the seashores, from where they were gathered. A fourteenth-century Muslim traveler in India, ibn-Batuta, reported that they were also cultivated by the natives in those islands. Leafy branches of the coconut palm tree were immersed in the sea, and upon them the shellfish spawned. After five to six months, the branches were removed from the water, the shellfish crop harvested and buried in sand pits along the shore to minimize the odor of decay when they died and putrefied. In two to three years, shells were dug up, cleaned, and sent in huge amounts in open native palmwood boats to Bay of Bengal ports in Bengal and Orissa, and to Bombay.

The islander seamen bartered the shells for oil, rice, and cloth. Except in these transactions, however, in their home territory they themselves never used cowries as currency, while in Bengal and Orissa cowries entered everyday commerce. This practice gradually diminished with the wider use of metal currency issued in the nineteenth century by the British in India. Cowries plummeted in value, and their low exchange rate made them impractical for continued use as currency.

From the beginning, cowries were put to other than fiduciary uses, but this monetary connotation, plus their ready availability at low cost, led to their decorative use as a symbolic display of wealth on the human body, on animals, and on utilitarian or decorative objects.

Cowries are particularly popular among Indian tribal people. They use them as button-type fasteners on jewelry; to decorate a hair-braid tassel, necklace, armlet, belt, apron, shawl, and a variety of other objects. Muria girls of Orissa wear them in masses on the bun at the back of the head, combined with pompons of brightly colored wool. The Bison-Horn Maria men of Bastar, Orissa, wear headdresses at their festivals that, besides the horns, include a headband with many attached strings of cowries that fall in a veil before the face. Almost all the Naga tribes of Nagaland use cowrie shells in a variety of body ornaments and to decorate parts of their ceremonial costumes. In many cases, the right to this use is reserved only for those who have earned it, which makes cowries in that place a symbol of power and prestige.

59. Madhya Pradesh
Folk dancers wearing amuletic cowrie-shell ornaments on head, chest, upper arm, waist, and calf

60. Jagdalpur, Bastar District, Madhya Pradesh
The so-called bison-horn Muria tribe is noted for its distinctive festive headdress of polished bull or buffalo horns and face veil of strings of cowrie shells worn as amulets against the evil eye, a universal Indian custom. Male animal horns used ornamentally are symbols of male potency, as are the black cock–tail feathers used in the Muria headdress ornament (gubha). They also wear cowrie shell–decorated bandoliers and armlets.

61. Andhra Pradesh
Bullock wearing an amuletic garland and head ornaments decorated with cowrie shells (Cypraea moneta) to protect it against the evil eye

When used in jewelry and on clothing, the shell must be pierced to be able to fix them to the foundation substance, or to string them. The substrate material to which they are attached can be woven fiber, heavy string, cloth, or leather. Normally, the cleft side is left visible because in repetition the resulting pattern is more decorative.

Cowries are also widely used in India for animal ornaments, a custom that symbolizes people's dependency on them. Cowrie-decorated collars, necklaces, leg ornaments, and trappings are made for bullocks, horses, and camels. In Rajasthan an especially attractive camel ornament is the *gorband*, a network of ropes decorated with cowrie shells, beads, mirrors, and tassels, spread out on the chest. Besides being decorative, cowrie shells used in animal ornaments always have the amuletic purpose of protecting the animal.

Only a few of the many examples of the use of cowries on objects can be mentioned. In Bengal, the outside of baskets traditionally made for the bride's dowry and used to hold jewelry or toiletries are completely decorated with cowries. In Rajasthan, the ring-shaped head pad (Raj: *idhoni*), placed on a woman's head to support her load, is frequently covered with cowries and ornamented with tassels ending in cowries and woolen yarn pompons. In Central India, Lamana gypsy women fixed cowries to the edges of blouses and around their skirt hems. Lamanas have used cowries for ornaments since Mughal times, when they were itinerant traders and suppliers to armies. Their peripatetic life-style helped to propa-gate and popularize cowrie use for decorative purposes.

In India, and elsewhere, the cowrie took on a powerful mystic symbolism linked to the cowrie's physical structure and the biology of the creature who inhabits it. Because of the almost indestructible nature of the shell substance, a form of calcium secreted by the mollusk's mantle, and its retention of a glossy, white surface, cowries symbolize immortality, an idea abetted by the fact that the cowrie gastropod is hermaphroditic. Its male and female procreative ability makes it appear to be magically self-multiplying, which contributed to its use in ornaments as a fertility symbol.

Most of all, it is the cowrie's physical appearance that gave rise to important symbolic interpretations. When held with its long axis vertical, the characteristic cleft of the underside of the shell suggests a resemblance to the human female pudendum, reinforcing its connotation as a fertility symbol. Seen with the cleft horizontally, the shell resembles an eye, which led to its widespread acceptance as a homeopathic amulet against the evil eye (*dristidosa*). This explains why it is often used in the ornaments of many tribal Indians and for animal trappings. The simple cowrie shell becomes a microcosm of Hindu metaphysics, encompassing the duality of sexuality, the mystery of fertility, and the continuum of the life cycle of birth, death, and regeneration —all concepts that form the basis of the Hindu worldview.

Snakes: Ophiolatry-Inspired Ornament

Snakes (S: *sarpa;* H: *nag;* Tam: *pambu*), are a frequent element in Indian jewelry design. Much of its popularity for this purpose developed out of religious belief and folklore, which in turn stemmed from the profusion of snakes indigenous to India. Fascination with snakes centers on their cold, scaly bodies, hypnotically fixed, unblinking eyes, flicking tongues, and the unpredictability and possibly dire effects of their attack—reasons enough to make the snake an object of both horror and admiration.

For millennia, snakes have been worshipped as minor deities by all classes of Hindus, and also by Buddhists, Jains, and followers of other Indian religions. (Snakes, *nagas,* have no relationship to the Naga tribes discussed ahead.) In general, the object of their worship seems to be to prevent the chance of becoming a victim of those snakes whose poison is deadly.

Also important to this reverence is the snake's form, which can be interpreted in terms of phallic symbolism, reinforced by the snake's prolificity in reproduction. Because snakes are connected with the concept of fertility, the belief prevails that when properly propitiated, snakes have the power to grant a wish for male offspring.

62. Andhra Pradesh
Bronze armlet (pambu-kappu) in the form of a hooded cobra, worn by a Jangam or Lingayat Shaivite priest or a dancer representing Bhadrakali Outer diameter 3½ in. (9 cm); height 5⁵⁄₁₆ in. (13.5 cm); weight 325 g Collection Mis, Brussels

Ornaments with snake-design motifs are especially common among southern Indian Dravidian people, which includes those speaking Kanarese, Malayalam, Telugu, and Tamil. A cup of a similar form is used to contain milk offered to cobras during the Hindu Nag Panchami holiday, when snake-worship (sarpa homa) ceremonies take place.

Seen against this broad background, the worship of snakes as sacred deities explains the widely prevailing custom of wearing jewelry bearing either symbolic reference to or actual representations of snakes. The highly adaptable snake form is used for head and braid ornaments, necklaces, earrings, armlets, bracelets, rings, belts, and anklets. It is found not only on images of deities but also in jewelry worn by all classes of people all over India.

The earliest physical evidence of serpent worship in India occurs in the Harappa Culture of the Indus Valley (c. 2500 B.C.). Seals discovered in Mohenjo-Daro and at other sites of this culture bear depictions of cobras, easily identified by their expanded hoods. Archaeologists and anthropologists believe they are connected with a proto-Shaivite deity who later, as Shiva, became a dominant deity in the Hindu pantheon.

Of all snakes indigenous to India, the one of special interest here because of its common representation in jewelry is the cobra (*Naja tripudians;* H: *nag;* Tam: *nagapambu*). The cobra is most commonly mentioned in Hindu mythology in connection with representations of Hindu gods, goddesses, and demi-gods, and

63. Ranchi, Bihar
Shaivite follower wearing a rudraksha-seed necklace (rudrakshmala) sacred to Shiva and two live cobras as a sign of his devotion to this deity

64. Tulunad, Karnataka
Cast-brass two-part belt, its top edged with cobra heads with expanded hoods; at the front is a cobra clasp.
Courtesy Rautenstrauch-Joest Museum für Volkerkunde, Köln

 63   64
 65   66

65. Hardwar, Uttar Pradesh
Shaivite fortune-tellers who chant predictions wearing silver head ornaments (nag mukut) with frontal cobra heads and central lingams, whose apexes spout black-dyed egret-feather crests and three sun discs

66. Kerala. 19th century
Gold marriage necklace (nagapadammalai) worn by Nayar women, consisting of forty-five stylized cobra heads represented by cabochon rubies and emeralds
Victoria and Albert Museum, London (1221-1872 IS)

as a design subject in Indian jewelry. Although it is the main snake of the snake cult, the cobra is related more to Shiva than to any other deity in the Hindu pantheon.

Cobras are peaceably disposed and seldom bite except in self-defense. When aroused, they raise their head from two to three feet above the ground and expand the hood, or capella. In nature this stance indicates a readiness for attack, but in Indian art, where it is commonly represented, the posture additionally signifies honorific protection of the subject with which it is associated. A single expanded cobra head or a group of heads in odd numbers of three, five, seven, nine, or eleven may form an overhanging canopy or shield that hovers over the head of a single deity, group of deities, a venerated subject or object such as the phallic symbol of Shiva (S. *linga*), or royalty. This posture, by implication, also protects the wearer.

The cobra is connected with Shiva in his aspect as the god of destruction. Most of the typical, iconographically correct ornaments he is represented as wearing are in the form of cobras, for which reason he is given the Sanskrit epithet Nagabhushana (the snake-decorated one). As a diadem, a cobra holds together the matted topknot piled on Shiva's head. His earrings, waist belt, and sacred thread are all formed of cobras. A person who wears jewelry in the form of cobras may be doing so as a means of indicating his or her devotion to Shiva.

Cobras are also associated with Karttikeya or Subramanya, the god of war and younger son of Shiva and Parvati. Subramanya is represented riding a peacock vehicle (*vahanam*), in whose talons a large, rearing, hood-expanded cobra is gripped, the peacock being a natural enemy of snakes.

The snake king Ananta, or Shesha, is associated with Vishnu. Ananta, whose name means "eternity," is represented in India as a coiled snake with its tail in its mouth. This circular form or an undulating line (as made by a snake in motion) lends itself well to use in jewelry forms, where they have the same symbolic meaning. A theme sometimes seen in jewelry is Ananta as a huge serpent with five, seven, or a thousand heads and hoods, floating on the eternal waters, upon whom Vishnu reclines while resting at the end of each period in the eternal cycle of creation, preservation, and destruction of the universe.

67. Tamil Nadu (opposite page)
Gold-braid ornament (jadanagam, braid serpent) worn by a Hindu bride or a Bharata-natyam dancer and formerly used by temple dancers (devadasis). This traditional head and braid ornament ensemble consists of six parts. At the top are the disc- and crescent-shaped units, together called the jadapillai. The disc symbolizes the sun (suriyan) and the crescent the new moon (amavasai). These are followed by the unit that represents the fragrant screwpine flower (thazhambu). The main body of the ornament, which is fixed on the triple braid, has the form of the multiheaded cobra Ananta-pambu, whose articulated, intertwined coils fall below. All units are ornamented with diamonds and cabochon-cut rubies. At the end is a three-part silk tassel (kuchcham or kunjalam), each part ending in a bell form (mani).
Courtesy Air India, Bombay

68. Madras, Tamil Nadu
Bazaar oleograph of Shiva or Mahadeva. Serpents are commonly worn as ornaments by Hindu deities. They are emblems of immortality because they are believed to be ageless. Shiva as depicted here is traditionally bedecked with serpents in his hair and around his neck, arms, wrists, fingers, waist, and ankles.

68

69. Maharashtra or Karnataka
Cast-brass ring (nandin-anguthi)
Private Collection, London

Worn by a Shiva Lingayat devotee, the ring depicts Shiva's vehicle, the bull, Nandin, who wears a lingayat amulet box containing a lingam, Shiva's most important symbol, flanked by three protecting hooded cobras.

69

◄ **70. Kerala**
18–19th century
Bronze female cuirass or body cover
Height 20 in. (51 cm)
Courtesy Sotheby's, London

Worn by a male dancer who represents the goddess Bhadra-kali, the cuirass is ornamented with two cobras, their heads on the shoulders and bodies falling between the breasts.

71. Tamil Nadu ➤
Gold-braid ornament (jadanagam) in the form of articulated, intertwined cobras
Collection Barbier-Mueller Museum, Geneva (2504-106)

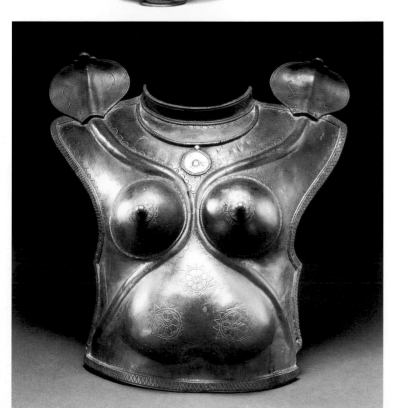

Mythic Nagas and Magic Gems

Vestigial instances of ancient serpent cults remain embedded in Hindu mythology. In the Hindu cosmological concept, the universe is described as being divided into three regions: the upper or heaven inhabited by the gods; the earth, inhabited by humans; and the netherworlds or hells below. Above the highest hells are seven lower worlds inhabited by various classes of beings. In one lower world, called Patala, the demigod Nagas reside in Nagaloka, the underworld sphere of serpents.

The mythological Nagas are ruled by three main chiefs: Sesha (Ananta), Vasuki, and Takshaka, a triad who also control their worldly counterparts: snakes on earth. Though Nagas are sometimes represented as normal snakes, they are also seen in Indian iconography—and therefore in jewelry too—as having a human torso to the waist, and a snake body below, with a cobra head or heads, hoods distended, protruding from their shoulders or the back of the head. Snakes are said to guard the mineral wealth of the world, and the capital of Patala, Bhogavati, possesses the richest collection of precious stones, more than the total in all other worlds. The Nagas, very much attached to this treasure, the envy of all the gods and demigods, assiduously guard it. From this idea comes the common belief in India that worldly serpents will always be found in the company of buried treasure and gemstones, which they guard, and also the unfounded belief that a cobra has a jewel embedded in its head. This idea may also be the origin of the use of the words nag *or* nagina *to indicate a stone set in a ring; and* nagina, *meaning a precious stone.*

72. Vishnupur, West Bengal
Gold armlets (nag taga) in the form of intertwined snakes with ruby eyes and central diamonds, referring to the myth that snakes, guardians of earthly treasures, including gemstones, have a gemstone in their head, which when secured is a remedy against pain and an antidote to poison

Naga Adornment:
Remnants of Neolithic Times

In an investigation into the origin and development of personal adornment worn by humankind, archaeologists are obliged to delve into the protohistoric past and formulate their conclusions from scant remaining evidence. Ethnologists and anthropologists who pursue this subject in India are far more fortunate because of the existence there of many aboriginal tribal groups (H: *adivasis*)—comprising about 25 million people—who live within its political boundaries. Their archaic cultures in many cases are probably not essentially different from that of Neolithic people who lived in India five thousand years ago, when the fundamental need for personal ornament, essentially for amuletic purposes, is presumed to have already been active. For centuries the practices and customs of these tribes have changed little from the time of their formation in past ages. These circumstances suggest that the ornaments worn by such groups are typical of kinds prevailing during the early development of Indian ornaments.

Exemplifying the democratic level of early cultural expression, which evolved from group sensibilities and later was under the influence of royal patronage, are the ornaments of the Naga tribes of northeastern India. The distinctive culture these people developed persisted almost intact into the mid-twentieth century, after which its decline becomes evident. A look at Naga ornaments from the period prior to that decline shows aspects of body decoration conceivably current at the naissance of personal adornment in India.

The various linguistically distinctive western (Angami, Sema, Rengma, and Lhota peoples), central (Ao, Sangtam, Yachumi, Chang, Phom, Tangkhul, Kalyo-Kengyu), eastern (Konyak), and southern (Kacha, Kabui, and Manipur) Naga tribes, totaling more than one million racially predominantly Mongoloid people, occupy a relatively small area in northeastern India and Burma (home to the Para and other Naga peoples). Ranging from the eastern Himalaya and the Assam Brahmaputra River valley, Naga territory extends southward toward the Bay of Bengal and separates Assam and West Bengal from Burma to the east. A varied terrain, it consists of mountains, high hills, narrow valleys, and jungles that sequester tribe from tribe, though not totally. Geography did, however, limit external contact, which reinforced the introversion of Naga cultural customs and concepts.

Also active in molding Naga culture was the fact that until the last century, Nagas were fundamentally self-sufficient in essential needs. Most of the materials they used for their ornaments came from local, relatively accessible sources, which accounts for their special character.

Religion has always been a factor in the development of ornaments. Those worn by the most primitive tribes in India generally show some evidence of Hindu cultural influence, but this is absent in the Naga ornaments, whose originality sprang from an early spiritual belief in animism. A primitive, superstition-based religion, its main precept is the idea that objects such as stones, plants, and living creatures possess a vital, natural energy principle or soul. Once a symbolic significance was ascribed to each type of material used, these ornaments became potent power objects.

Dramatically illustrating this concept was the Nagas' ornamental use of human hair harvested from the severed heads of male and female enemy Naga victims. The spirit of the former owner was believed to energize the wearer of the hair ornament with additional vitality. This gruesome practice was totally alien to Hindu, Buddhist, or Jain ideology.

Each Naga tribe declared its group identity with the distinctive ornaments they invented. In the general discussion of Nagas that follows, however, the reference is not to any particular Naga tribe, but is an abstraction of information meant to suggest the common essence of Naga cultural traits shared by all tribes.

No universal Naga language exists, as each tribe has its own dialect. The vernacular terms given here are those used by the Sema Nagas, a Western tribe (the third largest in number after the Konyak and the Ao), because Sema published references to the special vocabulary of ornament are the most extensive.

Naga Ceremonial Dress: Manifestations of Group Identity

Naga ornaments are one component of the elaborate ceremonial dress (*api*) assumed by Nagas at festival times, when the object is to win the favor of crop spirits or success in war. Each Naga tribe has its own ceremonial attire, which always includes a requisite complement of ornaments. A striking aspect of Naga festivities is the uniformity of dress and ornament, especially that worn by warriors (*kivimi*), which is far more decorative and elaborate than that of the women. Daily dress is simpler, though some ornaments are always worn.

In essence, the purpose of this more-or-less-uniform tribal livery is to bond the individual to solidarity with tribal membership. Any special status a person may possess in the group hierarchy is indicated by ornamental details and the design symbolism embodied in the artifacts worn. The motivation to acquire the right to own and wear costume and ornaments becomes the aspiration of every young person in the tribe. Their possession marks an individual's maturity and full entrance into tribal life.

Probably the most distinctive item of Naga ceremonial dress is the headdress worn on festive occasions by all male participants in warrior group dances. The head, according to Nagas, is the locus of the body's spiritual essence or soul (*abhongu*). The materials, colors, manufacture, and the manner in which each Naga tribal headdress is worn distinguish tribe from tribe and bond the wearer to the ideal clan image.

Ceremonial dress also required traditional shawls, baldrics, kilts, and aprons in specific formats in use by each tribe. Women wove these cloths on hip-tension looms. The man's shawl (*akhome* when plain; *asukedapi* when ornamented), still an important item in ceremonial dress today, was generally made in two joined lengths. A narrow baldric (*amlakha*), an

73. Kohima District, Nagaland
Angami Nagas at a festival wearing brass armlets and bracelets, headdresses of bamboo, colored yarns, and hornbill tail feathers. Each Naga tribe has distinctive festive ornaments and costumes worn to appease crop spirits.

74. Nagaland
Tangkhul Naga Chief Somra Tract, 1953, wearing a headdress (luhupa) used for special tribal occasions. It is decorated with red crab's-eye seeds (Abrus precatorius), the same seed universally used by Indian goldsmiths as weights when weighing precious metals and gemstones (see 679). Additionally, Job's-tears seeds, white-glass seed beads, black human-hair fringe, and hornbill tail feathers are fixed to a canework and cloth armature.

ornamental cloth used by several Naga groups, is worn diagonally across the chest, or crossing at the front in matching pairs over both shoulders. Its surface usually displays complex geometric patterns in designs made with the tabby weave of which the hip loom is capable. Some are fringed with woolen yarn, or red tie-dyed goat's hair, or are bound at one edge with bright yellow orchid stalk.

Ornaments (*anyhemoga*), essential to ceremonial dress and worn in profusion, were made of the highest quality materials and workmanship available. Not all the ornaments were made by the wearer, his family, or even the tribe. Some Naga groups made no ornaments themselves but purchased them from other Naga tribes who established specialty occupations in their manufacture. In this category are hats and helmets, armlets, gauntlets, leggings, and dance baskets. Also included are ceremonial spears (*angussah*) measuring approximately four to five feet in length and inventively ornamented with color-patterned cane plaiting; dyed human, goat, or dog hair; and orchid stem. These were never taken on head-hunting raids for fear they might be lost to an enemy. Ordinary spears were shorter and less profusely decorated. The *dao* sword (*aztha*) and the shield (*aztho*) could also be plain or ornamented for use in ceremonies. The fact that these items became objects of inter-Naga trade accounts for their similarity when they appear in use by different tribes.

Because of their important status significance, the prerogative to wear particular ornaments continues to be strictly controlled. Specific ornaments, or the configuration of decorative materials applied to the costume, may indicate a wearer's hereditary right to their use. Others require a socially approved means of earning that right. The fact that rights can

75. Nagaland
Chang Naga warriors, Tuensang Division, in ceremonial dress, which always includes special ornaments. They are wearing plaited canework helmets ornamented with a hornbill tail feather, red-dyed goat or bear hair, and two wild boar tusks. The chin strap is decorated with the ten claws of a tiger's two front paws. The tiger is held in superstitious awe by Nagas, and its claws can only be worn by a successful head-hunter. The cast-brass trophy-head pendants symbolize their success in head-hunting raids. The blouse is decorated with cowrie shells in a design permitted only to head-takers.

To designate taboos, Nagas in general use the Assamese loan word *genna*, meaning "forbidden," but each tribe has its own word. Taboos that concern only an individual, family, or a part of the community are termed *kenna*, and those that involve everyone *penna*.

Most taboos are concerned with the need for fertility in the annual agricultural cycle, the preservation of individual, family, and community health, and special individual circumstances at various stages of life. During these times the favor of supernatural spirit forces, upon which life and prosperity are believed to depend, is solicited by the performance of proper sacrifice.

Important individual or communal *gennas* are celebrated by several days of feasting, drinking, and animated communal dancing. The latter calls for wearing full ceremonial dress and the regalia of splendid ornaments, with special emphasis on the headdress.

Naga Ornaments: Symbols of Status and Power

The overriding purpose of practically all Naga warrior ornaments has been to display a language of power symbols understood by the particular tribe, and to a great extent by the entire Naga world. In this male-dominated society, body ornament proclaimed man's superiority over real or imagined human enemies and displayed visual evidence of male supremacy over both docile and dangerous, predatory animal adversaries.

These goals are understandable when such threats to existence have substance. However, much of this confrontation was invited, and one must conclude that, though partially theological in motivation, the pursuit of prey was fueled mainly by the males' need to evoke the esteem of their peers, both males and females, who by conditioning were not immune to the message. The lavish public display of symbolic ornaments at festivals proclaimed the wearer's manhood and status as a full-fledged member of the warrior class. Striving to achieve this goal dominated the efforts of all men who reached maturity in Naga society, and both men and women cooperated toward this realization. Not to own them meant relegation to an intolerable social position, not only for the individual, but his entire family.

In some Naga tribes, women acquired the right to wear certain ornaments because their male relatives had earned it. In general, however, women's ornaments had none of this direct warrior significance. Women did contribute their technical skill to the creation of men's ornaments, but their own objects were more concerned with aesthetics, social status, and value prestige.

be earned allows for a degree of social mobility and advancement to a higher status—a powerful motive for ornament possession.

At an earlier time, achieving these rights might necessitate a display of prowess in the hunt, success in head-taking, or (especially after the suppression of head-taking by the British administration of Naga territory early in this century) the sponsorship of Feasts of Merit (*sekrengi genna*), for which a certain number of domestic animals are sacrificed.

The entire community is invited to attend the ensuing feast. Only a wealthy man can act as sponsor, since earning the right to wear some ornaments might require up to five such feasts.

An important concept central to the Naga life-style is the periodic observance of traditional taboos that forbid certain practices and require the enactment of sacrifices. Strictly enforced, any violation is met with strong disapproval since transgression is believed to release evil forces.

76. Nagaland
Naga cast-brass trophy-head pendant worn on a necklace by a successful head-taker
Private Collection, Brussels

The face pattern simulates the tattooing on a Konyak-Thendu Naga man, the decapitated victim commemorated here.

Head-Taking: Interclan Ritualized Aggression

Of prime importance to the community and individual warrior, and central to the character of Naga ornaments, was the practice of beheading (*akutsu lulo*) an enemy, referred to in Naga literature as "head-taking." Though now banned, its symbolism is alive today. Not due to any personal vendetta, the incentive to commit this violent deed was the enactment of ritually institutionalized aggression intended to fulfill religious and social purposes. A human enemy head was believed to contain beneficial magical forces, relating to fertility or life essence, that could be manipulated by appropriate rituals to serve the living. Its presence meant the assurance of good crops, prosperity, and the prevention of human and domestic-animal illness.

A successful head-taker gained the right to wear specific ornaments whose form, or the materials of which they were made, symbolized his attainment of this status. Powerful communal and personal motives such as these condoned and perpetuated clan and village feuding and confrontation, whose ultimate purpose was head-taking and not territorial gain. Normally feuds did not pit one entire tribe against another, but generally involved the males of one or more of the village men's dormitories (*deka chang; morung*). Acquiring the right to wear prestigious ornaments did not end the desire for additional head-taking. Each subsequent success was commemorated by an additional cast-brass or carved-wood head worn like earned medals on a pendant, necklace, or hair ornament.

Head-taking, or an acceptable substituting act, was also essential to marriage. Without this accomplishment a man would not be entitled to wear the necessary ornaments of a warrior at festivals, for lack of which girls would consider him a coward, ridicule him, and refuse a marriage alliance.

On returning from a successful raid, the head would be placed on a special sacred rock in the village, or hung from a sacred tree outside the village, and a head-receiving ceremony performed involving all males in the village. The next day, all the village men in full ceremonial dress performed other rituals followed by group dancing and feasting. About a month later, the skull would be stored in racks in the men's dormitory along with others from past raids. From there the beneficial influence they exuded spread to the village and its occupants.

Inheritance Ornaments

Naga men generally marry between the ages of twenty and twenty-five, and women fifteen to twenty. When arranging a marriage, a bride's parents try to receive the highest possible "bride price" for their daughter, which always includes ornaments whose value is nearly half the total. In a woman's dowry (*akhu*), the beads and ornaments she brings with her become the husband's property.

Should a wife become an adulteress, her husband can divorce her and keep her ornaments. When a husband, due to incompatibility with his wife, divorces her, he returns the bride-price ornaments she brought with her. Should a husband mistreat his wife and, as a result, she leaves him, her ornaments also are returned to her.

Upon a man's death, the deceased is provided with objects and ornaments for use in the next world. Burial ornaments involve eschatological beliefs about death, resurrection, and immortality in which the deceased must have the same possessions in the next world that were owned while living. Women are buried with only a few beads.

Ancestral property, land or movable, is handed down in this patrilineal society from father to son(s). Heirloom ornaments are considered valuable movable possessions. When not in use they are normally kept in storage in a tightly woven, well-covered basket hung from rafters in the house loft. On suitable occasions they are taken down, washed with sand, and worn with evident pride. Ancestral jewelry is treasured by owners partly because some of it includes materials no longer available, such as old, long, or faceted carnelian beads, *deo mani* beads, old conch-shell beads, and some types of glass beads.

Upon a man's death, each of his sons receives an equal amount of movable property. As a woman generally cannot own land, her share is usually ornaments, and a widow is entitled to one third of the husband's movable property. Should there be no sons, a daughter can be the recipient. A dead woman's ornaments go to her father's heirs. Should a woman die in childbirth, her ornaments are thrown away as they are believed to be possessed by bad-luck spirits.

Spirits in Material Objects: Endowing the Inanimate with Soul

As Nagas were formerly animists, they believed the earth and sky were inhabited by spirits who possessed the power to affect the human condition. The Creator Spirit (*alhou*) determined man's earthly wealth in the form of his possessions.

Nagas also gave credence to the existence of a personal spirit (*agahu*) or "soul" that was attached to all their possessions, including ornaments. For this reason, according to tribal practice, when used jewelry passed as an inheritance or gift to another person, before the object was worn it was first placed on a dog to divest it of its old spirit, which might be antagonistic to the new owner, and transfer it to the animal. For the same reason, it was also common for the giver of an object to first wipe it on his or her body before passing it on. Should a bead necklace be stolen, its disapproving soul was said to depart in disgust, and if it were recovered, an offering would have to be made to it to persuade its soul to return.

Materials Used in Naga Ornaments

The choice of materials Nagas employed to create their ornaments, whether local, subcontinental, or imported, predetermined the forms these ornaments took. The distinctive imagery evoked by Naga ornaments can be taken as typical of the kinds used by many primitive, aboriginal tribes in India.

In selecting the materials Nagas turned to relatively durable substances that could to a degree withstand the damaging effects of exposure to humidity, sunlight, heat, cold, dust, smoke, fire, ravenous insect appetites, and other destructive natural forces that in India continually conspire to return man-made objects to elemental matter.

Most of these materials were used simply because of their physical qualities or attractive appearance. In some cases rarity placed a high value upon them. Ancient *deo-mani* glass beads and old faceted carnelian conch-shell beads are examples.

In the following discussion, objects incorporating several materials are mentioned under the one that dominates.

Local Materials: Exploiting Environmental Resources

Local materials used in Naga ornaments can be classified into organic and inorganic substances. Both are found in the immediate environment, or within the Naga Hill area. They could be gathered directly from the source or purchased by barter or for currency in the inland trade among Naga tribes.

Organic Vegetable Substances

Wildflowers (*akupu*) are used as ear ornaments, particularly by boys and young men who have not yet earned the right to use other materials. Placed in an earlobe opening (*akhamunu*), they are worn especially on *genna* days, and a favorite is the orchid. The ear hole is progressively distended to increase its size, first by rolls of cotton-wool, then bamboo sections. Eventually the opening becomes large enough for the insertion of metal, ivory, or rock-crystal ornaments.

Although today synthetic dyes have supplanted them, natural plant dyes were widely cultivated among the early Nagas, or were imported from plains sources. The main permanent colors used were red, blue, black, and natural, undyed white.

Blood-red dye is most admired by Nagas for coloring fibrous materials used for ornaments, artifacts, and clothing. Derived from a locally grown variety of madder (*Rubia sikkimensis*), its chief coloring principle, alizarin, a permanent red dye, is extracted from the plant's red roots. Although alizarin was synthesized in the West in 1869, the natural dye continued in use into the twentieth century in remote places such as Nagaland.

Indigo, an indigenous wild plant (*Strobilanthes flaccidifolius*) was cultivated as a source of blue dye. The vat dyeing method used was essentially the same as that employed for centuries in Indian indigo dyeing. Black was achieved by redyeing several times with indigo.

Of the many kinds of seeds (*atipithi*) used in Naga ornaments, particularly favored are the hard, shiny seeds commonly known in the West as Job's tears (*akithi; Coix lachryma*). The white variety were probably the predecessors of cowrie shells, and later they were used as cowrie substitutes when the latter were not available, or unaffordable. Like cowries, they are pierced and sewn to objects and clothing. Black plantain seeds (*Musa paradisiaca*) are strung into necklaces. Crab's-eye seeds (*Arbus precatorius*), red with a black spot, are used as beads and by the Tangkhul Nagas to decorate their headdress (*luhupa*) by mounting them on a background cloth spread with resin (*asutha*, see 74).

Bamboo (*akao; Bambusa*) in several varieties (common, little, large, and giant bamboo), each suited to different functions, is gathered from profusely growing wild sources. Widely used in making hats and headdresses,

it is also used as a supporting armature material for ornaments made of fibrous substances. The festive headdress of the Angami Nagas, among the most spectacular of all, is made on a bamboo structure woven basket fashion with bands of colored yarns.

Cane (*akkeh; Calamus*) a wild plant, is actually a scandent palm whose ropelike stems can reach a length of up to four hundred feet (102.5 m). Hollow, slender, flexible, very durable, and easy to dye, this material is used by Nagas for a variety of decorative and functional objects.

Hats (*akutsu 'kekkoh*) made of woven cane and bamboo seasoned for strength are a form of ceremonial helmet or headdress worn by most Naga tribes and other peoples of northeast India.

Cane hats made of tightly woven split-cane strips, a product of specialists, were acquired by barter from the Naga tribes who produced them. What makes a tribal hat distinctive is its ornamentation, which might include hornbill heads and casques, wild boar's tusks, horns, bear's fur, boar's bristles, or long switches of black human hair or hair dyed red. The right to wear such helmets was confined to warriors.

Cane armlets decorated with seeds, cowries, and hair were worn by a warrior who had taken a victim's whole arm as a trophy. After a head was taken, cuts were made in the victim's arms and legs to earn the slayer the right to wear armlets and leggings.

Cane belts of several strands, tightly pinching the waist, were worn by Konyak men. Formerly they were worn without an apron so that the genitals were exposed, a custom still practiced in remote places.

Cane upper leg rings (*pissoh*) dyed red or black, worn by men, are placed tightly just below the knee on the upper calf of both legs. Claimed by Nagas to be an aid when climbing hills with heavy loads, in time they cause varicose veins.

Cane leggings (*apkuki*) that go from below the knee to the ankle are worn as a part of festive dress to symbolize the taking of a human leg trophy. In these, narrow cane strips are tightly plaited, in a diagonal pattern, directly on the leg and ankle and conform to their shape. Those purchased by barter are made by the Angami or Kalyo-Kengyu Nagas, who sell them for high prices. To make them usable for any leg conformation, commercial leggings either have a slit at the narrow end near the ankle or are constructed entirely open at the side for ease in removal and storage.

Orchids abound in the moist, hilly jungle areas of Nagaland. The stem (*arozi*) of a wild orchid (*ayi-khwo*), admired for its lasting bright yellow color, shining surface, and durability, is gathered, pressed flat, dried, and then plaited, woven, or wrapped on many fibrous ornaments and objects (see 81).

Local woods (*asu*) of various kinds are used for decorative purposes, especially close-

77. Nagaland
Konyak-Thendu Naga man with tattooed face and blackened teeth. The ornaments worn here consist of glass-bead necklaces, a transverse wooden hair ornament passed through the hair knot, inserted with mirror pieces, and a woven cane hat. The ear ornaments are the polished horns of the Himalayan serow (Naemorhedus thar), a long-haired goat-antelope with short, slightly curved, black horns. Wearing the horns of a male animal symbolizes male virility. Originally the tattooing occurred only after taking a trophy head, but the practice has broadened. Other tribes that practice tattooing include the men of the Chang Nagas and the women of the Ao, Phom, and Sangtam Nagas.

grained varieties suited to carving, done by men. Hair ornaments of carved wood, often in the form of a long, flat, rectangular stick shape with end ornaments of human heads or hands, indicate that the wearer has taken their equivalents or assisted in killing an enemy. Worn by men, they are placed horizontally through a loop of knotted hair at the back of the head. Armlets made of a light, ivory-colored, densely grained wood are used as a substitute for armlets of real ivory, which it closely resembles. Pendants carved in wood or cast in metal, representing a human head or heads taken, are worn by warriors. In some tribes, combs of wood with incised ornaments are still given by young men to girls.

Cotton (*asupha*), formerly cultivated by Nagas and hand-spun into yarns, was woven into shawls, baldrics, and other garment cloths. Cotton cord (*asupa akoghi*) or thread (*ayeho*), hand-spun from locally grown cotton, was used for stringing beads and in the construction of ornaments. Very strong and durable, it served these necklaces through many generations of use. Today all the cotton yarn Nagas use is Indian mill-spun and imported to Nagaland by dealers. Mill-made cotton cloth in predyed

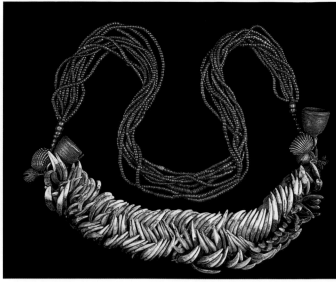

79

78. Nagaland
Konyak Naga man's head ornament of glass seed beads (also used for overhead supporting strings), tie-dyed goat-hair tassels, and red cloth ornamented with brass circular bosses
Collection Ghysels, Brussels

79. Nagaland
Naga pangolin claw bandolier, worn diagonally on the body
Collection Torbjörn and Judy Carlsson, Art Expo, Washington, D.C.

78

colors is used in ornament construction and decoration as well as for garments.

Cotton wool (*akinsupha*) wads are worn by several Naga tribes in the ear hole to enlarge the opening in order to make possible the use of large-diameter ear plugs. A ball of cotton wool is also used as a substitute for the immature, downy feathers of some variety of birds, often used for ear pompons.

Nettle (*apoghu; Urticacaea debregasia*), a common wild plant of the stinging variety, is a source of a very strong fiber used by Nagas to make string for threading and supporting heavy bead necklaces. Its use probably predates cotton.

Organic Animal Materials

As already mentioned, head-hunting (*ipfughelo*), to take a human head and its hair (*akutsuasa*) in a raid by decapitating the fallen victim, was formerly the aim of every young male Naga, who by this act attained the status of a warrior.

The importance of human hair lay in its symbolic meaning. The belief prevailed that the potency, vital life principle, and fertility of the slain enemy resided in that person's head and hair. When the hair passed to the slayer, it acted to fortify his own. This idea imbued human hair with an especially potent and powerful symbolism. Most highly valued was a woman's hair because it was often long and harder to obtain as women were less frequently encountered in a raid than men. Using hair

taken from a living person by their consent or by force was rare. Unwillingness to allow their hair to be cut and so used was based on the belief that misfortune, and possibly the death of its owner, would ensue.

When a supply of human hair was unavailable, an acceptable substitute was the hair of domestic animals such as the dog (*atsu*), especially a long, white-haired variety, (*atumatsu*), or goat (*ahya*) whose preferably white, therefore dyeable hair is sufficiently long for this purpose. Black animal hair was also used, but red-dyed hair was favored because it suggested blood spurting from the body of a decapitated victim. White goat's hair was commonly tied at intervals before dyeing it red, and the result is a horizontally striped effect of alternating red and white.

Hair was left long in irregular lengths, or trimmed to an even, brushlike fringe (*samogho*), an effect to which the stiff hair of a goat lent itself. The black hair-bristles of a wild boar and the long hair on the back of a serow goat antelope were also used in decorating hats and ornaments.

Skin and hair (*ayikwo*) of the black Himalayan bear is used in body ornaments, especially for decorating a helmet, or on leggings. This too had symbolic value associated with the fierceness of the animal, who aggressively defends itself when hunted. A headband of black Himalayan bear fur, supported by a cane armature to which hornbill tail feathers are attached upright, is worn on ceremonial

occasions by the Sema and the Yimchungr Nagas. The fur of long-haired monkeys, such as that of the langur, is also used in ornaments.

The claws (*aoumtsu*) of fierce animals such as the tiger, leopard, and bear were considered to be powerful amulets (*agha*), but so were the long, curved claws of the lethargic pangolin, a local anteater. It was believed that the strength of the former two and the sagacity of the latter would be imparted to the person who acquired them.

Tiger (*angshu; abolangshu*) claws, like those of the leopard (*anyenju*), are normally retracted, bared only when attacking. Possessing them was obvious proof of a man's stamina, bravery, and superiority over wild beasts. Tiger's claws were set in necklaces and, among the Kalyo-Kengyu Nagas, attached to the chin straps of a helmet to frame the wearer's face.

The claws of the unique scaly Indian anteater, or pangolin (*ashephu*), may be mistaken for teeth when seen in a distinctive style of long necklace or baldric made by Nagas. Each front paw grows five long, curved claws used in this necklace, which typically contains approximately three hundred pierced and strung claws; thus, at least sixty animals must be sacrificed for one necklace. Pangolins are not abundant, and accumulating sufficient claws for such a necklace may take a considerable time. As a result of indiscriminate killing, Nagaland pangolins are a threatened species. A powerful protective amulet, the necklace is worn as a baldric over one shoulder by a shaman whose tribal function is to manipulate spiritual power for human benefit.

Using an animal's horns (*aikibo*) for personal adornment probably originated as a form of totemism in which the material distinguished a family, clan, or tribe. No such practice exists today among Nagas but possibly did in the past, as evidenced by the horn motif connected with the idea of sacrifice commonly appearing in the wood-carved decorations of men's dormitories, textile decoration, the ornamentation of shell earrings, and in men's chest tattoos.

Animal horns used for body ornaments and the decoration of artifacts include those of wild and domestic buffalo, the bison, the mithan or gayal, the Himalayan goat antelope or serow, several variety of deer, and the single-horned rhinoceros. The small, end-pointed horns of the serow are smoothed and used in pairs as ear ornaments placed in stretched earlobe holes (see 77). Narrow, straight, rectangular-sectioned horn lengths, pierced with holes at regular intervals, are used as strand separators in bead necklaces and girdles such as those worn by Sema women. In some cases the entire horn is used. A pair of buffalo horns placed on a helmet signifies the leader of an attack.

Because human skulls (*akutsu paghe*) are too large for use as ornaments, to commemorate the event of acquiring one, substitutes in the form of smaller animal skulls are worn. Among the animal skulls most commonly used was the monkey, including the Bengal monkey, the tailless, arboreal gibbon, the hill monkey, and the long-tailed langur, whose skull is somewhat larger than that of the others mentioned. For ritual reasons some skulls were painted white.

Animal bone (*aghu*) was often carved into beads. Deer bone was used for square-sectioned bead-strand spacers (see 94), their upper surface occasionally decorated with a burned-dot design made with a heated, pointed metal tool. Flat bone lengths about one foot long (30.5 cm), used as hair ornaments placed through a topknot at the back of the head, were similarly decorated.

The teeth (*ahu*) of carnivorous, predator animals such as bears and tigers were highly valued because their possession indicated the wearer's bravery in the hunt. Pierced, they could be strung into a necklace or fixed in a metal wire mount and used in a pendant.

The wild boar (*a-li; amini*) is ferocious when attacked and therefore a proper adversary to prove bravery. The large, lethal tusks (*a-hu˙ a-li*) that curl alongside the head of a mature boar were used for ear ornaments, collars, and necklaces, as well as to ornament cane hats or headdresses worn with ceremonial dress. The right to wear one pair was earned by taking the head of an enemy; "touching flesh," i.e. spearing a victim; or killing a tiger or leopard. A common Naga necklace worn by several tribes was a collar (*aminihu*) of two to six boar's tusks matched for size and degree of

curvature, root ends bound with cane, ornamented at the front with a concave, rounded piece of conch shell into which a carnelian bead is placed, and closed at the back with a large conch shell bead.

Attractive parts of various birds that inhabit Nagaland jungles, especially feathers, wings, heads, and casques, are commonly used as elements in Naga ornaments. Down, the soft, fluffy, white, decomposed feathers of immature birds, is used by the Amgami and Sangtam Nagas to make pompons worn by both sexes singly or in pairs in each ear hole. Other feathers used in Naga headdresses come from several kinds of birds, including pheasants such as the tragopan, cock (the male of gallinaceous birds), including domestic fowl, green parrot, bulbul, male scarlet minivet, green pigeon, and the black drongo.

Entire bird's wings (*akichibo*) are used for ear ornaments, spread out like a fan for maximum display. Favored for this purpose are the wings of the Indian roller or blue jay (*Coracias benghalensis*), with its brilliant, iridescent blue feathers, but other bird wings are similarly used.

Hornbills, venerated by all Nagas, are probably the most symbolically significant bird in reference to Naga ornaments. Some Naga tribes claim mythic descent from the hornbill, which may have been a totem symbol. Their veneration, however, does not prevent Nagas from hunting it for its tail feathers, bill, head and casque—all used whole or in parts in Naga body decoration.

The genus *Hornbill* constitutes several large nonpasserine birds of the family Bucerotidae. Those inhabiting Nagaland jungles include the great hornbill (*wongsorai; aghacho; Dicnoceros bicornis*); rufous-necked hornbill (*awutsa; Aceros nepalensis*); Malayan wreather hornbill (*shefu; Rhytidoceros undulatus*); and the pied hornbill (*ghaboshutoki; Anthracoceros albirostris*). Different species inhabit extensive areas of northeast India, Nepal, Burma, and southern Asia in general. All these big birds are remarkable for the enormous size of their curving bill (*aghao-kechi*), in the largest variety surmounted by an almost equally immense, solid, hornlike process or casque.

The most sought after species of hornbill found in Nagaland is the great hornbill (*wongsorai*), which has the largest beak, head, and casque, measuring about one foot (30.5 cm) in its greatest dimension. Its characteristic white tail feathers, marked by a distinctive two- to four-inch (5–10 cm)-wide black band that crosses them near the extreme end, are about one foot long (see 74).

These tail feathers (*aghachomhi*), which Nagas consider to be most attractive, are the bird's most desirable part because of the symbolic significance Nagas attribute to them. The right to wear from one to three in a headdress was earned, according to different tribes, only by having taken an enemy's head, or having "touched flesh" in a raid, or performed a certain number of feats of merit. This feather, regarded by all as an indication of prowess, is the most important insignia of a warrior successful in head hunting and, therefore, a prized status symbol. Hornbill feathers were never worn in a raid for fear they might be lost to an enemy.

The great hornbill's head, beak, and casque and those of smaller hornbills are used by several Naga tribes to embellish the front-top of a ceremonial canework hat-helmet or split longitudinally in half and worn as addorsed decorations at its sides.

The greenish iridescent wing cases, the elytra of certain species of beetles, especially *Chrysochroa bivittata,* are used whole or in parts to decorate head ornaments, hats, hanging earrings, necklaces, and objects such as baskets. They are surprisingly durable and retain their color indefinitely (see 44). According to a common Naga eschatological belief, the souls of the dead enter insects such as beetles and butterflies. Consequently, wing cases are used to embody the souls of departed ancestors.

Imported Materials: Resources Beyond Nagaland

Imported materials can also be divided into organic and inorganic groups, and they came from Indian or foreign sources. Since the early nineteenth century, the isolation of the Nagas was relative, not absolute. Despite intertribal hostilities, a pattern of commercial relations among tribes was established, especially with those tribes in which Naga craftsmen practiced specialty arts and produced products of adornment for barter or sale. Because these were purchased, they can be thought of as imports from other Nagas.

Well before Naga cultural capitulation commenced in the mid-nineteenth century, intrepid Nagas emerged from their hill territories to travel for the purpose of trade. Commercial entrepots established in the nearby plains areas of the Hinduized Brahmaputra River Valley of Assam, and in Manipur, were owned by Indian Marwari merchants who stocked products that catered to the Naga taste for self-adornment. For example copper, brass, and iron were available in half-finished forms of wire, sheet, and bulk for transformation into ornaments and functional objects.

Motivated by a sense of adventure, groups of Naga men, usually including one who had learned Hindi, the Indian *lingua franca,* or an Assamese dialect, made annual cold-weather journeys as far as Calcutta. There they located the bazaar sources of nonlocal cowrie and conch shells, yarns, and cloth and carried them back home for their own use and resale. The commercial success of such journeys assured their seasonal repetition but contri-buted to the establishment of an increasingly money-oriented Naga economy that ultimately replaced barter.

One find to which Nagas responded was the ready-made Bengali cast-brass box whose cover bore a representation of the head of the Bengali Hindu snake goddess Manasa. Its traditional Bengali function is to hold sacrificial red powder. Eminently suited to the Naga purpose of serving as a surrogate severed-head symbol, it was worn as a pendant by successful Naga head hunters, as documented in many photographs.

Ivory

Elephant (*akaha*) ivory (*akahahu*) is the most expensive material used for Naga ornaments. Elephants do not normally live in Naga hill territories but when because of hunger they are forced up into the hills, they are not liked because they greatly damage crops. The ivory used in Naga ornaments originally came to them by hunting, but since the last century it has been purchased by Angami Nagas from plains traders, or from Calcutta or Varanasi.

Armlets of ivory (*akahaghi*) are the most highly valued of Naga ornaments; only warriors are entitled to wear them. Made of wide sections of elephant tusk, they are normally worn in pairs above the elbow, or one on the right arm.

These armlets typically are from two and one half to three and one half inches (6.3–8.8 cm) deep and have a thickness of one inch (2.5 cm) or more. The diameter of the central opening occurs naturally in the tusk—it is the space formerly occupied by the tooth nerve, which is removed. Only the upper part, where

82. Nagaland
Upper armlets of ivory-tusk sections (ketoh or chethoh), usually worn in pairs, indicating success in head-taking (see 75). Second from left: Angami Naga; others: Konyak Naga Height of largest 5⅞ in. (14.9 cm); diameter 4½ in. (11.4 cm) Collection Ghysels, Brussels

83. Nagaland
Sema Naga leather belt ornamented with cowrie shells and tassels
31⁵⁄₁₆ x 1³⁄₈ in. (80.5 x 3.4 cm); length of tassel 5½ in. (14 cm)
Collection Mis, Brussels

84. Nagaland
Ao Naga breast ornament, with central, now-crazed mirror, stitched paddy
grains, cowrie shells, and red glass beads. Used for a ritual purpose
Diameter 9⁵⁄₁₆ in. (23.7 cm)
Collection Museum of Mankind, London (1934 As–78)

Cowrie shells (*kedah*) are used in earrings, necklaces, bracelets, and belts and on garments such as kilts, aprons, and shawls. Most Naga groups restricted their use to men because their specific symbolism on particular objects referred to men. An exception was their use in belts by Sema and Rengma women. Their presence indicated a warrior of great prowess—someone who had speared an enemy, taken a head, burned an enemy village, killed a tiger, earned a reputation for amatory conquests—or the performance of an important animal sacrifice such as that of a *mithun*.

When cowrie shells are mounted on an object used by a man, they are sewn to it by the wearer, not by a woman. To prepare it for mounting on a flat surface such as a warrior's apron, the cowrie is ground on a stone to make it flat at the side opposite its opening. This permitted multiple shells to be mounted more regularly in series.

Cowrie-decorated gauntlets (*aouka-as'uka*), the shells placed closely together on a cloth or cane ground, are worn by the Konyak and Sema Nagas. Upper and lower gauntlet edges are frequently ornamented with a short, stiff, or long loose fringe of red-dyed hair. Only a warrior who has taken an enemy head or a hand trophy had the right to wear these gauntlets.

a suitably sized opening occurs, can be used for armlets. In time, the armlet, like all ivory, acquires an attractive natural yellow-to-brown patina often checked with a network of cracks. When ivory armlets are not affordable, substitutes made of a densely grained white wood resembling ivory are used.

Ivory ear plugs are worn by some Naga groups. Circular in form, about two inches in diameter and one inch in thickness, they are simply placed in an enlarged ear-lobe opening and held there by the lobe that passes around them.

Shells

Nagaland is landlocked hill territory relatively far from any sea. Kohima, its capital, is nearly 300 miles (475 km) from the Bay of Bengal as the crow flies and farther by roads. The nearest place with established markets for conch and cowrie shells is the port city of Calcutta, 400 miles (650 km) away. The actual origin of cowrie shells is more than six times that distance, in the Maldive and Laccadive Islands (see page 47). Contributing to their attraction is the fact that formerly they were used as a type of exchange currency, especially in Bengal, but also throughout tribal India. The prolific use of cowrie shells to decorate a variety of Naga ornaments and objects essentially symbolizes a display of material wealth.

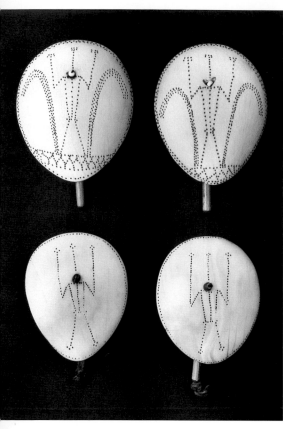

Belts (*kheki*), such as one decorated with cowries (*asiasakikheki*), worn at the waist often include ornamentation with red-dyed goat hair and yellow orchid stem. Men's aprons decorated with cowrie shells (*lapuchoh kuhu*) are the sign of a warrior and reserved only for those who had earned the right, either by inheritance, social position in the tribe, or by achievements in battles and raids. They could also be worn by an upper-echelon person who had performed ceremonial village feasts of merit.

Shoulder ornaments called *aghugu* (meaning, literally, "enemy's teeth") approximately 4 inches wide, of wood ornamented with an abstract design of two opposing curved rows of cowrie shells, its ends and bottom fringed with red hair, are said to represent blood pouring from the grimacing toothed mouth of an enemy whose head was severed.

Conch shells are commonly used in Naga ornaments. (For discussion of their origin, see page 175.) Shells can be used whole, such as those worn as a pendant by an aged warrior of renown. Half-shells are placed as a counterpoise at the back of a large, heavy bead necklace to balance its weight (see 94). Cross sections and whole shells with the inner structure removed are used as wrist ornaments.

This inner structure, called the columella (the central column or axis of a spiral univalve shell, such as the conch), removed when making a conch-shell bangle, was used primarily to make beads. They were made mainly by the Angami Nagas of Khonoma and widely traded among most Naga tribes. The longer the better, biconically tapered and highly polished, they were placed in a grooved wooden block to hold them down on a saddle-shaped stone. Pierced longitudinally, they were strung in graded lengths in several rows in a necklace called an *ashoghila*. Their presence considerably increases the value of that ornament. Conch-shell beads are rarely made today, which increases the value of those in old ornaments. Imitation conch-shell beads made of white agate or white milk glass are manufactured in India and used in the same way as the original.

Conch-shell ear ornaments, formed into convex ovals from shell pieces large enough to cover the ear, are often decorated with dot-drilled figurative motifs or abstract designs, such as the ubiquitous V-form symbolizing buffalo horns. Conch-shell buttons are commonly used as a closing device on a necklace or to fasten a loin cloth holding belt or girdle (see 97).

▲ **85. Nagaland**
Konyak Naga conch-shell ear covers
3⅜ x 2¹⁵⁄₁₆ in. (8.5 x 6.8 cm); weight of pair 46 g
Collection Ghysels, Brussels

The covers can be worn as shown or with attached long tassels of red-dyed hair or fur. The hot-poker-work dot-decoration design represents anthropomorphic figures, here probably warriors.

▼ **86. Nagaland**
Pair of dyed canework cuffs ornamented with cowrie shells
Collection Linda Pastorino, New York

Metals

Naga culture used metal objects but did not develop an indigenous technology of metallurgy in the mining and extracting of metals from ores (hence their designation as a Neolithic culture). Raw metals in the form of wire, sheet, and bar ingots came to them from outside Naga territory.

In some Naga groups, metal artisans today possess the necessary skills to earn their livelihood by making metal jewelry and implements. Most of the metal ornaments they used in the past and today, however, are made by non-Naga metalworkers established outside the community, either in the Assamese plains area of the Brahmaputra River Valley to the west of Nagaland or in Manipur to the south. Nagas went there to purchase ready-made Naga ornaments or, as in the case of the cast-brass pendants and necklaces Nagas wore to commemorate heads taken, to commission objects in which they specified the desired numbers of heads to be depicted. Some metal objects were also made by itinerant Hindu metalsmiths who went into and worked in Naga territory.

Brass (*asapui*), an alloy of copper and zinc that melts at a lower temperature than does copper, was preferred by Nagas for their metal ornaments. Three basic methods are employed in Naga ornaments: sheet metal fabrication, forging, and lost-wax casting. In none of these objects is any soldering technique employed, but in some, cold joining systems such as rivets are used.

The Konyak and the Kalyo-Kengyu Naga are proficient in sheet-metal fabrication. The most characteristic product is the round-bell metal gong or disc (*ai*) with a small, raised central boss pierced by a small hole for mounting, placed at the center front of the ceremonial apron used by Chang, Rengma, Sema, and Konyak Naga warriors. Brass plaques were also used in the decoration of a man's girdle worn by some Konyak Nagas, the overlapping plates cold-joined by rivets. An armlet made of sheet metal with regularly spaced projecting points, formerly worn by Konyak Nagas, is no longer made and hence a valued ancestral object.

Brass wire and rod were used to make various types of ornaments used by both men and women. In most the wire is round, but it could also be forged flat, then formed into a spiral.

Brass-wire finger rings (*asaphu*) were not originally worn by Nagas, but the practice is growing. These are generally made of round brass wire or white metal.

Brass wire in spiral form is used for several ornaments. Ao women wear brass spiral temple ornaments supported by a cord that passes over the head. Angami and Konyak women wear spiral earrings, often two in each ear. Chang and Konyak women wear upper armlets made by hammering brass wire flat, then wrapping it around a wooden mandrel in at least fifteen turns to form a cylindrical helix spiral.

87. Nagaland
Konyak Naga cast-brass pendant of six trophy heads
Private Collection, Brussels

The mouth markings indicate that they were stitched closed to retain the potent spirit of the deceased.

88. Nagaland
Cast-brass wristlets worn by eastern Chang Nagas in Lunghao Village, northern Burma, and southern Konyak Nagas
Outer diameter 3¹³/₁₆ in. (14.8 cm); inner diameter 3⅛ in. (8 cm); weight of pair 206 g
Collection Ghysels, Brussels

Presumed to be made in northern Burma, the wristlets probably were brought to the Nagas through barter. Spiked wristlets worn by men are intended for use as weapons in hand-to-hand combat.

89. Nagaland.
Late 19th century
Forged-brass bracelets with dot-punched patterns on the expanded terminal heads, worn by Angami Nagas
Outer diameter 3½ in. (9 cm); inner diameter 2⁵/₁₆ in. (6.6 cm); weight of pair 1,384 g
Collection Ghysels, Brussels

Their heavy weight was meant to be useful in combat. These were probably made in Manipur and are heavier than those made in this form today.

90. Tuensang District, Nagaland
Ao Naga girl wearing a three-strand necklace of carnelian beads alternating with cast-brass, trumpet-shaped units

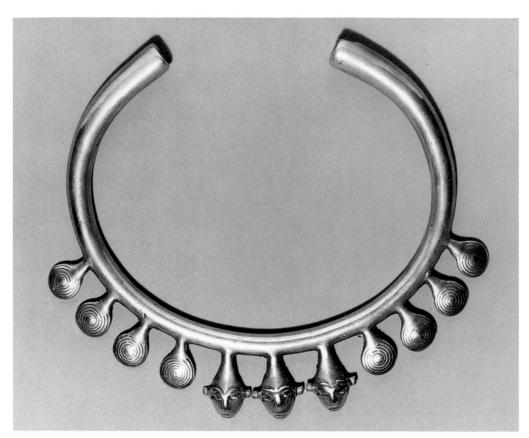

91. Nagaland
Cast-brass torque worn by Konyak and Kalyo Kengyu (Panso) Nagas to commemorate three trophy heads taken in a raid by the warrior-owner
Courtesy Susana Bacharach, London

Such necklaces indicated the social status of the wearer and were made to order from plains metalworkers as the number of heads to be represented on them varied with the success in head-taking of individual warriors.

Brass armlets (*akusha* for men; *aksa* for women), said to be made in Manipur, worn by Ao and Kubui men and women, consist of round-wire spirals with expanded terminals whose convex ends are ornamented with punched-dot patterns. Those of the women are lighter in weight than the men's.

Penannular bangles and upper armlets in a variety of weights are worn by many tribes. A large, very heavy bangle with overlapping ends that terminate in trumpet shapes is forged from thick brass rods. An archaic type, it is still made today.

The lost-wax casting method is used to form several Naga metal (brass) ornaments. First, a model of the object is made using a wax-resin composition. This is invested in a thick clay mold that, when dry, is heated to allow the composition within to be drained or "lost" through a downward-pointing opening, leaving a void formerly occupied by the model. The casting metal is heated in a crucible and, when liquefied, is poured directly into the now upward-pointing mold opening to fill the void. When cool, the mold is broken away and the metal casting exposed. Finishing and polishing processes may follow. Because the mold is destroyed in the process, each object cast this way is unique.

Cast-brass beads are an important component in Naga ornaments. Small cast-brass bells are often placed at the lowest strand of large necklaces, spaced out by hardstone or glass beads. Konyak women use them at the ends of a bunch of bead strands formed into a tassel and worn hanging from the bead belt at the sides. Larger cast-brass bells are worn strung in two or more crossing baldrics by Ao women in dancing dress. Women of the same tribe and the Sangtam wear a necklace of carnelian beads alternating with cast-brass trumpet-shaped units.

Cast-brass pendants suspended by a cord from the neck are worn by many Naga tribes. A common type already mentioned is a cast-brass head, or heads, symbolizing heads taken by the wearer. Konyak men wear a cast-brass pendant whose form resembles a longitudinal section of a conch shell terminating at the bottom with a fishtail shape.

Cast-brass torques, or collars, worn by Konyak warriors, consist of a rigid, curved rod at whose lower edge are joined sun-disc and head-form symbols, the number of heads representing those taken in raids.

Cast-brass bangles in as large a number as possible are worn by women on the wrist and upper arm. They may be plain or ornamented with punched dots and chiseled line patterns. The Wangpo Naga casters are noted for a version with an outer edge of dentated forms, worn on the upper arm in any number in graduated sizes.

Cast-brass bracelets (*asu'ukeka*) and armlets are generally worn in pairs. Simple ones may be forged; those with more elaborate forms are cast. A cast-brass cuff with palmated end flanges, made by the Tangkhul Nagas, is decorated with geometric-dot punched patterns that resemble Naga body tattoo designs. Worn in pairs, one on each wrist, the design is used by both men and women; those of the latter are of smaller size and lighter in weight.

Cast-brass wide cuffs of different designs, now obsolete, were probably made by plains jewelers or by Burmese metal workers. They are believed to be ancient, though their exact age cannot be ascertained, and therefore are treasured heirlooms. Because they do not appear in old photographs of Nagas, they may well be more than one hundred years old.

Money (*aurang*, the Hindi word for "throne") was not used in early Naga culture, where barter was the basis of commerce. Today a monetary economy in which Indian currency is used generally prevails. Silver (*aurang-i*) was not used for Naga ornaments,

92. Nagaland. *Probably 19th century*
Cast-brass bracelets worn by Angami and Zemi
Naga women with their palmated terminals
turned out (see 73)
Inner diameter 2 in. (5 cm); length 4⁷/₁₆ in.
(11.2 cm); weight of pair 788 g
Collection Ghysels, Brussels

Today commonly made by Tangkhul Nagas, the
bracelets' dot-punched pattern ornamentation
resembles the hot-poker work used on conch-shell
earrings and head ornaments of wood and bamboo.

93. Nagaland
Cast-brass ancestral, heirloom cuff (thado kuki),
one of a pair, with chased diagonal lines
Pitt Rivers Museum, Oxford University, Oxford.
Collected by J. H. Hutton, donated in 1931
(1923.85.716.1)

Hutton ascribed the cuff to the Thado Kuki,
Naga Hills.

as was the case of other primitive Indian tribes who had easier outside contact. Silver coins with an affixed loop for stringing, commonly used in Indian rural ornament, are occasionally worn in a Naga necklace, but this is not an original Naga concept.

Earrings of many kinds are worn by men and women, and only a sampling of the materials used for them can be mentioned. Down, cottonwool, bird's wings (see 81), cowrie shells, and white-glass beads are used. Others are made of bamboo slips covered with cloth and decorated with seeds. Brass wire bent into a U-shape with upturned ends, or formed into a large single or double spiral, are also worn.

Men's ear ornaments vary by tribal usage. Disc forms of bamboo, or wood decorated with plaited cane, orchid stem, and cowries, some fringed with a brush of goat's hair; tassels of dyed hair attached to carved wooden heads or brass discs; serow's horns; boar's tusks; conch shell and glass beads are all used for this purpose.

Hardstone Beads

Hardstone is a term used for any precious or semiprecious gemstone of a hardness of more than 6 on Mohs' scale of relative stone hardness. Hardstone beads (*athu achi*), completely hand-made, are an important material long appreciated by the Nagas and imported for use in necklaces and earrings. Due to the lack of written records, it cannot be determined exactly how far back hardstone bead import to Nagaland began. All hardstone beads came from Cambay, Gujarat, at the extreme, opposite western side of the country, more than fourteen hundred miles (about 2,240 km) away (see The Hardstone-Bead Trade, page 74). It is awesome to ponder that despite this great distance, this trade could exist. In the *Census of India, 1961*, Shri Kesarisingh Mavinh Thakor, one of the many Cambay manufacturer-dealers in hardstone agate beads, reveals that he and his descendants (and one assumes also those of other manufacturer-dealers) regularly

sent a representative with samples and a supply of finished beads to towns such as Dimapur, the former capital of the Kachari kingdom, on the Manipur Road, and Lakhimpur in Subinpur District in Assam in the plains to the west of Nagaland. They either cooperated with established Marwari dealers or themselves founded shops that sold agate beads wholesale or retail directly to the Nagas, who regularly came to these trading centers to make their purchases.

Hardstone beads are finished products, ready for use, and simply require stringing and assemblage. Because necklaces (*ala*) in the form of short (*yikwonhe*) or long (*kushuwa*) strings of beads are considered by Nagas to be important signs of social distinction, Nagas paid great attention to their design organization. Many assembly systems were invented, and color and form combinations were carefully considered. Typical of these necklaces is their use of spacer bars of bone, ivory, or metal that allow the multistrands to fall on the body in adjacent catenary curves.

Carnelian of a red-brick color is the hardstone bead material most favored by Nagas. The two forms preferred in Gujarati are called *chhasai*: an oblong, bitapered bead with six planes and edges, hexagonal in section; and *loi*: a long, bitapered, smooth-surfaced, barrel-shaped bead. Both types, horizontally pierced, could be from two to five inches (5–13 cm) or more in length.

Some Naga groups showed a preference for other kinds of hardstone, such as gray-banded agate shaped into a long barrel form. Still made today, in appearance these suggest conch-shell columella beads of the same form.

Nagas showed great discrimination when purchasing beads. They never bought irregular or low-quality beads and were fully prepared to pay the high price dealers demanded for beads of superior quality. Dealers knew this and always sent only the best quality beads to Nagaland, where they were prized as status-symbol objects given by parents to their daughters at the time of their marriage. In necklaces made with a combination of materials, the hardstone beads are always placed at the front where they are best seen.

Rock-crystal earrings are worn by women of the Ao and Tangkhul Naga tribes. Their place of manufacture is said to be Burma. Typically they are round-cornered, two- to three-inch (5–7.5 cm)-long squares, rectangles, or circles, approximately one-quarter- to three-eighths-inch (6.3–9.5 mm) thick, with a central, round hole from which a slot about one-quarter-inch (6.3 mm) wide extends to one outer edge. To wear this, the bottom of a stretched earlobe with a large enough hole is forced through the slot into the central round hole space, and the slot is turned downward so the earlobe, now in the hole, supports it. Some earrings in this style are of glass in imitation of rock crystal.

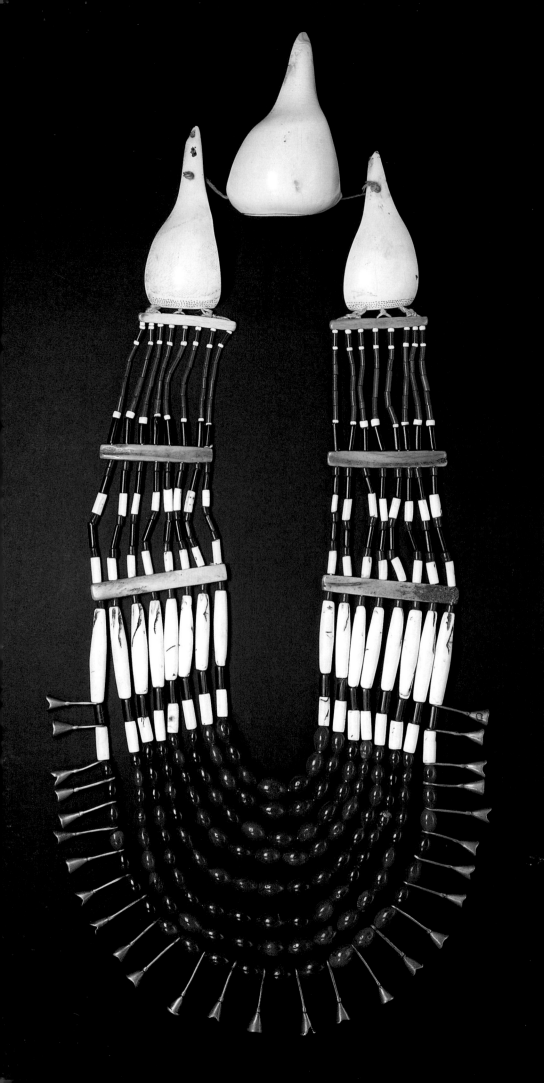

94. Nagaland
*Angami Naga necklace
using glass beads,
conch-shell columella
beads, carnelian beads,
and cast-brass trumpet-
shaped pendants
Length 47¼ in. (120 cm);
weight 1,020 g
Collection Ghysels,
Brussels*

95. Nagaland
*Tankul Naga women
wearing headpieces
and necklaces of glass
seed beads*

96. Nagaland
*Konyak Naga glass seed-
bead necklace. The
upper part of braided
strands are joined to
the lower flat band of
square-weave construc-
tion in which warp and
weft elements cross each
other at right angles.
Collection Harry and
Taila Neufeld, Gwynedd,
Pennsylvania*

*The geometric color
patterns found in such
jewelry are created by
carefully counting the
beads, which preferably
are of uniform size. The
resulting geometric pat-
terns derive from the
inherent possibilities of
this structural system.*

97. Nagaland ➤
*Angami Naga ceremon-
ial necklace of glass
beads, wound-glass beads,
a fringe of cast-brass
bells, brass spacer
units, and a conch-shell
button-back closing
Collection Harry and
Taila Neufeld, Gwynedd,
Pennsylvania*

Glass Beads

A variety of types of glass beads (*achi*), large (*akizhe*) or small (*kitila*), have for centuries past been used by the Nagas for ornaments. All available colors are used, though particular tribes show a preference for special colors and forms. Glass beads are an important item in every woman's dowry. Their value and amount are proportionate to the price the husband paid for the bride.

Multistrand small-bead necklaces (*achi ala*), generally of one color, are worn in hanks by men and women in most Naga tribes. The great regularity in dimensions and the accurate central opening of these beads indicate their foreign origins, from either Jablonz, Czechoslovakia, or Venice, Italy. Strands are interwoven at their terminals, and the necklace is closed by a shell button and loop (see 77). Glass-bead girdles (*tsoga-mini*) of a distinctive kind were worn by Sema women to hold up their cotton loin cloth, over which the girdle falls from the waist to well below the hips. In these, multistrands are held in place at intervals by long strand spacers.

Highly valued old *deo-mani* (spirit-god) beads, considered to be precious by all Nagas, are of glass although they resemble stone. As the Nagas possessed no glass-making technology, these beads must be foreign. Hutton describes them as dark red, flecked with black, and says they came from Nepal. Bower says they are a dull golden-yellow-brown color, and claims they were made by the Siemi, an ancient aboriginal race now extinct, which seems unlikely. They probably were imported in the unremembered past from an origin outside Nagaland along with other glass beads which have long been in use. Found at old grave sites where they were interred as valued possessions of the dead, they are considered to be miraculous gifts from ancestors, and are carefully preserved.

98. Nagaland
*Konyak Naga or Sema Naga
girdles of glass seed beads, conch
shell, and bone spacer bars
Top: 33⅛ x 5⅛ in. (84.2 x 13 cm);
weight 688 g; bottom: 33¹⁵⁄₁₆ x 5⅛ in.
(86 x 13 cm); weight 686 g
Collection Ghysels, Brussels*

*Seed beads, imported to Nagaland
via traders, probably originated in
Bohemia, whose glass-bead manufacturers had a considerable trade
with India. Today Indian-made
beads are used.*

Naga Ornaments in Decline: A Clash of Symbols

British intrusion into the hidden Naga world began in the 1830s, during the early time of the British Raj in India. British District Commissioners and their battalions controlled about half of these dangerous territories. From the beginning, government policy was characterized by paternalistic pacification meant to counteract the Naga practices of internecine wars and head-hunting. Trade and enlightened governing, it was hoped, would guide the Nagas toward more acceptable norms of civilization.

One event that brought about a fundamental change was the levying of a house tax on the Nagas, to be paid in currency. Its dramatic effect was to force the Nagas into a market economy. Growing dependence on government-issued money encouraged modern systems of trade and made possible the purchase of manufactured goods. Trade also brought about more peaceful intertribal relationships. Roads were built to facilitate access to the "interior," but while they made communication easier, they had the detrimental side effect of eroding tribal cultural individuality. Inevitably, Naga territory was flooded with industrial products that triggered changes in Naga life-styles. With their acceptance came an accelerated impetus toward general acculturation, as external cultural concepts challenged their own. In a move toward contemporary existentialism, in 1963 the numerous Naga tribes inaugurated their own political state in the Indian Union, called Nagaland, though small separatist groups still agitate for total independence.

Simultaneously at work, and perhaps even more potent, was the battle for spiritual dominion over the Nagas. The way was paved gradually in the 1870s by determined missionaries; by the 1950s American Baptist Christianity was established in Naga territories, and today about 90 percent of the Nagas follow that faith.

As intertribal feuding and head-taking gave way to the ideals of Christianity, old values and the symbolic significance given to many forms of Naga ornament and costume lost their original urgency. They became simply a decorative form of tribal identity. This loss of purpose and interest in the pursuit of ornaments led to a rapid deterioration of traditional Naga culture.

Also helping to promote the abandonment of traditional ornaments is the delusion many tribal people have that their own culture is inferior to that of more technologically advanced outsiders. Once general acceptance of change begins, the process swiftly accelerates. As many observers have witnessed, the cultural achievements of millennia can be wiped out rapidly, no matter how ancient or apparently entrenched they formerly seemed to be.

Conditions were ripe for Nagas to convert their cast-off ornaments into cash. Sensing this change in attitude, dealers in the antique markets of India's large cities, always on the alert for new areas of merchandise, made the most of it. With the help of local agents, by the end of the 1970s, treasured heirloom ornaments emigrated in quantity from Nagaland to New Delhi, Bombay, and Calcutta emporiums.

When they suddenly appeared on the Indian antique scene, these bold, striking ornaments were virtually unknown, even to most Indians. In no time Naga jewelry became an international item of interest, purchased by discerning, appreciative collectors and museums. Rejected by their creators, these orphan ornaments, which otherwise might have passed into oblivion, have found a permanent, safe home where they are being preserved for posterity. It now seems that future generations of Nagas interested in examining a significant aspect of their ancestral heritage will have to make a pilgrimage to the museums of Europe and America.

The Nagas have not totally abandoned the use of ornaments and on festive occasions still wear the distinctive dress that distinguishes one tribe from another. The quality of these new ornaments, however, has degenerated. They have become shrunken, simplified, lightweight caricatures of the old and often are made of substitutes for the materials formerly used.

FORMULATING THE INDIAN JEWELRY TRADITION

Rosaries of India

The use of rosaries in India is widespread among followers of the major religions and by others. The rosary is believed to have been the invention of Brahmanical Hindus (as early as 1,500 B.C.), from whom the concept passed to the Buddhists. Around the tenth century A.D., conquering Muslims came into contact with Hindu and Buddhist practices and in turn adopted its use from them. Among Christians, the employment of the rosary (which in English means "a garland of roses"; its equivalent in most Indic languages is *mala*, "a garland of flowers") is thought to have begun during the eleventh to thirteenth centuries A.D., when the Crusaders went to the Holy Land in an attempt to recover it from Muslim control. Upon their return to Europe, they brought with them the Muhammadan idea of rosary use.

As in all religions, the rosary functions as a counting device by which the number of prayers recited by a devotee can be noted. In all cases, this practice is considered to be a form of worship that will gain the reciter favor with the Divine.

Though primarily religious in function, a rosary worn as a necklace, as it commonly is in India, becomes a form of devotional jewelry. At the same time, it can also serve a practical purpose as a device for mathematical calculations.

The Hindu Rosary

The antiquity of the Hindu rosary is confirmed by its frequent inclusion with ancient Hindu deities represented in sculpture and painting. Held in a hand, the rosary is meant to symbolize some aspect or attribute of the particular deity, but its meaning is not the same in all cases. Rosaries are included in the depiction of the Hindu deities Agni, Agastya, Ahirbudhnya, Ardhanarisvara, Bhadrakali, Bhringin, Brhaspati, Gauri, Kamantaka, Lakulisa, Manasa, Parvati, Rati, Risi(s), Shiva, Subramanya, Surya, Uma, and Vayu, among others. Lesser spirits are believed to dwell in rosary-bead perforations.

Because rosaries are commonly used by the Hindu laity throughout India, every bazaar of any size features merchants who sell rosaries, which are either hung up or displayed spread out on a ground cloth. When worn visibly by a Hindu, the material used for the rosary bead can indicate the Hindu deity or sect to whom the rosary and its wearer are dedicated. Those not wishing to display such information wear it out of sight under clothing.

The ideal Hindu rosary has fifty beads, which corresponds with the number of characters in the Sanskrit alphabet, starting with *a* and ending with *ksha*. These two letters, combined with *mala*, form the word *akshamala*, which means "rosary." In Sanskrit, *aksha* also means grain, seed, or nut—of which many rosaries are made—and *mala* means a string of beads, garland, or necklace. Reciting or repeating the rosary is called in Hindi *mala japna* (S: *japa*, the mental or oral repetition of a prayer [*mantra*] accompanied by meditation); and consequently a rosary is also called a *japamala*.

In actuality, the total number of rosary beads may vary among different Hindu sects. For instance, Shaivites often use 32, or double that—64. A common Vaishnavite rosary has 108 beads. There are many other variants.

The Hindu rosary is used as an aid to meditation, to keep the mind from wandering in order to make it concentrate, without distractions, on the meaning of the prayer being recited. Recitation is usually murmured, or silent. Normally when saying the rosary, a Hindu will repeat the name of his or her self-selected deity (*ishtadevata*). It also may be the *mantra* that was whispered to a boy by his *guru* on the day he was initiated into his caste and invested with the sacred thread; thereafter, it is forever kept a secret. The receiver is regarded as the disciple of that *guru*, who is more revered than a Brahman priest. The *guru* guides him in all religious and spiritual matters for the rest of his life. The phrase, name, or sound (the latter termed a seed [*bija*] syllable), is repeated 108 times daily, keeping count with the rosary.

To prevent others from observing the act, and to eliminate personal risk of injury from the possibility of the evil eye falling upon both the rosary and counter, it is common among some Hindu sects to place the rosary and the hand holding it into a small, sometimes embroidered cloth bag while reciting. The bag is called *gaumukhi*, which means "cow's mouth." These bags are made and sold to pilgrims at the holy city of Varanasi, which gives their ownership a certain prestige.

99. Himachal Pradesh. *c.1720*
Miniature portrait of Raja Sidh Sen of Mandi (detail)
Gouache on paper
7⅞ x 7⅞ in. (20 x 20 cm)
Fondation Custodia (Collection F. Lught), Institut Néerlandais, Paris

The raja is depicted performing the daily puja of reciting the Gayatri mantra, the holiest verse of the Vedas, addressed to Surya, the sun god. The raja's head and neck are bedecked with other rosaries. During this recitation, his hand, which holds the counted rosary, is placed in a cloth rosary bag (gau-mukhi) to shield it from others' view.

The *Gayatri Japam*

A widely used Hindu rosary prayer is the *Gayatri Japam*, repeated twice a day at morning and evening devotions. It is addressed to the sun (Savitar), the supreme generative force and ruler of the planets, to propitiate hostile planets or angry gods. The greater the number of repetitions, the greater their blessing. The favored number of repetitions are 27, 54, or 108 times, without break. Through this repetition, the reciter strives to accumulate an inner force originating from the sun, which illuminates his mind and results in knowledge, energy, and blessings in one's undertakings.

The reciter sits in a quiet place on a seat (S: *asana*) made of a sacrificially pure substance, reserved only for that individual's use. It can be a *darbha*-grass mat, a plank of wood of certain trees, wool or silk cloth, a deer or tiger skin.

101

100. Khajuraho, Madhya Pradesh
*Vaishnavite sadhu wearing a rosary (akshamala)
of rock crystal (sphatik), wood (lakri), and other
beads. (See 106; the fourth rosary from the left is
this one.) His forehead bears the sectarian mark
(tilaka or pundra) of a Vishnu follower.*

101. Puri, Orissa
*Hindu rosaries (akshamala) displayed for sale
before the Jaganath Temple entrance. Those with
beads of the stems, branches, and roots of the
aromatic basil (tulasi; Ociumum sanctum) are
particularly prized.*

102. Vellore, Tamil Nadu ➤
*Young Shaivite acolyte wearing a rosary (Tam:
jebamalai) as a necklace. It has a central medall-
lion of Ayappan, a goddess whose cult is growing
among south Indian Hindus.*

103

During meditation, an eight-petaled lotus flower is pictured in the mind. Each petal represents a deity (*dikpalaka*), each of whom is a guardian of the four quarters and the four intermediate quarters, with the sun at the center. The deities invoked are: Surya (or another of the many Hindu names for the sun), Indra, Agni, Yama, Niruthi, Varuna, Vayu, Kubera, and Isana.

Materials Used for Hindu Rosaries

Materials approved for use in Hindu rosaries are perhaps the most varied of those used among all religions. A wide variety come from the vegetable world and include seeds, berries, fruit, nuts, drupes, dried plant stems, and wood. From the animal kingdom come bone, ivory, horn, coral, shells, and pearls; and from mineral sources come glass, semiprecious or precious stones, and metals.

A rosary of gemstones or gold is considered to be one hundred times as auspicious as any other material. A costly rosary (*vijayanti-mala*, victory rosary) is made of any kind of hardstone such as crystal, ruby, emerald, sapphire, cat's eye, and even diamond, as well as combinations of these. Glass has also been used in rosaries for centuries. Colors of glass are often chosen because they simulate that of precious stones (see The *Nava-ratna* Rosary, page 309). Today plastic beads whose color also simulates natural materials have become ubiquitous because of their low cost.

Various materials are believed to embody particular properties. Silver and gold fulfill wishes; coral brings wealth; crystal, good luck; pearls, glory; and shell helps one to achieve fame. Many traditional materials will always continue in use because of their association with a particular Hindu deity. Devotees of that deity believe that the use of these substances is particularly pleasing to the deity concerned. Among different sects devoted to the worship of the same deity, however, the use of a particular material is not uniform throughout India.

103. Tamil Nadu
Rosary of rudraksham seeds or nuts from the drupe of the utrasam tree (Elaeocarpus ganitrus) Victoria and Albert Museum, London (1176–1874)

The utrasam tree is sacred to Rudra, the Vedic god of storms, and especially to Shiva, with whom Rudra is identified. Such rosaries are also used in other deity worship. The tubercled nut develops from two to eleven segmented divisions or "faces," each delineated by a ridge extending from pole to pole; most have five or six such faces. Those with five (panjchaksharam, five eyed) are used for rosaries sacred to Shiva as five is his sacred number, corresponding to his five faces (panjchmukam). Those with six (arava-thanaksharam, six eyed) are sacred to Karttikeya. Celibate yogis use very rare and highly valued eleven-faced seeds (egathaksharam). Twin seeds (two joined together) (irattaippillaigalilonruru-draksham) are used in necklaces worn by priests.

▲ **104. Maharashtra**
Seeds used in the All Saints Mission, Mazagon, Bombay, for making rosaries and ornaments. Top to bottom: Fever nut (Caesalpinia bonducella); babul (Acacia arabica); cane (Saccharum officinarium); lal eval or red-weed seed; white cassia (Acacia farnesiana); kumbli (Gmelina arborea); Indian laburnum (Cassia fistula); quille (black); gul mohr (Poinciana regia); Job's tears (Coix lachryma jobi); rudraksha (small) (Eleocarpus lanceolatus); quille (gray); chiku velaga (Dicliptera parvibrac-teata); senna family tree (Cassia gigantus); guinea grass (Paranarium); Job's tears; teak (Tectona grandis); flame of the forest (Ixora coccinea); litchi (Nephelium litchi); betel nut (Areca catachu); rudrakshra (large) (Eleocarpus ganitrus); nukte, or Indian teasel

105. *Hindu rosaries of (left to right) lotus seeds, ivory, smoothed rudrakshas, Job's tears, black wood, tulasi stems, sandalwood, and black seeds*
Collection the author, Porvoo

106. *Hindu rosaries of bone, colored glass, silver, rock crystal and wood, clear glass, colored gemstones, and ivory. Sikh rosaries (mala, not shown) are of cotton and have 108 knots and two tassels.*
Collection the author, Porvoo

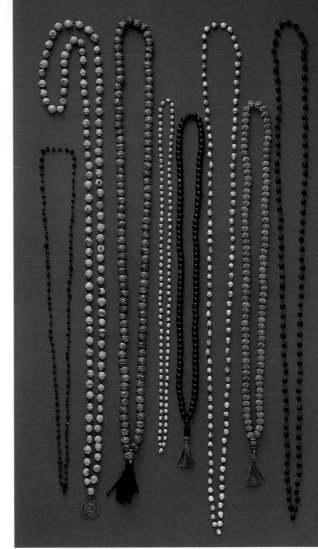

105
106

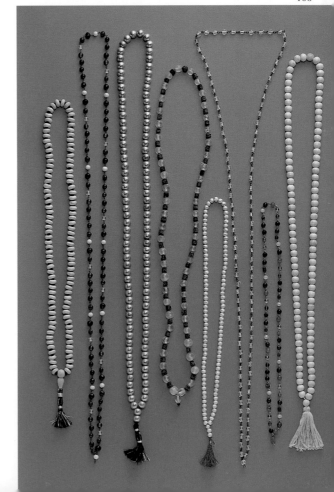

The Muslim Rosary

In India, a Muslim rosary is called *subhah* in Persian, or *tasbih,* in Arabic. Counting the rosary is termed, in Urdu, *subhah gardani,* or *tasbih parna.* If the reciter (A: *tasbihkhwan,* singer of praises to Allah) does this at least each morning and night, as the Prophet said, he or she atones for that person's sins, no matter how numerous or great.

Muslims commonly use rosaries and are frequently seen holding one in their right hand, even when engaged in other activities. Counting the beads of a rosary also becomes a calming method of coping with anxiety or mental stress. The recitation ceremony (A: *zikr*) is done as an act of devotion, either aloud, in a low voice, or silently, at all leisure moments while meditating (*tilawah*) on its meaning. Because they are used when the person is not otherwise occupied, these rosaries are often referred to in the West as "worry beads."

The Muslim rosary has 33 or 99 beads. When there are 99, they are frequently divided into three groups, usually by an additional "counter" bead placed after the 33rd and the 66th bead. Its function is to give the reciter a way of keeping track of the number of recitations said and to allow two rest pauses to be taken in one total round of recitations. This marker can be considered equivalent to the round mark or dot (*ayat*) in a Qur'an text, where a reader may optionally pause. The two *extra* counter beads are usually larger than the others, of a different shape, or made of a different material or color to give them distinction. When a shorter strand of 33 beads is used, the entire set is counted three times to arrive at the required total of 99.

At what may be considered the beginning or end of the rosary is often placed an elongated cylindrical bead made with a baluster-like profile. This is called the pillar (in Arabic, *situn* or *rukn*) or leader (*imam*). Also pierced through like a bead, it is threaded with the rest, and at its bottom there usually hangs a tassel (*jhabba*) of black or brightly colored silk, metallic silver, or gold thread, at times mixed with the colored yarn, and tied by a stringer and tassel maker (H: *patu'a*) with an artistic knot. Tassels are said to repel the evil eye, which is believed to dislike tassels and fringes.

The 99 beads represent the 99 beautiful names and attributes of God, *Asma'u'llah* (Qur'an, Surah vii 179). Muhammad said, "Verily there are 99 names of God and whoever recites them shall enter into Paradise" (Mishkat, Book cxi). Also commonly recited are one hundred repetitions of the *Tasbih:* "O Holy God" (*Subhaha'llah*); the Tahmid: "Praises be God" (*Alhamdu l'illahi*); or the Takbir: "God is Great" (*Allahu akbar*).

When reciting the 99 names of God, the 100th "ineffable name of God: *Allah*," is said either first when starting at the pillar, or last on finally arriving at the pillar.

Muslim rosaries are made of beads from a variety of materials in uniform size; their forms can be round, oval, melon, or gadrooned. The choice of material depends on the owner's relative wealth.

Siah rosaries are sometimes made of earth from the Karbela at Meshed and are acquired upon performing the Hajj pilgrimage to Mecca. Seeds, bone, and ivory are also used. Wooden beads are used by all Muslim sects. Rosaries of sandalwood (*Santalum album*) are sold in large numbers to Muslim pilgrims who go to Ajmer in Rajasthan to visit the famous shrine of Khwaja Saheb, a Muslim saint. They are used whenever a customary religious duty (*wazifa*) is performed. More expensive are rosaries of coral, amber, and hardstone beads such as carnelian (a favorite), lapis lazuli, and rock crystal. Sunni rosaries are usually a dark-colored stone.

In Mughal times, and frequently mentioned in the various accounts of the lives of the Mughal emperors, rosaries of pearls, rubies, emeralds, or sapphires were used and often given as gifts of favor. Today inexpensive plastic beads are common, frequently of a yellow color that simulates amber or of black to imitate black coral; beads of colored glass suggest a particular semiprecious stone. Very special are the rosaries carried by some Muslim mendicants (*fakirs*), which are made of snake vertebrae, a sign that they know a charm to cure snakebites.

107. Khambhat (Cambay), Gujarat
Muslim rosaries of faceted carnelian (left) and carved rock crystal (right). The latter has counter beads after the 33rd and 66th beads. Collection the author, Porvoo

The Buddhist Rosary

The Buddhist rosary described here is used by Tibetan Buddhists, the main Buddhist group living today within the political boundaries of India. Tibetan cultural influence and religion have always been strong among Indian groups who reside along the lengthy Indo-Tibetan Himalayan border area, especially as far as religion and jewelry are concerned.

Buddhist rosaries are used by Lamas or Buddhist priests and all the laity. It is common to see them either worn as a necklace or wrapped as a bracelet around the left wrist. Their constant presence makes them always available for use in leisure time, which is frequently devoted to rosary recitations. Even when occupied with other routine tasks, a Buddhist will commonly count the beads of his or her rosary. They keep accurate count of the number of times each round of rosary

108. Kham, Tibet
Tibetan rosary (sin-'phen) worn as a necklace by an East Tibetan Khampa warrior and used in the worship of Tam-din (S: Hayagriva), the Red Tiger-Devil, who is a fierce defender of the faith. The warrior's head ornaments include an ivory thumb ring (tre-kho, see 275), two silver "saddle" rings (ga tshi-ko) set with coral (see 274), and a long silver Kham earring (alung) with a large coral bead.

this center, are short strings that tightly hold ten small metallic rings or counters. Though variants occur, one of the strings often ends in a miniature thunderbolt (*dorje*), and this string is used as single unit counters (*drabg dzir*), each ring representing one round of the rosary. The other string ends with a miniature metal bell (*dril-bu*) and the rings on it are used to indicate units of ten recitations. In keeping count, when one round of the rosary is completed, one ring on the thunderbolt side is pulled down; when ten on that side are completed, they are all moved back upward, and on the bell side one ring is moved down. It works somewhat in the manner of an abacus. When all counters have been used, a repetition of 10,800 prayers have been said.

Each day a member of the laity may complete from five to twenty cycles; priests, who have more leisure to recite them, say many more. The friction of frequent handling smoothes and wears the beads down; worn beads, more apparent when the rosary is made of an irregularly surfaced organic material such as seeds, are a sign of great piety, obvious to all.

The beads of a Lamaist rosary are made either of mineral or natural organic materials. In the former group are round gold, silver, and hardstone beads, which can be of the most valuable kind, including rubies, emeralds, sapphires, rock crystal, turquoise, and agates. These are used by high Lamas and the wealthy. In the organic natural material group are hard seeds, such as those of the lotus and the *rudraksha,* and woods such as sandal. Especially favored is wood from the so-called Bodhi tree (*Ficus religiosa*) under which Buddha sat and attained Enlightenment at Bodh Gaya in Bihar, India. Other organic materials used for beads include pearls, coral, amber, conch shell, ivory, animal and human bone, and, in some cases, snake's vertebrae. A highly prized type used by Tantric Buddhists consists of flat discs of uniform diameter made from human skull bone, that of a Lama if possible. Tibetans do not bury their dead but expose them to be devoured by vultures and dogs; therefore, human bones are available. Different materials are used to distinguish various sects. Some materials are associated with a particular deity or its manifestation and are used only when they are worshiped. Combinations of different substances may also occur.

Telling the beads, usually by repeating a mystic formula said with a person's tutelary deity in mind, in Tibetan is called *tan-c'e*, which means "purring like a cat," a reference to the continuous *sotto voce* murmur of prayer repetitions. The most common Buddhist prayer is the *mantra, Om mani padme hum!,* usually translated as, "Hail to the jewel in the lotus." The "jewel" refers to Buddha's representative, the Bodhisattva Avalokiteshvara (also called Padmapani), the personification of the self-generative, creative cosmic force, reincarnated on Earth in the Dalai Lama.

recitation has been completed as a means of gaining merit and to influence an improvement in status in their next incarnation.

The Tibetan rosary (*oren-be,* a string of beads) normally contains a total of 108 beads, often divided into four groups of 27 each. Sectarian variants may have as many as 111 beads. The extra number above 100, which is considered basic, are there to assure a full count of the prescribed 100-time recitation, allow for any inadvertent miscount, and provide replacements for the loss of beads should a bead or the string of the rosary break. The

number 100 corresponds with the original 100 volumes in the Lamaic scriptures, the Kah-gyur, now extended to 108 volumes. The number 108 has other mystic significance in Buddhist thought.

At the bottom center of the Tibetan rosary are usually three beads (*do dzin,* retaining beads), larger than the rest, the central one the largest of the three. These *in sequence* symbolize the Buddhist trinity: the word (*dharma*), Buddha, and the Buddhist church (*sangha*). Attached at anyplace to either side of the rosary, but often at the 8th and 21st bead from

The Hardstone-Bead Trade

Early Interest in Hardstones: Khambhat, Gujarat

The earliest body ornaments were probably plant and animal products, but, at a very early time, stones were also put to this use. Hardstones are believed to have been discovered during the Stone Age, when man first searched for flint and other stones suitable for implements and weapons. Many other, relatively rare stones came to the searchers' notice. Initially their attraction may have been their hardness, but what made them exceptional was their color, degree of translucency or transparency, or a uniquely patterned surface.

Vast deposits of hardstones exist in India. Because of the human proclivity to give meaning to unusual objects, particular stones were attributed with magical qualities or supernatural powers. These "magical" stones were shaped and worn as beads. Hardstone beads are believed to be, if not the first, then certainly among the earliest of humanity's fabricated amulets. As archaeological finds at ancient sites in India have proved, hardstone beads were in use all over the subcontinent.

Quasi-religious beliefs about hardstones fortified the desire to possess them. As a result, there developed a complex network of people engaged in gathering, selling, setting, and otherwise using these stones for ornamental and religious purposes, a robust industry that continues today.

In its connection with the hardstone bead-making industry, Khambhat, or Khambhayat (the original name for Cambay, which is a British corruption), in Gujarat, and places in the surrounding area, have a history that covers more than five thousand years. In the vicinity are inexhaustible natural deposits of siliceous minerals, such as agates and related hardstones, suited for manufacture into beads. Today, descendants of the original bead makers continue to fabricate hardstone beads here by the same archaic manual processes established in Neolithic times.

Local physical evidence of this ancient manufacture and trade has been uncovered by archaeologists at Mohenjo-daro and other sites. One of great relevance is Lothal, a Harappan city related to the Indus Valley Civilization.

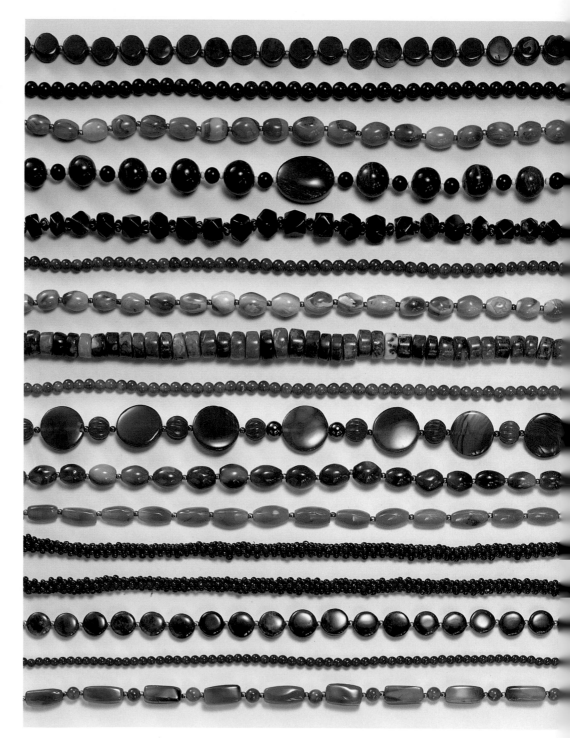

109. Khambat, Gujarat
Typical forms of contemporary hardstone beads manufactured here
Courtesy Thakorlal Chunilal Akikwala, Krishna Pole, Khambat

Natural Stone Forms of Aniconic Hindu Deities

The *Shalagrama*

Some Hindu deities are worshiped in the aniconic forms of natural fossil stones and tumbled river pebbles. An example of the former is the ammonite (shalagrama), a fossil mollusk (Ammonoidea, of the Cephalopoda class) common during the Mesozoic era, 65 to 390 million years ago. Ammonites are abundant in the beds of Himalayan rivers that eventually join the holy Ganges. Those from the confluence of the Gandaki River and the Ganges at Bankipur, Patna, Bihar, are highly prized. Their connection with Vishnu derives from their spiral configuration, which relates to one of Vishnu's main symbols, the sundarshana chakra, or wheel, a lethal instrument he throws at an adversary, its form representing celestial and cosmic order. Shalagramas are mounted in series in openwork gold or silver settings to form a long, garland-type necklace placed on a Vishnu image installed in a temple. Hindus recognize eighty-nine types of shalagramas, each associated with a different deity. The black one sacred to Vishnu is of basanite, and its form must be perfect and complete. Others not perfect are used by goldsmiths as a touchstone for testing gold quality.

111

The *Banalinga*

The banalinga is a natural orbicular stone or pebble formed by nature. It is not a fossil but is created by tumbling for millennia in a riverbed. Of oval form, it represents the phallus of Shiva and is his universal aniconic symbol in its movable as opposed to its fixed form. Banalingas created by nature are considered by Hindus to be auspicious and desirable, but they are also manufactured by lapidaries from clear quartz (the most preferred) or other hardstones. Both are acceptable for worship. They may be placed on a separate metal stand, and small ones are put inside an amulet container such as those used by Lingayats (see page 132). They are also placed at the apex of the chak head ornament worn by Gaddi women (see page 414). Banalingas (called rori or chorlia in Rajasthan) of different stones are connected with other Hindu deities.

112

◄ **110. Tamil Nadu**
Silver-mounted ammonite necklace (shalagramamalai) for ornamenting an image of Vishnu
Length 36½ in. (92.7 cm)
Victoria and Albert Museum, London (IM 92-1911)

Sixteen black basanite ammonite fossils (shalagrama) are encased in pierced work and chased silver. Such ammonites are believed to contain Vishnu's essence, indicating his capacity to assume any form, therefore his omnipotence.

111. Khambat (Cambay), Gujarat
Manufactured agate banalingas, made for Shaivite worship
Average length 1¼ in. (3.2 cm)

Modeled after natural banalingas found in the Narmada River, which, like these, are used in home worship, or as an amulet carried on the body within a metal container (see 233). An aniconic form of Shiva, they also represent "the Self-originated" (Svayambhu or Brahma, the creator). Unanchored in space and time, they do not "stand" or "arise" from anything but are rounded top and bottom like an egg, a reference to the Cosmic Egg (Hiranyagarbha) of Creation. A similarly shaped red stone (svarnabhadra) found in the Kosi River at Arrah, Bihar, is also auspicious as an aniconic form of Ganesha.

112. Bihar
Black basanite ammonite (S: shalagrama) from the Kali-Gandak River, Nepal, which emerges from the Himalayas into northern Bihar
Diameter 2¼ in. (5.7 cm)
Collection the author, Porvoo (Ex-Coll. Linda Golden, Berkeley)

Ammonites of basanite are commonly used by Indian goldsmiths as a touchstone (H: kasauti).

The author of the *Periplus* describes a contemporary network of sea routes between Egypt and the Gujarati ports of Khambhat and Barygaza (as Ptolmey called Baroch) and mentions the trade products at each port of call. To India came perfumes and unguents, as well as brass, copper, tin, and lead, Mediterranean coral, and rarities such as glass objects, gold and silver vessels, and musical instruments. It was always necessary to bring quantities of gold and silver coins: precious metals were demanded by Indian merchants as payment for Indian goods foreigners purchased as return cargoes.

The Roman trade with Khambhat included banded agates and chalcedony used for cameos and small objects made from agates, chalcedony, carnelian, and rock crystal, such as sword and dagger handles, boxes and cups.

The hardstone trade centered at Khambhat because from there these products were ready for immediate shipment. Thus Khambhat developed a monopoly on the export of all hardstone products to foreign destinations, including China, Africa, the Near East, and Mediterranean Europe.

On the westward return journey, sailing boats headed for ports in the Persian Gulf and Arabian and Red seas. Merchants knew which types of hardstone products each destination preferred and catered to those preferences. Beads of particular shapes or of specific stones were brought to wherever they attained highest prices. Arabs preferred agates, bloodstone (also called heliotrope), carnelian, and jasper. Flat, tablet-shaped stones, meant for use as sealstones, were always in demand in Persia and Muslim Africa where seals were commonly used by nonliterate people as an accepted, valid form of signature on documents. Carnelian beads in great amounts were offloaded at Aden, then shipped to Red Sea or other ports. In trade parlance, they were referred to as *Yemeni akik*, an example of how the actual origin of a product often was obscured because it took its name from the last place of shipment.

Cairo was one of the main Muslim trading points for the distribution of Khambhat hardstone beads to Africa, especially the Niger River basin area. Beads destined for Cairo originally were shipped in an unperforated round form and there faceted and perforated. After 1930, beads for this destination were shipped as finished products.

As an important commercial seaport during the fifteenth and sixteenth centuries, Khambhat became a principal embarkation point for Muslim pilgrims making their once in a lifetime *Hajj*, or pilgrimage to Mecca (Makkah) in the month of *Zu 'L-Hijjah*, the twelfth month of the Muhammedan lunar year, appointed for this purpose, any other time having no pilgrimage merit. During this time a stone archway was constructed in Khambhat. It was called the Mecca Gate (*Makkah Darwaza*) because

113. Raisen District, Madhya Pradesh.

c. 1st century B.C. Sanchi Stupa, eastern gateway (torana), buff sandstone, north pillar, south face

The guardian (dvarapala) wears a five-strand necklace of beads and chains with two rectangular side spacers—a basic form of necklace still in use (see 783, 784)—and beaded bracelets.

Located near Khambhat and the Sabarmati River, Lothal is only twenty-nine miles (46 km) from present-day Ahmadabad, the burgeoning capital of Gujarat, on the same river. Contemporary with Mohenjo-daro, the largest Indus Valley urban center, Lothal flourished about 2400 B.C. to 1700 B.C. A walled city, typical of early urban cultures, a large part of its enclosed area was devoted to residences and factories. Excavations have uncovered evidence of a substantial hardstone bead-making factory using carnelian, agate, crystal, and other hardstones.

Besides supplying an Indian market, these products were also exported to stone-poor Mesopotamia, already in decline by then. This claim is substantiated by finds of Indian-made hardstone beads and some Indus Valley seals excavated at various Mesopotamian sites.

The earliest literary reference to the Gujarati hardstone trade is recorded by Westerners such as Pliny, who in A.D. 77 stated that the Babylonians used Indian agates set in rings

because they believed this stone to possess medicinal properties.

Ancient trade with Khambhat is also mentioned by the unknown writer of the popularly titled *Periplus of the Erythraen Sea.* Mainly concerned with navigation of the waters of the Red Sea, as well as the Arabian Sea and the Persian Gulf, this book, written c. A.D. 80, illustrates how the monsoon winds affected seaborne trade between India and the world beyond.

From late April to mid-October, seasonal winds come from the southwest toward India; from October to April, they reverse their direction and blow away from India. Called the monsoon (after A: *mausim,* a time or season), this meteorological phenomenon could be depended upon by wind-driven boats to convey them seasonally to destinations in either direction. This wind pattern was well known to Arab sailors who in their dhows dominated sea trade of the entire area until the fifteenth century, when they were superseded by Europeans.

Indian Muslim pilgrims passed through it at the start of their *Hajj* to Mecca. It still stands south of the city facing the sea, but now, due to river siltage, is four miles inland.

Khambhat agates, carnelian, and rock crystal beads were made into Muslim rosaries and exported in quantity to Mecca. Indian Muslims purchased them there at a much higher price than they could be bought for at home because their association with that holy place increased their value considerably. Because Muslims from several countries convene at Mecca at each *Hajj* period, the Khambhat hardstone rosaries they purchased there were distributed over the extensive area of Muslim countries.

Khambhat agate beads were exported in quantity to Africa, which even now remains a major market. Red carnelian beads especially were used as a form of currency in the late seventeenth and eighteenth centuries by Arab slave traders in West Africa to purchase black slaves, who were resold to European seamen and brought to the New World. These beads came to East Africa on Arab ships in huge quantities and were distributed all over Africa. This trade was carried on by a network of Arab middlemen who supplied specific areas, each with a preference for beads of particular stones and shapes.

As a result, some of these beads, retained by slaves, found their way to the West Indies and the Caribbean Islands, where slaves were sent and resold to work British-owned sugar plantations. Indian carnelian beads and Indian indigo-blue dyed cotton cloth called "blue jean," were standard slave dress in the West Indies.

Europeans Expand the Hardstone-Bead Market

The Portuguese were among the first Europeans to come to India by the sea route and to establish permanent trading centers at Diu, Goa, and elsewhere on the west and east coasts, followed by the Dutch and the English, also great maritime powers. Khambhat, already a great entrepôt as a result of the additional European trade at the end of the fifteenth to the beginning of the seventeenth century, reached its summit of prosperity as a port city.

Many European source references give us glimpses of the contemporary Khambhat hardstone trade. A few can be mentioned here to indicate its importance and development. In 1514 a Portuguese traveler in India, Duarte Barbosa, cousin of Ferdinand Magellan, whom he had accompanied on his epochal circumnavigation of the globe, wrote a book describing his Hindustan adventures. He gives a detailed account of the trade in precious stones such as diamonds, rubies, and emeralds. Khambhat, he says, was inhabited by artisans in many trades, and he confirms that

agate articles made there were a part of the prosperous Arab trade with Arabian and African seaports.

That the hardstone trade prospered into the seventeenth century is indicated by Pietro della Valle, an Italian traveler in India from 1614 to 1626. Pietro della Valle visited Khambhat in 1623 and mentions the hardstone trade in his records: "A few cos from the city of Barocci [Baroch] is a mine of calcidonus [chalcedony, a form of agate], and agates, white and green, but these stones are carried less into Baroch than to Cambaia, although it is further from the mine, because there is a seaport and a greater concourse of foreign merchants; and in Cambaia they are wrought into little globes, either round or oval, to make coronets or necklaces."

Beginning early in the seventeenth century, siltage deposits from the Mahi and the Sabarmati rivers accumulated, threatening to destroy Khambhat's function as a port. Realizing this, foreigners established factories (trading posts) at other nearby open ports on the Gulf of Khambhat, such as Baroch, Surat, and Vallabhipur, which then rapidly increased in importance. Khambhat's port ultimately became useless, and it sank to a low status as a maritime power. Today, amazingly, Khambhat is stranded some ten miles (17 km) inland from the seashore. Even so, although some of the bead cutters moved to these other places, the majority of the agate cutting industry continued at Khambhat.

Competition from a faraway source arose in the nineteenth and twentieth centuries with the introduction of inexpensive Czechoslovakian glass beads imitating hardstones, which severely diminished indigenous hardstone-bead sale. Foreign demand, however, continued. In the last quarter of the nineteenth century, nearly the entire hardstone export trade came under the control of the active, enterprising Bohra Muslim merchant community concentrated in Gujarat and Western India, especially in Bombay, dominating the European, Arab, and Chinese hardstone export markets.

Present-Day Khambhat and the Hardstone-Bead Trade

The cutting and polishing of hardstone is one of the few industries that has survived in Khambhat, now shrunk to a population of some fifty thousand. Strong international competition from Idar Oberstein in Germany, Hong Kong, and China exists, but at those centers, hardstone beads are made by mechanical methods. Their products are therefore more regular and perfect in shape and hole penetration, the piercing now often done by laser beams. Because Khambhat's hard-

stone beads are still manufactured mainly by hand, its beads are generally less perfect, which accounts for part of their charm and gives them an air of antiquity. The still-low labor costs allow the continued sale of these beads at low prices.

Export continues to be the main market, and today 75 percent of Khambhat's total hardstone bead production still goes to tribal Africa. The rest is sent mainly to Europe and America. In India a small but growing percentage still supplies Indian tribal people, especially in Nagaland, Mizoram, and the Khasi-Jaintia Hills area in Assam.

At urban centers, the growth of foreign tourism has increased sales to foreign visitors. Indian urbanites generally do not appreciate these beautiful and inexpensive beads because from time immemorial they have been conditioned to favor precious stones and pearls. This idea is slowly eroding, however, and the use of hardstone beads in Indian urban centers is increasing.

The Khambhat bead trade is dominated by dealers who own about fifty factories. They finance the entire industry, from the purchase of raw materials to merchandising and shipping the finished product; regulate production; and decide what is to be made based on current market demand.

Hardstone-Bead Manufacturing

Agate Sources

Chalcedony/agate deposits found within a radius of approximately 120 miles (192 km) of Khambhat and Baroch are the main source of raw material for the hardstone bead–making industry of Khambhat. Deposits were laid down in the Mesozoic Era, the age of dinosaurs and marine and flying reptiles, when a series of huge lava flows of amygdaloidal basalt traprock covered an immense area of the Deccan. Before the rock solidified, cavities were created by internal steam pressure expansion. Upon cooling, such spaces were ultimately filled with deposits of different minerals, especially colloidal crypto-crystalline silica, primarily in the form of chalcedony, anhydrous quartz, and jasper, forming rounded solid nodules or hollow geodes, usually lined with interior crystals. These deposits were subsequently dislodged when the traprock disintegrated and transported by water and sand into the immense catchment area of the Narmada River, which passes Rajpipla and Baroch and disembogues into the Gulf of Khambhat. Covered in time by silt and gravel, the nodules and geodes became concentrated secondary alluvial deposits and are now found in riverbeds, sporadically scattered in nearby fields, and on hill slopes—all formerly under water.

Gujarat hardstones belong to the crypto-crystalline quartz-chalcedony silica group of quartzose minerals, to which in India the over-all generic term *agate* (from the Arabic *akiik,* for river) is applied. They include agate, basan-ite, bloodstone (heliotrope), chalcedony, car-nelian, chrysoprase, jasper, moss agate, onyx, plasma, sard, and sardonyx, all of which have a waxy luster when polished. These types can occur both in isolation or in combinations in which one may predominate.

Color primarily differentiates one stone from the other and is due to the presence of a metallic oxide such as iron, manganese, cop-per, nickel, or others. Color distribution can be homogenous, or may occur in spots, clouds, layers, or, as in moss agate, in dendritic forma-tions. All these stones have a similar specific gravity of between 2.6 to 2.65, and a relatively high degree of hardness from 6.5 to 7.5 on the Mohs' scale.

In chalcedony/agates, the interior nodule or geode structure may be either concentrical-ly layered or in straight, parallel bands. One of the former is orbicular or eye agate, which has concentric round layers and, when cut with the circle centrally placed, resembles an eye, a form highly valued and imported by Romans for use as an amulet against the evil eye and set in rings for this purpose. In the latter cate-gory are banded or stratified layer agates used for cameos.

From earliest times, Gujarat has been the main source of agates in India, and the chief source there is the Rajpipla Hill Range in the former princely state of Rajpipla, Gujarat, the area called *pathar khestra,* or "land of agates." Best deposits occur near Ratanpor village on the left bank of the Narmada River, about 29 miles (46.4 km) from Baroch, and 75 miles (120 km) from Khambhat. The trap beds of this place contain the best quality carnelian, found especially on a hill called Vaidurya Par-vat (Agate Mountain).

Another outstanding source of carnelian, of which the best quality comes from India, is the Bawa Ghori or Bawa Abbas Hill at Ratankhode in Rajpipla. Bawa Ghor, the sanc-tified patron of agate workers, was an Abyssin-ian merchant who in the sixteenth century established an agate manufactory at Limodra near Rajpipla. His brother, Bawa Saban, super-vised the lucrative export branch of the busi-ness at Khambhat. To be nearer the point of export, the factory was moved to Khambhat. The three main types of stone mined are *mora* or *Bawa Ghori; chashmedar* or *dola;* and *rori* or *lasaniyo.* Three grades of raw agate are recog-nized: first quality (*tukdi*); second quality (*gar*); and a third, inferior quality (*khadya*). In com-memoration of Bawa Ghor's great commercial success, today superior types of carnelian are called *Bawa Ghori akik,* a term still used in East Africa. His tomb at Ratanpor is visited annually by many agate craftsmen who pay homage to his memory.

Heat Treatment of Agates

Carnelian, a form of agate, is almost always heat treated to improve its red color, as are other agate stones known to react favorably to heat treatment. When found, agate composi-tion is generally not uniform. Some parts con-tain more color than others, and their relative density and porosity also varies. Most stones have a milky-white tinge, or are a pale color, ranging from white to yellow to cloudy brown. In carnelians, the deeper the original color the darker the red achieved after heat treatment. Because of variations in color and structure, results in a single stone are rarely uniform.

Most stones in the crypto-crystalline quartz group contain varying percentages of some form of iron or manganese oxide. When heated to the correct temperature, their color becomes reddish or brownish, its depth depending on the percentage of iron or manganese oxide pres-ent. Color change is due to *dehydration,* in which hydrogen and oxygen as chemically combined water are eliminated by heat, and a change in the *valence* (a measure of the extent to which an atom is able to combine directly with others) of its hydroferric content. After heating, orange-colored stones become white; maize yellow stones become rose colored; cloudy yellow or brown stones develop dis-tinctly marked areas of red and white; red car-nelians vary from pale red to deep blood red; light brown tints become white, and dark tints deepen to chestnut brown.

Carnelian is the most desirable and valued of all heat-treated agates. The best quality is free of defects and a translucent, uniformly deep red, though paler reds and deeper red-browns are also sold as carnelian. This deep red color is not common in nature, and most red carnelian has been made so by heat treatment. When dark brownish red, the stone is called sard.

Sun heating (*surya garmi*), a preliminary heat treatment process, takes place during the hot, dry season of March and April. Stones are spread out on terraces or corrugated iron sheets placed on house roofs and exposed to the sun for one and one half to two months, and turned every four or five days for even exposure. Sun heat eliminates the stone's external, and some internal, moisture content to avoid the pressure of trapped moisture con-verted to steam that will crack the stones dur-ing the following fire-baking process.

Baking (*bhatthi api,* to give fire) to devel-op the potential reds in agates is done by one of two methods. In either case, the tempera-ture necessary to affect the color change is from 572 to 752° F (300 to 400° C).

Bhalsal, the slow-firing method, requires a trench two feet deep by three feet wide (61 x 92.5 cm) dug in dry ground. At its bottom, about one and half inches (3.75 cm) of ash are spread, upon which the sun-dried agate stones are placed and covered with three or four alter-nating layers of ash, dry-goat and cowdung cakes, charcoal, and sawdust; these are ignited and consumed. After three days of an even heat, the stones are removed and examined. Those that require further heat treatment to develop full color are rebaked. The *bhalsal* method is preferred today because slow heat-ing reduces stone waste.

Handla, the pot-trench baking method, is a faster alternative to the above. Heat applica-tion is short and quickly reaches peak temper-ature. This process is done in May, directly after sun treatment. Overheating will cause stones to turn an irreversible white, or even to crumble into a white powder. Insufficient heat, on the other hand, leaves the stone an underdeveloped pink-orange or salmon color.

Stones are placed in black earthenware pots (*chatli*). If no hole exists, one is broken in the pot bottom to allow moisture to escape. Pots are placed over the stones, mouth downward, and a shard covers the hole. Clay pots act as a "muffle," and, when surrounded with fuel, cre-ate a reducing atmosphere inside that excludes oxygen to assist in red color development.

Rows of pots separated by bricks and fuel spread around and over them fill a cement-lined, compartmented trench. The fuel is ignited and burned continually in one day from sunrise to sunset, or one night from sun-set to sunrise. After the pots are removed, the stones are examined. Yellow or black stones are rebaked or kept for firing the next year, and those with too many flaws are discarded.

Hardstone bead–making in Khambhat is a vertically organized, integrated trade. Work-ers are drawn from the community without restriction of caste or religion. Each process involves artisans possessing specialized skills, formerly passed from father to son, now no longer always the case. Specialists workers include knappers; lapidary wheel workers; pol-ishers on stone; polishers on wood; and bead drillers. Mutual cooperation among the vari-ous specialist artisans is essential, and generally speaking, group relations are harmonious.

Master craftsmen oversee production and supervise the training of apprentices, who work for six to eight months before they can qualify as skilled artisans. Some work in the factories, and others at home. Both earn wages mainly on a piece-work basis.

Cutting and Shaping the Stone

The labor-intensive hardstone bead–making process begins with the examination of the raw material by a sorter (*bangiya*). First the outer skin (*chal*) of the geode is removed by a stone cutter (*kapnar*), who positions the stone on a pointed iron spike in the floor and, by ham-mering it with a mallet removes pieces from the mass. These results are split (*chirnaa*) either traditionally by hand, or (more often today) cut to a size usable for a bead on a mechanical stone sawing machine (*karvati*). The rough results are passed to the knapper.

Knapping (*khandiya*) is the process of chip-dressing the stone to shape it to its basic form, a process still similar to that used by Paleolithic stone tool–makers. Because of the innate structure of agate, when struck, stone fragments are easily removed by conchoidal fracture.

In the workshop is an earth and cowdung platform, one to one and one half feet (30–46 cm) above ground level, its area depending on the number of knappers it accommodates. The knapper sits on spread gunnysacks, placed to catch flying stone chips. Implanted in the platform floor before each worker is a two to three foot (61–91.5 cm) iron spike, fixed at an angle of sixty degrees with its sharply pointed end projecting about nine to ten inches (23–25.5 cm) above the ground toward the knapper.

Knapping a bead is done in two stages: rough-shaping (*phara parna*, broken pieces to fall), and full shaping (*chiria parna*, stripping pieces). Both require skill, the latter especially.

In rough-shaping, the stone, held in the left hand, rests against the spike end. Using a chipping mallet whose head, made of goat or buffalo horn, is fixed to a handle of springy, thin bamboo, the knapper chips away at the stone against the pointed spike until the rough bead shape is achieved, in two to three minutes. Final bead-shaping is achieved in about two and one half minutes using a lightweight, small knapping hammer with a nail-shaped iron head. The bead surface (*phala*) is still unsmooth, but the bead is now closer to a basic bead form.

Finishing a rough bead surface by smoothing can be done by hand-grinding on a grooved sandstone slab; hand-grinding on an electrically powered grinding wheel; or hand-grinding on a hand-operated grinding wheel.

Round beads (*golia*) are smoothed on a Porbander sandstone slab (*pattimar*) with a series of U-shaped grooves. The oldest hand-grinding method, today it is practiced by only a few craftsmen. Bead stones are held tightly in series in a long wooden clamp (*bhinthi*) at a right angle to the groove direction. Each clamped bead enters one of the lengthwise grooves in the sandstone, fixed at an inclined plane before the worker. Clamped beads are moved back and forth in the water-lubricated grooves, which rounds the contacting area. At intervals the beads are turned to grind all surfaces equally.

In the second method, the knapped bead blanks are ground on a vertically operating lapidary or grinding wheel (*vajar* or *sana*), whose design has remained unchanged for centuries. The wheel is a disc whose composition contains emery or corundum abrasive distributed in a binding medium. (Corundum, or *korund*, used in India since antiquity, is a grayish-black granular alumina found in the former state of Rewa in the area of Pipra and Kodopani.) Two grades of lap-wheel coarseness are used, the coarser one for quick cutting action, the finer one to give the bead a matte, prepolished surface (*gar*).

The wheel is vertically fixed on the lapidary frame axle, and the lapidary sits on the floor before it. The leather string of the driving bow is wrapped several times around the axle, and the bow is held in and operated by the left hand. The bead, held in the right hand, is occasionally dipped in water. Pushing the bow forward and backward makes the wheel rotate reciprocally while the stone is pressed and moved against it when it rotates toward the worker.

Hand-operated lathes are fast disappearing in Khambhat and are being replaced by electrically driven grinding wheels, with a motor connected to the wheel by a pulley. Grinding workshops equipped with one to thirty such machines are scattered throughout the city.

On ready-made grinding wheels, fast speeds are used for rough grinding and slow speeds for smoothing. Two or three workers use the same wheel fixed on the mechanism's frame. To form a completely round bead, a grinding wheel with an edgewise half-round concave depression is used. The bead is held and forced against the wheel edge with a simply constructed holder. The process takes only a few seconds.

Polishing the Beads

Any of three methods are practiced at Khambhat to polish hardstone beads. Two of them are manual and one mechanical. Once polished, agate retains its surface luster for a very long time, as witnessed by the agate beads found at various Indus Valley Civilization sites that date from 2500 B.C. This is partly explained by the fact that agate does not react to any acid but hydrofluoric acid, which is not found in a natural state.

To polish beads by hand, the polisher (*opiya*) holds each bead against a groove in a stationary wooden polishing board, applies a fine abrasive, and moves it up and back using water as a lubricant. Another method employs a revolving wooden polishing wheel mounted on a lapidary lathe, used in the same way as already described when using a grinding wheel. In an ancient, prewheel manual polishing method mentioned by early observers, hundreds of beads are placed in a strong leather bag (*chamrani kothri*) about two feet long and twelve inches wide (61 x 30.5 cm), into which a slurry containing a fine particle abrasive such as emery and powder gathered and saved from hole drilling are placed with water. The bag mouth is tied tightly and a flat leather strap is passed around the bag center. Two men seated on the floor some distance apart each hold one end of the strap, and drag the bag up and back between them, in shifts of ten to fifteen work days, during which the bag is kept moist with applications of water. As the beads tumble over each other, friction causes the stone's surface to become polished. Beads are removed, washed, and passed to the hole driller.

A relatively new innovation, polishing with a mechanical tumbling drum was until recently kept secret as it was thought knowledge of it would be detrimental to the trade. In principle, the leather bag system and this method are the same; here manpower is replaced by electrical power. The leather bag containing a batch of about 45.5 pounds (100 kilos) of beads plus abrasive and water is placed in a metal drum made to rotate by a motor. A sequence of two or three stages follow, each using an even finer abrasive. Polish tumbling takes from two to three days.

Drilling Holes in Hardstone Beads

Drilling the bead hole is achieved by the same method evolved ages ago for making a hole in a stone tool, a technique used since late Upper Paleolithic and Mesolithic times. The holes of ancient hardstone perforated beads found at many archaeological sites in India are often small and finely made. We can conclude that in prehistoric India complete mastery over this very specialized process had already been established.

In Khambhat today there remain only five bead-drilling establishments, although, in villages in a surrounding thirty-mile area, about three hundred cultivators, ages nine to forty-five, do drilling as a part-time occupation. Hole-making (*surakhi* or *kanu padavu*) in stone is accomplished here by rotary grinding, boring, or drilling.

Because hole-making employs rotary drills, hardstone bead holes are always cylindrical or conical. Three basic hole types are recognized, the first two being the oldest: *hourglass*, two-directional boring with a ball-ended solid-steel tool and diamond dust, done in two steps, from opposite ends toward a common central point; *conical*, two-directional boring with a pointed tool; and *cylindrical*, one-directional boring done either in a continuous action or in two steps from opposite poles, both using a hollow drill for large beads or a diamond-pointed drill for small holes.

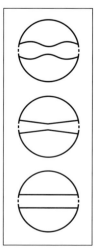

114. *Hand-Drilled Hardstone-Bead Hole Types*

Hourglass
Biconic
Straight cylinder

Normally Khambhat beads are drilled from opposite pole directions, and the result is a biconical hole, made to avoid chipping around the break through hole, which can happen in one-directional drilling unless great care is taken to ease pressure on the drill when it approaches exit.

Most Khambhat bead holes are made with a bow drill ending in a drill bit with a filed slot into which is émbedded one or two small carbonado diamond chips (*hira ni sharadi*) (depending on hole size), set in the bit by the driller, who carefully peens the metal over them.

The drill is operated by means of a short crosspiece to whose ends a string is attached and wound several times around the shaft. Moving the bow up and down imparts an alternating rotary motion to the drill. The top end of the shaft is held by a separate "handle" device, which acts as a bearing and protects the driller's palm from the friction of its rotation. In Khambhat this is a concave piece of coconut shell.

The driller grips the beads firmly in a wooden clamp held together by an iron ring. The drill haft is held in the right hand and, for greater control on the downward force, the left hand is passed under the left knee. (Due to the constant pressure on the shell and under the left knee, an occupational deformation of the muscles at these places can result.)

Small beads are drilled through in one continuous action. Large and long beads must be drilled halfway through, reversed, and drilled from the opposite direction. Agate sludge and diamond particles resulting from drilling are saved by occasionally dipping the bead into a bowl of water nearby.

Drilling a bead approximately a quarter of an inch (0.05 cm) in diameter takes about twenty seconds. Beads with long holes (1¾ in.; 4.5 cm) may take up to seven minutes to perforate. Drillers on the average perforate from 500 to 600 beads per day.

Because most Khambhat hardstone beads are drilled in two operations from opposite bead ends, nonconcentric inaccuracies occur when perforations do not meet in a straight line. Sharp edges may be left in the hole, which eventually fray the stringing thread and sever it. Other factors aside, relative bead quality is judged by the precision with which the two perforations meet and by hole centrality. Beads with off-center holes do not hang true because of unbalanced weight distribution. Such beads are rejected in the final sorting or are used in low-quality merchandise. Finished beads, inspected and sorted for color, size, and quality, are either sold in bulk or as ready-strung necklaces.

115. Khambat (Cambay), Gujarat
In hardstone-bead hand manufacture, the hole is drilled through the bead (held in a wooden clamp) from both ends using a hand-pump drill mounted with a drilling bit terminating in two diamond splinters.

Hardstone Names and Bead Forms

(The terms given below are Gujarati-Hindi.)

Agate	*akik*
banded agate	*doradar akik; jajemani*
eyed agate	*chashmedar akik; hadid*
milky white	*mansur*
moss agate	*suva bhaji*
Amethyst	*jabu; kataila*
Aventurine	*markaz*
green and blue	*bhura markaz*
red	*lal markaz*
purple	*lila markaz*
Bloodstone	*pitonia*
Carnelian	*lal akik; Bawa Ghori*
Cat's eye	*lasaniya*
Chrysoprase	*salan*
Citrine	*sunhela*
Coral	*munga*
Crystal, rock	*phitak; sphatik*
Diamond	*hira*
Emerald	*panna*
Garnet	*tamda*
Goldstone	*taramandal*
Jade	*echav*
Jasper, red	*zabarjad*
Lapis lazuli	*lajavarat*
Moonstone	*godanta*
Opal	*gomed sannibh*
Ruby	*manek*
Sapphire	*nilam*
Sard	*rathia*
Senimen ruby	*gomedak*
Smoky topaz	*dhuneila*
Sodalite	"sodalite"
Topaz	*pokhraj*
Turquoise	*firoza*
Yellow sapphire	*guru*
Zircon	*gomed medak; tursava*

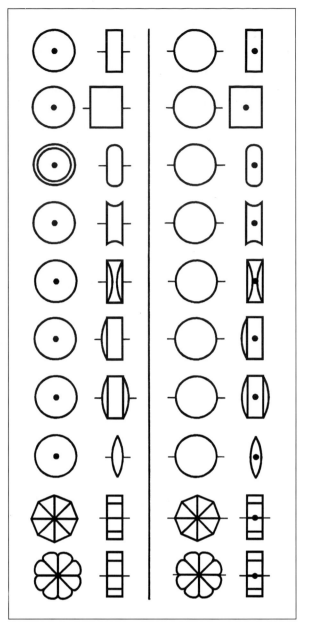

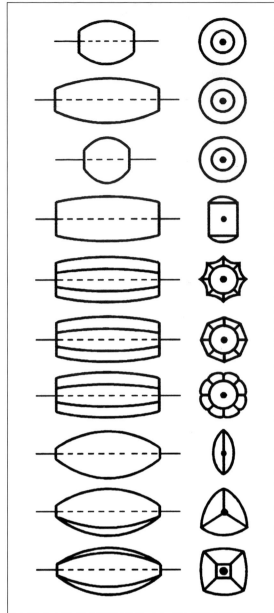

116. *Flat-Disc Beads*

*Perforations facewise and edge-
wise. Fabricated in all sizes; used
without or with lugs or collars*

*Flat-sided disc, round tabular
Thick button
Convex edge
Concave grooved edge
Concave-sided disc
Plano-convex
Convex-sided disc
Lenticular disc
Hexagon
Flower*

117. *Barrel and Related-Form
Stone Beads*

*Barrel (lohi)
Elongated barrel (lamba lohi)
Round barrel (gol lohi)
Flat barrel (hamwar lohi)
Concave-fluted, oblate (kholar
    kamrakhi)
Flat-faceted, oblate (hamwar
    kamrakhi)
Ribbed, oblate (paslidar kam-
    rakhi)
Two-sided, faceted (badam)
Three-sided, faceted (tin pasia)
Four-sided, faceted (chopat daria)*

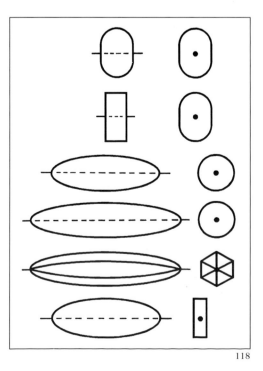

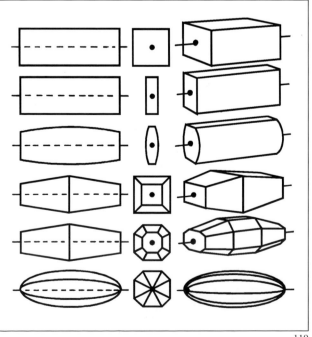

118. *Ellipsoid Beads*

*Vertical ellipsoid
Flat vertical ellipsoid, oblate
Round ellipsoid, horizontal
Round ellipsoid, long horizontal
    (khildar lohi), sold to Nepal
    and Tibet
Faceted ellipsoid, long horizontal
    (chassai: 6 or 8 facets, sold to
    Nagas)
Flat ellipsoid, horizontal*

119. *Rectangular (modandana)
Beads*

*Rectangle, square section
Rectangular panel, rectangular
    section
Rectangle with swelled sides
Rectangle with acute-cut sides
    (kandora)
Hexagonal (jorrat modan)
Hexagonal, faceted oval*

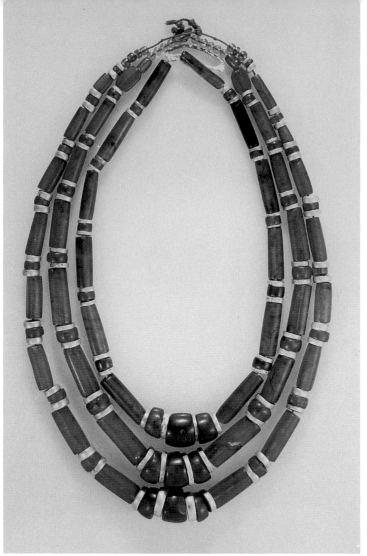

120

121

122
123

Popular Beads of Organic Substances

Red Coral

For millennia, red coral (S: pravala; P: murjan; A: bussud; H: parvara; munga; Guj: parvala; Mar: povale; Kan: havala; Mal: poalam; Tel: pagadamu; Tam: pavalam) has been widely used in Indian jewelry, primarily as beads. Not a mineral, coral is an organic substance manufactured by living, minute, soft polyps who multiply by budding and who live in colonies supported by a solid, medial, internal core required for growth and created by extracting calcium carbonate from seawater. Coral is in effect the internal skeleton, which in time develops a treelike form, its rootless foot a flat disk, permanently cemented to a rock or other solid at the sea bottom. If allowed to live to maturity, under favorable conditions up to thirty years, the main coral trunk can achieve a diameter of around two inches, although pieces of this size have always been rare.

The popularity of coral in India is a curious phenomenon because, although some exists in Indian waters, it was not regularly fished there. What probably attracted Indians to coral initially, as in the case of carnelian, was its auspicious deep red color (light orange, also used, is less favored). Other red stones (before the recent invention of synthetic gemstones) include the ruby, which is rare, very expensive, and beyond the means of most people, and garnet, whose deep red color is generally too dark to be considered auspicious. The availability and relatively low cost of Italian red coral contributed to its wide acceptance, and, until recently, most of the coral seen in India, Nepal, and Tibet was imported from Italy as ready-made beads.

Equally active in the popularity of red coral is its long-established place in Indian folklore. It is connected with one of the nava-grahas, *the planet Mars, or Mangala, associated with Karttikeya, the god of war, which makes it one of the auspicious* nava-ratna *planetal gemstones. (The word* mangala *also refers to anything that is regarded as auspicious, such as an amulet.) Coral is believed to have the power to dispel the malignant effects of the evil eye, which accounts for its very popular use as an amulet in bead form, a few strung on a cord and placed on the neck of women and children. Coral beads are also often used for Hindu rosaries.*

Because overfishing and water pollution have brought coral to near extinction in the Mediterranean, coral for Indian jewelry today comes mainly from Japanese and northern Australian waters. Also, a considerable industry now exists in India in the manufacture of all sizes of colored-glass beads meant to imitate coral.

120. Mizoram
Bead necklace (thihna or puan chei mala) of Burmese amber (burmite), worn by Mizo tribal women. Some have aluminium disc spacers that alternate with the amber beads.
Longest strand 31½ in. (80 cm); longest bead 3⅛ in. (8 cm); total weight c. 700 g
Collection Thorbjörn and Judy Carlsson, Art Expo, Washington, D.C.

The fossil resin burmite, a succinite type of amber, has been known to the Chinese since the Han dynasty (206 B.C.–220 A.D.). Until World War II, almost all Burmese amber went to China, but it was also long in use by the Mizos of the neighboring Indian hill areas. Mizos prize burmite for its reddish to dark-brown color and mottled appearance.

121. Aizawl, Mizoram
Mizo woman wearing a burmite necklace along with a necklace of coral and turqoise beads

122. Tandi or Gosha, Lahul and Spiti District, Himachal Pradesh
Lohar woman wearing a pair of amber temple ornaments (böschel) inset with coral, strung on cord, and tied to the hair

123. Chamba, Himachal Pradesh
Hindu Gaddi woman wearing two necklaces (lau mala) of imitation amber (H: naqli kahruba), coral (munga), and Tibetan dZi beads, the latter evidence of a cross-cultural influence. She also wears a silver blouse-stud ornament (sangli) connected with chains; silver hoop earrings (bali); wide, rigid silver bracelets (toké); and a woolen cord girdle (un ka dora) over her traditional dress (paswaz).

Amber

Amber (H: kahruba; A: 'anbar; Tam: ambar) is the hardened resin of coniferous trees that flourished millions of years ago. Amber is often described as fossilized resin. Yet unlike a traditional fossil, whose original structure has been replaced by minerals, amber remains organic, its composition essentially unchanged, and can be found in beautiful translucent colors ranging primarily from deep red to yellow. Perhaps because of its seemingly miraculous properties, amber has long been used as a natural amulet or in religious ceremonies as a purification incense. Amber is also commonly sold by medicine vendors in Indian bazaars. Beads of amber are supposed to prevent sore throats and goiters, and yellow amber is said to act against jaundice.

Amber's popularity in ornamental beads can be attributed partly to its warm, tactile quality, light weight, and the belief that it is a prophylactic substance. Long the focus of a competitive and far-ranging trade, amber used in India and Tibet comes primarily from the Baltic region via the Middle East. Amber is often used in both Buddhist and Muslim rosaries and is the preferred material for the latter (see pages 145 and 147).

124

125

126

SEED BEADS

124. Andhra Pradesh
Glass seed-bead necklace worn by Gondh women
Length 45⅝ in. (116 cm); weight 932 g
Collection Ghysels, Brussels

125. Junagadh, Gujarat
Rabari man wearing a necklace (limbori) of glass and wood beads strung on silver wire links. Pinned to his chest is a silver snuff container (H: nasdani), and in his ears are gold granulated earrings (see 697).

126. Kondhan Hills, Koraput District, Orissa
The Bondo, a tribal group of about eight thousand, live in sixty to seventy villages at an altitude of over 3,000 feet (c.1000 m). Among the typical ornaments worn by their head-shaven women are multicolored glass seed beads, strung with spaced-out coins, and silver- and brass-wire necklaces and bangles. Beads and metal are brought to them by Dombo plains traders, in exchange for local products. A typical Bondo woman's dress includes masses of these beads, which are worn as an upper "garment," along with a 9–10-inch (23–25-cm) cloth strip on the loins and a palm-leaf headband.

127

WOUND-GLASS, LAMP-WORKED BEADS

127. Gwalior, Madhya Pradesh
The process for making wound-glass lamp-worked beads as done at the Glass Bead Centre, Chattri Bazaar, Gwalior, and other centers, such as Purdalpur, Uttar Pradesh, and surrounding villages, where it is a cottage industry. Not a traditional Indian process, it was introduced from Czechoslovakia in the late 1930s. To begin, an 18-gauge iron wire (loha tar) is dipped into a slurry of kaolin, lime, and glue, then dried. The bead maker sits facing a battery of three to eight flames converging to one point. Holding the wire in one hand and a glass rod with a high lead content (to assure a low melting temperature) in the other, she heats the glass to viscosity. Rotating the wire, she wraps some molten glass around it and shapes it with a tool. The result—a wire holding finished beads—is placed upright in a container of sand and left to cool. Beads are removed from the wire by soaking the entire assembly in water to loosen the kaolin compound, then stretching the wire with pliers at each end. Under tension, the metal wire stretches sufficiently to permit the beads to be slipped off.

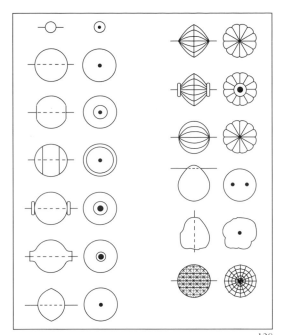

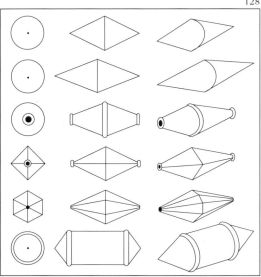

128. Metal, Hardstone, and Glass Bead Forms
Round-Spheroid (M = metal; S = stone;
G – glass; all Hindi terms)

Top to bottom: *Seed (dana):* Micro or pound
bead of ³⁄₁₆ in. (2 mm) or less (G)
Oblate sphere: With flattened or depressed
poles (SMG)
Composite sphere: Of contrasting-colored
stones cemented together (S)
Sphere with lugs, attached or separate (MG)
Spheroid: Acacia-seed form (babul bij) (MG)
Less than hemisphere: Two parts, joined (M)
Musk melon (kharbuza): Less than hemisphere,
ribbed (SMG)
*Flattened sphere, gadrooned (hamwar amalaka
mohan)* (SMG)
Drop (bunda) (SMG)
Baroque, tumbled (kadakar) (S)
Faceted (phuli kharbuza) (S)

METAL BEADS

129. Biconic Metal Beads

Bicone, short
Bicone, long
Bicone, truncated
Double pyramid
Double hexagon
Cylinder with conical caps

130. Northern India
Traditional silver-bead forms used in a necklace
(chandi moti mala)

131. Chamba, Himachal Pradesh
*Gujar woman wearing a silver torque (sira or
hansuli); a necklace of silver, grooved beads
(kamrakhi mala; the name kamrakh comes from
the carambola fruit [Averrohoea carambola],
which it resembles). In the Kullu area, similar
silver-bead necklaces are called doad mala when
the beads are spheroid, jau mal when oval, dar
mal when flat discs, and makhawaji mal when
oval with horizontal end lugs at openings.*

◄ **132. Purdalpur, Uttar Pradesh**
*Handmade furnace-wound-glass beads, used most
often in necklaces made for the decoration of domestic animals. Such beads produced at this center are
sold all over India, especially at cattle fairs.*

The Hardstone-Bead Trade • 85

133   134   135

Papanaidupetta, Andhra Pradesh: Making Glass Seed Beads

133. *The glass-block (gajuraye) melting furnace (bhatti) contains a crucible (thotti) with molten glass. The worker gathers as much as 110 pounds (50 kg) of molten glass on a tube-rod (ladi) and then shapes the mass (mudda) to a cone form by rolling it on a flat-surfaced marver.*

134. *A long iron rod (salakku) with a rounded end is inserted in the ladi to pierce the cone horizontally. This air space will eventually become the bead hole.*

135. *From the other side of the furnace, a worker using a glass-covered iron hook closes the opening on the pierced cone and, pulling the attached molten glass behind him, runs down the tube-drawing lane, away from the furnace. The result is a long glass tube that lies on the floor of the drawing lane, where it cools and becomes rigid. This basic tube-drawing process is repeated until all the glass on the pierced cone that is rotating in the furnace is depleted. This takes about three hours. Drawn-tube lengths can reach 490 feet (159 m), but generally they are shorter.*

136. *The round, perforated drawn-glass tubes (seliga) are broken into lengths of about 6.4 feet (2 m) or less, then sorted into bunches, each having approximately the same outside diameter.*

137. *Tied bundles of glass tubes of the same color and diameter stand ready to be processed into seed beads.*

138. *The manual bead-chopping process still used in Papanaidupetta is said to have originated in Venice, but, in the mid-nineteenth century, the system described here was replaced with machinery in Europe. The chopper (narakatam manishi) holds a handful of drawn-glass tubes resting equidistantly over the tooth-edged surface of a broad, soft-steel, chisellike tool (ari), whose long tang is fixed in the earthen floor. In a continuous action, tubes are slowly fed forward manually, then chopped into more or less uniform bead lengths by a sharp, wedge-shaped tool (badisa). The beads fall onto a cloth spread before the chopper or on the floor. Because the chopped bead length is judged visually in this process, bead size varies.*

136   137   138

139

140

141

139. To round the chopped edges, the beads are placed in a shallow, iron roasting pan containing sand and cowdung ashes, which fill the bead holes to preserve them. The pan with beads is placed in the roasting oven. While being heated, the beads are stirred to prevent them from sticking together. Heat softens the glass and causes bead edges to contract and become rounded (gundu). Heat also fire-polishes the beads, leaving them with a shining surface. After cooling, the pan's contents are poured from a height into a basket to separate beads from ashes. To further remove ash, the beads are transferred to a sieve and shaken.

140. To dislodge any remaining ash that would obstruct bead holes, two women alternate in gently "pounding" the beads in a wooden mortar.

141. The finished beads (pusalu) are strung by an ingenious system. About ten stiff steel "needle" wires, their gauge smaller than that of the bead holes, are fixed with a fine thread at one end. Held at one end, their other, free ends are jabbed into the bead mass, here placed in a winnowing fan, and the beads gradually accumulate on the wires.

142. When the wires have become sufficiently loaded, the beads are simply passed onto the thread attached at the other wire end. The process is repeated until a strand of about fifty beads is achieved. Strands of the same color and size beads are then tied together to form a bunch.

143. Bead stringing is normally done by women at home in their spare time. Strung beads are returned to the factory and weighed. The stringer is paid by bead weight, not by the number of strings she completes.

144. Bundles of seed beads of the same color and size are packed in paper, tied with a cord, and labeled. A bundle generally contains two bunches, each with twelve strings of fifty beads. The bundle therefore contains one hundred dozen, or twelve hundred, beads.

142

143

144

Amulets:
Semiotic Symbols of Supernatural Power

The motivation for amulet use stems from a distant time, when humanity's concepts about the surrounding natural environment developed in relation to a common belief in *animism,* in which nature as a whole, and all natural phenomena, whether inanimate objects or living bodies, are thought to possess life-vitality or be endowed with material or immaterial souls. Included in this general belief is *atavism,* or the idea that the spirit of a recently deceased ancestor or animal in the form of an aggressive ghost can be active in its possession of the living, unless propitiated. Other animistic concepts are *fetishism,* a belief in the magical power of a natural object, such as a claw or tooth of an animal, as an abode of a supernatural power, which can be transferred to a consecrated object fashioned in such a form; and *phallicism,* the worship of the reproductive power of living creatures.

Today the term animism refers to one of the earliest and most superstitious forms of religion that humans have created to satisfy their spiritual and physical needs. In support of this system, the amulet became the material instrument believers used to satisfy these ends. Amulets are power objects invented to help the living to cope with negative forces in nature, over which they realize they have no control, and which are therefore mainly interpreted as the actions of malignant spirits. Essentially, the amulet is a protecting device rising from the natural human instinct for self-preservation.

Animism eventually developed into a more sophisticated supernatural deism, a belief in a multiplicity of divine gods who possess miraculous powers above and beyond nature. This concept is given wide credence in India today among Hindus, Jains, and Buddhists, as well as rural and tribal people. The amulet is also a part of this system. Once amulet use was overtly or tacitly condoned for a religious purpose, its adoption spread. As a consequence, the use of the amulet as a power object meant to propitiate or coerce the divine and counteract the malicious influence of the spirit world is now universal throughout the Indian subcontinent.

Despite the evolution of cultural changes and the growth of modern education with its emphasis on rationality, many "enlightened" people have not completely abandoned belief in amulet efficacy. An explanation for its persistence may be that the use of an amulet provides the wearer with a decided feeling of identity with the community that shares such beliefs and practices. These ideas are so rooted in the Indian psyche that, even though amulet use established by previous generations may change over time, or explanations be lost, the fundamental reasons for wearing them remain unaltered.

Faith in its working power is the essential element that gives the amulet the capacity of functioning for the wearer, particularly at times of psychological stress when a believer is in a receptive state of mind. By self-suggestion, an amulet worn on the body gives the wearer a consoling sense of well-being through the belief in its protective power, permitting that person better to cope with life's problems.

How Amulets Work: Negative- and Positive-Acting Amulets

The dominant basis for amulet use on the body is the widespread fear of the hostility of negative or evil forces believed to be constantly active against humankind. In repelling such powers that may possess and harm an individual, the amulet acts as a physical, energized object that the user believes is capable of effectively nullifying or destroying the threatening evil force and, in so doing, provides protection. Even Hindu gods and goddesses recognize the power of an amulet, and many are commonly depicted wearing them.

An amulet can have the power either to repel or to attract, depending on which of these may be desirable. A very common repelling amulet is one worn against the inadvertent sorcery of the evil eye, which in effect is an expression of the ill wishes of a jealous person, of which the possessor may not be consciously aware. Intentionally malignant spirits are also rebuffed by an appropriate amulet, such as the one placed on children to propitiate Sitala, the goddess of smallpox, who may inflict or avert this disease. Another amulet is used to repel or slay a demon attempting to take possession of a pregnant woman and cause abortion.

On the positive-action side, some amulets are believed to be efficacious in the creation of harmony, order, and happiness in life. This can be accomplished by interceding with or propitiating the divine by wearing a suitable amulet. Amulets exist that can effect the promotion of fecundity, virility, the begetting of children, and the preservation of family health. Amulets can also effect the protection of personal and family material possessions, including land, cultivation products, houses, cattle, valued possessions such as jewelry, and to assure prosperity in an uncertain future.

Amulets are commonly used in connection with religious ritual, such as the celebration of the rite-of-passage events in the life stages of a male or female Hindu. At each of these stages, ceremonies are performed for which specific amulets are required. Perhaps the most important of these are observed after a child's birth (*jatakarman*); when a child is named, accompanied by an earlobe-boring ceremony (*namakarana*); at the initiation of a young man into the Brahmanical community (*upanayana*); when a pupil finishes his Brahmanic studies and leaves the house of his teacher (*samavartana*); and at the wedding ceremony (*vivaha*). Amulets can be classified by the way in which they are intended to be used.

Propitiatory amulets belong to the category of personal amulets that have a general function and are worn as a means of conciliating or pacifying a spirit or deity to render it generally more favorable to the individual before any misfortune has occurred. This amulet serves as a form of sacrifice to a deity, which helps to reconcile the individual with the god or goddess.

Apotropaeic amulets also have a general preventive purpose in that they are meant to avert the action of evil spirits before they have a chance to attack and possess an individual. As such, they are shields against evil.

Prophylactic amulets offer a more specialized kind of protection against specific ailments and diseases by warding off the particular malevolent spirit or deity believed to possess the power to withhold or induce that illness, or even death. This kind of amulet acts to neutralize the spirit's evil action and intention.

Homeopathic amulets have a specific medicinal function, which is to cure an already existing disease. Wearing one of these may be preceded by a ceremony performed by an exorcist, who tries to expel the particular evil spirit believed to be already in possession of the wearer. The amulet itself may be used in the process of exorcism.

Ancient Vedic Amulets: Magic in the Guise of Religion

Amulet use in India probably dates back to prehistoric times, but the earliest written references to them occur in the ancient Sanskrit writings called the Vedas. The three main books are the *Rig-Veda,* a collection of sacred songs or hymns of praise; the *Sama-Veda,* melodies chanted by a priest at a sacrifice; and the *Yajur-Veda,* which consists of sacrificial formulas. Later a fourth book, the *Arthava-Veda,* was added.

The Vedas frequently cite the use of amulets for which the word *mani,* broadly meaning "jewel or ornament" but more specifically meaning "amulet," was used. In later Sanskrit literature, the amulet is also referred to as *kavacha* (cuirass), and *raksha* (preservation, guardianship, support). Formerly, and to a great extent today, practically *all* body ornaments were worn for an amuletic purpose and were in fact considered to be a form of amulet.

The *Arthava-Veda* was written as a result of the assimilation of Aryan and indigenous Dravidian cultures, and it includes archaic magic formulas, myths, and legends of the common people. The last of the four Vedas, the *Arthava-Veda* (knowledge of magic formulas) contains abundant citations of amulets whose use by that time was already fully developed and established. It is believed to incorporate ancient ideas from the time of the Indus Valley cultures, as well as Dravidian magico-religious practices, and its appearance greatly influenced the subsequent development of early Aryan culture. It also gained general attention because it was concerned with the popular side of religion, whose main aim was to secure the immediate fulfillment of all desires. By the time of the *Arthava-Veda,* all the present basic concepts connected with the use of amulets were recognized, and they have not changed much since.

Activating an Amulet

It has never been sufficient for a person simply to acquire an amulet and wear it with any expectancy of its maximal potency. Among Muslims, amulet activation is performed by a mulla or dervish deemed capable of this act. To activate a Hindu amulet, it must be consecrated (S: *abhiseka*) in the same way in which a man-made image of a Hindu deity must be consecrated before it is considered to have spiritual life (S: *prana*) and divine energetic power (*shakti*).

In Vedic times, amulets were given generative power by the performance of sometimes elaborate rites that a priest carried out over them. (In the case of natural amulets, the intention was to reinforce any power the amulet already possessed.) Descriptions are given in Vedic texts of the material to be used for the amulet and the time it should be used. General rules (*paribhasa*) had to be followed in the consecration ritual. The person for whom the ceremony was performed (*karayitr*) stood behind the priest, who touched him with sacred *darbha* grass. Upon completion of these rites and ceremonies, the priest, while reciting an appropriate hymn, tied the amulet on the receiver's body.

Today, to energize a Hindu amulet and cause it to commence its beneficent activity against evil (S: *manas-papman*) and destructive powers (S: *nirrti*), it is brought to a priest (H: *purohit*) or shaman (A: *kahin*) who has a reputation of being able to perform the proper rituals. Such a person may also be a vendor of amulets.

Amulet activation today, as in Vedic times, still involves the incantation of magical formulas and the performance of various rituals whose nature depends on the type of amulet and its relative importance. Ritual purity (H: *safi*; A: *khalisi*; P: *parsai*) of the amulet and the receiver at the time when the amulet is activated are the chief conditions required for them to work. The process of purification may involve the priest's recitation of the words of a written charm and an effective proscribed *mantra* that provides protection against general or a specific danger. Every *mantra* includes a proper mystic syllable (S: *bija; kavacham*), which adds to its power.

All recitations and rites such as those for averting evil (S: *mahashanti*) must be performed with absolute correctness in accordance with established practice; any error may cause the amulet's power to recoil upon itself or adversely affect the user. The same condition of correctness applies to any written charm, and to the execution of a magic diagram such as a *yantra,* or a magic-number square on the amulet, and the iconographic depiction of a deity on the amulet.

Activation rituals usually involve a symbolic sacrifice (*yajna*), oblation (*odana*), or offering (*bali*) of a non-living substance such as rice or pulses to the deity (*deva*), spirit (*bhuta*), or ghost (*preta*) involved. The officiating priest is generally rewarded with a monetary gift (*dakshina*).

Amulets can be worn on any part of the body. In some cases, to preserve their potent power, they must be hidden within clothing or hats, turbans, or other headgear. When hidden, the private knowledge that they are pres-

145. Sanchi, Barhut, and Amaravati
Necklace of auspicious amuletic symbols, a type often represented on images, or alone, depicted on stupas built during the second century B.C.–third century A.D. Some of these symbols, such as the wheel (charka), lotus (padma), two fish (matsya), and trident (trishula) are still in use.

ent is enough to reassure the individual of their ability to protect.

In the generally warm climate of India, where clothing can be minimal, amulets are often visible on the wearer's body. There is usually no objection to their being visibly exposed, and they are worn without self-consciousness, since nearly everyone understands their function and concurs in their use.

Amulets are often placed near the several natural human orifices in order to deflect malignant spirits from possible entry into the body via the particular opening. The nose ring or stud is an example of this type, and, in addition to its other meanings, can be thought of as an amulet with this function.

The neck is probably the most common place for the suspension of an amulet, but they are also worn on the breast, chest, or attached to the sacred thread. Amulets may be placed on the specific body part they are meant to protect, such as under the left arm near the heart, fixed over the umbilicus by a cord, or attached to the genitals. They can be worn on the top of the head, forehead, and ears. They may also be tied to the outer upper arm, placed on the wrist, fingers, on the leg below the knee, and upon ankles and toes.

Any amulet without proper consecration is considered to be without life, not a working amulet but simply a decorative object. Even after correct consecration, an amulet that has become disassociated from its owner by being lost, stolen, or sold loses its power and is considered to be dead (H: *mara*). Lost or stolen amulets, if recovered, can be reactivated by repeating the required procedures. If it becomes necessary to sell a container-type of amulet, its magical contents are removed and kept by the original owner for whom they worked.

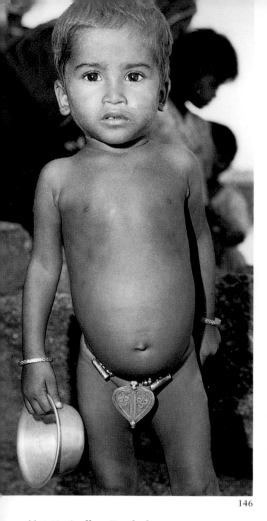

146. Nellore, Andhra Pradesh

Telugu girl wearing a silver cache-sexe plate in the shape of a yoni or leaf of the sacred fig tree. In Tamil Nadu this ornament is called mudi-thagadu, meaning "to cover metal plate," or aramudi. Besides serving modesty, this amulet guards a body orifice that otherwise would be exposed to the entry of evil spirits and is frequently worn with two flanking cylindrical amulet cases containing mantras, which fortify its power.

147. Andhra Pradesh

Silver cache-sexe, pubic ornament-amulet (marugu billa) for a young girl, worn as a substitute for a loin cloth, fabricated by repoussage and chasing 2⅜ x 1¾ in. (6 x 4.5 cm); weight 25 g
Collection the author, Porvoo

The design on the surface represents the tree of life, a symbol of fertility.

148. Uttar Pradesh

Vaishnavite sadhu Radha Das wearing a never-removed, cylindrical, solid-wood chastity belt (arbandh; H: ar, modesty; H: bandh, belt or band) with brass appliqués, and attached metal cache-sexe (langoti, which actually refers to a cloth worn between the legs of a celibate man), weighing 11 pounds (5 kg). The metal cache-sexe part can be unhooked and is sand scoured twice daily. At night, he digs a hollow in the earth to accommodate the arbandh form and allow him to sleep.

146

147
148

▼ ### 149. Andhra Pradesh

Silver cache-sexe ornaments (marugu billa)
Largest ornament 2⅓ x 2⅛ in. (6.3 x 5.5 cm); weight 21 g
Collection Ghysels, Brussels

Of yoni shape, these ornaments often bear designs such as sun or moon and flowers, symbols of fertility and the life force. Similarly shaped ornaments for the same function, but with two loops or a horizontal tube at the top, called caping in Malaysia, are also used in Sri Lanka and Indonesia.

Basic Amulet Forms

Amulets can be divided into basic types according to whether they are natural or fabricated. Natural amulets are the most ancient of those used for amuletic purposes. They can be used unaltered, as found in nature, such as animal claws, whose distinctive form is preserved and elaborated because of the claws' ingrained symbolic power. In some cases, the form itself can have the power by association, which permits the natural original to be substituted and fashioned from another, perhaps more easily available material. In other cases, the fragile nature of the power substance or object is such that it must be preserved within a special amulet container.

Amuletic substances can be vegetable, animal, or mineral. Objects and substances from the vegetable world, some but not all used in an unaltered state, comprise the largest source of amuletic substances. Varied in nature, each is believed to be capable of achieving a general or specific result. For example, rice (H: *chawal*) or barley (H: *jau*) placed in an amulet container act generally against disease, prolong life, and increase fertility. These substances themselves are frequently given as offerings to deities. Berries, seeds, nuts, fruits, and the stems and roots of certain sacred grasses and plants are all used as amulets as well as in rosaries.

Natural vegetative substances and forms, such as leaf, seed, bud, and flower of sacred plants, are often interpreted in stylized forms of wood, stone, or metal. Properly activated, they can perform the same functions as the originals and have the additional advantage of permanence.

Tiger-Claw Amulets

It has been noted that animal teeth and other body parts often carry strong amuletic powers. In this category are, most commonly, the claws of the tiger but also those of the cheetah, leopard, lion, bear, and pangolin.

The tiger (H: *bagh;* P: *sher;* Tam: *puli*), somewhat larger than an Indian lion, uses the extended claws of its powerful forepaws in self-defense, causing great damage to a victim. Claws are considered to be a highly potent amulet and are believed to impart to the wearer the prodigious qualities of the animal. After its death, by common Indian custom, a killed tiger's claws are immediately removed to insure against its possible vengeful return in the form of the widely dreaded tiger demon (*bagh-bhut* or *bagheswar*), who, if still in possession of its claws, will seek out and attack its killer.

Amulets of tiger's claws (P: *nakhun* or H: *panja,* an aggregate of five, the number on each paw) are used throughout India. In local vernacular languages they are known by vari-

ous names. In the north they are generally called *viagranakha ta'wiz* and, in Tamil Nadu, *pulinagam ratchabanthanam.*

A single claw may be used, but the usual form of this amulet includes an addorsed pair of matching-sized claws, usually mounted with their bases together and inserted into a metal holder, their ends pointing outward. Settings are often gold or silver and can be simple or elaborately ornamented, even with valuable gemstones, the choice depending on the buyer's financial resources. Among the most unique of indigenous Indian jewelry forms, the tiger-claw amulet's main function is to deflect any evil spirit that may approach and attempt to attack the wearer.

Amulets of this kind appear in ancient representations in bronze and stone of Hindu deities, wherever Hinduism was practiced. Such an amulet, worn as a pendant, or as a central unit in a necklace with a series of claws on both sides, is often depicted on representations of the ancient Dravidian folk deity and the Hindu god of war, known in the north as Skanda-Karttikeya and in the south as Subrahmanya, whose worship began as early as the fifth century A.D.

150. Rajasthan

Tiger-claw amulet (shernakh jantr), *the claws simulated in silver, ornamented with foil-backed glass stones and hanging bells*
3⅜ x 4¾ in. (8.3 x 12.1 cm); weight 140 g
Collection the author, Porvoo

In the absence of real tiger claws, a metal amulet whose form simulates tiger's claws can be used, provided the amulet is sanctified and its power activated by proper ceremony.

152

153

151. Arunachal Pradesh

Silver tiger-claw amulet (H: shernakh jantr) decorated with turquoises, clear glass "stones," and hanging silver bells (ghungrus)
2¾ x 2⅝ in. (6.7 x 7.1 cm); weight 163 g
Collection the author, Porvoo

The upper box is a container for charms. The attached claws encased in silver mounts are used for magical protection and as a cure for nightmares.

152. Tamil Nadu

Gold tiger-claw ornament with diamonds, rubies, emeralds, and pearls, the claws similarly overlaid
1⅞ x 1⅜ in. (4.8 x 3.5 cm); weight 50 g
Collection Mis, Brussels

153. Madras, Tamil Nadu

Gold tiger-claw amulet (Tam: pulinagam), with repoussé swami work depicting Shiva and Parvati, protected above by a makara, or guardian kirti-mukha (glory head)—often depicted at the top of an aureole (prabha-mandala) placed behind Shiva images and in jewelry—and flanked by peacocks (mayil). The tiger claws are tipped in gold.
Courtesy Chhote Bharany, New Delhi

Tigers are found throughout India in large grassland tracts or jungles. Past uncontrolled hunting has resulted in a decrease in their numbers. To prevent their extinction, the government has designated reserve areas where they are protected. Tigers in the wild are most commonly seen by aboriginal and rural people who live in remote areas near jungles. Among such people, tigers and representations of them are objects of veneration. They commonly wear an amulet depicting the goddess Durga, whose vehicle is a tiger, in which form she is called Bagheswara Mata, the "tiger-riding Mother," to indicate her invincibility. Nevertheless, rural people also hunt tigers and bring their claws to sell to jewelers in most large city jewelry bazaars.

154. Karnataka. *16th century*
Child Krishna in ivory with traces of polychrome and gold
7½ x 4⅛ x 2⅞ in. (19.1 x 10.5 x 7.3 cm)
Los Angeles County Museum of Art, Los Angeles. Purchased with funds from the Louis and Erma Zalk Foundation and Dr. and Mrs. Joseph Pollak (M.84.43)

Krishna wears a protective tiger-claw amulet (S: vyaghranakha) pendant set in gold and suspended on a gold chain, a practice that still prevails among children. Around his hips is a belt of bells, another child's ornament, its sound intended to frighten away evil spirits. He also wears a child's bell anklets (painjani) and other traditional ornaments. In his hands he carries two butterballs, which, according to legend, he stole from those prepared by his foster mother, Yashoda, a cowherdswoman who raised him.

155. Northern India. *19th century Gold necklace set with the ten claws of a tiger's front paws, mounted in graduated sizes*
Private Collection, Brussels

The idea of using many tiger claws in one necklace may have been inspired by a traditional necklace in this form commonly represented on images of Karttikeya, Hindu god of war. This one is made for a Western woman's use and is a form of trophy jewelry.

Victorian Tiger-Claw Jewelry: A Cross-Cultural View

We must digress here to discuss the use of tiger's claws in a type of jewelry popular in Great Britain during the late nineteenth-century era of the British Raj in India. In that period, intercultural contact in the field of jewelry had greater impact on contemporary British jewelry than is generally recognized (see pages 388–92). One interesting cross-cultural development occurred when the British adopted the use of tiger's claws as a form of trophy jewelry for women, a use that spread to European-made jewelry.

Judging from the amount of tiger-claw jewelry extant in Great Britain, they enjoyed more than little popularity. Their use is contemporary with the trophy jewelry of Continental Europe, where teeth, horns, and talons of other unfortunate, less fierce victims of the hunt were often mounted in elaborate settings. Today it seems surprising that an object such as a tiger's claw, which speaks of violence, blood, pain, and death, could have been so readily accepted by proper Victorian Englishwomen. Perhaps the explanation lies in the Victorian tendency to repress unpleasantness.

The Indian use of tiger-claw amulets was certainly familiar to the British who served in India. Tiger hunting then was "the sport of kings." It was very fashionable in the cold season for Indian maharajas who resided in areas inhabited by tigers to invite visiting British and other royalty, important government officials, and other guests to participate in a hunt (shikar), an old sport as indicated by many Mughal miniature paintings. For a Westerner to be invited to such a hunt was a symbol of the individual's high social status. And what better way of remembering the event than taking the twenty claws each animal could provide and transforming them into a memento in the form of jewelry.

Perhaps through such hunts, and the less glamorous poaching by peasant or aboriginal hunters, tiger claws were exported to Britain and China, where they were used in Western-style jewelry for women. Supply could never satisfy demand, and the smaller claws of leopards and cheetahs, indigenous to India, were also used.

Despite present-day revulsion for such seemingly frivolous slaughter, one has to admire the ingenuity and skill in the design and techniques used to arrange and mount these beautifully formed claws into ornaments such as earrings, pendants, brooches, necklaces, bracelets, and belt buckles. Complete parures of tiger-claw ornaments were created, the claws carefully matched and graded not only for size but color. Some were left in their natural state, others polished to a pearly gloss. Silver and gold were used for their mountings, and settings were often enriched by intricate engraving, wirework, canetille filigree, and precious stones. These Western design treatments were emulated in India by skilled goldsmiths.

The Indian versions were purchased by foreign tourists, who took them home as objects of exotic Indian craftsmanship. Because India had no unified system of hallmarking, it is possible that some of the unmarked Victorian claw-set pieces found today in British jewelry shops, at auctions, in antique supermarkets, and open-air flea markets may in fact have been made in India. Complicating identification of provenance is that not all British-made mounts were hallmarked either. Some gold- and silversmiths evaded the marking system to avoid payment of the tax levied on each object submitted for hallmarking. In other cases, the amount of precious metal used, for example when mounting a single claw as a brooch, was below that required to be stamped.

156. Tamil Nadu
*Gold necklace (ponnamalai) with a
central swami-style pendant
Length 23 in. (58.5 cm); weight 240 g
Collection Barbier-Mueller Museum,
Geneva*

The image is of Shiva and Parvati
mounted on Nandin, their bull vehicle
(vahanam). A composite amulet-
ornament, the necklace includes
green-glass tiger-claw forms (pachchai
palingku pulinagam) and a gold sun
disc (suriyan mandalam) with a central ruby, the planetal gemstone of the
sun god Surya.

Hindu Plaque Amulets

In a distinct category are manufactured amulets that do not possess *any* power to act for the benefit of the wearer until they have been properly consecrated. An outstanding example of this type is the Hindu metal plaque-pendant stamped with an image of a deity or deities.

The custom of wearing metal plaque amulets prevails especially among the rural people of Rajasthan and Gujarat, but also occurs elsewhere in northern India and Maharashtra (see 549). Such amulets bear a representation in relief of a Hindu deity, usually accompanied by its animal vehicle; a group of deities; or only the symbol associated with a deity, for example the footprints of Vishnu (see 177, *Vishnupada*), or Shiva's trident (*trishula*). Amulets of this kind are normally worn on a cord or chain suspended from the neck, and ordinarily they are visible on the person.

In Sanskrit literature the general term for amulets is *kavacha*, from which comes the Hindi *kavach*; in different locations this type of amulet is known by various names, among which are *mandaliya*, *phul deota*, *patri*, and *kathla*.

Central to the use of a two-dimensional plaque amulet representing a deity is the idea that every Hindu god and goddess is believed to possess divine powers that, upon request from a devotee, they will dispense. Such an amulet is a visible indication of the wearer's commitment to the particular deity, who, pleased by this show of faith, is favorably disposed to comply with requests for assistance. The amulet is activated by a priest or shaman who, for a fee, acts as a trusted intermediary between the deity and the devotee by giving it life (*prana sthapana*). Just as the deity's power is eternal, so is the potential power of the amulet.

Simple body contact with the amulet is a passive form of worship, but most Hindus perform daily worship (*puja*) to the deity depicted and possibly others. If at that time the amulet is worn, the omniscient deity immediately gives approval of whatever is requested of it. Prayers are often accompanied by a boon request of the deity. Common solicitations are fulfillment of a desire for male offspring, immunity to illness, prosperity and success in enterprise, and the destruction of enemies. To help in activating the deity's blessing and the amulet's power, the devotee learns spells to be recited during *puja*.

Selecting the Plaque-Amulet Deity

Deciding which plaque amulet to select and wear depends on group or individual preference or custom. Often the deity (H: *kul devata*) is the principal patron deity chosen by a family (H: *kul*), or it can be a hereditary ancestral family goddess (*kul devi*). The practice observed (*kul dharam*) is peculiar to a particular caste (S: *jati*) or tribe (S: *gotra*).

An individual can choose a male or female tutelary deity (S: *istadevata; ista*, desired, approved, cherished; *devata*, god) in whom he or she has trust and faith, and to whom he or she pays mystical devotion. In return, the deity guides and assists the worshiper to attain his or her goals.

Either of these is invoked during a *puja* on any occasion considered to be auspicious, or at prescribed times during festivals held in their honor. At such times, worship may also include common ancestral worship (S: *pitra puja; pitr*, father, or paternal ancestors), during which gifts may be presented to the deity (*pitrapan*) in the name of the ancestors.

Another class of amulets bear a representation of a local chief, leader, or hero (S: *vira; vir*,

157. Rajasthan
Gold-stamped amulet (madaliya) pendant depicting Ganesha and Lakshmi under an honorific umbrella (chhatri)
2 x 2¾ in. (5 x 7 cm)
Collection Michel Postel, Bombay

Plaque amulets could be made to order in gold but normally were of silver. A few copper and brass plaque amulets—the most economical options—also exist.

strong, brave) famous for his heroism (virata). An example is Ramdeoji, a deified Rajasthani hero to whom temples are dedicated, and whose story is repeated by traveling bards (Bhopas) who illustrate it with a long, episodic narrative painting (Ramdeoji ki par). (They also tell the stories of several other subjects, each with its own painting.) Hero worship (vira puja) of such an amulet is possible but could also involve images of the personage or his symbol. In the case of Ramdeoji, it is his horse, Kamala, on which he rides as always depicted in amulets, rider and horse making an easily identifiable symbolic image. Clay and cloth images of the horse alone, some life-sized, are offered at Ramdeoji Temple in Ramdeora, near Pokaran in Jaisalmer District, Rajasthan.

Plaque-Amulet Shapes

The shapes in which flat plaque amulets are fabricated can be grouped into a few basic categories. In most cases the outer amulet shape is not restricted for use by any one deity, group of deities, or symbols, although the general configuration of a particular subject may dictate a specific shape. Some shapes seem to be preferred regionally, which may help in identifying a plaque's origin.

Specific shapes may have a significant importance to the meaning of the subject. Others

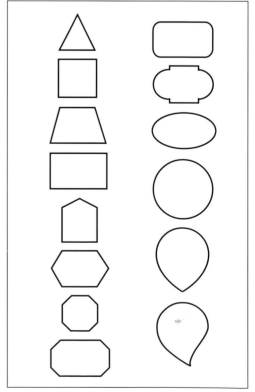

158. Rajasthan
Silver necklace (hainkal in Punjabi) of die-stamped amulets strung on a knitted wire chain with clasp. Included are the basic amulet forms: yoni, house, temple, and mandala.
Collection the author, Porvoo

Subjects: 1, 2, 9: Bhumiya Raj hero with consort on a horse.
3, 8: Durga on a lion. 4, 7: Vishnupadaka. 5: Ganesha and Lashmi. 6: Tree of life symbols

159. Basic Amulet Forms

Top to bottom: *triangle (shrine); square (house); trapezoid (house); rectangle (house); pentagon (temple); hexagon (emerald); octagon/long octagon (emerald); round-cornered rectangle; cartouche (shield); oval, circle (mandala); yoni;* and *mango*

160. Rajasthan and Gujarat
Silver die-stamped amulets in yoni form
Collection the author, Porvoo

Bhils call this form nama (from S: naman, obedience or salutation). The subject of several of these (1–4, 7–12) is Bheru or Bhairava, a form of Shiva, accompanied by his vehicle, a dog (S: shvan), the deity widely worshipped by Bhil tribals, one of the largest tribal communities in India. Another (13) shows the footprints (paglia) motif that can symbolically represent a god (S: deva) or goddess (devi); 14, 16, and 17 represent heroes (S: vira), a common one in Rajasthan being the Ramdeoji ke paglia. Also represented are a Naga deity (5), Hanuman (6), and addorsed peacocks (15).

161. Rajasthan and Gujarat
Five-sided, temple-shaped, silver, die-stamped amulets. The form is called patri in Rajasthan, the image called chagdu in Gujarat
Collection the author, Porvoo

Subjects: 1, 2, 3: Bhumiya Raj hero on a horse.
4: Durga as Mahisasuramardini, slayer of Mahisa, the buffalo demon.
9: Shiva. 10, 11: Devi.
12, 13, 14: Durga on a lion.
15, 16: Vishnupadaka.
17, 18, 19: Hanuman

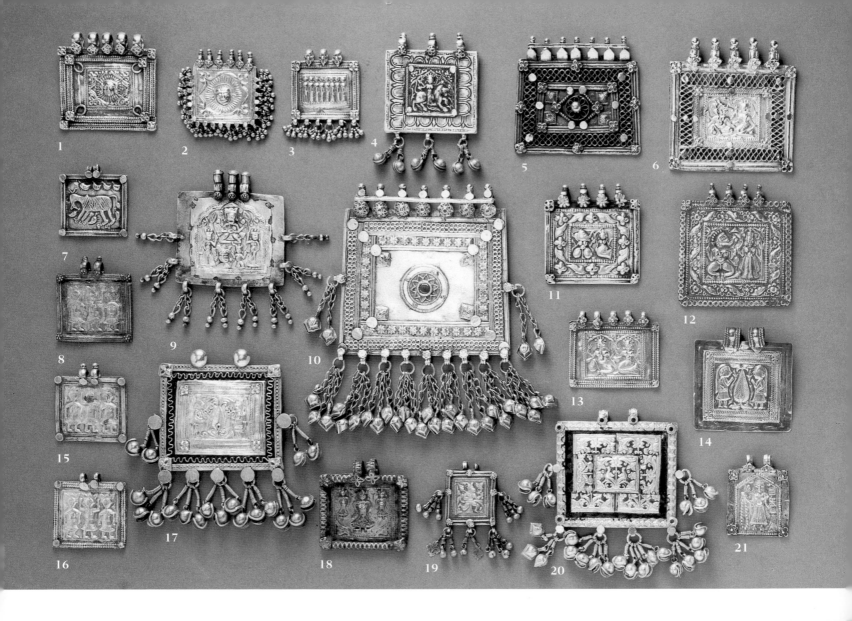

162. Rajasthan, Gujarat, and Himachal Pradesh

*Square and rectangular silver die-stamped amulets,
the form symbolic of a house plan (S: vastu)
Collection the author, Porvoo*

Subjects: 1, 2: The sun god (Surya). 3: The seven mothers
(Sapta Matrikas). 4: Durga on a lion. 5, 10: Sun symbol.
6, 11, 12, 13: Ganesha and Lakshmi. 7: Animal with
many offspring (fertility symbol). 8, 15, 16, 18: Hoi Mata.
9: Raja with attendants. 14, 17, 20: Tree of life
(S: kalpavrksha) flanked by guardians. 19: Hanuman.
21: Shiva with trident

163. Rajasthan and Gujarat ➤

*Round form (S: mandala), silver, mainly die-stamped
amulets. Circular forms repel evil spirits who dare
not enter them.
Collection the author, Porvoo*

Subjects: 1: Jain miniature painting of a Tirthankara,
under glass. 2 and 3: Vishnu's footprints (Vishnupadaka).
4: Tejaji, a Jat hero on a horse, with applied wire
snakes, one biting his tongue, worn to prevent a fatal
snake bite. Tejaji daily gave milk to a snake but one day
forgot. As punishment, the snake informed him that he
must be bitten. Tejaji agreed on condition that he first
be allowed to visit his father-in-law. Though severely
wounded by cattle robbers during that visit, he returned
home. The snake found his tongue to be the only clean
biting place. Tejaji died, was deified, and his main
shrine is at Kishengarh. 5: Three repeated Shiva images.
6: Five mother deities

are devoid of meaning and simply frame the subject. In some amulets, one shape is placed within a different shape. The basic shapes with symbolic meaning are the square or rectangle, representing an enclosure or house; the peaked pentagon, which symbolizes a temple (*mandir*); the circle (*mandala*); the bottom-pointing ovule (*yoni*); and the arrowhead (*tir*).

Making a Plaque Amulet

An individual may purchase a ready-made plaque amulet from a usually small selection in stock or, more probably, commission one to be made by a goldsmith. Discussions take place in which the subject, size, approximate metal weight (gold or silver), and degree of elaboration are agreed upon, all depending on what the person is willing to pay for the result.

Making a jeweler's stamping die, from which the plaque image is made, is the work of specialists. Throughout India are places where die makers prepare dies for regional use. For example, in Kantilo, Orissa, are many artisans engaged solely in making dies for use by goldsmiths, and their results are distributed all over eastern India. The subjects and patterns that appear on dies depend on what is in local or regional usage. The amulet maker keeps a stock of intaglio brass-stamping dies (H: *thappa*) with subjects of deities he knows are in demand by his normal local clientele.

A sheet of gold or silver (large enough to cover the die and allow for some extra space beyond the image) about 18 gauge (0.040 in.; 1.016 mm) in thickness is annealed to redness, then quenched in water to render it malleable. To stamp the die image on this sheet and form a die-stamped impression (H: *thappa naqsh*), it is placed on the negative die image, and over this is placed a thick sheet of lead (H: *sisa patra*) large enough to cover the die. With a heavy, broad-faced iron sledgehammer, the sheets are hammered with sharp blows, taking care to avoid moving them, which would cause an unclear, blurred image. The soft lead sheet acts as a shim that, under hammering, forces the silver into the die depressions. When the image area has been covered with repeated blows, the metal sheets are removed from the die and separated. A successful result will bear a cleanly made, distinct die-stamped impression (P: *naqsh*) on the silver sheet. The unwanted surrounding silver is trimmed away with shears to achieve the basic amulet shape.

164. Rajasthan
Bronze-plaque-amulet stamping die (ta'wiz thappa)
2⅜ x 2 in. (6 x 5 cm)
Collection the author, Porvoo

Used to make stamped sheet-metal amulets, this die portrays a local hero and his wife on a horse.

165. Rajasthan
Silver Bhumiya Raj die-stamped amulet
2¾ x 2 in. (7 x 5 cm); weight 20 g
Collection the author, Porvoo

This type of amulet subject (phul deota) is worn chiefly in western Rajasthan by Hindu Rajputs, Jats, and others. Depicted is a deified Bhumiya Raj hero, a landed, military proprietor or chieftain who died in defense of his property, including villages and their inhabitants. The term bhumiya is from bhum, meaning "land." Trusted and feared, the deified spirits of these local heroes protect their community by nightly riding a horse around the village to dispel enemies or evil agents.

▼ **166. Rajasthan**
Silver house amulet
3½ x 3⁹⁄₁₆ in. (8.9 x 9 cm); weight 27 g
Private Collection, Brussels

A symbol of family unity represented by a walled-in rectangle, the amulet uses stamped floral units to cover joins.

164

165

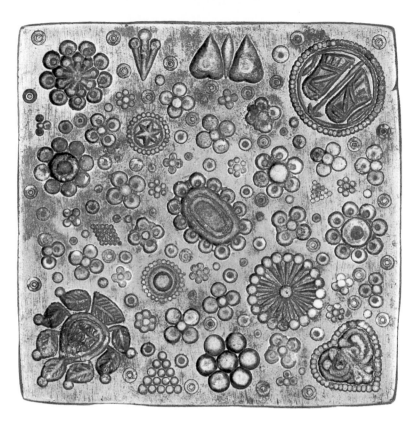

167. Northern India
Bronze goldsmith's square intaglio stamping die (H: thassa; thappa; chota naqsh thappa; Or: chhancha; Tam: kambattyamulai)
3½ x 3½ in. (8.8 x 8.8 cm)
Mingei International Museum of Folk Art, San Diego

Stamping dies of this kind, with many different small designs in one die, are used to make identical repeats of small sheet-metal units commonly used in Indian jewelry, especially to cover joins. Most often this die has a round form.

168. Tamil Nadu
Brass convex, positive-relief or goldsmith's cameo-stamping die (kambatta-mulai), for use when creating a back-of-head ornament (rakkodi).
Diameter 3⁹⁄₁₆ in. (9.1 cm); weight 446 g
Collection the author, Porvoo

An impression is made by hammering the sheet metal placed directly over the die. The result is then worked from the outer surface with chasing tools.

The main decoration of the plaque amulet is its applied border, which also has the practical function of reinforcing the constantly worn plaque. Some amulets are reinforced on the back by soldering on a central wire rib, often tapered toward the bottom.

Borders are made of various kinds of plain, die-stamp-patterned, beaded, or coiled and flattened wire. After being shaped to the amulet contour, they are soldered in place. In straight-sided plaques, joins occur at corners, and in curved ones, where the wire ends meet, usually at the top or bottom.

In all forms of Indian jewelry, a typical means of covering these joins is to solder over them a small die-stamped unit usually bearing a flower subject or a geometric form. For this purpose, every village goldsmith has a special, usually round die (H: *chota naqsh thappa*), on which appear a variety of small unit designs from which a selection can be made.

All that remains is to add a top loop, or a series of loops from which the plaque amulet will be suspended. Their number depends on the amulet shape and size.

Weapon-Shaped Amulets: Apotropaic Protection

An amulet is said to have apotropaic value when its purpose is to avert evil from the wearer. An ancient amuletic source of this kind is an actual weapon that has long been used in defense of threats from animals as well as humans. Among man's earliest weapons were stone arrowheads, spearheads, and knives. The power these lethal instruments possessed to cause the death of a threatening foe was highly respected by the ancients, and the weapons themselves came to be regarded as magical.

Arrowheads have been found in ancient tumuli, where it is believed they were placed as protective offerings to the deceased. Consecrated arrows were thought to possess the power to destroy an invisible enemy. To serve this function for the living, an amulet in the form of an arrowhead was tied around the neck of the wearer. Simulated arrowheads retained the form of the original, functional one and were believed to be no less effective. As ideological arrowheads, they did not have to be made of the flint commonly used in making actual arrowheads. What mattered was that their arrowhead form be unequivocally recog-

nizable to both humans and spirits. Sharpness became a visual metaphor implied by the form. Scale did not necessarily have to be realistic, and miniaturization or enlargement were both possible without any risk of loss in effectiveness.

As physical function no longer mattered, the object could be executed in any decorative stone, such as agate, jasper, onyx, or nephrite. Besides stone, other materials could also be used; in time, metal gained prominence. Indian necromantic beliefs held that particular metals such as iron copper, and alloys such as bronze, were imbued with mystical significance. Combined in one object, form and material together augmented the amulet's potency. At the same time, the use of metal at a relatively higher cost became a matter of prestige.

Eventually, the simple arrowhead evolved into more elaborate decorative forms. Embellishments were inevitable but had the effect of obscuring the identity of the arrowhead as the origin of the form. New meanings were given to the amulets, even when the original form was used. For example, often in India today the ancient arrowhead form is said to represent a *pipal* tree leaf (*Ficus religiosa*) associated with Hinduism and Buddhism, both of which developed at a much later date than when this form originated. Such an idea is an

169

170

170. Khambhat, Gujarat
Contemporary carnelian amulets in tanged arrowhead (A: sahm) form
Height approx. 1¼ in. (3.2 cm)
Collection the author, Porvoo

These amulets are a survival of an ancient type. Their tangs are pierced for stringing and placement on the body.

171. Delhi. *18th century*
White-nephrite amulet pendant
2⅜ x 1⅞ in. (6 x 4.7 cm)
Collection Special Treasury, Oriental Department, The State Hermitage, St. Petersburg (V3-408)

The amulet's tang is transversely pierced for hanging; its obverse is decorated with a flowering tree of life set kundan style in gold with thirty-three rubies, one emerald, and three beryls. Until 1921 it was in the collection of Prince Argutinski Dolgoruki.

171

◄ **169.** *Arrowhead Amulet Forms*

Top to bottom:

Without tang: Triangle, transverse or broad chisel head; leaf

Tanged: Tanged triangle, tanged leaf; tanged lunate

Tanged and barbed: Triangle; leaf or shield; square barb; pointed barb

Regional forms: Cambay, Gujarat; Punjab; Bihar; Gujarat; Rajasthan; Rajasthan; Himachal Pradesh

Mughal-developed forms

172. Northern India
Gray nephrite arrowhead-shaped Muslim amulet pendant with ruby, bearing an inscription meaning, MAY GOD PRESERVE US. THERE IS NO POWER OR STRENGTH EXCEPT IN GOD, THE GREAT, THE EXALTED, YEAR 1029 A.H. *(1619 A.D.)*
Chester Beatty Library, Dublin (CB81-221101)

The date occurs during the reign of Jahangir, and it was possibly made for that Mughal emperor. Nephrite from Khotan was considered a precious stone by the Mughals. From the Muslim belief that the surfaces of natural materials bear signs of the mystic properties they possess came the idea of inscribing astrological, religious, or magical inscriptions on an object's surface.

173. Rajasthan
Silver amulet in barbed arrowhead form (chagda), fabricated with densely arranged ornament, including gold-foil-backed glass inserts and silver pendants
3½ x 3¼ in. (9 x 8.3 cm)
Private Collection, Ojai, California. Courtesy Beatrice Wood

174. Bujodi Village, Kachchh, Gujarat
Rabari girl wearing a silver necklace (hulara or madalio no har) with a central, barbed arrowhead-shaped amulet pendant (chagda) and flanking tube-amulet cases (madaliyo) containing mantras. She also wears loop earrings (bhamaria), a nose ring (nathni), and a wire necklace (velo). Young girls nearing puberty are often heavily ornamented to enhance their attractiveness as possible brides. Amulets are universally worn in the lifetime battle of subduing external and internal evil spirits.

175. Rajasthan. *19th century*
Silver die-stamped amulet (madaliya)
4⅛ x 3¾ in. (10.3 x 9.5 cm); weight 61 g
Collection the author, Porvoo

Hanuman is depicted within an arrowhead form, flying through the air to bring the healing Himalayan herbs to cure the wounded on the Sri Lanka battlefield, as related in the Ramayana (see 182).

example of an accretion that supplants the original, often forgotten meaning.

The use of stone for an arrowhead amulet today is an instance of atavistic, ritualistic conservatism, harking back to ancient values. This is often the case when superstitions and ceremonial practices are involved, as in the consecration of an amulet.

Making a stone arrowhead involves chipping, polishing, and perforating, processes identical with the manufacture of hardstone beads produced at Khambhat, where hardstone arrowhead-shaped amulets also are still made. Arrowheads became hafted weapons, meaning they often have a projecting tang designed to allow the arrowhead to be fitted to the hollow end of a reed or wood shaft of the arrow and held in place by lashing with some fibrous material. Since Neolithic times, many arrowhead tangs were perforated to facilitate their being fixed in the shaft. As in the case of hardstone beads, the earliest holes made were hourglass shaped due to alternate side drilling. The presence of such a hole sim-

plified the transition of stone arrowhead to suspended pendant amulet.

When the stone arrowhead was translated into metal, refinement and development of forms became inevitable. Metal permitted arrowhead amulets to be thinner, broader, more complex in form. From simple triangular, almond, and chisel shapes sprang tangs and barbs, at first two, then several. With the use of sheet metal, the arrowhead amulet now had a surface that could be embellished by the lexicon of decorative metal processes available in the goldsmith's vocabulary. Besides purely decorative elements, magical additions such as inscriptions, diagrams, palindromic squares, and images of deities were possible. All such additions acted to multiply the amulet's power.

Over time, the flat plaque became a three-dimensional container, providing an inner space for additional magical elements. A proliferation of such objects, from *mantras* written or printed on paper to myriad charms or other objects believed to possess spiritual power, could be carried within.

173

174

176. Rajasthan and Gujarat
Silver amulets in arrowhead form
Collection the author, Porvoo

Subjects: 1: Devi. 2, 17: Two peacocks.
3, 7, 11, 12: Tree of life guarded by confronting
lions. 4, 10: Two birds (worn by an elephant).
5: Inscribed name of a deity. 6: Ornamented
arrowhead. 8: Durga on a lion. 9: Eight
Mothers, or Seven Mothers and a guardian.
13, 14: Hanuman. 15, 16: Vishnupada.

Vishnupada: Sacred–Footprint Amulet

The use of symbols to represent a deity dates back to the ancient Brahman practice of avoiding the representation of Vedic deities in the form of mortal persons, substituting instead a cult symbol for worship. This practice was gradually replaced during the last five centuries B.C. by the introduction of cult images of gods in human form, clearly set apart from ordinary people by their attributed supernatural or mystic powers. The old practice of using cult symbols, however, was never completely abandoned, and it continues today.

One such symbol is the side-by-side footprints (S: *pad*) of a standing deity, generally termed *sripada* (divine footprints) or *charan chinh* (footprint symbol). It came into use for worship among Hindus and Buddhists to symbolize the deity's presence. Several Hindu gods, and Buddha, have been and are represented by such a symbol. Carved in stone, or formed in metal, the footprints depict what appears to be an impression of the soles of the standing deity's feet, upon which appear several symbols, all with specific reference to that deity.

From this concept evolved the idea that similar symbols may appear on the soles of feet (and also the palms) of living saints and eminent persons as a sign to others of their sanctity.

Of all the footprint cult symbols, Hindus consider the *Vishnupada* (Vishnu's footprints) to be the most sacred. They are commonly depicted on a gold or silver plaque-amulet pendant or on belt buckles. A sacred, powerful charm, it is believed to offer the wearer protection against all calamities.

Vishnupada amulets, and footprint amulets of other deities, find a wide audience, especially in northern India. They are often enameled on gold and silver. Those on gold were, and still are, made in the important enameling centers of Jaipur and Nathdwara, both in Rajasthan. In Nathdwara they are often purchased by pilgrims visiting the local temple of Srinathji. Silver enameled Vishnu footprint pendants formerly were also made in Kangra, in Himachal Pradesh, and widely worn throughout that sub-Himalayan area.

In what seems to be a carryover of Hindu influence, among Muslims in India, the footprints of Muhammad (A: *kadam-rasul*) printed on paper are a revered amulet.

177

177. Nathadwara, Rajasthan
Gold pendant (Shri Nath-ji novami), polychrome enameled
Ashmolean Museum, Oxford

Worn by a Shri Nath-ji devotee, the pendant bears a representation of the footprints (charan or padaka) of the deity, a form of Krishna who is worshiped in the Shri Nath-ji Temple at Nathadwara by the Vallabhacharya sect. The soles of the feet of deities are believed to bear auspicious symbols, which differ according to the deity. Here Shri Nath-ji's left footprint includes the sun, bow, lotus, and conch; the right, the moon, banner, mace, and swastika. On the other side of the pendant is the name Shri Nath-ji in Devanagari characters.

178. Rajasthan
Silver die-stamped amulet with Vishnu's foot-prints within a cusped arch, under an honorific umbrella (chhatri)
5½ x 4⅝ in. (14 x 11.7 cm); weight 179 g
Collection Ghysels, Brussels

▼ **179. Uttar Pradesh.** *2nd–1st century* B.C.
Buddha's footprint (Buddhapada), greenish gray schist
2¹³⁄₁₆ x 1¼ ft (7.2 x 3.3 m)
Prince of Wales Museum, Bombay

The toes each bear a swastika, a pre-Aryan sun symbol, now a symbol of good luck, the sole a dharma wheel (chakra), and the heel the three-gem (tri-ratna) symbol. Footprints of Muhammad and Muslim saints are also shown great reverence, as are those of the Prophet at the Kadam Rasul Hill near Secunderabad, Andhra Pradesh.

178

The Hanuman Pectoral Plaque

Hanuman, the celebrated celestial monkey chief and devoted follower of Rama, is held in great veneration all over India by Hindu Shaivas and Shaktas, but especially in the south by Vaishnavas, because of his humility, loyalty, and assistance to Ramachandra, the seventh of the ten incarnations (dasavataras) of Vishnu. Devotees believe that his worship imbues them with physical energy, fearlessness, and mental enlightenment. Like Ganesha, the elephant-headed son of Shiva, he is also worshiped as the remover of obstacles, which, in Hindu mythology, he never failed to overcome.

Hanuman appears on amulets (mandaliya) commonly used by rural people, on armlets (bazuband), and even belt buckles (kamarband baksha). A special type of Hanuman amulet-ornament-badge deserving particular attention is the large, round, lost-wax-cast brass pectoral plaque in which he is the central subject. This is worn by ascetic devotees to Hanuman, especially in Karnataka (though encountered elsewhere), suspended from the neck on a cord that passes through an integral loop at the back.

The traditional iconography of these plaques is fairly uniform, incorporating many symbols. Its outer, circular form is a mandala that serves as a frame surrounding the image. It represents conventionalized flames (prabhavala), implying a mystic radiance or aura that emanates from the subject. At the top of the frame is the five-headed, hooded cobra-capella variously called Ada-sarpa (first serpent), Ananta (the infinite), Nagaraja (snake king), or Shesha (remainder—a reference to

its creation from the residue after the world was formed from chaos), hovering over Hanuman's image to protect it. Because of Hanuman's association with Vishnu, at either side of the mandala frame often appear Vishnu's main symbols: the conch (shankha) on the right, and the flaming discus (chakra) on the left.

Hanuman, the central image, is represented in an archaic posture: head in right-facing profile, body frontal, arms frontal, and legs apart with the feet in right-facing profile. The pose suggests running, but is intended to represent him in flight in air. Hindu mythology explains that Hanuman inherited the power of flight from his parents, who were Vayu, the wind, and Anjana, an apsaras, or type of celestial nymph who, among other attributes, symbolizes clouds and often is similarly represented in a flying posture. On Hanuman's head is a crown or tiara, and a miniature standing figure of Rama, his master, is sometimes included.

Hanuman's flying pose refers to a specific incident described in the Ramayana, the great Hindu epic story in which, as an ally, he faithfully served Ramachandra. Because in this story Rama was motivated by an exemplary high morality, he is much loved by Hindus, and Hanuman's devotion to him to a great extent accounts for the reverence paid to this monkey god by the masses all over India. Other elements in the iconography of this pectoral plaque can be explained by relating Hanuman's role in the Ramayana.

Ravana, the King of the Demons (Rakshasas), who lived in Lanka (Sri Lanka) abducted Sita, Rama's wife, while the couple were in exile. Clutched in Ravana's twenty arms while flying in his chariot to Lanka, Sita, unobserved, managed at intervals to drop some of

180

180. Nashik, Maharashtra
Sadhu wearing a cast-brass Hanuman pectoral (bajrang bali, strong monkey)

181. Northern India
Cast-brass belt buckle (baksha) bearing an image of Hanuman flanked by lions
4 x 6 in. (10 x 15.2 cm); weight 238 g
Collection the author, Porvoo

182. Maharashtra (opposite page)
Cast-brass pectoral plaque (bajrang bali) of Hanuman or Maruti
9½ x 7½ in. (24 x 19 cm); weight 1,022 g
Private Collection, London

181

the ornaments she wore to indicate to Rama, who she knew would soon follow in pursuit, the direction in which she had been carried. Finally installed in Ravana's palace, she was visited there by Hanuman, sent as Rama's emissary to reassure her of her imminent release.

Anticipating Sita's doubt as to Hanuman's true identity, Rama had given Hanuman his signet ring (see 603). From a tree where he sat in the garden in which he found Sita, Hanuman threw the ring at her feet. She immediately recognized it as belonging to Rama, irrefutable proof of Hanuman's veracity when he relayed Rama's message to her. In return, she gave Hanuman one of her seemingly inexhaustible supply of jewels to bring back to Rama, along with a message from her.

During the ensuing battle with the Rakshasas, no mean adversaries, many of Rama's followers, including Laksmana, his devoted younger half-brother, were mortally wounded. The only known way to restore Laksmana and the others to well-being was to procure a magical flesh-healing herb called *sanjivani buti* (some say *visalya-karani*, or *laksa*), which was known to grow on Dronachala Mountain (or, variously, Mount Gandha-madana, or Mount Dunagiri) in the Himalayas in the far north.

Because of Hanuman's ability to fly rapidly through the air, Rama asked him to procure this herb. As an act of devotional service to his grand master, Hanuman undertook the task with alacrity, bounding in one leap from Lanka to the Himalayas. But his task was not accomplished without difficulties.

Aware of Hanuman's mission, Ravana instructed a giant called Kalanemi to kill Hanuman as he searched for the herb. Hanuman saw through the giant's disguise, and, being his superior in strength, grabbed him by a leg and threw him whirling toward Lanka, where he fell dead before the throne of Ravana. In this plaque, Kalanemi is depicted falling helplessly through space at the bottom of the circular *prabhamandala*.

At the mountain, Hanuman searched impatiently for the herb. Unable to distinguish it from others, he assumed gigantic form and uprooted the entire mountain. Holding it aloft in his right hand, he started his aerial journey back to Lanka. In plaques and pendants, the upheld right hand may hold a conventionalized representation of the mountain, or it may be empty, the simple gesture considered to be sufficient as a visual reference. In his left hand, he often holds a stylized depiction of the herb, which was supposed to be a vine with a leafy, flowering head and a long, trailing stem that descends, then curves upward to the left.

Upon his arrival at Lanka with the mountain, the healing herb was identified and administered, and Laksmana and his fallen associates were restored to health. Hanuman then returned the mountain to its place of origin. Rama's reward to Hanuman was the gift of life for one million years.

Palindromic "Magic Squares" in Hindu and Islamic Amulets

A common Islamic amulet type (A: *ta'wiz*) is a stone or metal plaque with a religious text, usually a quotation from the Qur'an, or a text composed by the wearer, on its surface. Another concept in use for at least seven centuries among Hindus and Muslims in India, and throughout the Islamic world, is a commonly used glass, metal, or hardstone amulet that has inscribed on its surface a diagram, popularly called a "magic square" or more exactly, a palindromic square. A typical configuration consists of a square grid of minimally three but more often a larger number of units. Within each square or unit is inscribed a number or letter. Reading in either direction—horizontally across in any row, vertically in any column, or along the two diagonals from corner to corner —the *sum* of the numbers within the squares adds up to the same odd (H., A: *'adad i taq*) or even (H., A: *'adad i juft*) number, or, in the case of letters, spells out the same word or name.

Such figures are called palindromes (from the Greek word *palindromos,* meaning "running back again") because the sum or word in these three directions can be read forward or backward. The term "magic square" applied to such configurations is too limited to indicate

their function because the sum, word, or name may have a deeply religious or mystic significance or association, and the same applies to the manner in which they are constructed.

That it was possible to create these squares placed them in great awe in India, not only by illiterate rural people but also among religious devotees and mystics. At the peak of its popularity in the nineteenth century, palindromic-square invention became something of an industry at Nasik in Maharashtra, a Shaivite center where specialist palindromist amulet-makers produced them in quantity. The squares were believed to be a source of universal power, at first associated entirely with religious symbolic meanings. The tradition has degenerated for the most part into simple magic, and their former spiritual meanings are forgotten. Today their main function is to avert the "evil eye" and prevent illness. For this reason, they are often found painted on either side of the entranceway to a village house.

It is now believed that such squares were known and used in India before they appeared in Islam. Possibly they came from China to India by way of the overland silk-trade route. Another source might have been Chinese Buddhist pilgrim monks who came to India from China during the fourth to seventh century A.D. to visit Buddhist shrines and learn more about Buddha's message of the *dharma* (moral and religious duty and custom); one

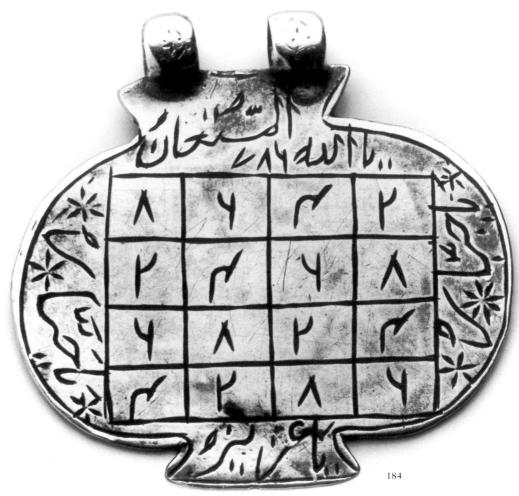

183. Northern India
Muslim ta'wiz of nephrite carved in the form of a polylobed heart or tanged and barbed arrowhead
2⁹⁄₁₆ x 2³⁄₁₆ in. (6.5 x 5.6 cm)
Bibliothèque National, Cabinet des Medailles, Paris (2276)

Both faces are inscribed, the side shown here with a central magic-number palindromic square.

184. Northern India
Muslim ta'wiz in a shield shape (takhti)
1½ x 1⅝ in. (3.9 x 4.2 cm); weight 8 g
Collection Ghysels, Brussels

In this palindromic square (A: wafq or wufq), flanked by the Arabic inscriptions
YA 'AZIZ (OH, ALMIGHTY GOD);
YA GABBAR (OH, ALMIGHTY GOD),
the numbers add up to 20:

8	6	4	2
2	4	6	8
6	8	2	4
4	2	8	6

185. Northern India
Muslim takhti-shaped silver ta'wiz with a central palindromic magic square of numbers and a border with a quotation from the Qur'an
3½ x 3⅝ in. (9 x 9.1 cm);
weight 46 g
Collection the author, Porvoo

184

185

such pilgrim was the famous Hiuen Tsiang (or Yuan-chuang), whose journey took place from A.D. 629 to 645. Indian Buddhist missionaries, who went to China to spread the gospel and then returned to India, could have spread the practice.

In the Islamic world, the earliest books discussing palindromic-square construction, with examples, appeared in the tenth century A.D. By the twelfth century, the squares were in popular use throughout the Islamic world as an amulet (A: hama'il), even though magic (sihr) was forbidden to Islam. After the thirteenth century, a number of books dealing with them were published in Arabic and Persian.

In India, there is no extant written document concerning the squares before A.D. 1356, when the first Hindu record appeared. Written by Narayana, it was called the *Ganita-kaumu-di* (S: *ganit*, the science of arithmetic; *kaumudi*, moonlight, a word commonly used in the titles of works). The squares included in this publication are highly sophisticated, which implies that, to achieve them, methods for their construction must have been known much earlier. Priority in publication does not automatically date their use to outside India prior to that time. Indian silence on the subject could be explained by the traditional Indian system of learning. Whether the subject was religion or magic, information was passed orally from the teacher (*guru*) to the disciple (*chela*). Thus, it is entirely possible that this subject was not recorded until well after its initiation.

The number of units on any one side of a palindromic square, either in a horizontal row or a vertical column, is termed the *base number*. For example, a square of four units has a base number of four, and the whole figure consists of a four by four block.

The so-called Arabic numerals include the nine digits and the cipher zero. Most of these, and in particular the concept of zero, were first used in India. The Arabs called them "Indian" or "Hindu" numerals and introduced this numbering system to the West, where it is in universal use since about the beginning of the ninth century A.D.

Metaphysical and Religious Symbolism

In his analysis of the construction of palindromic squares, Schuyler Cammann found that methods differed in each of the three main areas where they were created: China, India, and the Islamic world. Methodology reflected cultural differences, and certain preferences, connected with religious beliefs and thought patterns, are evident in the mentality of particular peoples. This is not to say that specific construction types were solely confined to one group. Ideas overlapped, and all methods used in square creation were known in each place.

Because of the sacred value and significance Muslims give to these squares, in old Islamic publications where they are discussed, one finds a certain reticence to explain the construction systems palindromists employed. Methods were highly guarded, and some were deliberately garbled. For instance, in some cases not all the numbers within a particular square were revealed. Someone who understands the method used, however, can correct such "mistakes." Cammann believes that purposeful errors were meant to confuse people who might misuse the magical properties the squares were believed to possess.

In some Islamic odd-numbered blocks, the central number of the block was given special reverence. Because of its position, devout Muslims considered it to be the symbol of Allah. For this reason, it was often given the value of one, to symbolize Allah as the source of all things. (According to orthodox Muslims, it is lawful to use an amulet with the symbol or name of Allah inscribed on it when the intention is to evoke Allah's help.) In other cases, this central number was omitted because it was thought to be too sacred to reveal, but it can be calculated. (Hindus showed no interest in the Muslim concept of the central number.)

In Muslim amuletic squares with a base of four, the letter/numbers often spell out one of the ninety-nine names of Allah that have four characters, which is believed to greatly reinforce the potency of the amulet. The numbers used in such a square become a symbol to be interpreted by the name, and, as in all palindromic squares, the numerical values they represent, when added from any direction, come to the same sum.

Muslim palindromic squares commonly employ Arabic letters, and each of the twenty-eight letters in the Arabic alphabet has been given a numerical value so that the characters can be interpreted either as numbers or letters, or both.

The Arabic arithmetical arrangement of the alphabet is called *abjad*, taken from the first four letters in this arrangement. Each letter has a power from one to one thousand. In sequence the letters spell out the words, *abjad hawwaz hutti kalaman sa'fas qarashat sakhaz zazigh*, said to be the names of the eight sons of Muramir ibn Murra, the inventor of Arabic characters.

Hindu Palindromic Squares

In medieval Hindu India, the interrelationships of the numbers within a square had a religious meaning that expressed ideas basic to Hinduism. In complex Hindu-square construction, the style was generally to begin at a point near the center, then cross over and back in a diagonal pattern. This movement suggested to Hindus the interweaving of warp and weft threads, analogous to the Hindu concept of the structure of the Greater Universe, which contains both active (weft) and passive (warp) principles. By this analogy the square became an important religious symbol, which furthered the spread of its popularity as an amulet.

Planetary Palindromic Squares

Planetary squares, whose function was not religious but magical, were a later, Islamic invention also taken up by Hindus. To Muslims, the fact that in all such blocks the rows, columns, and the main diagonals added up to the same figure was symbolically interpreted as God's regulation of the length and width of the Universe, in which all is sustained by Divine order. Muslims, like Hindus, believe in the effect of the planets on the lives of every person on Earth. Magical planetary palindromic squares were invented as a means by which an individual could harness the propitious influence of a particular planet, or the entire planetary system.

Muslim planetary palindromic square sets consist of seven squares corresponding to the seven planets in the traditional Muslim concept of the universe. A Muslim set includes a square of three for Saturn (Zuhal); four for Jupiter (Mushtari); five for Mars (Mirrikh); six for the Sun (Shams); seven for Venus (Zuhrah); eight for Mercury ('Utarid); and nine for the Moon (Qamar).

The Hindu universe contains nine planets. The following is an example of a Hindu set of three base nine planet squares, the order shown here following the arrangement of the *nava-ratna* gemstones (see page 304).

6	1	8	7	2	9	8	3	10
7	5	3	8	6	4	9	7	5
2	9	4=15	3	10	5=18	4	11	6=21
9	4	11	10	5	12	11	6	13
10	8	6	11	9	7	12	10	8
5	12	7=24	6	13	8=27	7	14	9=30
12	7	14	13	8	15	14	9	16
13	11	9	14	12	10	15	13	11
8	15	10=33	9	16	11=36	10	17	12=39

37	78	29	70	21	62	13	54	5
6	38	79	30	71	22	63	14	46
47	7	39	80	31	72	23	55	15
16	48	8	40	81	32	64	24	56
57	17	49	9	41	73	33	65	25
26	56	18	50	1	42	74	34	66
67	27	59	10	51	2	43	75	35
36	68	19	60	11	52	3	44	76
77	28	69	20	61	12	53	4	45

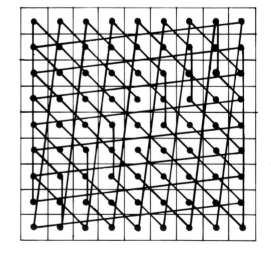

186. Northern India
Hindu magic-number palindromic square. The imposed line diagram below it shows its Hindu construction pattern, which suggests an interwoven textile, or warp and weft. The sum of the numbers is 369.

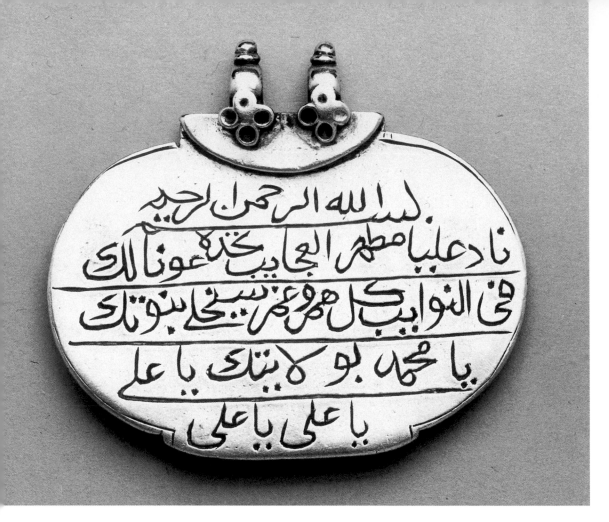

187. Northern India
Muslim takhti-shaped silver ta'wiz
(P: Nad-i-'Ali)
2⁹⁄₁₆ x 2¹³⁄₁₆ in. (6.5 x 7.2 cm);
weight 46 g
Collection the author, Porvoo

*Amulets of this type are always
inscribed with a prayer to Ali, a
cousin and adopted son of Muhammad who married Muhammad's
daughter Fatimah and by her had
three sons, Hasan, Hussain, and
Muhsin. Ali became the fourth
Khalifah (A.H. 35–A.H. 40) and died
at age fifty-nine after being struck
with a poisoned sword. The conflict
that developed concerning his right
to succession to the Khalifate gave
rise to the Shi'ah–Sunni schism
that created the two main Muslim
sects. The Shi'ah faith, or "followers
of Ali," is the national religion of
Iran. In India, Muslims constitute
about 11 percent of the population,
and, with the exception of Avadh
where Muslims for the most part
are Shi'as, are mainly Sunnis of the
Hanafi sect, though in some places
practices peculiar to Shi'ahs pre-
vail. The Nad-i-'Ali amulet is much
used by Shi'ah sectarians.*

*The inscription, here rendered in
five lines, is translated at left:*

IN THE NAME OF GOD, THE MERCIFUL, THE COMPASSIONATE
CALL ON ALI WHO SHOWETH FORTH MIRACLES. THOU WILT FIND HIM A HELP TO THEE
IN ADVERSITIES. ALL CARE AND GRIEF SHALL VANISH
BY THY HOLINESS OH ALI
OH ALI, OH ALI

188. Northern India
*Muslim amulet (takhti-ka-ta'wiz)
of etched green glass mounted in
a silver frame ornamented with
turquoises*
2⅛ x 2¹⁵⁄₁₆ in. (5.3 x 7.5 cm);
weight 41 g
Collection the author, Porvoo

*The glass bears Qur'anic inscrip-
tions invoking Allah. Its color and
shape suggest an intention to simulate an inscription-carved emerald
(see 748).*

189

190

189, 190. Deccan (Dakhan), Southern India.
17th–18th century
Two-part, octagonal, gold, niello-decorated
container-pendant to hold a matching-shaped
miniature Qur'an. Front (above) and back views
Diameter 2¾ in. (6 cm)
Courtesy Sotheby's, London

Worn on the neck suspended by three attached
cornerless cube loops, this form dates to the 10th
and 11th centuries in central Asia. Against a black
niello ground, Arabic calligraphy in gold includes
an invocation to God and His Attributes (Qur'an,
Chapter 56, 79–80); magic letters; and the Shi'ah
eulogy quatrain to Ali (the Nad-Aliyan), which
gives the container an amuletic function of protecting its contents and indicates its use for protection
by Shi'ah Muslims. The prototype of such Qur'an
cases dates to the 10th–11th century in central
Asia. They were also produced in Qasvin, Iran,
until recent times.

191. Iran. *19th century (opposite page, above)*
Miniature illuminated octagonal format Qur'an
(open) made to fit inside a container such as
the one at left
1⁵⁄₁₆ x 1⁵⁄₁₆ in. (4.1 x 4.1 cm)
The Nasser D. Khalili Collection of Islamic Art,
London. Acc. No. Qur 315 A,B. Courtesy of
the Nour Foundation

191

192

193. Delhi. *19th century*
Muslim amulet (haldili) of pale green nephrite or lizardite serpentine
Width 2¼ in. (5.7 cm)
Courtesy Sotheby's, New York

Worn to control heart palpitations (P: tapidan), the amulet is ornamented kundan style with rose-diamond-set crescent and green-foiled crystals set in Muslim symbols: three stars, leaves of the tree of life, and four birds that inhabit it. The reverse side has an Qur'anic inscription, NO GOD BUT ONE GOD / MUHAMMAD IS THE PROPHET OF GOD, *surrounded by invocations to Allah.*

The *Haldili:* An Islamic Nephrite Amulet

An elegant jade (nephrite) Muslim pendant amulet, still used mainly in northern India and the Deccan, is known by several names. In use probably since Mughal times, when the technology of fabricating jade objects decorated with inlays of gold and precious stones reached a height of perfection, its most usual format is approximately two inches (50 mm) long, flat slab or tablet, with a distinctive contour. This flat form accounts for its Persian name—*takhti,* a small tablet, or throne, the latter with the implication of a governing place that exerts influence. In Jammu, Kashmir, it is called an *ordhali* (from the Hindi *orna,* to protect oneself, or to ward off a blow with a shield, and *dhal,* shield). *Ordhali* therefore designates an amulet that offers shieldlike protection. (The term *shield* is figurative and has no reference to the typical *haldili* form; Indian shields were almost invariably round.)

Haldili, its most widely used designation, emphasizes its religio-mystic function, which relates to the heart and magical qualities attributed to jade (in India nephrite). The spiritual significance of the word *haldili* derives from the Arabic word *hal,* a transient fleeting condition that comes upon the heart of a man without his intention or desire, and a state or condition of ecstasy induced by the continued contemplation of God, considered to be a prognostication of direct illumination of the heart by God, to which is added the Persian *dil,* or "heart."

The amulet's more prosaic power is to control involuntary palpitations of the heart. Another traditional belief, of Persian origin, is that the *haldili* has the power to divert lightning from striking the wearer. Others say it is an alexipharmic antidote against poison, which it either counteracts or expels, a belief connected with miraculous qualities attributed to jade.

The typical *haldili* contour is probably derived from decorative cartouche forms often found on Mughal buildings, manuscripts, or on objects framing an inscription (P: *kitaba*), usually religious in nature, as is often the case with *haldili* inscriptions. Similar contours are used for flat, usually silver Muslim amulets, and also those of glass, sometimes encased in silver (see 184, 185, 187). Metal plaque and glass amulet types with this form are less expensive substitutes for the jade *haldili,* which is the paragon of Muslim amulets.

Making a *Haldili*

The *haldili* is a miniature version of the larger and far more elaborate jade objects, inlaid *kundan* style with gold and precious stones, that were popular in Mughal times (see page 366). As in practically all Indian crafts, the specific skills involved in its creation are performed by specialists, the object passed from one to the other at various stages of its fabrication. The description that follows is based on interviews with the craftsman Mahendra Singh Talwar of Jaipur, contact with whom was kindly arranged for by the proprietors of Surana Jewelers in Jaipur, Rajasthan.

The initial nephrite slab is prepared by Jaipur lapidaries, called *hakkak* in Arabic. Cutting is done by the ancient method: with a bow cutter that has two parallel, tautly stretched copper wires, necessary to create a flat slab and maintain equal slab thickness. The abrasive used must be a substance harder than nephrite, and the most usual one is crushed and powdered diamond mixed with oil to make an abrasive slurry that will adhere to the cutting wires and the stone. Other hard materials such as crushed and powdered quartz, corundum (ruby), and garnet, can also be used. The

slurry is either dripped on the cutting line, or, when the object is small, as in this case, the entire piece is dipped into an abrasive compound kept in a nearby bowl.

Because of the *haldili*'s small size, and the fact that nephrite is valuable, that jade used for the *haldili* comes from pieces cut from a large mass of nephrite that has been shaped in preparation for making a larger object, such as a cup, bowl, dagger handle, comb, mirror back, or Qur'an stand. The same can be said for archer's rings (see page 267).

The basic *haldili* contour form is achieved by the use of cutting wheels mounted on a hand-bow-driven horizontal stone-cutting lathe (P: *char-e-hakkak*) mounted on the workshop floor, before which the worker squats. The same procedure is carried out later when carving lines, depressions, and making holes in the surface of the *haldili* slab to receive the inlay of gold and stones. A similar lathe and grinding system is used when a lapidary cuts and polishes gemstones, or a seal engraver excavates the characters on a seal stone. Each type of work requires different kinds of abrasive wheels, from very large to tiny.

Normally, there is no three-dimensional relief on the *haldili* nephrite surface—it is simply flat. To polish the surface, the same abrasives used for slab cutting, reduced to a much finer particle size, are employed. Final polishing is achieved using an impalpable abrasive such as whiting or chalk.

The projection at the top of a stone *haldili* is usually drilled with a hole to allow its suspension from the neck on a cord or chain. Some are left undrilled, in which case the entire object is mounted within a gold frame or casing that covers and protects the stone edges and includes a suspension system.

Haldili Surface Ornamentation: Jeweled and Inscribed

Following the established tradition of using predominantly floral and plant motifs in Mughal arts, the upper, visible plaque surface of the Muslim *haldili* is normally decorated with a motif invested with special iconographic meaning. This is a linear, conventionalized, bisymmetrical branching tree-of-life pattern, its trunk sometimes emanating from a vase (P: *guldan*) below, a common Eastern conception. Flanking the tree frequently are two birds in profile, facing the tree in veneration. In some cases they may be replaced by stars, or other symbolic images.

An ancient motif, the tree of life (S: *jeevan vriksh;* H: *vriksh*) was in use as long ago as in Mesopotamia and Safavid Persia. For Muslims, it represents the tree that grew in the middle of the Garden of Eden and bore twelve kinds of fruit that, when eaten, gave the eater everlasting life. According to Hindu concepts, it is the cosmic tree that supports the Universe and, in so doing, preserves life.

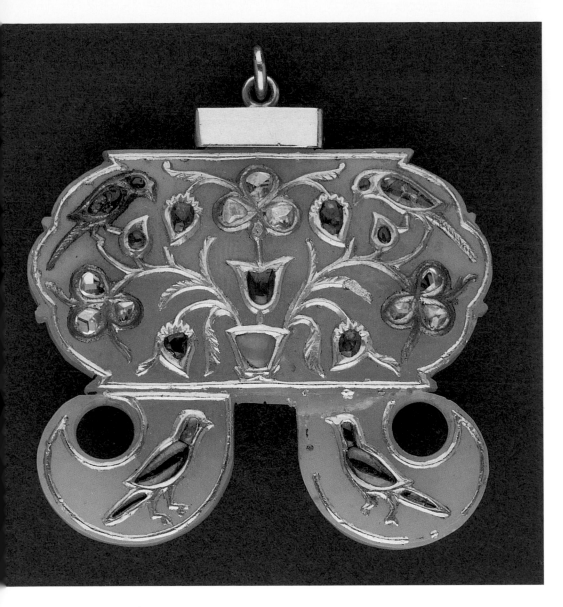

194. Delhi. *19th century*
Muslim haldili in white nephrite
1⅞ x 2 in. (4.8 x 5.1 cm)
The Nelson-Atkins Museum of Art, Kansas City,
Missouri. Gift of Mrs. Jacob L. Loose (34-236/103)

This double-purpose, cross-cultural (Islamic-Hindu) haldili is unusual because it incorporates stylized tiger-claw forms. Also depicted is a tree of life, whose branches bear fruits and flowers of gemstones inlaid kundan style.

195. Bhera, Shahpur District, Pakistan
Nephrite plaque-amulet blanks, such as this and others of lizardite serpentine, were made in Pakistan by lapidaries (see 197) and decorated at Delhi with kundan-set gemstones. The shield shape was most favored; other forms included the polylobed heart. This one is ready to be decorated (H: kundan-jarao).

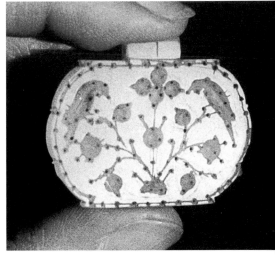

The *Kundan* Inlay Process

The trunk and branches are represented on the *haldili* in lines of inlaid gold. Their ends are often bedecked with multicolored cabochon-cut gemstones, probably a forgotten reference to the abovementioned fruits on the tree of life and an example of how symbols change over time. If there are nine, and they are the correct gemstones associated with them, they have become the Hindu *nava-ratna* planetal gemstones (see page 304). If seven, they could represent the Muslim seven planets (P: *saba'-saiyara*). In other cases the gemstones have lost all symbolic significance and are simply decorative.

The reverse side of a *haldili* can be plain, which may mean it was intended for use by a Hindu, or, if for a Muslim, it may never have been inscribed. After fabrication the reverse side of the *haldili* is often left blank so the client can select a desired inscription (P: *kitaba*). Muslim *haldili* inscriptions commonly are a pious phrase, often from the Qur'an. Carving this on the stone is the work of the seal engraver (H: *khatamkar*), a specialist in carving calligraphic inscriptions on stone and metal. Unlike the reverse, mirror-image inscription

on a seal, those on the *haldili* are *positive* and easily read because this amulet is not used as a seal. Another possible inscription could be a magic palindromic square with enclosed numbers or letters.

Contrary to metal Muslim amulets where the inscription is intended to be visible, the inscribed side of the *haldili* amulet is not seen when worn, and that side lies flat on the body. Contact with the wearer's skin is important because proximity of the inscription to the body is believed to increase its benefit to the wearer.

In achieving the *haldili* decoration, the surface design is drawn in lines on the stone with a scriber (H: *salai*), then ground out with a small grinding wheel. The depth and width of depressions intended for gold inlay are about half the stone's thickness. At spaced intervals along lines to be inlaid with gold, small holes (P: *kani*) are drilled perpendicularly into the slab surface but are not allowed to penetrate it. Their function is explained ahead. At positions where stones will be set, cup-shaped depressions are ground out with a round-ended wheel of appropriate size.

The gold used for inlay must be as pure as possible for a functional reason explained ahead. To achieve gold of near purity (H: *khalis sona*; 24 karat) it must be processed by annealing it several times, each time hammering it flatter and larger and immersing it in a special acid menstruum that dissolves into solution any other metals it may contain, such as copper or silver. The process of beating, flattening, and acid submersion is repeated until a flat piece of virtually pure gold leaf (H: *sona ka warak*) results. This is folded lengthwise several times to form a narrow strip (*sona ke patta*).

While it is worked upon, the *haldili* blank is fixed design-face-up in a shellac stick (H: *hundi*) whose round, upper surface is spread with the resinous substance lac (H: *lak*). It has a handle below to be able to hold the work in progress. The lac is heated over a charcoal fire to soften it sufficiently for the *haldili* to be pressed into its now-plastic surface, which upon cooling hardens and holds it securely.

The artisan uses a tweezer (H: *chimti*) to manipulate the gold strip into the groove lines, pressing it down with the help of a scriberlike tool (H: *kundan salai*) that has a pointed end, and a diagonally shaped spatula end resembling a small chisel.

Because of its purity, the gold is in a highly malleable state, and the pressure of the tool compresses it into a self-welded solid, without heat, much in the manner in which a dentist fills a tooth cavity. The *kundan* process would not otherwise be possible on jade because in normal inlay, as in metal damascene work, the wire inlaid must be hammered down, an obvious impossibility when working with a stone that would shatter upon impact.

With the pointed end of the tool, the gold is compressed to form a line and simultaneously is forced into the holes drilled along inlay lines, in effect forming miniature integral rivets all along the line to hold the gold in place. In one style of inlay work, only enough gold is used to make it flush with the stone surface. In another, the gold is shaped with the chisel-shaped tool end, dressed (H: *kundan pakana*), and then polished with an agate burnisher.

Stone-Setting in Jade

Before setting gemstones on nephrite (H: *kundan jarai ysheb par*) into the prepared depressions, the setter (*murassakar*) melts some lac, and the gently heated gemstone is pressed into the lac to melt it and shape it to conform with the gemstone's underside form. Over the solidified lac he puts a shaped piece of gold or silver foil (A: *waraq*), depending on gemstone color, and again heats the gemstone, which is pressed down to join the foil to the lac. These foil pieces back each translucent stone, reflect light through them, and brighten their color.

More of the pure gold strip is forced around the stone perimeter to wedge it in place and, by slightly overlapping the stone edge, secure it. When the gold inlay is completed, the gold is manually polished with a burnisher, which compresses it further. No other polishing is required.

The jade *haldili* amulet was a minor Mughal object as compared with the large three-dimensional achievements in nephrite. Yet its small size and affordable cost assured its survival. Its production in the twentieth century tapered off but did not end. Craftsmen in Delhi and Jaipur still can and do produce them and are fully capable of executing the delicate work of inlaying jade *haldili* amulets with gold and precious stones. The survival of this technique can probably also be attributed to the similarity between it and the skills needed for the *kundan* technique used in setting gemstones in traditional enameled gold jewelry, whose production flourishes. Today there seems to be a revival of interest in the *haldili* amulet. As there are not enough of the old ones available on the market, new ones are being made, some of which supply a clandestine market in pseudo-antiquities. It is almost impossible for an outsider to observe their guarded production.

Jade: Origins and Characteristics

Until recently, jade, of which the haldili *amulet is made, was not found in India; despite this lack, it became a medium for a uniquely Indian form of creativity involving not only flat tablet-shaped amulets but also three-dimensional objects. Since Neolithic times, jade has been recognized for its density and was once used for ax heads. Jadeite beads were found in Mohenjo-daro in what is now Pakistan (3,000–2,000 B.C.), but the source of this type of jade is unknown, possibly Burma. The jade the Mughals used is found in river beds in what formerly was Chinese Turkestan, now Sinkiang Province. Around Khotan in Yutien State (yu means "jade"), and Yarkand is the world's largest deposit. An important specific source is at the confluence of the White Jade River (Yurung Kash) and the Black Jade River (Kara Kash) that both issue from the Kunlun Mountains. When the river waters recede seasonally, jade is found in the river beds as tumbled boulders, stones, and pebbles whose weathered and discolored brownish skin must be removed to expose their true interior color. Since the eighteenth century, jade has also been mined at its source in the Jade Mountains at Belurtag.*

The journey of jade to India was made by established tedious overland trade routes, loaded on camels led in caravans. Jade was one of the standard products of trade or barter. In the return direction, after the Qing regime's expansion into and control of Sinkiang, by the same route, magnificent mid-eighteenth century Mughal period finished jade objects traveled to Yarkand and beyond. The best of them went as tribute gifts from Central Asian vassals to the Qianlung emperor (1736–1796), an ardent Mughal jade-object admirer, who called them the technical feats of "wizards." More than 150 of these Mughal jade objects have survived and are in the collection of the Palace Museum at Taipei; others are still in China.

Two similar but distinct stones are popularly called jade: jadeite and nephrite, the latter known as "true jade." (Nephrite, derived from the Greek nefros, *meaning "the kidney," was so called because it was reputed to be useful in renal diseases. The Romans called it* lapis nephriticus.) *They are never found together but are deposited in two distinctly separate areas. The jade of Sinkiang is nephrite, and jadeite deposits are mined by the Kachins in North Burma near Taminaw in the Mogaung Subdivision of the Myitkyina District, on the right bank of the Uru River. Although the Mughals knew jadeite, they did not use it. Mughal jade objects, including the* haldili *amulet, are all nephrite. Central and Southeast Asian terms for jade do not differentiate between the two types.*

The terms for nephrite in Central Asia are etymologically derived from the same root: in Persian it is yashm; *in Urdu,* yasaf; *in Arabic,* yashb; *and in Turkish,* yesim. *In early Mughal times the same word (*yashm*) was used for both jasper and jade, the latter then believed to be a rare, fine variety of jasper, though in fact it is a distinct stone. Bowenite (called in Hindi* sang-i-yeshm*), a very pure form of serpentine, is said to be available in the Punjab, and light green plasma and lizardite, which resemble jade, are found in Afghanistan.*

Nephrite and jadeite have similar physical properties. Both are very hard. On Mohs' scale (introduced by Friedrich Mohs in 1820 and universally in use) of 1 to 10 (10 being diamond, the hardest of stones), nephrite is 6.5, jadeite 6.75. Nephrite is a calcium-magnesium silicate and jadeite a sodium-aluminum silicate. Like jadeite, nephrite ranges in color from white to various shades of green from light to dark, the color due to the presence of iron as ferrous silicate. Jadeite is also found in other colors such as blue, lavender, and pink, which are not found in nephrite.

Because of its dense, almost textureless nature, jade is very durable. It can be carved with great precision and detail and is capable of having very distinct-edged depressions excavated into it. This is important in allowing the haldili, *other amulets, archer's rings, and other objects made in jade in India to be inscribed and inlaid with gold and gemstones. Nephrite can be polished to achieve an unctuous, translucent glow, and it has a warm, tactile quality, agreeable when it is used as an amulet such as the* haldili, *which is worn in contact with the skin.*

Translucent, monochromatic white nephrite was the type of jade the Mughals preferred, and this preference continues today in India. The best quality of white nephrite in the West is called "mutton fat" jade because it resembles congealed fat. In India it is called "pearl jade" (H: motiya yashab), and it is the type most commonly used for the haldili.

As yet, no reference in Indian literature has been found concerning the working of jade. Some historians say its use was possibly introduced by the Central Asian Muslim invaders as early as the thirteenth century, although no Indian jade objects datable to that early time exist. The cultural impact of Central Asian courts at Yarkand, Samarkand, and Bokhara cannot, however, be overlooked.

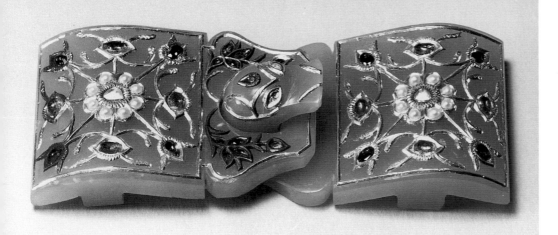

196. Northern India, probably Delhi. Mughal, 18th century
Carved nephrite belt clasp (chapras or baklas) encrusted with gemstones set kundan
style in gold, the form influenced by Chinese or Turkish belt clasps
Length 3⅝ in. (9.3 cm)
Asian Art Museum of San Francisco (B62 J28)

**197. Bhera, Shahpur District, Punjab,
Pakistan**
Indo-European three-strand (tin lara) necklace with
almond-shaped (badami) beads, formerly thought to
be pale green, translucent plasma, but now known
to be lizardite serpentine
Length 23⅝ in. (60 cm); weight 200 g
Collection Ghysels, Brussels

Often mistaken for jade, lizardite serpentine also
has a waxy luster but is softer. Mined at Kandahar,
Afghanistan, it was formed into beads and objects at
Bhera. Necklaces such as this, strung in various systems, were carried by peddlers (boxwallas) to be sold
at north Indian hill stations, where, in the hot season, Europeans stationed in India in the last century
went to escape the plains heat. The pendant cross
here is a clear indication of a European sales target.

By the sixteenth century, admiration for things Persian was
rampant at the Mughal court and its cultural influence was strong.
Generally speaking, during the sixteenth and early seventeenth
centuries, Persian design concepts, at least initially, dominated all
work produced in Mughal workshops. Their models were Persian
objects that came to the Mughal court as official gifts. Several
examples of such objects, engraved with the names of their
appreciative Mughal recipients, are extant. In an effort to
develop and improve the quality of indigenous production, for
the greater glory of the Mughal court and to satisfy an innate
love of luxury, Mughal emperors constantly enticed skilled
craftsmen, from Persia, China, and even Europe, to establish
themselves in India. It is entirely possible that Persian and
Chinese craftsmen who worked in jade in India could have
been among these émigrés.

By the end of the sixteenth century, Mughal administrative stability encouraged an unprecedented production of a
variety of decorative objects in all media. India continued to
look toward Persia for inspiration, but the Mughal emperors
did not neglect their own craftsmen. As is often recorded in the
memoirs of Akbar (Akbar Nama), Jahangir (Tuzuk-i-Jahangiri),
and Shah Jahan (Shah Jahan Nama), artisans were constantly
rewarded when they personally presented their masterworks to the
emperor at court. These accounts are replete with references to official presents, for example, daggers with jeweled jade handles, a type
commonly given as a political reward to the deserving, including members of the royal family. Objects in jade reached a peak of perfection in
the reign of Shah Jahan (1628–58) and represent a mature, indigenous
accomplishment: by successfully synthesizing Persian and Indian design elements, Mughal carvers realized what became a distinctive and recognizable
Mughal design style.

Even after the decline of the Mughals following the puritanical, repressive rule of
Aurangzeb (1658–1707), and the disastrous 1739 raid on Hindustan by Nadir Shah, jade
object manufacture unfalteringly continued, in part to supply increasingly important provincial courts that rose up and prospered while the center declined. Craftsmen at Amber-Jaipur,
Lucknow, and Varanasi took up the craft. Perhaps these were craftsmen who deserted
the declining Delhi court and moved to work for more stable patrons. Until the mid-nineteenth
century, increasingly florid examples were produced, elaborately decorated with gold and gemstones to satisfy a desire for ever greater ostentation. After 1857, the Mughal Dynasty ceased to
exist, and, to a great extent, production faltered with the decline of royal patronage.

Coins as Amuletic Jewelry

Pieces of metal, whose weight is certified by a mark stamped upon them by the authority of a government, we call coins (P: *sikka*, a die; to stamp). Since they were first minted in India, by the Sah dynasty group (180/170 B.C.–about 50 B.C.), coins have been used by people of all economic levels as elements in jewelry. For those who could afford it, gold coins were used, and others had to be satisfied with silver.

This practice persists in India, where old silver coins no longer current are commonly used for ornaments. Even remote tribal people who trade mainly by barter and are less involved in a money economy follow this practice. The idea came to them from other urban and rural people, an example of a frequent pattern of influence in which tribal people adopt outside customs they consider to be more "progressive" than their own.

Coins might at first appear to be purely decorative elements in Indian jewelry, and on costumes; however, as is typical of Indian culture, almost every component in jewelry has more than a decorative significance, and this also applies to coins. Obviously, coins are a symbol of wealth. Presumably, a person who uses coins as ornament possesses a surplus. Because coins in jewelry are seen by others, they contribute to the wearer's prestige, a calculated objective. Further, by using government-minted coins in jewelry, the wearer is tacitly admitting his or her support for that prevailing government. Coins in jewelry thus came to symbolize state protection, from which evolved the idea of the mystic, amuletic power superstitious people often attribute to coins.

The British-Indian government used precious metal coinage until 1947 and did not oppose the use of coins in jewelry; in fact, they encouraged the practice as a form of governmental propaganda. The increased decorative use of coins in the nineteenth century manifested itself at a time of relative political and economic stability, when precious metal coinage was available in sufficient quantity to permit this use, even though when coins are used for ornamental purposes they are withdrawn from circulation and lose their function as exchange currency.

Coin ornaments are more common among the lower economic sections of Indian society, who are most vulnerable to drastic fluctuations in economic circumstances. When these groups use their surplus savings for this purpose, they are declaring their relative economic well-being. This circumstance probably explains the wide use of silver coins in rural Indian jewelry, especially during the time of the British Raj. In the latter part of the nineteenth century, and continuing up until the time of Indian independence in 1947, more silver currency was in circulation than ever before, which reflects favorably on the stability of the paternalistic British-Indian administration.

199

200

◄ 198. Kullu, Himachal Pradesh
Silver necklace (pathachong; kachong; or kath mal). Each strand (kanthi), always in odd numbers, has a central pendant (tikra: the largest, lowest one; tikri: other smaller ones). Here coins are used as pendants, but others may have arrowhead or leaf-shaped, enameled pendants.
Courtesy The Studio, New Delhi

199. Andhra Pradesh
Lambadi woman wearing a necklace (rupaya har) of authentic silver coins and other ornaments traditionally worn by this group. Similar coin necklaces are used throughout India, each having its particular local name.

201. Belugunta, Ganjam District, Orissa
Lost-wax-cast brass ritual image of a Maliah-Kondh woman holding a child
5¼ x 3⅛ in. (13.4 x 8 cm)
Victoria and Albert Museum, London (IS 52-1955)

As is the custom, this image is given as a dowry to a bride, and symbolizes fertility. In a surprising display of verisimilitude, the maker has carefully depicted the Kondh woman's traditional tribal ornaments, including the coronet of coins, torques, and a coin necklace. The face pattern simulates the tattoos commonly placed on the face of a girl in a tribal initiation ceremony.

202. Baligurha; Orissa
Maliah-Kondh girl wearing an heirloom coronet of British-Indian silver rupee coins depicting George V (ruled 1910–36). Her face is tattooed in the traditional manner of her tribe.
Courtesy Rautenstrauch-Joest Museums für Volkerkunde der Stadt Köln

200. Rajasthan
Reverse side of a stamped silver amulet (madaliya) to which three British Indian silver rupee coins have been soldered as an offering to the deity depicted at the front, after said deity has fulfilled the requested favor. The promise to do so is a vow (vrata). In some cases, the amulet is removed after the vow has been realized. The coins are of Queen Victoria as Empress of India and Edward VII, her son who succeeded her and inherited the title of emperor. This dates the amulet to the early twentieth century.
Courtesy Alby Nall-Cain, Frontiers, London

Coins' round form and size range make them eminently suited to use in jewelry, especially in necklaces. Also, because the coins were of precious metal, they could be manipulated as metal permits. It is only in the last hundred years or so that the Western idea was established that a coin is disfigured if it is altered by a hole or if additions are joined to it by solder. Though this practice decreases its numismatic or actual monetary value, such coins are no longer currency but essentially looked upon as precious metal.

A hole-pierced coin is suspended by an inserted jump ring from a cord or chain in a necklace or can be sewn to a supporting material in a costume or accessory. A more common suspension system used in India is a half-round wire, U-shaped silver loop whose ends are hammered flat in parallel. Soldered to the coin, the flattened parts are joined like a clip to front and back. Often the loop terminal contacting the coin is ornamented with added elements such as shot and wire. A bezel could be added to the coin face to hold a small hard-stone, or a glass "stone." Decorative elements placed on the more important obverse side bearing the main field image, or inscription, enter the decorative scheme. On British-Indian silver coins, the image was always a British ruler: William IV (1830–1837), Victoria (1837–1901), Edward VII (1901–1910), George V (1910–1936), and George VI (1936–1952). In effect, coin ornaments become a form of commemorative jewelry marking the reigns of the various British monarchs related to Indian history. It did not matter to Indians that most inscriptions on these coins were in English, which the majority of Indians could not read. When the original system of mounting the coins in a necklace is still intact, which happens more often when

202

201

they are joined to a chain and not strung on a cord (cords may have been replaced and the coins restrung by a *patu'a,* at which time more recent coins may have been added for length), it becomes possible to date the necklace. The date of such a necklace would be that of the most recently minted coin.

Coins used in jewelry are commonly conceived of as amulets, partly because of attitudes toward the metals of which they are made, and in some cases because of the images stamped upon them. Examples of the latter are the old coins minted by the southern Indian kingdom of Vijayanagar, on which figures of Hindu deities and/or their symbols were depicted (see 207).

Most of the coins struck in Indian principalities formerly dominated by the Mughals, or ruled by a Muslim, had no figural subjects but used Arabic or Persian inscriptions. Frequently these were a quotation from the Qur'an or another quotation of Islamic religious importance. For Muslim people, when such a religious inscription appears, it adds greatly to the coin's value, a circumstance responsible for the common Muslim use of such coins as amulets.

Several forms of traditional Indian jewelry employ coins. They may be the sole element or used in combination with other elements such as metal, hardstone, or glass spacer beads; pendants; and amulet cases.

Necklaces use the greatest number of coins in one object. They can be widely spaced on a cord that is knotted to keep them in place or closely strung in consecutive or overlapping series. Often these necklaces have a large central pendant. Coin necklaces are known by various names in different parts of the country. In the Punjab, necklaces of rupee coins are *henkal* or *hamail;* in Rajasthan, *rupaya har.* In Tamil Nadu the term is *kasumalai,* a necklace with thirty to forty gold coins the size of a quarter-rupee joined to a gold chain. The latter name also applies to any necklace in which coins (*kasadi*) dominate. Ancient gold and silver coins issued by various rulers have been found with attached loops, a clear indication of their early use in ornaments such as a necklace.

Coins with loops soldered to their reverse side are used as shirt buttons or studs. In some a permanently joined safety chain is passed through the back loop of all of them.

Coins are commonly used for rings, the shank soldered to the coin back of one or several solder-joined coins. They can also be set in the bezel of a signet ring.

A particularly interesting use of coins in jewelry was that of the "pagoda" gold coin, current in Madras and the South until 1818, when the British ceased the minting of gold coins in India. The original unit of weight there, the coin which contained 42.048 grains of fine gold, was called a *pagoda* by the British, a term generally used by Europeans to designate Hindu and Buddhist temples, because on the pagoda's reverse side a pyramidal temple

203

203. Northern India
Silver necklace (rupaya har or hullar) with British-Indian rupee and half-rupee coins with the images of Edward VII and George V as emperors of India
Length 38³⁄₁₆ in. (97 cm); weight 528 g
Collection Mis, Brussels

204. Orissa
Old silver coins with solder-attached beads, used in an armlet (rupaya bazu) strung on cord
Total length 17½ in. (44.5 cm); weight 256 g
Collection Ghysels, Brussels

Coins with Arabic, Persian, or Urdu inscriptions were used by independent Indian principalities, which issued their own coinage.

205. Padadhari, Rajkot District, Gujarat
Silver necklace (kanthilo or hullar) of sixteen die-stamped simulations of old silver coins with Urdu inscriptions and a central pendant (jibro) in yoni shape, strung on knitted wire tubes (kajuri), with back hook (pench)
Courtesy Krishna Nathan, Krishna Gallery of Asian Arts, New York

206. Junagadh, Gujarat
Mehr man wearing a gold necklace (jhuman) of gold sovereign coins, arrowhead and yoni-shaped pendants, and a gold choker (tumpio), which may have been borrowed from a female relative for a special occasion.

207. Tamil Nadu ➤
Gold coin necklace (kasumalai). Originally made with a gold coin issued by one of the Chola rajas in the name of a toddy drawer (sanar) who discovered gold and secretly amassed great wealth. Upon being discovered, he was condemned to death, but, before his execution, the raja granted his request that his name, Sanar Kasu, would be perpetuated by the issue of a pure gold coin. This necklace, now made of gold kasu coins—or imitations—continues in Tamil Nadu and elsewhere. It is often seen on representations of southern Indian female Hindu deities (see 367). The term kasu is included in all compound names of any southern Indian necklace that includes coins.

205

206

208. Dumbur, South Tripura
Rai women, Marsum tribe, wearing necklaces (rathai) of kampani British-Indian silver rupee coins

was depicted. Locally it was known as the *bhagavati,* a reference to one of the epithets of Parvati as Durga, whose image formerly appeared on the face of this coin.

Several pagoda coins were issued at different places and times. Some of them can be mentioned here: pagodas of the Chalukya dynasty, the Gajapati dynasty, the Lingayat pagoda, and those of Vijayanagar, Gandikota, Chittuldroog, Travancore, Adoni, Mysore, and the East India Company pagoda. The *pon,* equal to half a pagoda, was also in circulation. These are the original coins used in the *kasumalai,* a coin ornament still popular today in Tamil Nadu.

Later British-Indian Coinage

The coins most commonly found today in traditional Indian jewelry are silver coins of strictly controlled weight and silver content issued during the time of British rule in India in the nineteenth century and up until the time of Indian Independence. The coins' weights and values based on their silver content were considered to be so reliable that throughout India, Nepal, and Tibet they received preferential acceptance. These coins were referred to as

kampani, the reference being to the British East India Company that governed India until the mutiny in 1857, followed thereafter by direct British administration. The designation persists today even when post-Company British Raj silver coins are referred to in jewelry.

The fact that its standard precious metal content (165 grains silver in a total weight of 180 grains troy) was guaranteed made it possible, when it became necessary, to sell old coins used in jewelry to refiners at their face value in terms of current precious metal prices, without testing their quality. Old coin prices are still published daily as a separate entry in the list of precious metal values in the major daily newspapers of India.

Because silver coinage of this time was so abundant, jewelers often used it as a source of raw material, melting it down when needed. They then normally debased the alloy by increasing its content of copper, the alloying metal. This reduced the actual value of the result by weight, but its bulk was increased so that a larger number of ornaments could be made. British-Indian silver coins, hoarded by ancestors who passed them on to heirs, still surface. In ornaments they are worn as symbols of ancestral patrimony.

Weight Conversions of British-Indian Silver Coins Found in Jewelry

One rupee	= 16 annas	= 180 grains
Half rupee	= 8 annas	= 90 grains
Quarter rupee	= 4 annas	= 45 grains
Eighth rupee	= 2 annas	= 21.5 grains

Those who cannot afford precious-metal coins use imitation coins in jewelry. Real or not, the meaning of a coin as a symbol of wealth persists. Imitations are made by casting duplicates from an original coin, actually a form of counterfeiting, though such coins are not intended to enter circulation as currency. Sheet metal can be stamped with an image to make it resemble a coin; the result is called a *bracteate.* Often base metal is used and plated in precious metal.

209. Bombay, Maharashtra. *Late 19th century* ▶
Gold necklace (ashrafi-ka-har or gathala) with stamped units simulating gold coins (ashrafi)
Total length 14⅝ in. (37.4 cm); widest width 1³⁄₁₆ in. (3 cm); weight 102 g
Private Collection, Brussels

Not a traditional style, it is a type made for a Western woman's use.

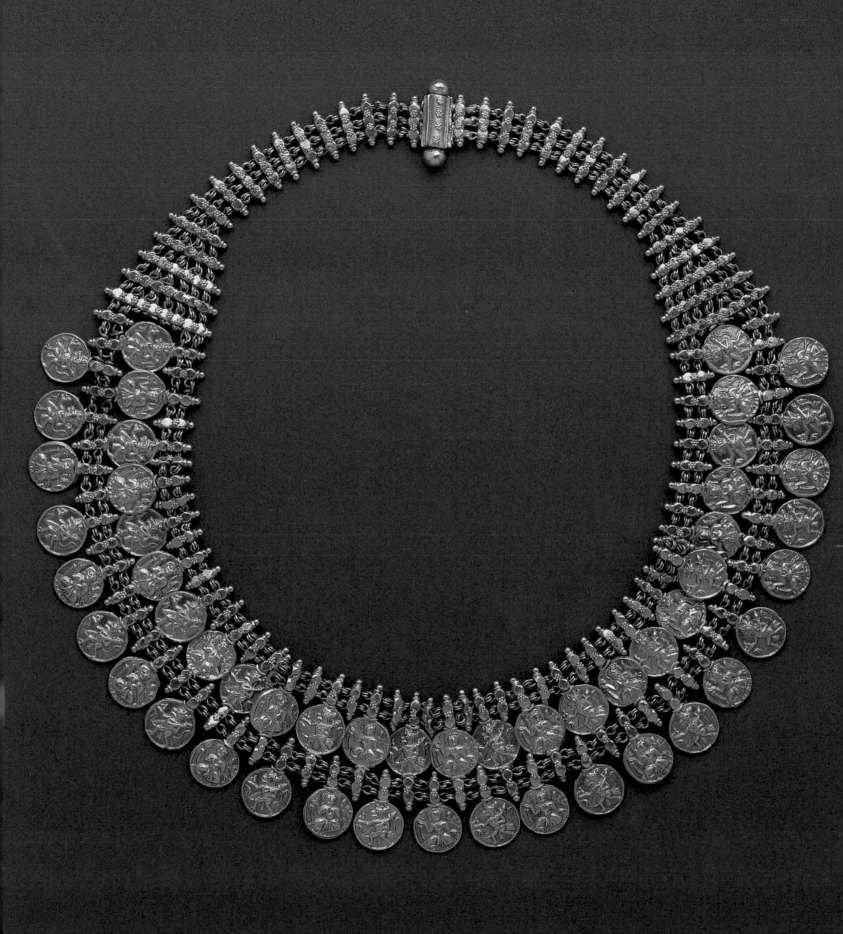

Amulet Container Forms: Protecting Magical Contents

The purpose of all three-dimensional amulet containers is to protect and prolong the efficacy of whatever magical objects they may enclose. Containers without any visible access are meant not just to hold but also to seclude the amuletic object(s) from view when this is considered desirable. According to some Indian religious beliefs, should such an object come into visual or physical contact with other objects or persons thought to be capable of defiling them, they become ritually contaminated and lose their power. The closed container also solves the problem of how to keep the magical or mystic object on the owner's body, where it will offer the most benefit.

For those with limited means, an amuletic object that requires protection or seclusion can simply be wrapped with cloth and tied into a small package, or placed within a cloth bag attached to the body with a cord. Far more durable are containers of any metal, base or precious. The actual form a metal container takes is normally determined by local cultural custom and, in principle, depends on what it is meant to hold. For instance, a container that is completely closed probably holds a paper amulet.

Written charms originated with the earliest development of Indian writing systems, in which materials such as palm leaf (S: *tala pattra*) or birch bark (S: *bhoj pattra*) were used as the surface inscribed or written upon with a stylus. These materials are still sometimes used for written charms, but paper has in general supplanted them.

The written charm was held in awe, especially among illiterate people. Uneducated people were apparently unconcerned by the implication that the evil spirit against whom the charm was written would have to be literate for it to be effective; its intention was sufficient for it to function. All charms lasted as long as they remained intact and continued to be used by the individual for whom they were consecrated.

Probably the most universally common amulet container form is the tube into which can be inserted any written or printed charm on a material that can be rolled up. Tube containers are made of sheet metal, most often a simple round cylinder, but they can also be made in a variety of polygonal sectional forms, such as square, pentagon, hexagon, or octagon. Such forms have been in use in India since as early as 100 B.C.

The closing at both tube ends can be flush and permanent, although, in many cases, one end is left removable to provide access to the interior. Most often the end-sleeve closing is a half-dome, conical, or other ornamental form held in place by an inner flange matched to and inserted into the opening. Once there, it is held in place by a tight friction fit. In large, tube-shaped containers, the end is often screwed on.

To suspend metal cylindrical containers, a metal loop (or loops) is attached, usually soldered or riveted in place. An old tube amulet form still in use in South India has only one end loop and is suspended vertically by a cord or chain. In this system, the container swings freely in its suspension from the neck. Horizontally suspended cylindrical containers—having a single central loop; one fixed at both ends; or a series of loops—are more stable.

Another category of Hindu amulet form is the flat, round, square, rectangular, or other-shaped three-dimensional box. Box amulets also can be permanently closed or fabricated with the capacity of being opened by removing either one end or the back, which fits into the front by an internal, surrounding flange. In some cases, front and back are hinged at the top. A subtype is provided with a front opening through which is seen the object it contains, such as a miniature painting of a deity, or, today, a photograph or print. The opening can have a protective glass or not.

All these forms may be unadorned or treated with a variety of surface metal-decoration techniques. They can be additionally ornamented with glass or semiprecious or precious stones. In this case, they become far more than simple amulets: they are elaborate forms of jewelry in which their ornamentation is meant to glorify their associated deities.

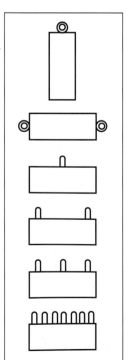

210

211

210. Gandhara, Afghanistan. *c.3rd–4th century* A.D.
Gray schist Bodhisattva Maitreya Buddha
Height 30¹¹⁄₁₆ in. (78 cm)
Courtesy Sotheby's, New York

Seated on a throne holding a lotiform water bottle, this bodhisattva wears typically Gandharan jewelry, including large, foliated armlets, a jeweled collar, ropework necklace, and another with a central pendant of two makaras holding a jewel between them (see 578). On a narrow cord are threaded cylindrical amulet boxes (like 211) of a form still in use. He wears kundala round earrings (see 450), and his chignon is secured by a beaded band.

211. Gandhara, Ahin Posh, Jalalabad, Afghanistan. *Gandharan period* (5th century B.C.–4th century A.D.)
Gold horizontal-tube amulet case (patri) found in a stupa
2⁷⁄₈ x 1³⁄₁₆ in. (7.3 x 3 cm)
British Museum, London (1880-29 099011)

Each of the amulet's faces is set with five garnets in alternating oval and leaf shapes. Strung on two suspension rings, its cylinder ends are flat and capped with beaded wire perimeters, and one end is removable.

◄ **212.** *Tubular Amulet Suspension Systems*

Vertical: *Top loop.* Horizontal: *End loops; single central loop; two end loops; three loops; multi loops*

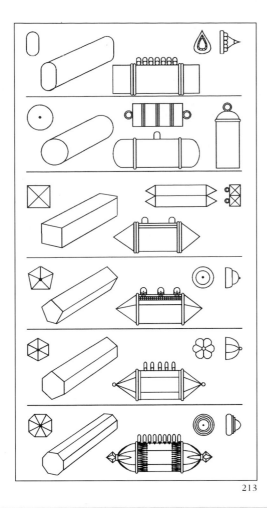

213

214

213. *Tubular Amulet Forms*

Oval; round; square; pentagonal; hexagonal; octagonal

214. Kerala. *19th century
Gold marriage necklace
(mangkaliyam) worn by
Nayar women
Total length 17½ in.
(44.5 cm); central vertical
tube units length 1¾ in.
(4.5 cm); thali ⅝ x 9/16 in.
(1.6 x 1.5 cm); weight 135 g
Victoria and Albert Museum,
London (03060 IS)*

*The marriage emblem (thali
or bottu) at the right side
bears an image of Devi. The
vertical tubes are receptacles
for mantras.*

215

216

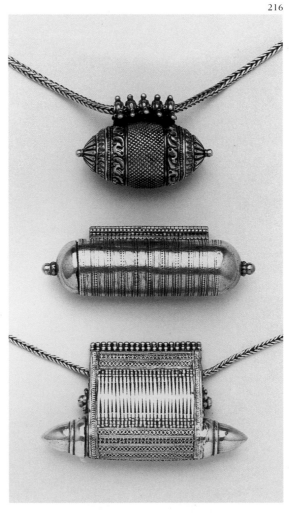

215. Kerala
*Silver belt (patti aranjanam)
whose base of braided silver-
wire cord (patti) is strung
with beads (mani) in round,
oval, half-moon, and other
shapes; and amulet cases
(elas) in series alternating
with beads
Collection Ivory, New York*

*The central crescent-shaped
amulet appears at the waist
in front. The belt is worn by
Kathakali male and female
character dancers as well
as for everyday use.*

216. *Silver amulet containers worn as a central unit in
a necklace*

*From top to bottom:
Harad (Bihar): 2¼ x 1⅜ in.
(5.6 x 3.5 cm); weight 56 g
Ta'wiz (Hyderabad):
1³/16 x 3¼ in. (3 x 8.2 cm);
weight 56 g
Kappu kuttu (Kerala):
1⅞ x 3⅛ in. (4.8 x 8 cm);
weight 26 g
Collection Ghysels, Brussels*

217. Bhuj, Kachchh, Gujarat
Silver necklace with strung units,
including four container-type
amulets, a central arrowhead-type
amulet plaque, additional decorative
units, and ghungrus
Courtesy Judy Margolis, Origins,
Santa Fe

The place of amulet cases in a
necklace relates conceptually to the
Gandharan use of such amulets and
exemplifies the continuity of ancient
regional prototypes.

218

218. Bangalore, Karnataka
Silver amulet box on a chain
Amulet 3 x 6½ in. (7.5 x 16.5 cm); chain length
30 ⁵⁄₁₆ in. (77 cm); weight 460 g
Collection Mis, Brussels

Ornamented with a central makara or kirtimukha flanked by birds and bands of floral creepers, the box unscrews at one end for the insertion of magical protective objects and mantras on sheets of metal or paper.

219. Gujarat
Silver necklace (ta'wiz ka kanthla) with three amulets, the central one mounted on cloth and trimmed with glass seed beads
Central amulet container 1⅜ x 3⅜ in.
(3.5 x 8.5 cm); weight 96 g
Collection Ghysels, Brussels

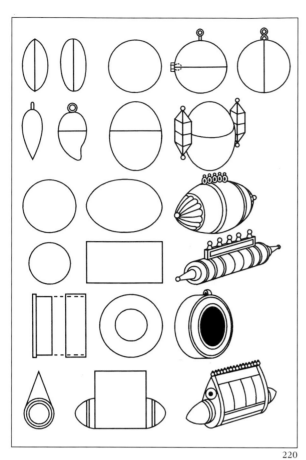

220. *Amulet Container Types*

Flattened circle; lentil; ball, horizontal opening, vertical opening; oval, vertical; mango; egg; oval, horizontal; cylinder; cylinder with opening; tear-shaped tube with enclosed cylinder

221. *Amulet Container Types*

Arrowhead-leaf (Bihar); triangle (Kodagu [Coorg]); lozenge-diamond (Gujarat); square (Bengal); rectangle (Rajasthan); rectangle-pillow (Punjab); octagon (Himalaya); hexagon-ogival (Ladakh)

222. Rajasthan
Lambadi or Banjara Indian gypsy women of a nomadic mercantile tribe, wearing silver necklaces (kanthla mala) with ten units of stylized double tiger-claw amulet forms and central arrowhead-form pendant. Similar ornaments are worn by Jat, Sikligar, Gujar, and Pinara women in Gujarat.

223. Bikaner, Rajasthan
Silver necklace whose main elements are three amulets: two in arrowhead or fan form (phanki), one in seed form (hard), separated by beads (goli), with back tassel (fumtu)
Collection Eleanor Smoler, U.S.A.

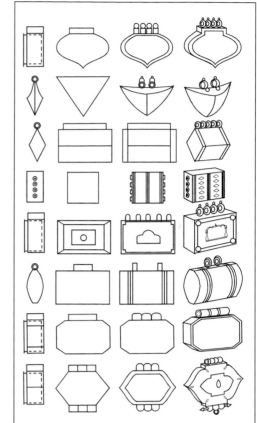

220

221

222

223

224. Rajasthan
The silver container amulet may hold charms to ward off the evil effects of others engendered by thought (soch), word (vach), or action (karm).

226

226. Rajasthan
Gold amulet box (chhedi ka jantar) with central Rajput-style cusped-arch opening through which an inserted image of a deity may be seen. The box is ornamented with a fringe of small balls (gajre). Courtesy Chhote Bharany, New Delhi

227. Delhi
Silver amulet container (chhedi ka jantar) 2⁹/₁₆ x 2⁷/₁₆ in. (6.5 x 6.2 cm); weight 56 g Collection the author, Porvoo

Under glass at the center is a lotus form cut from colored foils. The border is set with foil-backed cabochon-cut glass "stones." A container-type amulet, it opens at the reverse side to reveal a miniature painting of a Hindu deity.

227

225. Rajasthan
Silver amulet box (chhedi ka jantar) with a frontal opening (chhedi)
3³/₁₆ x 2⁵/₁₆ in. (8.1 x 6.9 cm); weight 56 g
Collection the author, Porvoo

Through the opening can be seen a flat or dimensional representation of a deity or deities. In this one, the reverse is embossed with auspicious agricultural subjects, alluding to fertility symbolism.

Yantras in Hindu Container Amulets

Yantras are Hindu geometric diagrams often combined with written mystic characters or individual *bija* letters believed to possess occult or magic powers. *Yantra* diagrams are normally used for the purpose of stimulating meditation (S: *samadhi*) upon the particular deity with whom that *yantra* or *bija* is associated. When used as an amulet printed on paper or inscribed on metal foil and inserted in a tubular or box type amulet container, its function is to invoke the assistance of that deity in protecting the individual against the influence of an evil spirit, or the evil eye.

Yantras used this way are generally worn by Hindus who worship Devi, the mother goddess, but *yantras* connected with other deities are also used. As an amulet, the power of the *yantra* diagram is believed by many to be superior to any written amulet. To render them maximally potent before use, the *yantra* must be consecrated by a priest, preferably one of a temple dedicated to the deity with whom the particular *yantra* is connected.

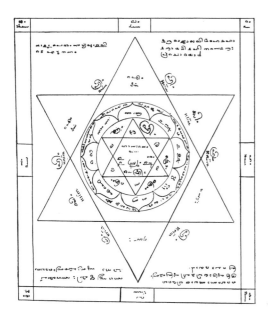

228. Kerala
Yantra of Subramanya (Karttikeya, Skanda or Murugan), god of war, with Malayalam inscription, some written in reverse, which augments their power

Lingayat *Lingam* Caskets: Ornamental Cult Objects

The *lingam* casket, developed for use as a container for the movable *lingam,* the main cult object worshiped by Lingayats, is a unique and striking design concept, even within the diverse world of Indian ornament. Its form is a prime example of how religious practice dictates what an ornament must look like and a good Indian example of the design truism that "form

229. Gudimallam, Chittore, Andhra Pradesh. *c. 5th century* A.D.
Granite Shiva lingam permanently installed in an inner shrine (garbhagriha lingam), Parasuramesvara Temple. The top section is marked with Shiva's symbol.

follows function." To understand the formal evolution of the *lingam* casket requires some background on aspects of Lingayat religious principles.

Lingayat is an anglicized form of *Linga-vant,* the vernacular term commonly used by members of this religious community to designate themselves. An individual is a *lingi.* A Shaiva sect identified with the Virashaiva (those who honor Shiva), it came about as a movement reacting against superstitious practices and established Brahmanism. The sect became prominent in the twelfth century A.D. at Kalyana, the capital of a western Chalukyan kingdom ruled by King Vijjala in the Karnataka region of southern India.

The founder of the sect was Basava, the king's minister, who used his high position to carry out religious reform. Rejecting Brahman authority, Basava replaced them with a new order of priests called *jangamas.* His radical views aroused Brahmans, and the king dismissed Basava and expelled him and his followers from the kingdom. In exile, the well-organized cult grew and attracted other Shaiva cults. Today many Lingayats live in Karnataka, Maharashtra, Andhra Pradesh, and Tamil Nadu, but the sect's main center remains the Kanarese country. Basava's sayings and those of his colleagues are collected in the *Vacana-*

shastra, and their sacred book is the *Basava Purana,* both in Kanarese.

Basava's purpose was to make humans realize their place in the universe. Among its tenets, this sectarian Shaivite cult includes the refusal to recognize the supremacy of Brahmans; a denial of polytheism, acknowledgement of only one god: Shiva; a rejection of Brahma and Vishnu, the two others of the Hindu triad; and a repudiation of the authority of the Vedas. Basava also denounced obscurantism; idol worship; and the creation of temples.

Lingayats disavow all aspects of what they consider to be Brahmanical tyranny. They do not recognize caste distinctions; do not believe in the doctrine of rebirth; and reject sacrifices, penances, pilgrimages, and the practice of fasts, all contrary to Brahmanical Hinduism. In addition, they object to child marriage; believe in the equality of men and women; approve of the remarriage of widows; and they do not practice cremation but bury their dead.

About two-thirds of all Hindus worship Shiva, and there are many Shaivite cults, of which the Lingayats are but one. The cardinal principle of their faith is an unquestioned belief in the efficacy of the *lingam,* the symbolic object that represents Shiva and is one of the most ancient symbols of worship in India, dating back at least two thousand years or more.

A *lingam* can be of two types. The fixed, immovable stone *lingam* (*sthavara linga*) installed in Shiva temples and worshiped by most Shiva sects is represented embedded in a *yoni,* the female generative organs, and varies in size from a small projecting knob to a round-topped cylinder of considerable height. Surrounding it in the *yoni* runs a gutter (*pranalika*) toward a projecting spout that drains the liquid libation poured over the *lingam* by a worshiper.

The other *lingam* type is the movable *lingam* (*jangama lingam*), which can be small

230. Jaipur, Rajasthan
Carved rock-crystal, stationary (stavara) Shiva lingam with protecting cobra, standing on a yoni, with projecting bull's-head spout to drain libation liquids. Used in home shrines
Courtesy Sotheby's, London

231. Karnataka
A compound encased, movable jangama lingam, *which is placed in a Lingayat's* ayigalu
Collection Torbjörn and Judy Carlsson, Art Expo, Washington, D.C.

232. Shimoga, Karnataka
Female Lingayat Virashaiva or layperson (linga banajiga) wearing a silver lingam casket (ayigalu) in modified egg form (gundgurdgi). Lingam caskets are also worn by men and women on the left arm or by a Lingayat Jangam priest on the top of the head under a cloth cap.

233. Karnataka
Three silver lingam caskets (ayigalu or shivadhara), in "round pot" shape, each containing a movable (jangama) lingam
Left: 2⅛ x 2¾ in. (5.4 x 7 cm); weight with chain 100 g. Center: 1⁵⁄₁₆ x 2¾ in. (4.2 x 7 cm); weight with chain 103 g. Right: 2⅝ x 2⅔ in. (6.7 x 7 cm); weight with chain 103.5 g
Collection Ghysels, Brussels

This is the most common type worn by Lingayat laypeople (pancham or linga banajiga).

enough to be carried upon the person; related to that is the *lingam* in pebble form (*ratnasabhapati*). As Lingayats are opposed to temple worship, they believe the movable type to be Shiva's only true symbol.

The Lingayat priest, or *jangam* (*jan*, knowledge, soul, essence; *gam,* care, concern), highly esteemed in the Lingayat community, is believed to be the reincarnation of the deity and god on earth. As the community *guru,* the *jangam* resides over Lingayat initiatory rites that do *not* include the normal Hindu presentation of the Brahmanical sacred thread, which involves caste distinctions to which they are opposed, but instead involve the giving of the *lingam* emblem. On achieving adulthood, a child is initiated by the *guru-jangam.* Initiation (*diksha*) is associated with the idea of rebirth.

While performing the ceremony, the *jangam* looks intently into the child's eyes and meditates on Shiva. Placing his hand on the child's head, he extracts the child's spiritual principle and replaces it in the form of a consecrated *lingam,* the child's for life and eternity, and created *only* for that individual. Because symbolically it represents the initiate's life (*pran*), the *lingam* must be very carefully guarded and protected. The need for a *lingam* casket is obvious.

All Lingayats, young and old, poor and rich, carry their *lingam* on the body at all times. It must never be put down. Its loss is regarded as spiritual death, although, with proper ritual, it can be replaced by a *jangam.* On the *lingi's* death, he or she is buried in a seated position with the *lingam* in the left hand.

The Lingayat *lingam* given to the initiate is made of soapstone (steatite) carved by specialist stoneworkers. The total height of this miniature stone *lingam* is about three-quarters of an inch (19 mm). The tiny *lingam* is covered with another substance called *kauthi,* to preserve it from harm, a process that illustrates the importance of this object for Lingayats. The *kauthi* composition contains lac, clay, and sacred cowdung ashes—said to be the *semen virile* of Shiva—as well as marking-nut tree (Kan: *ger-kayi; Semecarpus anacardium*) fruit juice, or black antimony powder (P: *surma*), the latter also used as an eye liner cosmetic. Either of the latter two account for its final black color. Heated and still malleable, the *kauthi* is plastered evenly around the *lingam* to form either a round shape (flattened where it stands), or a slightly truncated cone that will stand upright, with the *lingam* at its center.

The spout of the *yoni* points to the right. During worship, this side must face the devotee. To be sure that this position is maintained, while the compound is still plastic, a permanent indention is made to mark the proper side. The prepared *lingam* is then wrapped in a white or red square of cotton and carefully placed inside the *lingam* casket in the proper upright position, spout right in relation to the wearer.

Lingayats are easily distinguished from other Hindus because in most cases the *lingam* casket is visible on the body. A Lingayat priest wears his *lingam* in a case wrapped in a cloth and tied on his head like a turban, in which it forms a visible bump. Cultivators wear it wrapped in a cloth tied around the neck; when they work, they tie it to the upper left arm; when they bathe, it is tied to the head.

Caskets were once made of sandalwood or copper, which is considered to be a ritually pure metal among all Hindus. Today, the wealthier mercantile class uses silver, and those who can afford it use gold. Silver or gold caskets are made in several distinct forms. The most usual one is ovoid and in Kanarese is called *gundagadigi* or *gundgurdgi,* meaning "round pot." Another term is *ayigalu.* Various other names are used by Lingayats at different locations.

The way in which the typical casket design functions is ingenious. At the center is a vertical egg form, a material metaphor for the *hiranyagarbha* (golden egg) representing the creator, the source of all life. Flanking it are vertically placed, elongated rectangular forms, square in section, joined at both top and bottom with a pyramidal form at whose apexes are a large ball finial. The bottom balls are solid, but the top ones are pierced through by a hole whose diameter is sufficient to allow a carrying cord (*sivadhara*) to be inserted. The whole object divides in half *horizontally.* Both parts fit together by internal flanges, and the united egg form is perfect and complete, with only a horizontal line to indicate the division between top and bottom. This construction allows the casket to be opened and closed

234. Karnataka
Gold Lingayat fertility necklace for the provision of male offspring
Victoria and Albert Museum, London (IS 30-1984)

The necklace consists of thirty pendants set in gold, each with symbolic meaning connected with fertility, most of them alternating with a long gold tube bead. There are six phalluses (lingam), five in gold, two with gemstone tips, and one of black coral. Four of these are combined with a twin-seed form suggestive of male reproductive anatomy. Of four point-ended forms (yoni), two are set with gemstones. Ten natural seeds symbolizing the germ of potential life, the life force, and conception, are mounted in cap bails with decorated gold bases. One bead is of auspicious red coral, bail mounted. A black-stone arrowhead form is set in gold. These subjects suggest that this necklace is from Karnataka, where Lingayats, a Shaivite sect, have a large community that worships the movable lingam.

235. Karnataka
Polychrome wood necklace made for use in rituals performed by Lingayats in the worship of Shiva and Parvati. The forms are alternating male and female genitalia (linga and yoni).
Collection Ivory, New York

234

235

236. Maharashtra ➤
18th–19th century
Cast-brass, hollow lingam cover (mukhalinga) in the form of the head of Shiva
Height 11⁷⁄₁₆ in. (29 cm)
Courtesy Rautenstrauch-Joest Museums für Volkerkunde der Stadt Köln, Köln

Shiva wears a Maratha-style turban and a lingayat amulet container of stylized bull's horns type around his neck (see 237).

237. Karnataka ➤
Silver lingam casket in square (chauka) form
4⅛ x 4¾ in. (10.2 x 12 cm); weight 602 g
Collection the author, Porvoo

The projections symbolize stylized bull's horns, a reference to Nandin, Shiva's bull mount, and Basava, the sect founder. In Hindu mythology, Basava is the lord of cattle and men and protects his devotees against evil.

easily, which must be done daily when the *lingam* inside is worshiped.

The carrying cord, which normally passes over the left shoulder to suspend the casket on the right side, is of round plaited silver wire. Its ends pass through the top holes in the aforementioned two upper balls, and descend through the rectangle to the lower half of the casket. Each cord end has an attached ring that engages a crossbar fixed in the lower casket half. As a result, the cord cannot be removed, and this arrangement also permits the upper casket half to slide upward and ride on the fixed cord. Because the upper half of the casket cannot be taken off the cord, it can never be lost or misplaced.

Another form of casket, called *chauka* in reference to its rectangular shape, consists of a rectangular box whose top cover rises upward at opposite ends to tapering points meant to suggest a bull's horns. The form is a metaphor for the founder's name: Basava is another name for the bull Nandin, who is the vehicle (*vahanam*) of Shiva. A symbol of fertility and strength, the bull is considered to be the theriomorphic form of Shiva and became his vehicle once Shiva was represented anthropomorphically. This casket form is additionally ornamented at its base with chased designs of foliage surrounding a central *makara*, a mythic aquatic animal associated with water, alluding to the usual custom of pouring a water or milk libation over the *lingam* during worship to honor the deity. As in the case of the egg-shaped casket, the top part of this one can slide upward on the fixed cords.

Yet another variation takes the form of a rectangular case or *lingam* stand surmounted either by a representation of a *lingam*, sometimes with attached Shiva heads (*mukhalingam*), or a representation of the seated bull Nandin, who is usually installed outside a Shiva temple facing the inner shrine that contains the *lingam*. His presence there immediately identifies that temple as being dedicated to the worship of Shiva. It serves the same function here. Another unique casket form is in the shape of an entire temple, which because it is portable, does not contradict the Lingayat proscription against fixed temples.

The *lingam* is used as a meditation device to allow the worshiper to concentrate on Shiva. In daily worship, the *lingam* is removed from its casket and placed upright in the left palm with the indented dot facing the worshiper, who pours a water or milk libation over it with the right hand while reciting appropriate *mantras*. The water offering (S: *tirtha*) or milk (*dadhi*) that falls into a tray placed below is collected and imbibed by the worshiper, since to drink this sacred liquid, which has theoretically contacted the *lingam*, purifies and strengthens the individual and expels all sin. After the ceremony, the encased *lingam* is dried, wrapped in cloth, and returned to the casket, ready to be worn again.

238. Andhra Pradesh
Silver ayigalu, in stupa form, containing a
movable lingam (jangama lingam)
Collection Anne Jernandier de Vriese, Brussels

239. Andhra Pradesh or Karnataka
Silver Lingayat yoni-shaped lingam casket ayigalu),
mounted with a five-faced (panch mukha) lingam
with confronting bull (basava), suspended by a
heavy, square loop-in-loop chain
5¹⁄₁₆ x 5⅝ in. (12.8 x 14.2 cm); chain length 33½ in.
(85 cm); weight with chain 1,470 g
Collection Mis, Brussels

Tibetan Ornaments: Sub-Himalayan Jewelry

The proximity of northern India to western Tibet, with which India shares a long Himalayan boundary, has resulted in a rich cultural exchange between the people living on both sides of the frontier. Thus, it is no surprise to find that in Ladakh, long called "Little Tibet" but politically part of India, most people follow a distinctly Buddhist-Tibetan cultural tradition. This west Himalayan area also includes parts of Kashmir, Lahul-Spiti, Himachal Pradesh, and Uttar Pradesh, and each group there has made its own cultural contribution that is distinctive and unique.

This richness is especially evident in the elaborate ornaments worn by women of the area. For example, the Tibetan woman's *ga'u* or amulet container, popularly worn throughout the sub-Himalayan geographic complex as a part of a total ensemble, is designed in configurations that can identify a particular geographic group.

Counter to the strong Tibetan influence is the impact of Indian, essentially Hindu, ornament concepts. Designs of distinctly Indian origin here mingle with those from Tibet. In some cases, ornaments actually made for Hindus in adjacent areas of India are adopted and used intact, often in a manner different from that originally intended (see 267). The subject is vast, and only a few examples of the ornaments found in this area can be discussed here.

Such cultural diversity can be traced to Tibet's larger history. The culture of Tibet, initially derived from that of India, also came under Chinese influence. Its cultural development was, however, seriously affected in 1951 by a Chinese army invasion of Tibet that extinguished its former independence, and designated Tibet as the Tibetan Autonomous Region of the People's Republic of China.

Since 1959, more than 60,000 Tibetan refugees have fled oppression, and now more than 120,000 in exile are settled in about fifty

240. Lahul and Spiti, Himachal Pradesh
Silver head ornament (kan balle in the Tandi-Gosha area; khul-kantaie in Kinnaur)
Courtesy Chhote Bharany, New Delhi

The loops are worn at the sides of the head. The chains pass to the back of the head, where they are fixed to a strip of cloth and hooked to the hair.

locations in India, Nepal, Bhutan, Europe, and America. Displaced Tibetans support themselves through cooperative societies and try to preserve the precious heritage of their religious and artistic traditions by the manufacture and sale of jewelry, metal objects, carpets, and other items that follow traditional Tibetan design styles.

A relief map of northern India reveals the highest, most stupendous mountain range on our planet—the *Himalaya* (S: *hima,* snow; *alaya,* abode), whose snow-covered peaks extend from Afghanistan in the northwest to Burma in the southeast, a distance of more than 1,500 miles (2,400 km). North of this range lies the sparsely inhabited high-altitude plateau (15,000 ft; 3846 m) of Tibet, and to the south are the people who live in the sub-Himalayan hill area that extends into India. Tibetans designate their country *Bod-yul* and refer to the Himalayan hill people as *M'hon.* Indians call Tibet *Bhot,* all Tibetan related people *Bhotia,* and hill people in general *Paharia* (belonging to the mountains).

The unique Buddhist culture of Tibet that dominated many of the peoples of the Indian sub-Himalayan hill area was disseminated unhindered by the relative isolation imposed on them by the highly irregular terrain between Tibet and India. Trade routes followed the deep valleys created by the melting Himalayan snows and glaciers that ultimately give rise to the many rivers that emerge from the hills and flow into India. All these rivers eventually join the three main subcontinental northern Indian rivers: the Indus, Ganges, and Brahmaputra, which together make cultivation and life possible in the entire region of north India, Pakistan, and Bangladesh. Along these trade routes also flowed Tibetan cultural concepts.

In the central sub-Himalayan area, independent Nepal (Hindu-Buddhist) and Bhutan (Buddhist)—between which lies Sikkim (Buddhist) now politically Indian—form a block that politically separates Indian sub-Himalayan inhabited territory into western and eastern sectors. Those areas within the boundaries of India that are occupied by Buddhist and other groups might be thought of as the extended ethnic and cultural boundaries of Tibet.

In the western sector bordering Tibet are Buddhists of Ladakh. To the south lies Himachal Pradesh, partially inhabited by the Buddhists of Lahul and Spiti, the Hindu Gujar and Bakarwal nomads, and the Hindus of Kullu and Chamba. Southeast, in Uttar Pradesh, are the Bhotia Mahals of Garhwal and Kumaun.

In the eastern sub-Himalayan sector, also bordering on Tibet, inhabited mainly by Mongoloid Tibeto-Burman tribes, some of whose ancestors migrated there from Tibet, is the recently created Indian sub-Himalayan Hill State of Arunachal Pradesh, formerly administered under the North East Frontier Agency (N.E.F.A.). Following Bhutan, from west to east, its five district subdivisions include Kameng

241
242

243

244
245

◄ **241. Shimla, Himachal Pradesh**
  Cast-brass, chased fibula (sti or bumni), worn in the hills north of Shimla
  6¹¹⁄₁₆ x 6⅞ in. (17 x 17.5 cm); weight 334 g
  Collection the author, Porvoo

◄ **242. Kaza, Spiti, Himachal Pradesh**
  Silver repoussé-work shawl fibula (tomukch or bamno)
  5⅛ x 4¹⁵⁄₁₆ in. (13 x 12.3 cm); chain length 4⅞ in. (10.5 cm);
  pinstem length 3⅞ in. (9.7 cm)
  Collection the author, Porvoo

The three circular forms symbolize the three gems (S: tri-ratna; Tib: dKon-mch'og-sum) of Buddhism (see 689, 692). Lotus forms set with gemstones are an allusion to the Tibetan mantra or dharani, OM MANI PADME HUM (Hail to the Jewel in the Lotus, i.e. Avalokiteshvara). A similar arrangement of three circular forms in a pyramid is the chintamani (Tib: norbu dgos-'dod-dbung-'jom), a protective, wish-fulfilling gem, according to Hindu mythology, kept in Manidvipa (Jewel Island), an epithet for the hood of the celestial cobra Ananta (see 72).

243. Lahul, Himachal Pradesh
Lahul Valley women wearing the chased-silver tomukch

244. Dirang Dzong, West Kameng Division, Arunachal Pradesh
Monpa tribal woman of high social status wearing a hat of felted yak hair with twisted fringe. Her silver ornaments include Tibetan-style ga'us (they live near the Tibetan border), bracelets, rings, a very long necklace of amber beads suspended from the head, and a central shawl clasp set with turquoises (Tib: digra).

245. Gameri Village, Kameng Division, Arunachal Pradesh
Aka or Miji tribal woman wearing silver ornaments and a number of glass-bead necklaces distinctive of this tribe. Influenced by Tibetan usage are the four silver charm boxes (melu). Additionally worn are the head fillet (lenchhi), ear plugs (rombin), garment clasp (digra), and turquoise- and coral-mounted bracelets (gejjui; Tib: drodung), all made to order by silversmiths in the Assam plains. The Mijis are subordinate to the Akas, who live closer to the plains area.

246. Eastern and Western Siang Districts, Arunachal Pradesh
Adi-Minyong, Abor, and Gallong women of Siang wear the benyop cast-brass ornament belt until the birth of their first child. The origin of the benyop is explained in a local myth: Gingor-Shingor, a spirit, fell in love with a mortal woman. Whenever they engaged in intercourse, he gave her a benyop disc. When a child was born, she removed the disc girdle.

247. Eastern and Western Siang Districts, Arunachal Pradesh
Locally made lost-wax-cast brass loop-topped belt ornaments (benyop or bayop), worn by Adi-Minyong women
Unit diameter 2¹⁵⁄₁₆–5⁷⁄₈ in. (7.5–15 cm)
Victoria and Albert Museum, London (04962 IS)

Three, five, seven, or nine such units are strung on a cane, screwpine fiber cord, or leather belt. The largest is placed at the center, the others arranged in graduated sizes.

(occupied by Monpas, Sherdukpens, Bugun, Daflas, Dhammai, and Aka-Hrussos); Subansiri (Apatanis and Miris); Siang (Boris, Adis, Minyongs, Padams, and Gallongs); Lohit (Chulikatas, Membas, Khambas, Taraons, Kamptis, Idu Mishmis, Zakhrings, Munyols, and Singphos); and Tirap (Tangras).

Since at least the fourth century A.D. and into recent times, these groups occupied all the habitable, Indian sub-Himalayan valley areas. Because the rugged terrain kept these groups relatively isolated, each of them developed indigenous civilizations, the result being that, within a relatively small area, an extremely diverse cultural spectrum exists.

Among the ornaments used by the eastern Himalayan groups, glass and hardstone beads are universal, but a few distinctly original forms of metal jewelry worn by different Arunachal Pradesh tribes are worthy of special mention.

Wealthy Aka women wear a silver fillet-headdress (lencchi) consisting of a large, central, repoussé-ornamented disc to which a series of link chains are attached, forming a broad, crownlike band that encircles the head. With this traditional ornament a pair of huge

trumpet-shaped silver ear discs (gichli) are worn, passing through stretched earlobe holes. Both items are made by nearby Assam plains silversmiths exclusively for use by this group. Dafla, Adi-Minyorg, Abor, and Galong women wear a distinctive, locally made ornament consisting of a cord belt on which is strung a series of five to eight large lost-wax-cast brass discs (hoffi; benyop), worn by girls and women until the birth of their first child.

The Tibetan *Ga'u* Amulet Container

The charm box pendant called the *ga'u* (a small box or container) originated in Tibet. Unlike other Arunachal Pradesh ornaments associated with a particular tribe, this form of jewelry is in wide use throughout the western and eastern sub-Himalayan area by tribes who follow Buddhism and others who emulate them, though the local term used to designate it varies with the group. (The following terms are Tibetan, unless otherwise indicated.)

The origin of the charm container-pendant in Tibet can be traced to the often inhospitable environment. Violent natural phenomena, such as seasonal floods, hail, wind, and sandstorms, affect the success of the crops upon which the people's very existence depends. An ancient, animistic Tibetan cosmography shared by most people in this region provides them with a means of coping with such natural disasters. Elemental in this system is the belief that the physical elements in the environment possess power attributed to the presence of natural spirits, some benevolent (trinchhem-po) and others malignant (sem ngem-po). They infest the air, water, earth, and stones, and those that are evil cause accidents, disease, and even death. To solicit the aid of benign spirits and evade or control malevolent forces, the former must be propitiated, and magical protection is secured against the latter.

The theology of Buddhism proliferated into several highly philosophical and esoteric orders and sects, yet older and more primitive folk beliefs, such as the use of protective charms (hrung-po) and amulets (ten), were never abandoned but were integrated into popular Buddhism.

Parallel beliefs exist among some of the previously mentioned western and eastern Indian hill groups that adhere to Buddhism. In the west are the Ladakhis and the people of Lahul and Spiti. In the eastern sector are the Sherdukpens, Monpa, Khamba, Memba, Zakhring, Munyol, Khampti, and Singpho groups. Other non-Buddhist people in the latter area who have been culturally influenced by the customs of their neighbors are the Aka-Hrusso, Begun, Dhammai, Idu Mishmi, and the Dafla. Racially similar, these groups favor the culture of Tibet over that of plains Hinduism.

Almost every man, woman, and child in Buddhist Tibet and the Himalayan area of India carries a variety of charms and amulets on the body, each intended for a different purpose. For an individual to be rendered invulnerable to the evil or illness against which such charms are ritually activated, it is essential that the charm be in physical contact with the body.

Ga'us worn by Tibetan children and women and by Indian hill people are generally suspended from the neck as a central pendant on a string of beads (*thrang-nga*). Tibetan men use *ga'us* in different ways. For example, in pre-Chinese Tibet, a small, roundish *ga'u* was worn by government officials of the fourth rank and above, fixed in their hair-plaited topknot (*pachok*) as an indication of high rank and distinction. Tibetan men, and sometimes women, use another type of *ga'u* when undertaking a journey in perilous mountain terrain. These are usually a box form, and most can stand on a flat base. Made in a wide range of sizes, they are often carried on the right side of the body suspended by a cord or strap that passes over the left shoulder. *Ga'us* of this type are not discussed here as they cannot rightfully be considered to be a form of amuletic jewelry.

The *ga'u* is a complex of form, function, and symbolism. It can be of copper (*zans*), brass (*ra-gan*), or bronze (*kar-ba*), and combinations of these. Many are made of silver (*nga*), which may be used for the entire object, or only its visible front, in which case the back half is usually copper, brass, or sheet iron (*cha*). In Tibet, silver objects may be partially or completely mercury fire-gilded (*gyim-bag-gis byug-pa*). Tibet is rich in gold (*yser*) and those who can afford it have their *ga'us* made of that precious metal. Because only a limited amount of gold is local, precious metals, as well as copper and brass, were also imported over great distances from India and from China via Mongolia by human and animal transport. Another source of silver was obtained by melting Indian and Chinese silver coins when silver currency was in circulation.

Because a *ga'u* functions as a container to hold and protect the various charms placed within, all *ga'us* consist of two basic parts that fit together by an inner flange, so that access to its inner space is possible. Parts are generally divided horizontally in a direction across the body, an exception being the cylindrical and

248. Kaja, Spiti District, Himachal Pradesh
Buddhist woman wearing the traditional ornaments of her community: enormous silver charm boxes (shtungma) suspended on a waist cord; shawl clasp (digra) resembling the front of a Tibetan woman's ga'u, backed by two hooks that are fixed into the woolen shawl; side-of-head ornaments (mul-u or mulmento) with a triangular, upper unit from which falls a cascade of chains hung with pipal- or bo-tree-leaf-shaped pendants (pipala); temple ornaments set with turquoise (Tib: pen-dap or e-kor), identical to those worn in Lhasa; a necklace (pat kachong) with beads of turquoise, coral, and amber, worn close to the neck, and long silver chains (shanglang). All these ornaments are made by local silversmiths (domang in Kinnaur-Lahul). The Buddhist Lahul people, called Kanet, who constitute the majority in the district, are of mixed Mongolian-Indian origin. Spiti people, who live in an outlying valley southwest of Lahul, are almost wholly Tibetan in origin. Their ornaments differ and reflect Tibetan and indigenous types.

square sectioned *ga'us* worn in the eastern Himalaya, which usually are vertically divided at the center. Once its contents are in place, both parts are often tied together by a cord or leather thong to prevent accidental loss.

Traditional *ga'u* forms can be classified according to their basic shape, some of which are regionally distinctive. In Ladakh, besides using the forms that are typically Tibetan, women wear a necklace consisting of a series of miniature, backless *ga'us* of double-sided-ogee and oval form (see 271). In central and western Tibet women show a preference for the square, some with projecting points on all four sides; the rectangle; trapezoid; diamond (*dorje*); octagon; and double-sided-ogee rectangular forms. Their size can range from small to enormous. The women of Lahul and Spiti wear *ga'us* up to ten inches (25.5 cm)

wide, suspended by a cord at the waist. In eastern Tibet the round (*gor-mo*) and the oval (*kerima*) forms are common.

No matter what the *ga'u* shape, its top is provided with either a single tube, or one made in three parts, two of which are attached to the front half of the *ga'u* and one to the back half, together acting as the lugs found in a conventional three-part hinge. Through all of these is often placed a copper tube, into which a bamboo tube is inserted, or one of bamboo only. Their purpose is to hold the parts together, as would a hollow rivet, and to reduce the hole size. Through its opening passes a string that suspends the *ga'u* and holds a few, or many, beads, which together make the ensemble a form of neck ornament (*ske-cha*).

At the bottom of most *ga'us*, attached to the front (or in cylindrical forms, divided into

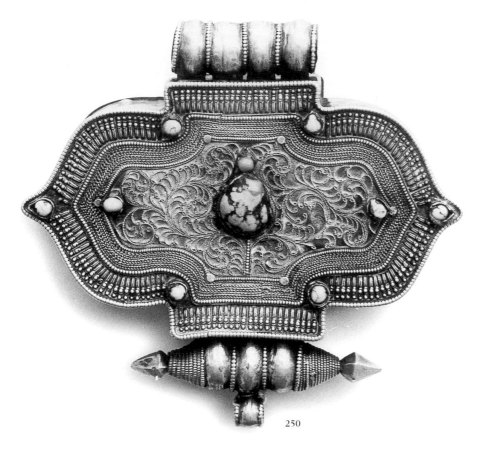

249. Lhasa, Tibet (opposite page)
Necklace with a central, round silver ga'u ornamented with gold filigree work, corals, and a turquoise. Placed on a strand of coral (byi-ru), turquoise (yu), and silver beads (ngu thrang-nga), with a silver back clasp set with coral. The shorter, inner coral bead strand supports the central ga'u weight, permitting the outer bead strands to fall in a wide curve. Ga'u diameter 3⅜ in. (8.6 cm)
Collection the author, Porvoo

250. Kinnaur, Himachal Pradesh
Silver amulet box (ngulgi ga'u) in double ogival form, its surface ornamented with wire work, stamped units, and turquoise stones
5½ x 6 in. (14 x 15.2 cm); weight 402 g
Collection the author, Porvoo

251. Tibet
Copper (sang) and brass (ra-gan) ga'u with a central chased kalasha or bum-pa motif (see 261), from which emerges a wish-granting tree of life (pag-sam-shin, or yond-'dus-sa-gtol)
Collection Ivory, New York

252. Tibet
Copper ga'u with pierced-work (tum-pu le-ka) brass overlay in scrolling vine forms, with central symbol, one of the seven world-ravishing gems (jigs-yons-gyi rin-po-ch'e)
4⅞ x 3¾ in. (12.5 x 9.6 cm); weight 270 g
Collection Ghysels, Brussels

250

251

252

halves), is usually found a double-ended, facet-pointed appending form that symbolizes the diamond thunderbolt (*dorje*) associated with several Tibetan Buddhist deities, or the Hindu god Indra, to symbolize their attributed powers. Often at the bottom center of the *dorje* a small loop, which has no set functional purpose, is attached. Many books in which illustrations of *ga'us* appear show them, incorrectly, upside down with the *dorje* at the top.

Ga'u Magical Contents

The importance attributed by Tibetans and others to the *ga'u* relates as much to its apotropaic contents as to its form. Describing what is placed within them reveals ancient, pre-Buddhist beliefs that express common anxieties and concerns involving the psyche of the people who use it. From this great variety only some typical examples can be mentioned.

Handwritten or printed charms, chosen for general or specific purposes according to the individual's need, are perhaps the most common *ga'u* content. In Tibetan Lamaism, charms written or printed on paper in Tibetan Lantsa characters are believed to possess magical or divine power and active psychic and cosmic energy. The common mystic charm diagram, the *yantra*, is a visual counterpart to a mental or spoken *mantra*. Another is a circular cosmological diagram (S: *mandala*)—at whose center a deity (S: *devata*) or its *bija*, or seed, emblem is placed—used for focusing concentration. Printed or placed in a *ga'u*, they function as amulets or charms (Tib: *srung*) that protect the carrier in a general or specific manner when carried on the body.

Many Tibetan charms are derived from Indian ancient religious texts or *yantra* diagrams, but their power is based on Tibetan Tantric-Buddhist belief and practice. Their use increased in Tibet with the development of Vajrayana Tantric Buddhism, which absorbed indigenous beliefs and practices of the more ancient Bonpo religion.

On a less spiritual, pragmatic level are special written or printed personal charms that express a desire for luck, prosperity, potency, and longevity. Others bind disease-causing demons or shield against illnesses such as cholera and plague. Some insure protection against dangers encountered when traveling; attack from eagles or other birds of prey, as well as mad dogs, the claws of wild cats, bears, and tigers; and against weapons and bullets. A person wishing to have a general or specific printed charm goes to the shaman, or *lama*, who possesses the printing block from which he makes an impression and consecrates the result.

Charm objects believed to have magical virtues constitute another category. Very popular is a small unfired clay image (*tsa-tsa*) of a deity, or a group of deities. *Tsa-tsas* are made by pressing clay into a metal mold (*par*); when

253. Dharmsala, Himachal Pradesh
Tibetan man wearing two protective charms (do or trung-nga) of magic formulas printed on paper, folded, bound with colored cotton thread tied in a controled geometric pattern around them (pal peu), and sealed with sealing wax at the four cardinal points to preserve the charm's efficacy and repel evil spirits from all directions. For protection, the result may be placed in a cloth or leather bag and hung from the neck.

dry, the result is frequently polychromed. Potent pills (*ri-pu*) made from the cremation ashes of *lamas* are often placed in a *ga'u*. Propitiatory food offerings to gods and demons such as grains of rice (*dre*) or barley (*ne*), or mustard seeds (*ke-kang son*), the latter with the power to repel evil beings, are also placed within.

Whatever its form, a charm is inert and powerless until it has been consecrated by a *lama*. To instill it with living force, the *lama* performs acts of consecration and awakens its potency. As in the case of all sympathetic magic, the charm works provided the owner is conditioned to believe in its power.

Should it ever become necessary to sell a *ga'u*, all of its contents are removed and saved. Before handing it over to the purchaser, the seller rubs the *ga'u* on his/her body to return to him/herself the spiritual good luck it contains, and a small recitational ceremony may be performed.

Ga'u Surface Decoration

Although the *ga'u* is primarily functional, it is also a decorative object, often one of considerable artistic merit. Its surface can be flat or

convex, and pristinely plain, sparingly decorated with a central motif, or charged with energetic and highly symbolic ornamentation. A variety of decorative treatments are used. The surface may be a pierced-work sheet-metal ornament of one metal placed over another, color-contrasting metal, such as brass on copper, or in other decorative techniques.

Many flat-surfaced *ga'us* follow a design format in which the outer perimeter is delineated by beaded wire, which also serves to reinforce the form. This is usually followed by a series of small abutting stamped, three-dimensional, lotus-petal forms placed side by side, the flower symbolizing purity as it rises unspotted from muddy waters.

Within the basic border, various treatments are possible. The space can be filled with backed gold or silver filigree wire work (*cha-ku le-ka*) in scrolling and tendril patterns that symbolize nature's life energy essence. At corners, granules (*nas-'bru*, barley grain) either round, or hammered flat to form a small disc, are used as accent points and to cover joins.

The surface of other *ga'us* is partially or completely worked in repoussage (*yar-kyak-pa*) and detail chasing (*tro-gyap-pa*). The forms created may be abstract, or of subjects such as the favored scrolling creepers. On the surface may be magic *bija* letters, or invocatory phrases (*dharani*) or *mantras* in Lantsa script such as the ubiquitous *Om mani padme hum*, "Hail to the Jewel in the Lotus," a reference to the Bodhisattva Avalokiteshvara or Lokeshvara. Another popular symbol is the composite symbolic monogram called the All-Powerful-Ten, which is composed of ten *bija* syllables in Lantsa script letters, and the *dorje*.

Traditional sets of graphic symbols may also be represented. Most common is the eight Buddhist lucky symbols, also called the Eight Glorious Emblems (Tib: *bkra-s'i-rtags-brgyad*; S: *ashta-mangala*). These include the following: the white parasol (Tib: *gdugs*; S: *chattra*); two fishes (Tib: *gse-nya*; S: *matsya*); the conch shell (Tib: *dung*; S: *sankha*); the lotus (Tib: *pema*; S: *padma*) and the vase (Tib: *bumpa*; S: *kumbha*); the standard (Tib: *rgyal-mts'an*; S: *dhvaja*) or victorious banner; the wheel (Tib: *'khor-lo*; S: *cakra*) and the endless knot (Tib: *dpal-be*; S: *shrivatsa*).

Certain gemstones are used to ornament the *ga'u* itself or as beads on the one or two hanging strands. Cabochon-cut gemstones, often a bead cut in half, may be placed at the center only or also in outer corners. Contour-shaped gemstones are used to compose figural mosaics, such as an open-lotus flower or a representation of the Hindu-Buddhist sacred *kalasa* vase. The Tibetan method of setting gemstones in *ga'us* and other ornaments, whether set individually or in a mosaic, is similar to that employed in India and Nepal and involves the use of lac, as described on pages 357 and 359.

Turquoise (*yu*) is said to be available in Tibet but is inferior in both color and hardness

254

255

256

to that which comes from Iran and China. Tibetans who are turquoise connoisseurs generally seek the best quality: a hard, bright sky-blue variety that comes from mines near Nishapur in Khorosan, Iran, where the type is called *Abu Ishaki firoza*. This variety retains its color and is said to have the power of averting the evil eye and banishing unpleasant dreams. Lesser turquoise qualities tend to discolor to a shade of green after exposure to natural skin oils or fats used in cooking. Because turquoise is hydroscopic, it also absorbs acids, musk, and camphor, which cause discoloration. A lavish use of turquoise is found in a common type of *ga'u* used in central Tibet in a square or double-*dorje* form (square with triangular projections on four sides), whose visible top surface is primarily or completely covered with a mosaic of small, closely placed turquoises.

Red coral (*ma-po ch'i-ru; Corallum rubrum*), the most esteemed coral type, came to Tibet after a long journey from the Red Sea or the Mediterranean, in modern times usually via Calcutta and Nepal. The Tibetan use of Italian coral in the thirteenth century was attested to by Marco Polo: "Coral is in great demand in this country and fetches a high price for they delight to hang it around the necks of their women and of their idols" (see 249). Coral is sold according to its size, density, color, and degree of flaws. In Tibet, unblemished deep red is most esteemed, and the best quality in large or even small sizes fetch enormous prices.

Amber (*pö-she*), the organic compound of hardened resin from ancient coniferous trees, is not used by Tibetans to decorate the *ga'u* but only as one of the traditional materials used for beads placed on the *ga'u* supporting bead strand. Though amber colors range from white through yellow to orange, red, and brown, and in degrees of transparency from clear to turbid, in general, Tibetans seem to prefer opaque yellow amber beads, preferably of large size (see 261). Most amber came to Tibet from an even greater distance than coral. Its ancient

257

258

254. Sikkim
Silver ga'u whose outer border has representations of twelve good-luck symbols (so-de ta), three on each side
Collection Thapar, New Delhi

The repoussage inscription in Tibetan Lantsa characters is transliterated from Sanskrit. It includes the invocations (dharanis) of the three transcendental bodhisattvas: OM ARAPACANA DHID (Manjushri); OM MANI PADME HUM (Avalokiteshvara); OM VAJRAPANI HUM HRIH (Vajrapani). The central cartouche reads EVAM (so, thus), meaning, "Thus may the contents be efficacious."

255. Tibet
Silver charm box (ngu ga'u)
3¹⁵/₁₆ x 4⁹/₁₆ in. (9.8 x 11.6 cm); weight 136 g
Collection the author, Porvoo

Depicted is Padmasambhava, the Indian Buddhist who, at the reigning king's invitation, visited Tibet in the eighth century A.D. and taught the people Buddhist principles. He is credited with founding the Tibetan Nyingma-pa School of Buddhism and is now venerated as a Tibetan Buddhist saint.

256. Lhasa, Tibet
Silver dorjema ga'u, parcel-fire-gilded (tsha-ser), with central ruby, turquoises, and pearls. The vertical symbol of lightning (dorje) is guarded by mythic lions (kyang).
5¼ x 5¼ in. (13.4 x 13.4 cm); weight 352 g
Collection the author, Porvoo

257. Tibet
Gold amulet box (dorjema ga'u) set with diamonds, rubies, carved turquoises, and pearls
Collection Jacques Carcanagues, New York

A form introduced in this century (see 258), this type is often given a red patina by covering the gold with a paste of copper acetate, cream of tartar (potassium tartrate), and salt and heating it. Not permanent, it remains in unabraded depressions and is much admired by Tibetans and Indians.

258. Darjiling, West Bengal
Tibetan woman wearing a necklace with a gold dorjema ga'u ornamented with contoured turquoises and rubies. On her right shoulder is a silver chatelaine (chap-chap), and in her hands is a rosary ('pren-ba) of 108 beads.

259. Tibet
Gold thumb ring (ser tre-kho) set with turquoises
Outer diameter 1¾ in. (4.5 cm); inner diameter ⅞ in. (2.2 cm); weight 24 g
Collection the author, Porvoo

Originally of ivory and simple in form (see 275), this type of ring became elaborated and was also made in precious metals. Its purpose is to protect the wearer against a malignant witch (sön-dre-ma) who appears at night in a deserted place, first as an attractive young girl, then as an old hag. Upon encountering the witch, the wearer must touch her head with this ring, which renders her harmless.

260. Sikkim
Silver ga'us in traditional forms, two of them ornamented with gold, set with coral and turquoise, and strung on necklaces of coral, turquoise, amber, mother of pearl, and dZi beads

source is the amber found in countries along the South Baltic Sea coast, including Estonia, Latvia, Lithuania, East Prussia, and Poland.

Since its identification in the Neolithic period, and thereafter into the Bronze and Iron Ages, amber was highly prized and used in Europe primarily for amuletic beads. Its desirability made it an early trade commodity, which resulted in the so-called Amber Route, a trade traffic network that connected the Baltic region with the south of Europe, and then by other routes to the Middle and Far East. It is not known when amber first came to Tibet, but this must have occurred at an early date. It is mentioned by Tavernier that, in the mid-seventeenth century, Armenian traders regularly went to Danzig and bartered silk carpets and textiles made in the Middle East for local raw amber and amber products such as beads, which they brought to the Middle East and India for trade with Bhutan and Tibet.

Burmite, called *ambeng* in Myanmar (formerly Burma), is a variety of amber found in Myanmar land deposits. It is generally a deep reddish-brown but can also be yellowish; it is harder than Baltic amber and has a tendency to be turbid rather than transparent. Burmite is mined at a depth of up to thirty feet (10 m) in the low hilly valley area of Hukong near the sources of the Chindwin (Kyendwen) River in northwest Myanmar, close to the Assam border of India, in an area occupied by the Singpho tribe. Burmite was formed into beads at Mandalay in Myanmar, near its source; their price varied with color and degree of transparency. Some of this amber went to Assam and Manipur, where it was and still is used by indigenous tribal people, and also to Sikkim and eastern Tibet.

Mother of pearl (*dur-dkar*) comes from the inner nacreous layer of mollusk shells that live in tropical waters of the Red Sea, the Persian Gulf, and near the Philippines. Thick shells are divided into cubes, then formed into round beads popular in Tibet for use on strands supporting *ga'us,* especially as this material resists splitting and cracking.

Pearls (*mu-ti*) of all types and sizes, in round or irregular forms, have always been very popular for use in Tibetan jewelry. It is interesting to contemplate that coral, amber, pearls, and mother of pearl—all sea products—were and still are so highly valued in this landlocked country because of their exotic nature.

Imitations of all the gemstones mentioned are also common. Stones are dyed to appear as turquoise and lapis lazuli. Coral is simulated by plastic and glass beads either imported from Europe, or from India as ready-made beads. Amber substitutes are commonly found in Tibetan bead necklaces. Spurious amber is made of copal resin and various plastics that closely resemble it in appearance. A form of genuine amber called *ambroid* is artificially formed into large masses by using heat and pressure to fuse small amber pieces.

The Tibetan *dZi* Bead

Beads in Tibet have always had religious or magical significance. The particular substance of which they are made and their color are often attributed with auspicious or magical properties. The quality and relative value of a bead may be based on its natural color and markings, its shape, and the degree of skill evident in its preparation, such as its regularity of form and surface polish. These factors contribute to a value system based upon the ideal

261. Lhasa, Tibet
Necklace with rectangular silver ga'u on a gold filigree ground, with a bead strand of coral, turquoise, amber, and dZi beads
Ga'u 3¹⁵⁄₁₆ x 2¹⁵⁄₁₆ in. (9.3 x 7.5 cm)
Collection the author, Porvoo

The central turquoises form a sacred vase (S: kalasa; Tib: bum-pa) that holds immortalizing magical ambrosia and stores all the hidden riches of the three regions of life.

and the relative rarity of the stone. Among Tibetans no bead is given greater prominence, scrutiny and value than the uniquely patterned Tibetan *dZi* bead.

The specific origin of authentic *dZi* hardstone beads is not clear. Tibetans say they miraculously fell from heaven. It has been claimed that they were produced at hardstone bead–making centers such as Khambhat in Gujarat, which has always had a large export market. If the patterns on these beads were produced there, however, they are unknown to present-day manufacturers (at least, no one would admit their manufacture there to this author). It is entirely possible that the basic bead form was made there and the creation of the distinctive patterns, a relatively simple process, was done elsewhere. Some scholars think they may have been produced in Tibet proper, or in Nepal, and others say we must look to Bhutan or some other place.

The sources of imitation *dZi* beads are more easily identified. Those made of glass probably originated in Bohemian or other European glass bead-making centers, or in India. Those made of plastic probably come from India, which has a sophisticated plastic industry. Substitutes such as these are in wide use among Tibetans who cannot afford real *dZis*, which can either be of a naturally striated banded agate or a hardstone whose surface has been patterned artificially.

Since the mid-nineteenth century, so-called etched beads—meaning hardstone, generally chalcedony quartz beads with a uniform ground color and a white or dark linear surface pattern—have been the subject of lively interest among archaeologists and bead scholars, and even more so since they became more easily available from Tibetan refugees in the 1960s and 1970s. Beads of this type have a nearly 4,500-year history of production. They have been unearthed at archaeological sites in Mesopotamia, the Indus Valley Civilization (2700–1700 B.C.), Iran, Taxila (550 B.C.–A.D. 200), and elsewhere. In this category belongs the commonly used Tibetan *dZi* bead, also in use by Tibetan-influenced people throughout the sub-Himalayan area in bead strands that support the *ga'u* amulet box pendant.

In all literature concerning these beads, the descriptive technological term *etched* is employed to designate this category. In the author's opinion, *etched* is an inappropriate term when the accepted meaning of that word is considered. To etch is to produce a figural or design image on a substrate substance such as glass, stone, or metal, by subjecting its surface to the action of a chemical reagent, in this case an acid solution in which the object is generally submerged for an extended period of time. The acid *corrodes* exposed areas on the object. In traditional etching, parts of the object meant to resist corrosive acid action are protected beforehand by the application of a *resist* material such as wax or resin, which creates a barrier against acid action while the area to be etched is left exposed. In the case of the *dZi* bead, the pattern is *not* obtained by submerging the bead in an acid solution, nor is a resist used.

To create the patterns found on *dZi* beads either of two basic technologies (and their variants) are used, and it is possible that both may be carried out on the same bead. One is by the action of an alkaline, oxidizing *bleaching agent* in a dry, hot atmosphere, and the other employs an organic substance, or a chemical metallic-salt *coloring stain* applied by immersing the bead in a nonacidic solution, followed by dry heating. In both cases, the bead's initial surface remains intact, and, in most cases, its original surface condition, which may be a high polish, is also retained.

The process of creating a white-line pattern on a colored bead is best described as *negative bleaching* since color is removed. When adding a ground color, the process is *positive staining*. Combinations of both processes result in *stain- and bleach-patterned beads,* a designation that follows the normal sequence of their design creation. When already appropriately colored hardstones are used (such as brown sard), only bleaching of the pattern is carried out.

The bead in question is usually a form of chalcedony, a type that encompasses the hardstone category that includes the quartzes agate, carnelian, fossilized wood (also called agatized wood, which can consist of chalcedony or, less frequently, opal, in which case it is called opalized wood), onyx, sard, and sardonyx. All these are porous to a greater or lesser degree. Substances used to create a permanent ground color on a bead by staining or a linear pattern on a colored ground by bleaching, do so by penetrating the hardstone's surface. The extent of the material's porosity and the duration of the time of treatment determine how far the stain or bleach penetrates the stone structure.

Chalcedony beads can be stained dark brown or black over their entire surface, or in controlled areas, the former by the use of a sugar solution, the latter with a gum-sugar paste. In India the sugar substance is palm sugar or jaggery (from the palm *Caryota urens;* H: *jagri*), or molasses (H: *gur*).

The stone bead is soaked in a sugar solution to allow the sugar to enter its pores. When it has dried and the bead is heated, the sugar impregnated in the stone carbonizes, leaving the stone a permanent brown to black color. Because heated sugar is used, this process has been popularly called carmelization. When the hardstone is sufficiently porous and uniform in structure, the result is an even color or stain. The bead can then be treated to create a white line pattern in the manner described below. These two basic processes, staining and bleaching, can be utilized in many different ways to achieve various effects.

The old Indian process of using an alkaline bleaching agent to create a white-line pattern on a natural or artificially colored hardstone bead may have originated in the Indus Valley Civilization. Patterned beads made there were trade products and have been found in Mesopotamia. A process that probably approximates the ancient one has been described by Bellasis as it was carried out in 1857 in Sehwan, Sindh, Pakistan (formerly India), 139 miles (222 km) from Karachi. One of the substances used, an organic gum, came from a small, low, prickly shrub or tree (*Capparis aphylla;* Sindhi: *kiral*) whose green, immature flower buds are the capers of commerce, preserved in vinegar. Young shoots were plucked and mashed to form a paste. To this an alkali was added, and the strained result was ready for use.

The alkaline substance used for this color bleaching process is a form of soda or sodium carbonate, a strongly alkaline salt, which is found in quantity in India as a salt efflorescence on soil (*reh*) that appears after the monsoon rains dry. To create line patterns on a bead, this preparation was here applied with a reed pen (H: *kalam*).

Beads prepared with a surface design were placed in a gas-permeable ceramic container, which was placed on an iron sheet and, for a period of about five minutes, heated over a charcoal fire. The container was removed from the fire and allowed to cool for ten minutes. The beads were then removed, and the carbonized surface gum and soda were wiped off, exposing the bleached design.

Chemistry explains what takes place. In chalcedony stones, color is due to the presence of black iron oxide, which is soluble in alkali. In the reduction atmosphere created by placing the beads in a closed container, when heated, the carbon left by the burnt gum assists in a local reduction on the bead. Heated carbon becomes carbon dioxide, whose oxygen content is given off as a gas that dissipates in the atmosphere. Under heat, which accelerates the process, the melted alkali on the bead penetrates the hardstone pores. In this reduced atmosphere the iron oxide becomes pure iron, allowing the soda or alkali to work better on the silicon dioxide and digest the iron by rendering it soluble. These areas then become lighter or white in color.

Patterns or markings found on *dZi* beads are quite varied. The design elements most frequently encountered include the already mentioned circle, commonly referred to as an "eye" (*mik*), which may occur from one to twelve times on a single bead. Other factors aside, to a Tibetan, a *dZi* bead's value may depend on the number of "eyes" it contains. Curved and straight lines commonly appear, both used to form stripes and geometric figures. Between these elements there may be symbolic figural formations. Among these is the *Om* symbol in Sanskrit, alone or within a cartouche. Other seed letters in Tibetan Lantsa characters, related to prayers, invocations, and

262. Tibet
Necklace of genuine, "pure" dZi (phum-dZi or tsang-ma-dZi) beads (thrang-nga), including three of rare, long barrel shape
Collection Ivory, New York

263. Mizoram
Necklace of beads (pumtek) of opalized Palmyra palm wood (Borassus flabellifer; H: tal)
Collection Ghysels, Brussels

The linear surface patterns on these beads are produced in the same manner as those on Tibetan dZi beads, which resemble the long barrel-shaped beads here. Mizoram borders on Myanmar (Burma), which accounts for the four Burmese coins in this necklace. Formerly valued heirloom possessions, they were—and still are—used by the Kuki in Mizoram and their relations, the Chin of neighboring western Myanmar. Originally they were made by the Pyu in Burma, who flourished during the third to ninth centuries and were absorbed by the invading Myanmar. Beads in cruder versions are still produced in Payagyi, Myanmar, and old ones, sold to the Indian Akas, appear in New Delhi antique shops.

magic spells, may also be found. Another pattern is a three-lobed (closed-cloverleaf) figure (*tri-ratna*) symbolizing the Buddha, Dharma, and Sangha.

The *Perak:* Ladakhi Woman's Head Ornament

In the area around Leh, the remote capital of mountainous Ladakh in the western Himalaya, established in 1533 by the Namgyals, women wear a unique traditional head ornament called a *perak*. Its astonishing size alone attracts attention, and, like most other personal ornaments in this part of the world, it has considerable significance.

The *perak* is the outcome of a variety of social, religious, and economic factors. One of these is the pan-Tibetan practice of polyandry, in which one woman marries all the brothers in a family. In such a household, the Ladakhi woman becomes the supreme head. As such, she is allowed to trade and accumulate her own earnings, whose surplus she invests in the several elements that constitute a good *perak*, which openly displays a woman's wealth. In this culture, a woman's material worth can be estimated at a glance, and the wearer is automatically accorded a relatively appropriate degree of respectability.

Several of the materials used in the *perak's* composition are local and readily available. The most valued elements, however, are exotic and come to Ladakh from great distances, probably the main reason they originally became esteemed possessions. Foremost among the latter is turquoise, the *perak's* dominant element. In fact, the word *perak* is said to be derived from the word *per,* an old Ladakhi term for turquoise.

In former days, the position of Leh near high Himalayan mountain passes, accessible during the summer season, made it a significant caravan terminus and entrepot of commercial activity. Situated at a crossroads, Leh flourished economically from the east-west trade between Tibet and Kashmir until 1962, when China appropriated Tibet, and also ended the north-south commerce route between Yarkand and Bokhara in Turkestan, and India. Among the products exchanged at Leh for millennia are gold, silver, turquoise, coral, amber, pearls, mother of pearl, and carnelian —all used in the Ladakhi *perak* and other ornaments.

Contributing to the considerable wealth that formerly, and now to a lesser extent, flows to Leh is its proximity to important Buddhist Lamaistic monasteries. Pilgrims in large numbers annually attend the great three-day summer festival celebrating the birthday of Padmasambhava, founder of Lamaism, at Hemis, Ladakh's largest *gompa,* 28 miles (45 km) from Leh. As at all Indian festivals, participants, especially

women, dress in their best apparel and wear their finest ornaments. In the temporary bazaar that always materializes on such occasions are dealers in turquoise and sellers of jewelry, *ga'us*, and other *perak* elements.

The *perak* is worn by young girls starting at the age of five or six, but these are small and simple. An unmarried woman's *perak* might include mother-of-pearl and glass beads, which generally are gradually replaced by turquoises. The full *perak* is the prerogative of a married woman, proudly worn as her most valued possession, if possible, until old age. The potential value of the *perak*'s turquoise stones acts as a form of old-age security. Should the need arise, they can be sold to a ready market. The *perak* also has a practical function: as part head covering and part cape, it offers the wearer some protection against the prevailing cold climate of the Ladakh area for a greater part of the year.

Ideally, if it can be preserved intact, the *perak* is a family heirloom and, in normal practice, a woman's *perak* will be presented to her eldest daughter when she marries. This custom accounts for the large collection of stones found on many *peraks*—they represent an accumulation of several generations. When a woman has no daughter, her *perak* can be inherited by a close female relative. In some cases, as an act of pious charity, a woman will give her *perak*, complete or piecemeal, to a monastery. Should a woman die intestate, as a burial fee, *lamas* who enact the last rites and arrange for cremation often manage to gain possession of the woman's *perak*, and, if not, then some of her other ornaments. These they sell to help support the *lamasery*.

Sadly, today one sees fewer of the large, elaborate *peraks*, and those in use seem to have shrunk in size and decoration. Many women, unable to afford them, have taken to wearing a front-split, brimmed black-felt hat (*tibi*) or one made of brocade (*gonda*).

Embodied in the *perak* is its religious symbolism. The typical *perak* has a base about thirty-nine inches (1 m) long, made of brown or red dyed leather or thick felt, covered with a layer of thinner red felt all stitched together. When laid flat, its configuration instantly suggests a spread-out snake skin, which it actually represents. This idea is reinforced by its decoration and the manner in which the *perak* is worn. Draped over the top of a woman's head, it projects forward over her forehead, like a cobra's head, and increases in width like the cobra's expanded hood. The rest of its body width diminishes and hangs down the back, tapering to a pointed tail. When a woman stands, the *perak* takes on the position of a rearing cobra poised to strike.

264. Ladakh, Jammu, and Kashmir
Perak with high-quality turquoises, worn by
a wealthy married woman
Private Collection, Brussels

The cobra (*nag*) is venerated by numerous snake cults all over Hindu India, particularly because of its association with Shiva (see also page 48). The snake also figures importantly in the complex symbolism and concepts of Yoga, and its associate Tantric Buddhism, as in the widespread Vajrayana cults of Ladakh and Tibet that dominate Lamaism. In Hindu and Buddhist iconography, the cobra with expanded hood is frequently represented hovering protectively over the head of a deity image, and the *perak,* by this analogy, figuratively offers protection to the wearer. Snakes (*nagas*) are said to be the guardians of the earth's mineral wealth, including gemstones, so the symbolic snake form of the *perak* and its turquoise decoration are singularly appropriate.

Except for the perimeter of the red-felt border, ideally, the rest of the *perak*'s visible surface as far as possible is covered with turquoise stones pierced and sewn or glued to the base. This means that between 100 and 400 stones are arranged in as many as seven lengthwise rows, their total weighing as much as 6.6 pounds (3 kilos). No attempt is made to alter any stone shape from the generally lumpy form in which they are purchased. More important than form regularity are maximum stone size and quality, which makes good stones of any shape acceptable.

The single biggest and best stone is usually placed at the very front point (the snake's head), followed by the next best, where they are most easily seen. Their position there relates to the Hindu-Tibetan mythological belief that the head of a snake is said to contain precious stones. From this narrow start, the horizontal rows increase to the chosen number at the widest place, the snake "hood," and continue as regularly as possible down the rest of the "body" in sizes that decrease toward the tapering "tail." From a distance, these closely placed stones create a pattern that resembles a snake's scaly skin, adding to the snake allusion.

Turquoise does not exist in Ladakh but comes there by overland trade from Tibet, China, and via India from Iran. Each source produces particular types of turquoise, which an expert (as all Ladakhi women are on this subject) can identify. By universal agreement, the best quality is from ancient mines near Meshed in Iran. These are uniformly bright sky-blue, free of matrix inclusions, and physically the hardest and therefore most durable among all turquoises. Chinese stones vary considerably in color and quality and generally do contain matrix, which, if in a dark spiderweb pattern,

is also desirable. Each woman tries to cover her *perak* with the best possible collection, a process that may take years to accomplish.

Besides turquoise (*yu* in Ladakhi), other stones may be included in the *perak* composition: carnelian (*lal akik*) comes from India; coral (*chi-ru*) came formerly from the Mediterranean, now Japan; mother-of-pearl beads (*nya-pyis*) come from the Philippines and China; and amber (*fi*) comes from the Baltic Sea area. If not already mounted in settings, these stones are sewn to the ground or strung. Pearls (*murik*), usually small and baroque, are generally not used in the *perak* but commonly appear in Ladakhi earrings, necklaces, and headpieces.

Metal ornaments are another element in *perak* embellishment. Most important is the gold or silver Tibetan *ga'u* box in any size, from miniature to huge. In Tibet, and also Ladakh, the *ga'u* is normally worn as a pendant hanging from a woman's neck, usually on a string of beads. In Ladakh they can also be attached to the *perak*. Centrally placed in the field of turquoise stones, the *ga'u* acts as an accent. Some *peraks* display a series of *ga'us,* usually the best one on top but also at the back. Because the *ga'u* functions as an amulet box, it may contain charms chosen to protect the wearer and so reinforce the *perak*'s protective function.

Also used is another exotic head ornament, the chain-constructed *daoni,* made in Mandi, Himachal Pradesh (see 417), where it is worn hanging on the head from the forehead down the sides of the face. *Daonis* come to Leh through trade and on the *perak* are incorporated intact, spread out like a trophy, or separated into two parts and attached to the *perak*'s side edges (see 264).

An indigenous silver ornament, often worn in pairs at either side of the *perak,* is an ornamented plaque that looks like the front part of a *ga'u* without the attached box at the back. It has a top loop and hook for suspension, and often a series of flat-element chains hang below, each ending with a small bell.

The richest *peraks* have an added strip ornament at the left edge. Starting about shoulder level, attached to a horizontal, ornamented silver spacer bar, is a series of five to ten rows of strung coral beads that descend in gradually diminishing sizes, ideally to the *perak* end. All these stones and metal ornaments make the *perak* rather heavy. In addition to the normal head strap, some must be supported by attached shoulder straps.

Completing this ensemble is an end-of-braid or -*perak* tassel (*chun-po*). The straight,

265. Leh, Ladakh, Jammu, and Kashmir
Woman wearing a perak; seed-pearl ear ornaments; necklaces of coral, turquoises, and glass beads; a central ga'u; and wool ear lappets (kundaz). Two ga'us are visible at the top of the perak.

266. Leh, Ladakh, Jammu, and Kashmir
Ladakhi woman illustrating the manner of wearing the perak. For protection against cold, many women wear a long-haired, white goatskin body cover.

◄ 267. Leh, Ladakh, Jammu, and Kashmir
Silver side-of-head ornaments (shunga) with connecting chain (tentak). The intertwined lucky-knot motif, a Buddhist long-life symbol (S: shrivatsa; Tib: dpal-be), is one of Eight Glorious Emblems (S: ashta-mangala; Tib: bkra-s'i rtags-brgyad). Looped below is a Himachal Pradesh daoni.

268. Leh, Ladakh, Jammu, and Kashmir
Cowrie-shell-decorated tassel (chun-po) worn attached to the end of the perak
Collection Ghysels, Brussels

As peraks become increasingly shorter, these formerly common tassels have become rare (see 264).

black hair (*spu*) of a Ladakhi woman is allowed to grow to a long length and is braided. Some continue to follow an old, traditional style in which the hair is braided into 108 narrow plaits, a number equal to the volumes of the Kangyur, the Tibetan Buddhist holy books, which makes this a power number, also used in Tibetan rosaries. Many wear two braids, into each of which is incorporated black woolen yarn that simulates hair and acts to lengthen the braid down to the calf.

All braids are combined and to their end is attached an elaborate yarn tassel made of a bunch of joined smaller tassels, each often ending with cowrie shells, bells, or coins. This is equivalent to the *paranda* (see 807) worn by women in India. Hanging near the end of the *perak*'s tail, it almost sweeps the ground.

Other Ladakhi Ornaments

A few additional Ladakhi ornaments, listed below, in descending order, are only a very brief testament to the richness of the Ladakhi ornamental tradition.

Not a form of jewelry, but used to support hooked-on ornaments, a highly distinctive feature of the Ladakhi woman's ensemble are the large lappets (*tsaru*) worn at the sides of the head. Made of black woolen cloth, they are edged or completely covered with black astrakhan lambskin of the karakul sheep, or brown otter skin (see 265).

One very special Ladakhi ornament (*chodpan*) is a hatlike arrangement of many strands of pearls, turquoises, and corals held by radiating spacers.

Earrings (*alung*) often consist of strings and clusters of beads, usually of coral, turquoise, glass, mother-of-pearl, and, most favored, small baroque pearls. A variety of arrangements exist. In some, bead strands are attached to a metal ear stud, which can be set with turquoises. A popular type of ear ornament, called *nam chokali,* has small strands of pearls that pass over the ear top, their ends fixed to the hair, and pearl tassels that hang below.

Ornaments worn on the neck (*skecha*) are of a variety of types. Strands in combinations of coral, turquoise, amber, and mother-of-pearl beads are common. One consists of a string of coral beads alternating with a series of miniature, open-backed *ga'us*. Another has a series of silver flower-bud forms strung with corals and turquoises. A distinctive neck ornament made in many variants is a biblike, cloth-backed form to which many combinations of coral, turquoise, amber, carnelian, pearl, mother-of-pearl, and other beads are attached, often surrounding a central *ga'u*. A tight-fitting neck choker (*sikaposh*) made of interlocking metal units backed by cloth is worn by women who do not have a *perak*.

Chest fibulas, used to secure a heavy woolen shoulder cloth or shawl, are often made of silver in round, rectangular, or lozenge form, the sheet metal ornamented with repoussage patterns, usually of good-luck symbols, wire work, or pierced work. At its back are two, large sharp-pointed hooks to fix them to the cloth. A pendant with a musk deer's tusk set in gold or silver is worn against the back as an amulet, to protect the wearer from the evil eye.

Worn hooked on the left shoulder, the chatelaine (*sundus; branshil*) starts with a decorative unit from which hangs a series of chains, each terminating with a small toiletry item, such as an ear pick or probe, tweezers, toothpick, or a head scratcher made of ivory. This ornament, which resembles chatelaines used in Tibet proper, is given by a mother to her daughter upon her marriage.

A large, round gold, brass, or copper disc (*docha*) in repoussage pierced work bearing the Buddhist endless-knot design, a symbol of longevity, is usually attached at the waist and hangs near the left hip. From it hang several rows of silver chains, each ending with a small bell or leather strips, to which are attached a series of amuletic cowrie shells.

On the wrist, solid silver penannular bangles with formalized animal head terminals are worn by those who can afford them. Buddhist and local Muslim women wear conch-shell bangles (*tunglak*). They are placed on a girl in her childhood, and, when they become too small, are sawn off and replaced by larger ones, which the woman wears for the rest of her life. As a means of showing respect (or thanks when receiving a gift), when women meet, they greet each other by one striking the shell bangles of the other. The wealthy may have them inlaid with silver or dyed red. In the past, porcelain imitations made in China were also in use.

Rings (*sirkop*) of many types are also worn. Most are of silver and mounted with a coral or turquoise stone surrounded by a bezel ornamented with shot. Rings are often given to a woman by her mother-in-law at the time of marriage.

270

271

272

269. Leh, Ladakh, Jammu, and Kashmir
*Silver left-side-of-chest amulet-ornament (also worn before the face),
symbolizing the sun and the moon, set with coral and turquoise; its
upward-pointing crescent-moon shape works against the evil eye.*
Courtesy Chhote Bharany, New Delhi

270. Tandi, Lahul, Himachal Pradesh
Silver plaque (dunkertsa or dun-dkar) with coral and turquoises
5⅞ x 5⅞ in. (15 x 15 cm); weight 179 g
Courtesy H. C. Mehra, Ellora, New Delhi

Worn at the back of the head, the form is a mandala with a chased central lotus flower
set with a gemstone.

271. Ladakh, Jammu, and Kashmir
Silver ga'u forms, open backed, strung with coral beads
Top: length 13⅞ in. (35.3 cm); six ga'us with gilded faces, each 1⅝ x 1⁹⁄₁₆ in.
*(4.2 x 4 cm); set with central turquoise. Bottom: length 13³⁄₁₆ in. (34 cm); seven egg-
form ga'us, each 1³⁄₁₆ x 1 in. (3 x 2.5 cm)*
Collection Mis, Brussels

272. Leh, Ladakh, Jammu, and Kashmir
*Silver clasp (chap-tse) backed with two end prongs (kug) used to secure a woman's
woolen shawl*
Courtesy Chhote Bharany, New Delhi

The central lotus motif with gemstone (missing here) is an allusion to the Tibetan
dharani, OM MANI PADME HUM.

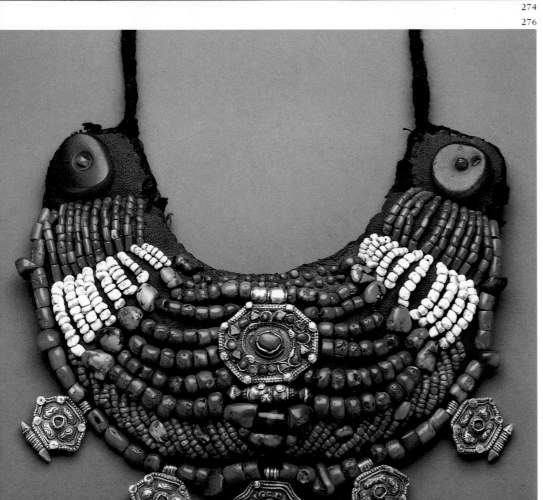

273. Leh, Ladakh, Jammu, and Kashmir
(opposite page)
*Seven-strand necklace (ultik) of coral, amber,
turquoise, cowrie, and silver beads, with repoussé-
worked silver terminal spacers and conch-shell clasp
Longest bead strand 19¾ in. (50 cm); weight 522 g
Collection Ghysels, Brussels*

274. Tibet
*Silver rings (ngü tshi-kho) worn on the fingers and
in the hair and headdress (see 108). This form,
here set with corals, the Chinese called a "saddle"
ring (ga tshi-ko), a name that persists in Western
terminology because its form resembles that of
a Tibetan horse saddle.
Collection the author, Porvoo*

275. Tibet
*Ivory thumb ring (pa-so tre-kho) worn as a
protective amulet (see 259)
Outer diameter 2¼ in. (5.7 cm); inner diameter
1⁵⁄₁₆ in. (2.4 cm); height ¾ in. (1.8 cm); weight 62 g
Collection the author, Porvoo*

276. Hemis, Ladakh, Jammu, and Kashmir
*Ceremonial gorget: a cloth ground on which beads
of coral, amber, turquoise, conch shell, and carnelian
(the most widely used bead materials of Tibet) are
fixed. At the center is a silver ga'u, and from its
lower edge is suspended six smaller silver ga'us.
Collection Ghysels, Brussels*

Marriage and Jewelry

A discussion of marriage jewelry is really an entry into the dynamics of Indian society, involving the fundamental relationships between men and women. Like most world cultures, Indians have devised and widely adopted an ornament, worn by a woman, and sometimes by a man, to signify to others that they are married. Because men dominate most Indian societies, the status and social role of a woman must be clear to all as this is the basis for acceptable behavior patterns between the sexes. Marriage ornaments help to convey this status.

No single ornament, however, serves this purpose throughout the Indian subcontinent, as, for instance, the wedding ring does in the West. Instead, regional types exist that, following local practice, are worn on different parts of the body, including the head, nose, neck, wrist, toes, and combinations of these.

A better understanding of this complicated subject may be arrived at by indicating a general, geographic division where primary types are worn. If an imaginary line is drawn between northern and southern India that follows the southern boundaries of Gujarat, Madhya Pradesh, and Orissa, *in general* it can be said that to the north of this division marriage symbol ornaments are worn on the head, nose, wrist, and toes; and to the south they are worn suspended from the neck. No sooner than this is said, however, exceptions could be mentioned, but basically this division holds. Further complicating this subject is that, in many places, secondary types of jewelry, commonly given to a woman at the time of her marriage, by custom may also be an indication of the wearer's married state.

All these matrimonial ornament forms have the basic function of warding off the malignant effects of evil spirits, and so act to protect the wearer. A socially useful by-purpose for others is that the forms may indicate the wearer's geographical place of origin, her religion, and also her caste—all subjects of great interest to Indians. In some areas, the primary marriage symbol ornament must be of gold, a metal considered to be ritually pure and sacred to the gods, while in others silver, also highly regarded, may be in wide use, especially among people of lesser means.

Regional Marriage Ornament

Northern India

In Kashmir, high-caste Brahman Pandit women wear the dejharu, *a pair of gold pendants that pass through a hole in both ear conchas and fall far below shoulder level to rest on the chest. This unique ornament is given by a father to his daughter at her marriage.*

A common Muslim Kashmiri form of marriage jewel is a silver ear ornament that consists of hanging bell-shaped earrings supported and connected by a chain that passes over the head (see 407, 456).

In the Kullu Valley, Dehra Dun, and northern Uttar Pradesh, a large, gold, septum suspended nose ring (bulak) *is worn (see 364).*

In the Kangra Valley and northwestern India, a large, circular, highly ornamented gold nose ring (nath or besar) *is worn, usually supported by an attached chain whose end is hooked into the hair or headgear.*

In West Himalaya and the Punjab, women wear a forehead ornament (tikka) *at the central hair parting. In general, among Hindus the forehead is regarded as the center of emotions (see 363).*

East Himalayan matrimonial ornaments include a large silver nose ring (nath), *and a necklace of silver coins (see 359).*

In Himachal Pradesh, Jammu, and northern Punjab, a top-of-the-head silver ornament (chak, *see 414) and natural white or red-dyed ivory bangles* (hathi dant ka chura) *are worn on the arms.*

Gujarati brides wear ivory, gold, and glass bangles (see 330, 338) and silver toe rings (bichhwa).

Rajasthan marriage ornaments include the nose ring (nath), *a central gold or silver forehead ornament* (bor), *silver toe rings on the middle toes, and silver anklets with attached bells* (paizeb).

Marwari women are distinguished by a gold nose stud (luang, *see 362), glass bangles* (churi), *toe rings, and a gold or silver belt with jingling chains* (kandora or kardani).

Southern India

Maharashtrian women are recognized by a necklace of small, black glass beads (mangalsutram) *with centrally attached gold marriage pendant* (thali), *and/or a necklace of auspicious units* (kolhapuri saj, *see 491); and a gold-wire nose ring* (nath) *often elaborately set with pearls, rubies, emeralds, and sometimes diamonds.*

Tamil Nadu women wear some form of gold thali, often a phallic symbol, either separately on the neck or in combination with other auspicious symbolic amulets.

In Kerala, a gold marriage necklace is worn without a phallic symbol; it usually consists of many unit repeats of the same design. Different designs are used such as serpent heads studded with stones (nagapadathali), *units with three grooves* (kuzhimani), *and others. A gold thali may be incorporated into such a necklace or is worn separately (see 492).*

Southern Indian Christians use a gold bangle and a gold thali similar to the Hindus' but bearing a cross, and, in some places, a gold penannular earring fixed through a hole in the fossa.

In addition to these ornaments, it is common practice almost all over India for a Hindu married woman each day to place some red pigment powder (S: sindur; P: shangraf; H: kumkum; Tam: jathilingkam) in the parting of her hair near the forehead. The pigment symbolizes the union of Shiva and his Shakti, indicating that the wearer's husband lives.

277
279

278
280

277. Srinagar, Kashmir South, Jammu, and Kashmir
Kashmiri Pandit Brahman woman wearing a distinctive ear ornament used by married women in this community. It consists of a gold chain (anther-ru) that passes through a hole at the center of the ear scapha, from which is suspended a gold pendant (dijhaharu or dejhar) having the same mystic shape as the figure (wegu) traced on the ground at the birth of a child. This ornament is a part of a woman's dowry (gulimuit) given to her by her father and is worn while her husband lives.

278. Sunehar Village, Bilaspur District, Himachal Pradesh
Large gold nose ring (besar), ornamented with gemstones, pearls, and enamel. Those of smaller size are called nath.

279. Jodhpur, Rajasthan
Forehead ornament (bhor-rakh-di) made of silvered glass beads and central mirrors, worn by a married woman. Her upper-front incisor teeth are inlaid with central gold studs (rekhan). Hindu belief holds that a person wearing gold in the mouth will not tell a lie. To do so would be sinful as it would defile that metal, which is sacred.

280. Pushkar, Rajasthan
Brahman woman of the Baniya or mercantile class wearing a gold forehead ornament (sona ka bhor) set with diamonds and edged with seed pearls and other gold ornaments

281. Jodhpur, Rajasthan
Silver forehead ornament (bhor), with foil-backed glass insets, worn by a married woman at the central hair part (mang) Collection Ivory, New York

Marriage and Jewelry · 157

282. Pudukkottai, Tamil Nadu

The kazhuththu uru gold necklace, as shown here, is worn again during the performance of another, major ceremony. According to a Hindu concept, the age of a man is 120 years. His sixtieth birthday (shashtipurti) theoretically marks the halfway point of his life. The occasion is celebrated among the Nattukottai Chettiars by a feast, attended by relatives and friends to thank the gods for this great achievement. Various ceremonies are performed, depending on particular community tradition. A reenactment of the wedding ceremony generally takes place, during which the original marriage necklace, and possibly one newly commissioned for this occasion, are worn by the wife. The groom wears the rudraksham seed and lingam pendant necklace (rudraksamalai). Both are visible here. This ceremony is not performed for the man alone if the wife has died beforehand. Courtesy Barbier-Mueller Museum, Geneva

283. Trichur, Kerala

Goldsmith's catalogue drawing of marriage ornaments (thalis) worn alone, with flanking cylindrical amulets (thayittu), or bead pairs, seen in the lower right. Shown here are front, side, and back elevations. The drawing is shown to a client, who then makes a selection for its fabrication. Each form is used by a particular religious sect or caste, to indicate the wearer's affiliation. For example, the double thali (irattaiyana thali) (2nd row, left) with an enthroned sectarian mark, is worn by Vaishnavite Brahmans. The plain, circular thali is worn by Sudras, and the round and heart-shaped ones with a cross by Indian Christians.

284. Pudukkottai, Tamil Nadu ➤

Traditional gold marriage necklace (kazhuththu uru) worn by a bride of the Nattukottai Chettiar community
Approximate length 18⅞ in. (48 cm); approximate weight 500 g
Collection Ivory, New York

The Nattukottai Chettiars are a devoutly Shaivite, wealthy mercantile caste including bankers. During the British colonial period, their expanded trade interests caused many to emigrate to south Asian countries.

This necklace is given to the bride (manavatti) by her parents as a part of her dowry jewelry (kaliyanamabaranam). At the wedding ceremony (kaliyanachchadangku), it is tied on the bride's neck by the groom (pagan). The cord (kayiru) on which the necklace units are threaded is tied with three knots (munru mudichcham) symbolizing the union of the self (tanakku), husband (kanavan), and God (kadavu).

The format of this necklace varies. The central, pierced-work (uduruvu) unit, the actual marriage badge (thali or tirumangalyam) can be up to 7 inches (18 cm) in length. Strung on the same cord can be a total of from fifteen to thirty-two gold units such as ornamental, round, or square section tube-shaped beads (kolai) and a back-hanging terminal tassel-pendant (kuchcham) fixed to cord ends. In some cases, two necklaces of similar form are worn together, each with two hands (see 282). In this necklace are four hand-shaped units (nalu viralkal) that are said to represent the two hands of the groom and those of the bride. Its four fingers represent the four Vedas: Rig, Yajur, Sama, and Atharva. The hands usually are surmounted by upright, sharp-ended "spires" (kumbam) that can be up to 3 inches (8 cm) in height. They terminate in a four-faceted double pyramid, symbolizing the four cardinal directions. These "spires," together with the domed form at their base, give this motif the appearance of a spired stupa.

Such necklaces can weigh from 43 to 75 gold sovereigns (or from 343 to 600 g or more). Older ones are generally larger and heavier. Large necklaces can still be commissioned but are worn only for ceremonial use, which explains their good condition. A smaller one (siru thali jodippu) is substituted for daily use.

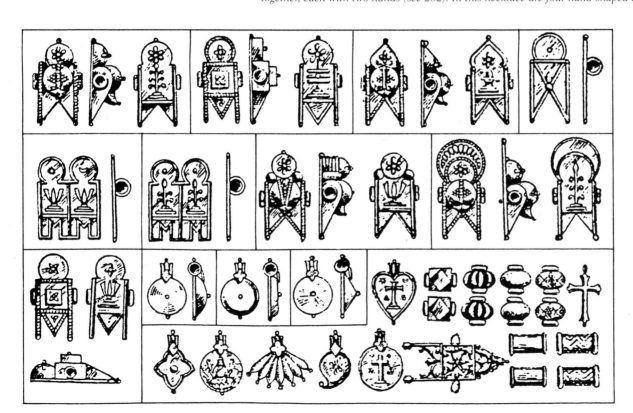

Hindu Marriage Custom and Ornament

Among Hindus (and surely other groups), the most important social event in the life cycle (S: *samsara*) is marriage (S: *vivaha;* H: *biyah;* Tam: *kaliyanam*), in which jewelry always plays a significant role. It is rare that an Indian woman remains a spinster. Among Hindus today, child marriage, now banned by law, is far less frequent than formerly. Most rural marriages take place soon after the girl reaches puberty, and the boy his teens. In urban societies, marriageable ages are generally later.

Love matches do occur, but the arranged marriage is far more frequent and is generally the responsibility of the parents who, in anticipation of the eventual necessity, are always on the lookout for a suitable mate for their children. If one cannot be found, the help of a professional marriage broker (H: *ghatak*) may be enlisted. Today the classified marriage-offer section of Sunday newspapers contains hundreds of entries for both men and women; they aim to locate a possible mate whose religion, caste, and social standing is compatible with that of the eligible party.

Normally the marriage proposal originates with the prospective bride's family. A representative of the boy's family—his father or guardian—goes to see the offered bride. A similar inspection visit is made of the boy by the girl's representatives. If reactions prove satisfactory, serious negotiations can commence.

A hired or family astrologer (H: *jotishi;* Tam: *jothishan*) compares the horoscopes of the couple (charted at birth and saved mainly for this occasion) to see if their respective planets and signs are compatible for a happy future. Should no conflict exist, the girl's parents grant permission for the marriage to take place. An auspicious date based on favorable astrological signs is decided upon. By tradition, marriages most frequently take place in spring. February, March, and April are considered to be the best months, but a marriage can occur at another time so long as the astrologer determines it to be auspicious. A betrothal ceremony is performed by the astrologer, priest, and male parents to solemnize the forthcoming contract.

At the foundation of both Hindu and Muslim marriage ceremonies is the formulation of an agreement or contract (H: *biyah jakarna;* Tam: *vakku-nichchayam*) drawn up by the two parties, usually after endless discussions and compromises. In effect, this is a deed of transfer for the possession of the bride, formerly her parent's property, to the groom. The agreement involves the price paid by the groom's family to the bride's, a practice more common among the less affluent classes; the bride's dowry; the number of feasts to be given during the several days in which a wedding is normally cele-

285

brated; and presents that must be given to relatives and friends on both sides. Each caste and social strata follows different arrangements in these matters, and expenditure varies according to economic status. The sums spent can be staggering and may result in financial ruin, particularly in families with several daughters. It may take years to recover financially.

The bride's dowry (H: *jahez,* paraphernalia; *kannyadan,* gift of a virgin; Tam: *sithanam*) is usually provided by her family. Agreements concerning its contents can be verbal, but when considerable amounts are involved, as they often are, it is usual to prepare a written agreement that specifies all the items deemed necessary to establish a household. The agreement includes the number of garments, and—very important—the amount in terms of *total weight* of the precious metals in the form of

jewelry that must be given to the girl, normally governed by the bride's social standing or caste. In some cases, particular traditional jewelry forms may be specified, especially among close-knit rural groups where religion, caste, and tradition are strictly observed.

There is always an interchange of gifts (H: *shagun,* a gift of good augury) between the two families. In this exchange, the bride often receives a fine *sari,* among other items, and possibly a rich ornament from her future in-laws.

Fulfillment of the requirements for the bride's jewelry usually involves several trips to jewelry shops, where the bride, her parents, and advisors spend many hours choosing ornaments appropriate to their social standing. The family's commitment to this obligation is de rigueur to avoid a loss of their social standing. During the pre-marriage season, the jewelry bazaars

285. Chirag-Delhi; Thekhand; Juliana Villages, Punjab

Clay image of Sanjhi-Devi (called Hoi in Haryana) created by girls on a house wall for the worship of Devi, the supreme Hindu goddess, during the Sanjhi-Devi Puja (September–October). The object of this worship is to find a good husband and make a successful marriage.

The larger figure is Sanjhi-Devi, the smaller her brother Sanjha. The units that compose the image are of unbaked clay fixed, while still plastic, to an exterior house wall. The importance of jewelry to village women is illustrated by the attention it is given here. This veritable lexicon of local traditional women's ornaments includes: head ornaments (bor; jhumar); earrings (karan-phul-jhumka); necklaces (hansli; mala; patli har; champakali); armlet (bazuband); and foot ornaments (paizeb; kara; lachhe; chura; jhanjhan).

286. New Delhi

Punjabi bride and groom. Tied to the bride's red-dyed ivory bangle (chura), given to her by her maternal uncle, are silver and gold half domes (kalirei; singular kalira)
Diameter c. 2 in. (5 cm) or larger

These symbols of fertility are given to the bride at the wedding by guests who approach her and tie them to her bangle. After the marriage ceremony, she playfully hits them on the heads of unmarried girls present to bring them good luck in their future marriage. After the wedding, the kalira bunch is hung in the couple's room.

287. South East Punjab and Haryana.
Early 20th century
Cotton ground, silk embroidered head cover (phulkari, sainchi type) worn by village brides
99 x 59⅞ in. (251.5 x 152 cm)
The Calico Museum of Textiles, Ahmadabad (1516)

Girls prepare these head cloths long in advance for use on this occasion. Here the central auspicious lotus flower is surrounded by wish-fulfilling symbol motifs: representations of the traditional regional jewelry given to a bride as a part of her dowry.

288. Nimkhera, Raisen District, Madhya Pradesh
Brahman bride receiving wedding gifts from the groom's family

289. Nimkhera, Raisen District, Madhya Pradesh
A Bagheli Thakur bride wearing her gold and silver wedding jewelry. Since males control most land and agricultural income, a woman's ornaments are often her most valuable possessions.

are crowded with men, women, and their companions making their decisions and selections.

Because traditional customs are an extremely powerful social force, a bride usually selects traditional jewelry forms for her dowry, a reminder of her connection with her community and ancestors and the main reason that so many of these forms survive.

Unless poverty prevents it, every bride brings to her marriage the agreed upon amount of gold and/or silver jewelry, recorded item by item in a legal document. In many cases, (especially in the past), this jewelry constitutes the only real personal assets or real property that she can legally own. Her jewelry and other possessions are termed *stridana*, from the Sanskrit *stri* (woman) and *dana* (gifts).

Stridana jewelry serves as a woman's insurance in case of need. Among rural people, under trying circumstances, a wife may offer them to her husband for disposal as a means of family survival. Should a woman be divorced, she retains her *stridana* jewelry. Upon widowhood, when she can no longer wear them, they remain her ancestral property and she is free to sell them or give them away as she wishes—usually to her daughter(s) and female relatives.

The Hindu Wedding

Weddings are as lavish as the economic circumstances of the parties permit. In many cases they become the occasion for a huge family reunion, possibly involving literally hundreds of guests who show their family solidarity by coming from long distances, today even continents away, to participate in this joyous family occasion.

All the married women present feel obliged (one suspects due to a certain sense of competition) to wear their best jewelry, most of which was probably acquired when they themselves married. Weddings consequently become a moving pageant of power symbols and one-upmanship.

At this most auspicious gathering, the bride must also look splendid. Every bride strives, as best as she can, to realize her community's ideal image of nuptial perfection. With great care and concentration, the bride's female relatives spend hours in ceremoniously dressing and adorning her, the process in Sanskrit called *shringara;* a term associated with Shri, the goddess of female beauty, good luck, prosperity, and fertility, linked with Lakshmi. Her

hands and feet are decorated with intricate designs stained with henna (*mehndi*), a nerve-soothing procedure performed by family ladies or professionals, over several hours (see page 26). She is bedecked with all the jewelry she now owns as a part of her dowry and possibly other ornaments borrowed for the event.

Several preliminary rituals have been performed in the two or three days prior to the marriage ceremony. On the day of the ceremony, the bridegroom, his face covered by a veil (*sehra*) and wearing a crown or turban with an *aigrette* (see 826) and possibly also necklaces and other ornaments, sets out in procession (H: *barat*) from his house. In village weddings, he may be mounted on a white horse, but in cities, he may only become a horseman at a predetermined place near the bride's house. The horse is also usually elaborately ornamented with silver trappings and jewelry, and, in recent times, may be draped with glittering trappings. As this procession usually takes place after dark, it is accompanied by several men bearing brilliant portable arc lamps on their heads, with a loud brass band leading the way, followed by a throng of male relatives and wedding guests.

290. Maharashtra
A Maharashtrian bride wearing a face-framing chaplet (mundavalya) of jasmine buds (ran mogri; Jasminum officinale); a mango-shaped gold nose ring (nath) of pearls and diamonds, cluster pearl earrings (kap); a pearl necklace (timani); a pearl collar (guluband) with a pendant bearing the auspicious Om (see pages 2 and 3); and a forehead mark (tilak) in crescent moon form. A strung jasmine flower ornament (H: gajra) is worn around the bun on social occasions.
Courtesy Air India, Bombay

Shringar (decoration) in Indian arts pertains to the romantic essence and may refer to decorated beauty in general or to a bedecked woman. Shringar also designates decoration of a temple deity with flowers, garlands, and jewelry to increase the pleasure of the viewer (H: darshan) when beholding the divinity. Some families do not approve of the common custom of decorating the bride with an ostentatious display of precious-metal jewelry at the wedding ceremony. Instead, they commission a mali to prepare an entire matching set (H: phul shringar) of ornaments made of flowers to be placed on the head, ears, neck, hair braid, upper arm, wrists, fingers, waist, and toes. Marvels of ingenuity, they almost always include sweetly scented jasmine buds.

291. West Bengal
Bride wearing a traditional crown (makuta) of shola pith. Shola (Ben: shola; Tam: netti; Aeschynomene aspera) is a unique wild plant used in several areas of India for creating various types of personal and festive ornaments. A small, water-loving bush, shola grows abundantly in Bengal marshy areas and on land inundated during the monsoon season. Its tall, straight stems are covered with a brownish-gray bark and achieve a diameter of two to three inches (5–7 cm). Inside is the white, lightweight spongy fiber called the pith. In the dry months of April and May, the thickest shola stems are harvested, cut into lengths, tied into bundles, and set aside to dry. When dry, each stem's bark is removed and the pith cut spirally with a special knife (kath-narul) to make large, flat sheets that can be pasted in layers for carving. All the forms of ornaments normally made in precious metals and used in West Bengal are duplicated in shola with great imagination and skill. Most common are the shola crowns (mukut, makuta, or topi) worn by grooms and brides in West Bengal wedding ceremonies. These may be unadorned or decorated with synthetic gold or silver threads, wire, or foils.

292. Puri, Orissa
Crown (makuta) with tassels (pentha), made of shola pith, paper, mica, tinsel, pigment, and dye, worn by a groom and bride during the marriage ceremony

293. Maharashtra
Hindu wedding scene from the film Padmini, produced by the Punjab Film Corporation, Bombay. Seated before the traditional sacred fire, the groom wears a face cover (sehra, see 297, 299) of strung jasmine buds, and the bride wears a flower headdress. The sanctified area in which the ceremony is performed (pandal) is strung with auspicious garlands of mango leaves and blossoms.

294. Rajasthan
Women applying mendhi (mendhi mandana) to each other's palms. The paste, prepared from the crushed leaves of henna (Lawsonia alba) is dribbled on with a stick to control the patterns, almost all of which have symbolic significance. The dried paste is scraped off and the hands rubbed with lemon juice, which, like a mordant, enhances and fixes the red color. After ten minutes, the hands can be washed. (See also 22.)

295. West Bengal
Hindu groom's traditional crown (topar) of shola pith, with attached side tassels (pentha)

296. Kachchh, Gujarat
Hindu Rabari bride-groom wearing a face veil (mod) of stiffened cloth decorated with glass-seed-bead (chidiya moti) embroidery (moti bharat) and topped with tufts of colored cotton yarn

297. New Delhi
Bridegroom (dulha) arriving at the wedding ceremony, traditionally seated on a white horse (dulha ka ghora) led by a syce (sayis). His face is covered by a sehra of gold tinsel whose purpose is to prevent the attack of the evil eye (bad-nigahi), the result of jealousy. His horse is also decorated with a forehead ornament (tikka), as well as necklaces, harness ornaments, and leg bracelets. An umbrella (chhatri) is held over the groom even though the ceremony takes place at night; its purpose is symbolically honorific.

296

298

297

299

298. Chhindwara, Madhya Pradesh
Gondh tribal groom's wedding crown (moad) of paper, palm leaf, bamboo, and tinsel yarn. It includes an upper print image of Ganesha and a central one of Krishna Murlidhar and Radha. The Dravidian Gonds are now acculturated Hindus.
Collection Tribal Research Institute, Chhindwara

299. Mandi, Himachal Pradesh
Hindu groom's face veils (sehra) ready-made for sale. During northern Indian marriage ceremonies, the groom and bride often wear face coverings intended to shield them from the malefic effects of the evil eye inadvertently cast upon them by a jealous guest.

300. Punjab and Himachal Pradesh
Silver groom's crown (umlakh)
Unit: 8¾ x 3⅜ x 16⅝ in. (22.1 x 8.5 x 42.3 cm); weight 866 g
Collection the author, Porvoo

Worn during the wedding ceremony, tied to the head of the groom by the attached silver chains, such crowns were probably inspired by those represented on images of Hindu deities, or multiunit crowns worn by Tibetan tantric priests. They are owned by bankers, money lenders, and goldsmiths who rent them out for the occasion. Each panel bears a representation of an important Hindu deity, here including Ganesha, Shiva, Karttikeya, Lakshmi, and Kali. Their represented presence at the wedding is considered auspicious.

301. Calcutta, West Bengal. *c. 1798–1804*
Watercolor painting of a Hindu marriage cere-
mony, made in Calcutta by a Murshidabad artist
Marquis Wellesley Collection

Bride and groom are wearing face veils and crowns (mukut). The wedding pavilion (pandal) is orna-mented with auspicious garlands of mango leaves and garlic to repel evil spirits. The couple is cir-cumambulating (phera) the central sacred wedding fire (vivahan) with seven steps (saptapada), the most important ritual in a Hindu wedding.

The groom's party is met outside the bride's house, or the place of marriage, by her female relatives. To honor the now dismount-ed groom, the bride's mother performs the oil-lamp ceremony (S: *arti*), waving the flame in a circle around his face as is done in a Hindu temple before the image of the deity. She also places a red-pigment auspicious mark (H: *tikka*) on his forehead. The groom is then met by the bride, who places a triumphant garland (H: *jaimala*) on him, and he reciprocates with the same. These flower garlands are worn dur-ing the following ceremonies.

The marriage ceremony is performed on the chosen auspicious day, time, and moment. It often takes place under a large, gaily pat-terned, colored cloth, sun-shading pavilion (P: *shamiyana*) erected outdoors to accommodate the large number of guests.

Within this a wedding canopy (S: *pandal*) has been erected and decorated with auspi-cious mango leaf and especially marigold flower garlands. A Hindu family priest (S: *purohita*) consecrates the area below it, offers suitable sacrifices to all the gods and invites them to come to the *pandal* and preside over the ceremony and feast to follow. The groom is brought under the *pandal* and seated, followed by the bride, who is seated to his left. Their fathers and mothers flank them, and all face East. The bride's father rises and places a *kusha*-grass amulet ring (see 24) on the groom's right-hand ring finger in preparation for the next rit-ual. While making offerings and repeating their names, the father invites the family ancestors, who relate the present to the past, to attend the wedding.

Married women bring in the sacred fire on an earthenware or metal tray and place it at the pandal center. Fire represents truthful Agni, the fire god, who witnesses the marriage ceremony. The priest consecrates the fire by scattering *kusha* or *darbha* grass. He propitiates the nine planets and eight directions with rice offerings and invites them to attend. The tutelary deities of both families are also propitiated and similarly invited.

During the ceremony, several marriage rituals are performed. In one, the groom ties a temporary marriage wristlet, the *kankana*, around the left wrist of the bride. Originally this was made of blades of kusha grass, but now it usually is a cord dyed yellow with saffron or turmeric and decorated with beads. The bride in turn does the same to the groom, placing the thread on his right wrist. This act, the *kankana-charana*, is one of those intended to symbolize the couple's acceptance of each other.

The most important of all the ceremonies is the *kanniyadan*, Sanskrit for "the gift of a virgin," which symbolizes parental renunciation of their authority over the bride and its transference to the groom. After many prayers and mantra recitations to the gods (S: *mangalashta*, eight marriage blessings), the bride's father places his daughter's hand into that of the groom. Gifts follow, including a *salagrama*, an ammonite fossil symbolizing Vishnu.

The *Mangalsutram*: Marriage Cord

All marriages require some prescribed form of marriage symbol ornament that is never removed by the woman during her married lifetime, until widowhood. A typical one is the auspicious, permanent marriage cord, or *mangalsutram*, from the Sanskrit *mangal*, "propitious, blessed, happy, successful, prosperous," and *sutram*, "cord," commonly used in western India but spreading elsewhere. Ideally it is made of 108 (an auspicious number) fine cotton threads twisted together and dyed yellow with saffron or turmeric. On it is normally a

centrally strung gold *thali*. Before this is placed on the bride, it is carried around to all the wedding guests who touch it, bless it, and wish the couple a long married life.

After other ceremonies, while he recites mantras and the guests sing and musicians play to drown out any inauspicious sound such as a sneeze or a cough, the groom (in the south aided by his sisters), ties the *mangalsutram* and *thali* on his bride's neck, securing it with three knots. This act of tying symbolizes the groom's acceptance of the gift of a virgin and signifies that from then on she is his property. Two women bless the pair by performing the *arti* ceremony of circularly waving lighted oil lamps over them.

The *mangalsutram* and its attached *thali* are regarded as an auspicious amulet and the bride herself is said to be auspicious (*sumangala*) because, by wearing this ornament, she becomes immune to the evil eye. By extension, anyone who sees her is automatically granted good luck.

The *thali* may not be alone on the cord. Mangala is also the name of the auspicious planet Mars, whose color is red, the same as the auspicious garment color worn by Hindu brides. Because of this association, it is common for a bead, or beads, of auspicious red coral (*munga*), the stone sacred to Mars (see 713), to be placed on the *mangalsutram* as a means of invoking his protection and averting the evil eye. In various places, several other good-luck or auspicious amuletic ornaments, each with special symbolic form and function, are also threaded on the *mangalsutram*. In Maharashtra, the *thali* on the *mangalsutram* is flanked by small black glass beads (*kala pota*) said to repel the evil eye.

302. New Delhi
The wedding of Chandradas Mathur and Punam Mago-Mathur. After the ceremony of fire circumambulation, other ceremonies may follow, some with a lighthearted, symbolic purpose. In this one, the kangna ceremony, the bride and groom untie the knots of the kangna, a cord around their wrists, on which is threaded a red bead symbolizing auspiciousness, a green bead for prosperity, and a small iron ring that guards against evil. The strings are immersed in a shallow bowl of water, into which is also placed cut kusha grass and a gold ring. Together the couple tries to fish out the gold ring; by tradition the groom retrieves it and places it on the bride's finger as her wedding ring.

303. Bombay, Maharashtra
The common Hindu woman's wedding ornament (tala; mangalsutram), used here today, normally consists of a gold pendant (taouli) in a variety of forms, which may be strung on gold wire chain but more usually is strung on cord with small, black-glass beads (pota or kalipot) believed to frighten away evil spirits and to dispel witchcraft (jadu). The type of mangalsutram illustrated here is now gaining favor, and its use is spreading to other areas.

302

303

304. Kerala
Gold marriage necklace (erukkilamptu thali) with red glass "stones," worn by some Nambudiri Brahman women. The design is derived from the flower of the gigantic swallowwort (erukku; Calotropis gigenta).
Pitt Rivers Museum, University of Oxford, Oxford. Collected by J. H. Hutton, donated in 1933 (1933.65.2)

305. Tamil Nadu
Silver marriage ornament (periya thali, great thali) in an anthropomorphic male figural form
5¾ x 1⁹⁄₁₆ in. (14.5 x 4 cm); weight 268 g
Collection Ghysels, Brussels

The top circle bears a rampant lion; the remainder is floral patterned. Some such thalis, set with rubies, are made for use by the wife in the celebration of the husband's sixtieth birthday (shashtipurti).

The *Thali:* Primary Southern Marriage Ornament

Today the term *thali* (also sometimes spelled *tali*) refers to the gold marriage ornament or auspicious amulet placed on the *mangalsutram*. Its use is especially common in southern India, but it is gaining acceptance elsewhere. The Sanskrit word *thali* is derived from the vernacular name of the palmyra palm (*thala; Borassus flabelliformis*), or the large-leafed talipot palm (*thali pat; Corypha umbraculifera*), both common in southern India. Originally it was customary there to tie a strip of either of these palm leaves around the neck of a married woman to indicate her married state. The custom and term were transferred to the gold ornament now placed on the *mangalsutram.*

A *thali* can be made in a great variety of forms and in any size, from very small to huge. In Tamil Nadu, they are usually phallic symbols. In temple sculpture, female deities are often represented wearing a *thali* ornamented with a representation of Ganesha. Perhaps from this idea comes the southern Indian *thalis* that bear representations of gods and goddesses, especially Lakshmi, the goddess of good fortune.

In the *Saptapada* ceremony, one of the rituals that concludes the Hindu marriage ceremony, the groom's lower garment is knotted to that of the bride (H: *ganth jorna*, to tie the nuptial knot). They stand up, and he takes her hand. To indicate that their acceptance of each other is irrevocable, they then perform the walking ceremony (H: *pherai*, circuits). After making a burnt offering (H: *ahuti*) to Agni, they take seven steps (S: *saptapada*) around the sacred fire, each step symbolizing force, strength, well-being, offspring, luck, wealth, and their eternal friendship. This rite solemnizes the marriage.

The bride takes all her jewelry with her to her new home (H: *sasural*, the home of the father-in-law), which may be some distance away. When she arrives, her marriage jewelry will be carefully examined by her new female relatives. Their value and number may be a factor in determining the future treatment she will receive from her female in-laws. Rural brides continue to wear their marriage ornaments at least until their first anniversary, since to remove them before that would be unlucky.

307

308

306. Tiruchchirappalli, Tamil Nadu
*Gold Hindu marriage necklace (kaliyanam anivadam) with a central marriage ornament pendant
(thali or bottu), on which the goddess Lakshmi is depicted, worn by Chettiar women in Tamil Nadu
Total length 7¾ in. (19.5 cm); thali 3⅞ x 1¹/₁₆ in. (9.7 x 2.7 cm); weight 100 g
Collection Ghysels, Brussels*

307. Tamil Nadu
*Gold thali with a central representation of Mahalakshmi enshrined in a hand form (astham)
3¼ x 1⅝ in. (8.2 x 4 cm); weight 25 g
Collection Ghysels, Brussels*

308. Tiruchchirappalli, Tamil Nadu
*Gold Hindu marriage ornament (thali) worn by Chettiar women as a sign of marriage; it is removed upon
being widowed. At the top are birds, apsarasas, and lions, surrounding a small seated image of Lakshmi.
In the center are deer, and in the lower area yalis and birds.
7½ x 5⅞ in. (19 x 4.8 cm); weight 140 g
Private Collection*

Married Hindu Women and Their Jewelry

Jewelry on a woman is always a happy omen, and it is worn on all important religious and social occasions. Its presence on her person guarantees its security, but pieces not in use will be carefully hidden to avoid robbery. After marriage, there are other traditional occasions on which a woman may receive a gift of jewelry, for example, when she is about to have her first child and returns to her parent's home for the delivery. After its birth and her recovery, her mother gives her a piece of jewelry, its value determined by her means, and she then returns to her husband's house. A woman may also be given jewelry at the time of an auspicious event such as the sixtieth birthday or the anniversary of her marriage.

When a woman's husband dies, the widow (S: *suhag-utarna: suhag*, good fortune; *utarna*, to pass over) by custom breaks her glass bangles (H: *churi thandi hona*) to mourn his death, the act symbolizing her entry to widowhood. After the funeral, as a widow she will normally dress in white for the remainder of her life and by custom will no longer wear jewelry (see 437). After a few days, during which her female relatives and friends share her grief, one of her nearest female relatives, while reciting mantras, cuts the *mangalsutram* cord on her neck. It must be *cut*, not *untied*, the act symbolizing the severance of her married state.

In former days—the custom was banned during the Governor-Generalship of Lord William Bentinck (1825–35), although it occasionally still occurs—when a woman's husband died, she could elect to sacrifice herself on his funeral pyre. Such a woman is called a *sati*, meaning "virtuous, true, pure" in Sanskrit, in association with the goddess Sati, who personifies the virtue of faithfulness in a wife. In effect, the act (*sati-hona*) was a meritorious suicide. The *sati* would dress in her finest apparel and, like a bride, bedeck herself with all her jewelry. She was led to the pyre, and before mounting it, was divested of her ornaments, which were given to her female relatives.

Second-Marriage Amulet

When a Hindu widower remarries, it is an ancient custom for the second wife to wear a special pendant amulet meant to propitiate the spirit of the dead first wife and allay any feelings of jealousy the spirit may bear. This ornament may depict either a face or a figure or symbol of the first wife.

In Gujarat, the amulet is called *shokpagunu* (*shoki*, sorrowful, sad; *pag*, footprint) and is usually a silver disk stamped with a pair of footprints that represent the husband's first wife. This amulet prevents the spirit of the deceased first wife (H: *byahta*) from harming the family.

309. Kerala: Cochin, Ernakulam, and **Alleppy area**
Gold hoop earrings (kunuk) worn at the top of the ear by Indian-Syrian Christian women. Now becoming unfashionable, these are only seen on older women. Her stretched earlobes indicate she once wore a second pair of heavy gold earrings.

310. Rajghat, Madhya Pradesh
1st century B.C.
Rock-crystal pendant (sautin, from sautiya, of or belonging to a co- or rival wife)
2⅜ x 2¾ in. (6 x 7 cm)
Private Collection, Philadelphia

Pendants with a similar purpose are also made in gold and silver. Represented on this one is a face symbolizing a Hindu man's dead first wife. The pendant is worn by his second wife (H: sauti, a rival), or a widow (H: rand) who remarries, to avert the possible jealousy of the ethereal form (H: preta) of the first spouse, who may return during the period between death and union with the ancestors (H: pitr). The second wife or remarried widow places such an ornament on her neck before applying vermilion (sindur) to her hair part (mang-tikka) for the first time as a sign of her being married. In the rare case of multiple marriages, more than one pendant may be worn.

Muslim Marriage Custom and Ornament

Muslims constitute about 14 percent of India's population. Muslim women have no special marriage ornament. In general, today Muslim jewelry usage in India has been heavily influenced by Hindu practices, understandable when they live in a Hindu-dominated cultural environment, and because many of their descendants, formerly Hindu, were forced converts to Muhammadanism. A Muslim bride *may* wear a head ornament (*jhumar* or *chamba*) on the left side, often designed in the form of a crescent moon and combined with other Muslim symbol ornaments such as a star, but this is a festive ornament, not worn daily. Like Hindus, they may also wear a nose ring and glass bangles.

Among Indian Muslims, marriage (P: *shadi*) is a civil contract and does not depend on any religious ceremony. Once the eligible bride and groom have given their consent, the marriage contract (A: *nikahnama*) must be settled by a Muslim agent, usually a legal guardian or other representative recognized by Islamic law. In this document, the husband settles a dowry (P: *jahez*) upon the girl, ostensibly to be given to her father. Its value has a significant place in the actual marriage ceremony. The possible amount is unlimited but must be in accordance with the social rank and economic position of the bridegroom.

The dowry is usually divided into two parts: prompt (A: *mu'ajjal*) and deferred (A: *mu'-akhkhir*). The first is theoretically owed a wife upon signing of the contract, before she enters her husband's home. The second is payable should the marriage end in divorce. In India, the prompt dowry is sometimes paid, but usually it is held in abeyance as a means by which the wife assures her good treatment by her husband. It is always payable on demand.

Among the two main Indian Muslim sects (Shi'ahs and Sunnis), marriage rites are similar, although there is no absolute uniformity. What is described here is general practice.

The legal Muslim marriage ceremony (A: *nikah*) is actually a celebration of the agreement of the marriage contract. This is followed by at least three days and three nights of festive rejoicing (P: *shadi*). In strictly orthodox practice, the bride is kept in seclusion (H: *parda*) during most of the wedding ceremonies. Invited guests appear in their best dress and wear their most valuable ornaments—often a spectacular sight.

On the second night, in elaborate procession, the bride sends her representatives with henna to the groom's house, along with presents, among which are his wedding costume and others for his family. The groom is dressed while all the women of his house watch, and the soles of his feet are dyed red with henna.

On the third night, the bride is prepared for the concluding marriage ceremony, which will take place at her parent's house or under a

311. Hyderabad, Andhra Pradesh
Muslim bride wearing typical gold marriage ornaments of that area, which are often similar to those worn by a Hindu

tent (P: *shamiyana*). Elaborate henna designs are applied to her hands and feet, often by a hired professional. The bride is ornamented with the nose ring (*nath*) presented to her by her husband's family and all her wedding jewelry. She is not seen by the groom or the guests present until the marriage ceremony is over.

The Muslim bridegroom (U: *dulha*) arrives at the place of the marriage ceremony riding a white horse (*duldul* in Urdu, the name of Muhammed's mule which he rode as a symbol of humility), accompanied by musicians and light bearers, a procedure similar to that described for Hindus.

The ceremony is performed by a Muslim judge or learned man, who asks the groom to tell the value of the wife's dowry. The groom replies with the amount, and the judge repeats this to all present. He then asks the groom to confirm his consent to the dowry. Without this mention of the dowry value, the marriage is not legal. After a prayer by the judge, the ceremony is over. The groom embraces his male family members and his friends and receives their congratulations.

The groom is then allowed to see the bride, in the case of traditional orthodoxy, for the first time. He enters a room where she has been waiting, dressed in her best finery. He sits down at her side and, in order not to appear brazen by looking directly at her, he regards her reflection in a mirror placed before them. After the usual feast, the bride is taken in procession, completely covered from public view, to the home of her husband.

The Bangle: A Universal Indian Marriage Ornament

From the remains of the earliest major city-civilizations of the Indus Valley Culture (c. 2500–1750 B.C.), such as Mohenjo-daro and Harappa, now in Pakistan, and other sites in India, archaeologists have excavated protohistoric ancestors of the bangle. Jewelry finds in this arena include complete bangles and parts or fragments from which technical deductions can be made. Terra-cotta and bronze images have also been found, some depicted wearing bangles. These ancient bangles or fragments are of gold, silver, copper, stone, shell, and fired ceramic. In the earliest strata, ceramic bangles are most common and were probably in widest use. In later levels, ceramic bangles are decorated in patterns painted in colored clay slips that contrast with the clay body color. Other examples are of glazed faience and easily worked steatite (soapstone), which could also be glazed. Infinitely varied in material and decoration, the bangle remains among the primary ornaments worn by Indian women and is often an important indication that the wearer is a married woman.

Lac Bangles

Bangles of lac (S: *laksha*; H, Pb, Mah: *lakh*; Tam: *arakku*) have been widely used in India since ancient times. Lac is produced by a unique scale insect (*Tachardia lacca*) indigenous to Indian forests. Secreted by the female during development and reproduction, lac is the only natural resin of animal origin.

The insect lives in aggregated masses on the young twigs of several host trees that grow wild in northern India but are also cultivated in large plantations for this purpose. About five million people, mainly local aboriginal tribals, are involved in all phases of the huge lac industry, which is centered in Bihar.

Tree twigs encrusted with lac secreted by the last generation of insects are collected and cut into lengths of four to six inches (10–15 cm). The lac is either scraped off by hand or the twigs are spread on a floor and passed over with a roller, which breaks off the resinous

312. Mohenjo-daro, Pakistan
Bronze statuette of a dancing girl, found by Sir John Marshall in the 1920s excavations at Mohenjo-daro, a major Indus Valley Civilization site National Museum of India, New Delhi (Inv. No. 195)

Probably made for a votive purpose, this is one of the few surviving cast-metal works of this ancient civilization. Standing nude in a natural pose, the girl wears a necklace and, on one arm, eleven upper arm and fourteen lower arm bangles; on the other she wears two upper and two wrist bangles.

313. Ahmadnagar, Maharashtra.
Mid-19th century
Set of thirteen red- and green-dyed ivory wrist bangles (chura jori or churian) with gilded and painted patterns
Victoria and Albert Museum, London (08308 IS)

Small: Outer diameter 2¼ in. (5.7 cm); inner diameter 2¹/₁₆ in. (5.2 cm)
Large: Outer diameter 3¹/₁₆ in. (7.8 cm); inner diameter 2⅞ in. (7.2 cm)
Total height 4¹⁵/₁₆ in. (12.2 cm); total weight 128 g

matter. The resulting *stick lac* (68 percent resin) is placed into water-filled tubs and trod underfoot (*dal marna*) or beaten (*raunda hua*) with a wooden pestle. Crushing and washing frees the resin of much of its impurities (and natural red color, which was traditionally used as a dye), leaving it in a granular state, the *seed lac* of commerce (88.5 percent resin), after which it is dried and converted into *shellac*.

In India it is common practice for goldsmiths to use a lac compound to fill hollow constructed parts of gold and silver jewelry (see page 364). It is left inside for the lifetime of the ornament to preserve its shape and prevent denting from impact during use. This practice dates back to the time of the Indus Valley Culture, from whose sites archaeologists have recovered gold bangles filled with a lac core. Lac is also used in the shaping, faceting, and polishing of hardstones; in setting stones into jewelry (see page 118); to fill a hollow object undergoing repoussage work; and for theatrical jewelry.

Lac Bangle Manufacture: Jaipur, Rajasthan

A considerable percentage of the lac produced in India goes into the making of lac bangles. In northern Bihar and Rajasthan alone, about one hundred tons of what is called *refuse lac* (called *kiri* in Bihar), which remains in the sack after squeezing, is used annually for bangle cores, saving the better quality lac for decoration.

Bihar

LAC PREPARATION

314. *The raw lac is placed in a cloth bag held over a fire at opposite ends by two men; the bag is stretched and twisted. Liquidized lac seeps through the cloth, and strains it of foreign particles. (A pile of finished sheet lac appear in the lower right.)*

315. *The lac is placed on a porcelain cylinder containing hot water, and, as it becomes viscous, it spreads over the cylinder's surface. Removed from the cylinder, the result is sheet lac, which is stretched while warm and piled up, as seen in the previous photograph. This cooled, rigid form, called shell lac, is broken into pieces for further processing.*

Shivpuri, Madhya Pradesh

LAC BANGLE MANUFACTURE

316. *Over a flat stone slab, the prepared cylinder consisting of a core of crude lac (kiri), made of lac mixed with talc to make it less brittle and covered with pigment-colored, better quality lac, is teased out to a suitable sectional diameter with a wooden tool (hatta).*

317. *A cut length is pressed in a wooden mold (khali) to give it the desired cross-sectional shape.*

Lac bangles (S: *lakshavalaya*; Raj: *lakh ki chudia*) in India have long been worn only by married women. This custom persists in some areas, especially among the aboriginal tribal people of Bihar and West Bengal, including the Bhumij, Ho, Munda, Oraon, and Santal. Formerly in very wide use by all classes of women, today they are mainly used by the poorer classes, who can only afford to purchase low-cost ornaments. They continue to be made in considerable quantity, but, compared with the past, the number of manufacturers has diminished drastically. Another reason for this decrease is the invention of the synthetic resins and plastics now widely used for bangles. Newer generations of bangle makers have entered more lucrative occupations. The unique skills developed over centuries in making and decorating lac bangles eventually may be lost entirely. Admirable lac bangles of the last century now in museum collections indicate the extent of the loss.

Throughout India are found Hindu lac bangle–makers belonging to the hereditary lac-workers caste, variously called Laheri, or Lakhera, living mainly in Bihar, West Bengal, Orissa, Madhya Pradesh, and Maharashtra. In Rajasthan and Hyderabad-Deccan, they are Muslims who call themselves Manohars. (The Hindi term *manohari* means "a beautiful, heart-ravishing woman.") In Jaipur, approximately two thousand persons belong to this group, which is divided into the Sanganeri, Shekhavati, and the Amarsari, so named after the places in Rajasthan from where they say they originated. Their working unit is the family; men prepare the lac and form the bangles, and women decorate them.

The age-old technique of making the basic lac bangle is the same, wherever in India this craft is practiced. Differences in the bangles among various production centers lie in their preference for a certain bangle dimension or form and the manner in which they are decorated.

Almost all lac bangles have an inner core made of the grayish-brown refuse lac, which is covered by a relatively thin layer of the better quality, colored lac. To further strengthen the core lac, a filler such as white clay (*safed mitti*) or talc powder (*abrak*) is added. The purer lac that covers the core is mixed with lithopone, a white, opacifying pigment consisting chiefly of zinc sulphide and barium sulphate, plus coloring pigment. When preparing either one, the dry ingredients are heated, mixed together, and quickly kneaded and pounded with a mallet, a process repeated until the mass is a homogenous, doughlike lump (*dala*).

Core lac and covering lac are heated separately, then each rolled into a cylinder. One end of the core-lac cylinder is fixed to the end of a three-by-twelve-inch (8 x 31 cm) wooden cylinder (*lui*), whose other end serves as a handle. The opaque (*dhundhla*) core lac, still malleable from heating, is shaped into a bluntly tapered cone form. The colored lac (*rangin lakh*) is spread over its apex and worked toward the *lui* handle end with a spatula until it completely and evenly covers the core lac.

While holding a heat-insulating cloth, the result is extended by hand into a long rod (*dandi*, length or handle) until its diameter is reduced to bangle thickness and finished by rolling it across a flat surface with a flat shaping tool (*hatta*).

The next step is to cut a series of measured bangle lengths from the rod until all the lac on the *lui* is consumed. In some locations, the long lac rod is wound spirally on a wooden forming mandrel. These spiral turns are cut and the results shaped into a bangle.

Before joining the ends, the straight bangle length is shaped into various sectional forms, made by pressing the length into contoured grooves on each side of a wooden forming block or mold (*khali*). The lac is forced into the groove with the *hatta*, and takes on the groove shape.

The result is formed into a circle over a conically tapered shaping mandrel (*muthiya*) whose diameter corresponds to a range of women's bangle sizes. Open bangle ends are joined by touching them with a flat-bladed, heated tool that melts the lac. The ends are

318. *Still soft, a length of lac is formed into a bangle over a wooden mandrel (muthiya) and is allowed to cool and harden.*

319. *Bangle ends are joined to make sets in graduated sizes and decorated with strips of tinsel, colored lac, and in many other ways.*

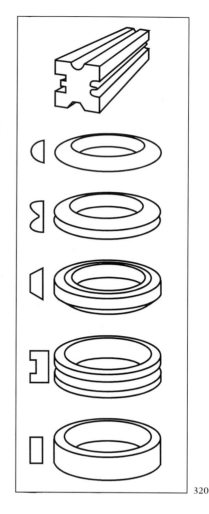

320

pressed together and smoothed out with a cool tool and cloth. To size the bangle, it is heated and pushed up the mandrel's larger diameter to the desired position, then quickly dipped into cold water to harden the lac and eliminate the chance of deformation. One advantage of a lac bangle is that it can be reduced to the smallest size on the spot by the seller by cutting it, then placing a sheet of metal under the join ends (to prevent the wearer's wrist from a burn), heating the ends with a tool, and pressing them together.

Separate narrow bangles (*chudian*) are often worn in a set (*muttha*). Five to seven bangles in graduated sizes are worn on each wrist, so ten to fourteen make a normal set. After their manufacture, sets are tied together to preserve their sequence for presentation to a client as they would appear on the wrist. In some cases the set for each wrist appears to be a series of

320. Top: *The wooden grooved block (khali) is used to create the various profile forms of lac bangles by pressing the still-plastic lac with the flat hatta into the groove selected.*

Below: *Basic profile forms for lac bangles include half-round (nim-gol), half-round with external central depression (gar), truncated pyramid (bangdi), U-shape (khappa), and flat.*

321. Calcutta, West Bengal. *c. 1798–1804 Watercolor painting of a peripatetic lac-bangle seller (left) and a village woman client (right) 7¹¹/₁₆ x 9¹/₁₆ in. (19.5 x 23 cm) Collection India Office Library and Records, London (47 ix. 137; Add. Or. 1234)*

Bangle ends are trimmed to size with a betel nut cutter (serota) (below), then heated sufficiently to soften them, and placed on the client's wrist. Ends are softened with a metal spatula heated over the charcoal fire in the ceramic dish (below), then joined by pressing them together.

322. Jaipur, Rajasthan
Lac bangle makers (manihars) here decorate a finished lac bangle with small, geometrically shaped mirrors and polychrome glass seed beads that are heated on an iron sheet placed over a small charcoal fire cooking stove (chulhi). Picked up with a tweezers, they are pressed while hot into the lac bangle, which melts locally, then cools and hardens to hold the implanted unit. Finished bangles are seen in the foreground.

321

322

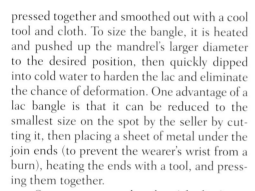

separate bangles but is permanently joined into one rigid group (*bandhachuri*). In other cases, the set is temporarily joined for presentation to a client and split apart after purchase.

The decorative treatment of lac bangles varies widely. Patterns can be created flat or stamped in relief in lac colored differently from the base. Several colors can be combined to form a cloud or marbleized pattern (*abrikam*). Small stamped metallic units or patterned metal strips can be heat-fixed to the base. Glass beads, decorative wire, small bits of geometrically shaped mirrors, or flower-shaped mirrors can be added. The possibilities are infinite.

In the rural "outback," bangles are sold on market days (*hat*), in the open market, and at special-fair (*mela*) markets. In cities they are purchased in shops, and many cities have special bangle bazaars. The one in Hyderabad-Deccan probably rates among the best.

Conch-Shell Bangles

The manufacture of bangles (S: *kadiam*; H: *bangri*; Tam: *kadagam*) and ornamental objects from conch shell (B: *shankha*; Tam: *shangku*) today, as in the past, is a specialty of West Bengal and, formerly, also of the area around Dacca in Bangladesh. An estimated twelve thousand artisans are still employed in the various stages of conch-shell bangle manufacture. Conch-shell bangles have long played a significant role in the traditional Bengali marriage ceremony. It is still common practice for the bride's father to present his daughter with at least one pair of conch-shell bangles, one for each wrist. During the marriage ceremony, the bridegroom places them on the bride's wrist as a symbol of his accepting her as his wife.

Until recent times, it was considered a religious obligation for all Bengali Hindu married women to indicate their married state (*aye stri*) by wearing these bangles. A woman was not believed "pure" unless she did so. Called in Bengal *sabitri shankha* (A: *sabit*, firm, permanent, enduring; Ben: *shankha*, conch-shell bangle), they symbolize the desire for a long married life.

Conch-shell bangles of the smallest possible diameter are worn because they will move least when on the wrist and this minimizes the chance of breaking. Once on, they are never removed. Normally they are worn for the duration of a woman's married life but are broken should she become a widow.

In West Bengal, conch-shell bangles are made by traditional Hindu craftsmen generally called Shankaris, of which Shankharakas are Shudras, and Shankha-banikas are Vaishyas. Records from the thirteenth century A.D. refer to Shankharakas as a guild, which implies that this craft is even older. Among the shell-bangle makers, a division of labor has always existed. Each phase of the process is the work of specialists—craftsmen who prepare the shell, cut the shell into sections, finish these sections, and decorate the bangles—using techniques that often require mastery in the use of special tools.

Production of conch-shell bangles is carried out at Bisnupur and Hatgram (Bankura District); Bhadreswar, Chandernagore, and Dasghora (Hooghly District); Ghoranas, Bagnapara, and Patuli (Burdwan District); Karidhya and Baram (Birbhum District); Ranaghat and Nabadwip (Nadia District); in Calcutta City in Jorashanko, Keshab Sen Street, and Baghbazar; and in other places in Murshidabad and twenty-four Parganas Districts. Formerly they were also made at Dacca, Pabna, Dinajpur, and Rangpur, now in Bangladesh, and Sylhet in Assam.

The shells used for bangles are spiral univalves of large marine snails: *Turbinella rapa*, *Turbinella pyrum*, and *Maza rapa*. Their maximum diameter of four to five inches (10–13 cm) is well suited to normal bangle dimensions.

323. Hyderabad, Andhra Pradesh
Glass bangles, lac covered, decorated with gold foil, wire, and glass seed beads, prepared in the famous central Lad Bazaar, an important bangle bazaar near the Char Minar monument, where a staggering amount and variety of bangles are sold. Those here are a Hyderabad speciality.
Collection the author, Porvoo

Lac-cum-Glass Bangles: Hyderabad, Andhra Pradesh

A unique, dazzling kind of bangle, produced in Hyderabad, Andhra Pradesh, uses a glass bangle core that is covered with lac, then decorated with glass beads (poth) and glass "stones." This technique is claimed to be a specialty of this place.

At the meeting of the four main roads in the center of Hyderabad City is a stately Mughal monument called the Char Minar (four minarets). Completed by the Kutb Shahi sovereign Muhammad Kuli Shah in 1591, each of its four high arches faces a street at the compass quarters. To the west runs the Lad Bazar, or "Street of the Beloveds" (lado means "beloved" in Hindi), so called because the houses on this street were formerly occupied by the ruler's numerous paramours.

Here are more than thirty bangle shops filled with a galaxy of glittering temptations, and above most of them are the workshops where the bangles are made. This craft is believed to have existed since Kutb Shahi times, and possibly earlier. Present-day bangle-makers are Muslims of the Mudraj and Munnur Reddi groups.

Today, particular designs are given the glamorous names of whatever Indian Hindi or Urdu movie star is currently popular and widely known by the huge audience of Indian moviegoers. A great variety of arrangements have been invented, some including colored stones as well as clear, and new arrangements are constantly being introduced to stimulate consumer interest.

324

326

327

328

A variety of these shells, called *doani*, found in coastal waters off Kerala in southern India, is especially valued for its uniform size and clear, white color. Others come from the coastal waters around Tamil Nadu, particularly in the Gulf of Manaar between India and Sri Lanka. The best find area is off Jaffnapatam in northern Sri Lanka.

The chosen conch shells are first deskinned or cleaned (*safai*) to remove any outer marine life accretions by soaking them in a detergent or a solution of hydrochloric acid. After rinsing, the shell is rubbed with sand, irregularities are filed away, and the conical top end is chopped off.

A unique saw is designed specifically to cut the shell sections. Made of a high-grade steel, it is manufactured only at Dinanathpur, Mauza Gopalpur, Burdwan District, West Bengal, and is used specifically for this purpose. The saw is an example of a tool whose form evolved over centuries to suit a special process and material. It is virtually indestructible and much less expensive than mechanical cutting tools. The cutter sits on the floor and immobilizes the shell in a viselike grip between the toes of both his feet, forcing it against an upright wooden post (*goj*) fixed in the floor. Its considerable weight allows the worker to achieve a rocking momentum in action that minimizes fatigue. Normally, it takes from three to five minutes to cut through the shell.

The saw's blade consists of a thick steel sheet about eighteen by ten inches (46 x 25.5 cm). At either blade end are two integral, upright handles. The convexly curved lower cutting edge is beveled to a thin, sharp edge, and a series of very fine "teeth" are formed by hammering along its length. The width of these tooth dents forms a kerf in the shell wide enough to prevent the blade from jamming in use.

Each shell is sliced into a series of parallel sections (*rek*) of equal width. Narrow bangle widths are called *choru*, wide widths *mota*. Ideally, four quarter-inch (6-mm) sections, the

324. *A finished wide conch-shell bangle (tunglas, this one from Ladakh) with a carved surface pattern. By Bengal tradition, a set of conch-shell bangles is given to every Hindu bride.*
Victoria and Albert Museum, London (959A 1874)

Vishnupur, West Bengal

Conch-Shell Bangle Manufacture

325. *Conch shells are prepared by chopping off their conical top ends to create an opening. Removed pieces are saved for processing into rings and large beads, the latter formerly worn tightly strung around the neck by Bengali sepoy (sipahi) soldiers, otherwise dressed in semi-European style.*

326. *The shell is cut into equal-width cross sections with a traditional, heavy, steel conch-cutting saw (shankeri korat) specially designed for this function. Normally grasped by its upright handles, it is rhythmically "rocked" over the shell to cut with minimum waste.*

327. *Sliced sections are filed on their edges and outer surface to shape them uniformly. Those from a single shell are kept together in sequence to make a set with perfectly fitting contours.*

328. *The bangle inner surface is filed by making repeated passes over a cylindrically shaped stick (danda) covered with a compound of carborundum or river sand and lac.*

329. Parlakimidi, Ganjam District, Orissa
Bangle of water-buffalo horn (moihinsi singha chuda), ornamented with inlays (munabati) of brass sheet-metal wire
Outer diameter 3¼ in. (9.5 cm); width 1 in. (2.4 cm); weight 25 g
Collection the author, Porvoo

Parlakimidi is the most important Orissan center for the manufacture of jewelry and objects made from water buffalo horn. Such bangles may also be inlaid with ivory, mother of pearl, or colored plastic.

width most commonly used, are cut from one shell. These are kept together in sequence as a set of four (*char gachi,* four strand). Five-strand (*panch gachi*), six-strand (*choi gachi*), and even seven-strand (*sat gachi*) bangles are possible, the latter when cutting an unusually large shell.

Bangles are most often worn in pairs—one on each wrist—and less often in sets of two or more on each wrist. In a set of four, normally the two middle sections are worn together as a pair on one wrist, with the two outer ones from the same shell also making a pair for the other wrist.

After sawing through the shell, remains of the bangle's interior columella volute are removed with a jeweler's saw. Any inner projections and sharp places must be ground away with an abrasive mandrel (*danda*) to make the inner surface smooth. The bangle's outer surface is also smoothed and its width equalized by rubbing it on a flat, rectangular stone (*sil*). In this state, the bangle is termed *bala shankha,* side-finished bangle.

The outer bangle surface then must be shaped to a predetermined form dictated by its planned decorative treatment. Some designs call for a flat surface and a square section. Others require a half- or completely round sectional shape. Shaping a bangle section is done with a file (*pas uko*) whose sectional shape depends on the result required. Normally, to make convexly rounded sectional forms, a flat file (*aspat uko*) is used, and, for inside rounding, a round file (*gol uko*) is used. Files are also used to make the notched edges commonly found on many shell bangles.

Relief carving (*khodai*), the repeat pattern on shell bangles, is the work of specialists who receive the bangles in their basic form. Most patterns are traditional and so familiar that it is unnecessary to draw them on the surface before carving. Others require a carefully measured divisional marking.

The carving process is done with files of different sectional shapes. Often small chisels (*chheni*) with variously shaped cutting ends are propelled by a hammer (*hathuri*). Grooves and details are made with gravers (*batali* for wide cuts, *buli* for narrow ones) similar to the burins used to engrave metal. Holes are created with a bow drill (*bhomor duali*). The carved surface is polished by rubbing it with a fine, wet abrasive such as brick dust, whiting, or chalk, which gives it a final degree of luster.

Most bangles are considered finished after polishing. Often in the past, but less frequently today, shell bangles were partially colored by picking out excavated details such as lines, circles, and holes in the design with red- and green-colored lac in stick form, applied by heating the stick end and pressing the lac into the depressions. After cooling and hardening, the surplus lac would be scraped, to bring the color level with the shell surface, and the bangle polished again.

It was once common to dye shell bangles red, an auspicious bridal color, by treating them with a mordant and immersing them in a natural or synthetic dye bath, then polishing. Colored bangles are termed *rangil shankha.* The practice is ancient and suggests an affinity with the similar coloring of ivory bangles (see page 179), which is still done in Rajasthan and Gujarat.

Also in the past, shell bangles were decorated with a cold application of gold leaf and glued-on glass beads. A set of four shell bangles lacquered red and decorated with gold leaf is called *shona mukhi.* Some bangles are made with a continuous external groove that encircles them parallel to the perimeter. Into this groove, a flat strip of 22-karat gold is fixed with rivets. If the design was carved spirally, two-ply, twisted gold wire would be wrapped in the groove. Shell bangles set with pearls and precious stones formerly were made but are now rare unless commissioned.

Ivory Bangles

For more than two thousand years, India has been a major consumer of ivory for use in ornaments and other objects. Some of this ivory came from Indian elephants (*Elephas indicus*) who inhabit jungle areas in the northeast and the south. Because of their immense size and the superior quality of the large tusks of the male (most female elephants in India are tuskless), elephants in the Garo Hills of Assam are considered to be the best in India. Other elephant habitats are in Orissa, Andhra Pradesh, and Karnataka.

Unlike the African elephant, *Loxodonta africana,* which struggles to survive in the wild, Indian elephants are domesticated and trained to do work for humans and are venerated in Indian culture. Further, because of widespread Hindu and other religious beliefs opposed to the taking of life, the major part of ivory from Indian elephants has been tusks found on dead animals or ivory cut from domesticated, living animals.

Most of the ivory used in India, however, in ancient trade between India and Africa, has always come from whole tusks from killed African elephants, and so the responsibility for the animal's death fell upon others. Indian products shipped to Mombassa, Mozambique, and Zanzibar were routinely exchanged for an annual average of more than two hundred tons of African ivory that entered India at Bombay and from there was distributed to all Indian ivory craft centers. Among those are Pali in Rajasthan, Delhi, Patiala, and Hoshiarpur in Punjab, Murshidabad in West Bengal, Cuttack and Puri in Orissa, Vishakhapatnam and Hyderabad in Andhra Pradesh, Mysore in Karnataka, and Trivandrum in Kerala. The style of work in ivory in each place is distinctive.

At the peak of its trade in the nineteenth century, ivory was delivered to an estimated ten thousand ivory craftsmen, many concen-

objects from India has ceased. Thus, the descriptions in this section refer to an industry whose demise seems imminent.

Elephant tusk or ivory (H: *hathi dant*), a greatly enlarged incisor tooth used by the animal for food gathering, and as a self-defense weapon, is composed mainly of a form of calcareous dentine, as opposed to bone. Like all mammal teeth, the tusk is embedded in a socket in the jawbone; only about half of it is visible.

A tusk's conically tapered form is solid for about half its length from tip to center. The rest contains a central, tapered cavity with the pulp or nerve, which is removed when the tusk is taken, usually by burying the tusk, allowing the pulp to decay, then washing it away. This characteristic structure is important in the manner in which ivory is utilized, and undoubtedly suggested its use for bangles and armlets.

Tusks taken from live elephants, called "green" ivory, are considered to be superior in quality to "dead" ivory, or ivory found after an animal has died a natural death. The latter term is also applied to ivory stored too long under high heat conditions, which cause it to lose its moisture and gelatine content and become brittle. When a tusk is cut from a domesticated elephant, normally the cut tusk end on the animal is capped with metal to strengthen it. The tusk continues to grow so that every two to five years an additional portion can be removed.

Indian artisans consider African ivory to be superior to indigenous ivory. An African tusk can average ten feet (300 cm) in length, while its Indian counterpart rarely reaches seven feet (180 cm). The diameter of an African tusk is also proportionally larger. Indian ivory has an opaque, dead-white color and a tendency to warp, check, and become discolored over time. African ivory has on oily, mellow, translucent tint, is less inclined to yellow in aging, and has a closer, denser texture than Indian ivory. African ivory exhibits a characteristic end grain with a translucent rhomboidal structural network, difficult to imitate in plastic, the most usual synthetic ivory substitute. This structure makes it ideal for detailed carving and piercing and suits it to lathe turning, methods used in making and decorating bangles.

Raw ivory is cured by storing it in a cool atmosphere, if possible for several years. During this time, a portion of its internal moisture is lost and it becomes denser, but it is then less likely to check when worked into objects than if worked fresh. To render it temporarily softer by increasing its moisture content and to reduce its brittleness, before carving and turning, ivory is wrapped in wet cloths for several days.

Pali, a small town near Jodhpur in Rajasthan, has for several centuries been a major center for the manufacture of ivory bangles (H: *hathi dant ka churi*), which are also made at Barmer and Merta in Rajasthan, Ahmadabad in Gujarat, and other places in northern India. By tradition, rural women in Rajasthan

330. Banni, Kachchh, Gujarat
Meghval woman wearing a full set (chudiyon) of sixteen upper-arm and twelve lower-arm ivory bangles, a total, on both arms, of fifty-six bangles, almost equivalent to one ivory tusk, plus others of gold and glass. She also wears a long silver chain necklace (chandan har or gallegi) with flower links (chinka), suspending a charm pendant (madaliya); and a silver spiral wire necklace (varlo).

trated in northwestern India, where ivory bangles were worn in profusion by rural women, a practice now in decline.

Today the import of African ivory to India has been severely curtailed, and the use of Indian ivory in India has been banned. The numbers of ivory craftsmen is now reduced to about two thousand. With the international adoption of restrictions against the import of all objects made of ivory, the export of ivory

Pali, Rajasthan

IVORY BANGLE MANUFACTURE

331. *Schematic system for cutting bangles from one average-length ivory tusk. Tusk divisions are (left to right): nok, point; mudiya, extremity or head; chatta, one quarter; banbu, open. Internal cuts (below, left to right): two cylinders; three cylinders; two cylinders; three cylinders. Total sixty-three bangles.*

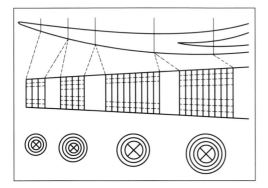

332. *Ivory bangles are turned on a hand-bow-driven lathe (sanghada). The cutting tool rests on an iron bar and is guided by the hand and toes. Cutting concentric bangles from solid ivory stock is accomplished with special lathe cutting tools with bent, pointed ends designed for this function.*

333. *Finished, turned ivory bangles tied together in sets of graduated sizes. The central group, dyed red, is decorated with strips of die-stamped gold sheet.*

and Gujarat wear a great number of ivory bangles because of a common belief that this will keep a woman healthy and assure her ease in childbirth. Throughout India, an old but dying custom calls for a bride's maternal uncle to present her with an ivory bangle, worn as an amulet and never removed during the first year of her marriage.

Today about two hundred Pali craftsmen produce ivory bangles to satisfy the demand of rural women, especially in Rajasthan and Gujarat but also in the Punjab, Central India, and parts of Uttar Pradesh. Their use, however, is declining due to the ever increasing cost of ivory, which accounts for the growing substitution of off-white plastic, similar in appearance to ivory.

In Rajasthan and Gujarat, an ideal set of ivory bangles includes seventeen (called *chura*) worn on the upper arm, and nine (called *muthia*) worn on the lower arm, a total of fifty-two on both arms. Some women wear only the *muthia* on the lower arm. Never removed, they are worn during a woman's entire married life.

The bangle makers of Pali divide the tusk into four parts as shown in the diagram. The *nok* is too small in diameter for bangles and has been removed and sold to other ivory makers, who manufacture small articles from it. The solid *mudiya* is used for *muthi* bangles, and the solid *chatta* for *chura* bangles. The hollow *banbu* is used for the manufacture of a multitude of carved objects.

To make ivory bangles, the tusk is first cut into sections of fifteen to thirty inches (38–76 cm) in length. From these are cut smaller lengths—three to three and a half inches (7.5–8.75 cm) for *chura* making, two to five inches (5–12.75 cm) for *muthia* bangles. Each of the solid parts is then divided into concen-

tric cylinders from which separate bangles are cut. On one *chura* section, for example, inside cuts are made (depending on the diameter of the ivory used) to create two or three cylinders, each of which is then divided by nine sectional cuts into ten bangles, each about a half-inch (10 mm) in width. A similar process is applied to each *muthia* section. The result is a complete range of bangle sizes.

All these cuts are made while the ivory, solid or cylinder, is mounted horizontally on a manually operated lathe (*jhindra* or *kharad*). Prior to cutting, the outer, barklike surface is shaved away to uncover the inner, usable ivory, the form is dressed to a true cylinder, and the positions for cutting the internal cylinders are marked with a compass. A specially designed tool (*singari*) with a small, angled, sharp end is used to make internal cuts.

After cutting, the surface of the bangle must be finished. To decorate it with incised lines or contoured depressions, the bangle is mounted on a conically tapered mandrel fixed between the lathe center points, and the areas to be removed are excavated with an appropriately end-shaped lathe cutting tool. To polish the surface, a rough leaf dipped in water or

chalk is used, the latter applied to a damp cloth and pressed against the rotating bangle, followed by washing in soap and water.

Bangles referred to today as *fancy churi* are those ornamented with carved linear patterns, or drilled with dots or small circles made with a hollow drill point mounted on a bow drill. As in the case of shell bangles, these depressions are filled with colored lac in stick form, simply by pressing the lac stick against the rotating bangle. Rotational friction melts the lac, which fills the depressions, and any surplus is removed by scraping while the bangle rotates. Bangles might also be ornamented with paint or dye, beads, and gold leaf so that little of the ivory is visible. As recently as 1903, there was a considerable manufacture in Pali of highly ornamental ivory bangles, but today this is rarely done.

Ivory bangles are, however, still made with a central depression into which a strip of gold, plain or stamp-patterned, is fixed. This type is usually dyed red. Red-dyed ivory bangles are considered to be auspicious and are given as a gift to a bride.

In earlier times, the primary source of a permanent red dye was the Indian madder plant

334. Gujarat
Two sets of red-dyed ivory bangles (dantin chudo ambadani) for upper and lower arm, given to a bride by her father. Their grooved surface has an inserted embossed strip of silver or gold.
Collection C. S. Grewal. New Delhi

335. Pali, Rajasthan
Ivory-bangle merchant arranging sets of bangles with gold-strip inserts

334

335

336

336. Saurashtra and Kachchh, Gujarat
Red-dyed ivory bangle (chudo), inset with a gold, relief-stamped strip of an exuberant, wish-fulfilling vine (kalpalata), fixed into a groove, worn by Kanbi women and other groups
Collection Ivory, New York

337. Bombay, Maharashtra
Ivory cuff (hathi dant ka chur) ornamented with elaborate pierced work and carving. Similar ones are now made here of plastic decorated with gold ornaments.
Approximate height 4 in. (19 cm)

337

Ivory bangles are made in Surat, Gujarat, and Pali, Rajasthan, by the Brahmakshatriya community, whose artisans (hathi-dant chudigars) produce them for the Hindu community. The number a woman wears, and their weight, are an indica-tion of her social and economic status. Today a diminished ivory-bangle production contin-ues and is busiest during the marriage season (November to May), when they are most in demand for a bride's dowry.
Collection Ivory, New York

338. Kachchh, Gujarat
*Ivory bangles (baloyun) dyed an
auspicious red*
Collection Ivory, New York

**339. Saurashtra and
Kachchh, Gujarat**
*Hourglass-shaped, red-dyed ivory
bracelet (baloyun), made in two
parts held together by three
vertically inserted metal rods*
4⁵⁄₁₆ x 3⅛ in. (11 x 8 cm);
weight 302 g
*Collection Jacques Carcanagues,
New York*

It is worn, until widowhood or
death, on the left arm by married
Dhebaria, Vaghadia, and Jhala-
vadi Rebari women.

340. Rajasthan
Carved Ivory Bangle Patterns

Top to bottom: Diamond cut
(hira); litchee fruit skin (litchi);
ripples on water (jaltarangu);
caterpillar (kira); paddy stem
(chawal); twisted rope (gathi);
points (gokhri); creeper (lata);
conch shell lotus (shankhu
padda); bangle protome terminals
of carved makara head

(*Rubia tinctorum*)—a perennial evergreen shrub whose dye principle, alizarine, is contained chiefly in the cortex of its long, slender roots—widely cultivated in India for this purpose for at least two thousand years. Porous ivory readily absorbs mordant and dye solutions. To achieve a brilliant, permanent red, alum was the necessary mordant. After a mordant bath, the ivory bangle was steeped in a boiling dye-bath solution. Upon removal, it was immediately plunged into cold water to prevent cracking. The dyeing process could be repeated to deepen the color and eliminate color irregularities.

Synthetic red dye whose chemical composition is identical with the natural dye was introduced to India from Europe about 1871. In combination with the same alum mordant, it can produce an even more uniform result than the natural dye and with far less trouble. Little wonder that synthetic red dyes were quickly and enthusiastically accepted and predominate today.

In recent years, old or broken bangles collected by merchants and divided or reassembled by joining the parts with metal fittings and a hinge, have become a popular fashion jewelry export item to the West. Many of these were red-dyed ivory bangles and still retain traces of reddish tones on their surface, even after surface abrasion has caused most of the color to wear away. Foreigners who purchase these bangles consider this worn color a part of the bangle's charm.

As mentioned, many workers in this traditional bangle craft have turned to using preformed tubes of white plastic for bangles, which are bought as substitutes by tradition-minded women who cannot afford the ivory originals and will not give up the custom of wearing such bangles. Their manufacture is carried out in essentially the same way as described for ivory. Wide ivory-colored plastic cuffs, elaborately ornamented with pierced work and even appliqués of 22-karat gold units riveted in place, are made in Bombay and probably represent the ultimate in the refined use of this synthetic material.

In a similar way, in Parlakimidi, Orissa, bangles are made of sections through water buffalo horn, highly polished. Most of these are left plain, but the best are carefully inlaid in geometric patterns with small pieces of ivory or white plastic, and brass units in the manner of giant piqué work.

Glass Bangles

In their excavations of Indus Valley Culture sites, archaeologists have unearthed bangle fragments of a material they termed "vitreous paste." A misnomer, this is probably a compound of colored frit added in powdered form to fine clay and made into bangles that were blue (with cobalt oxide), green (with copper oxide), or another color with the appropriate oxide added. These bangles were either rolled out or formed in a clay or wooden mold, dried, and fired at a relatively low temperature. Their color is not just on the bangle surface—as in glazed clay or steatite bangles—but is uniform throughout the bangle body, and their surface is smooth. If this material had been heated to a high enough temperature (above 1260° F; 685° C, the point at which vitrification occurs), the result would have been a kind of glass, but this was not done. As a result, the composition was only partially fused, so by definition it was not vitrified and does not quite qualify as true glass. Still, frit-paste bangles must be looked upon as the ancestors of the true glass Indian bangles that appeared in the next millennium.

It is significant that the earliest known glass objects made in India were beads and glass bangles, both of which do not require glass-blowing technology. At sites such as Hastinapura (1100–800 B.C.) and Taxila (700–300 B.C.), fragments of true glass bangles have been found. The Mauryan Stratum II at Taxila (c. 400 B.C.) produced composite-colored glass-bangle fragments, with green and yellow, blue and yellow, and black and white combinations predominating. The use of color and the glass manipulating techniques of twisting, swirling, dotting, stratifying, and folding with which these glass bangles were formed and decorated indicate a fairly advanced glass technology (blowing not included), whose sophistication implies an earlier development.

The wide distribution of later archaeological sites where glass beads and bangle fragments have been found, such as Kausambi, Maheshwar, Nagda, Patna, Paithan, Sravasti, and Ujjain, tells us that glass technology must have rapidly spread throughout the entire subcontinent. By the eighth or ninth century A.D.—known as the early Indian medieval period—glass bangles were virtually in universal use. Glass bangles from the twelfth to thirteenth century A.D., excavated at Sirpur, Andhra Pradesh, exhibit advanced decoration technology. The Muslim invaders reached India in the twelfth century. From then on through the Mughal period, important developments occurred in indigenous glass technology, particularly in blown-glass forms.

Mughal rulers lavishly patronized all the arts, and their style and high standard of excellence had profound impact on Indian cultural life. The reigns of Jahangir and Shah Jahan were especially conducive to cultural developments. They encouraged the immigration of foreign craftsmen with special skills—such as glassmakers and enamelists from Persia—to work at the royal workshops. In the seventeenth century, Aurangzeb augmented the Muslim bangle-making community in northern India by his forceful conversion to Muhammadanism of Hindu bangle makers of the Maniar caste. In the South, bangle makers generally remained Hindu.

In the nineteenth century, indigenous glass-bangle manufacture was threatened by

341. Pochampalli, Andhra Pradesh
A married woman of this weaver community wearing a typical assortment of glass bangles (palingku kadagam). She is preparing a warp for the yarn-dyed, tie-dyeing technique, a weaving specialty of this place.

the import of enormous quantities of cheap glass bangles from China, followed by glass-making centers in Czechoslovakia and Germany. The competitive price of their products undercut even the low cost of Indian glass bangles (H: *desi bangda*, home country bangles), and their manufacture foundered until, ironically, relief came during World Wars I and II, when competition from imports ceased. In those times, Indians had no recourse but to buy indigenous products and the Indian glass-bangle industry flourished.

Today, the vicissitudes of the industry have greatly reduced the number of Indian glass-bangle producing centers. Another unprecedented threat to its existence has appeared: plastic bangles, a product of modern chemical technology. Bangle-making centers such as Tarapur, Maharashtra, are in a state of incipient disappearance; however, one remains healthy and active at Firozabad in Uttar Pradesh.

Firozabad, a shabby but bustling town of about 120,000 in the Agra District of Uttar Pradesh, is the largest center of Indian glass bangle–making, an industry that engages about 95,000 of its inhabitants and many more in the surrounding villages. In this century the industry has grown considerably there. In 1932 the town boasted of 23 glassworks; now there are more than 150 separate factory units, the largest employing about 150 men. Firozabad also has the largest concentration of wholesale dealers in glass bangles.

A visit to Firozabad is an amazing encounter. Glass bangles are visible literally everywhere. The main street and side lanes are lined with bangle-making and decorating factories. Streets here are simply extensions of the factory premises. Uncountable numbers of finished bangles tied together are piled high on the ubiquitous wood-framed, cord-strung Indian beds (*charpai*) (used at night for sleeping by some of the workers), awaiting transport to local decorating factories or to be sorted, packed, and loaded onto trucks that each day take them by the millions to bangle merchants at bazaars all over India and abroad.

The Firozabad glass-bangle industry, like others, is divided into specialties, each group supplying the other at various stages of manufacture and decoration. Some factories make only the basic block glass; the largest number create the glass-bangles; particular factories weld the bangle ends together; and decoration is the specialty of others. Work is farmed out to small units in the city or in the surrounding villages.

In the past hundred years, the survival of the indigenous glass bangle–making industry was threatened by cheap foreign imports. Total dependence upon hand power nearly spelled its doom. Today, wherever possible, modern equipment and mechanized power are used, although many processes must still be done by hand. Thus, of the two basic types of glass bangles, jointless and jointed, jointless bangles, made by an old technique rarely used today, are not described here. The majority of contemporary glass bangles are made by mass-production methods in which jointing is necessary.

Block glass, the raw material for glass bangles, is locally produced in various translucent and opaque colors. Placed in a crucible in

a furnace whose seven circularly arranged openings each contain a crucible with glass of a different color, the block is melted.

In the most common method used for bangle manufacture in Firozabad, the bangle maker (*churigar*) gathers a lump of molten glass on the end of a hook-ended pontil (*ankri*) and smooths it into a cone-shaped parison by rolling it on a marver. This is passed to another worker, who draws out the end of the lump into a rod or cane. Its end is attached to a hook at the small diameter end of a tapered fire-clay mandrel, and while the glass remains viscous, the cane is wound upon the four-foot-long (122 cm) fire-clay mandrel (*kulbut*) to form a continuous spiral several feet long. About 180 to 200 turns, each one a future bangle, can be made on a standard mandrel whose tapered diameter corresponds to standard inside-diameter bangle sizes. These sizes start at one and one-eighth inches (2.8 cm) for a child, and progress at intervals of one-eighth of an inch (3 mm) to the largest inside diameter, which is three inches (7.5 cm). The greatest production of bangles have inside diameters that range between two and one-eighth and two and a quarter inches (5.5 and 5.7 cm). The spiral is allowed to cool and is removed from the mandrel and annealed, a process of slow cooling in a chamber to temper and strengthen the glass and eliminate internal stresses that could cause the glass to spontaneously fracture later.

Specialist cutters (*kataiya*) divide the spiral into single bangle units by line-scoring the glass along the dividing point with a diamond-pointed scribing tool. Each turn of the spiral is broken at the scored line to make a single bangle. These are passed to the joiner (*juraiya*), who heats the two ends in the flame of a jet kerosene lamp to bring the glass to the necessary state of viscosity. With a small tongs (*chimti*), he presses the two ends together to make a joint (*jor*) that welds them into a bangle. Bangles that do not require any surface decoration are now finished.

Bangle decoration can be of two basic types: those done on hot glass and those carried out on cold glass, the latter in some cases followed by reheating. Each process is done in a separate factory by specialists in that technique. Because of the heat generated, hot-glass decorators generally work at night, and cold glass decorators by day. Particular types of bangles are made for specific kinds of decoration techniques.

Each decoration technique has several variants, most of which are also used in glass-bead manufacture. Because they are labor intensive, decorated bangles are more expensive than ordinary ones and are considered to be the superior products of the industry.

Among the bangle decorating techniques that require the use of heat are the following:

Press-pattern molds with intaglio patterns are stamped (*chapna*) over the hot glass cane to impart a design in relief.

Firozabad, Uttar Pradesh

GLASS BANGLE MANUFACTURE

343. *Glass bangles are prepared by the cutter (*kataiya*) at center, who scores the whole coil length with a diamond-tipped tool, then passes them to a man who breaks them apart at the place scored. They are then passed to the man at upper left, who ties them into bundles to be sent to the joiner (*juraiya*).*

344. *The ends of the glass bangles are welded together by applying heat from a kerosene torch, after which they are placed on a shelf to cool.*

Pinching (*nochna*) or nipping the glass cane with a small tongs raises ribbed forms in relief.

Folding (*lapetna*) creates a pattern on a two-or-more-color layered cane. By folding one over the other, an undulating pattern results that is then marvered to create a flush, smooth surface.

Two-ply twisted strand bangles are made by twisting together (*batnai*) two polychromed elements while the glass is viscous. The result, called *rassi* (a thin rope), is like a twisted rope or cable.

342. Varanasi, Uttar Pradesh. *c. 1815–20*
Watercolor painting, labeled, "Choorey walla's Bhaultey (furnace) for making Glass Jewells"
9⅞ x 7½ in. (25 x 19 cm)
Collection India Office Library and Records, London (89 i-c xxi; Add. Or. 141)

One of one hundred illustrations, bound in two volumes, depicting traditional craft occupations. This shows glass bangle makers with their glass-melting furnace, working in a manner little changed from that of present-day Firozabad, the center for glass bangle making in India.

345

346

347

Externally cased glass canes are made of two colors, one overlaid on the other in distinct layers of approximately equal thickness. When the outer layer is thin, it is called flashing. The cane can be left this way to make a solid colored bangle, or used for cold cut decorations that expose the inside color.

Internally cased glass canes are made with a pattern encased within a solid glass rod. For example, a cane may contain two opaque colors twisted together, encased within clear glass.

Internally mirrored canes are made of hollow tubes (khukhla nal), used to make a very popular kind of glass bangle called reshmi, "like silk," because of its satinlike, shining appearance. The process combines cold- and heat-requiring techniques. The cold tube is cut into bangle lengths. The inner space is silvered by drawing into it a silver nitrate solution, the procedure the same as when making a mirror. Reshmi silvered tubes can be used round or heated and flattened to form a wider bangle. Joints are made with heat.

Color layering (rang rakhnewala) is a technique in which one color is melted (ranga-hona) on top of another. This kind of cane does not require more than joining to finish the bangle, but it can also be subjected to other processes, such as cold cutting, to reveal the lower color.

Trailing is a method by which a colored glass thread is drawn from the molten mass and trailed over the surface of a second colored glass. Trails can be left in relief on the surface, or the surface can be smoothed level with a tool. The trailed color can be tool swirled while hot to manipulate it into various patterns. Cane lengths are also spirally wrapped

with a trailed glass thread, the result left in relief or smoothed.

Prunting is the technique of making colored spots or small beadlike blobs on the surface that stand out in relief. A contrasting colored glass cane is heated to redness with a kerosene torch (the technique is called lamp-work), and the heated glass is touched to the surface and quickly withdrawn, leaving a raised spot. These may be applied to the bangle in many different arrangements.

Enameled glass (mina, colored enamel) involves the use of this glasslike substance for decoration. Enamel ground to a fine paste is mixed with an oil base, painted on a finished bangle, and allowed to set. To fuse the enamel to the glass, the bangle is fired in a muffle kiln at a temperature lower than that needed for fusing the glass bangle itself and then cooled slowly. Opaque enamel colors are generally used, and the result appears in low relief on the bangle.

Gilded bangles, termed sonabai (sona, gold), are very popular in western and southern India. In gilding, the surface must be clean and grease free. The design is painted on with a liquid gold luster containing fine particle gold suspended in an oil. The result is allowed to dry, then fired in a muffle kiln (pajaya) at a low temperature. During firing, the oil binder burns away leaving a gold deposit on the glass.

Cut-grinding (san-katna), the major cold decorating process, uses small rotating grind-stones and is carried out on thicker, better quality bangles so the cutting does not weaken them. Cutting is normally done on round-sectioned (gola) bangles, the form best adapted to both faceting and linear cutting processes. Sometimes cased glass bangles are cut to ex-

345. Basic Glass-Bangle Sectional Forms

Top to bottom: Round (gola); flat strip (patti); equilateral triangle (kamp or tri-kona); knife or isoceles triangle (chhuri); square (chaupela); half-round, or "pure" (nirala); thin rope (rassi, two colors twisted together); flat metallic yarn (badla, flat metal wire wrapped around a supporting thread core)

346. In a final decoration process, gold luster, prepared in the two cups below, is mixed with an oil medium in the bottle and poured into a tube applicator. This is applied to the glass bangle, dried, then heated to fix the luster to the glass.

347. Typical glass bangle factory, one of many in Firozabad, that specialize in cut-glass-bangle decoration. All the lined-up grinding wheels operate on a common motor-driven shaft.

▼ **348.** Traditional Cut Patterns on Glass Bangles

Top to bottom: pillar (khambha); scissors qainchi); net (jal); cup (donchi katori); and diamond (hira).

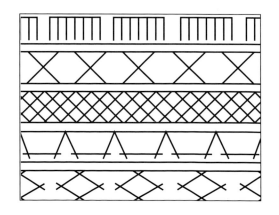

pose the color below the surface color. Cut-grinding glass is a technique essentially derived from lapidary work.

According to cutters here, there exist more than one thousand possible design cut patterns. To achieve them, the cutter presses the bangle against a small rotating grinding wheel with different profiles: flat for facet cutting; U-shaped for flutes; or V-shaped face for grooves or mitres. Cutting leaves the cut surface matte, so the cuts are polished with a fine abrasive, which restores brightness.

Glass-Bangle Symbolism: *Subhagya*

An important concept associated with glass bangles—and in some places also with those of lac, shell, ivory, and iron—has been crucial in keeping this industry alive. This is the universal Indian idea that glass bangles identify the wearer as a married woman (S: *subhaga*), who ideally is a favorite wife beloved by her husband and the honored mother of a family, including sons. *Subhagya* represents the state of being a woman in those happy circumstances, and *subhagi* is an adjective meaning "lucky."

The death of a woman before that of her husband is interpreted as a reward for her goodness; however, when a woman's married life ends with her husband's death, she enters the sad condition of widowhood (S: *vidhava*), and bangle symbolism again comes to the fore. By tradition, the lamenting woman breaks her glass bangles (H: *churi thandi hona*), as much in anticipation of her enforced circumspect future as a widow as for her loss.

This custom was already common during the Mughal period, as confirmed by statements in the writings of contemporary European travelers in India. For instance, Johan Huyghen van Linschoten, a Dutchman in India in 1588, recorded in his journal that in Malabar (Kerala), "When a husband dies, a Brahman wife breaks all her jewels [bangles] ... for they are mostly of glasse."

Glass bangles are available in every bazaar. Some bangle sellers (H: *churi faroshinda*) cater to women who live in purdah (P: *parda,* behind the curtain), traveling from household to household in cities and towns, or farther afield to nearby towns and villages in the "interior," to dispose of their wares. In the lives of secluded women, the seller's arrival was, and still is, an exciting event. All the ladies and girls of the household flock around the seller to examine bangles, make their purchases, and have them placed on their wrists. A male bangle seller is the only one of his sex allowed to touch a woman who is not his wife or daughter, which he must do when placing the bangles on the client's wrist. In some houses, even this is not permitted, and only women sellers are allowed entry.

Glass bangles are worn by women of all classes of society, rich and poor. They may also be worn by girls, but, for a married woman,

A Mannilla or Glass Bracelet maker

349. Firozabad, Uttar Pradesh
Glass bangles (churi) of superior quality are made in an immense variety of colors and surface treatments.
Collection the author, Porvoo

350. Thanjavur, Tamil Nadu.
Late 18th century
Occupational (Company) painting of an itinerant glass-bangle seller and his wife
9⅞ x 7⅝ in. (25 x 19.3 cm)
British Museum, London (1974-6-17-07.30)

The bangle seller holds his stock of bangles in a cloth bag slung over his left shoulder. Others, strung on a cord, are held in his right hand. His arms and torso are marked with Vaishnavite sectarian symbols. His wife holds bangles displayed on cloth cylinders and wears bangles and gold ornaments in use by her caste group (Manihars).

351. *Glass-bangle merchant and his wife in the Firozabad bangle bazaar*

352. Bhopal, Madhya Pradesh
Woman having a new set of glass bangles placed on her wrist by a bangle seller (manihar) in a street bazaar. This is the only time in which an unrelated man is permitted to touch another man's wife.

their symbolism makes them a necessity. Generally between eight and twelve glass bangles are worn on each wrist, twenty-four in two matching sets, but no rigid rules about numbers exist. Today glass bangles are often combined with those of gold.

Buyers wear bangles of the smallest diameter size that will pass over the hand onto the wrist and hold the bangle in place in the approximately six inches (15 cm) between the wrist and the forearm. Loose bangles that fall toward the elbow when the arm is raised are not considered elegant or attractive. Besides, glass bangles are relatively fragile, and looseness would simply increase the chance of breakage.

Purchasing glass bangles has its hazards. Because of their closed form and small diameter, placing bangles on a wrist by the seller can be a painful experience. Even though the woman's outer hand and wrist are lubricated with oil to help in sliding them on, the seller must fold back her thumb and its fleshy part over the palm to force the hand into as small a sectional circumference as possible. Starting with the largest, which will go highest on the arm, each bangle is slowly pushed inch by inch (or millimeter by millimeter) over the widest place until it passes safely onto the wrist. The client often suffers afterward from hand swelling and develops black and blue marks as temporary mementoes of the experience.

If during this process a bangle breaks, some take it as a sign of bad luck or an omen

of an unhappy event to come. More immediately, a broken bangle can cause a gash so that blood is shed in the fitting process. All such dangers and pain are willingly endured as a necessary sacrifice to achieve *subhagya*, not to mention the satisfaction of personal vanity.

The range of colors available in glass bangles today is enormous. Women of various groups favor bangles of a special color or colors considered appropriate for a particular time of the year or for a special occasion. Hindus tend to prefer tones of pink at the time of the Holi festival or Spring Saturnalia, or yellow in recognition of wild spring flowers. Muslims prefer green, a color commonly associated with that religion. Among sophisticated urban women, bangle color is chosen to match the sari of the day. Brides, of course, wear red bangles, their auspicious color. In some communities, widows are permitted to wear black bangles.

Metal Bangles

Metal bangles, popular because of their durability, are worn in pairs, alone, or combined with bangles of other materials. They can be made of gold, silver, copper, bronze, brass, and zinc alloy (bidri), the choice of metal reflecting the buyer's social rank and status. The whole range of metal fabrication and decoration are used in their creation, including casting (355), sheet-metal fabrication and pierced work (354), and enameling and gemstone setting (356).

353. Bikaner, Rajasthan
Woman wearing pairs of silver guard bangles (khatria or bangri gokru) with ball perimeters (pacheli, a regional variant of 354) and others between them. Using powdered rice, chalk, and colored pigments, she is preparing a traditional floor decoration (mandana) for the celebration of the Lakshmi Puja.

354. Jodhpur, Rajasthan
Gilded-silver guard bangles
Outer diameter 3¹⁵/₁₆ in. (10 cm); inner diameter 2½ in. (6.3 cm); weight of pair 269 g
Collection the author, Porvoo

Worn above and below a series of bangles or bracelets placed between them (see 294). Similar types are made elsewhere in Rajasthan and Gujarat.

355. Rajasthan
Cast-brass guard bangles (khatria), worn in pairs on each arm, above and below a series of bangles or bracelets
Outer diameter 4¾ in. (12 cm); weight 316 g
Collection Anne Jernandier de Vriese, Brussels

356. Punjab
Punjabi woman wearing gold bangles, enameled and set with gemstones, and other gold ornaments typical of the area. Punjabi Sikh men wear a plain steel bangle (kara) as one of the five external symbols (panj kakke), all beginning with the letter k, worn by male members of the sect, a practice introduced by Guru Govind Singh (1666–1708) that continues today.

353

355

354

356

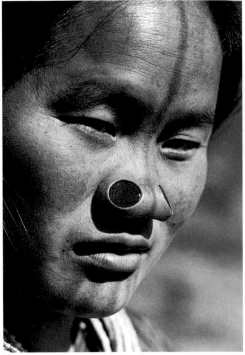

357

358

359

Nose Ornaments as Marriage Symbols

The concept of boring the nose (one nostril, both nostrils, the septum, or combinations of these) for the insertion of a nose-held ornament seems to have been current in Central Asia and Persia before the custom appeared in India. The earliest references to nose ornaments in India occur in Sanskrit literature after about 1250, which corresponds with the time of the Muslim invasions.

Once the custom of its use was established, the nose ring acquired substantial significance in Indian culture. Most generally, when worn in the left nostril it symbolically indicated that the wearer was a married woman, a meaning that still prevails especially in northern India. Because the nose ring symbolizes *subhagya*, it is worn only while a woman's husband is alive and must be discarded when she becomes a widow.

Nose rings do not appear in lists of ornaments given in ancient treatises that describe jewelry, nor are they found on Indian sculpture until about the sixteenth century. They are known to have been in use at the Mughal court, based on several references to them in contemporary European writings and in miniature paintings. Perhaps at first Hindus considered them to be a Muslim ornament. With their eventual acceptance, however, their use spread over the entire Indian subcontinent.

Superstitions evolved connected with the custom of nose-ring use. It became common, especially among rural people, for the nose of a newborn girl child to be bored (H: *nak bindhna*). By so doing, the child acquired an

357. Ziro, Lower Subansiri District, Arunachal Pradesh
Apatani woman wearing two wooden nose plugs (dat). Women's faces here are traditionally tattooed with a central vertical line from forehead to nose end and on the chin.

358. Orissa
Kondh tribal woman wearing a pair of large, gold-disc nose studs (kailegi) and a septum ornament. Her forehead and chin are tattooed with linear patterns.

359. Tatiana, Sirmur District, Himachal Pradesh
Married woman wearing a gold nose ring (nath), whose heavy weight is supported by three silver chains with end hooks fixed in the cloth head covering. A broad chain goes to the back-of-the-head, circular ornament (leju). In the opposite nostril (not seen), she wears a small nose stud (laung). Additional ornaments include the choker (gera) and earrings (kante).

360

360. Kachchh, Gujarat
Gold nose ring (nathadi) ornamented with granulation, stamped units, and gemstones
Diameter 2 in. (5 cm)
Collection Michel Postel, Bombay

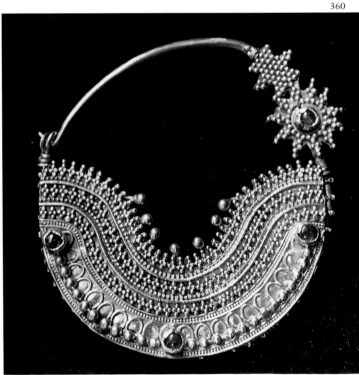

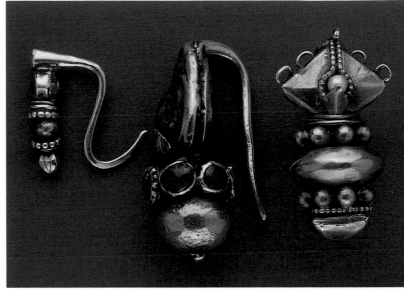

361

362

361. Chamba, Kangra, Mandi District, Himachal Pradesh
Gold nose ring (balu), set with diamonds and pearls, worn by upper-class Hindu women
Courtesy Roopchand Jewellers, New Delhi

362. Southern India
Gold nose studs (mukkuththi), in the north called laung (clove)
Left to right: 2¹⁵⁄₁₆ x ³⁄₁₆ in. (2.2 x 0.5 cm);
1⁹⁄₁₆ x ⅞ in. (4 x 2.2 cm);
1½ x ¾ in. (3.8 x 1.8 cm)
Collection Ghysels, Brussels

363. Punjab ➤
Bride wearing traditional Punjabi ornaments: forehead pendant (chand-tikka); nose ring (nath) supported by a pearl-strung chain hooked to the hair; earrings (karanphul); and necklaces. All are set kundan style with diamonds, rubies, emeralds, and pearls. Typically, the head-cloth (dopatta) worn by brides in this area is ornamented with gold thread ribbons and tinsel appliqués.

365

366

unattractive "deformity," which made it less vulnerable to attack by evil spirits, illness, or death.

In India ornaments for the nose are of three basic types: the stud, the nose ring, and the septum ornament. In the north, the stud is generally called *laung,* Hindi for "clove," which it resembles, or *phuli,* meaning "little flower." In the south it is given the Tamil term *mukkuththi.* Studs can simply be a gold hook with a small, decorative head, or even a diamond; or a flat disk whose surface is elaborately decorated and whose reverse side has a post that passes through the hole in the nostril. Inside the nostril, a nut is screwed on the threaded post end to secure the ornament.

The general northern Indian term for a nose ring is *nath,* with many regional variants. In Sanskrit, *nath* means "Lord, master, protector, husband"; in Hindi, besides indicating a nose ring, *nath* also refers to a rope passed

through the nose of a draft animal. The inescapable implication is that the *nath* nose ring is a symbol of a man's control over a woman after their marriage.

The *nath* can be of any size, from a simple, small wire ring to an extraordinarily large and profusely decorated one, depending on local cultural customs and economics. Large, heavy nose rings lie on the cheek and must be supported by an attached chain or chains and hook that pass to the hair, head cloth, or hat into which it is hooked; otherwise, they would distort the shape of the nose, as they sometimes do in any case.

The ornament that hangs below a hole pierced through the septum is known by the Hindi term *bulaq* in the north, and in the south by the Tamil term *bulakku.* This too can range from a modest ring to a very large, elaborate ornament that hangs over the mouth and must be lifted up when eating.

364. Jogindar Nagar, Mandi District, Himachal Pradesh (opposite page)
Married woman wearing a gold nose ring (balu) ornamented with gemstones and pearls, and a septum ornament (bulak) hung with leaf-shaped pendants (jhamkan). Its heavy weight is supported by a chain hooked to the head covering. Diameter 5½ in. (14 cm)

365. Kachchh, Gujarat
Mutwa woman wearing a gold septum-nose ring (chand-ko-bulaq or buladi) of crescent-moon shape, a side-of-nose stud (phul), and other traditional silver ornaments

366. Rewalsar, Himachal Pradesh
Gold granulation-decorated nose-septum ring (bulaq or kundu) worn by local married women in conjunction with the side-of-nose stud (phul)

Unique Vernacular Ornaments

Temple Jewelry

The Hindu Temple Complex and Treasury

A spiritual map of India would indicate many major and minor Hindu temple complexes (S: *kshetra,* sacred place) scattered all over the country but concentrated especially in the south, where they are called by the Sanskrit term *mat'h.* Within a surrounding wall are the main temple shrine (H: *dev-mandir*), sacred to the particular deity worshiped by the sect (H: *panth*), and residences for the monastic community, which includes the senior temple priest or superior abbot (H: *mahant;* S: *mat'h-dhari*) and his resident disciples (S: *chela*). Also present may be a shrine to the sect founder (A: *samadh*) and one or more buildings to accommodate pilgrims (S: *dharamshala*).

Temples of any size also possess a treasury (S: *dhanasthana*), controlled by a treasurer (S: *dhana-adhyaksha*). In it is kept all objects of value owned by the *mat'h.* The amount of jewelry and precious objects accumulated by a temple over the years can be immense. Unfortunately, as history has shown, owning such riches has repeatedly made temple treasuries the targets of rival kingdoms, foreign marauders, or militant Muslims bent on suppressing the idol-worshiping infidels. Temple treasuries were periodically pillaged by vandals and zealots and their entire contents carried off as booty. Surviving accounts describe such raids on the well-known temples at Dwarka, Modhera, and others. Because such raids no longer take place, in modern times reputed temples, such as that dedicated to Shri Venkateshwara (a form of Vishnu who grants salvation to all) in Tirupati, Tamil Nadu, have acquired immense storehouses of wealth.

The existence of this accumulated wealth can be traced to the Hindu concept of pilgrimage (S: *yatra;* Tam: *thirththayaththirai*) to one or several temples, or sacred places such as the Ganges River at Varanasi, in order to achieve salvation (S: *mukti*). The pilgrimage makes possible a more favorable rebirth, eternal life in the hereafter, and ultimately the attainment of Nirvana or Absorption with the Divine. The vow (S: *vrata*) to undertake such a pilgrimage (S: *yatra diksha*) and its fulfillment may, how-

367. Madurai, Tamil Nadu
Bazaar oleograph of Minakshi-Devi (the fish-eyed goddess), consort of Sundareshvara (Shiva), and the main deity of the temple complex at Madurai. She wears the high crown (kiriti mukuta) of a major deity and traditional ornaments of a wealthy south Indian woman, including: a tight necklace (adigai, with a central thali); a necklace of gold pagoda coins (kasumalai, see 207); and a necklace (chilaka haram) with a central pendant in the form of a two-headed bird (antarantapatcippatakkam, see 372). The practice of decorating the image of a deity with jewelry (shringar), flower garlands, and the waving of lights in front of it is believed to make its beholding a great pleasure and blessing.

ever, be motivated by other than spiritual reasons. Pilgrims solicit divine intervention in effecting solutions to the difficulties resulting from daily problems and human relationships. Among these are the promotion of domestic felicity or conjugal happiness; the achievement of relief from illness; the prolongation of one's earthly life span; or the removal of obstacles to business success. Infertile women or men or those with only female offspring make pilgrimages to solicit divine assistance in the conception and bearing of a male child. A considerable portion of the women who go to Tirupati do so for the latter reason.

Making a donation (H: *dan*) to the temple visited is a meritorious deed that blesses the donor (H: *dani*) with peace of mind, and fosters an individual's sense of spirituality by cultivating a nonattachment to the world of objects and material possessions. As in the case of a worldly contractual agreement, the donation in effect becomes advance payment for the hoped for conclusion to be achieved by miraculous celestial intervention. Donations come not only from the wealthy but also from a broad spectrum of society, including those with lesser means who, as a material act of faith, give whatever they can afford. For instance, at Tirupati poor women donate their long, black, lustrous hair, which is carefully shaved from their heads by permanently employed barbers who ply their trade in large salons outside the temple walls. The considerable accumulation is sold by temple authorities to the international wig-making industry, and the proceeds represent considerable additional temple income.

More valuable are votive offerings of jewelry of precious metals and gemstones as well as unmounted gemstones, occasionally of great value. According to Hindu belief, in which ritual purity is a dominant concern, all precious-metal jewelry and gemstones are believed to be ritually pure (H: *saf*); any pollution or contamination they may inadvertently possess is removed simply by washing. Such donations are often the property of older persons who wish to enter a recognized final stage of life in which material possessions are renounced in favor of spiritual pursuits. Jewelry that belonged to a departed relative is given in that person's name in order to facilitate the deceased soul's progress in the afterworld.

All such offerings are acceptable, although not all jewelry is deemed suited to actual temple use. Donated jewelry of lesser merit is usually dismantled, its gemstones—if any—are removed, and the metal is given to a refiner to be melted down into an ingot. This precious metal becomes a resource for temple authorities, who may commission a goldsmith to create a splendid, new ornament to decorate an image—especially those carried in procession. It may also be used for the manufacture of ritual objects used in worship, temple shrine doors, or other embellishments.

368. Ahmedabad, Gujarat
Jain white marble image of Santi (one of the twenty-four Tirthankaras worshipped by Jainas), whose identifying symbol, the antelope, appears at the base. His silver-sheet-metal body cover (kavacha) simulates all his requisite ornaments, executed in repoussage.

Types of Temple Jewelry

Founders of and donors to a Hindu temple customarily also presented ornaments for use in the decoration of installed deity images. Fixed and movable processional images were provided with sets of jewelry for all body parts. Gifts like these are recorded in epigraphic inscriptions at famous temples in Chidambaram, Kanchipuram, Madurai, Srirangam, Thanjavur, Tiruvanamalai, and others. Of these ancient gifts none survive, but their equivalents can be surmised from contemporaneous representations on temple images. All donated jewelry is loosely included in the category of temple jewelry. Strictly speaking, however, only the jewelry commissioned specifically for use on a deity image can properly be so designated.

Although an image of a deity in stone, metal, or other material almost always incorporates representations of jewelry, the ancient custom of daily adorning an image with actual jewelry continues as part of the daily ritual of dressing and ornamenting the deity as if it were alive. The deity is treated like a terrestrial ruler for whom sixteen ceremonial acts of daily worship are enacted in every major Hindu temple. Among them, the deity is bathed, clothed appropriately for the season, fed, and adorned with flower garlands and jewelry selected from the large temple treasury collection. When the image is smaller than life size—often the case—jewelry scaled to human use when placed upon it seems outsized, but this sometimes startling discrepancy does not disturb a worshiper's aesthetic sensibilities.

Today, the most showy and valuable donated jewelry is preserved and becomes the festive ornaments (H: *teohar jawahirat*) placed on the image at special times such as the *Holi* and *Diwali* holidays and on the occasion of the deity's birthday. After use they are returned to the temple treasury and replaced by the jewelry (P: *ma'muli jawahirat*) used on ordinary days. Jewelry in former contact with the deity image is believed to acquire a special sanctity (S: *prasadi*). When jewelry is damaged or broken, therefore deemed no longer worthy for use, it is sold or given away. Because of its former proximity to the image, it will probably gain a higher price than its actual market value. Persons who, as a meritorious act, purchase such jewelry may redonate it to a Brahman priest or give it to a mendicant (*sadhu*), who in turn may sell it and use the money for personal purposes.

From the priest's point of view, temple jewelry embodies a religious theatricality that

369. Madurai, Tamil Nadu.
*Nayak Dynasty, 18th century
Carved ivory figures, formerly
polychromed, of a Nayak Raja
and Nayaka Rani
Raja 19⅝ x 3½ in.
(27 x 8.9 cm); rani 10⅛ x 3½ in.
(25.7 x 8.9 cm)
Virginia Museum of Fine Arts,
Richmond (81.192.1/2)*

*They probably represent the
famous Raja Trimalai Nayak,
the seventh king in this dynasty,
who ruled from 1623 to 1659,
and his wife, the Thanjavur
princess. He was responsible for
the construction of the magnificent Minakshi Temple in
Madurai. Nayak rulers contributed many ornaments for
the decoration of deity images
in the temples they constructed
in their kingdom.*

369

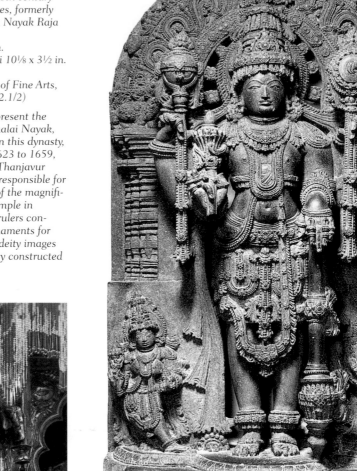

▲ **370. Somnathpur, Karnataka.** Hoysala Period,
c. mid-13th century A.D.
*Image of Keshava, a name of Vishnu-Krishna, worshiped to
counteract bad omens. Made of chloritic schist
41 x 21¼ in. (104 x 54.5 cm)
Asian Art Museum of San Francisco. The Avery Brundage
Collection (B70 S5)*

*The sculpture that decorates temples constructed during the
Hoysala Period in Karnataka reached a pinnacle of elaboration in
the representation of jewelry in stone. Every body part bore its
traditional ornament, depicted here in incredible detail. This was
technically possible because all Hoysala sculpture and temples were
made of a close-textured greenish or bluish-black chloritic schist.
The resulting headdresses, necklaces, girdles, bracelets, rings, and
ankle bracelets represented on deity images are not only a tour de
force of the stone carver's art but also illustrative of the work of
skilled goldsmith-chasers. With justifiable pride, some sculptors
even signed their work.*

*Keshava's name is derived from the Sanskrit word kesha (hair),
where, it is believed, an individual's soul and procreative substance
reside. The reference is to Krishna's origin from a black hair.*

◄ **371. Surat, Gujarat**
*Life-size bronze image of Amba ("Mother," a form of Durga) installed
in a temple. She is spectacularly arrayed with secular ornaments
donated by devotees, and wears an elaborate gold, gemstone-encrusted
crown (mukuta) made especially for this image.*

Ratna Darshana: Viewing a Gemstone-Bedecked Deity

The ancient Hindu idea of viewing or contemplating something sacred or revered (S: *darshana*) incorporates the philosophical concept that, by that act, the viewer becomes receptive to the spiritual and/or material benefits that emanate from the object or person. This idea accounts for the gathering of enormous crowds when, for instance, it is known that a famous spiritual or even a political leader will be present. The benefit derived from such a viewing increases as the distance between the object and the viewer decreases, hence the typical crush of humanity toward the revered object or individual.

This concept is also active when an individual views the sacred image of a Hindu deity in a temple. The words used to designate such a viewing (S: *shringara darshan utsava*) can be loosely rendered as an ordered occasion for viewing an ornamented image of a god or goddess. *Shringara* can mean "adornment," or "erotic excitement." *Utsava* is "a festival to order." The power believed to emanate from the image can be increased by making arrangements beforehand for temple staff members—usually priests—to adorn the deity with a full set of ornaments (S: *shingara*) taken from the temple treasury. When these contain precious stones, the occasion is called a precious-stone viewing (*ratna darshana*).

For a viewing, which is either paid for by the viewer or arranged for a person or persons who have made a substantial contribution to the temple, it is possible to specify that the image be ornamented with jewelry containing any of the *maharatnani* gemstones. In this case, only ornaments with those gemstones will be used. They may have been donated to the temple as votive offerings or made especially for the image using donated unmounted gemstones.

In many large temples, upon payment of an appropriate fee, temple authorities will arrange a private *darshana* of the deity adorned in diamond, ruby, emerald, sapphire, or pearl jewelry. Indian pilgrim guidebooks list the current cost of various types of deity *darshana*, and the most costly and beneficial is the diamond *darshana*. At such a time, in the inner sanctum where the image is installed, a ritual worship (*puja*) takes place only in the presence of the officiating priest and the person or persons who have ordered and paid for the *darshana*. Worship before the dazzlingly ornamented image involves the offering of flower garlands, the recitation of sacred texts, waving of lighted oil lamps (*arti*) before the image, and the ringing of bells to attract the deity's attention. Money or jewelry presented in the ritual is placed on a platter or stand before the deity. In return, the devotee is given a spiritual gift (S: *prasad*) of holy water; red powder, which is placed on foreheads in a form of blessing; and a garland.

372. Madurai, Tamil Nadu
19th century
Gold crown (mukuta) with gemstones, for an image
Approximate height 11 in.
(28 cm)

The Treasury of the Minakshi Temple contains many ornaments used to decorate the stone and metal images of deities installed there. These ornaments often incorporate traditional secular ornaments donated to the temple by devotees. For example, this gold crown includes an armlet (kadagam); below it, a two-headed bird pendant (antarantapatcippatakkam); and above it, center, a circular head ornament (rakkodi) flanked by sun and moon ornaments worn by dancers (see 419).

is designed to give the devotee a dazzling impression of a deity's otherworldly grandeur. Romanticized ideas concerning these ornaments, and fabulous descriptions of them, are found in old publications, but truth is more difficult to discern.

Connoisseurs of artistic and technical merit privileged to have examined temple treasury objects observed that the precious metals used are genuine but, surprisingly, the quality of the workmanship and gemstones in these ornaments is not invariably the highest. Many gemstones contain flaws and are in irregular cuts—conditions acceptable in most traditional Indian jewelry. It must be pointed out also that the laity sees this jewelry some distance away from the image, which is installed in an inner sanctum on a temple altar that is not approached by any but the priesthood.

Thus, although undeniably lavish in appearance, much of this jewelry would have a lower commercial value than one might imagine. This does not imply that the jewelry is less artistic or attractive than other Indian traditional jewel-

ry. What matters most in its use is the impression it makes on the mind of the viewer, often an unsophisticated person to whom such a show of wealth is awe inspiring. This jewelry therefore serves its function admirably.

Art historians date temple jewelry mainly on the basis of style and design. Due to the nature of traditional jewelry, in which styles and designs are perpetuated over extended periods of time, however, judging age by these criteria alone is treading on shaky ground. Judging approximate age therefore becomes an inspired act of artistic intuition.

Dating temple jewelry is compounded by the fact that little or no records exist, and many ornaments have undergone repair, or have been altered due to changes in style, and therefore may not be in their original state. Some temple jewelry is actually a pastiche of various donated ornaments created at different times and incorporated into one object, such as the crown above. In other cases, deliberate copies of old-style ornaments have been fabricated for use in the present.

Theatrical Jewelry

India's rich, vital theatrical traditions—including classical and folk theater, pure dance, and dance-drama—with their ancillary stage arts, costume and ornament crafts, continue to thrive in the specific locations where each developed its unique visual and performance style. Examples of what have become classical schools include the *Chhou* masked dance-drama of Seraikala, Singhbhum, Bihar; the *Ras* dance-drama of Imphal, Manipur; the *Yakshagana Badagatittu Bayalatta* dance-drama of Karnataka; the *Bharata-natyam* dance style of Tamil Nadu; and the *Kathakali* dance-drama of Kerala.

Theatrical themes are pan-Indian, often based on episodes in the major Indian epics, for example the *Mahabharata* and the *Ramayana,* whose subjects are religious, and the pure-dance *Nritya,* which is secular. Besides affording pleasure, these theatrical forms educate and perpetuate ideal Hindu cultural values. Traditional drama and dance is performed publicly on temporary stages during lunar holidays, seasons sacred to a divinity, religious festivals, or privately at the time of a marriage, or in celebration of the birth of a son.

Encouraged in part by the National Academy of Dance, Drama, and Music (*Sangeet Natak Akademi*), and popular patronage, the abovementioned classical theatrical dance and drama forms today have all developed audiences beyond their places of origin. Especially during the winter season, traveling troupes give performances attended by urban audiences in permanent theaters and outdoor locations in the major Indian cities. Established companies even perform abroad.

The unique character of each of these established forms is based not just on their content or distinctive style of acting or dance movement, but also to the use of masks or traditional makeup (P: *taiyar karna*), which can be varicolored, startlingly patterned, and mobile, as well as the marvelous costumes (H: *pahirao*) and ornaments (S: *abharana*) they utilize. Each school has its basic classes of characters, whose traditional costumes and ornaments transform the performer into a superhuman, heroic, royal, mortal, or evil being, as well as a host of unclassifiable types or individuals. In some cases, special costume materials such as silk, satin, velvet, or cotton have become associated with a particular dance-drama form, or even an individual character. The variety of ornaments and costumes is immense; only a few examples can be represented here.

It is not unusual for the ornaments worn by a dancer or actor to be made of genuine precious metal and gemstones. In the past, this was often the case, as when dance-drama performances were given on temple grounds or at a court. Private jewelry is still worn by *Bharata-natyam, Odissi,* and *Kathak* dancers, the

373. Cheruthuruthy, Trichur District, Kerala

Kathakali costume, ornament, and makeup are meant to reveal character. Here a performer wears the pea-green face makeup (theppuh) of a Satvik character, which could be a god, Nayaka hero, or noble king. Facial structures are clearly deliniated to assure greater communication between dancer and audience. This character has a band on the forehead (nettinada) and a white-paper (kadalas) facial frame (chutti) attached to the skin with rice paste (adri-koram), which dries in one hour. The most common Kathakali ornaments (abaranam) are the crown (kiridam) with halo (prabha mandalam) or headdress without halo (mudi), both carved of a lightweight wood and decorated with colored cloth, paint, and the white pith of calamus stems from peacock feathers (pili thantu). Also worn are round earrings (kundalam or thodu); concave, elongated circlets above the ears (chevi-pukuttu); a chest piece (channa-vira or kotalaram); breastplates (marumala) adorned with gold glass bead necklaces (kazhutharam), worn by men playing female characters; shoulder caps (tolvalla or tholput); armlets (vala or thanapathipu); wrist bracelets (katakam); bangles (vala); a silver belt (avanjanam) with a series of amulet containers; another belt (padiaranyal) for males; long, clawlike, silver nail rings on the left hand (naglam damshtram); rings (angulitra); and bells (mani) tied on the legs and below the knees. All ornaments can be decorated with colored glass, mirrors, imitation gold foil, iridescent beetle elytrae (wanda otu), and colored yarns.

374

375

376

374. Maisur (Mysore), Karnataka
Actor in the traditional Yakshagana Badagatittu Bayalatta dance-drama of Karnataka. Characters wear elaborate costumes and oversized ornaments made of a lightweight wood covered with lac and imitation gold leaf. The headdress of a character indicates his role and status. The type shown here (mundasa), in the form of a lotus petal, is the headdress of heroes. Its relative size is an indication of the importance of the character. Headdresses are covered with red and black cloth, ornamented with gold and silver tinsel ribbons and lac decorations covered with imitation gold leaf.

375. Kerala
Teyyam dancer wearing the facial makeup, crown, and ornaments of a character in this style of dance-drama, whose purpose is the glorification of the goddess Bhagavati (Kali) and the Bhagavati cult. Performances are celebrated at Bhagavati shrines.

376. North Malabar, Kerala
Male dancer impersonating the goddess Bhagavati, a form of Kali, at the Tirayattam dance festival. The dancer taking this role is often from a community of priests, called Malayans or Munnuttas, who practice exorcism. On his head is a silver diadem of small serpent heads, crowned with red flowers. Most of the ornaments are of soft wood, with covered lac, and decorated with imitation gold leaf. Other ornaments include a huge gold necklace, earrings, a carved and decorated breastplate, silver armlets and bracelets, and flower garlands.

latter a Muslim pure-dance form. In the world of Indian cinema, "star" dancers and actors on occasion also wear real jewelry, although reproductions of classic traditional forms and amazing, fanciful inventions are more common.

By far, however, the majority of theatrical ornaments are made of a variety of nonprecious materials. For example, in southern India, the striking, oversized headdresses and body ornaments worn by the all-male *Kathakali* and *Yakshagana* performers are generally carved from lightweight wood decorated with paint, colored cloth, felt, colored yarn, metallic ribbon, real or imitation gold and silver leaf or foil (see 798, 799), metal elements, mirrors, and colored-glass stones. The use of these materials brings into play a host of specialist craftsmen skilled in the manipulation of particular mediums.

In northern India (terms in Hindi), especially at Mathura, Uttar Pradesh, a large industry exists in the manufacture of theatrical ornaments for regional needs. Generally these are made of a papier-mâché or canvas substrate, covered with paint or cloth, and most characteristically ornamented with brilliant, low-cost metallic yarns (*zari*), whose manufacture centers mainly in Surat, Delhi, and Varanasi. Originally genuine gold, gold-plated silver, or pure silver yarns were used. Today, metallic yarn is generally gold- or silver-plated

copper *lametta* or synthetic metal-anodized plastic yarn.

The outstanding Indian decorative art of *zari* decoration uses filaments created from narrow, flattened (*badla*), broad (*diwali*), or thicker wire (*mukaish*). These may be used in their original, untreated condition for fringes (*jhalar*), "lace" (*jali*), or embroidery (*zardozi*). From this basic material is also made fine wire spirals (*salma*), created by coiling the flat or half-round *zari* around a thin, needlelike wire mandrel whose sectional shape may be round, square, pentagonal, hexagonal, or octagonal. Each spiral type is different and its appearance can be varied by using highly polished or matte wire. The resulting smooth or angled coil, cut into a desired length, like a bead, is passed through by a needle and thread and stitched to the surface of the ornament—such as a crown —which may have a base of velvet or satin. An especially rich effect is created in this method of overlaid or couched embroidery (*zardozi ka kam*) by first cushioning particular motif areas with heavy thread or cut out cardboard shapes that are then covered with padding yarn and *zari* to create three-dimensional effects.

Tinsel wire is also used to make spangles or sequins (*sitara*) and metallic cord (*dhat ka dori*). Specialist weavers (*kinaribafs*) use the wire as weft to make cotton- or silk-thread

warp metallic ribbon (*gota*: gold, *sonai gota*; silver, *nuqrai gota*), in narrow, broad, or stamp-patterned forms.

Punjabi women and widows, as a home industry, use *gota* ribbon to make ingeniously folded and stitched floral and star-shaped units in many designs. These are sewn to ornaments and on garments such as head cloths (*dopattas*), bodices (*cholis*), and petticoats (*ghaghras*) and used to make long bands sewn on saris as borders or on a costume for a bride.

These materials are used to make masks, headdresses, tiaras, turban ornaments, earrings, necklaces, shoulder ornaments, upper arm, wrist, breast plates (for males impersonating females), and belts and girdles for both male and female dancers and actors. The gorgeous glitter of these outsized creations, viewed from a distance, especially in the case of the lavishly decorated headdresses, communicate a sense of drama and excitement as well as information. Because even theatrical jewelry used in classical dance and drama is traditional in nature, devotees of a particular theatrical form are familiar with the distinctions they imply.

Less bound by classical traditions, folk dancers may use many of the same abovementioned materials for ornaments in an even more varied and unconventional way. Their ornaments acquire greater variation because

377. Cheruthuruthy, Kerala
(opposite page)
Kathakali traditional dance-drama ornaments and props used by various characters at the Kerala Kalamandalam. They are made of carved wood, yarn and cloth, gold foil, mirrors, glass beads and gemstones, feathers, and paint.

378. Vrindavan, Uttar Pradesh
Polychromed-marble images of Vishnu and his consort Lakshmi, adorned with a full set (shringar) of miniature ornaments of gold yarn, sequins, and imitation seed pearls, all made in Mathura Height approx. 19¾ in. (50 cm)

379. Varanasi, Uttar Pradesh
Young boys wearing crowns (zari mukut) and ornaments made of metallic tinsel and imitation stones, created in Mathura. They are dressed to represent Rama and his consort Sita and are performers in the Hindu classic epic drama the Ramayana, or Story of Rama. Episodes of this story are enacted nightly in the Ramlila during the nine-day Rama Navami holiday. Performances are especially popular in Uttar Pradesh, where Rama is reputed to have ruled in Ayodhya.

378

379

380. Probably Delhi. c. 1878
Collar of (now tarnished) silver yarn (zari) applied to a stiff, sized buckram ground
Total length approx. 40 in. (101.6 cm)
Courtesy Henry Brownrigg, London

This startling object, supposedly made for a provincial Indian ruler, simulates a British-Indian Order Collar, perhaps longed for but not awarded. It probably was made after the state visit of Edward, Prince of Wales to India (1876–77), when the awarding of British orders was given much publicity. Not an exact duplication of an existing order collar, it naively draws its design elements from them, including the star-shaped central pendant bearing the confronting lion and unicorn of the British royal coat of arms, surmounted by an arched crown surmounting an escutcheon, and linked with an openwork chain embodying stars, the United White and Red Roses of Great Britain, and Indian lotuses. It is an outstanding example of the zari style of laid or gimped embroidery in which shaped pieces of vellum are applied to a buckram ground, the flat, raised, or padded elements then covered with couched metallic yarns. The same technique was used to decorate the uniforms of British Indian officers.

382

◄ 381. Mathura, Uttar Pradesh
Necklace (zari mala) of gold metallic yarn (zari), ornamented with imitation seed pearls, sequins, and red glass "stones"
Total length 30 in. (76.2 cm)
Collection the author, Porvoo

Backed with stiffened red cloth, such necklaces are made for use on the image of a deity installed in a household shrine.

382. Kerala
Dancer representing the demon Darikasura, the king of evil titans, whom the goddess Bhagavati fights and kills at the climax of this most important, sacred, evening dance-drama called Mutiyettu, performed before a Bhagavati temple or shrine in celebration of the Bhagavati cult. Kali destroys the demon by thrusting the claw of her big toe into his ear and then severing his head. The demon's silver eye covers and large cloth mouth with protruding tusks indicate his evil nature.

383. Palghat District, Kerala
The Parayanthira dance performed by Pariya trib-als is a ritual pageant that celebrates the goddess Bhagavati of the divine mother cult. This character is Cheria Tamburatti, popularly interpreted as Bhagavati's daughter. As it is performed by a male dancer, to indicate femininity "she" wears brass breasts. Other ornaments include a large, circular crown-headdress (kiridam), a large bronze torque-necklace (see 475), and a belt with many bells (see 523).

383

they draw upon a larger variety of materials, all locally available and of comparatively little or no cost. As previously shown, folk dance-drama performers still depend widely upon nature's resources to provide seeds, leaves, *shola* pith, flowers, straw, bamboo, gourds, shells, feathers, feather quills, beetle-wing cases, horns, and many other substances for costume and ornament.

Some of these materials become an indication of relative importance of a character because the audience, familiar with them, realizes their rarity, the difficulty in their procurement, or the labor that must have been invested in their utilization as elements in the fabrication of ornaments. (See additionally 11, 15, 33, 40, 41, 44, 51, 52, 55, 60, 70, 73, 95, and 408.)

Ornament for Animals

Probably as numerous as the human population in India, animals are depended upon in varying degrees by nomadic, tribal, rural, and urban people for transport, as draft animals, and as food. A sign of their importance is their presence in many of the religious and secular events that punctuate the Indian religious and social calendar. It is common practice at such times to honor these animals with decorative ornaments and color.

Animal reverence in India is partially explained by the fundamental Hindu philosophical doctrine of metempsychosis, or the transmigration upon death of the immortal soul or spiritual essence of a human to another body, in some cases also human and in others possibly mammal, reptile, fowl, or insect. In this hierarchy, the specific incarnation depends upon the balance between the individual soul's lifetime commitment of virtuous or sinful acts. Among the most auspicious animals are cows, bullocks, horses, and elephants.

Images of domestic and wild animals are seen in Hindu temple sculpture and painting, where they are often represented wearing honorific jewelry. Augmenting their significance is the Hindu mythological tradition in which some of these animals have the role of conveyance (*vahanam*) of greater and lesser Hindu gods and goddesses.

Jewelry on living animals primarily has an amuletic function and therefore appears daily in some form on the animal. Ornaments of greater intrinsic value are stored and brought out for occasional use. Its amuletic purpose is primarily in the interest of the humans these animals serve: it guards the animal by warding off the malefic effects of the evil eye and diseases that may affect their productivity. Contrary to amuletic jewelry worn by humans, which often is made of or includes dead animal parts attributed with magical power—exceptions being the yak tail (*chamar*) and feathers—the jewelry placed on animals is made of other materials. Metal ornaments for animals can be divided into two classes: those that emulate types worn by humans, although appropriately increased in scale; and those without human jewelry counterparts, whose form is determined by the particular animal's anatomy. Always popular in such ornaments is the use of small metal bells, which in some cases function to locate strays but in general act to frighten away evil spirits. Nonmetallic animal ornaments are primarily made of yarn, cloth, or leather, each employed or decorated in a manner suited to the particular material. Embellishments often include cowrie shells and glass beads, both also used separately to create animal necklaces (see 132).

Decorated animals can be encountered by chance, but the best place to see an enormous, lavishly ornamented, zoological display is at pan-Indian annual animal fairs (H: *janwar ka mela*) attended by thousands of rural people. Astonishing in this respect are the Pushkar fair in Rajasthan (October–November), and one at Sonepur, Bihar, at approximately the same time. At such events, vast numbers of well-groomed domesticated animals are offered for sale. Certain natural animal markings (Tam: *suli*) are considered auspicious and therefore are sought by a potential purchaser. A common one is a natural, circular whorl of hair at a particular place on the animal's body. Geometric patterns are sheared on the bodies of shaggy animals like the camel. Animals with smoother fur, such as the cow, bullock, horse, and elephant, are frequently pattern-painted with pigments and dyes.

384. Madurai, Tamil Nadu
*The goddess Ganga, a jewel-bedecked water spirit personifying the Ganges River, represented at a portal of the Minakshi Temple. She stands on her vehicle (*vahanam*), a makara, or mythic aquatic animal inspired by the crocodile and having occult and magic powers relating to lake, river, and sea fertility.*

385. Junagadh, Gujarat. *19th century*
Silver dog collar (H: kutta-guluband) made for a favorite pet of the Maharaja of Junagadh. The dog (S: shvan) is the vehicle of the Hindu god Bhairava, a form of Shiva
15 x 1¼ in. (38 x 3 cm); weight 174 g
Courtesy Maharukh Desai, London

Cow, Bullock or Zebu, and Buffalo

In India, the cow (H: *gae*) and water buffalo (S: *bhains*) are kept for milking and milk products. They also draw the plows, wagons, or two-wheeled, often-canopied travel vehicles whose form varies regionally. In the latter occupation, they are frequently gaily decorated. Common adornments on cattle are flower garlands, forehead ornaments, and a tight necklace of colorful handmade, wound-glass beads, or cowrie shells (see 61), to which may be added a central brass-bell pendant or one of arrowhead shape. A longer necklace of brass bells may fall on the chest. Often a brass ring by which the animal is led dangles from its pierced septum. In southern India, pairs of doughnut-shaped hollow brass ring ornaments containing sounding pellets, which frighten away malefic spirits, are placed on their horns, and tapered cylindrical brass terminals decorate horn ends. Water buffaloes are less likely to be decorated, perhaps because of their association with Mahisa, who was slain in buffalo form by the goddess Durga after his hostile confrontation with the gods.

Bulls that are spared castration at birth are generally allowed to roam freely, and, because of their association with Shiva, a Shaivite pious follower may provide them with ornaments that embody Shaivite symbolism. Foremost among Hindu-sculptured representations of zebu bulls is Nandin, "giving delight," the vehicle of Shiva, whose symbolic function in Hinduism is the establishment of universal order (*dharma*) in cosmic and worldly spheres. Found facing a Shaivite temple shrine mainly in the south, and especially in Karnataka, is a three-dimensional, couchant Nandin wearing traditional ornaments and trappings, usually carefully delineated. Most elaborate in ornament representation are the

386. Karnataka. *Hoysala dynasty, 13th century*
Chloritic schist sculpture of the bull Nandin, vehicle (vahanam) of Shiva and Parvati
23 x 31¾ x 14 in. (58.5 x 80.6 x 36 cm)
Philadelphia Museum of Art. Joseph E. Temple Fund (66-123-1)

As befits a deity vehicle, Nandin is honorifically ornamented with a series of elaborate headbands (see 389), three necklaces (the lowest a chain), a series of threaded bells that hang on his chest and join a belly strap and ornamental haunch band at the top of the back, and leg ornaments on the front feet and ankles.

387. Saurashtra, Gujarat
Two pairs of Gujarati bullocks, a superior breed, belonging to Kadwa Kanbias, who love to decorate them. Brought for sale to a cattle fair, they wear cotton trappings embroidered with silk and liberally set with small, round mirrors (abla or kanch) from Kapadvanj. Trappings include forehead (matharoti-yum), face (khobhra), muzzle (makkiyah), and horn covers (shingadia) and a large back cloth (jhul).

388. Saidapet, Tamil Nadu
Bullocks wearing brass horn-ring ornaments (van-dayam) with internal pellets. These rings, along with attached or neck-suspended bells (salangu), are common bullock ornaments whose sound is intended to frighten away harmful spirits.

387

388

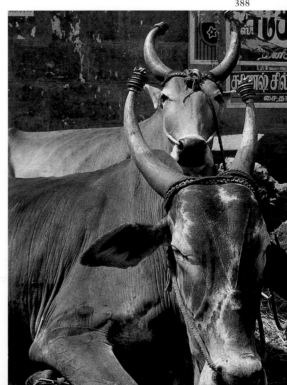

390

391

389. Nagpur, Madhya Pradesh. *19th century*
Cast-brass forehead ornament for a bullock, with Shaivite symbols and peacocks
Length overall 22¾ in. (58 cm); weight 586 g
Collection the author, Porvoo

The ornament is placed on the bullock as a decoration for the pola festival (August–September), at which time draft animals are thanked for their help in plowing the fields.

390. Southern India. *18–19th century*
Bronze Nandin mask
Height 14⅝ in. (37 cm)
Courtesy Sotheby's, London

The mask image features end-of-horn rings (vandyam), a beaded ropework halter, and, on the forehead, sun and moon symbols associated with Shiva.

391. Tamil Nadu
Cast-brass ornaments fixed to the bullock (eruthu) horn ends (kombu-nuni), which include terminal representations of Shiva's head
Height 4⁵⁄₁₆ in. (11 cm); diameter 1⁹⁄₁₆ in. (4 cm); weight of pair 384 g
Collection the author, Porvoo

392. Tamil Nadu
Hollow bronze ornaments (vandyam or vattam) placed on a bullock's horns
Outer diameter 2¼ in. (5.6 cm); inner diameter 1⁷⁄₁₆ in. (3.6 cm); weight of pair 290 g
Collection the author, Porvoo

Metal pellets (sittundai) inside the ornaments sound in movement. The bull is honored as the vehicle of Shiva.

images associated with Karnataka Hoysala Shiva temples. On Nandin's head are a multitude of ornaments, and his neck bears a sequence of several tight necklaces. On his body, three main ornaments converge at the center of the back: a long chain of bells falls over the chest; an ornamental cincture girds the belly and sometimes anchors a saddle cloth, and a swag chain passes under the tail, encircling his haunches.

At festive times, the horns of bovine animals are often pigment enameled in shining, bright colors and their bodies splashed with auspiciously colored dyes. Cows are imprinted with their owner's extended-finger red pigment (formerly the blood of a sacrificial animal) handprints, a barrier symbol that repels the evil eye.

Camel

Like other animals, the camel (H: *unt*; A: *ibil*) is revered by Hindus. Most popular among the mainly nomadic Rabari in Kachchh is the mother goddess Mommai, whose vehicle is the camel. They were also ridden by some apotheosized local heroes at whose shrines votive offerings of camels in cloth or clay are presented by devotees. At the center or outskirts of villages throughout this area one finds rows or groups of upright mounted, carved stone-pentagonal or shrine-shaped memorial tablets (*khambha* or *palaya*), some placed on a common platform (*pedharan*), bearing a hero image. Their equivalent in the form of an amulet-ornament is the silver-stamped image of similar heroes, worn by men and women in this area (see 165). Some of these tablets show horses, but those of Rabari heroes depict a camel in profile, or camel with rider-hero (*surapura*) who, according to oral tradition, generally died as a result of protecting the village inhabitants and its animals. Tablets usually face east or north, confronting the historic direction from which racially recalled past invasions occurred. These tablets are erected to appease the hero's ghost, who haunts his place of birth or death, and to ward off sickness or other threats to the village inhabitants.

Only the dromedary or one-humped camel is found in India. They are raised for use as human transport, as work animals who carry caravan goods, or to draw carts. Of equal importance is their employment for military purposes. Famous for their fitness and elaborate, full livery ornaments, they participate prominently in the annual January Republic Day Festival Parade in New Delhi, and dominate the much admired Tattoo that traditionally summons soldiers to quarters at night and closes these weeklong celebrations.

Abu l'Fazl, biographer of the Mughal Emperor Akbar, noted a long list of camel's ornaments, most of which have their contemporary equivalents. In present-day Bikaner, Jaisalmer, Jodhpur, and other Rajasthani desert

393. Bikaner, Rajasthan. 1891
Drawing by John Lockwood Kipling of a lead camel with elaborate head and neck decorations of colored cord, silver appliqués, and cowrie shells

394. Chhaya, Junagadh District, Gujarat
Carved-stone memorial tablets bearing images of Rabari heroes riding ornamented camels. Camels are traditionally associated with these nomadic shepherds, who raise them.

cities, a number of camels are assembled at an annual Desert Festival, which always features camel races. Proud owners compete in grooming and ornamenting their favorite camels with brightly colored cotton and woolen yarn bands, tassels and pompons. These occur on the head strap (*sartang*), neckstrap (*gardanband*), and the chest strap (*sinaband*). A special, unique camel ornament that hangs from the neck across the chest consists of an elaborate yarn network (*jajajil*) adorned with cowrie shells or its present frequent substitute—white buttons—mirrors, and bells. Wood-framed riding saddles (*kantho*) are often elaborately mounted with rivet-held brass and white-metal piercedwork appliqués. As mentioned, the hair on their exposed flanks is shaved in intricate geometric patterns.

395

396

Horse

In Hindu India, a white horse (H: *ghora*) is a sun symbol associated with Surya, the sun god, and its head represents knowledge. India's Muslim Mughals hailed from Central Asia, where the horse was essential to daily nomadic life. This probably accounts for the Mughal passion for the horse. The best of Mughal-bred horses, mainly tractable mares who were valued more than stallions, were kept by rulers and their nobility solely for use on state parade occasions. At such events, as a form of power symbol display, these horses were caparisoned with sets of accoutrements of gold and silver embellished with diamonds, emeralds, rubies, and turquoises. The ornaments placed on horses ridden to battle always included a pair of bangles, one clasped to each foreleg. These symbolized the rider's vow to be victorious or to die in battle. The mount of the supreme military commander was hung with white yak tails (*chamar*) as a standard (*tugh*) symbolic of his high status.

Elaborately caparisoned horses of both types are frequently depicted in Mughal, Rajput, and southern Indian miniature paintings. Idealized and romanticized, they typically are shown with a small head and large eyes, a tremendously arched neck, fat body, slender legs, and a tail that sweeps the ground.

Today horses are less in use but are still important to those whose occupation requires them. In cities and towns, horses draw a variety of two-wheeled taxi-gigs such as the *ekka* and *tonga*. Ornaments placed on such horses (*ghore ka saz o saman*) include an upstanding feather or tinsel head ornament (*turra*) similar to one worn by a prince or bridegroom, and necklaces of strings of glass beads or the ubiquitous cowrie shells and bells. Leather horse trappings are often much decorated with embroidery and polished metal studs.

In a more lavishly ornamented class are the preferably white horses ridden by a groom to his wedding ceremony (see 297). Using a horse for this purpose is probably a relic from the past, when as a sign of his virility, a mounted groom abducted his bride, a type of marriage termed *rakshasa*. It is still symbolically reenacted by some Rajputs in Rajasthan. Common ornaments include those placed on the forehead, chest, and neck, the latter hung with silver necklaces, and the haunch and croup, which are covered with a tasselated silver network (*jali*). Mane and tail may be dyed an auspicious henna red and the hair braided or banged. Large, elaborate saddle cloths, pro-

(see 297)

395. Thanjavur, Tamil Nadu. *c.1820*
Miniature portrait of the Maratha ruler Raja Sarabhoji of Thanjavur (1798–1832) depicted in full regalia riding an elaborately caparisoned black charger, a mount for parade
Courtesy Artemis Fine Arts (UK) Limited, London

In northern India similar ornaments worn on a horse include (Hindi terms) a head ornament of gold tinsel and feathers (turra); a silver necklace strung with many pendants (padak mala); a neck amulet set with gemstones (Sulimani manka); a tiger-claw ornament (shernakh jantr); a metal leg rattle (ghagri); yak tails hanging below (chauris); and silver bangles (chura) placed on the forelegs. The latter in times past signified that the rider was honor bound to conquer or die in battle.

396. Rajasthan. *19th century*
Horse ornaments of gold-plated silver, including parts of an amulet necklace (two units below), body ornament of small lions that slide on straps, central peacock turra holder, articulated lozenge-shaped unit, and triangular forehead ornament
Courtesy Sotheby's, London

397. Tamil Nadu
Elaborately ornamented, permanent temple horse (ayyankoil kuthirai) connected with a local, indigenous village deity (grama devata) named Ayyanar. Painted plaster

The son of both Shiva and Vishnu, Ayyanar actually rides a white elephant, but his many generals, the Palaiyakarar, ride horses. Temporary (life-size or smaller) horses in terra cotta are made to order by local potters (kuyavan) and carried from their place of manufacture to the temple. At the initiation (sthapana) or installation of the horses for worship (kanthirapu), a rooster's toe is cut off, and the issuing blood is smeared around the horse's eyes to give it life (jivaraththam). As the god of field watchmen, Ayyanar and his mounted generals protect gardens, fields, and villages by riding nightly round their perimeters to prevent the entry of evil spirits.

398. Jaipur, Rajasthan
A bridegroom's traditional caparisoned white horse (dulha ka ghora). Riding a horse to the wedding ceremony is a vestige of the ancient custom of marriage by abduction. The horse is decorated with silver amulets, including a network (jala) of strung beads, pendants, and tassels.

397

398

fusely and splendidly decorated with a glittering display of tinsel embroidery, sequins, and beads, have recently come into use.

Elephant

Elephants (S: *hathi*; P: *fil*), the largest of all land animals, are indigenous to India. The Indian elephant's head is surmounted by two pronounced forehead lobes, while that of the African is lower and tapers backward in profile. This physiological characteristic makes a difference in the form of ornaments placed on the Indian elephant's head. In the hierarchy of religious and domesticated animal mounts for deities, the elephant has an exalted standing. The famous multitrunked white elephant, Airavata, ridden by the Hindu god Indra, is a symbol of might and the prototype of the terrestrial, resplendent royal processional elephant, as well as those used in military pageants.

Of great importance to every Hindu is sagacious Ganesha, the elephant-headed pot-bellied, dwarf son of Shiva and Parvati, represented with one intact and one broken tusk.

In times past, elephants in numbers up to three thousand or more, protected with steel armor (*pakkar*) that was often gilded and decorated, comprised an army's chief strength as a fighting machine. Besides forming a formidable front line, its power was utilized as a battering-ram to force the gates or portals of a fort or city during a siege, and to carry or draw heavy cannon and tents. Formerly, and still occasionally, in times of peace, fitted out with a magnificent litter (H: *hauda*), an elephant is ridden by a raja in a military, state, or religious procession. Its impressive size and majestic gait befits a monarch's dignity and adds considerably to the pomp of the occasion.

The appearance of a processional elephant was greatly enhanced by the variety and size of the splendid ornaments (H: *fil ka zebaish*) placed upon them, as often depicted in Indian Mughal and Rajput miniature paintings. Where such ornaments or their descendants survive today, they are still used. For instance, famed for their magnificence are the ornaments placed on the parade elephants of the Maharaja of Mysore, Karnataka, who participate annually in the procession celebrating the Dussera festival (September–October). Equally impressive, although in another style, are the ornaments of the Vedakkunathan Swami (Shiva) Temple elephants at Trichur, Kerala. As many as thirty to more than one hundred of them, all magnificently ornamented, form a long, impressive enfilade before the temple at the Pooram Festival (April–May).

In a Rajasthani folk-art display, the heads, ears, and trunks of parade elephants are painted with brightly colored linear patterns of flowers, vines, and geometric forms, and some also bear a forehead sectarian mark. Fixed over pads on its back is the *hauda* in which the rider sits. Large, rectangular, decorative hangings (*jhul*) extending well below the belly, are attached to the *hauda* sides.

In northern India, a variety of silver or sometimes gold or gold-plated silver ornaments are used. The crown of the elephant's head may bear a feathered *sarpech* or another head ornament. At the temples are hung a cascade of six-foot-long (183 cm) multiple-chain ornaments (*sankal*), to which light-catching leaf-shaped silver petals (*pata*) are fixed. Around its neck pass one or more necklaces (*fil ka har*), a typical one consisting of a series of arrowhead-shaped amulets (see 176). Silver festoons passing from saddle cloth to under the tail hang on its sides, often bearing small bells (*ghungrus*). Larger bells (*ghanta*) are hung from the neck or sides at the end of long, swinging chains. The often trimmed tusk tips are provided with silver, brass, or iron terminals or ornamental rings (*bangri*), which for strength may be placed at intervals along the length of the tusk. Around the animal's legs are enormous silver anklets (*payal*), some with attached bells, a type clearly derived from those worn by women.

399. Madras, Tamil Nadu
Bazaar oleograph of Ganapati (Ganesha), the elephant-headed god of wisdom, bedecked with the ornaments of a major deity. Ganesha assists in overcoming any obstruction or difficulty and therefore is worshiped before undertaking any important venture.

This universally popular, most-worshiped Hindu god functions as the remover of all obstacles to success. Consequently, he often appears on the lintel above the entrance door of a house whose occupants and visitors invoke him on entering and leaving. Popularly thought of as the god of prosperity, his assistance and blessing is sought at the inauguration of any new enterprise. Goldsmiths and merchant jewelers open their annual new account book (*bahi*) and perform a ceremony (*puja*) before his image. Ganesha is first to be acknowledged when the construction of a new house commences, when setting out on a journey, at the start of a marriage ceremony, or when first placing an ornament on the body.

400

401

400. Trichur, Kerala

Ornamented, central, caparisoned elephant, of which from three to more than fifteen are lined up before the Parama Kao Temple in Trichur during the celebration of the Vela Puram Festival in honor of Bhadrakali. Decorations include a special forehead covering (anaipattam) ornamented with three central balls (mun-komala) representing the Hindu triad: Shiva, Vishnu, and Brahma; crescent-moon shapes (chandrakalas) and half domes (komala) symbolizing the sun, all fixed to a cloth ground, with edge fringe (pudipus) and bottom tassel (kalanchi). Resting on his forehead is an upstanding plaque (kolam), at whose center may be a representation of Shiva, Krishna, or Bhagavati, surrounded by floral bosses (pu). Seated on each elephant is his guider (yanaivazhikatti) and two or four other men who hold aloft a ceremonial umbrella (koda), mounted yak-tail whisks (venchamara), or a peacock-feather-decorated round ceremonial fan (alavattam), the latter two raised up at intervals during loud drumming sequences performed in front of the elephants.

401. Delhi or Agra. Mughal, Jahangir period (1605–27)

Elephants Fighting. Paint on paper
17½ x 12 in. (44.5 x 30.5 cm)
The Metropolitan Museum of Art, New York. Rogers Fund, 1912 (12.223.2)

Staging this spectacle was the prerogative of the emperor Jahangir, who watches on horseback in this scene. Despite the violent "sport," the two tusk-cut elephants wear typical necklaces, body ornaments, bells, and tusk rings.

402. Jaipur, Rajasthan. 1891

Drawing by John Lockwood Kipling of ceremonial elephant decorated with a necklace of amulets, a turra, tusk rings, bells, and elaborate trappings surmounted by a howdah (hauda), in which the raja would sit

3 INDIAN JEWELRY TYPOLOGY: FROM HEAD TO TOE

Ornaments in India are infinitely varied. An attempt has been made to bring some order to this heterogeneity by presenting on the following pages a pictorial overview of forms in traditional Indian jewelry, organized according to their use on the human body: from head to toe. Within each area, objects are grouped according to particular physical features they have in common, such as their systematic design plan or their basic construction.

This typological grouping has one decided advantage above other systems: it emphasizes the basic morphological or formal and structural relationship between these widely diverse objects, especially since these examples of more than rudimentary interest hail from geographically far-flung locations or are in use by culturally diverse groups. In effect, typological classification slices through and sweeps aside compartmentalizing barriers thrown up by geographical or communal groupings, which although also useful in other contexts, tend to fragment more than unify the overall subject. This system also has the advantage of allowing us to compare regionally diverse objects and see how their design and construction concepts have been interpreted and developed, often by people outside their probable place of origin. Variations such as these provide us with insight into the subtlety of the creative capacity of Indian jewelers as applied to traditional ornaments.

403. Uttar Pradesh
Gold regal crown (mukut) presented by the Talukdars of Oudh (Avadh) to Edward, Prince of Wales, during his visit to India in 1875–76. The gold circlet is composed of a series of openwork floral tablets set with a large central diamond surrounded by smaller, irregularly faceted and shaped ones, the band edged top and bottom with pearls. Frontal sarpech (kalgi missing) and leaf-shaped, diamond-encrusted crestings terminate in pendant emeralds and are richly counter-enameled. Eight gold arches ornamented with diamonds converge at a sunken, diamond-set rosette in the center. The purple velvet cap is encrusted with gold-set diamonds and pearls.
The Royal Collection Courtesy Her Majesty Queen Elizabeth II

404. Bikaner, Rajasthan
Marwari married-woman's silver foot and toe ornaments, including: anklets (jurd) containing sounding pellets; upper-foot ornament (pagpan); big- and small-toe rings (naklia) joined by five crossing chains (sankali); and three small-toe rings between, all ornamented with jingling bells (ghungru) and balls (goli)

405. Bhopal. Madhya Pradesh
Her Highness Nawab Sultan Jehan Begam Sahiba. Born in 1858, she ascended the throne (masnad) in 1901. She wears a jeweled crown (mukut) ornamented with three turras, always seen in her official portrait photographs. As a Muslim ruler, she governed from behind the curtain (parda) and in public appeared covered from head to toe with a burqa. She also wears the British-Indian orders and collars of the Grand Commander of the Star of India and Grand Commander of the Indian Empire (see 742).

403

404

406. Kullu, Himachal Pradesh
Miniature cast-bronze mask (mohra) of the goddess
Mujuni Devi
11½ x 10½ in. (29.2 x 26.6 cm)
Los Angeles County Museum of Art.
Gift of Dr. and Mrs. Pratapaditya Pal (M.76.-147.1)

To assure village prosperity, the goddess mask is carried
in procession in the annual October celebration of
the Dussera and Shivaratri festivals in Kullu and the
vicinity. The mask incorporates a typical Himachal
Pradesh–style crown with peaked elements, a type
found on local images of deities since the ninth
century A.D. The goddess also wears kundala-type
earrings and a torque necklace. The snake symbolizes
her connection with Shiva.

407. Srinagar, Kashmir South, Jammu and Kashmir
Woman's hat (topi; tomara; galtan; kasab) with circular gilded-silver ornaments stitched to
the cloth as a kind of protective amulet (ta'wiz or tawati). From the hat hang silver side-of-head
ornaments supported on chains. Over the hat goes a head cloth (putz or daj). The top of her
garment (feran) is embroidered in gold yarn (tila) in couched or laid work.
Courtesy Air India, Bombay

Top-of-Head Ornaments

408. Khasi Hills, Meghalaya
Young woman participating in
the annual Khasi Nongkrem
Festival, at which a group of girls
dressed alike and wearing these
crowns dance to honor the ruling
goddess, Ka Blei Synshar, to
assure crop fertility. She wears
other traditional ornaments,
including the necklace of huge
coral (paila) and lac-filled gold
(ksiar) beads, silver chains (kynjri
shabi), a collar (rupa-tylli), and
gold earrings (kurneng).

409. Khasi Hills, Meghalaya
Silver crown (pansngiat)
Crown diameter 7¹/₁₆ in. (18.2 cm);
width 2½ in. (6.3 cm); finial
8¼ x 2 in. (20.9 x 5.2 cm);
weight 292 g
Collection the author, Porvoo

Seen here is the rear view with
the upward projecting spire
(u'tiew lasubon) worn at the
back of the head. Its inner, reverse
side is covered with flowers.
The crown closes in front by the
removable central boss (visible in
photograph) that slides into three
lugs on the pierced-work crown
band. Made by goldsmiths in
Karimganj, Assam, it is worn by
unmarried Khasi women during
the spring Nongkrem Festival
dance.

408

409

410

411

410. Palampur, Himachal Pradesh
Gaddi girl wearing a silver forehead ornament (chiri-tikka; chiri means bird)

411. Kangra, Himachal Pradesh
Chiri tikka enameled blue and green, the colors favored by Kangra enamelists, with an elaborate fringe of silver balls (goli) and leaf forms (pipal patti). Smaller versions are called bindi.
4¹⁵⁄₁₆ x 5⁵⁄₁₆ in. (12.5 x 13.5 cm); weight 126 g
Collection the author, Porvoo

◀ **412. Panjim, Goa**
Silver hair combs (kanghi), some central flowers set with a red gemstone. Inspired by mid-nineteenth-century prototypes from Europe
3⅛ x 2¹⁵⁄₁₆–4⁵⁄₁₆ x 3¹⁵⁄₁₆ in. (8.3 x 7.5–11 x 10 cm); weight 28–32 g
Collection Ghysels, Brussels

◀ **413. Santhal Pargana, Bihar**
Santhal tribal man wearing a decorative wooden comb (kunghi or kakai) in his hair during the celebration of the Sorae harvest festival. The use of hair combs by men and women prevails among other tribal people of the area, including indigenous Dravidian tribes such as the Mundas of Chota Nagpur. Also worn are a silver rupee coin necklace (rupiya har) and a glass seed-bead necklace (motimala).

414. Himachal Pradesh ▶
Gaddi woman wearing a silver, domed top-of-head ornament (chak) with attached side chains joined to two smaller side-of-head domes (chak-phul). Called chadura when worn by women in the Punjab plains, it normally is not visible as it is covered by a head cloth (dopatta).

415

416

Side-of-Head Ornaments

415. Chamba, Himachal Pradesh
Gujar woman wearing a pair of silver side-of-head ornaments (sirka chamkuli) of elaborate construction

416. Himachal Pradesh
Silver side-of-head ornaments (sirka chamkuli), to be worn in pairs at the sides of the head, with their end hooks fixed in the headcloth 11¾ x 3⅛ in. (28.3 x 8 cm); weight (one) 119 g
Collection the author, Porvoo

417. Mandi, Himachal Pradesh ➤
Silver head ornament (daoni-tilak) with central turquoise-and-coral-set round forehead unit (tilak), from which radiate (upward) the hook for attachment to the hair; (downward) the central, crescent-moon-shaped enameled forehead ornament (chand); and (sideways) two broad side-of-face, multiple-joined chains edged with a fringe of pipal-leaf-shaped pendants. Additional hanging earrings (karanphul-jhumka) are often fixed to the two ends.
Collection Viscount and Viscountess Scarsdale, Kedelston Hall, Derbyshire

418. Shahpura, Rajasthan
Bhil woman wearing a silver head ornament (chhoga), loaded with bunches and borders of hollow balls (goli), and silver upper and lower arm bangles (bangri) worn in sets (see 334)

419. Tamil Nadu

Bharata-natyam *dancer Swapna Sundari wearing traditional gold head ornaments set with rubies and pearls, also worn by brides: The sun (*suriyan*) ornament (right side); the moon (*santhiran*) ornament (left side); diamond nose stud (*besari* or *mukkuththi*); septum ring (*bulakku*); three-part head band (*thalaikkachchu* or *thalai-saman*) with forehead pendant (*vakchutti*); and earrings (*thodu*) on the lobe with hanging dome-shaped part (*jimiki*) and attached chain (*mattal*). At the back of her head (*unseen*), she would wear a round ornament (*rakkodi*) or a braid ornament (*jadanagam, see 67*). In her hair is a floral ornament of fragrant screwpine flowers (*thazhambu*), and around her neck is a tight necklace (*addigai*) with a ruby-set pendant (*padhakkam*). The long necklace is a silver substitute for the gold equivalent (*mangamalai, see 494, 495*). To complete the traditional set (*not seen here*), she would also wear V-shaped armlets (*vanki, see 544, 546*); another armlet (*naga vodthu*); bangles (*valai*); rings (*modiram*); a tight waist belt (*oddiyanam, see 524*); and ankle bells (*salangai*).*

▲ 420. Jaipur, Rajasthan

*Woman's gold head ornament (*phuljhumka binda suda*), consisting of two strips (*jhalas*) and a central ornament (*ek kalangi sarpech*) attached to earrings (*karanphul-jhumka*), set with diamonds, cabochon rubies, emeralds, and pearls. Similar to the sarpatti worn by a man (*see 832*), it is distinguished by the attached karanphuls at either end.*
The Royal Collection Courtesy Her Majesty Queen Elizabeth II

Among the ornaments presented to Edward, Prince of Wales, in 1877 by the Maharaja of Jaipur, it was formerly on display in the Indian Room at Marlborough House, London.

421. Palampur, Himachal Pradesh ➤

*Gold head ornament (*mor patti*) attached to heavy earrings, the opposite end fixed to the hair to support them; also called damani-karanphul when the earring is a large, round shape, or phul-jhumka when the earring is a karanphul-jhumka type, or binda suda*
Courtesy Air India, Bombay

422. Lucknow, Uttar Pradesh

Bride wearing a head ornament (jhumar, also called chapka). Some were made with obverse and reverse sides (do-rukh), each ornamented with different gemstones to be reversible. She also wears a forehead ornament (mang tika) with a pearl-strung support (mang patti) and a nose ring (nath), both symbolic of marriage in northern India.
Courtesy Air India, Bombay

423. Lucknow, Uttar Pradesh

Silver head ornament (jhumar)
Disc diameter 1½ in. (3.8 cm); chain length 3⅛ in. (8 cm); lower unit length 4⅜ in. (11.2 cm); weight 72 g
Collection the author, Porvoo

This object is rare because of the design subject in the upper roundel: two fish (mahi-maratib, honor of the fish), a symbol of the former Muslim court of Avadh, now Uttar Pradesh. In Mughal times, this symbol was carried in state processions as a standard, held aloft by a person attending the Nawab. From the roundel is suspended a barque, with peacock prow and stern, and hanging bells (ghungru).

424. Northern India

Gold head ornament (jhumar) with diamonds, rubies, and pearls. It attaches to the hair by a top hook (missing).
Courtesy Spink and Sons Ltd., London

425

426

Back-of-Head Ornaments

425. Sitamarhi, Bihar
Silver end-of-braid tassel (chhoti or chunti), normally attached to three hanks of black silk or cotton thread, braided into the back-of-head braid, the ornament hanging at its end (see 807)
Length 5⅝ in. (14.4 cm); weight 259 g
Collection the author, Porvoo

426. Mandi, Himachal Pradesh
Silver braid-end tassel (bini band), worn by brides in the nineteenth century, now obsolete

427

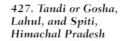

428

427. Tandi or Gosha, Lahul, and Spiti, Himachal Pradesh
Silver back-of-head ornament (kirkitsi or kyir-byir-tea) with a central turquoise and four corals
Diameter 3½ in. (9 cm); weight (approx.) 180 g

Fixed to the back of the head by passing some hair through a central back loop, it is worn constantly by older women and often by many women on festive occasions, usually in conjunction with two side-of-head large amber (böschel) beads (see 122).

428. Bangalore, Karnataka
Flat, repoussé-decorated silver hair ornament (jadaibillai or phirkiche phul) backed by a copper wire spiral (kambisuriyulla) that is "screwed" into the hair braid or bun at the back of the head to hold it in place
Diameter 2¼ in. (5.9 cm); weight 49 g
Collection the author, Porvoo

This and a more dimensional form (koppe) are also worn in Andhra Pradesh.

Ear Ornaments

429. Anatomy of an Ear

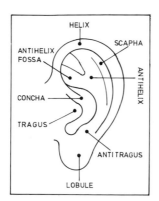

In India, the ear of a woman, and sometimes a man, may be pierced at any of the designated major positions (and others) for the insertion of an earring. The particular place is determined by religious and social customs or economic factors, and the custom in practice by a particular community.

430. Tamil Nadu

Tamil Nadu ear ornaments are generally of 22-karat gold. Goldsmiths there have developed an elaborate ear-ornament tradition, which often necessitates piercing the ear at several locations and distending the hole made in the earlobe to accommodate them. The attention to detail evident in these ornaments, some of which are very small, illustrates the local goldsmith's outstanding skill.

    These drawings have been culled from thirty of the many volumes of Village Survey Monographs, published in connection with the Census of India, 1961, Madras (Tamil Nadu), 60, part 45, 1963, in which, among other subjects, the traditional jewelry worn by women and men in each of the villages studied is discussed and illustrated. Ear ornaments have been arranged in horizontal rows by concepts, from simple to complex. In the caption, the village of origin appears first, followed (from left to right) by their Tamil vernacular names. Unless designated otherwise, they are all worn by Hindu women.

Row 1
1. Pappanaickenpatti: kammal
2. Thadagam: olai thodu, or katholai (with attached ring called kundolai)
3. Kadambangudi: kadukkan (worn by men)
4. Aladipatti: kaddukkan
5. Thiruvellari: kaddukkan

Row 2
1. Athangarai: thattu (Muslim)
2. Kottumangalam: visala murugu
3. Ariyur: koppu (stick); thattu; kammal
4. Pappanaickenpatti: koppu (top); kammal (lobe)
5. Athangarai: koppu; thodu (Muslim)

Row 3
1. Sirumalai: koppu (top); thattu (middle), clover thattu; kammal (lobe)
2. Thiruvellari: koppu; lolakku (stud with pendant); thallukku (stud); kammal
3. Thadagam: koppu (top); visalamurugu (left); pottu (right)
4. Villangulam: koppu; "S" thattu (left); plain thattu; clover thattu; kammal
5. Visavanoor: kathuvala (set of twelve rings, Muslim); kammal

Row 4
1. Arkavadi: thattu (left); mattal with kammal; lolakku (pendant); talukku (two types)
2. Aladipatti: koppu (top); kurungathu thalukku (bird); mattal (strip); clover thalukku; kammal
3. Vilangulam: mattal; kammal; thongattam (hanging bell)
4. Thadagam: visalamurugu (left); mattal; thodu (lobe stud); and jimikki (bell)
5. Kadakkara: mattal; kammal-jimikki

Row 5
1. Kadambangudi: thongattam or thodu
2. Kadathuchery: kammal-jimikki
3. Ravanasamudram: kathuvalli (set of twelve rings, Muslim)
4. Athangarai: urukkumani
5. Aladipatti: ananthamudichu

Row 6
1. Visavanoor: koppu; onnappu-thattu (small stud)
2. Kanakagiri: thanduvetti
3. Kanakagiri: ananthamudichu
4. Iswaramoorthypalayam: thanduvatti
5. Iswaramoorthypalayam: koppu; visirimurugu; ananthamudichu

Row 7
1. Villangulam: koppu; thattu; puchikudu
2. Kutumangalam: assorted
3. Ravanasamudram: pampadam
4. Kottuthal Azhamkulam: murichi (top stud); lollakku; thallukku; thandatti
5. Kottuthal Azhamkulam: pampadam; ananthamudichu

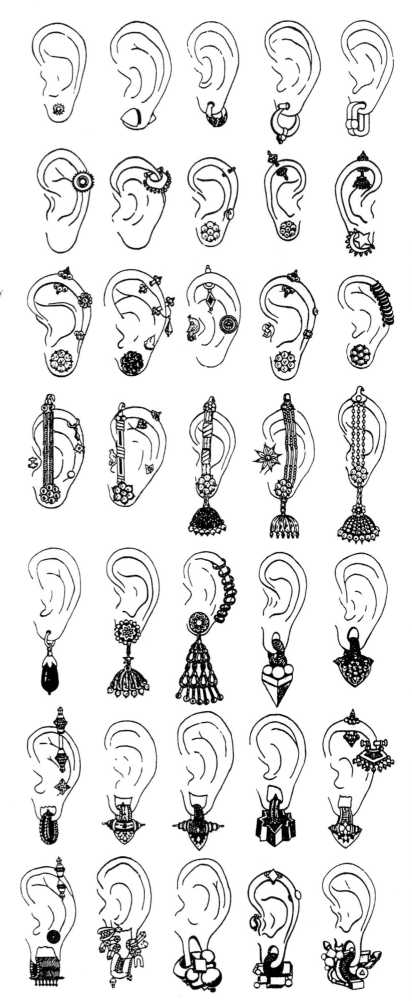

432

Top-of-Ear Ornaments

431. Sam Village, Jaisalmer District, Rajasthan
Young girl wearing silver pendant earrings (panddi) that hang from the top of her ears and sets of ivory bangles

432. Kachchh, Gujarat
Silver earrings (patina loriyan) worn by Rabari women hanging from the top of the ear
Each 2¼ x ¾ in. (5.7 x 2 cm); weight 17 g
Collection Ghysels, Brussels

431

433. Dumbur, Southern Tripura, Tripura ▲
Rai Marsum tribal woman wearing silver top-of-ear studs (wari), her lobe distended by a silver tube, through which passes the loop of a hanging earring (berbali). She also wears a coin necklace (rathai) and strings of glass beads (mani).

434

435

Ornaments Along Ear Edge

434. Kullu, Himachal Pradesh
Woman wearing a series of ear hoops (bhadarian or dandiah; bali or gosh-wara in the Punjab), along the ear perimeter, and hoop earring (bala) through the lobe (see 454)

435. Orissa
Silver earrings (nagula) in the form of a spiraled cobra, worn by screwing the tail end through a series of four to five holes at the ear perimeter, the number corresponding with its number of coil turns
Length 2 in. (5 cm)
Courtesy Chhote Bharany, New Delhi

Earrings Hanging from Lobe

436. Junagadh, Gujarat
Bhopa woman wearing gold earlobe ornaments (vedhla), edge-of-ear ornaments (vat). She also wears a gold arrowhead-shaped neck pendant (ramnami) bearing the stamped name of the god Ramachandra.

437. Andhra Pradesh
Female religious mendicant (gosavin), who, having arrived at the state of widowhood, has adopted an ascetic life-style. Her stretched, pierced earlobes indicate her former possession of heavy gold earrings. Her absence of ornaments publicly communicates her renunciation of worldly possessions and the adoption of an attitude of detachment from material objects, concepts common to Hinduism, Buddhism, and Jainism.

436

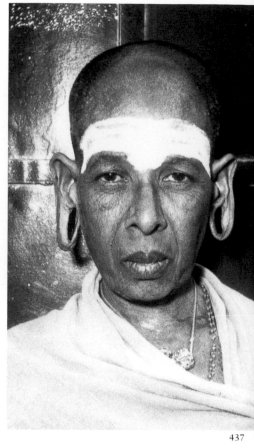

437

Earlobe Hole Dilation

In a custom prevailing among the Kollar, Maravar, Pallar, Paravar, Pariah, Shanar, and Vellala castes, especially around Tirunelveli, Tamil Nadu, the ears of a girl child are pierced on or about the third day after birth. A man of the Koravar caste, whose traditional occupation is bird-catching, pierces both earlobes with a triangular-bladed knife and inserts a piece of cotton wool to prevent the holes from mending. This is changed daily, and, each time, the quantity used is increased in order to stretch the earlobe hole. Healing takes place after about one month, when, for a few days, rolled cotton-cloth plugs replace the cotton wool. Finally, a lead ring is inserted in the hole and, gradually, more rings are added until there are as many as eight in each hole. By the time the child is one year old, the rings' weight has established the stretching process. At this time, the several rings are combined into one of equivalent weight, which is retained until the girl reaches about thirteen. By then, the lobes have become stretched to their utmost, "ideal" limit—almost to the shoulders.

Probably inspired by ancient representations of similarly stretched earlobes on images of Buddha and male and female Hindu deities in temple sculpture, the groups who follow this practice considered stretched earlobe holes a sign of respectability and wealth, and a woman without them was suspected of being a prostitute. Only gold ornaments, as part of a bride's dowry, are used.

The death knell for this custom began to toll when Christian missionaries active in the Tirunelveli area of southern India in the nineteenth century decided to eradicate this "barbarous" fashion. Many converts had operations performed on their earlobes to shorten them. Today the practice is gradually dying out, probably for economic reasons. When the custom ends, so will the manufacture of all earrings meant to be so worn.

◄ 438. Tirunelveli, Tamil Nadu
Kondayan Kottai Maravar woman wearing traditional gold earrings: (top) poodi, (edge) murugu; konapu thattu; (anti-helix) kurututhathu; (earlobe) pampadam, thandotti, mudichi ulakku, and arisithadupu. She also wears a marriage necklace (chutturuvum thaliam or thirumangaliam), each of whose variously shaped units has a particular symbolic meaning.

▼ 439. West Bengal. 19th century
Gold earring (one of a pair) set with gemstones. At the top are two flaming conch shells, symbols of Vishnu, one with a ruby, the other a diamond. Wire loops are threaded with many flat gold, pierced discs.
Each 2⅜ x 2¼ in. (6 x 5.7 cm);
weight 94 g
Victoria and Albert Museum, London (03150 IS)

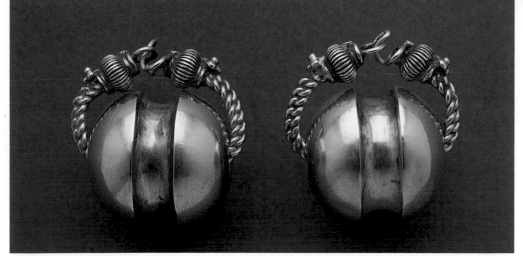

440. Tamil Nadu
Gold earrings worn by Tamil Brahmans, called elai thodu when without attached hooked ring; katholai when with it; the ring is called kundolai.
Each ¾ x ⅝ in. (2 x 1.9 cm); chain length 1¾ in. (4.5 cm); weight 11 g
Collection Ghysels, Brussels

441. Tamil Nadu
Gold tubular earrings (puchikudu)
Tube length ¾ in. (1.9 cm); outer diameter ⅝ in. (1.6 cm); bottom projection length 3/16 in. (0.5 cm); side projection length 3/16 in. (0.5 cm); weight of each 8 g
Collection Ghysels, Brussels

442. Tamil Nadu
Gold earrings (thandatti) of sheet-metal geometric forms filled with a lac composition to prevent denting. The design suggests a three-dimensional yantra.
Each 1¾ x 1½ in. (4.5 x 3.7 cm); weight 114 g
Collection Barbier-Mueller Museum, Geneva (2504-118 A & B)

443. Tamil Nadu
Gold earrings (pampadam), with hollow balls (kundu) and a hollow square (thattu)
Height 2 1/16 in. (5.2 cm); weight 63.5 g
Collection Ghysels, Brussels

The design of purely geometric forms is said by some to represent an abstract bird and, by others, a serpent. All parts are hollow and lac filled to prevent denting (see 438).

444. Madurai, Tamil Nadu
Maravan woman wearing traditional gold ear ornaments. Top: murugu and pudi; center: konnapu or onnappu; hanging: tandatti

444

443

445

446

Studs in Enlarged Earlobe Hole

445. Shekawati, Rajasthan
Woman wearing gold earrings (jarau karanphul-jhumka)
Courtesy Kanjimull and Sons, Scindia House, New Delhi

The double strand of pearls and gemstones that pass over the ears help to support its weight. Attached to one edge of the disc is a projecting peacock. This old design has persisted until today.

446. Shekawati, Rajasthan. *Mid-18th century*
Gold earrings (jarau karanphul-jhumka)
Diameter 1⅞ in. (4.7 cm); total width 2³⁄₁₆ in. (5.5 cm)
Rijksmuseum, Amsterdam (AK-NM-1057)

Probably the most widely used northern Indian type, this large, round earring and its many variants evolved from the earlier kundala. In this version, all parts are set with diamonds, rubies, emeralds, and pearls. Attached perpendicularly to the side of the circular, frontal unit is an ornament in the form of a peacock.

447. Saurashtra, Gujarat
Silver ear ornaments (akota) with parcel-gilded stamped units, front and back view, worn by Ahir, Rabari, Bharwad, and Mer women
Disc diameter 2 in. (5 cm); pendant 2⅛ x 1⁵⁄₁₆ in. (5.5 x 3.4 cm); depth 1³⁄₁₆ in. (3 cm); weight of each 39 g
Collection the author, Porvoo

448. Ahmedabad, Gujarat ➤
Front and underside/back view of a pair of gold ear ornaments (akota) set kundan style with rubies, rock crystals (simulating diamonds), green glass (simulating emeralds), and pearls
Disc diameter 2⅝ in. (6.8 cm); lower projection length 3¼ in. (8.2 cm)
The Nasser D. Khalili Collection of Islamic Art, Acc. Nos. JLY 1105; JLY 1106.
Courtesy of the Nour Foundation

These elaborately decorated gold earrings, based on the form normally made in silver for use by rural women, was made for a rural woman who, though wealthy, wished to be identified with her group origins.

447

449

450

449. Madhya Pradesh
Silver earring (tarkulia) with decorative
hanging chains (one of a pair)
Disc diameter 2⁵⁄₁₆ in. (5.9 cm);
projection length ¹⁵⁄₁₆ in. (2.4 cm);
longest chain 5½ in. (14 cm);
weight 18 g
Collection Ghysels, Brussels

451. Maharashtra
Gold earrings with a cluster of seed pearls (kap)
Pearl cluster each diameter 1³⁄₁₆ in. (3 cm);
weight 11 g
Collection Ghysels, Brussels

The ingenious system of construction is illustrated
with a sequentially disassembled unit at right.

452. Bangalore, Karnataka
Two pairs of gold studs, with removable domed plug
that engages a corresponding tube joined to the back of
the front unit. Made of stamped units variously ornamented with red stones and pearls. (Some in this style
have attached pendants, jimikki.)
Each approximately 1⅜ x 1³⁄₁₆ in. (3.5 x 3 cm); weight 10 g
Collection Ghysels, Brussels

450. Junagadh, Gujarat
Silver earrings (kundal or pokhaniu) worn
by Kanbi, Bharwar, Patel, and Totiyu women.
A classic Indian type called an ear reel in
Western jewelry literature, it is commonly
depicted on ancient Indian frescoes, paintings,
and images of deities. Originally it was made
of a strip of palm leaf formed into a spiral, a
style still worn by tribal women in Bihar.

451

452

Earrings with Support

453. Srinagar, Kashmir South, Jammu and Kashmir
Muslim woman with silver ornaments. The weight of the many earring units (kana vaji) is supported by a fancy link chain (alka hor) passing over the crown of the head and attached to the hair. Each hoop is ornamented with stamped floral units. The granulated silver beads of the necklace are gold plated.

454. Kullu, Himachal Pradesh
Silver earring (bala) with pendant green-glass bead, two flanking red-glass beads within wire caps, and attached chains hooked to the hair for support (one of a pair)
Diameter 2⅛ in. (5.3 cm); pendant length 2⅛ in. (5.3 cm); chain length 4½ in. (11.5 cm); weight 28 g
Collection Ghysels, Brussels

455. Delhi
Gold enameled earrings (bale jhabbedar) set with diamonds, with attached crescent- (naya chand or hilal) and fish-shaped (machhli) pendants and fringe pendants
Private Collection, Brussels

An ornamental chain (sankali) is fixed at the top and supplied with an end hook for attachment to the hair to support its weight. This popular design originated in Mughal times.

◄ **456. Srinagar, Kashmir South, Jammu and Kashmir**
Silver head ornament (dur) consisting of a pair of earrings joined by a chain that passes over the top of the head to support them. A Muslim ornament, it incorporates the Muslim crescent-moon symbol (A: hilal).
Length 19⅛ in. (48.7 cm); weight 110 g
Collection Mingei International Museum of Folk Art, San Diego, California

457. Bargarh, Orissa ►
Gold earrings: vertical, attached to the helix (karanphula); horizontal, attached to the antihelix fossa (jalka); nose stud (phulli); and gold necklace (thali mala)

Earrings that Hang from Lobe with Pendant

458. Chhaya, Gujarat
*Mehr woman wearing gold pendant earrings
(loriyan). Her neck, arms, and hands are tattooed
with symbolic religious patterns.*

459. Porbandar, Saurashtra, Gujarat
*Gold pendant earrings (panddi), surface ornamented
with a border of flattened spiral wire, wirework,
and granules
Each 2¹⁵⁄₁₆ x 1½ in. (7.5 x 3.8 cm); weight 8 g
Collection Ghysels, Brussels*

460. Cochin, Kerala
*Gold earrings (andi bhaden kathija) worn by
Muslim Malayalam women in Cochin Division
Height 2⁷⁄₁₆ in. (6.2 cm); weight 41 g
Courtesy Chhote Bharany, New Delhi*

461. Tamil Nadu
*Gold earrings (ananthamudichu) with pendants
Each 1⅞ x ⅞ in. (4.7 x 2.2 cm); weight 7 g
Collection Ghysels, Brussels*

462. Kachchh, Gujarat
*Gold twin-pendant earrings (nagalah) worn by
married Dhebaria Rabari women
Height with loop 2½ in. (6.3 cm); each unit width
1⅛ in. (2.9 cm); weight of each 17 g
Collection Ghysels, Brussels*

458

459

460

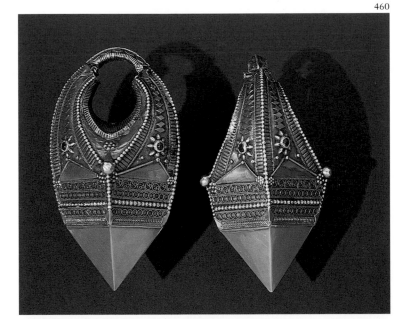

461

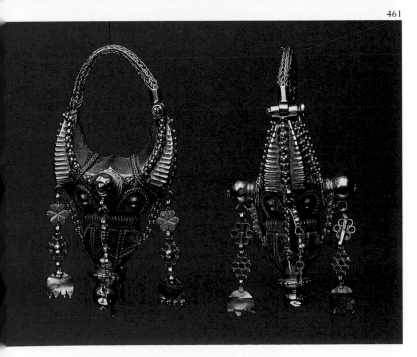

462

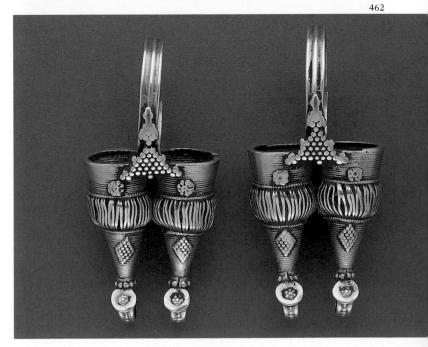

463

464

465

466

463. Kachchh, Gujarat
Gold pendant earrings ornamented with
granulation and set with red glass
Above: diameter ⅞ in. (2.2 cm); Below: diameter
1⅛ in. (2.7 cm); height 2⅛ in. (5.3 cm);
weight of each 9 g
Collection Ghysels, Brussels

464. Kozhikode (Calicut), Kerala
Gold shot-decorated earrings (kattilakal) worn by
Syrian Christian women
Each 2 x ¹⁵⁄₁₆ in. (5 x 2.4 cm); weight 13 g
Courtesy Ghysels, Brussels

465. Cochin, Kerala
Gold earrings (koppu) worn by Muslim
Mappilla women
Each length 2⅜ in. (6 cm); diameter 1³⁄₁₆ in.
(3 cm); weight 11 g
Collection Mis, Brussels

466. Jaipur, Rajasthan
Gold enameled earrings (minai karanphul-
jhumka) with white zircons and pearls,
a classic example of this type
Courtesy Bhuramal Rajmal Surana, Jaipur

Ornaments Covering
Entire Ear

467. Cuttack, Orissa ➤
Silver-filigree ear ornament (kan or kanphul)
that covers the entire ear and is supported
by a chain that either passes over the ear top
or hooks to the hair (one of a pair)
3 x 1¾ in. (7.6 x 4.5 cm)
Collection the author, Porvoo

468

469

Bead Necklaces

468. Udagamandalam (Ootocamund), Nilgiri Hills, Tamil Nadu
Silver bead necklace (sarad) used to decorate the semidomesticated water buffalo they raise and sacrifice at a funeral. The central bead, 5 x 2 in. (12.7 x 5 cm), has a form inspired by the indigenous carambola fruit (Marathi: karambal; Averrhoa carambola). The discs covered with cowrie shells hang at the back and act as a counterweight.
Total length (metal part) 30½ in. (77.5 cm); weight 1,255 g
Collection the author, Porvoo

Most of the jewelry made for the Todas is created by Asaris from Malabar who work in Udagamandalam.

469. Yepparshkood, Nilgiri Hills; Tamil Nadu
Toda woman wearing traditional silver jewelry, including a sarad necklace, a smaller version of 468
Courtesy Air India, Bombay

Rigid Torques

470. Udaipur, Rajasthan
Man wearing a solid silver torque (hansuli), choker (chirpatti)

471. Rajasthan
Rigid silver torque (hansuli, referring to the collarbone, where it rests) of hollow (pola) construction, with chasing and dot-punch stamping
Diameter 5⅛ in. (13.1 cm); center width ¹⁵⁄₁₆ in. (2.2 cm); weight 135 g
Collection the author, Porvoo

This basic torque form, preferably of one, solid (thos) piece of metal, is worn throughout the Gangetic plain area. In each region it has a different name: serin in Jammu District, Kashmir; sutya in West Bengal and Bihar; kanti in Andhra Pradesh. Engraved in Urdu on the right is the name of the former owner, a common practice throughout India:

470

471

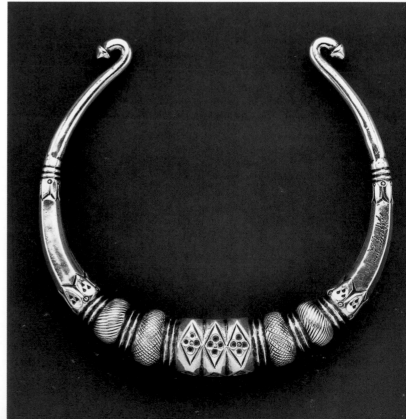

472. Rajasthan
Hollow (pola) silver torque (hansuli), which opens at right rear by an internal hinge. A typical form, its central square section tapers to round at the end.
Highest diameter 6⅝ in. (16.8 cm);
widest diameter 6¼ in. (16 cm); weight 180 g
Collection Ghysels, Brussels

473. Pali. Rajasthan
Silver torque (hansuli), solid except for the sheet-metal-stamped ball-patterned parts to simulate small balls (gajre)
Approximate diameter 7 in. (7.9 cm)
Collection Linda Pastorino, New York

474. Gujarat
Solid (thos) silver torque (hansuli) with patterned punch stamping
Widest diameter 6¼ in. (16 cm); highest diameter 6¼ in. (16 cm); weight 138 g
Collection Ghysels, Brussels

475. Kerala
Cast-bronze pectoral gorget-torque, simulating a series of necklaces, worn by Kerala devil dancers (see 383)
8⅝ x 9⅛ in. (22 x 23.2 cm); weight 436 g
Collection Mis, Brussels

476. Lucknow, Uttar Pradesh
Silver necklace (chamel) of repoussage-decorated sheet metal, with hinged back units and wirework floral pendants
Diameter 7½ in. (19 cm); weight 210 g
Collection Museum für Volkerkunde, Staatliche Museen Preussischer Kulturbesitz, Berlin (IC 44044)

472

473

474

475

477

476

477. Lucknow, Uttar Pradesh
Rigid silver-wirework torque (chamel) with pendants in sun and moon forms
Diameter 8¾ in. (22.3 cm); weight 280.5 g
Collection Chandless, New Jersey

479

478

Wire Neck Ornaments

478. Rajasthan and Gujarat
Silver wire torque (varlo), the wire wrapped and braided, with stamped-flower appliqués
11 x 7¹⁄₁₆ in. (22 x 18 cm); weight 480 g
Private Collection, Brussels

479. Kachchh, Gujarat
Silver-wrapped spiral, continuous-wire torque (vadlo or vaidlah), worn by Vaishnavite Hindu Meghval, Mutra Muslim, Hindu Rabari pastoral, and Harijan women
7½ x 7¹¹⁄₁₆ in. (19 x 19.5 cm); weight 910 g
Collection Ghysels, Brussels

An important item in a bride's dowry, it is normally given to her by her father, or future father-in-law.

480. Horka, Banni District, Kachchh, Gujarat
Jat woman wearing a silver wire necklace (vadlo or varlo) made of five wires of different guages. Jats are famous for the refinement of their embroidery and the small size of the mirror inserts they place in it. The result suggests a gemstone set in a textile.

480

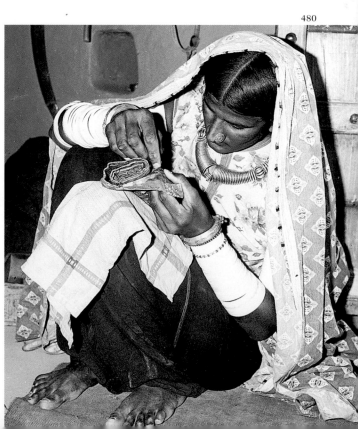

481

481. Rajasthan
Coiled and wrapped silver wire torque (hansuli). Its entire wire decoration consists of one continuous wire length wrapped and coiled over a solid-core wire.
Diameter 6⅛ in. (15.5 cm); central spiral diameter 1³⁄₁₆ in. (3 cm); weight 270 g
Collection the author, Porvoo

482. Andhra Pradesh
Silver torque (hanswi) with three pendants (bottu), worn by Lambadi or Sugali women as a marriage symbol
8⅛ x 8⅛ in. (20.5 x 20.5 cm); pendant length 5⅞ in. (15.5 cm); weight 800 g
Private Collection, Brussels

483. Bikaner, Rajasthan
Silver torque (hansuli) in a distinctive Bikaner design, in which the hollow, tapered tube form is completely wrapped with fine wire and the surface then ornamented with braided wire, die-stamped floral units, granules, and turquoise stones
Outer diameter 6³⁄₁₆ in. (15.7 cm); inner diameter 5⅛ in. (13 cm); front width 1¾ in. (4.3 cm); weight 200 g
Collection the author, Porvoo

483

482

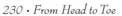

484. Barabanki Village, Uttar Pradesh
Woman wearing a silver choker (katesari) along with other silver ornaments

485. Bahraich, Uttar Pradesh
Silver choker (katesari), each lower unit containing a foil-backed clear-glass "stone" with a central, auspicious red dot (tikka)
Total length 9½ in. (24 cm); back chain length 4½ in. (11.5 cm); neckband width ¾ in. (2 cm); pendant length 1¼ in. (3.2 cm); weight 203 g
Collection the author, Porvoo

Multiunit Chokers and Necklaces

◄ **486. Jaipur, Rajasthan**
Gold necklace set with diamonds, rubies, and pearls (timaniya; tin mania, *three gems*). The name refers to the three central ball-shaped units typical of this basic type. One with five balls is panch mania. Typically supported at the sides with multistrands of glass seed beads (kanch bija mania), it is presented to a bride as an auspicious gift. Courtesy Gem Palace, Jaipur

487. Ranchi, Chotanagpur, Bihar
Oraon boy of Dravidian origin wearing a choker (khambia) of silver spacer units and strung red-glass beads, as well as a glass-seed-bead collar made for him by a female admirer. Similar bead necklaces are made by Mundas.

Necklaces of Strung Units

488. Kozhikode (Calicut), Kerala
*Gold necklace of sixty-seven long units with
attached stamped pendants and clasp*
Total inside length 15¾ in. (40 cm); total outside
circumference 32¼ in. (82 cm); unit length 2½ in.
(6.5 cm); weight 80 g
Collection Mis, Brussels

489. Kerala
*Silver necklace (puthali) of thirty units in two
alternating flower patterns, strung on black cord*
Length 7⅞ in. (20 cm); unit width 2 in. (5 cm);
weight 51 g
Collection Ghysels, Brussels

490. Ambasamudram, Tamil Nadu
*Gold marriage necklace (uru or chuttuvurum thali-
um) with a central thali and other amuletic pendants, some set with coral stones, presented by the
husband to the bride at the wedding*
Length 8⁷⁄₁₆ in. (21.5 cm); weight 240 g
Collection Mis, Brussels

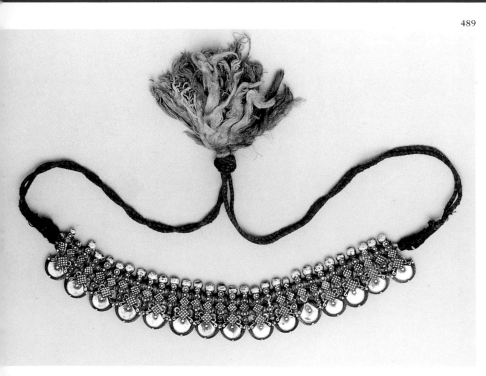

491

492
493

491. Kolhapur, Maharashtra
Gold wedding necklace (kolhapuri saj) with twenty-six pendants, each with a different Vaish-navite symbolic meaning, and a central marriage ornament (thali)
Length 15 in. (38 cm); weight 22.4 g
Private Collection

492. Kerala
Nayar woman wearing, according to custom, simultaneously three traditional gold marriage necklaces (mangkaliyam anivadam): Top: flower units (puthali); center: tiger-claw-shaped units (pulinagathali); bottom: (kuzhimanithali); and gold earrings (thoda)
Courtesy Air India, Bombay

493. Delhi
Necklace (kathla) of nine units on a braided silver wire chain, interspersed with melon-shaped beads
Length overall 18½ in. (47 cm); central unit: 1⅝ x 2½ in. (4.1 x 6.2 cm); smaller unit: 1¼ x 1⁹⁄₁₆ in. (3.1 x 4 cm); weight 148 g
Collection the author, Porvoo

These pendants employ a common Mughal deco-rative device: a highly polished, concave oval or other geometric form, which, by the way it reflects light, gives the false impression of being a silver foil-backed, transparent, cabochon-cut stone, when actually none exists.

494

494. Madras, Tamil Nadu. *19th century*
Gold necklace (gembu rattinamangamalai, ruby-set garland of mango-shaped units), each one with a central diamond (vairam)
Height as pictured 11¾ in. (30 cm)
The David Collection, Copenhagen
(33-1981)

This intricate style of gemstone incrustation (izhachakkai) is still made, though in modern versions the gemstones are generally synthetic.

495. *Reverse side of 494 showing the regionally employed system of holding a series of units in sequence by the use of two flat (thattaiyana) knitted-gold (ponnulla) wire chains (saradu) that pass through loops at the back of each. In this case, an additional, narrower one also passes through the hollow mango-shaped units.*

496. Ajmer, Rajasthan
Banjara woman wearing a necklace (mala) of silver discs (jhalara), each one called a patti, and a central square pendant (chauth). At its terminals are tapered tubes (nali) with attached melon-shaped beads (halde). This necklace is also worn by Lohar, Jat, and Gadolin women.

494

495

Chains

497. Rajasthan and Gujarat
Bhil chain necklace (limbori) with silver wire links and black wooden beads
19¾ x ½ in. (50 x 1.45 cm); weight 96 g
Collection Mis, Brussels
It is called limbori because the wooden beads resemble the seeds of the fruit of the neem tree (Guj. limbo; Melia azadirachta), held in great esteem by all Indians.

498. Northern India
Silver locket (dibiya) on a double, square, four loop-in-loop pair of chains
Length 36¼ in. (92 cm); locket 3¹⁵/₁₆ x 1¾ in. (9.2 x 4.5 cm); weight 346 g
Collection Ghysels, Brussels

499. Terai, Uttar Pradesh
Silver three-strand necklace (tin lara har), worn by Tharu women in the Terai, a sub-Himalayan foothill-jungle area bordering Nepal
Length 22⅞ in. (58 cm); weight 157 g
Collection Ghysels, Brussels

Necklaces with end-spacer terminals such as this almost always have an odd number of strands. The "star" (tara) is worn at the back. Tharu women are often tattooed (lilla) with geometric patterns.

497

498

499

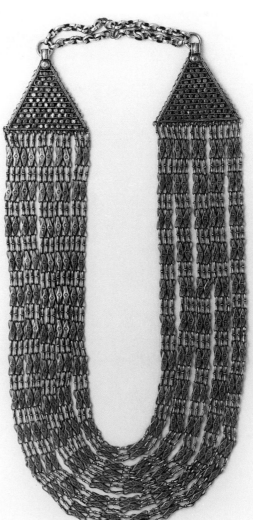

◄ **500. Punjab and Uttar Pradesh**
Silver chain necklace of five strands (maulsari har or panch lara chandan har), widely worn by Hindu and Muslim women
Length 39 in. (99 cm); triangular spacer width 2¾ in. (6.9 cm); weight 426 g
Collection Ghysels, Brussels

501

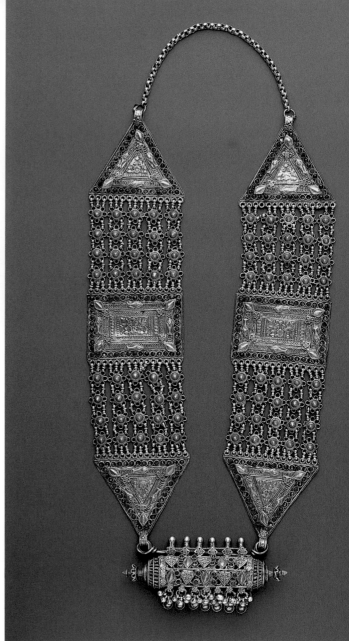

502
503

501. Mandi, Himachal Pradesh
Silver necklace with three main units edged with
stylized snake forms, decorated with die-stamped
units, connected by single loop-in-loop chains, and
hung with bells (ghungru)
Length 23⅝ in. (60 cm); central ornament 1⅜ x
2⅜ in. (3.6 x 6 cm); weight 141 g
Collection the author, Porvoo

502. Jaisalmer, Rajasthan
Silver necklace (chandan har; gallegi) consisting of
top triangular spacers (tekra), connecting chains
(sankhal) of flower links (chinka), and loops (kula-
ba), with central amulet container (madaliya) and
bells (ghungrus). Applied stamped units are gold-
plated and set with red- and green-glass faceted
"stones" (see 330).
Patti length 13 in. (33 cm); amulet container
length 4¾ in. (12 cm); back chain length 6¼ in.
(16 cm); weight 470 g
Collection the author, Porvoo

503. Patna, Bihar
Silver necklace (panch lara har) whose pendant
units are set with foil-backed, cabochon-cut glass
and represent strung flower buds
Longest strand length 20½ in. (52 cm); unit height
⁹⁄₁₆ in. (1.5 cm); back spacer unit 1⅜ x 1⅜ in.
(3.5 x 3.5 cm); weight 219 g
Collection the author, Porvoo

Pendants

504. Tamil Nadu
Gold pendant (ponnulla kadukkan)
with a swami relief representation
of a four-armed Vishnu seated on
a cobra throne (anantasanam)
wearing traditional ornaments of
Tamil Nadu, ornamented with five
pendant rubies
Approximate height 3⅛ in. (8 cm)
Courtesy Krishna Nathan, Krishna
Gallery of Asian Arts, New York

505. Lahore, Pakistan
Gold pendant (jugni; dhuk-dhuki;
nam) depicting two parrots flanking
a flowering plant, with hanging
pearl. The foil-backed, kundan-set
gemstones are cut to form body
parts. It was formerly used on a
baleora-type necklace (see 763).
1¹⁵⁄₁₆ x 1⅜ in. (4.9 x 4.2 cm);
weight 22 g
Collection Ghysels, Brussels

506. *Pendant Bells*

The charming tinkle of these small
bells (ghungrus), commonly
attached to many Indian ornaments, elicits an erotic response in
most Indian men.

507. Madurai, Tamil Nadu
Late 18th century
Gold pendant (kilikadukkan) in
the form of a parrot (kili), set with
diamonds, emeralds, rubies, and
foil-backed rock crystal, with two
integral suspension loops and
pendant pearls. The reverse is
engraved with floral motifs.
3¹⁵⁄₁₆ x 2⅜ in. (10 x 6 cm)
Courtesy Spink and Son Ltd.,
London

504

505

506

507

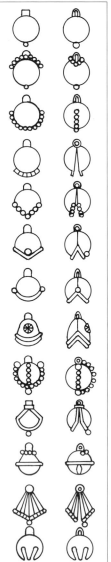

Shoulder Ornaments

508. Jaipur, Rajasthan. *Late 19th century*
Gold navette-shaped epaulet (khag or kandha ka gahna), the obverse set with white sapphires in floral designs; the reverse polychrome enameled
5 x 2¼ in. (12.8 x 5.2 cm)
Courtesy Sotheby's, London

Worn by Maharajas such as those of Varanasi and Bundi, this epaulet originally had a pearl fringe hanging from the integral perimeter loops. An ancient type of Indian epaulette (bujakirudu) is depicted on sculptures of Hindu deities from the twelfth century onward. The present type was inspired by European military models and worn in pairs. Under the one on the right shoulder went the ribbon, to which an Order badge was attached or on which an ornamental clasp was threaded (see 521).

509. *Reverse side of the epaulet, enameled with six red poppies on a white ground (safed chalwan), the central pair flanked by birds. The light blue ground is surrounded by a green-enamel lobed border. The many integral side loops were meant to hold a missing pearl fringe.*

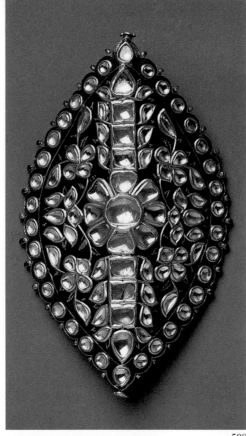

508

509

510. Kullu, Himachal Pradesh
Silver shoulder pins (khanda sui) and connecting chain worn to secure a woman's woolen wrap-around garment
Pendant 3⅛ x 2⅝ in. (8 x 6.8 cm); chain length 6⅜ in. (16.3 cm); pin length 3½ in. (9 cm); weight 79 g
Collection the author, Porvoo

511. Varanasi, Uttar Pradesh
His Highness Maharaja Sir Prabhu Narayan Singh Bahadur G.C.I.E. of Varanasi, wearing a pair of gold gemstone-set and enameled epaulets with attached pearl and emerald fringe. He is also wearing the collar and badge of the Most Eminent Order of the Indian Empire (see 742).

512

Torso Ornaments

512. Junagadh, Gujarat
Bridegroom wearing a silver shirt-stud ornament
(hare) and matching silver belt (kandora)

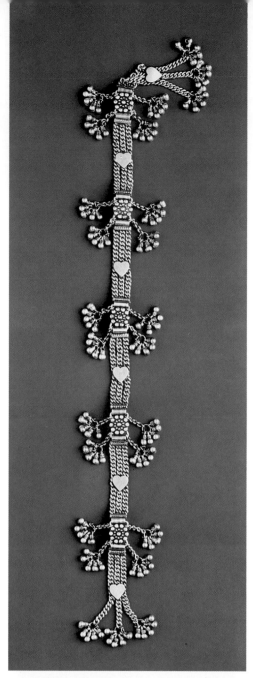

◄ **513. Gujarat**
Man's silver shirt-stud
ornament (hare or
camp, rural name;
ser, urban name)
18⅛ x ½ in.
(46 x 1.3 cm);
weight 149 g
Collection the author,
Porvoo

Behind each floral
unit is a stud that
passes through two
corresponding eyelets
in a shirt or tunic. The
chain (sankal or zanjir)
and stud (phulli) tops
remain visible at the
garment front. Similar
types are worn by Gujar
women in Himachal
Pradesh to close their
upper garment (kurta)
and are there called
ta'wiz- janzir.

514. Delhi ➤
Silver openwork shirt
ornament (kurta
zewar) made of many
small applied units,
joined by links, with
three circular studs
and a bottom "fringe"
Length 10¼ in.
(26 cm); weight 45 g
Collection Jay and
Jean Gang, New York

515. Golconda, Andhra Pradesh
Early 18th century
Wall hanging of a woman wearing a cross-chest
torso ornament (baddhi)
Painted cotton, 48¾ x 33 in. (123 x 84 cm)
The Museum of Far Eastern Antiquities, Stock-
holm. Gift from the Ernest Erickson Foundation
(ÖM 1989:82)

516. Himachal Pradesh. 19th century
Silver cross-chest torso ornament (baddhi) made
of round and flat beads (gol aur hamwar dar)
in the form of flower heads, and two strung
amulets (jantra)
Each strand length 46½ in. (118 cm); unit
diameter ⅝ in. (1.7 cm); center unit diameter
1⁹⁄₁₆ in. (4 cm); amulet length 1⁹⁄₁₆ in. (4 cm);
weight 188 g
Victoria and Albert Museum, London (03490 IS)

Worn by both men and women, this ornament
is depicted in sculpture as early as the second
century B.C., as in the ceramic figurines of Mother
goddesses (see 691). It was also popular among
Mughals and Persians.

515

516

517

518

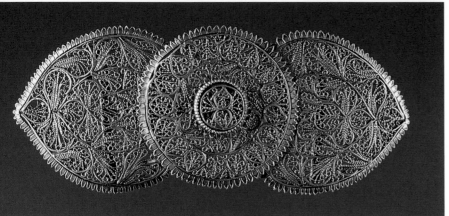

519

520

Belt Buckles

517. Northern India. *18th century*
Steel, silver inlaid (koftgari) belt buckle (baklas)
4⅝ x 2⁹/₁₆ in. (11.7 x 6.5 cm); weight 47 g
Collection the author, Porvoo

Buckles of this design were used on a sword suspension belt
(yakbandi or nijad).

518. Kotli Loharam, Pakistan
Steel belt buckle (faulad baklas) with a damascene inlay of
gold and silver on a hatched ground (teh-nishan style)
4⅜ x 2¼ in. (11 x 5. 7 cm); weight 131 g
Collection the author, Porvoo

The design has the form of two plane tree (chinar; Platanus
orientalis) leaves.

519. Karimnagar, Andhra Pradesh
Silver filigree (tarkashi) belt buckle (baklas)
4½ x 2⅜ in. (11.5 x 6 cm); weight 30 g
Collection Torbjörn and Judy Carlsson, Art Expo,
Washington, D.C.

520. Jaipur, Rajasthan. *19th century*
Gold belt clasp (P: girift) with central lotiform rosette set
with diamonds, rubies, and emeralds; polychrome enameled,
the reverse in floral design, in translucent colors on an
opaque white (safed chalwan) ground
Length 4½ in. (11.4 cm)
Courtesy Sotheby's, New York

521. Northern India. *19th century*
Three gold shoulder-baldric buckles (H: patka sath or parkar) and a belt clasp (baklas),
gemstone set and enameled
The Royal Collection. Courtesy Her Majesty Queen Elizabeth II

Presented to the Prince of Wales (later Edward VII) during his tour of India in 1875–76.
The top three are worn on the chest supported by a broad ribbon, diagonally placed from
left shoulder

Brass Belts

522. Jagdalpur, Bastar, Madhya Pradesh
Cast-brass tribal belt of eight openwork and nine linking units
33½ x 1⅛ in. (80.5 x 2.7 cm); weight 678 g
Collection Mis, Brussels

523. Irinjalakuda, Kerala
Cast-brass belt (aramani) hung with bells (mani), seven units decorated with geese (hamsa)
33 x 2 in. (84 x 5 cm); pendant bell length 2¼ in. (5.7 cm); weight 730 g
Collection the author, Porvoo

The belt was made for use by local theatrical and devil dancers.

Rigid Belts

524. Madras, Tamil Nadu
Rigid gold belt (oddiyanam), two part, hinged, held by a clasp encrusted by diamonds, emeralds, and cabochon rubies; the inner surface, unseen when worn, is elaborately pierced and engraved with floral patterns.
The Royal Collection. Courtesy Her Majesty Queen Elizabeth II

Tight belts are much liked by Indian women because they accentuate the hips. Particularly among Dravidians, large hips are considered to be a sign of feminine beauty and fertility, as indicated by many south Indian temple sculptures of goddesses. This belt was presented by a maharaja to the Prince of Wales in 1875, to be given to Alexandra, his slim-waisted wife.

525. *Smt Yamani Krishnamurty, Bharata-natyam dancer, wearing a rigid-waist belt (oddiyanam) of silver sheet metal decorated with pierced-work floral designs*

Flexible Chain Belts

526. Honava, Karnataka
Silver loop-in-loop belt (kamardani), with hooked closing
Length 23⅝ in. (60 cm); diameter ¾ in. (2 cm); weight 940 g
Collection Ghysels, Brussels

The finished chain is drawn through a drawplate to make it smooth. A new belt is termed "virgin" (H: kori). Through wear over the years it becomes smooth and supple (H: chikna, greasy, polished, shiny).

526

527

527. Nashik, Maharashtra
Silver double-braided wire-chain belt (getha)
Length 36 in. (91.5 cm); belt width ⅝ in. (1.7 cm); knob end width 1⅝ in. (4.2 cm); weight 549 g
Collection Ghysels, Brussels

Provided with seventy-seven sliding bands ornamented at front with alternating large and small die-stamped floral rosettes to hold two loop-in-loop chains together. One end terminates in a large ornamental knob (ganth) that passes through the loop (phanda) at the other end to close it.

Linked Belts

528

528. Kozhikode (Calicut), Kerala
Silver belt (arapatta), made of large, double interlocking wire links, with buckle and hook-end extensions elaborately decorated in wirework, used by Muslim women
33 x 2 in. (84 x 5 cm); weight 600 g

The belt closes by passing the end through the buckle, then engaging its inverted hook into the chain links.

529

529. Bombay, Maharashtra. *19th century*
*Silver chain belt (pon) with half-round wire links,
formerly used by Son Koli fishermen of the Bombay
area, who wore it below the navel over the dhoti
(lower garment) to hold the dhoti up*
*Length 23⅝ in. (60 cm); clasp width ¾ in. (2 cm);
chain width ⅝ in. (1.5 cm); weight 951 g*
Collection Ghysels, Brussels

530. Bombay, Maharashtra
*Silver chain belt (pon) with square, multiloop wire
link construction*
*Length 31⅞ in. (81 cm); clasp width 1 in. (2.5 cm);
chain width ⅝ in. (1.5 cm); weight 949 g*
Collection Ghysels, Brussels

531. Gwalior, Madhya Pradesh
*Silver belt (kardhani) of four rows of decorated links,
two-paneled clasp with central screw forming a hinge,
unscrewed to open the belt*
28⅜ x 1¾ in. (72 x 4.5 cm); weight 590 g
Courtesy Ellora, New Delhi

532. Madhya Pradesh
*Silver belt (kamarband) of thirty-one six-linked pierced-
work units, with screw clasp*
32¼ x 1¾ in. (82 x 4.5 cm); weight 612 g
Collection Ghysels, Brussels

530

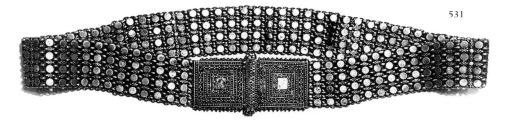

531

532

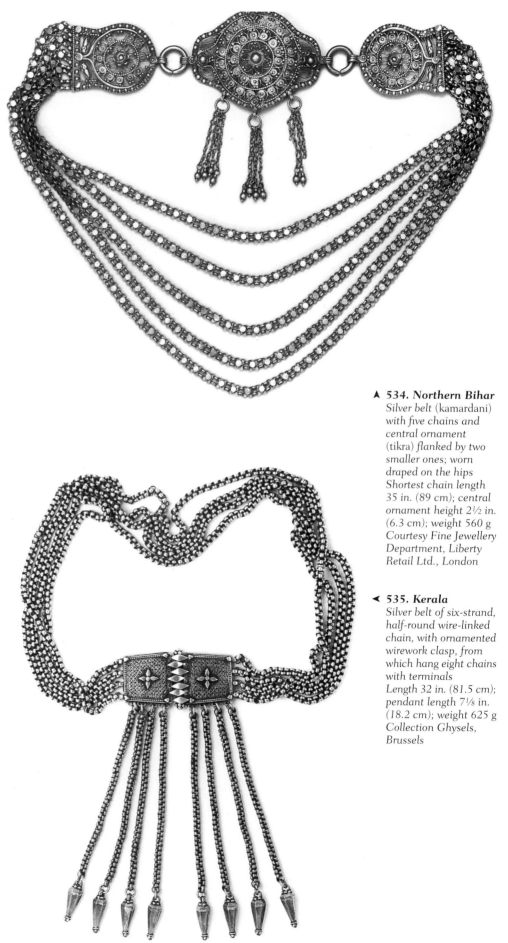

533. Didarganj (Patna), Bihar
Maurya Period, 3rd century B.C.
Yakshi or fertility goddess (generally called a "fly-whisk
[chauri] bearer"), in polished sandstone
64¼ x 19¼ in. (163.2 x 49 cm)
Patna Museum, Patna (134)

A very early representation of an ideal Indian female,
she wears a belt (kamardani) of five chains joined by a
lotuses-in-profile clasp. Draped on the hips in the same
manner as 534, this representation indicates the antiquity of this design.

▲ **534. Northern Bihar**
Silver belt (kamardani)
with five chains and
central ornament
(tikra) flanked by two
smaller ones; worn
draped on the hips
Shortest chain length
35 in. (89 cm); central
ornament height 2½ in.
(6.3 cm); weight 560 g
Courtesy Fine Jewellery
Department, Liberty
Retail Ltd., London

◄ **535. Kerala**
Silver belt of six-strand,
half-round wire-linked
chain, with ornamented
wirework clasp, from
which hang eight chains
with terminals
Length 32 in. (81.5 cm);
pendant length 7⅛ in.
(18.2 cm); weight 625 g
Collection Ghysels,
Brussels

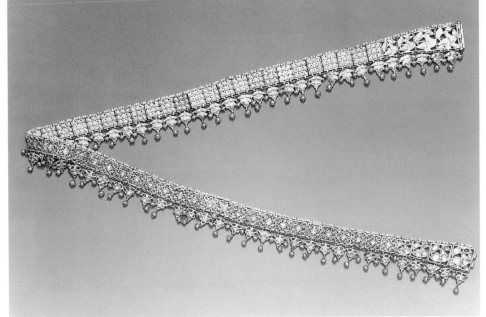

Hinged Belts

536. Tamil Nadu
Gold belt (araippattigai) with fifty-eight small, square, floral units hinged together, fifty of them embellished with cabochon rubies, and a central diamond
Approximate length 26 in. (66 cm)
Courtesy Spink and Sons Ltd., London
The front eight units are decorated with a procession of eight geese (hamsa), in ascending sizes (see 625), on a pierced-work ground and pendant pearls.

536

◄ **537. Hyderabad, Andhra Pradesh**
Silver belt (kamarsal), with forty Garuda-head units hinged together, worn by Vaishnavites
30⅞ x ⅞ in. (78.5 x 2.3 cm); weight 702 g
Collection Mis, Brussels

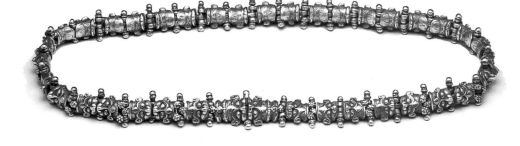

Braided-Wire Belts

538. Pune, Maharashtra and Hyderabad, Andhra Pradesh
Silver belt (kamarpatti or kandora) of four-strand braided silver wire
Length 33½ in. (85 cm); weight 700 g
Collection Ghysels, Brussels

539. Vellore, Ambedkar District Area, Tamil Nadu
Silver belt (araipatti)
27½ x 2 in. (70 x 5 cm); weight 650 g
Collection the author, Porvoo

Ornamented in the front with four repoussé-worked lotus-flower design panels. The central square, stepped-pyramid unit suggests a Hindu temple tower (sikhara), topped by a green glass insert. All are joined by five-lugged hinges. At the back, a series of integrated, knitted-wire units are joined to form a broad band, held together by seven sliding clasps (mattukai), each ornamented by a repoussé-worked floral design.

538

539

Knitted Belts

540. Madras, Tamil Nadu ➤
Silver belt (peti or araikkachchu)
with knitted (pinnayasthiram)
fabric band of very fine-gauge
wire. The belt tip is ornamented
with an image of the goddess
Devi, the buckle with two female
guardians, the guard slide with
one, all in the swami style of the
mid-19th century.
28 x 2 in. (71 x 5 cm); buckle
2¾ x 1½ in. (7 x 3.8 cm);
weight 150 g
Collection Samuel and Laurel
Beizer, New York

541

542

Waist Ornaments

541. Himachal Pradesh
Gaddi leather pride purse (man-
dua or bagalu) worn by shepherds
and local women. Ornamented
with leather appliqué, embroidery,
mirrors, buttons, shells, beads,
and leather spiralettes, by custom
they are exchanged in friendship
with relatives and friends.
Collection Jacques Carcanagues,
New York

542. Himachal Pradesh
Gaddi shepherd blowing on a silver trumpet (narsingha or kahala)
of a unique, local form, used at
temple services, to call assemblies,
at ceremonial dance festivities,
and in marriage processions. His
costume includes an ornamental
leather pride purse (bagalu) at his
waist, and a Tibetan-style tinder
purse (mer-cha).

◄ 543. Rajkot, Gujarat
Silver chatelaines (judas) used to
hold a woman's household keys
(chabi) at her waist, each one
backed by a large, flat hook
(pakara) to catch it in place at the
waist, and a keyring (chabi ka
girda). The visible, ornamented
front covers the keys. They are
used by merchant class (Baniya)
Marwari women as a prestigious
sign of their ownership of possessions that must be secured.
Length 4 to 6 in. (10–15 cm)

544

Upper Armlets

544. Madras, Tamil Nadu
Rigid gold armlet (vanki)
Approximate inner diameter 3 in. (7.5 cm)
Courtesy Air India, Bombay

The design has a central lotus (kamalam) *flanked by*
addorsed peacocks (mayil) and a pendant of two geese
(hamsa), all parts set with diamonds, cabochon-cut rubies,
and emeralds.

545. Gujarat
Rigid silver armlet (bazu-ta'wiz) with attached amulet case
Height 1 in. (2.5 cm); outer diameter 3¼ in. (8.3 cm);
amulet case length 2¼ in. (5.6 cm); weight 92 g
Collection Ghysels, Brussels

546

546. Tamil Nadu
Rigid gold armlet (vanki) set
with diamonds and rubies; with
pendant pearls in an openwork,
meandering floral-creeper
(padarkodi) design
Inner diameter 2¾ in. (7 cm);
weight 102 g
Courtesy Spink and Son Ltd.,
London

545

547. Tamil Nadu
Rigid twisted-and-wrapped-wire, silver upper armlet vanki)
Height 2¹⁵⁄₁₆ in. (7.5 cm); diameter 2⅞ in. (7.2 cm);
weight 116 g
Collection Ghysels, Brussels

The armlet's V-shaped form permits size adjustments by
stretching it apart or compressing it.

548. Maharashtra

Lost-wax-cast copper bangle (virkangan; vir, hero or powerful; kangan, bangle)
Outer diameter 4 in. (10.1 cm); inner diameter 2¾ in. (7 cm); weight 118 g
Collection the author, Porvoo

Worn as a bangle or an armlet by a Shaivite ascetic (bairagi). Represented around the perimeter are symbols associated with Shiva and his relatives: the lingam with four heads (charmukhi linga); bull (Nandin); trident (trishula); Parvati, Shiva's wife, his sons Ganesha and Karttikeya, their symbols and incarnations; the goddess Devi or Bhavani; foot impressions (Shivapadakam); serpent (samp); sun (suraj); moon (chand); rattle drum (damaru); five piled-up balls (panch pindi) representing the five elements of life (panch krida); and others.

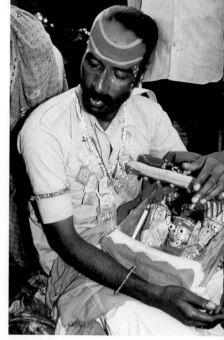

548

549. Kala Am Khurd, Kandwa District, Maharashtra

Shaivite devotee wearing an armlet (virkangan) and several necklaces, each with many die-stamped silver and gold amulet plaques (see 158). He carries a box (pitari) containing deity-image plaques and a lost-wax cast brass head of a goddess ornamented with a gold nose ring.
Courtesy Rautenstrauch-Joest Museums für Volkerkunde der Stadt Köln

549

550. Indore, Madhya Pradesh

Rigid silver armlet (vauk) worn by Mahratta and Gujarati women of the Raval community. The semiflexible body of broad braided wire has a central floral ornament, behind which is the concealed closing device.
Height 2¾ in. (7 cm); outer diameter 4¹⁵⁄₁₆ in. (12.5 cm); inner diameter 2⁹⁄₁₆ in. (6.5 cm); weight 368 g
Collection Ghysels, Brussels

550

551. Dumka, Santhal Pargana, Bihar

Rigid silver upper armlet (bank) with silver tassel (ghundi), worn by Santhal tribal women
Outer diameter 3¹⁵⁄₁₆ in. (10 cm); inner diameter 2¹⁵⁄₁₆ in. (7.3 cm); tassel length 2¾ in. (7 cm); weight 102 g
Collection the author, Porvoo

551

552. Indore, Madhya Pradesh

Silver-wire, two-part, hinged armlet (vauk) made essentially of two uniformly bent wires held in place by soldered rings at top and bottom, ornamented at front with wirework strip and retaining screw
Height 2⁹⁄₁₆ in. (6.5 cm); outer diameter 3½ in. (9 cm); inner diameter 2⅜ in. (6.1 cm); weight 261 g
Collection Ghysels, Brussels

552

554

553

553. Tarbha, Sonapur Taluk, Balangir District, Orissa
Pair of rigid silver-wire armlets (nagmuri) with an undulating, serpentine motif and a flower clasp (phula). Also used around Raipur, Madhya Pradesh
Height 1³⁄₁₆ in. (3 cm); outer diameter 2³⁄₄ in. (7 cm); weight (one) 83 g
Collection Ghysels, Brussels

554. Jodhpur, Rajasthan
Bhil woman wearing local silver ornaments, including earrings (karanphul jhumka), necklace (panchmaniya), amulet (madaliya), rigid armlet (baju-chur), hand ornament (hathphul), cuffs (bahi-chur), ring (chhalla), and glass-bead necklaces (kanch moti har)

555. Vidyadarpur, Orissa
Pair of rigid silver armlets (tada) ornamented with shot, stamped units, stamped wire and strip, and small cast forms
Height 1³⁄₄ in. (4.5 cm); outer diameter 3⁵⁄₈ in. (9.2 cm); inner diameter 2⁷⁄₈ in. (7.2 cm); weight (one) 365 g

The central projections suggest the tower (shikara) of a Hindu temple. The two-part, hinged construction is opened by winding an ornamented screw head clockwise. Indian jewelry screws generally turn in a direction counter to that used in the West.

556. Shillong, East Khasi Hills, Meghalaya
Pair of rigid silver armlets (baju-chur), worn by Khasi women
Outer diameter 3¹⁄₂ in. (9 cm); inner diameter 2³⁄₄ in. (7 cm); weight (one) 174 g
Collection the author, Porvoo

The armlets are worn during festival dances performed before the Siem priestess to the ruling goddess Ka Blei Synshar, who controls the success of crops (see 408).

555

556

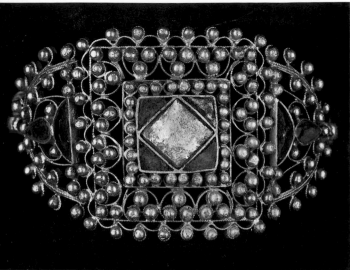

557. Rajasthan
Three-part gilded-silver armlet (bank) with red and green glass "stones"
Length 2¹⁵/₁₆ in. (7.5 cm); weight 40 g
Museum für Volkerkunde, Staatliche Museen Preussischer Kulturbesitz, Berlin (IC 3831)

558. Rajasthan. c.1750
Miniature painting of mother and child, in which the mother wears a pair of bank-type three-part armlets (see 557)
6³/₈ x 5⁹/₁₆ in. (16.2 x 14.1 cm)
British Museum, London. Gift of P. C. Manuk & Miss G. M. Coles, through N.A.C.F. (1949-10-8-023)

557
559

558
560

559. Jaipur, Rajasthan
Pair of gold, three-part, hinged armlets (bazuband) set with rubies
4¹/₈ x 2 in. (10.5 x 5 cm); weight (one) 65 g
Courtesy Bhuramal Rajmal Surana, Jaipur

560. Delhi
Gold three-part armlet (bazuband) in the classic Mughal armlet format of three flexible, hinged units, each set with gemstones
4³/₄ x 1¹/₂ in. (12.2 x 3.8 cm)
Courtesy Sotheby's, London

Here, flower petals and leaves of a central ruby, carved emeralds, and diamonds are used. The reverse (below) is polychrome enameled in a floral design.

561. Tarbha, Sonapur Taluk, Balangir District, Orissa
Flexible silver armlet (bahasuta) made of units strung on a flexible, multistrand, braided chain band
Width 2³/₈ in. (6 cm); outer diameter 4¹/₈ in. (10.5 cm); inner diameter 2⁹/₁₆ in. (6.5 cm); weight 456 g
Collection Ghysels, Brussels

A highly work intensive ornament, it is usually worn on the right upper arm, with the tada (see 555) on the left upper arm.

562. View of armlet 561 showing the inside of the front part and the back sliding units on the braided-wire chain band.

561

562

563. Jaipur, Rajasthan. *19th century*
Gold armlets (bazuband):
Above: Flexible with twenty interlocking vertical units, each set with diamonds; the semicircular ends are set with diamond birds on a blue enamel ground.
Length 5¹¹/₁₆ in. (14.4 cm)
Below: Three-part, hinged, set with diamonds, kundan style
Length 5½ in. (14 cm)
Courtesy Sotheby's, New York

564. Udaipur, Rajasthan
Woman wearing flexible silver armlets (bazuband) of multiple, interfitting, abutted units, each with a top and bottom loop through which cord is threaded and tied to the arm. She also wears a gold necklace called charmania (four gems).

565–67. Rajasthan
Flexible silver armlets (bazuband, called bahutta by Muslims). Three versions of a basic design concept:
Top: 6⅞ x 2¼ in. (17 x 5.7 cm); weight 200 g
Center: 5 x 1⁵/₁₆ in. (12.7 x 3.3 cm); weight 62 g
Bottom: 7¾ x 3 in. (19.7 x 7.5 cm); weight 288 g
Collection Ghysels, Brussels

▼ **568. Mandi, Himachal Pradesh**
Woman wearing flexible silver armlets (bajuband) with elaborate hanging silver tassels (sar ghundi or sumbala) attached to the loose cord ends
Tassel length c. 15 in. (38 cm)

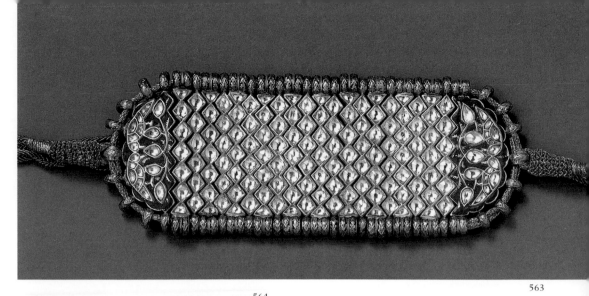

563

564

565, 566

567

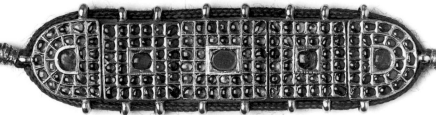

569

569. Tamil Nadu
Flexible gold armlet (bujam ponnabaranam), with rubies and a central emerald in each of the five units (one of a pair). See 851 for a Western interpretation.
3¹/₁₆ x ⅞ in. (7.9 x 2.2 cm); weight 23 g
Collection Mis, Brussels

▲ 570. Rajasthan
Knitted-wire, flexible-tube silver bracelet (bala),
the tube joined by a chased-sheet-metal closing
Outer diameter 3½ in. (9 cm); inner diameter
2½ in. (6.5 cm); approximate weight 80 g
Private Collection, Brussels

Bracelets

▲ 571. Rajasthan
Pair of rigid, penannular solid-silver bracelets (kara)
Outer diameter 3¼ in. (8.2 cm); inner diameter 2 in. (5.1 cm);
weight (one) 237 g
Collection Ghysels, Brussels

◄ 572. Madras, Tamil Nadu. *19th century*
Pair of one-part bracelets (pattil or kadiyam). The flat band opens by
a screw under the flower head and supports two horizontally projecting,
lozenge-shaped, flat plates with engraved borders, each mounted by a
three-dimensional paroquet (orsirukili) with ruby-set eyes; and a central
lotus flower with ruby-set petals.
Outer diameter 1¾ in. (4.4 cm); ornament length 2⅜ in.
(6 cm); weight (one) 47 g
Victoria and Albert Museum, London (IS 1014-1872)

The bracelets were shown at the International Exhibition, Paris, 1872.

573. Madras, Tamil Nadu ►
Rigid hollow-silver bracelet of shell-
like forms with teaslelike hooked
projections
Outer diameter 4½ in. (11.5 cm);
inner diameter 2 in. (5.1 cm);
width 1⁹⁄₁₆ in. (4 cm); weight 111 g
Collection; Ghysels, Brussels

574. Coimbatore, Tamil Nadu
Gold bracelet (raksha kadakam), two-part, hinged, worn by a Konga
Vellala Tamil Brahman woman
Outer diameter 3¼ x 3⅜ in. (8.3 x 8.6 cm); weight 120 g
Collection Ghysels, Brussels

This mainly agricultural caste community of the northern Coimbatore-
Salem area includes wealthy landowners as well as merchants,
accountants, and other occupations, all with a reputation of having
become wealthy through frugality. The central motif in this bracelet is
an abstraction of a double-headed yali (a mythic animal, conventionalized beyond recognition), which acts as a raksha (an amulet used to
avert the evil eye and protect the wearer against witchcraft).

575. Hyderabad, Andhra Pradesh
Silver bracelet (shown opened)
Outer diameter 2⅛ in. (5.5 cm); inner
diameter 2 in. (5 cm); weight 96 g
Collection Anne Jernandier de Vriese,
Brussels

The central lotus motif is flanked by four
peacocks. The linear chased side units
simulate a wide, multi–link-in-link band,
possibly used in earlier bracelets in this
format.

**576. Tarbha, Sonapur Taluk,
Balangir District, Orissa**
Pair of two-part, hinged, hollow-silver
bracelets (bandaria or kharu)
Outer diameter 4¾ in. (12 cm); inner
diameter 2⅝ in. (6.7 cm); weight
(one) 302 g

The sharp spikes can be used in self-
defense.

577. Barpali, Orissa
Weaver-caste woman wearing a pair of
spiked silver bracelets (bandaria)

574

575

576

577

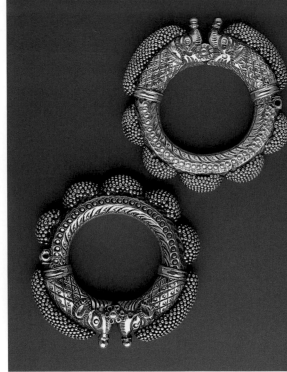

580

Bracelets with Makara-Head Terminals

578. Madras, Tamil Nadu
Two-part, hinged, hollow-silver bracelet with makara-head protome terminals;
opens by the top, central screw
Outer diameter 3⁵⁄₁₆ x 3½ in. (8.5 x 8.7 cm); inner diameter 2⅜ x 1¾ in.
(6 x 4.4 cm); weight 62 g
Private Collection, Brussels

Between them, in their mouths, the makaras hold a magical "jewel." Also made
in gold, the bracelet is worn by Rajas and given by them to male subjects as a
mark of favor.

579. Northern India. 19th century
One of a pair of two-part, hinged, gilded-silver bracelets with makara head
protome terminals
Outer diameter 4⅜ in. (11 cm); inner diameter 2⅝ in. (6.7 cm); weight (one) 126 g
Victoria and Albert Museum, London (03009 IS)

580. Rajasthan
Pair of silver, two-part bracelets (nogri or gajredar bangri) with central makara heads
Outer diameter 3½ in. (9 cm); inner diameter 2½ in. (6.3 cm); weight (one) 175 g
Collection Ivory, New York

The bracelets are ornamented with bunched hollow balls (gajre) rigidly fixed to the
main body by threading a wire through their attached integral loops. This work is
called moti ke gajre kam; the effect of bunching is guchchedar. A silver ball bunch
is called chandi ke gajre ka guchchha; gold, sone ka gajre ka guchchha. They are
placed on bangles, bracelets, necklaces, pendants, earrings, belts, and anklets.
A simplified effect is simulated in stamped sheet metal (see 473).

581

582

581. Jaipur, Rajasthan
Gold bracelet with elephant-head protome terminals (hathi-ka-kara),
polychrome enameled and set with Mughal-cut diamonds, the style called
kundan jarwana-mina kam (kundan-set gemstones with enamel work).
Opens by unscrewing the diamond headed screw to the left. (See also
635, 860)
Courtesy Fred Leighton, New York

582. Sonkh, Mathura, Uttar Pradesh. c. A.D. 100
Makara depicted on a carved-sandstone lintel fragment
Height 11¾ in. (30 cm); length 31½ in. (80 cm)
Mathura Government Museum (SO.1V.37)

The makara, a mythic water monster combining the features of a crocodile,
reptile, elephant, and fish, is the vehicle of the goddess Ganga, the Ganges
River personified, and Varuna, the god of terrestrial waters, and its magical
powers relate to the fertility of water life. Makara heads in matching pairs
frequently appear on the protome terminals of Indian penannular
bracelets and anklets.

Hinged Bracelets

583. Rajasthan
Two-part, hinged, hollow-silver bracelet (charkha), triangular in section
Outer diameter 5¾ in. (14.6 cm); inner diameter 3¼ in. (8.2 cm); weight c. 360 g
Private Collection, Brussels

584. Madras, Tamil Nadu
Two-part, hinged, hollow silver (also gold) bracelet with twenty-six projecting tapered cones, each with an apex of a granulation cluster
Outer diameter 5½ in. (14 cm); inner diameter 2 in. (5.1 cm); weight 107 g
Collection Ghysels, Brussels

The design represents the sun with rays.

585. Orissa
Two-part, hinged, hollow-silver bracelet (kataria), worn in pairs
Outer diameter 7⅛ in. (18 cm); inner diameter 3¹⁵⁄₁₆ in. (10 cm); weight 325 g

The bracelet's form is inspired by Vishnu's or Krishna's serrated-edged weapon (chakra): a steel disc with central hole and sharpened edge, twirled rapidly on a forefinger and hurled at an adversary.

586. Bombay, Maharashtra
Two-part, hinged, silver bracelet (vala), with hollow front, solid shank
Front unit 1½ x 7⅛ in. (3.7 x 18 cm); outer diameter 3½ in. (8.7 cm); inner diameter 2½ in. (6.2 cm); weight 164 g
Collection Ghysels, Brussels

Worn on the right wrist by the Thalkar community of Son Koli fisherwomen about fifty years ago, the bracelet is now obsolete. Wealthy women wore two, some of gold, others of silver with gold balls.

587. Banswara, Rajasthan
Woman wearing a multitude of local traditional silver ornaments and a gold nose ring (nath). On her neck are two enameled gold pendants bearing Ram's footprints (Ram novami padaka, see 177).

588. Rajasthan
Silver, two-part bracelet (naugari) with projections of simulated gajre balls made from stamped sheet metal (see 580)
Collection Ivory, New York

583

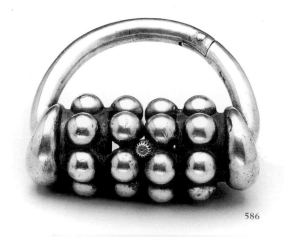

586

584
585

587
588

589. Gujarat or Rajasthan

Cast-brass bracelet of four hinged units, worn by Bhil tribals
Square form 2⅝ x 2⅝ in. (6.6 x 6.6 cm); height 1¾ in. (4.5 cm); approximate weight 225 g
Collection Thorbjörn and Judy Carlsson, Art Expo, Washington, D.C.

The head represents Bhairava, a form of Shiva associated with the village godling Bhairon.

590. Delhi

Flexible silver-chain bracelet (jarao-pahunchi) with hinged clasp and spacers at intervals, set (jadia) with glass "stones"
Approximately 7⅞ x 1¾ in. (20 x 4.5 cm); approximate weight 100 g
Courtesy Fine Jewellery Department, Liberty Retail Ltd., London

589

590

591

Cuff Bracelets

591. Sibsagar, Assam
Khasi woman wearing a pair of gamkharu silver cuff bracelets

592. Jorhat, (Sibsagar), Assam
Two-part, hinged, silver cuff bracelet (gamkharu) with parcel-gilded stamped-sheet-metal ornament; opened by a removable pin
Height 2¹³⁄₁₆ in. (7.2 cm); outer diameter 2½ in. (6.3 cm); inner diameter 2 in. (5 cm); weight 127 g
Collection Mis, Brussels

Made in Sibsagar, the bracelet is worn in pairs by dancers at festival celebrations.

592

593. Shillong, Meghalaya
*Two-part, hinged, silver cuff (syngkha),
worn by Khasi women
Height 4½ in. (11.5 cm); outer diameter
2¾ to 3¼ in. (7 to 8.2 cm); weight 280 g
Collection the author, Porvoo*

594. Vidyadharpur, Orissa
*Two-part, hinged, silver cuff (kalai-churi)
with applied wirework ornament
Height 2⅜ in. (6 cm); outer diameter 2¹⁵⁄₁₆ in.
(7.4 cm); inner diameter 2³⁄₁₆ in. (5.4 cm);
weight 210 g
Collection Ghysels, Brussels*

593

594

595

596

597

595. Vidyadharpur, Orissa
*Two-part, hinged, silver cuff (bahi-churi)
Height 3¼ in. (8.2 cm); outer diameter 3 in.
(7.5 cm); inner diameter 2¼ in. (5.7 cm);
weight 252 g
Collection Ivory, New York*

596. Gujarat. *19th century*
*Two-part, hinged, gold cuff (baluya), worn by
Ahir women
Height 2⅝ in. (6.7 cm); upper diameter 2½ in.
(6.4 cm); lower diameter 2³⁄₁₆ in. (5.6 cm);
weight 113 g
Victoria and Albert Museum, London (IS 1986-1883)*

597. Gujarat
*Pair of rigid silver cuffs (kambi-kadla), worn by
Rabari and Mehr women
Height 3 in. (7.5 cm); outer diameter 3¾ in.
(9.5 cm); inner diameter 2½ in. (6.4 cm);
weight (one) 250 g
Private Collection, London*

Strung-Unit Bracelets

598. Punjab
Flexible silver bracelet of many units (lahsan ke pahunchian), each representing a clove of garlic (lahsan)
Unit ½ x ¼ in. (1.1 x 0.5 cm); total length (without cords) 5⅞ in. (15 cm); weight 155 g
Collection Ghysels, Brussels

Units are closely strung on a black cotton cord, in ten parallel rows. Closed with end loop and ball, the bracelet is worn in pairs, one on each wrist.

598

599

599. Uttar Pradesh
Silver bracelet (chuadanti pahunchian, rat's teeth bracelet) with tooth or tusklike forms, each unit with its own integral loop, strung on cord, then wrapped with silver thread (zari)

600. Himachal Pradesh and Punjab
Woman wearing lahsan ke pahunchian bracelets, along with others

600

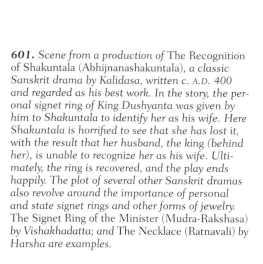

601. *Scene from a production of* The Recognition of Shakuntala (Abhijnanashakuntala), *a classic Sanskrit drama by Kalidasa, written c. A.D. 400 and regarded as his best work. In the story, the personal signet ring of King Dushyanta was given by him to Shakuntala to identify her as his wife. Here Shakuntala is horrified to see that she has lost it, with the result that her husband, the king (behind her), is unable to recognize her as his wife. Ultimately, the ring is recovered, and the play ends happily. The plot of several other Sanskrit dramas also revolve around the importance of personal and state signet rings and other forms of jewelry.* The Signet Ring of the Minister (Mudra-Rakshasa) *by Vishakhadatta; and* The Necklace (Ratnavali) *by Harsha are examples.*

Signet Rings: Sigillographic Power Symbols

*S*igillography (the study of seals) in India is most closely associated with the signet ring, a special form of personal body ornament, incorporating a hardstone or metal seal. Some signet rings also function as a kind of amulet.

A seal is an impressing or printing device, usually small but sometimes very large, with a flat or slight to highly convex face. On this surface is carved or engraved in the negative, or intaglio, a word, phrase, name, title, date, graphic image, symbol, or a combination of these, to be imparted to another substance by impression or printing. The term seal applies to the seal itself as well as the result.

When the seal design is meant to be readable, it must be carved as a mirror image, in reverse, so that, when impressed or printed, it will appear positive and legible. In cases where the inscription on a seal has been created in the positive, the object was meant to function not as a seal but as an amulet. True seals, however, may also have an amuletic purpose.

When the seal face is impressed on a tenacious, plastic material capable of taking an impression, such as clay, sealing wax, resin, or lead, it imparts a positive, relief reproduction of its negatively carved intaglio subject. Unlike clay or lead, many of these substances must be heated to render them plastic, at which time they are impressed with the seal; when cool, the substance hardens and retains the impression indefinitely. To be made permanent, a clay impression must be fired, but, with sufficient pressure, lead, which is naturally soft, can be impressed cold. The plastic material used can be applied directly to a document or over a ribbon, cord, wire or chain, all meant to contribute to the sealing's security and its authenticity, or to act as a means of attaching the seal to the document.

The sealing wax (H: chap-ka-lac) used on documents and packages in India generally contained little or no wax but consisted primarily of lac plus a coloring pigment such as vermilion (P: sangarf) or lamp black (H: kajal), and sometimes perfume (A: 'atr). Formed into a stick while plastic, it is heated, imparted to the object, and, while still hot, the seal is impressed into it.

Seal printing on a flat surface, as opposed to impressing in a sealing medium, was more commonly done in India where the prevailing hot climate limited the use of sealing wax. When ink is spread onto the seal surface, it does not enter the engraved grooves so that, when the seal is imprinted, only the flat plane makes contact with the surface and the depressed, engraved areas in the impression remain colorless. To print a seal (H: muhr chhapna), its surface is smeared with ink spread by the finger. The area of the document to be stamped is first dampened to assist in making a clear impression (H: muhr ki chhap). The ink in general former use in India was prepared from the juice of the marking nut (H: bhela; Tam: sehnkottai), produced by the marking nut tree (Semecarpus anacardium) and is waterproof and permanent in color.

Seals were and still are put to a variety of uses. Their main function is to serve as a form of control in administration and trade. A seal may belong to an individual or an institution and, in the latter case, represents their authority. The impression or print from a seal is a power

602. Northern India
Silver royal signet ring (P: khas mohr, personal seal) in flower form, the seal face line-chased on brass, with a silver mount and shank on the reverse
Diameter 2 9/16 in. (6.5 cm); weight 56 g
Private Collection, Brussels

The mirror image inscription in Sanskrit, Kaithi script, has been translated by Professor Asko Parpola, Helsinki, Finland (uncertainties in the readability of some letters prevents a complete translation): I, KING RAMACHANDRA OF VAIKUNTHADHALA . . . PLACE HERE THIS SEAL, indicating its use by the said royal person. Such seals were in common use till the end of the nineteenth century.

603. Jaipur, Rajasthan. *19th century*
Image of Hanuman, white Makrana marble
13⅜ x 5⅞ in. (34 x 15 cm); diameter 3¹⁵/₁₆ in.
(10 cm)
Collection the author, Porvoo (Ex-Collection
Eugene and Lee Shapiro)

*Hanuman is depicted holding in his left hand before
his chest the signet ring (muhr) of Rama, his master,
which Rama had given to him to deliver to Sita,
Rama's abducted wife, imprisoned in Lanka (Sri
Lanka) by Ravana, its king, to assure her of his
imminent arrival and her rescue. As historian
Romila Thapar has pointed out, this incident in
the epic Ramayana is an accretion to the earlier
story and dates to a period after the first century
B.C., when Indo-Greeks popularized the Greek
use of signet rings in India.*

symbol, accepted by those concerned as legally and officially confirming whatever purpose the owner intended. A sealed document therefore had the force of a verbal message, a command, or a legal statement, and was equivalent to the sender's physical presence. Private seals (H: muhr-i-khass), until recent times in India, were commonly used by all strata of society in lieu of a signature, especially when, because of illiteracy, a person was unable to sign his or her name; however, the practice was also extended to the literate because the seal was officially acceptable as a signature substitute. Seals, whether used by officials, soldiers, or even servants, usually took the form of a signet ring.

The belief that an inanimate seal engraved with a religious precept or moral sentiment had the power to generate credence in a reader and result in a desired action probably accounts for their wide acceptance as a type of amulet possessing magic potency. This idea was reinforced by the widespread belief in India, among both Hindus and Muslims, that a name or phrase inscribed in the positive on any enduring substance such as stone or metal has the power to be active eternally.

The early importance of state seals in Hindu society is well illustrated by the classic Sanskrit play Mudra Rakshasa (The Signet Ring of the Minister), written by Visakha Datta in the eleventh or twelfth century A.D. Its events relate to the history of Emperor Chandragupta, the Mauryan ruler, fourth century B.C. The minister's seal ring plays a significant part in its plot. Another which centers on a personal seal ring is Shakuntala by Kalidasa presumed to be written in the second to fourth century A.D. Generally, Hindu signet rings are all metal—gold, silver, bronze, or copper—and do not employ mounted, engraved hardstone seals, which seem to have been associated with established Muslim practice. Hindu seals are of two basic types. In one group are those bearing an inscription, not in Arabic letters but in one of the many vernacular Indic languages. Others have a geometric pattern, which may have symbolic significance, or depict a vegetal subject such as a flower or branching plant, the latter usually interpreted as a symbol of fertility and the life force. Some are in intaglio and others in relief, the latter, as mentioned, suggesting their use primarily as an amulet.

Although signet rings (S: anjulimudra; H: mudra; Tam: muththirai) have been used by Hindus all over India since ancient times, their employment was greatly augmented through the widespread influence of the Mughal Muslims. According to orthodox Muslim practice, a gold ring was considered unlawful for use by a man, but a silver or bronze signet ring was acceptable. There exist many Muslim gold signet rings (A: khatam) that date from early Islamic times (ninth–tenth century A.D. and onward). The Prophet Muhammad is said to have worn a silver ring with the signet turned under his little finger against the palm of his left (some say right) hand. On the signet was engraved Mahammadun Rasulu'llah (Muhammad the Messenger of God). Muhammad's specific sanction of the use of the signet ring undoubtedly explains its almost universal use in Islam. Some women, especially those in high positions in society, or those connected with offices concerned with the seraglio, could also possess signet rings.

Many contemporary Muslims continue to wear a silver signet ring on the right-hand little finger or, less frequently, on the middle finger. The signet is engraved with the wearer's name, to which is often added the word 'Abdu (His servant), meaning the wearer is a servant of God. Additionally, it might have a religious phrase from the Qur'an, or one alluding to it. In the eighteenth and nineteenth centuries, inscriptions became longer and more elaborate.

Seals for Buddhist use were made in India from the first through tenth century A.D. These were probably made by Buddhist monks in monasteries, and a large number of seal impressions on fired clay have been excavated at various Buddhist sites such as Nalanda, Bihar. The earliest are believed to have been for monastic use, but they eventually acquired an amuletic function among the laity. The obvious care expended on these seals is an indication of the importance given to them. Early Buddhist seals can be divided into four groups:

Possession seals were used by the monks of the great monasteries to denote the ownership of an object by the monastery, and also for monastic transactions. Creed seals bear a statement concerning Buddhist law. They were used to consecrate an object, such as a miniature clay stupa presented as a votive offering to a monastery or temple. Votive seals depict an image of a Buddhist deity, or a stupa, and may also have an inscription. Impressions on clay were used by monks and others for personal worship, or were purchased by pilgrims visiting a shrine as a talisman for use in home meditation and worship. Verse seals bear a short formula of verses or words (dharani) generally attributed to Buddha. Impressions from these were probably carried in a bag upon the person as they had no suspension hole. They were believed to possess great magical protective power and were worn to propitiate or coerce a deity or spirit; as a protection from evil; or as a good-luck amulet.

604

605

606

607

608

604, 605. Southern India
Top and side views of gold signet ring
(muththirai) inscribed in Nagari characters
with an invocation to Rama. Side shoulders
bear kirtimukha (face of glory) heads, a magically protective mask; the shank bottom
includes a rosette.
Height 1 in. (2.5 cm); weight 47 g
(Ex-Collection Derek J. Content)

606. Maharashtra
Gold signet ring (muhr) with floral motif,
probably used by a Hindu
Outer diameter ¾ in. (2 cm); inner diameter
⅝ in. (1.8 cm); weight 15 g
Collection Ghysels, Brussels

**607, 608. Bangalore, Karnataka,
or Maharashtra**
Front and back views of silver "winged" signet
rings (muhr). Also produced in gold.
Bezel dimensions (left to right):
¾ x ⅝ in. (1.9 x 2.2 cm); weight 22 g
1¼ x 2⅛ in. (3.1 x 4.7 cm); weight 47 g
⅝ x ⅝ in. (2.3 x 2.3 cm); weight 33 g
¹¹/₁₆ x ¹¹/₁₆ in. (1.8 x 1.8 cm); weight 26 g
Collection Ghysels, Brussels

609. Delhi. 19th century
Silver signet ring (muhr or chhap)
Height ⅞ in. (2.2 cm); bezel
⁹/₁₆ x ¹¹/₁₆ in. (1.4 x 1.7 cm);
weight 6 g
Collection the author, Porvoo

Set with a black-onyx seal stone
inscribed with its former Muslim
owner's name, and the date: Hajji
Ismail Abdul Sattar, 1304 A.H.
(A.D. 1886), carved on the stone
after he made the Hajj pilgrimage
to Mecca. Applied as a signature
to documents on which it is
stamped.

When not of metal, the seal on a signet ring is made of a durable substance such as a hard-stone because a seal was meant to be used for a relatively long time period, as in the case of a seal created for a particular post of officialdom, or, at the least, for the lifetime of the owner. Unlike precious metals, which can be melted down and reused, a hardstone seal generally has no intrinsic value. Most were made of thin stone sections, and it was not worthwhile to grind away the inscription and reuse the stone as the result would be too thin and fragile. Since the seal had a particular owner's name, it was of no use to someone else. For these reasons, many have survived from ancient sites and have come down to us unmounted from their original precious metal ring. In today's antique market, it is often difficult to determine whether a signet stone is from India or Persia as they are often similar. One must search for clues in the style of writing or the meanings of the inscription.

The choice of hardstone used for a seal depended on the relative wealth of the owner or the symbolic, magical, or apotropaic connotation of a particular stone, which added to the mystique of its use. Carnelian was probably the most common of the stones used and remains the favorite. When cool, agate (the stone group to which carnelian belongs) characteristically will not pull away any of the sealing wax into which it is impressed. The stones used are given here in order of their increasing hardness according to Mohs' scale, in which diamond, rated 10, is the hardest, along with their Arabic names, standard in the seal trade: steatite (jaharat), 1.5-2; coral mirjan), 3.5; lapis-lazuli (lajward), 5; turquoise (firoza), 6; garnet (mehtab), 6.5; agate or quartz (akik; babaghuri), bloodstone (tahnani), amethyst (nilavarn), carnelian (lal akik; yamani), onyx (sang-i-sulimani), rock crystal (billaur), and magnetic iron ore (chamak), 7; emerald (zumurrud), 7.5; and diamond (almas), 10.

The outer contour of a hardstone seal mounted in a signet ring could be round, oval, pointed-oval, tear-shaped, square, rectangular, octagonal, or variants of these. Generally the upper surface is flat, which best suits it for engraving with characters and for use as a printing seal. To facilitate mounting a stone seal in the bezel of a metal ring, the sealstone generally has a beveled edge over which the metal bezel is forced to hold it in place.

The rings on which seals were engraved were made entirely of metal. Those using a seal-stone had a variety of forms. In some places, distinctive forms evolved, such as the Maharashtra "winged" seal ring (see 607, 608).

Until the beginning of this century, when the custom declined due to growing literacy, a private seal, or muhr-i-khass, as mentioned, was a necessity in the form of a signet ring. Seal engravers (H: muhr-kand) plied their trade in this special branch of lapidary work in every major city and in provincial government centers. In Delhi, the Dariba Bazaar, which remains a center of the jewelry trade, was the place where generations of superior seal engravers made this work a local specialty. The same stone engravers who made seals also executed the texts on Muslim stone slab amulets such as the haldili (see page 116).

The seal engraver's lathe (H: muhr kharad) comprises a thick rectangular wooden plank fixed with three upright wooden slabs. The first and third of these are immobile, but the center one can be moved by sliding it along a horizontal wooden rod that passes through all three and is then fixed in position by a screw. Above this rod is a second, thinner metal rod or spindle, mounted only between the center and right uprights, with its end projecting beyond the right upright. To this end is fixed the engraving tool: changeable, small, thin-edged copper discs (H: barma) of various dimensions, from quarter-inch (6.3 mm) to smaller sizes, with different profiles.

The engraver, who sits on the floor before the lathe, and often uses his bare feet to steady it, like other Indian craftsmen, is quadrumanous (having four hands) and uses both hands and feet to accomplish the work. In Indian hand lathes, the spindle is made to rotate by the use of a hand bow which has an attached loose string that is wrapped around the spindle rod before it is fixed to the second bow end. The bow is operated with the left hand (or by an assistant) and moved forward and backward, causing the spindle to rotate reciprocally. Carving takes place when the mounted cutting wheel rotates toward the operator.

The stone to be engraved is mounted face up in a shellac stick (H: hundi), below which is a handle used to manipulate the stone during cutting. In a small cup nearby is the stone-cutting abrasive and lubricant medium, usually a mixture of oil and corundum or diamond dust, which is applied to the rotating cutting disc. As the disc rotates, the stone is pressed smoothly against it and the required cuts are made following the design drawn on the seal surface. The basic cuts are: straight (H: khatt-i-mustaqim), curved (khatt-i-munhani), circular (khatt-i-mustadir), and a dot (khatt-i-nuqta). Depending on its use, the seal inscription, normally a signature or name, is either in reverse (ultana), or positive (sidha). The result is mounted in the ring bezel by a setter of stones in rings (khatimband).

610

610. Delhi. *Late 19th century*
A seal carver at the Dariba Bazaar, Delhi, sits behind his weighted carving lathe before which, to illustrate his skill, is a framed paper bearing imprints of seals he has made. The Delhi sealstone carvers were the most famous in India because of their skill in making highly aesthetic calligraphic Persian and Urdu inscriptions in Arabic characters.
Collection the author, Porvoo

611. *Signet Ring Seal Forms*

Top to bottom: Square, rectangle, octagon, long octagon, long hexagon, hexagon, rounded rectangle, oval, tear, ogival, circle, flower

611

612. Northern India
Man's silver signet ring (muhr or katm)
Bezel ⅞ x ¹¹⁄₁₆ in. (2.3 x 1.7 cm); weight 23 g
Collection Ghysels, Brussels

The inscription, translated by Salme Martikainen, Helsinki, reads 1276 A.H. (A.D. 1859), SAYYID HUSSAIN, DESCENDANT OF THE PROPHET, SLAVE OF THE PROPHET.

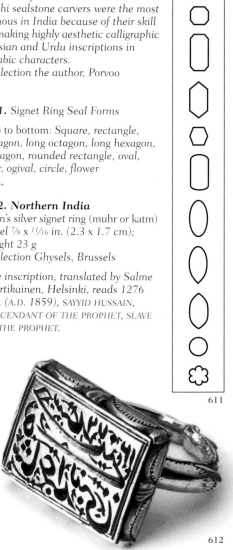

612

Ritual and Secular Rings

613. Bastar, Madhya Pradesh
Cast-brass ritual rings, worn by Muria tribal men
Height 2⅛ to 2⅜ in. (5.4–6.2 cm); width ½ in.
(1.7 cm); inner diameter ¾ to ⅞ in. (2–2.1 cm);
weight c. 52 g
Collection Mis, Brussels

Used as a male fertility symbol at the time of
plowing and sowing crop seeds. The earth (Tallur-
Muttai, mother earth) is conceived of as female,
which a male cultivator plows symbolically,
injecting his seed from which grows a rich harvest.
Typical subjects depicted standing on the band
are a farmer with a pair of bullocks drawing a
plow; a field of growing grain; and a water well.

614. Bastar, Madhya Pradesh
Ritual, patinated cast-brass crop fertility bracelet
Outer diameter 5⅜ in. (13.5 cm); inner diameter
2⅜ in. (6 cm)
Courtesy Bodhicitta, London

The subject and concept in the rings (above) are
the same as in this bracelet. An additional fertility
symbol is depicted here: beside the cultivator is
his wife holding a baby.

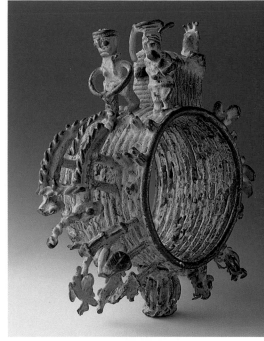

615

615. Patna, Bihar
Silver ring (angusthi) with lotiform
top and attached bells (ghungrus)
Height 1⅝ in. (4.2 cm);
outer diameter ¾ in.
(2 cm); inner diameter ½ in. (1.7 cm);
weight 24 g
Collection the author, Porvoo

616. Karnataka or Maharashtra
Cast-copper ring in the form of the
sacred bull Nandin, Shiva's vehicle.
Worn by Lingayats for ritual use
Height 1⅞ in. (4.7 cm); outer
diameter 1⅛ in. (2.8 cm); inner
diameter ⅞ in. (2.2 cm); weight 72 g
Collection Mis, Brussels

616

617

617. Bihar
Silver ring (dibbi ka angushta) whose top opens for access to a container
Approximate height 2⅛ in. (5.4 cm)
Private Collection, Ojai, California.
Courtesy Beatrice Wood

618. Srinagar, South Jammu and Kashmir
Silver ring in architectonic form
Approximate height 2 in. (5 cm)
Collection Ivory, New York

619. Rajasthan
Silver ring for two fingers (vesya or davano)
Outer diameter 1¾ in. (4.3 cm); inner diameter ¾ in. (1.9 cm); weight 22 g
Collection Ghysels, Brussels

620. Delhi
Top and side views of silver thumb ring (angushtana, or arsi) with mirror (arsi; aina), set with foil-backed, cabochon-cut glass "stones"
Diameter 2 in. (5 cm); mirror diameter ¾ in. (2 cm); weight 33 g
Collection the author, Porvoo

The crescent-moon motif indicates its use by Muslims.

620

618

619

Arsi: The Right-Thumb Mirror Ring

This special ring with a round format has set in its center a small, usually round but sometimes heart-shaped mirror. Worn on the right thumb, it is called arsi in northern India. Although this is originally a Muslim ornament, like other forms of Mughal jewelry, it was accepted by Hindu women and is still very much in use by both.

This type of ring has been worn for more than three hundred years, as attested to by visitors to the Mughal court. One such individual was Niccolao Manucci, a Venetian traveler who spent sixty years (from 1656 to 1717) of his life in India and died near Bombay. A part-time physician and soldier, he personally witnessed events in the reigns of Shah Jahan, Aurangzeb, Bahadur Shah, and Farrukhsiyar. On many occasions, he was able to observe court life closely, and he was even admitted to the women's quarters to administer medical care.

In his first-hand account, Storia do Mogor (1653–1708), an extremely valuable store of information, he wrote, "I have not relied on the knowledge of others; and I have spoken of nothing which I have not seen." He gives us a vivid description of court women's jewelry, including the following: "On [the seraglio women's] fingers are rings, and on the right thumb there is always a ring, where, in place of a stone, there is mounted a little round mirror, having pearls around it. This mirror they use to look at themselves, an act which they are very fond, at any and every moment."

The arsi can take on many variations. It can be of gold, silver, copper, or brass, with the mirror surrounded by gemstones, colored foil–backed glass units treated en cabochon or enameled, or it can be entirely of metal, without stones. Its diameter can reach extraordinary dimensions. It is commonly used also in the northern Indian compound hand ornament called hathphul (hand flower), worn on the right thumb in an ensemble of five rings, one for each finger, joined by chains to a reverse palm ornament and wrist chain.

621. Jaipur, Rajasthan
Gold dorsal hand ornament (hathphul; ratan chur; panchangala), consisting of a central flower unit to which eight chains are attached, three passing to a bracelet, and five to each of the fingers to secure a finger ring (angushtari), each with a different flower motif. The left hand thumb ring (arsi) contains a mirror. The reverse of all parts is polychrome enameled. Hands have been pattern decorated with henna (mehndi).
Courtesy Air India, Bombay; Ornament: Courtesy Kanjimull and Sons, Scindia House, New Delhi

622. Rajasthan
Silver thumb rings (arsi) with mirror inserts in the form of a heart (dil). Clockwise from lower left:
1¾ x 1¼ in. (4.5 x 3.2 cm); weight 67 g
3¼ x 2½ in. (8.2 x 6.5 cm); weight 69 g
2⁵⁄₁₆ x 2⅛ in. (6.7 x 5.4 cm); weight 50 g
2¼ x 1¾ in. (5.6 x 4.4 cm); weight 24 g
Collection the author, Porvoo

623, 624. Delhi
Front (623) and back views of a silver ring (angushta) set with glass "stones," each in a bezel (ghar). The ring covers four fingers; its shank (dandi) is soldered on the back.
Diameter 3⅜ in. (8.5 cm); weight 121 g
Collection Marjatta Svennevig, Helsinki

621

622

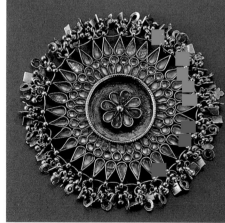

623

624

625

625. Tamil Nadu
Gold ring (ponnulla angkuliyam) whose shank is mounted by a white goose (hamsa; Anser indicus), vehicle of Brahma, god of Creation
Height 2⅜ in. (4.6 cm); weight 34 g
Private Collection

This goose is associated with the sun, as is gold, and with male fertility as well as knowledge and purity. Its name is derived from the exhalation of the Sanskrit sound ham and the inhalation of sa, together constituting the return of the life force to brahman, its cosmic source.

626

627

626. Jaipur, Rajasthan
Gold ring (murassa ka angushta or mundri), set with diamonds. Polychrome enameled by master craftsman Kudrat Singh, Jaipur
Outer diameter 1⅛ in. (2.7 cm); inner diameter ¾ in. (1.9 cm); weight 15 g
Collection the author, Porvoo

627. Ahmadabad, Gujarat
Silver dorsal hand ornament (hath hakalu) that includes, in addition to the usual elements, ornaments for the finger ends
Length wrist to tip 1⅞ in. (20 cm)
Collection Musée de l'Homme, Paris
(M.H. 61.121.198; C. 62.742.494)

The Hololithic Archer's-Thumb Ring

The archer's right-thumb ring, or archer's thumbstall (P: zihgir; zih, bow string; gir, seizing; P: shast, to aim at; a large hook), was designed specifically to aid in achieving improved target accuracy and greater travel distance for the flight of an arrow released from a bow. This type of ring was in use as long ago as the Han dynasty (c. 206 B.C.–220 A.D.) in China, from where it was adopted by the nomadic Mongols who eventually brought the concept to Persia, Turkey, and India with the Muslim conquest of India starting in the last quarter of the twelfth century.

This ring is an ancient example of form following function in jewelry. Its unique format, and the fact that it was made to be worn on a man's thumb, unequivocally identifies it. At its front, the ring has a high point that develops in smooth transition as a kind of hook. This form is derived from the method the Mongols adopted for releasing a bowstring, one quite different from that used in Europe.

When on the thumb, to protect it from the pressure and friction of the string as it is drawn and released, the point projects upward toward the wrist in the space between the thumb and index finger. To use it, the bowstring is hitched behind the point, and the space between thumb and index finger is clamped closed. The index finger around the string is pressed against the ring point to prevent string release until desired, while the rest of the fingers are curled closed. When the hand is pulled back, the bowstring, firmly hooked behind the ring point, is brought under tension at a single point close to the arrow nock. To release the string tension and propel the arrow, pressure on the ring is removed simply by separating the fingers. The bowstring immediately slides smoothly off the ring, pulls it forward, and with a twang the arrow is launched on its trajectory toward the target.

Archer's rings were immensely popular throughout the Mughal dynasty. Their explicit representation in Mughal miniature paintings informs us that one or several such rings of different materials—indicated by color—were worn dangling from a belt by a cord or cords. Possession and display of these rings, which were a part of the royal regalia, identified the wearer as a person of high rank.

Several intrepid survivors bear inscriptions of the names of their former owners, persons of rank including Mughal emperors. Two hololithic jade (nephrite) rings in the collection of the Bharat Kala Bhavan, Varanasi, have inscriptions that indicate they belonged to the Emperor Jahangir. In the Salar Jang Museum, Hyderabad, is a dark green jade (nephrite) ring with an inscription of the titles of Shah Jahan, and the date 1040 A.H./1631 A.D. One of white nephrite in the Victoria and Albert Museum, London, also belonged to this emperor, as its inscription says, SECOND LORD OF THE AUSPICIOUS CONJUNCTION, *his personal astrological epithet, and it is dated 1042 A.H./A.D.1632–33. Nephrite ring inscriptions generally appear on the inner-shank surface behind the point, flush-inlaid in gold, kundan style (see page 366).*

Those made of gold for upper-echelon persons are usually set with diamonds, rubies, and emeralds, the latter two usually cut en cabochon or flat. Following the Mughal predilection for sculptural forms and richness in surface decoration, even in miniature, rubies could be detail carved as flower petals—the poppy (P: kokinar) and the tulip (P: gul-lala) were favorite subjects —and emeralds were used for leaf forms. These stones were generally not of high quality, and often crystal or glass backed by colored foil was used to simulate them.

Most of these rings that have survived are made of durable hardstone, and some of ivory, bone, or horn also exist. Unlike gold, these other materials cannot be reclaimed and recycled, and undoubtedly many of gold were fated to oblivion in the gold refiner's crucible. This probably explains why more rings of this kind in nonmetallic materials have survived than any other form of Mughal jewelry.

Hardstone rings were always made in one piece, hence the term hololithic. The favored stone was jade (nephrite), but a variety of other hardstones were also used, including agate, almandine garnet, carnelian, chalcedony, rock crystal, coral, and one of a hololithic emerald is known to exist. Working hardstone into this form was no mean technical feat of fabrication in the lapidary art. Far softer and easily worked, ivory, bone, and horn could be elaborately carved and drill-pierced for ornamentation.

Hardstone rings exist with a puritanically plain, smooth surface, but nephrite, other hardstone, and gold rings were frequently decorated with kundan-style gold inlay and gemstones, as on the haldili *amulet. One suspects that the highly ornamented rings were meant only for display since their uneven surface might interfere with proper function.*

628. Northern India. Mughal, 17th century
Banded-agate hololithic archer's thumb ring (zih-gir).
Carved to allow its natural varicolored strata to
appear as a central, circular "eye" form
1¼ x 1⅛ in. (3.1 x 2.9 cm)
Victoria and Albert Museum, London. From the
Collection of Sir Andrew Fontaine (1676–1753) of
Narford Hall (IS 42-1981)

630

629. Delhi; or Agra, Uttar Pradesh. *Mughal,
c. 1625–50*
*Gold archer's thumb ring (zih-gir, string grip) with
six Mughal-cut diamonds, twenty-one flat and
cabochon rubies, and fourteen emeralds, all foil-
backed and mounted kundan style*
Diameter 1⁹⁄₁₆ in. (4 cm)
*Special Treasury, State Hermitage Museum,
Oriental Department, St. Petersburg (V3-703)*

*After his rapacious conquest of Delhi, the Mughal
capital, in 1739, Nadir Shah, ruler of Persia, to
inform them of his victory, sent emissaries to Russia
and Turkey bearing diplomatic gifts selected from
the vast confiscated Mughal Treasury, of which this
ring was a part. All gifts to Russia remain in the
State Hermitage Museum, St. Petersburg. Aside
from their historic interest and intrinsic value, they
provide us with rare datable examples of jewelry,
as in the case of 631; its inscription includes the
date of manufacture.*

630. *View of archer's thumb ring (629) showing
its inner surface. Engraved in Persian, within a
cartouche, is the honorific title of the Mughal
Emperor Shah Jahan:* THE SECOND LORD OF THE
AUSPICIOUS CONJUNCTION.

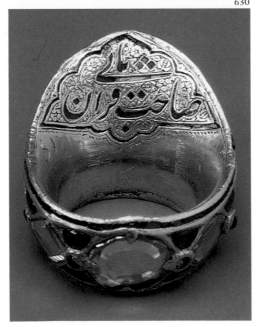

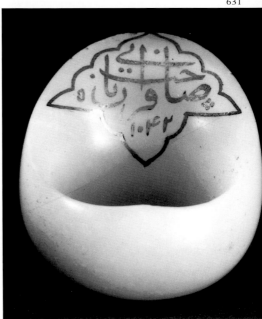

631. Delhi; or Agra, Uttar Pradesh. *Mughal, second quarter, 17th century*
White-nephrite hololithic archer's thumb ring (zih-gir)
1⁵⁄₈ x 1¼ in. (4.1 x 3.2 cm)
Victoria and Albert Museum, London (1023-1871). From the Waterton Collection

Engraved and flush-inlaid in gold with an honorific title of the Mughal Emperor Shah Jahan, THE SECOND
LORD OF THE AUSPICIOUS CONJUNCTION, *and the date, 1042 A.H. (A.D. 1632). The First Lord of the Auspicious Conjunction was Jahan's ancestor, the Mongol conquerer Timur Lenk (Tamerlane), 1336?–1405.*

632. Northern India. *c. 18th century*
Ivory archer's thumb ring (zih-gir or ustana),
relief carved, stained brown
Height 1⁹⁄₁₆ in. (4 cm); weight 8 g
Collection Mis, Brussels

Ivory archer's rings were sometimes carved
by ladies of the Mughal court as gifts to their
menfolk. When not in use, an archer's ring
was worn suspended on a string tied to the
waist sash (patka).

633. Northern India. *18th century*
Two views of a white-nephrite hololithic
Mughal archer's thumb ring (zih-gir) inlaid
with diamonds, rubies, and emeralds set
kundan style in gold
Courtesy Unicorn Oriental Gallery,
Scottsdale, Arizona

632

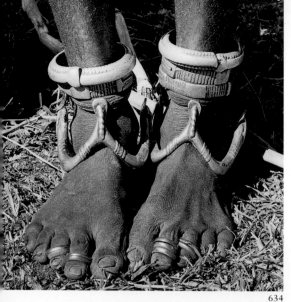

Anklets

634. Secunderabad, Andhra Pradesh

Bottom: Cast-brass, one-part anklet (wankidi), worn by a Lambadi or Banjara gypsy woman
Diameter 3⁹/₁₆ to 2⁷/₈ in. (9.2 to 7.3 cm); height 2³/₈ in. (6 cm); weight (one) 199 g

Related in form to the V-shaped armlet (vanki), this form fits comfortably on the ankle. The body (jereka) rises at the front to a projection (gundu) with a series of applied ball ornaments (cheyu). Above it are two brass hinged anklets and a rigid penannular one that must be hammered closed on the wearer's foot by a blacksmith.

634

635

636

▲ **635. Rajasthan**
Rigid silver anklet (kara) with makara-head protome terminals
Height ¾ in. (2 cm); outer diameter 4⁵/₈ in. (11.8 cm); inner diameter 3¼ in. (8.2 cm); weight 142 g
Collection the author, Porvoo

Similarly ornamented forms in bracelets (also called kara, hard) may have tiger-head terminals (nahar-ka-kara); elephant heads (hathi-ka-kara); or snake or dragon heads (azhaka-ka-kara). They can be solid or hollow, as this anklet, in which case the interior may contain sounding pellets. Bracelets with the archaic theme of confronting pairs of animal-head protomes that guard the opening are believed to have originated in the Near East in the eighth century B.C., and the concept spread west and east from there. In India this design persists, and in the West it became very fashionable during the Art Deco period (see 860).

636. Bihar ▲
Cast-brass one-part anklets (pairi), plated with a white metal, zinc-lead alloy (kathir), worn by tribal women
Height 3⁹/₁₆ in. (9.3 cm); diameter 3¹⁵/₁₆ to 3¹/₈ in. (10 to 8 cm); weight (one) 654 g

▼ 637. Chhindwara District, Madhya Pradesh
Cast-brass, two-part anklets (chura), worn in pairs by Gond women
Diameter 2 to 3¼ in. (5 to 8 cm); weight (one) 249 g
Collection Ghysels, Brussels

After casting, the anklets' surface is turned on a hand lathe and the two parts joined by inserted rods.

638. Khajuraho, Madhya Pradesh
Rigid silver anklets (neori kara) worn by female cultivators

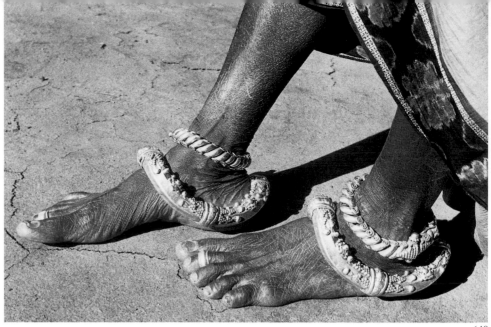

▼ 639. Rajkot, Gujarat
Rigid one-part silver anklets (bedi)
Outer diameter 4⅜ in. (11.3 cm); inner diameter
2⅜ in. (6 cm); weight (one) 216 g
Collection Mis, Brussels

640. Kantilo, Puri District, Orissa
The lower ornaments seen here are silver, one-part
rigid anklets (goda bala) ornamented with decorative balls (rua).
Outer diameter 4⅜ to 3¹⁵⁄₁₆ in. (11.3 to 10 cm);
inner diameter 3⅛ to 2½ in. (8 to 6.3 cm); weight
(one) 110 g

641. Irinjalakuda, Kerala
Pair of cast-bell-metal anklets (kal chilampu) worn
by a priest (achari)
Outer long diameter 7⅛ in. (18 cm); inner long
diameter 5⁵⁄₁₆ in. (13.5 cm); length 7¹⁄₁₆ in.
(18 cm); weight (one) 780 g
Collection Ghysels, Brussels

The anklet is ornamented with symbols: (left) sun;
deity; (right) moon; sacrificial sword (baliyagiya
katam); stamped C.K.N.

642. Irinjalakuda, Kerala
Rigid cast-bell-metal anklet (kal chilampu or
pujari kai chilabu), one of a pair worn on the legs
of a priest or seer-oracle (velichapad) in a temple.
A pair of similar types (chilanka) are also held in
each hand. These are made by bell-metal casters
using the lost wax casting method.

640

641
642

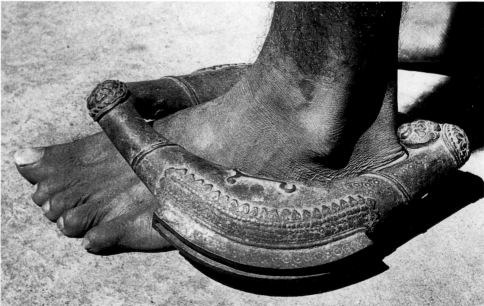

643

643. Punjab, Himachal Pradesh

Rigid silver anklet (jhanjar, tinkling), the name a reference to the sound made by its internal shot pellets (gujri)
Outer diameter 4¹⁵/₁₆ in. (12.7 cm); inner diameter 3¹⁵/₁₆ in. (9.9 cm); terminal diameter ⅞ in. (2.1 cm); weight 157 g
Collection Ghysels, Brussels

644

644. Bhopal, Madhya Pradesh

Rigid, hollow-silver ankle bracelet (bavthira), with stamped and chased patterns, containing sounding shot (charra)
Height 1¹/₁₆ in. (2.8 cm); outer diameter 5⁵/₁₆ to 4⅜ in. (13.5 to 11.1 cm); inner diameter 3⁹/₁₆ to 2⅞ in. (9 to 7.3 cm); weight 239 g
Collection Ghysels, Brussels

645

645. Rajasthan

Silver, two-part, hollow anklet (kara) made with stamped sheet metal imitating gajre balls (see 580). One quarter-hinged part can be opened by a central screw.
Height 1 in. (2.4 cm); outer diameter 4 in. (10.1 cm); inner diameter 2½ in. (6.3 cm); weight 174 g
Collection Ghysels, Brussels

646
647

646. Probandar, Saurashtra, Gujarat

Pair of two-part, hollow, cast-silver anklets (jeram damgi or kadla) worn by Harijan, Koli, and other women. Its two parts are held together by a screw.
Weight (one) 980 g
Collection Ghysels, Brussels

647. Vadodara (Baroda), Gujarat

Pair of sheet-silver, two-part, hinged anklets (kadla), pattern-punch decorated
Front height 4½ in. (11.5 cm); outer diameter 5⅛ in. (13 cm); inner diameter 2¾ in. (7 cm); weight (one) 870 g
Collection Ghysels, Brussels

This type was exported to Zanzibar and Oman for use by expatriate Indian women.

▲ **648. Dabhoi, Vadodara (Baroda) District, Gujarat**
One of a pair of silver, hollow, two-part anklets (todo, singular; toda, plural; or kalla) worn by Maldhari women and others
Height 4¼ in. (11 cm); outer diameter 4¾ in. (12 cm); inner diameter 2⅝ in. (6.7 cm); weight 850 g
Collection Viscount and Viscountess Scarsdale, Kedelston Hall, Derbyshire (No. 7)

A masterpiece of repoussage and chasing, the design represents two addorsed, highly stylized makara heads. Because these immense, heavy anklets cause discomfort and even limb injury, women tie rags around their legs to protect the skin.

◄ **649. Dabhoi, Vadodara (Baroda) District, Gujarat**
Hollow-silver two-part anklet (kalla or athasia) with two frontal stylized makara heads and attached clusters of hollow silver balls (gola)
Height 3¹⁵⁄₁₆ in. (10 cm); outer diameter 4½ in. (11.5 cm); inner diameter 2⅛ in. (5.5 cm); weight 998 g
Collection Mis, Brussels

650. Gumsur, Orissa
Cast-brass, two-part, white-metal-alloy-plated anklet (godu, a type of pradi dorbo, or ancient valuables)
Outer diameter 4⅞ in. (12 cm); inner diameter 2³⁄₁₆ in. (5.5 cm); weight 700 g
Collection Anne Jernandier de Vriese, Brussels

One of a pair, each anklet can weigh from 20 to 30 pounds, carved in diagonally fluted patterns. Kondh tribals formerly placed them on a bride's ankles to prevent her from running away. Once she was reconciled to her new status and surroundings, the anklets were removed and kept as a family heirloom for use on another such occasion.

650

651

Flexible Chain Anklets

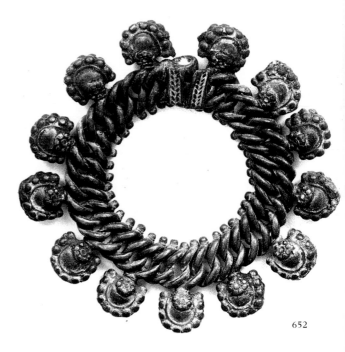

651. Sawai Madhopur, Rajasthan
A mud casting mold prepared to create a pair of flexible chain anklets (laung ke santh)
The Metropolitan Museum of Art, New York. Gift of Sir Casper Purdon Clarke, 1908 (07.207)

Left: A part of the mold has been removed after casting to show the anklet's placement. Right: Finished flexible chain of 60–70 links. Also made by this method are other types of santh: with plain links (sutwan santh); or with small top-edge projections (chaktidar santh). They are fastened by a screw (kil-kunda-ki-santh). Castings may be of silver or brass, the latter often plated with white metal (a zinc-lead alloy).

652

652. Sawai Madhopur, Rajasthan
Cast-bell-metal, flexible-chain anklet (santh) with integral cast bells (ghungru) and clove chain (laung-ki-santh)
Chain outer diameter 4⁵⁄₁₆ in. (11 cm); inner diameter 2⁹⁄₁₆ in. (6.5 cm); bell height ¾ in. (2 cm); weight 170 g
Collection Genevieve Prillaman, Paris

◄ **653. Bundelkhand, Madhya Pradesh**
White cast-metal chain anklets
3½ x 2¹⁵⁄₁₆ in. (9 x 7.5 cm); inner diameter 2⅜ in. (6 cm); weight (one) 205 g
Collection Anne Jernandier de Vriese, Brussels

654. Uttar Pradesh

Flexible silver chain anklet (sankali or paizeb) with a fringe of hollow balls (goli)
Height 1¾ in. (4.5 cm); weight 230 g
Private Collection, Brussels

655. Northern India

Gold chain-link anklets (jarao ka paizeb) set with diamonds, kundan style. The feet are decorated with mehndi (see 22). That gold is rarely used for ankle bracelets indicates that a privileged person once owned these bracelets.
Courtesy Tribuvandas Bhimji Zaveri, Zaveri Bazaar, Bombay

654

655

656. Rajasthan

Flexible silver anklet (paizeb) with screw closing (pech se kasna) and fringe of balls (goli jhaladar)
1⁵⁄₁₆ x 15¼ in. (3.5 x 38.6 cm); inner diameter 3⅛ in. (8 cm); weight (one) 316 g
Collection Ghysels, Brussels

657. Rajasthan. *19th century*

Hereditary chain anklet (ta'zim, honor, respect), gold with diamonds, worn on the right ankle of a noble or Rajput vassal (Thakur, a chief among certain Rajput castes)
Height 1¼ in. (3.2 cm); outer diameter 4¼ in. (10.8 cm); weight 490 g
Private Collection, Brussels

The anklet is given by a Maharaja to an eligible person such as a noble, landlord, or village headman as a sign of special recognition, the recipient called a tazimi sirdar. In later times it was also granted to an important merchant (mahajan) or banker (sarraf or seth). Less often, as a sign of high honor, permission was given to wear a pair of such anklets, one on each ankle. The anklet entitled the wearer to a certain position at a court durbar (formal reception) and rendered the grantee exempt from custom duties, search and seizure, and criminal processes. Anklets were originally of gold but later adapted in silver by lower classes; even today, a village bridegroom may wear a silver one on his right ankle (see 742)

656

658. Hyderabad, Andhra Pradesh

Silver anklet (milna payal) made of a series of floral-stamped interlocking units, with a central truncated cube containing the closing mechanism, worked by a screw topped with a conical ornament
Body height 1¼ in. (3.2 cm); clasp height 2¾ in. (7 cm); weight 320 g
Collection Jacques Carcanagues, New York

657

658

Multiunit Anklets

659. Rajasthan
Pair of silver child's anklets (painjin), with units in an auspicious mango (am) shape
6³⁄₈ x ⁵⁄₈ in. (16.3 x 1.4 cm); unit length 1 in. (2.5 cm); weight (one) 54 g
Collection Ghysels, Brussels

660. Udaipur, Rajasthan
Cast-brass ankle bells (gajjalu). Fixed to a leather strip, they are worn by a male dancer to mark the rhythm while performing.

661. Rajasthan
Detail of flexible silver-chain anklet (golidar paizeb) with hundreds of attached balls (goli)
10 x 1³⁄₄ in. (25.7 x 4.5 cm); weight 298 g
Collection Ghysels, Brussels

662. Jammu, Jammu and Kashmir
Silver anklet (machchhi ka paizeb)
Height 1³⁄₄ in. (4.5 cm); inner diameter 2⁹⁄₁₆ in. (6.5 cm); weight 110 g

Each unit is a fish (machchhi) form, a fertility symbol as fish breed prolifically.

659

660
662

661

Toe Rings

663. Rajasthan and Uttar Pradesh
Cast–white metal toe rings (panw ki ungli
anwat; bichhiya)
Length 2⅞ to 3¾ in. (7.3–9.4 cm); width
1½ to 2⁷⁄₁₆ in. (3.9–6.2 cm); weight 22
to 62 g
Collection the author, Porvoo

The rings are worn on the middle toe with
the ornament pointing upward, lying flat
on the foot. Those with bells contain
sounding pellets.

**664. Rangareddi District, Andhra
Pradesh**
Cast–white metal toe rings (anwat), with
double bells, worn by a Lambadi gypsy
women along with cast-brass anklets

**665. Madikeri (Mercara), Kodagu
(Coorg), Karnataka**
Silver ankle-foot-toe ornament, worn by
a bride at the Coorgi marriage ceremony
(kanni mangala, virgin-bride marriage)

666. Madhya Pradesh
Cast–white metal big-toe ring (anwat)
Ornament height 2 in. (5 cm); shank
outer diameter 1⅜ in. (3.6 cm); inner
diameter 1¹⁄₁₆ in. (2.6 cm); rod length
1³⁄₁₆ in. (3 cm); weight (one) 35 g
British Museum, London (59.6-17.17)

The projecting rod passes under the
small toes.

667. West Bengal
Set of three silver toe rings, joined by chains (bichhiya),
worn with the point toward the toe end
Chain length 1¾ in. (4.5 cm); diameter ¾ in. (2 cm);
weight 95 g
Musée de l'Homme, Paris (6.78.735.493)

668. Rajasthan
Three-unit silver toe-ring set (bichhua or phulri),
ornamented with bunches of small balls resembling fish
roe, a fertility symbol
Height 1¹¹⁄₁₆ to 1¾ in. (4.3–4.5 cm); width ⅞ to 1 in.
(2.3–2.5 cm); weight (total) 107 g
Collection Ghysels, Brussels

663

664

666

667

668

665

4 GOLD AND S...
MAKERS' MEA...
USERS' OBSESSI...

Gold and silver—the first, according to Hindu belief, a sacred metal symbolic of the warm sun, the other suggesting the cool moon—are the quintessential metals of Indian jewelry. Pure gold does not oxidize or corrode with time; consequently, it does not diminish in bulk, and it survives undamaged even after suffering long interment in secret hiding places. Perhaps this is why Hindu tradition associates gold with immortality.

Gold imagery occurs frequently in ancient Indian literature. In the Vedic Hindu myth of cosmological creation, the source of physical and spiritual human life originated in and evolved from a golden womb (*hiranyagarbha*) or egg (*hiranyanda*), a metaphor of the sun, whose light rises from the primordial waters. When the womb split in two, one half, of gold, became the heavens, and the other, of silver, formed the earth. Because gold is inherently sacred, either a ritualistic symbolic mention or an actual offering of gold is made in all Hindu rite-of-passage ceremonies, from birth to marriage to death.

Gold has also found a place in ayurvedic medicine, the Hindu Vedic science of health that uses medication derived from indigenous plants and natural mineral substances. Gold leaf (*sona varak*) and gold ashes (*sona bhasma*) in the purified form of a fine dark-brown powder are used as an aphrodisiac, to increase sexual powers and cure impotence, or as a tonic to augment natural beauty and strength in general and to improve the intellect and memory.

According to folkloric belief, gold has the power to purify water passed over it. Related to this concept is the custom of placing gold studs in one's two upper front teeth as visual evidence that the person who reveals them with a smile cannot tell a lie, as to do so would be sacrilegious to the metal (see 279). It is also said that the thief who steals gold is doomed to remain in Hell for as long as the sun and moon exist.

In India, the symbolic sacredness of gold and silver is transferred to jewelry made of metals. As gold is considered to be a metal possessing maximum potency, it is commonly used for amulets and amuletic jewelry meant to repel disease and evil spirits. Losing a gold ornament is interpreted as a prophesy of an impending personal disaster.

Gold was the first metal to be universally used for decorative purposes. Besides its warm and unique yellow color, its *ductility* and *malleability* permit great economy in its use. Another attraction is that it can be altered and reworked by goldsmiths, almost without loss, in seemingly endless ways, which accounts for the recycling of precious-metal ornaments throughout Indian history.

During the period of Mughal reign, Indian royalty established sumptuary laws limiting the use of gold ornaments to themselves and those they favored. To further emphasize their high status, only royalty and a few others to whom they granted permission could use gold ornaments on their feet, which normally would be considered to be defiling this sacred metal, an idea the Mughals probably acquired from their Hindu subjects.

Hindu rebellions and dynastic struggles in the late eighteenth and early nineteenth centuries weakened the once-mighty Mughal Empire. With the diminution of Muslim Mughal patronage (H: *murabbi-gari*), upon which the Indian jeweler had long depended, came a rise in Hindu culture and growing Hindu patronage, especially by the developing middle class of mainly Hindu merchants, bankers, traders, landowners, lawyers, and civil servants, a segment of society that acquired the position and wealth to be able to contribute to the ensuing proliferation in gold and silver jewelry production.

After the Indian Mutiny of 1857–58 (referred to in India as the First War of Independence), the government of India was transferred to the British Crown. The ensuing relative peace and stability allowed Indian people to accelerate their practice of purchasing jewelry as security against the risk of future economic crises. Natural disasters such as floods, plagues, and local famines nevertheless occurred regularly in various parts of the country, reinforcing the message, especially to rural people, that while they prospered they should invest in precious-metal jewelry to insure their survival. (An unfortunate corollary to these disasters was that an enormous

...
for...
whole...
atively h...
production...

Fortuitou...
was discovered in...
Australia (1851). Th...
harvest increased eno...
of gold on the world...
became available in large qu...
of intensive exploitation of the...
Mexico and Peru. Adding to the...
the discovery of the Comstock Lode...
da in 1859, which made the United Sta...
world's largest silver producer until 1...
when the lode ran out and leadership wa...
taken by Mexico.

Demand increased and as in the past, in the nineteenth century, a large percentage of the precious metals, especially silver, that appeared on the world market went to India, where it was made into jewelry and was also used in an augmented production of silver coinage. The upsurge in both the gold and silver industries was abetted as well by a doubling of India's population in the nineteenth century, with the result that the rural classes in India acquired silver jewelry to an unprecedented degree.

The abundance of precious metals has always been accompanied by a higher standard of artistry and technology, and this accounts for the high quality of the middle range of jewelry produced in India in the nineteenth century. In his *Monograph on the Gold and Silver Works of the Punjab*, published in 1890, E. D. Maclagan reported: "Of late years . . . the use of precious metals has largely increased . . . in the better class of work (and) better forms of ornaments. . . . More ornaments are worn now than were a generation ago. . . . Some people say that the amount is twice, others three, four, or as much as six times as much as formerly." Maclagan concluded that "the use of ornaments appears in this country [to be] universal, and to most minds excessive. . . . The actual amount of potential wealth that the native locks up in jewellery is something beyond conception."

Gold Fever

Alluvial gold is found in river sands in almost every state in India, but the amount recovered has always been small. Ancient gold mines existed in Mysore, Hyderabad, Chota Nagpur, and Dharwar, as well as other places in southern India. Today the most active mines are the Kolar Gold Fields of Mysore (Karnataka), the Hutti Gold Field in Hyderabad (Andhra Pradesh), and the North Anantapur Field (Tamil Nadu); of these, 99 percent of the gold recovered comes from the Kolar Field. Even after modern mining methods were adopted in the last quarter of the nineteenth century, the annual yield is slightly fewer than 100,000 ounces of gold, a fraction of the huge demand for gold in India. This relatively small total places India as seventeenth among the world's gold-producing nations.

All Indian-mined gold, and a good portion of the world's annual production of gold—and silver—are consumed in Indian jewelry. It is true that hoarding precious metals as jewelry is a time-honored practice in other places, but Indians easily surpass all others in preeminence.

Today's rampant inflation convinces many people that only the precious metals retain a universally unwavering fiduciary value, and its ownership provides them with a psychologically satisfying sense of security. Consequently, the fluctuation of precious-metal prices in India has become an accurate barometer for gauging the extent of popular political and economic anxiety. Rural people, especially, remembering the lessons of history, have developed a pragmatic, conservative outlook.

The difficulties encountered in effecting social reform in a culture dominated by traditional values is illustrated by what took place when the Indian government attempted to shake the universal Indian faith in the survival value embodied in high-karat gold jewelry. In the early 1960s, the decision was made by Finance Minister Morarji Desai to try to liberate some of India's much-needed undeclared gold reserve, believed to be the largest of any country in the world. Despite the booming capital market and the continuous rise in individual purchasing power, gold more than ever was being hoarded by middle-class Indians. To counteract this practice, a Gold Control Order was introduced in January 1963. As reported in the Indian newspapers, its longterm objective was "to wean people away from the use of gold, and free at least a part of the vast accumulation of gold frozen in the form of ornaments for use in the economic development of the country, and build adequate gold reserves to insulate the economy against fluctuations in foreign trade."

The central provision of the order, by which it was hoped to effect a major change in people's thinking, was that jewelry could no longer be fabricated in the usual Indian standard of 22 karats (24 karats represents pure gold) but must be no higher than 14 karats, a quality and quantity reduction of almost 35 percent. The government believed that, when the reason for this order was made clear, people would be convinced of its necessity and eventually come to accept 14-karat gold.

Another provision of the order stated that persons possessing primary gold in any form other than ornaments (which actually comprised about 85 percent of the total) were required to declare holdings of more than 50 grams per adult and 20 grams per minor for taxation purposes.

Soon after the order was passed, goldsmiths, refiners, and dealers countrywide staged mass demonstrations that continued for more than three years. The Indian populace adamantly refused to accept 14-karat gold as the standard for jewelry, and goldsmiths suffered a drastic reduction of business, which threw many of them out of work. Protesting goldsmiths were arrested, and scores of them committed suicide, some by public self-immolation. As a consequence, in September 1963, the law was relaxed. Goldsmiths were permitted to make ornaments of a higher quality than 14 karats by using gold given to them in the form of existing 22-karat ornaments. Although partially mollified by this concession, goldsmiths continued their agitation, demanding that the entire order be rescinded.

The census of 1961 reported about 1,000 gold refiners in India, 27,000 dealers in gold, and 300,000 goldsmiths. All told, about 450,000 goldsmiths, silversmiths, dealers, and others in related jewelry trades such as gemstone processors and merchants, were working in India. Such a large work force could not be sustained under existing regulations without dependence upon smuggled gold.

A gold-smuggling syndicate centered in Dubai brought contraband gold into India via Pakistan and countries in the Persian Gulf. The problem was exacerbated by the Indian government's setting of high import duties on precious metals.

The gold, chiefly in the form of 3.7 ounce ingots, the bullion type preferred in India, was crated and placed on dhows equipped with high-powered diesel engines that enabled them to travel twelve hundred miles across the Arabian Sea to India, where they were met by fishing trawlers. Though government patrols were constantly active, smuggling was, and still is, difficult to control because of India's extensive coastline and land frontiers. The circulation and disposal of the gold ingots in India was facilitated by the stamps they bore indicating their international origin and standard of purity. These stamps are accepted without question in India.

To determine whether its law was producing the desired result, the government organized an Informal Committee of Officials on Gold Control, whose function was to investigate and evaluate the law's effect to date and to make recommendations. Their results, submitted on August 30, 1966 (published in the Hindustan *Times Weekly,* September 4, 1966), stubbornly concluded that the order should be upheld and even strengthened: they recommended that the 14-karat-gold requirement be reenforced and cautioned that to alter such a deeply ingrained attitude in people's thinking would require more than three-and-a-half-year period that had passed. Even so, on September 2, 1966, Prime Minister Indira Gandhi yielded to popular pressure and removed restrictions on the fabrication of gold ornaments of more than 14-karat purity.

It was still prohibited to possess primary gold in the form of bars, ingots, slabs, billets, shot, pellets, rods, and wire. Those who owned such were given a reasonable time to dispose of it to dealers or have it converted into ornaments. A limit was levied on the possession of gold ornaments, however, and those who exceeded this limit—or who still owned primary gold—would be required to make a declaration for purposes of taxation.

Thus, the middle and lower classes successfully defended their centuries-old custom of investing in gold jewelry for use in times of domestic contingency. The mysterious gold fever that infects the Indian psyche continues unabated, and no cure is in sight. Today gold is the preferred precious metal for ornaments among urban people while silver dominates the world of rural jewelry. Silver's working qualities compare favorably with those of gold, and its relatively greater abundance and availability has always placed it in a lower price category. Until recently, no self-respecting urban woman would wear silver jewelry for fear of being considered by others to be provincial or low caste. That attitude, especially among the younger urban generation, is changing, due in part to the high cost of gold in India and also because of the rise in the value of silver, which perhaps makes it more "respectable."

669. Dariba Bazaar, Delhi
A typical gold and silver retail shop (zewarat ka dukan), open to the street

670. Srinagar, Jammu and Kashmir
A street jeweler's stock-in-trade display of traditional silver ornaments

671. Bombay, Maharashtra
The active, sophisticated Bombay gold bazaar consists of many large, elaborately installed gold jewelry shops, such as this one.

669

670

671

Jewelry Purchasing

Purchasing jewelry, especially in rural communities, often takes on the quality of a ritual. The winter marriage season, September to March, is the year's most active jewelry buying period. Acquisitions are normally made by a group of people that may include the head man of the family, the matriarch, female family members, relatives, friends, and the eventual recipient—the bride-to-be. Decisions are made by a consensus of opinion after much discussion on the merits of one item versus another. In rural agricultural communities, which is to say the greater part of India, jewelry purchases are also tied to the seasonal harvest, whose relative success or failure determines the decision to purchase or dispose of jewelry.

Jewelry shops (H: jawahir ka dukan) concentrate near each other in the bazaars of even small towns, generally on a street whose name designates it as the local jewelry bazaar. The simplest and most numerous shops consist of an open cubicle whose street side is without windows and is nightly closed by a steel roll-down security barrier locked with a stout padlock.

Raised considerably above street level, the floor is covered wall-to-wall with a padded mattress over which a clean white cloth is spread. On it sit the barefoot merchant (H: dukandar) and his clients (H: jajman), their dealings exposed to the observation of all casual passersby. More sophisticated shops have interior glass-covered wall and counter showcases and client benches. Some silver jewelry may be on display on wall hooks or in cases, but most of the stock, including gold, is generally kept in a safe in a back room.

In all such shops, visible against the rear wall is a standard metal, two-doored, shelved cabinet that can be locked. At its bottom are two metal drawers used to store used silver jewelry purchased from clients. Periodically this tangled accumulation is sent to the local refiner, who melts it down, passes it through a refining process, and casts it into ingots, one of the mainstays of the Indian bullion market.

At the other extreme, large cities such as Bombay, Calcutta, New and Old Delhi, Hyderabad, Bangalore, and Madras boast of a sizable gold and silver bazaar, in some cases contiguous, in others separate. In close proximity are very large shops splendidly fitted with attractive, modern display and counter cabinets in which ornaments are organized by types. Most likely a khaki-uniformed guard, often a Nepali Gurkha, a group noted for fierceness, ominously bearing a well-polished rifle, stands at the heavy plate-glass, bullet-proof door and scrutinizes incoming clients. In the air-conditioned interior, the well-groomed, young sales staff politely and attentively caters to customer needs. Yet even large shops with considerable sales personnel, especially at the marriage season, are thronged with clients who must patiently wait their turn to be served.

Raw Forms of Precious Metals

672. Jhaveri Bazaar, Jaipur, Rajasthan
Silver merchant (chandi farosh *or* sarraf) *with his scale* (tarazu), *weighing a stamped silver ingot (right pan) with standard weights* (tolne ke bat) *(left pan).*

In the jewelry trade, the basic form in which gold and silver are available is the ingot. (The terms that follow are in Hindi.) *Asli* is a general term for superior quality gold ingots, stamped with the percentage of their fineness and the name of the place where they are cast. *Passa*, a block or bar-form ingot from the United States, Europe, Australia, or South Africa, has an average weight of 25 *tolas*. *Desia passa* is an Indian ingot made of melted-down gold ornaments. *Patra* or *tezab ka rava* (*tezab*, nitric acid or aqua regia) is gold refined by the use of acid and is usually a four-inch (10 cm) square in sheet form. *Nakli* is an unstamped ingot of inferior quality. *Gori* is gold dust collected by people who pan for it in rivers. *Kundan* is the purest gold of all, sold in sheet form and used in gemstone setting.

Int ke chandi is a general term for a silver ingot from a foreign source. *Thobi* is a silver block marked off into equal weight divisions and is prepared from inferior refined silver. *Sil ki chandi* is a high-quality silver. *Raini* is a cigar-shaped ingot. *Kurs* is a loaf-shaped, especially pure European ingot.

Among the trade names for silver are *anguri ki chandi*, a highly refined silver made from *sil ki chandi* and used for silver leaf placed on food and *pan* (spices wrapped in a leaf and chewed as a digestive). *Phuldar chokla* is a highly refined silver from old ornaments. *Tapia ki chandi* is also made from melted-down ornaments and can be of varying quality. *Rupa* is a general name for an inferior quality of silver alloyed with copper or zinc.

The alloys of gold used for Indian jewelry contain silver or copper, or both. Most of the silver used for jewelry is alloyed with copper or zinc or both to improve its mechanical strength and resistance to wear and tarnish.

Precious metals available on the Indian bullion market come from primary (mined) and secondary (recovered and refined) sources. These raw forms are categorized and reported with their current prices in the daily newspapers of India, where gold prices are quoted per 10 grams and silver prices by the kilogram. The primary categories for trading gold and silver in India are as follows:

New York Metal Gold (0.999): The highest international standard, sold in New York
Standard Mint Gold (0.995): Indian Government–minted gold, produced in Bombay
Ornaments Gold (0.917, or 22k): Gold already alloyed for use in making 22-karat gold ornaments
Sovereign Gold (0.917): in the form of the British sovereign gold coin, weight 8 grams
Gold Vitur (0.999–0.900): Unofficial gold refined secretly, and, despite its illegality, reported in the newspapers
Silver (0.999): The highest international standard, refined by the most scientific means
Silver (0.996; 0.994): Also available in these qualities
Silver Spot (0.916): *Spot* refers to the quoted price and indicates the silver is ready for immediate delivery after sale, for cash payment.
Silver Tenderable: Silver purchased on a futures contract, to be delivered at a definite future date, in contrast to the immediate delivery of *spot* silver
Silver Gaddi or *Takiya* (0.960–0.800): *Gaddi* (bun) is a round ingot; *takiya* (pillow) describes this ingot's shape. Both are from old jewelry refined by quasi-scientific means and are generally used by village jewelers.
Thobi Silver (0.960–0.800): A Punjabi term, essentially the same as *gaddi* and *takiya*
Karawal Silver (0.960): *Gaddi* form, good-quality silver from old ornaments, alloyed with zinc
Silver Tezabi (0.960–0.920): Also called *raw tezabi*, or *desi tezabi*. Refined by primitive methods using nitric acid, or aqua regia (a combination of nitric and sulphuric acid)
Old Coins Silver (0.900): Made from old silver rupee coins, or silver coins of known standard used by any country in the past

Various factors affect the price fluctuations of the precious metals. Primary among them is the international exchange rate of the U.S. dollar, which changes almost daily, as does the price of gold and silver, which is tied to it. Foreign manipulations of gold and silver stocks on the world market also affect the highly sensitive Indian price of precious metals. Other factors causing prices to rise include large-scale seizures of contraband gold; the annual approach of the winter marriage season and the ensuing demand for dowry jewelry; and periodic anxiety concerning foreign and/or domestic situations.

673. Dariba Bazaar, Delhi
Jewelry bazaar refiner (H: nyariya; P: musaffi) who buys used gold and silver for refining. His most important, visible tools are a touchstone (kasauti), to test metal quality, and a scale (tarazu). In the foreground is a pile of old gold yarn (zari) to be burned and the gold recovered.

The Indian Goldsmith

Goldsmith.

674. Bhuj, Kachchh, Gujarat. *August 1856*
"Company" painting in gouache of two goldsmiths
at work. One of seventy-two paintings bound in
two volumes depicting trades and crafts of Kachchh.
Painted by a local Indian artist.
9 x 5½ in. (22.8 x 14 cm)
Collection India Office Library and Records,
London (198 i-xliv; Add. Or. 1555)

The hearth (chulera) is a red clay pot (ghara). The
goldsmith (right) is working on silver anklets; a
completed one is under his right knee. The
goldsmith at left is soldering an object inside the
hearth, by blowing air through a blowpipe. He
manipulates the work with hand-held spring tongs
(chimta). Below his hand, sunk in the earthen
floor, is an anvil (nihai).

The Goldsmith Guild

Prior to the Industrial Revolution, which reached India in the latter half of the nineteenth century, to avoid anarchy and insecurity in their trade, jewelers and goldsmiths formed occupational caste associations or corporations (H: *sreni*; P: *jama'at;* A: *firqa*) loosely comparable to Western guilds, which in effect acted as economic trade unions.

Although guild membership was open automatically to members of hereditary goldsmith castes (H: *sonar*), any qualified person who had completed a proper apprenticeship (H: *shagirdi*) and paid an initiation fee could join. As a result, today many practicing goldsmiths came from other artisan castes. Blacksmithing, carpentry, coppersmithing, stone cutting, and goldsmithing comprise the five traditional Hindu artisan castes (*panch-salar*). Goldsmiths, silversmiths, and workers in each of the base metals all belonged to different subcastes and had separate guilds.

Guilds in India were organized and operated in much the same way as those of medieval Europe. They regulated the craft by establishing a code of professional ethics and morality, determined hours of work, estab-lished a fair wage scale to workers (H: *mazduri*) for various kinds of work, settled disputes among members, imposed fines on violators, and paid taxes. Consumer patronage was encouraged by the guild's maintenance of standards of skill, a guarantee of good workmanship and the stated quality of materials, and of a fair price for their products. Guilds also performed social functions, such as supporting needy members by loans and salary advances and providing pensions to widows of deceased members. Guild leaders were socially prominent and invited to participate in all state functions. As a group, the guild joined community religious functions, and epigraphic inscriptions record guild contributions to temple construction. Many of these original guild functions survive in the practices of present-day trade organizations, which supplanted guilds in the Industrial Age.

It was traditional for a family member already engaged in an artisanal profession to pass his knowledge on to a younger member. Also possible, a child became an apprentice to an unrelated master craftsman (H: *karigar;* P: *ustad*), lived with the master's family, and worked in his workshop (H: *karkhana*). Learning was (and is) informal. It commenced by observation and the assignment of simple tasks that in time increased in difficulty and degree of responsibility. Training concentrated on the basic techniques required to produce the regional jewelry types favored by the local clientele. Technical competence in selected skills was stressed above design originality, which was less in demand because traditional jewelry styles were perpetuated. When necessary, team members of other specialist goldsmith guilds, such as those of the engravers, enamelists, and stone setters, were called upon at the proper time to contribute their expertise.

After an indefinite number of years, training ended when the apprentice proved himself capable of satisfactorily executing work of an expected standard. Usually the trainee then became a staff member of the workshop in which he was trained, or, more rarely, he started his own establishment. When the relationship was father and son, the latter eventually inherited his father's capital and credit as his patrimony.

Historically, the artisan guilds protected consumers against unfair practices, mainly involving the quality of precious metals and gemstones. The guilds censured transgressors by levying fines. Although no quality-control hallmark stamping laws existed, and identifying manufacturer's marks on jewelry and objects were (and still are) rare, in general, the

675. Jaipur, Rajasthan
Family of goldsmiths in their open-fronted bazaar workshop (jawahir karkhana), a type essentially unchanged for centuries. At the center is the hearth (chulera): an inverted red-clay pot with one portion removed, the remainder acting to retain heat. Inside, its floor is spread with ashes; outside, the pot is coated with clay for reinforcement and insulation. By tradition, goldsmiths work squatting on the workshop floor.

jewelers' ethics were high. With the decline of the guilds, however, corrupt practices have increased. While many artisans undoubtedly are honest, well-known Indian folkloric aphorisms—deserved or not—cleverly express the prevailing viewpoint. An example from Uttar Pradesh: *Sat bar sunar ke jawe usi ka ho jawe* (Send an ornament to a goldsmith for repair seven times and there will be nothing left).

As an outcome of this attitude, it became common practice for a client to provide a goldsmith with precious metals and gemstones of known quality and weight, usually in the presence of witnesses who, if need be, can be called upon to confirm the material's original, recorded weight and quality. Clients normally expect the finished ornament to have the same weight as the gold given and the return of any surplus. In all goldsmith work, however, a 2 to 3 percent metal loss is normal. If this is not understood by a client who agrees to such a loss, a goldsmith may resort to unscrupulous means to increase the weight of the gold by alloying it with a base metal such as copper.

Even today, the goldsmith may be asked to come to the client's home with his tools and set up a temporary workshop there so that his work could be carried out under the watchful supervision of the client, a trusted family member, or a servant. Because jewelry-making tools are comparatively few and portable, this is done easily. Even so, a dishonest goldsmith, by means unknown to persons unacquainted with the trade technology, could indulge in sharp practices without detection.

676. Northern India. *19th century Detail of an engraving after a colored lithograph, Sonnah Waller, "drawn from Nature and on stone by Capt. J. Luard." Two women assigned by the house proprietor watch a goldsmith work to be sure he does not cheat while he prepares a commission of jewelry on the client's veranda (H: baramada). Indian goldsmiths can work anywhere because all their tools are portable. Collection Maria de Lisitzin, Porvoo*

677

677. Andhra Pradesh
Copy of a cast-brass founding tablet, the original inscribed with the date 1110 Saka Era (A.D. 1188) Height 11¾ in. (30 cm)

The subject is dedicated to Vishvakarman, the Hindu deity who represents supreme creative power. As artificer of the Universe, he is the father of all artisans. Below the upper two registers, where Hindu gods are depicted, are five registers in which appear his five sons—Manu, Maya, Tvastr, Daivajna, and Vishvajna—who represent the five major Hindu artisanal castes, three of which involve metalwork (iron, copper, gold-silver). Tools of their trade are depicted.

Duplicates are now used as a commemorative award to outstanding Indian artisans, thereafter designated as Mastercraftsmen and Mastercraftswomen, given during the annual Republic Day celebrations in January. The major occupations are as follows:

Occupation	Hindi	Marathi	Kanarese	Telugu	Tamil
Blacksmith	lohar	lohar	kambara	kamr uru	karuman
Carpenter	barhai	sutat	bargia	wad'l uru	thachchan
Coppersmith	thatera	tambatgar	kantsagara	kantsar uru	kannan
Stone cutter	sang tarash	gondi	kassigara	kassi uru	kalthachchan
Gold- and silversmith	sonar	sonar	aksala	aosal uru	thattan

678. Ajmer, Rajasthan
Goldsmith (sunar) at work using the simplest of all soldering tools; a blowpipe (nali) through which he blows air to intensify the heat of the oil lamp (tel ki batti) flame (ag). By increasing the rate of oxygen flow, the flame heats the object enough to melt the solder and join parts. For ease in manipulation of the object, the work is placed on a hand-held charcoal block (zugal lakkar).

Two main categories of goldsmiths exist today in India: those who are independent and those who work for others. Independent artisans who own their own workplace and tools —and often are capable of carrying out all phases of the work without recourse to specialists—are most commonly found in small towns. Theoretically, they are free to sell their own products directly to the public or to any jewelry dealer. Usually, however, they sell to a single merchant with whom they have a long-standing relationship. The average goldsmith has little or no business skills and depends upon these merchants for access to wholesale (H: *thok*) and retail (H: *phutkar*) outlets.

Particularly in rural India, but also in large cities and central towns, the goldsmith-jeweler, who rarely possesses the capital necessary to operate his own business, often works instead for a financier-entrepreneur known as a *mahajan* (H: "great person"), or a *sarraf* (A: rural banker, money changer or lender who also sells precious metals). Many own a jewelry manufactory (P: *jawahir-ka-karkhana*) and employ an overseer (P: *karkhandar*), often a master craftsman, who hires goldsmiths, generally of the same religion as his, and usually works alongside them. Based on current market demand, to which he pays close attention, the *sarraf* decides what is to be manufactured, its quantity and quality, and often supplies the goldsmith-jeweler with designs. In this system the goldsmith works for a contracted monthly wage, and any specialists needed are hired and paid on a piecework (H: *pai wandkari*) basis.

Tools, materials, and supplies are provided by the workshop owner. *Sarrafs* often also own large, modern retail goldsmith shops with a varied, ready stock of jewelry available for immediate purchase, and they arrange for the creation of commissioned (P: *farmaish*) ornaments.

Practically every independent goldsmith has a connection with a *sarraf* as either a supplier or outlet for his products. The *sarraf* may sell precious metals to him at a profit or advance him precious metal bullion to be paid for at an agreed date. If payment is late, as is often the case because most goldsmiths operate in a state of continuous financial arrears, the interest rate (P: *sud*) is substantial.

In general, the *sarraf* is considered a responsible, trustworthy person, but, because of the prevailing system, the average goldsmith, whether independent or a hired worker, is constantly in debt to the *sarraf* and therefore under his control. Exacerbating this condition is the *sarraf's* paternalistic role as personal money lender. Loans to provide a daughter with a dowry, or pay for wedding, medical, or funeral expenses, often put the goldsmith under long-term obligation to the *sarraf,* who then controls his livelihood in virtual perpetuity.

Indian Goldsmith Weights

In the past, and to a considerable extent even today in rural India, the system of weights and measures varied from place to place. With the unification of the various Indian provinces during British rule, to avoid possible deceit by the use of false or unstandard weights, local weights and measures were gradually abandoned in favor of common standards that more or less became universal throughout India.

Basic to the weight system adopted was the Indian silver rupee initially issued by the East India Company after 1793 and minted at Bombay, Surat, Farrukhabad, Varanasi, Calcutta, Murshidabad, and Arcot (Madras). From 1835 onward, all Indian silver rupee coins contained a purity of 165 grains fine silver within their total weight of 180 grains troy, or had a purity of a 0.916 (91.6 percent). On May 19, 1836, the standardized weight of the *tola* at 180 grains troy was adopted. This remains its ponderal value, and it is the basis of all Indian goldsmiths' weights.

Silver coinage continued in India until 1956, when its value as precious metal exceeded its face value. All through its time of issuance, and today, silver rupee coins were and are commonly used intact as ornaments because of their known, reliable silver content (see page 120). They were also melted down to fabricate ornaments.

In 1956, after Independence, the Standards of Weight and Measures Act established the metric system as the standard of weights and measures. In this the primary length unit is a meter, the primary mass unit is the kilogram, and the unit of capacity is the liter. This act has since been amended by additional laws that do not affect the discussion here.

Abrus precatorius, a seed produced by the Indian wild licorice root, jequirity bean, or crab's eye shrub, has been used by Indian goldsmiths since antiquity to weigh precious metals and gemstones and is still in use today, despite the introduction of modern, international weight systems. Round, very hard and durable, scarlet red with a distinctive black top, the seed is produced by a beautiful, wiry, climbing shrub found throughout the Indian plains and in the Himalayas up to three thousand feet (c. 900 m). The variety with the rose-colored flowers generates the scarlet seed with the black "eye," collected when the climber's fruits have withered and the seed pods open.

The universal use of the seed by goldsmiths in India is attested to by its widely dispersed regional names: Sanskrit *raktika;* H: *ratti;* Mah: *gunja;* Tam: *gundumani.* The Hindi term *ratti* will be used for the purposes of this book. Its nearly uniform size and weight makes the *ratti* eminently suited to this purpose. Actually, its weight can vary from 1.75 to 1.93 grains troy, the mean weight being about 1.84 grains troy. *Ratti* weight values are higher in the south, where the seeds are larger: about 2.14 grains troy. Dishonest goldsmiths use the heavier *ratti* for buying and the lighter one for selling. (One carat is a twenty-fourth of an ounce, or 3.17 grains troy).

679. *Red-and-black-spotted jequirity, or crab's eye seeds (H: ratti or gunja; Abrus precatorius). Because of its remarkably uniform weight, this seed has been used since antiquity for weighing precious metals and gemstones. It is therefore colloquially called "the weighing seed" (H: tula-bij). Its weight is about 1⁵⁄₁₆ grains troy, the factitious weight about 2³⁄₁₆ grains.*

680

681

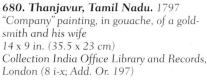

680. Thanjavur, Tamil Nadu. *1797*
"Company" painting, in gouache, of a gold-
smith and his wife
14 x 9 in. (35.5 x 23 cm)
Collection India Office Library and Records,
London (8 i-x; Add. Or. 197)

In this genre of painting, couples of various
castes and occupations were depicted in their
traditional dress and ornaments with the tools
of their trade. Here the goldsmith holds a
blowpipe (uthukural), tongs (ilaikkurathu), and
hammer (chuttiyal). His wife carries a typical
brass-bound goldsmith's box (thattan thai-
yarpetti). Thanjavur, a center of traditional
painting, was the first to produce such minia-
ture paintings. By the nineteenth century
the idea had spread all over India, each place
developing a more or less local style.

681. Southern India. *19th century*
Brass-bound goldsmith's box (thattan thai-
yarpetti) with a sliding cover
3 x 15 x 9 in. (7.5 x 38 x 23 cm); weight 1710 g
Collection Mis, Brussels

The box is used to store a gemstone and
precious-metal weighing scale (taddan tarasu),
weights (padikkal), a touchstone (uraikal), and
small hand tools. During the last three days
of the nine-day Dussera holiday (September–
October), all traditional caste craftsmen, in
a special ceremony (Tam: ayutham vazhiadu;
H: ayudha puja), worship the tools by which
they earn their livelihood. Goldsmiths clean
them and scatter over them red powder or
vermillion (Tam: jathilingam; S: sindur) as a
substitute for a blood sacrifice; some perform
an actual small animal or fowl sacrifice.

682. Dariba Bazaar, Delhi
Street gold-electroplater (sona tanda mulammakar)
with all the tools of his trade visible. Clients bring
jewelry and objects to him for instant, while-they-
wait replating.

Goldsmiths have another use for this seed. They crush it to a fine powder and mix this with water to make a strong adhesive gum used to hold delicate parts of jewelry together before the applied heat fuses the solder and joins them.

Ratti seeds are also used extensively for rosaries or necklaces, made into ear orna-ments, and for the decoration of objects such as baskets. Their use for rosaries suggested their botanic designation *precatorius*, Latin for "precatory," the act of requesting, entreating, or wishing, as when reciting a rosary. In India, the seeds are sometimes taken internally as a purgative, but an overdose can be fatal because their red coating contains a potent poison closely analogous to snake venom.

Indian Jeweler's Traditional Weights

The *tola* is used chiefly in weighing precious metals and coins. *Mashas* and *rattis* are used chiefly by goldsmiths and jewelers and in the evaluation by assay of the precious metals.

Payment for jewelry by tradition is based on the per-*tola* weight of the finished object. Each class of ornament has a different per-*tola* rate, depending on its construction and its degree of technical complexity. For example, one rate applies to solid cast objects, another for hollow work, and yet another for very

demanding fine work (H: *barik kam*). The pay-ment for specialists who may be called upon to contribute their skill to the execution of a sin-gle object is incorporated in the per-*tola* price.

This rate is calculated to include so-called working charges (P: *gimat*), which, compared to Western goldsmith practice, are low in India. In the West, labor costs often constitute a greater factor in the price of an object than the material costs because labor charges are usually calculated on an hourly rate basis. In India, where skilled craft labor is abundant and wages low, and time of less consequence, piecework is more common. These circumstances explain why prices are primarily expressed in terms of weight of the material used.

Conversion of Traditional Indian Goldsmith Weights (Northern India)					
1 *ratti*	= 8 *jau* (barleycorns)	= 8 *khaskhas*	= 1.75 grains troy	= ~ 0.122 gram	
1 *masha*		= 8 *rattis*	= 15 grains troy	= 0.976 gram	
1 *tanka*	= 4 *mashas*	= 32 *rattis*	= 60 grains troy	= 3.904 grams	
1 *tola*	= 12 *mashas*	= 96 *rattis*	= 180 grains troy	= 11.712 grams	= 1 silver *rupee*
5 *tolas*	= 1 *chhatak*				
16 *chhataks*	= 1 *ser*				
40 *sers*	= 1 *maund*				

Distinctive Goldsmith Techniques

Granulation: A Multicultural Technology

Granulation (P: *rawa-kam; rawa,* a grain of sand; *kam,* work) is an ancient jewelry decoration process employing small, solid balls of gold or silver with a diameter of from one-sixtieth to one-eightieth of an inch (0.4–0.14 mm) to ornament jewelry and objects. The manner by which these are joined to the work is one of the great technological achievements of jeweler goldsmith-silversmiths. In this delicate technique, the granulator (H: *charmkar*) manipulates minute, solid orbs into grouped and linear patterns and figures.

The technique seems to have originated in Ur, Mesopotamia, around 2000 B.C., from where it was dispersed westward via the Middle East, Syria, and Egypt (c. 1900–1600 B.C.) to the Mediterranean area and eastward to Iran. Jewelry historians who trace the development of the granulation process eastward from Mesopotamia generally have proceeded no farther than Sassanian Iran and hardly mention India or areas farther east or south. The eastern world of jewelry granulation virtually becomes terra incognita, forcing one by implication to assume that it either did not exist there or was of no consequence. Facts prove otherwise.

Exactly how far back granulation was first established in India, and its specific source—probably more than one place and time—is conjectural due to the paucity of surviving, datable examples before the second century B.C. However, the high degree of technical excellence displayed in those works that have miraculously survived implies an even earlier development and a connection with sources where it is known to have been in practice prior to this date. Extensive trade existed between India and ancient Greece, Achaemenian Iran, and Rome, and jewelry was among the luxury export-import commodities. It is reasonable to assume that distinctive technical aspects of foreign work, such as granulation, would have been noticed in India and adopted within its own culture.

Direct contact between the cultures and Indians occurred with the campaigns of Alexander the Great, called Sikander in India, king

683
684

of Macedonia from 336 to 323 B.C. After uniting Greece, Alexander's next quest was the submission of the Achaemenian Persians, longtime enemies of Greece. To accomplish this he invaded Asia in 334 B.C. and overthrew the Achaemenian Empire by defeating Darius III in 330 B.C. Alexander then proceeded eastward and entered Indian territory by crossing the Hindu Kush Mountain Range (327 B.C.) and the Indus River (326 B.C.), the latter considered to be the westernmost demarcation line of India proper. The area it drains is called the Punjab ("five rivers"), after its five main tributaries.

Both Persians and Greeks used gold ornaments and objects as diplomatic bribes to gain the fidelity of surrendered leaders. In Greek and Roman histories we are told that in 326 B.C. Alexander presented submitting chiefs, such as Ambhi of Taxila, with lavish presents that must have included some of the granulated Greek jewelry and objects so typical of Greek goldsmith work. Conceivably, the style and technology of the conqueror's gifts provided a point of reference for local jewelers to emulate. Greek design influence and techniques such as granulation appear in the jewelry excavated at Taxila.

During his three-year campaign, Alexander's deepest penetration into India was the Beas River in northern Punjab. Unwilling to face the unknown farther east, or increase the already great distance from their homeland, his troops refused to advance farther into India. In great frustration and disappointment, Alexander was forced to begin his retreat to Greece, which he never reached; he died in Babylon in 323 B.C., at the age of thirty-three.

In retrospect, perhaps Alexander's greatest achievement was his breakdown of the barriers between West and East. After Alexander left India, trade by land and sea continued among India and Greece and the places in between, resulting in a considerable cultural and commercial interchange of Hellenic, Iranian, and Indian concepts and technologies, especially evident in the field of the arts.

From the fourth century B.C. onward, trade with Greece and Rome grew. Particularly in demand were hardstones for intaglio seals carved in the West and mounted in rings.

Greek motifs incorporated into Indian jewelry included the scrolling and angular meander, creepers, the acanthus leaf, the palmette, and the use of animal and figural subjects. It is possible that the technique of granulation was introduced to India at this point via Greek models. (However, the additional possibility cannot be totally ruled out that the process of producing small round balls of gold or silver may have been developed independently in India.) If not then new to Indians, granulation may have gained in importance by the example of its common use in Greek jewelry, to which India had access via Bactria and Greek culturally dominated centers such as Taxila.

Extant Gandharan Jewelry: Taxila

A considerable quantity of extant jewelry has been excavated at Taxila, as it was called by the Greeks and Romans (S: Takshasila), whose capital of the same name was founded c. sixth century B.C. 20 miles (32 km) northwest of Rawalpindi, now in Pakistan. Although the center of the Gandharan culture was probably closer to Swat, Taxila participated in its development. An important archaeological site, Taxila is a complex of several subsequent relocations, such as Sirkap (second century B.C.). In the course of its history, Taxila passed from the rule of the Achaemenians to that of Alexander (326 B.C.), Chandragupta (317 B.C.), the Bactrian Greeks (305–303 B.C.), Ashoka (274 B.C.), again the Bactrians (c. 175 B.C.), the Parthians (A.D. 20–30), the Scythians, or Sakas (A.D. 78), and the Kushanas (A.D. 125). Finally it was demolished by the invasion of the White Huns or Ephthalites (fifth century A.D.), whose descendents include several Rajput clans, Jats, and Gujars.

As a result of these successive rules, Taxila became a wealthy and populous international city and kingdom with extensive surrounding territories. Several waves of Greek influence, and commercial contact with the West, fostered a noteworthy Greek-dominated material civilization there in which, following a pattern prevailing in Hellenistic Greece and Imperial Rome, whose culture Taxila emulated, gold jewelry became an important luxury in demand by a wealthy clientele.

Jewelry found in Taxila, Sirkap, Sirsukh, and in neighboring monastery and temple remains during the last and present centuries included diadems, earrings, torques, necklaces, pendants, medallions, lockets, amulets, many hardstone beads, the X-shaped torso-crossing ornament (stanabhinna hara), bangles, bracelets, finger rings, and anklets. Some of the jewelry recovered came there through its extensive trade with the West, especially with Greece and Rome. Others were created in Taxila by resident Greek goldsmiths who either emigrated there or arrived with Parthian or Bactrian invading armies, some of whose members settled there. Still others must have been made by local Indian jewelers, who either were trained by Western jewelers or who adopted and worked in styles demanded by their Greco-Roman–oriented patrons.

The Hellenistic element in this jewelry occurs in its forms and subject matter and the highly skillful techniques of the surface decoration processes they employed, such as granulation, repoussage, chasing, stamping, wirework, gemstone cutting, polishing, and inlay, and the use of loop-in-loop chains and straps. Yet the Greco-Roman style of this jewelry did not translate in toto into contemporary or later Indian work. As is typical of Indian jewelers when exposed to foreign design or work concepts, they interpreted these foreign models for use by their Indian clientele in a manner peculiarly Indian. Identifiable elements of Hellenistic influence on Indian jewelry that followed were mainly of a technical nature, such as the use of granulation and filigree work, and only sometimes thematic.

Some direct connections between Taxilan jewelry and that of later Indian design can, however, be mentioned. Perhaps of greatest importance is the Taxilan use of amulets, whose subjects—such as the lion (simha), tortoise (kurma), goose (hamsa), three jewels (triratna), two fish (matsya yugma), and crescent moon (naya-chand)—were of Indian origin and significance. Among the Taxilan finds was a gold tiger-claw pendant amulet decorated with granulation, an outstanding example of the application of that process. Also recovered from stupas were amulets in the form of arrowheads, spearheads, and pipal-leaves.

Besides the use of granulation, another Taxilan goldsmith technique worthy of special notice is the common Indian practice of filling finished hollow jewelry units with lac or resin to support the form. Sir John Marshall, archaeologist and late Director General of Archaeology in India during the British Raj, claimed the concept is of Greek origin, but lac-filled metal bangles were found in the much-earlier Indus Valley Culture, and lac is an indigenous Indian product. Its use as a filler probably originated in the practice of working sheet metal in the repoussage process by fixing the metal over a supporting substance, such as lac resin combined with a filler, to give it resilience and plasticity.

683. Coimbatore, Tamil Nadu
Gold earrings (kammal) with rows of high-quality granulation (maniyakkugai), using small-sized granules (oremani) alternating with right- and left-twisted wire (kambi)
Each diameter 2¾ in. (7 cm); weight 40 g
Collection Mis, Brussels

684. Ahmedabad, Gujarat
Gold earrings (akota, see 447), ornamented with granulation (rawa), held on the ear by a cylindrical-stud backing
Courtesy Egon von Lixfield, Jewel of the Lotus, Scottsdale, Arizona

685. Kashmir (probably). *9th–10th century* A.D.
*Three-piece gold diadem, repoussé decorated
with four half-avian kinnaris or minor mythical
spirits and inset with a central garnet. Edged
at the bottom with nineteen pendants, the central
one with a leaf-shaped terminal, the side one
with a concave disc
Height (central panel, less pendants) 2⅛ in.*
(5.4 cm); length 11⅞ in. (30.2 cm)
*The Metropolitan Museum of Art, New York.
Gift of the Kronos Collections, 1988 (1988.395)*

*The design treatment is influenced by the Greek-
inspired gold jewelry of the Gandhara region.*

686. Junagadh, Gujarat
*Woman wearing a granulated-gold, reel-shaped
earring (totiyu in gold; kundal in silver) in a
stretched earlobe hole. This earring is popular
among Bharwar, Kanbi, and Patel women. She
also wears upper gold rings (pandi or boria).*

687. Gujarat, Rajasthan
*Gold earrings (karanphul) intricately ornamented
with granulation, braided wire, and set with rubies;
with back stud
Each diameter 2½ in. (6.4 cm); weight 39 g
Collection Mis, Brussels*

688. Barhut, Andhra Pradesh. *Shunga* ➤
Dynasty, 1st century B.C.
*Stone sculpture on a post (stambha) railing
(vedika) that surrounded the Barhut Mahastupa
Indian Museum, Calcutta*

*Depicted is a yakshini wearing the ornaments
of contemporary times. These include (in modern
terms) the forehead ornament (tikka); earrings
(kundala); three necklaces: a long one (hara), on
top of which is an eight-strand bead necklace
(moti mala) and, over it, a third necklace (identical
with 689), the one that mainly concerns us here.
On a round, loop-in-loop chain is strung two
granulation-decorated tri-ratna bead-pendants,
flanking a similarly ornamented large central
barrel-shaped bead.*

Mauryan Jewelry

Alexander's fiery destruction of Persepolis, the
Acheamenian capital, led to the dispersal of its
numerous artisans. Some migrated to the
northern Indian kingdom of Magadha, ruled
by Chandragupta Maurya I (322–298 B.C.).
The excavated remains of the Mauryan capital
of Pataliputra (near Patna, Bihar), recall the
audience halls (*apadanas*) of Achaemenid Persepolis, Susa, and Ekbatana. These displaced
artisans undoubtedly made aesthetic and technical contributions to Mauryan culture by introducing Persian design concepts, probably in all
mediums.

Further evidence of Achaemenian influence is seen in the style, form, and finish of
the still extant Mauryan monolithic pillars (S:
lats; stambhas) with Buddhist animal and other
symbol capitals, obviously inspired by Achaemenian prototypes. These pillars were installed
at many locations in India by the third Mauryan
emperor, Ashoka. On them were inscribed the
Buddhist *dharma*, the essential moral precepts
of Buddhism, which Ashoka had adopted and
attempted to make universal in India.

Another Persian contribution may have
been the use of granulation in jewelry at which
the Achaemenians were masters. (Achaemenian jewelry itself is an amalgam of several cultural influences, including that of Mesopotamia, Egypt, and Greece. Subject and design
elements characteristic of those places, creative-
ly adapted, frequently appear in this work.) If,
indeed, this technique did enter Mauryan jewelry by this route at this time, that would
explain the proficiency of its practice in the
later Sunga and Andhra examples discussed
ahead. In any case, from this period onward,
the granulation process became an important
decorative component of Indian jewelry.

As actual examples of Mauryan jewelry are
not available, we must look to other sources to
form an idea of their appearance. That Mau-

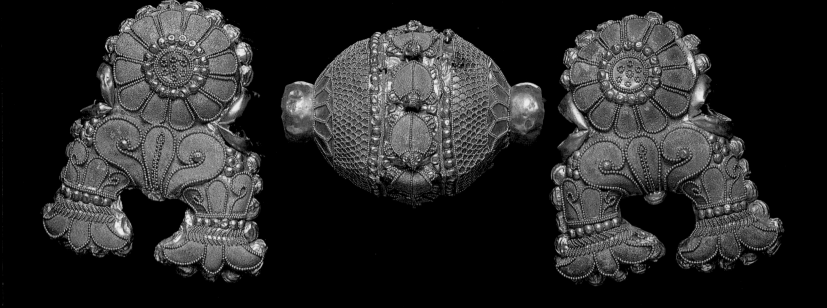

689. Northern India. Shunga Dynasty, 185–72 B.C.
Gold necklace (mala) of three main units (tri-ratna)
Tri-ratna pendant height 2¼ in. (5.7 cm); central bead length 2¼ in. (5.7 cm)
The Cleveland Museum of Art, Cleveland. John L. Severance Fund (73.66-68)

690. Detail of 689 showing granules of three distinct size groups, an indication that they must have been graded by the use of sieves

Kautilya's *Arthasastra*

Because it sheds light on the early development of jewelry in India, the contemporary Arthasastra (S: artha, purpose, wealth; sastra, treatise), a famous Indian work on government written sometime between 321 and 300 B.C. by Chanakya, alias Kautilya, is of prime interest here. Kautilya served as prime minister to the last Nanda king of Magadha. Because of Nanda misrule, sometime around 322 B.C. Kautilya overthrew and murdered the Nanda ruler and his family and installed Chandragupta Maurya, the first historic emperor of India, on the throne of Magadha at its capital of Pataliputra, present-day Patna, Bihar. He became the emperor's chancellor.

The fifteen books of the Arthasastra *make up the oldest extant Indian treatise meant as a guide for a ruler. A compendium of older Arthasastras, plus Kautilya's additions, it deals with the traditional elements of a political state: king, minister, fortress, territory or subjects, treasure, army, and allies. Systematically organized, it discusses political science, methods of government administration, fiscal management, economic relations among social groups within the Mauryan Empire, and trade relations with neighboring empires. For instance, it specifically mentions the advisability of establishing trade with southern Indian kingdoms, where gold, conch shells, and diamonds, pearls, and other gemstones, were abundant.*

Also included are all aspects of human relationships and practical life, which together give us an accurate picture of conditions and practices at this early time. Of particular interest in connection with jewelry are its extensive references to mining, the treasury, the goldsmith, jewelry technology, and ancient laws regarding property and inheritance, which always involve jewelry. Taken together, they clearly indicate the immense importance and significance that Mauryans attached to gold, precious stones, and jewelry. The many references to technology lead us to believe that by the fourth century B.C., Mauryan jewelry had already achieved an advanced state of development, which explains the high quality of later jewelry finds.

691. Tamluk (ancient Tamralipta), Medinipur District, West Bengal. *c. 200 B.C. Terra-cotta plaque of Shri (Mother Goddess), symbolic of fertility and abundance 8 x 3¹⁵/₁₆ in. (21.3 x 9.9 cm) Ashmolean Museum, Oxford, Department of Eastern Art (X-201)*

Shri is still universally worshiped throughout India. Similar terra-cotta images were made in Gangetic cities (4th–2nd centuries B.C.) and have been found in large numbers. This one, the most magnificent of them all, was found in 1883. Sumptuously adorned, the goddess eloquently illustrates the highly developed state of personal ornament style and manufacture at this early date. All body parts are ornamented, but most spectacular is the two-bun headdress, the one on the left ornamented with five hairpins whose terminals bear female energy (shakti) symbols: elephant goad (ankusa); trident (trishula); axe (pharshi); thunderbolt (vajra); and banner (dvaja). The jewelry appears oversized in relation to figure size, but this was probably done deliberately to emphasize them and add to her grandeur.

ryan men and women made profuse use of jewelry is indicated by its common representation on surviving images from that period, in terra-cotta and stone, such as those from Mathura and later Shungan sites. Their variety of form, design, and use on all body parts indicates that by the mid-third to the first century B.C., the art of Mauryan jewelry fabrication had reached a high technological level. With the heirs to the Mauryan dynasty (322–185 B.C.), the Shungas and the early Andhras, we come onto firmer ground concerning the use of granulation, as extant examples from these periods exist and are discussed, described, and illustrated ahead.

Post-Mauryan Granulation

The earliest examples of Indian jewelry employing granulation—aside from those recovered at Taxila—have miraculously appeared in this century. With their discovery, the history of granulation in India becomes more than conjecture. Two superb examples profusely and expertly ornamented with granulation exist in museum collections in the United States.

One, a necklace in the Cleveland Museum of Art, is a masterwork dating from the Shunga dynasty (185–72 B.C.). Successors to the Maurya, the Shunga emperors relinquished the northwest but also ruled Magadha from their southern capital at Vidisha (now Besnagar). During this rule the great Buddhist stupas at Sanchi and Barhut, including sculptural subjects wearing contemporary jewelry, were created. The Cleveland necklace consists of three hollow gold units: two Buddhist *tri-ratna* or "three-jewel" forms, each symbolic of the Buddhist Trinity—faith in the Buddha, his doctrine (*dharma*), and the Buddhist Order (*sangha*)—separated by a large, barrel-shaped bead. Its assignment to the Shunga period is based upon its close correspondence to very similar necklaces depicted on sculpture from the Sanchi and Barhut stupas. Although some scholars disagree, the contemporary practice

692. Sanchi Stupa, Raisen District, Madhya Pradesh. *Shunga Dynasty, 2nd–1st century* B.C.

Northern torana, *east pillar, east face. Detail showing the tri-ratna symbol ornamented with floral designs. The same form, inverted with the points downward, was used in the tri-ratna necklace.*

of representing actual ornaments substantiates the belief that the ornaments depicted in Shunga sculpture were not inventions of the sculptor's fantasy.

Shown on page 289 is an image of a *yakshini*, or female tree spirit, one of many represented in the railings from the Barhut stupa (c. 100 B.C.) who, among others extant, wears an identical type of necklace. In this sculpture, the visible surfaces of these three units are carved with a regular pattern of small circular forms, not intended to represent pearls—as some sources claim—but meant by the sculptor to signify granulation, although the scale is far coarser due to the limitations of the stone medium.

The other example is a magnificent pair of gold earrings from the Kronos Collection at The Metropolitan Museum of Art in New York. Also hollow in construction, almost all of the earrings' surfaces are decorated with granulation. Extremely rare survivors from the past, they have been attributed to the early Andhra (Shatavahana) dynasty (c. 72 B.C.–c. A.D. 225), which supplanted that of the Shungas in the northwest Deccan and southeast India. The date of these earrings is also based on their sculptural representation. During this dynastic period, the four gateways (*toranas*) of the Sanchi stupa (c. 25 B.C.–A.D. 25) include a multitude of figures, many wearing ornaments, and the stupa at Jaggayyapeta (first century A.D.), 30 miles (48 km) northwest of the Amaravati site, were built. A good example of an image wearing similar earrings is the figure of the universal monarch (*cakravartin*) on a panel from Jaggayyapeta, but others exist.

The symbolic subjects depicted on these earrings, including the vase of abundance (S: *purnaghata*), the lion (*simha*), and the elephant (*gaja*), are all associated with royalty, and suggest that they may have been made for a royal personage. Similar earrings in less decorated forms appear in other sculptures, where they are worn by women.

Both outstanding examples of the granulation technique, these objects indicate that Indian goldsmiths at this early date already possessed outstanding skill in the granulation process. Their mastery in the highly controlled use of several distinctly calibrated granule sizes to form clearly defined images informs us that they were obviously mature works. It is highly unlikely that products of such a high degree of technical excellence could have sprung suddenly into existence. Their presence therefore is an indication that a long development in the acquisition of this skill must have preceded them, probably dating back to Mauryan times.

Since this early period, in one place or another in India, granulation has always been one of the traditional jewelry decoration techniques employed by Indian goldsmiths. As a living decoration process, the technique today is perhaps best accomplished in Gujarat in

693. Andhra Pradesh. *c. 1st century* B.C.
One of a pair of gold granulated earrings (prakaravapra kundala), known as the Kronos earrings
1⁵⁄₁₆ x 3⅛ in. (3.4 x 7.9 cm); diameter 1½ in.
(3.8 cm) (The other of the pair has similar dimensions)
The Metropolitan Museum of Art, New York. Gift of the Kronos Collections, 1981 (1981.398, 3, 4)

Each earring was fabricated in a traditional twisted form in which the central curving cylinder becomes transposed into terminal squares convex at both ends. Among the most important finds of ancient Indian jewelry, these ear ornaments were excavated in central Java in the late 1970s. They probably came there through the well-developed trade between India and countries in Southeast Asia and may have been worn by early Buddhist-Hindu rulers there who looked toward India as an inspirational source of cultural concepts. This earring form is often represented on Indian sculpture from this period.

694. Above: *Underside of the left earring.* Below: *Top view of the right earring, showing two purnaghata vases of abundance, from which flow triratna–type symbols*

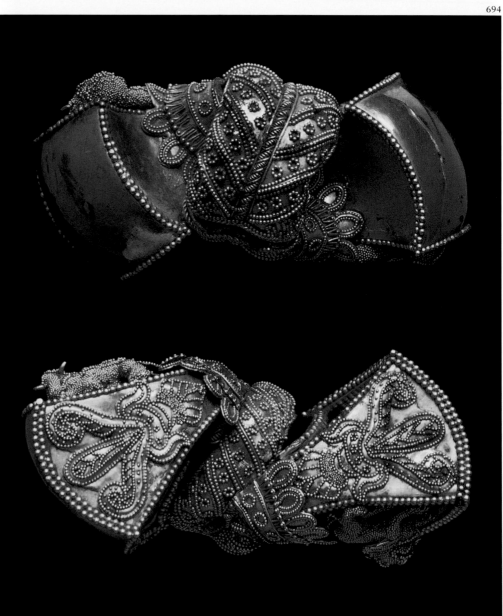

695

696

northwestern India. Granulation done there on traditional ornaments as late as the nineteenth century, and the present century, can be of great technical complexity. Important production centers are Ahmadabad in Gujarat, where unique jewelry forms are often decorated with granulation; Coimbatore in Tamil Nadu; and Kozikhode in Kerala.

The Granulation Process

The manufacture of tiny, solid gold balls in small sizes called granules (H: *rawa*) is a natural outcome of metallurgical and thermal principles. When enough heat is applied to a small amount of gold, it liquifies. At this point, due to the cohesive force of surface tension, the metal will automatically draw itself into a form having the smallest possible surface area, which is a round, solid ball.

Obviously, an efficient method for producing hundreds of gold or silver balls in calibrated sizes was necessary to be able to apply them as decoration. To accomplish this, Indian goldsmiths prepare a small ceramic or metal container with a layer of charcoal dust, which when burned creates a desirable reduction atmosphere that aids the granule-forming process. Over this, a piece of gold is filed with a coarse cut file, and the more-or-less-uniform resulting particles fall onto the charcoal, but are not allowed to touch or they will join and

form a larger ball. Layers are similarly prepared, each one consisting of particles covered with powdered charcoal until the container is full. By an alternate method, generally used to produce balls of larger diameter, gold wire or narrow strips of sheet metal are cut into small snippets with a hand shears, then dropped into the charcoal.

Using forced air from a bellows, the container is heated to a temperature sufficiently high to transform the particles into round granules (pure gold melts at 1945.4° F, 1063° C, and pure copper melts at 1981.4° F, 1083° C). The container is cooled, filled with water, and stirred. The gold balls sink to the bottom, and the floating charcoal and ash are removed. To calibrate the results, the dried granules are sifted through a series of sieves, from small to large mesh, which grades them by sizes, each stored separately.

In a single object, granules can all be the same size or a combination of two, three, or more sizes. They can be used in massed or geometric arrangements or in linear patterns, the latter especially as borders. Granules of small size are often used to fill spaces made of balls of a larger size, or of the same size, arranged to outline a figure, as in the Kronos earrings.

The granulation process consists of fixing the granules to the base metal of the object and to each other by a form of fusion welding, without the use of solder. In general, fusing

695. Gujarat
Gold amulet-pendant decorated with granulation, twisted wire, and flattened shot
2 x 2½ in. (5 x 6.4 cm); weight 55 g
Courtesy Chhote Bharany, New Delhi

Worn by Shaivites, this form represents the horns of a bull, Shiva's mount.

696. Kodki Village, Kachchh, Gujarat
Granulated-gold amulet (jibi), worn as a central pendant on a traditional silver necklace (seer or adaliyun), usually flanked by two gold beads (gora)
Diameter 2⅝ in. (6.7 cm); weight 43 g
Courtesy Alby Nall-Cain, Frontiers, London

Symbolizing the spirit of the Mother Goddess, represented only by her breasts, the necklace is worn by Dhebar Rabari women and others. The circular flat forms placed at intervals around the border are granules hammered flat.

the granules in groups is more easily accomplished than joining them singly to the base. In some cases in India, solder is used to join granules, but this work cannot be called true granulation. The difference between the two can be seen easily by using a 10x magnifying loupe to observe the join between the balls and the metal substrate. If any metal has partially crawled up the sides of the balls, leaving their outline shape incomplete, then solder has been used. When the metal at the point of contact between ball and base is minimal and most of the ball form can be clearly seen, the joining process is true granulation.

To accomplish true granulation, the clean granules are coated with a pastelike mixture of organic gum or glue combined with a powdered natural chemical containing some form of copper. The gum holds the balls in place on the object, but it also has another function. When the object is heated over a charcoal fire with a soldering blowpipe, as is normal in India, the gum carbonizes, allowing the two metals—gold and copper—to melt at a temperature lower than that normally required to melt either metal separately. At the proper temperature and critical moment of fusion welding, an instantaneous chemical reaction occurs in which the thin copper coating the granule melts, breaks, and by capillary attraction flushes to the small point of contact between the granule and base, forming an alloy with the molten surface gold that strongly joins the ball and base where, upon cooling, the atoms recrystallize. The heat source must be removed instantly (or the work from the heat) at the moment of fusion or the object will collapse. The object is then cleaned in an organic acid solution, such as one made of green mangoes or a citrus fruit, to remove all signs of residual surface copper oxide. This basic fusion process can also be used to create the joins of parts of precious-metal jewelry and objects.

697
698

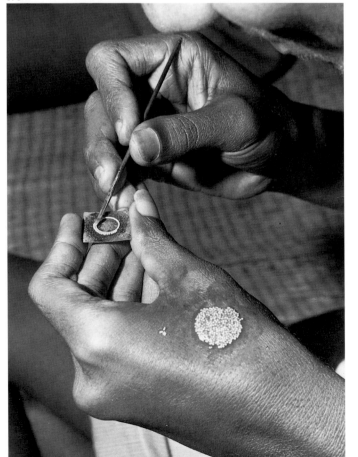

697. Junagadh, Gujarat
Mehr man wearing a set of three granulated-gold ear studs, each passing through a hole at different locations in the ear. Top to bottom: bhungri or phul, through the antihelix fossa; sisoria or theliya, through the concha; and champva or chapva, through the earlobe

698. Ahmedabad, Gujarat
In the granulation process, the goldsmith here places the granules on gum applied at the base of his thumb. From there he picks them up one at a time and puts them in position on the object, which rests on a sheet of mica (abrak), on which the object will be heated to fuse the granules in place.

699. Delhi. *19th century* ➤
Gold brooch (P: poshak zewar) with babul-kam work decoration
Diameter 2¹⁵⁄₁₆ in. (7.5 cm); approximate weight 20 g
Victoria and Albert Museum, London (IS 03332)

The visual similarity of the babul effect to the acacia flower is best seen in the lower round forms, but it was also applied to other forms such as crescent and tear shapes.

700. Delhi. *19th century* ➤
Silver necklace (kanta mala) of nineteen units, decorated with babul-kam work, threaded on two braided wire chains, with clasp
Length 17¾ in. (45 cm); unit length 1⅜ x ¾ in. (3.6 x 1.5 cm); weight 138 g
Collection the author, Porvoo

699

700

Babul or Kikar Work: Delhi

A unique, ancient form of jewelry decoration—mainly of gold but sometimes using silver—formerly done in Delhi and the Punjab but extinct since the early twentieth century, took its name from its resemblance to the yellow ball-shaped flower found on the acacia tree (H: *babul*; *Acacia arabica*) of the mimosa family. From this comes its designation *babul kam*, or *kikar kam*, meaning "acacia work." The sweet scented flowers of this tree grow in bunches; each blossom is round and covered with fine filament pistils that project outward in all directions to form the ball. Babul work imitates the flower's convex form and projecting filaments.

In this technique, a semicircular, oval, or tear-shaped dome, or a hollow spherical ball, is first made from a gold or silver alloy of lower quality than the points will be. The entire surface of the form is covered with minute, perpendicularly projecting, attenuated cone-shaped forms of a high-karat gold (or high-quality silver), made by hammering uniform, short lengths of wire into a mold that has depressions of a corresponding form.

The process of joining the miniature cones to the base resembles the heat-fusion granulation technique in which no solder is used. Prior to their placement, the forms are dipped into a mixture of organic glue, flux, and a powdered substance containing copper oxide, then positioned apex up, base down, as closely together as possible to completely cover the substrate surface. When the object is heated, the glue in the compound carbonizes, and the metal on the dome or base starts to melt. The higher quality points, which withstand the heat because of their higher melting point, become fused in place, whereupon the flame is instantly withdrawn. The result is boiled in an acid solution that produces a "bloom" or matte surface on the gold or silver, which contributes to its resemblance to the acacia flower.

The technique was especially used to decorate traditional Indian earrings of one, two, or three balls. It was noticed and appreciated by resident foreigners for whom goldsmiths used the process to create and decorate European-style ornaments, such as pendants, brooches, earrings, and bracelets, or to make a border around a central stone or a miniature portrait painting set in a frame. The same treatment was used for units in a necklace. In a bolder form, in which the points are larger in scale, this style of work was called *gokhru kam*, meaning "thorn work," and was used on earrings worn by Punjabi Jat men.

701. Cuttack, Orissa. *19th century*
Pair of filigree (malida or tarkashi kam) bracelets (pahunchi)
Each 8⅝ x 1¾ in. (22 x 4.4 cm); weight 28 g
Victoria and Albert Museum, London (IS 03375)

The rose (Or: chalu) motif with ball-ended pistils appears in many forms
of jewelry made in Cuttack and is one of its characteristic motifs.

Filigree:
Objects of Wire and Air

Filigree work in northern and central India is called by the Persian term *tarkashi kam* (*tar*, wire; *tarkash*, a wire drawer), or *melilakamsari-gaiyizhaippu* in Tamil. The European term *filigree*, or the older *filligrain* (L: *filum*, wire; and *granum*, grain) came into use because in this work, characteristically, the object is made with wire and small metal balls or grain, though today this is not always the case either in India or the West.

In this delicate, time-consuming style of metalwork, jewelry is made entirely from gold or silver wire of high standard. Wire has long been used in jewelry throughout India as it is one of the basic forms of metal available to the jeweler. Early jewelers used strips of sheet metal formed into a coil and rolled tightly to produce a wirelike form that was not true wire. With the invention of the *drawplate*—a rectangular steel plate drilled with holes of graduated size through which the wire is pulled to reduce it in section and simultaneously increase its length—very long lengths of solid metal wire became possible. Exactly when this tool first came into use in India is uncertain, especially because of the paucity of extant ancient jewelry. In Europe, where evidence is more plentiful, the use of the drawplate is believed to have been established around the tenth century A.D.

Some specialists claim that the drawplate originated in the East, however, so it seems likely that its introduction to India was earlier.

With today's iron or steel drawplate, still used as a hand tool in the filigree industry, a relatively small amount of metal can be transformed into a surprisingly long length of wire. Reduction to an unbroken hairline filament is possible because the precious metals are inherently high in *ductility*. When gold or silver wire is diminished in thickness by a half, third, or quarter, its length is increased, respectively, four, nine, and sixteen times. One ounce of gold can be drawn into a single, hairline filament 35 miles (21.8 km) long. From one *tola* of silver, up to four thousand feet (1025 m) of wire can be drawn. Ancient Indian literature speaks of "cloth of gold," meaning cloth woven with fine gold wire. To produce the prodigious amounts of fine-gauge wire required for weaving this type of cloth, it is reasonable to suppose that the drawplate must have been used. If so, drawn wire would also have been available for use in jewelry fabrication.

What makes the filigree jewelry technique attractive to both jewelers and their clients is that a minimal amount of precious metal is consumed to create an object of maximum size, important in India where precious-metal jewelry is sold by weight. Even though filigree work is highly labor intensive, a skilled artisan in India earns a low salary by world standards. Thus, the cost of filigree products stays relatively low.

Filigree work was a specialty of Dhaka (Dacca), now in Bangladesh; Cuttack in Orissa; and Karimnagar in Andhra Pradesh. The industry seems to have reached a peak of excellence by the mid-nineteenth century. Representative examples were shown and admired at the London Great Exhibition of 1851, as well as the series of international exhibitions that intermittently followed in European and American cities. Some of the best pieces shown at some of these exhibitions fortunately survive in the collection of the Victoria and Albert Museum in London.

The filigree industry now centered at Karimnagar and the nearby villages of Elgandal and Manakondur in Andhra Pradesh has been traced back more than two hundred years. The technique seems to have come there from Persia, where it was known as *melilehkari* (P: *melileh*, fine gold and silver wire), and was practiced especially at Isfahan. No written records exist, but it is said that the Karimnagar founders belonged to the Telegu Hindu traditional Kamsali gold- and silversmith community, some of whom saw this filigree work when traveling in Persia.

Filigree work from Karimnagar was first patronized by the ruling Nizam of Hyderabad, his family, the wealthy, and local landholders (P: *jagirdars*). Craftsmen produced fanciful, high-quality luxury objects and toys for ceremonial and social occasions among the upper classes. To a lesser extent, they also made products intended for a broader public. Those times have passed, and the craftsmen now doing this work have diversified to include a range of less expensive, and perhaps not as technically challenging, objects, including a variety of jewelry intended for both Indian and foreign use.

In an effort to perpetuate this industry, around 1885 the Nizam offered filigree craftsmen and their families free land for housing. According to the 1961 Indian Census, about thirty-five families, or about one hundred and twenty artisans, now live and work in Karimnagar and neighboring Jagtiyal. They have formed a cooperative and a marketing agency in Hyderabad City.

Cuttack (from S: *katak,* a royal residence) in Orissa was founded in the tenth century A.D. by Nripati, also known as Makar Kesari, as the capital of his kingdom of Kalinga. The Kesari (lion) dynasty ruled from the second to the twelfth century A.D., followed by the Ganga dynasty, which ruled until 1803, when the Cuttack Fort was taken by the British under Marquis Wellesley.

Cuttack filigree craftsmen were first patronized by local rajas, who often gave filigree objects to visiting dignitaries. Cuttack today is the largest center of Indian production of filigree jewelry, its main product now. Many shops in the Nayasarak Bazaar sell a wide range of filigree articles.

The largest of the many factory units in the city is the Kalinga Cooperative Silver Filigree Works Ltd., located in an Industrial Estate at Madhupatna. About one hundred and fifty other establishments are clustered in the city areas of Alisa Bazaar, Bania Sahi, Dagharbara, and Muhammaedia Bazaar. The work process described here is based mainly upon procedures carried out at the abovementioned cooperative but in general is typical of all filigree manufacture here.

Filigree work, like many other jewelry-making processes in India, has always been a technology of specialization. Involved in its production are wire drawers, wire twisters, filigree object fabricators, solderers, and polishers. As with many mass-production systems, every object produced incorporates the input of each of these individuals.

At the cooperative factory, wire drawing is divided between men who draw heavy gauge wire (*kandlakash*) and those who make fine-gauge wire (*tarkash*). Production is carried out by about fifty working units of ten persons each, or a total of about five hundred craftsmen. Each team is headed by a skilled artisan (*karigar*), who works as a team member but also directs the work of others and assigns work to group members according to their experience and ability. Almost all filigree craftsmen are Hindus, mainly of the Brahman, Bania, and Karan castes.

More than three-quarters of the filigree industry is controlled by private brokers (*dallal*), or persons who do assaying, banking, and money-lending. They act as middlemen who make contractual agreements with private filigree workers, whom they employ in workshops established by them. They usually give their workers advance money, which is deducted from their future earnings, and supply them with wire on credit against a return of finished filigree work. The artisan receives an agreed-upon fee for his work based on the weight of the finished objects he delivers. Readymade wire when used is purchased by the entrepreneur from wire manufacturers in Bombay, Surat, Varanasi, or Calcutta. These middlemen are also wholesalers of filigree products, distributing finished jewelry and objects widely in India, as well as exporting them abroad. They supply the craftsmen with the designs they wish them to execute and are alert to changing fashions and consumer response. Many filigree artisans can make the basic objects from memory, consulting drawn designs only for size and pattern.

Wire: The Raw Material

(Terms used here are Hindi, Oriya, and Telugu.)

The silver wire (*chandi tar*), the main material used in Indian filigree work, and discussed here, manufacturers claim, is better than 92.5 percent pure (the international standard of sterling silver), the rest consisting of copper to strengthen the alloy. Gold filigree is only made to order. In Cuttack each year about 5,000 kilograms (11,000 pounds) of silver are consumed annually by this industry.

702. Cuttack, Orissa
Workshop in the Kalinga Filigree Factory, Cuttack, the largest filigree workshop of the many in this city. Workers (karmakars; tarkashikars) sit on mats spread on the floor, six within each low-partitioned cubicle. The only mechanically aided work is wire drawing, done here on electrically powered wire-rolling mills, seen at the back.

703. Varanasi, Uttar Pradesh
The heavier gauge wire is made by the kandlakash, *who draws it from an ingot and passes it to the fine-gauge wire drawer (tarkash), who here uses an ancient method of drawing (khinchna) silver wire (chandi tar) to lengthen it (tar barhana) and simultaneously reduce the gauge. Mounted on the workbench is a small spool (charkhi) to hold the wire, which passes from there through a vertically placed drawplate (jantri) held against two upright iron bar supports, and is wound around a hand-turned large spool (charkha), whose larger size increases the pulling power.*

To make wire, the silver ingot is divided, melted, and cast into a smaller, round ingot bar (*chandi-kadi*). Its end is tapered by forging to prepare it for drawing into heavy-gauge wire. The steel drawplate (O: *janta*; H: *jantri*; Tel: *kambechchu*), mounted on a large drawbench (H: *tarkash ki jantra*), has a series of holes in diminishing diameter sizes. The bar is reduced in diameter gradually by drawing it with tongs (*chimta*) through each smaller hole. The process can be done by hand or mechanically. Fine-gauge wire is produced manually by the ancient traditional method of using a table-sized draw-bench mounted with two reels. From the larger one (*charkha*), wire is passed through a fixed draw-plate to the second, smaller reel (*charkhi*). The process is repeated, each time drawing the wire through a progressively smaller hole in the draw-plate until wire of the desired gauge is achieved.

Anatomy of a Filigree Object

Three types of wire are needed in filigree work: each has a specific function. First is the outer frame wire (O: *bita tara*), which is the heaviest (14 gauge) and is square in section. The frame wire outlines the basic design and supports everything within it. The second wire is a lighter (18–20 gauge) square wire that divides the space within the outer frame into smaller units. It defines the main lines of the design subject, such as a flower, leaf, or creeper pattern. The third wire is made of two strands of 36-gauge round wire spiraled together, then either flattened by hammering on an anvil or by passing it through the rollers of a rolling mill. From the result are made all of the many types of units used to fill the remaining space within the frames.

The outer frame (O: *farma,* form) of a filigree object is made with a tweezers and the joints soldered. Similarly, inside frame divisions (O: *sika*) are fitted into the outer frame and soldered to it at points of contact. The solder (H: *tanka*; O: *patia*) is an alloy of 16 tolas of pure silver and one anna of zinc (H: *jasta*; O: *khapara*), equivalent to Western hard solder. The flux used in soldering to assist in metal flow under heat is borax (H: *sohaga*).

Filler Units: The Vocabulary of Filigree

Filler units are formed with a tweezers (H: *chim-ti*) from lengths cut with a nipper (H: *katna ka chimti*). Standard shapes are prepared in advance and stored in glass jars ready for use. Filling the frame with them is called *jali kam* (net work), or *jhanjhridar kam* (making a lattice work). That all filler wire shapes have flat sides is of great importance in filigree work. Within the outer frame, flat sides abut and support each other even before they are soldered together, which allows the finished but still unsoldered work to be handled without falling apart. The small units that fill the interior frame space are based mainly on the spiral. What follows is a listing of basic forms:

704. *Filigree Units*

Top to bottom: Chakri; pherpharua; dui chakri; dui; sat; malda; murudi; binnadini; paduka; belpatti; phula patar patti; metro; kanwal phanka; dhankei

Among single-unit forms are the *chakri* (wheel), a tight, round spiral form, and *dui,* a unit in the shape of the number 2 in Oriya script. Any design made with *dui* units is called *dui kam; dui chakri* consists of two round spirals made with one piece of wire. *Malda* is a double, joined spiral; *pherpharua* (H: *pher,* turn or coil; *pherphar,* alternations or repeated changes) is an ellipsoidal spiral form; and *sat* is a form in the shape of the number 7 in Oriya script. The latter is also called *dhakei,* after Dhaka, where it was in use.

Compound filigree units include: *binna-dini* (from *binna,* to twine), fine wire work done with twisted wire, used for flowers; *murudi,* which uses only *dui* units or *dui* and *dhanki* to make a curling leaf form; and *paduka,* a bud.

Border patterns include: *belpatti,* a leaf and scroll strip; *dhankei* (from H: *dhankar,* a hedge) consisting of small semicircles on top of *dui* work, next to the frame edge; *kanwal phanka,* "water-lily leaves"; *metro,* a crenelated pattern; and *phulka patar patti,* a flower-leaf strip.

Granules, or *chandra* (moon), are spherical shot balls flattened with a hammer on an anvil to make a disc; *duba* is a length of wire whose ends are heated and automatically form a ball there. These are used, folded in half, combined in bunches, and placed at the center of a flower, where they stand upright in imitation of flower pistils. *Gajara* is the practice of using small shot balls at the juncture of crossing wires in a wire network. *Ravaa* (granule, seed) balls are made in various sizes by heating coarse silver fillings, traditionally placed on top of wire units and compounds and at joints to conceal them.

Before filler units are inserted into the object, they are heated to anneal or render them soft, then cleaned by soaking in an acid solution and rinsed in water. Into the outer frames, using a tweezers, the filler units are picked up and placed, packed in tightly until all the units hold together simply by the pressure of one against the other.

All the filigree parts must be joined by solder, and two grades are used. The first melts at a higher temperature and is used at joins in frames when made. The second melts at a lower temperature and is used to join the filler units to the frames after placement. A paste is prepared from borax and ground red crab-eye seeds (H: *lal ratti*; O: *kaith*), the same seed used by Indian goldsmiths for weighing precious metals. Here, its purpose is to act as a gum that holds the filigree parts together. The object is lifted with a tweezers and dipped into this solution. Over it is dusted a mixture of fine solder filings and borax. The object is then lifted with tweezers and placed either on a sheet of mica (H: *abrak*), when soldered over a charcoal fire, or on an asbestos sheet, when soldering is done with the flame of a blowpipe.

In the first case, after object and support are placed upon the charcoal bed, the heat level is brought up with a hand bellows (H:

dhaunkni). When a blowpipe is used, its end is pointed through a flame of an oil or kerosene lamp, and the oxygenized, thus heat heightened, extended flame is directed toward the object being soldered. The solder melts and runs into all points of contact and joints, whereupon the flame is immediately withdrawn. The object is lifted with tweezers and quenched in cold water, then cleaned in a dilute sulphuric acid solution. From this it emerges with the typical dead-white color commonly found in finished filigree objects.

Final cleaning is done using a brass wire handbrush (H: *pithal tar ki kanchi*) and a soapnut (H: *ritha*) and water solution. Because of filigree work's delicate nature, no machine polishing is done. The visible upper edges of the heavier wires are hand burnished to brightness with a highly polished agate or steel-tipped burnisher (A: *saiqal*; O: *maskala*), the polished wires making a contrast with the others that are left matte white.

Filigree Objects

All the standard forms of jewelry are produced in filigree: bangles, brooches, bracelets, earrings, ear tops, hair pins, coat pins, necklaces, pendants, chains, rings, tie pins, and buttons. Characteristic designs in Cuttack filigree are the *juhi* flower and the rose (O: *chalu*), a many-petaled rose with upstanding ball-ended pistils. One of the latter takes about three hours to make.

Nonjewelry filigree objects include: betel-leaf box (*pandan*), container for lamp black or collyrium for eye-lining (*kajalauti*), vermilion pigment box (*sindurdani*), anise-seed box (*saunfdani*), spice box (*masaladan*), cardamum-seed box (*elaichidan*), tray (*thali*), scent container (*attardan*), rosewater sprinkler (*gulabdan*), miniature replicas of Hindu temples (*mandir*), and deity chariots (*ratha*). Also, in the attempt to broaden their market, a goal since early contact with foreigners, filigree manufacturers made and continue to make many objects especially for foreign use.

707

705. *Dried, fleshy berries of the north Indian soapnut tree (H: ritha; Sapindus mukorossi; in southern India called Tam: ponan-kottai; Sapindus trifoliatus) is used universally by goldsmiths to make a natural detergent for cleaning and polishing metal objects. The skin and pulp of the dried fruit (from which the seed has been removed) are soaked in warm water for half an hour, then bruised to create a frothy lather containing the principle saponine. The object is immersed in this and worked over with a brass wire brush (H: pital tar kanchi), then rinsed.*

706. Khambat (Cambay), Gujarat
Agate burnishers (A: saiqal)
Average length 2 to 2½ in. (5–6.3 cm)
Collection the author, Porvoo

Used by goldsmiths to create the final polish on jewelry and objects of precious metals. Their surface is rubbed with this hardstone, often using spittle (thuk), or a soapnut (ritha) solution as a lubricant. Most traditional Indian jewelry is still polished this way, although mechanically operated buffers are coming into more general use in finishing modern, nontraditional jewelry.

707. Kozhikode (Calicut); Kerala
Gold necklace (valaippinnal) mainly in filigree (sarigaiyizhaippu) work with stamped units, made for the Great Exhibition, London, 1851
Inner circumference 22¹⁵/₁₆ in. (58.2 cm); outer circumference 30⁷/₈ in. (78.5 cm); clasp height 2¹¹/₁₆ in. (6.8 cm); weight 224 g
Victoria and Albert Museum, London (IS 124 1852)

Thewa Work

The *Thewa* Technique: Background

Partabgarh (in past literature also called Pertabgarh and Pratapgarh; from *partab,* bow-shot, the range of an arrow's flight; and *garh,* city), in Rajasthan, was formerly a small Rajputana principality with its own ruler. It was established by the Maharawat (a title originally granted by the Mughal emperor Shah Jahan) Partab Singh and named after him at the beginning of the eighteenth century. In 1818, Partabgarh passed under British control.

According to the craftsmen in Partabgarh, who call themselves Raj Sonis, this unique technique, practiced only by the men of a related family, originated approximately seven generations ago with Nathuni Sonewalla, a goldsmith relative of the present extended family of craftsmen who still practice *thewa* work. He is said to have created this style of work in 1767, during the reign of the Maharawat Samant Singh of Partabgarh, who employed him. The source of his inspiration, however, is unknown as the process resembles no other practiced in India. As with all established traditional skills, its technology passed from father to sons, who start learning it at age five. The craft flourished, especially during Victorian times when an important Western market had developed. Many of these objects set in gold were sold to British women living in or visiting the country and were taken to Europe as souvenirs. Some now find their way to the British antique market, and the work is recognized by European jewelry historians for its distinction.

The local name for this technique is *thewa,* which in Rajasthani-Hindi means "setting." Curiously, *thewa* work was practiced only at this location in India and made no permanent foothold elsewhere. T. N. Mukharji of the Calcutta Indian Museum in the late nineteenth century and Sir George Watt, director of the comprehensive exhibition and catalogue, *Indian Art at Delhi,* 1903, recorded that it was also done at Ratlam and Indore in Madhya Pradesh, cities just across the present state border from Partabgarh in Rajasthan, but it is unknown in those places today. It seems likely that it was practiced there by members of Partabgarh families who had migrated there, possibly due to marriage alliances. Its concentration in Partabgarh, as so often happens in the case of specialist crafts in India, is due to the fact that the craftsmen successfully secreted their techniques and (aside from the above-mentioned) continued to reside in this one place. To preserve its secrecy, daughters and sons-in-law are not allowed to come to their workplaces.

During the end of the nineteenth and the early part of the twentieth centuries, much Indian craft work was officially investigated by British Indian government employees. Partab-garh *thewa* craftsmen, however, never revealed *all* the details of *thewa* work to researchers, and this accounts for the inaccuracy of their descriptions. Many of those errors have, unfortunately, been repeated ever since. This we hope to correct here.

In a late nineteenth-century text, *Art Manufactures of India,* 1888, T. N. Mukharji says, "*Opinions differ* (author's italics) about the mode of manufacture, which is a family secret." He then quotes Sir George Birdwood, who in his pioneering work, *The Industrial Arts of India,* 1880, gives the following fancifully inaccurate account of this process (author's italics below). It is

> *apparently* done by melting a thick layer of green *enamel* on a plate of burnished gold, and, while it is still hot, covering it with thin gold cut into mythological, or hunting and other pleasure scenes.... After the enamel has hardened, the gold work is *etched* over with a *graver* so as to bring out the characteristic details of the ornamentation. In some cases it would seem as if the *surface of the enamel* was first *engraved,* and then the gold *rubbed into* the pattern so produced, in the form of an *amalgam* and fixed by fire.

Sir George slipped badly here, and although this account reveals a surprising unfamiliarity with basic technology, it nevertheless has been repeated subsequently, without verification, by many writers.

In the *Handbook of Indian Arms,* 1880, Wilbraham Egerton stated, also incorrectly, "In the *enamels* produced at Partabgarh in Bengal [*sic*], delicately *etched* gold figures are *inserted* on a background of transparent green or blue *enamel,* while it is still in a fused state." Sir George Watt, in *Indian Art at Delhi,* 1903, guardedly described this work as "a form of *enamellings*. The article is made of a piece of green or red coloured glass, or thick layer of *enamel,* the crude material for which is imported from Kashmir."

These descriptions gave rise to the terms encountered in Victorian and Edwardian literature to designate this work, such as "quasi-enamel," "imitation enamel," and even "quasi-gold enamel," an absolutely meaningless term used by Watt. Misleading misnomers such as these must have delighted the secretive *thewa* workers —if they ever saw them. They are perpetuated even by contemporary writers, who diligently research these sources when discussing what they claim to be European-set Victorian jewelry containing *thewa*-work plaques, the settings for which in fact were made in India.

It must first of all be emphasized, therefore, that as a technical process, *thewa* work has no connection whatever with enameling. The result may *appear* to utilize enamel; however, enamel, which *is* a glasslike substance, is applied in a granular or powdered form to a metal ground to which it is permanently fused by heat. The reverse takes place in *thewa* work, in which a thin gold-foil sheet is heat-fused to the visible surface of an already existing sheet of glass.

Another difference lies in the way light is reflected through enamel and *thewa* glass. Indian transparent enamel is done over a substrate of precious metal engraved with a linear pattern that helps to hold the enamel and reflects light through the enamel layer above it. In the case of transparent *thewa* glass, light is reflected from a *separate* sheet of metal foil placed below the physically separate *thewa* glass unit. The latter method is also used when setting gemstones in closed-setting traditional Indian jewelry, and *this* is the source of the practice in *thewa* work. Here probably also lies the reason for the choice of the word *thewa* to designate this work. This name, however, emphasizes the comparable traditional method of stone setting and has no reference to the *technique* used to make a *thewa* plaque, as one might expect. Perhaps even the designation was deliberately ambiguous.

At the time of the writer's interview with these craftsmen, in 1965, five families were producing *thewa* work in Partabgarh. The outstanding craftsmen were Ram Vilas Muthuralal, Beni Ram Muthuralal, Shankar Lal Muthuralal, and Ram Prasad Ramaljee (the latter the person interviewed most extensively), all living in or near Jhanda Gali (Flag Alley) in Partabgarh. The craftsmen were willing to answer questions—up to a point. Thereafter, they politely refused to reveal the "secrets" they have successfully guarded for more than two hundred years. The process described ahead is based in part on the information they did divulge, plus a careful examination of many *thewa* works with a 10X loupe, and logical deductions based on what is technically feasible. Today's work is still skillfully executed, but, due to a decrease in patronage, the manufacture of large objects such as those made in the past containing many *thewa* units has become rare. They can, however, still be commissioned.

708. Partabgarh, Rajasthan. *19th century*
Gold thewa-work parure
Courtesy Sotheby's, New York

Matching thewa-work plaques are mounted in a rare, surviving parure, which includes a necklace (thewa ka mala), pair of bracelets, earrings, and a brooch. All depict hunting scenes (shikar).

709. Partabgarh, Rajasthan
Thewa work in progress. The four gold sheets (thewa-ki-patti), each intended for a thewa unit, are fixed to a lac-resin compound spread on a board. Following a design previously inscribed in line on the gold, using very fine cutting chisels (tankla), an openwork pattern is pierced through the sheets.

710. Partabgarh, Rajasthan ➤
August 17, 1902
Drawing of thewa workers by Percy Brown. Sketched from life for use in George Watt's catalogue Indian Art at Delhi, 1903. At right, a worker is chiseling out the openings in the gold sheet mounted on a lac-resin covered board. On the left, the thewa plaque has been placed on charcoal in a small crucible. The worker is fusing the gold pierced-work sheet to the glass base by blowing through the blowpipe to raise the temperature. Tongs are held ready to remove the crucible at the point when the heat fuses the metal to the glass. At the center, above, is an example of a thewa plaque showing Krishna and the Gopis. Small prepared thewa-glass units appear on the table at left. At center, below, are a belt with thewa units, and a thewa-ornamented box. Brown errs in designating these workers as "enamellers."

The *Thewa* Process

Thewa work can be described as the fusion-appliqué of a pierced-work–patterned sheet of gold foil onto transparent colored glass to create a unit that is then mounted with a separate foil backing into a bezel in jewelry or an object. Each unit consists of a flat piece of transparent red, green, or blue glass, the colors intentionally suggesting ruby, emerald, and sapphire. Units also have the same geometric contours —round, oval, drop-shaped, square, rectangular, or octagonal—used for regularly cut gemstones. They can be in any size, but in their greatest dimension, none is larger than about two and a half inches (63 mm). (All vernacular terms ahead are in Rajasthani.)

The patterned metal sheet (*sona ki chadar*) is pure, 24-karat gold. To create the pierced-work design, several blank foil sheets somewhat larger than the final result are fixed side by side, one after the other on a working surface, a board covered with a layer of lac. The lac is warmed and the metal pressed lightly into it. When cold, the lac hardens and holds the metal, its resilience supporting the pressure on the metal during work.

Traditional design subjects are carefully drawn in outline on the gold surface with a pointed steel scriber (*sui*). The designs commonly used can be divided into two main groups: mythological or religious, and secular. Popular subjects among the former are Srinathji, a form of Krishna installed at nearby Nathdwara and continually visited by pilgrims; and Radha-Krishna. Another is the Ram Panchayat—a group of five figures including Rama; Sita, his wife; his half-brothers, the twins Lakshmana and Shatrughna (or a guru

instead of the latter); and Hanuman the monkey god—the main characters in the epic *Ramayana*. Others are Mahadev, an epithet for Shiva; and Mataji, the mother goddess. Secular subjects include *shikargah,* a hunting scene depicting animals in jungle foliage filled with flowers, some with a stream of water; *jhonpra patti,* a scene with a hut and domestic animals; *bungala,* a scene with a house; and *phul patti,* a scene with flowers, foliage, and birds. Special subjects such as portraits (*taswir*) were also made on order.

Details within the subject outlines are created not with gravers but with small chasing punches (*chheni*), each face having different shapes and patterns, such as straight and curved lines, circle, dot, and textures. The punch held vertically over the desired place is lightly tapped with a small metal rod. Slight pressure is enough to impart an impression on the thin gold foil.

Leaving a surrounding frame intact, the entire internal background of the design is then removed by piercing, and through these openings the colored glass is seen in the result. Piercing is accomplished with tiny, sharp chisels (*tankla*) made by the craftsmen themselves in the common shapes that suit their needs. The miniature scale of the best work seems almost miraculous. The finished pierced-work sheet (*thewa ki patti*) is heated and carefully stripped from the lac surface, cleaned, and dried. Surplus metal outside the design frame is trimmed away and reclaimed, as are the small removed background pieces of gold.

Watt mentioned that the glass ground (*kanch ki patti*) came from Kashmir; the craftsmen interviewed said that until recent times it

came from Germany, but that now, due to import restrictions, Indian sheet glass manufactured in the glass center of Firozabad is used. Transparent and bubble-free, the glass is purchased in sheets three by four and a half inches by one-sixteenth inch (76 x 102 x 3 mm) thick and cut into a shape corresponding with that of the decorated foil.

Absolutely clean, the glass is placed on a sheet of mica, to which glass will not adhere when heated. On top of it the finished gold foil is placed, and together they are transferred to a small, open, clay crucible (*kuthali*) filled nearly to the top with sand and ashes. Using long, U-shaped tongs (*dast-pansa*), the open crucible is placed in the heat source—the center of a prepared open hearth containing glowing charcoal and ash—leaving the *thewa* unit visible and exposed to air.

To bring the temperature high enough to fuse the metal to the glass (well below the melting point of gold), the craftsman introduces a stream of oxygen by blowing air through a long brass tube blowpipe (*punkna*). He intently watches the condition and color of the glass to judge its state of fusibility. As soon as the heat turns the glass red hot, it has done its job of fusing the metal to the glass surface. Heat is withdrawn, and the work is allowed to cool slowly in order to leave the glass stress-free. If cooled too quickly, the glass might later shatter due to internal stress caused by an unequal rate of contraction between glass and metal. Because the gold is 24 karat, no discoloring surface oxide forms during heating, as would happen if it were a gold alloy containing copper.

The finished unit must be mounted or set (*jadana*) into a bezel that has been prepared by a goldsmith to receive it. Before this is done, a flat sheet of brightly polished silver or tinfoil (*varak*) cut to the contour of the unit and bezel is placed in the closed-back setting below the *thewa* unit to reflect light through the glass and intensify its color and brilliance. Pure silver or tinfoil is used under green, blue, and red glass. In old work sometimes yellow glass was used, and the foil was colored red to make the glass appear red.

In most of this work, the bezel and mounting metal are a silver alloy above 90 percent in purity, a type commonly referred to among Indian silversmiths as "pure" silver (*shudh chandi*). After seating the unit in its setting, the upstanding collar bezel edges are forced down over the unit with a burnisher to hold it in place and conceal and protect its edges. Since the setting is closed and backed, the foil inside is permanently sealed against direct exposure to air so that it resists oxidation and remains bright for a considerable length of time. To harmonize the gold-foil *thewa* unit and the silver setting (or sometimes, an entire object) when this metal is used, the silver is goldplated and burnished to brightness.

Goldsmiths of the last century who worked with *thewa* unit makers often prepared elaborate settings in gold wire in the *canetille* style, so called after a contemporary European type of embroidery. In this popular early to mid-Victorian style of wirework, tight coils of gold wire in the form of miniature flowers and foliage were built up in a dimensional filigree. Contrary to what some historians say, these gold-wire settings on such jewelry found in Europe are probably Indian and not European. Many Indian goldsmiths were well aware of contemporary European jewelry styles and technology. Europeans frequently brought jewelry for them to copy. It is unlikely that unmounted *thewa* units were brought to Europe for mounting or that they were remounted by taking them out of Indian settings. It is true, however, that in India *thewa* units were mounted as a *backing* in some Jaipur and Banaras enameled jewelry, but examples are few. In some cases, the front of the unit was set with stones and backed with *thewa* work.

Thewa Objects

Jewelry with *thewa* units in gilded-silver settings is still produced at Partabgarh. The jewelry shown here, however, is nineteenth-century Indian, made for European use, evident because their forms follow contemporary European jewelry fashion. Brooches, buttons, cuff links, hairpins, and earrings with *thewa* work generally were not used by Indian women who might, however, use belts, necklaces, and pendants, especially if the *thewa* units employed traditional Hindu subjects. Many of the non-jewelry *thewa*-decorated objects were made in traditional Indian forms such as trays (*thals*), betel-nut containers (*pandans*), and rosewater sprinklers (*gulabdans*), but again, other forms such as cigarette boxes, calling-card boxes, and flower vases were made specifically for Europeans. Many forms, including sword, fan, and umbrella handles, shields, flower vases (*gul dasta*), spoons, perfume bottles, jewel boxes, and cigarette cases were produced, and *thewa* units were incorporated in the trappings of elephants, camels, and horses.

Today, the most popular forms of jewelry include hair pins (*bal pin*), chokers (*gale ka har*), earrings (*top*), lockets (*dibiya*), cuff links (called *cuff ka buttons*), watch chains (*jebi ghari ki chain*), coat buttons (*coat ka buttons*), tunic buttons (*kamiz ka buttons*), bangles (*churi*), rings (*anguthi*), and belts (*peti* or *kamarband*). The use of English terms illustrates the extent to which Angloisms have penetrated the Indian craftsman's vocabulary. Indians also buy various boxes (*dibbi*), including the rectangular *pan* (spice) boxes (*choras dibbi*) and a box to hold the image of the Jain deity Chanda Prabhu (*sidh chakra*), which is always kept under a cover (*dhakkan*); and large round plates (*tashak*) used for *pan supari*, spices prepared in a betel leaf.

710

.ENAMELLERS. PERTABGARH·RAJPUTANA. PERCY·BROWN. 17·8·02

GEMSTONES

Nava-ratna: A Celestial Palladium

(Vernacular terms are Sanskrit, unless otherwise designated.)

Hindu cosmology conceives of the universe as containing seven planets and two personifications of the moon cycle, all designated as celestial deities. Early Hindu references to these deities appear in Vedic and post-Vedic texts, especially the *Puranas*, and in several others that deal with astrology and ancient Hindu beliefs concerning planetary influences on gemstones.

The importance of these deities to the field of Indian jewelry involves the particular gemstones associated with each of them. The idea of celestial deities and gemstones connected with them is believed to have come to India from Mesopotamia, where it existed in the third millennium B.C. Originally in India, all gemstones were used for preventive, antidotal, and therapeutic purposes. Combined in a single ornament, their traditional arrangement (and the jewel itself) is called the *nava-ratna* (nine gemstones). As a symbol that describes celestial relationships, the nine gemstones become a powerful Indian amulet by polarizing all space in relation to the sun, the giver of life, and humankind in relation to the universe. In so doing, the *nava-ratna* becomes a manifestation of the divine plan for every living creature and a symbol of the universe. Augmenting their combined power is the fact that the number nine is itself considered to be magical because, as the last of the single digits, it contains all numbers in one digit but is contained in none of them. The magic of numbers has long caught the imagination of Indians, as it has elsewhere. Coincidentally or not, nine is also the number of months of human gestation.

Understanding the *nava-ratna's* multiple levels of meaning requires a discussion of the basic concepts of Hindu astrology (also adopted by Jains, Buddhists, and some Muslims, though the science of astrology is not considered lawful in Islam); the connection between planets and celestial deities; the latter's special functions; the gemstones associated with particular deities; and the format and significance of their arrangement in this amulet. In effect, the *nava-ratna* amulet represents a summation of these concepts, which all have had profound and lasting impact on the Indian psyche. Through its symbolic arrangement of the uni-

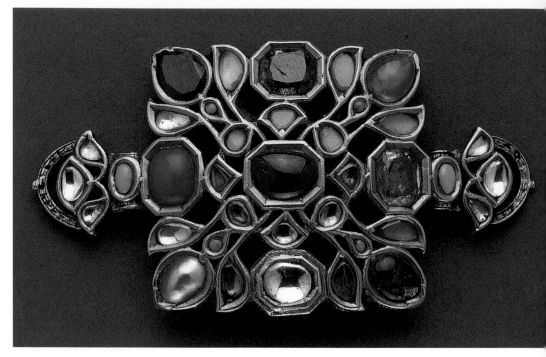

711. Jaipur, Rajasthan
Gold armlet (bazuband) with the classic Hindu planetal gemstone (nava-ratna) arrangement
2¾ x 1½ in. (7 x 3.9 cm); weight 40 g
Collection Mis, Brussels

The nava-ratna gemstone concept embodies a symbolic analogy between the microcosm (humankind) and the macrocosm (the universe).

verse and space, this charm in jewel form allows the wearer to manipulate celestial forces for personal benefit.

The Great and Lesser Gems: *Maharatnani* and *Uparatnani*

In Sanskrit, *ratna* refers to a precious stone or object and is used as a play on words in old Sanskrit dramas. *Mani,* another word meaning specifically "precious stone," is also used to describe an ornament employing precious gemstones, such as *mani-mala,* a precious stone necklace or garland.

In terms of earthly commerce, and therefore in the minds of most people, some *nava-ratna* gemstones were considered more precious than others because of their relative rarity.

Consequently, at an early time, the nine were divided into two groups: the great stones (*maharatnani*) and the lesser stones (*uparatnani*). The oldest reference to the *nava-ratnas* as classified into the great and lesser gems appears in the *Agastimata* (*shlokas* 327–28:131). These nine gemstones are the basis upon which all subsequent ancient writings (*shastras*) on the subject of gemstones were composed, although they also discuss other stones.

The *maharatnani* encompass the diamond (*vajra; hiraka; pavi; bhidura*); pearl (*mukta; muktaphala; jalabindu*); ruby (*manikya; padmaraga*); sapphire (*nila; indranila; mahanila*); and emerald (*marakata; tarksya*). The *uparatnani* are the topaz (*pusparaga*); cat's eye (*vaidurya*); coral (*pravala; vidruma*); and hyacinth (*gomeda*); or zircon (*rahuratna*).

The *maharatnani* are standardized, but the *uparatnani* may vary in later writings and in popular usage, which accounts for the differences found in their use in the *nava-ratna* group of ornaments. Some vary with the source, as does their attribution to a particular astral deity. Too many such differences exist to be mentioned. The attributions given here are the earliest and by their precedence should be considered to be correct.

Nava-graha: The Nine Celestial Hindu Deities

The nine celestial deities corresponding to the Hindu universe are called the *nava-graha,* or "nine seizers." This term is used because Earth's sun and moon, as well as five planets and two "nodes" (together loosely referred to as nine planets), and their corresponding deity, are believed to seize upon humans and influence their destiny. The *nava-grahas* are: the Sun (Surya); Moon (Candra); Mercury (Budha); Venus (Shukra); Saturn (Shani); Mars (Mangala); Jupiter (Brhaspati); Ascending Node, or Dragon's Head (Rahu); and the Descending Node, or Dragon's Tail (Ketu).

Though applicable to all the deities, the epithet *seizer* is particularly appropriate for Rahu, deity of the Ascending Node, who is said to seize the sun or moon during an eclipse, an event whose outcome excites fear in many Hindus; and to Ketu, the deity of the Descending Node, responsible for comets, whose appearance may also have baleful significance. The planets Uranus, Neptune, and Pluto, discovered after the Hindu cosmological system was established, do not belong to ancient Hindu astrology or astronomy.

All nine celestial entities are represented anthropomorphically as male deities, and most have several names that differ according to the particular ancient sources in which they are mentioned and described. The name given here is the most common one. Like all other Hindu deities, each *nava-graha* has a special color (*varna*); rides a vehicle (*vahana*); and during worship is offered special propitiatory ritual foods (*naivedya*). (See table, page 306.)

The names of seven of the *nava-graha* deities have been applied to the Hindu names for the days of the week. Over each weekday, the celestial deity of that day presides. (The Tamil day names given are equivalent to the Sanskrit day names (from *vara*, day) and are also the deity names).

Day	Sanskrit Name	Tamil Name
Sunday	*Ravi-vara*	*Nayiry-k-kilamai*
Monday	*Soma-vara*	*Tinkal*
Tuesday	*Mangala-vara*	*Cevvay*
Wednesday	*Budha-vara*	*Budhan*
Thursday	*Brhaspati-vara*	*Vyalam*
Friday	*Shukra-vara*	*Velli-k-kilamai*
Saturday	*Shani-vara*	*Cani-k-kilamai*

Ancient Hindu astrologers believed in a heliocentric concept of the universe, as described in writings such as the *Vishnu Purana,* believed to have been written in the eleventh century A.D. or earlier. The sun as the source of life and chief of the other heavenly bodies, over whom he rules, radiates his rays of light and energy to all the spheres. As undifferentiated light, sunlight contains all the colors of which white light is composed; light passing through a prism is broken into the seven principal colors of the spectrum. The consistent color arrangement of the spectrum and the rainbow is interpreted as prime evidence of the seven cosmic rays within the universe. According to the *Kurma Purana,* the seven planets associated with the seven prismatic colors are actually condensations of the seven cosmic rays. The same applies to the seven gemstones associated with them.

Upon absorbing sunlight, each planet radiates to Earth its particular colored light ray. The transmission of these light rays through space, accompanied by the energy powers of heat, electricity, and magnetism, are believed to affect the lives of every living creature.

On Earth, all physical forms contain matter centers, which are penetrated by these celestial rays. Upon absorption, rays are diffused within the body and also appear outwardly as a radiating emanation or aura (*prabha*), a subtle energy flow that imparts its influence on anyone within range. Its color in an individual depends on the dominant one he or she reflects, and its degree of brightness is greater in more than in lesser developed persons.

The nine *nava-grahas* can be worshiped at home or in a temple. In southern India their images are usually found in Shiva temples, where they are often installed in an enclosed veranda around or near the main, central shrine. The sun, placed at the center and facing eastward toward the sunrise, is flanked by the others, arranged in a specific order at the cardinal and intermediary points with which they are associated. Few temples in India are dedicated exclusively to Surya, the sun, and his attendant planets, but this apparent relegation to a lesser status as deities does not diminish their importance to the average person.

According to Hindu astrology, the moon, Jupiter, and Venus are believed to be beneficent and lucky bodies (*somyagraha*). Mercury by itself is lucky but can be unlucky, depending on its position in relation to the other planets. Others, including the sun, Mars, Saturn and the Ascending and Descending Nodes are maleficent, or unlucky (*kruragraha*, or *papagraha*). The influence of the maleficent bodies, in particular, must be counteracted by proper propitiatory action. Also, the conjunction of the planets in particular spatial relationships in the universe at various times of the year can be maleficent; when this happens, their evil influence must and can be averted. If neglected, the celestial deities are believed to become

angry and cause all sorts of personal and communal difficulties, epidemics, hysteria (*grahapasmara*), or even war.

To placate the *nava-grahas* and render them favorable, individual or professional rites variously called *grahabali* (ground offering), *grahashanti* (pacification), or *grahayajna* (sacrifice) are performed by Brahman priests (*purohitas*). In these propitiatory ceremonies, specific flowers, plants, grain, or burnt offerings acceptable to the deity are given, while suitable *mantras* are recited. The most common goals of these ceremonies are the prevention of illness or regaining of health; the attainment of longevity; success in personal or commercial achievements; and general prosperity. The propitiatory burnt offering to *all* the bodies is last, and these are placed on the ground, as described in the *Matsya Purana* (3:5–20), in the same positions as the equivalent placement of the *nava-ratna* gemstones.

All Hindu festivals that take place every year are timed to the movements of planets and stars. No matter how properly the ritual is otherwise carried out, the outcome can be successful only if a religious ritual takes place *at the right time.* Timing is especially important when performing rituals celebrating the significant rite of passage events in the life of every individual, such as conception, birth, puberty, initiation, marriage, and death. The same applies to lesser, even apparently trivial events, such as ascertaining the auspicious moment to put on new jewelry.

Every year, information concerning the positions of celestial bodies is made available in the form of the Hindu almanac (*panchangam*), published by Brahman *purohitas* with the input of astrologers and astronomers (*jyotisi*). By studying the almanac, one can calculate and fix auspicious days for important events. The almanac is also used in deriving the horoscope (*janapattra*) of every Hindu child. Recorded at birth, the horoscope includes the constellation or natal asterism (*janma-naksatra*) under which the infant is born, and which of the planets, whose positions at that moment are ascertained, will thereafter have a special influence on the course of his or her future. In light of all this, the importance of the correspondence between the deity and the gemstone representing him can readily be appreciated.

Relating *Nava-ratna* Gemstones to *Nava-graha* Deities

The manner in which each *nava-graha* deity became associated with a particular gemstone is described in a myth about the origin of gemstones, which appears in full form in Buddhabhatta's *Ratnapariksa.* According to this myth, the demon Bala (or Vala), who possessed great strength, decided to go to Heaven with

The *Nava-grahas* and Their Attributes

Nava-graha	Vehicle	Color of Deity	Right Hand	Left Hand	Metal	Element	Propitiatory Burnt Offering	Worship Grain	Sacred Plant
Sun (malefic) *Surya*	Chariot (*ratha*) with seven red mares (*radaba*)	Red	Open lotus (*padma*); sun disk (*chakra*)	Open lotus (*padma*); sun disk (*chakra*)	Copper	Fire	Rice cooked with sugar	Wheat	China Rose *Hybiscus rosa-Sinensis* (*java*)
Moon (beneficent) *Candra*	Chariot (*ratha*) with ten horses (*ashva*)	White	White water lily (*kumuda*); moon disk (*chandra mandala*)	White water lily (*kumuda*); moon disk (*chandra mandala*)	Silver	Water	White rice; ghee; and sugar	Paddy	Water lily *Nymphea Lotus* (*kamala*)
Mercury (beneficent) *Budha*	Snake (*sarpa*); lion (*simha*)	Yellow	Shield (*karacha*); club (*khatvanga*)	Sword (*khadga*); arrow (*bana*)	Gold	Earth	Milk and rice	Green gram	Rough chaff tree *Achyranthes aspera* (*apanarga*)
Venus (beneficent) *Shukra*	Mole (*akhu*)	White	Rosary (*aksamala*)	Treasure (*nidhi*); beggar's pot (*kamandalu*)	Silver	Water	Coarse sugar and rice	Beans	Cluster fig *Ficus glomerata* (*udambara*)
Saturn (malefic) *Shani*	Crow (*kaka*); tortoise (*kurma*)	Black	Rod or staff (*danda*)	Beggar's pot (*kamandalu*)	Iron	Air	Rice, sesamum, pulses; cooked in milk	Sesamum	Mesquite *Prosopis spicigira* (*shami*)
Mars (malefic) *Mangala*	Goat (*aja*)	Red	Mace (*danda*)	Beggar's pot (*kamandalu*); severed human head (*munda*)	Brass or copper	Fire	Grain	Lentil	Black catechu *Acacia catechu* (*khadira*)
Jupiter (beneficent) *Brhaspati*	Goose (*hamsa*); frog (*manduka*)	Yellow	Rosary (*aksamala*)	Beggar's pot (*kamandalu*); book (*shastra*)	Gold	Ether	Yellow rice and curds	Bengal gram	Sacred fig *Ficus religiosa* (*ashvattha; pipal*)
Ascending Node or Dragon's Head (malefic) *Rahu*	Chariot (*ratha*) with eight black horses (*kalashva*)	Smoky	Sun (*surya*)	Moon (*chandra*)	Lead	—	Mutton	—	Couch grass *Cynodon Dactylon* (*durva; dub*)
Descending Node or Dragon's Tail (malefic) *Ketu*	Chariot (*ratha*) with eight green horses (*haritashva*)	Blue	Sword (*khadga*); club (*khatvanga*)	Noose (*pasa*); snake (*naga*)	Bell metal	—	Colored rice	—	Sacred *kusha* grass *Poa suroides* (*kusha*)

712. Eastern India. *11th century*
Kubera, buff sandstone
24¼ x 13½ in. (62.2 x 34.2 cm); diameter 4¹⁵⁄₁₆ in. (12.6 cm)
Asian Art Museum of San Francisco (B63 S8)

Kubera, the Hindu god of wealth, is represented as a squat, stout figure holding a lime (jambhara, symbol of abundance and riches) in his right hand, and a mongoose (nakula) in his left. Whenever he squeezes the animal, it vomits a stream of gemstones. Kubera is the leader of the yakshas, guhyakas, and rakshasas who guard his nine divine treasures (nidhis) and the precious gemstones hidden in the earth. The lord of riches, Kubera dwells in the womb of jewels (ratna-garbha). His vehicle is a man (nara).

the intention of conquering Indra. The gods requested him instead to "become the beast in our sacrifice." Bala, thus propitiated, agreed to this meritorious act. In the sacrifice, the gods slaughtered and dismembered Bala, each grabbing a part of his body, which was immediately transmuted into various precious gemstones. From Bala's blood came ruby; from his teeth, pearl; his bile, emerald; his bones, diamond; his eyes, sapphire; his flesh, coral; his skin, topaz; marrow, chrysoberyl; body fluid, beryl; fingernails, cat's eye; fat, rock crystal; semen, *bhisma*, an unspecified stone.

The particular gemstone held by the deity became associated with him; thereafter, the stones were termed "the preferences of the planets." Because the gods were nine in number, this particular gemstone group associated with them became known as the nine gemstones (*nava-ratna*). As a group, they are said to be an amulet of great defensive and remedial advantage. They possess exceptional magic power by providing a sympathetic medium for the transmission of stored energy from the planets, which then cast their influence on the wearer. These concepts, reiterated in the tenth-century manusript *Agastimata* (*shlokas* 343–44), have become firmly implanted in Hindu thought.

The gemstones themselves are considered to be repositories of cosmic rays, which they discharge eternally. Like a battery, the stored energy of each gemstone is constantly renewed by emission from its corresponding planet. A gemstone's cosmic ray color, however, is not necessarily the same as its apparent physical color. This can be seen in the chart (713) on page 308.

Nava-ratna Arrangement: A Universal *Mandala*

The arrangement of the *nava-grahas* and the *nava-ratna* associated with them (shown here as described in the *Navaratnapariksa*) creates, in effect, a metaphor of the universe. As such, it takes on profound significance as its intention in principle is to awaken consciousness of the individual's identity, and the play of cosmic forces upon each person. Since each celestial deity controls a particular direction, the stone that represents him does the same. In this arrangement, the stone becomes a locus into which the deity can descend when occasion demands his presence and protection. If the wearer of a *nava-ratna* ornament is endowed with truthfulness, and good moral conduct, the *nava-grahas* will never harm him or her but in combination will offer protection against the approach of evil from all directions.

As regents of the sky and space, each celestial deity has been assigned the guardianship of a specific direction, which includes the center, the four cardinal points, and the four intermediary compass points. The concept of spatial points permits humans to better understand their place in the design of creation. Because Hindus worship the sun (Surya), the cardinal points are named in reference to the east, where the sun rises daily. When this worship takes place, the east is *aspara,* "the front"; the west, *apara,* "behind"; the north, *vama,* "the left hand"; and the south, *dakshina,* "the right hand."

The chart at right includes the names in English and Sanskrit of the celestial deities; the gemstone associated with each; its physical and cosmic color; and the cardinal and intermediary direction each deity controls.

Following this cosmic directional pattern, a square grid of nine gemstones, with three stones on each square side and one in the center, becomes the *nava-ratna* locus classicus. Fixed by cardinal points, the square is believed to be a final, unequivocal form, indicating the Absolute. The arrangement also mirrors a zodiacal palladium. The square is often the form of a Hindu temple, which is built on the pattern of the universe, its plan conceived of as a *mandala* (a circle enclosing or enclosed by a square). As in every *mandala,* all parts relate to the center (in this case, the Sun-ruby), from which power flows to all other parts (the other stones). Once consecrated and ritually purified, a properly arranged *nava-ratna,* gemstone-set ornament, like any *mandala,* by design provides its owner with potent protection against malevolent forces. Combining the influence of *all* the celestial bodies in one amulet, the *nava-ratna* gains the wearer maximum possible benefit.

The *nava-ratna* grouping of gemstones is used in rings, pendants, armbands, and other forms of jewelry worn on different parts of the body. In addition to the primary arrangement within a square, various other configurations become necessary due to the particular ornament form. The gemstones can be placed in a circle, the most common *mandala* form, which symbolizes infinity, as in an earring (*nava-ratnakundala*). Related to both square and circle is an arrangement of two overlapping squares, one with the cardinal and the other with the intermediary points, the stones forming either an octagon or circle. When the stones are used in a strip or a choker-type neckband (*graiveyaka*), by necessity they are placed in a long rectangle with the ruby at the center and the eight other stones placed four on each side, the arrangement corresponding to a common linear arrangement of the celestial deities in a temple. In a long, garland-type necklace (*nava-ratnamala*), the same series can be repeated on each side and support a *nava-ratna* set pendant (*lambaka*) at the center. The same linear arrangement can be used in a stiff bangle (*valaya*) and flexible bracelets (H: *pahunchaband*).

When an extended linear arrangement is used, the major stones may be alternated with other stones, such as diamonds, turquoises, or pearls. In other arrangements, these additional stones can be used as space fillers. No matter what the format or the ornament size, the

Jupiter	Descending Node	Mercury
Brhaspati	Ketu	Budha
Topaz (*pusparaga*)	Cat's eye (*vaidurya*)	Emerald (*marakata*)
Physical color: yellow	Physical color: gray	Physical color: green
Cosmic color: blue	Cosmic color: infrared	Cosmic color: green
Northwest (*vayava*)	North (*uttara*)	Northeast (*aisana*)
Saturn	Sun	Venus
Shani	Surya	Shukra
Sapphire (*nila*)	Ruby (*manikya*)	Diamond (*vajra*)
Physical color: blue	Physical color: red	Physical color: white
Cosmic color: violet	Cosmic color: red	Cosmic color: indigo
West (*pascima*)	Center (*madhyadesa*)	East (*purava*)
Ascending Node	Mars	Moon
Rahu	Mangala	Chandra
Hyacinth or Zircon (*gomeda*)	Coral (*pravala*)	Pearl (*mukta*)
Physical color: yellow-red; red-brown	Physical color: red-orange	Physical color: iridescent white
Cosmic color: ultra-violet	Cosmic color: yellow	Cosmic color: orange
Southwest (*nairrita*)	South (*dakshina*)	Southeast (*agneya*)

nava-ratna stones appear dominant. Tradition stipulates that each of them should be the same size to give equal importance to each deity (though sometimes the Sun-ruby is largest). Each should also be as nearly flawless as possible and of good color. Stones of better quality have greater efficacy than inferior ones, which might even be harmful to the wearer.

In some arrangements there may be more than nine major stones. An explanation in one instance is that sometimes the moon is metaphorically represented in triform with three stones: moonstone for the waxing moon, pearl for the full moon, and cat's eye for the waning moon. Other irregularities may simply be due to the jeweler's lack of knowledge on the subject.

The *Nava-ratna* Finger Ring: An Apotropaic Amulet

A finger ring (*anguliya*) set with the *nava-ratna* stones is a much-favored ornament. Usually the stones are in a square, but, as mentioned, they might also be set in a circular or an oval arrangement. In any arrangement, their correct relative order is maintained.

Before commissioning such a ring from a goldsmith, one first brings the selected stones to a priest, who blesses them. At an auspicious time, they are then given to the goldsmith, who will set them in high-quality gold (22 karat). According to orthodox practice, when the gold setting is ready, each of the stones corresponding to a planet is set in the correct order of priority and position, at a time auspicious for that planet. If this procedure is followed, the process might take a year or more to complete. The finished ring is given to the owner at a propitious time, determined by an astrologer-*purohita*. It is first worn at an auspicious time (*muhurta*), also ascertained by an astrologer or a Brahman priest, who performs an initiatory ceremony during which a *mantra* or sonorous form of a divinity (or divinities) appropriate for the occasion is chanted. When the ring is not in use, an orthodox person keeps it in a box containing aromatic herbs, placed near the household family shrine.

An alternative to a single *nava-ratna* ring mounted with all the nine stones is a set of nine rings, each fixed with one of the stones. The rings can be worn together or separately on the particular day of the week appropriate to the celestial deity of that day. This latter use heightens the individual stone's power as an amulet, especially important when it is used as therapy in the treatment of illness. Because their power is believed to lie in their emanation of cosmic rays, using the *wrong* stone for this function may *become* the cause of another, otherwise unexplainable illness.

◄ **713.** *The nine planetary deities (nava-graha) in their traditional arrangement, each in a specific direction and position*

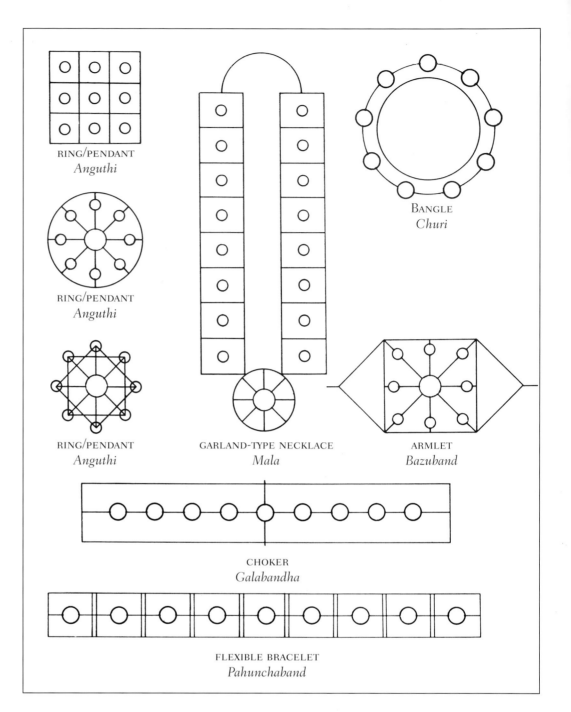

RING/PENDANT
Anguthi

RING/PENDANT
Anguthi

RING/PENDANT
Anguthi

GARLAND-TYPE NECKLACE
Mala

BANGLE
Churi

ARMLET
Bazuband

CHOKER
Galabandha

FLEXIBLE BRACELET
Pahunchaband

The *Nava-ratna* Rosary

In Dravidian southern India, especially in Tamil Nadu, *nava-ratna* gemstones are used in a rosary (S: *nava-ratnamala*), which can be expensive or not, depending on whether the beads are genuine gemstones or colored glass intended to simulate them.

The standard *nava-ratna* rosary consists of nine gemstone beads, repeated in twelve units, making a total of 108 beads. The twelve repeats are an allusion to the twelve months of the year. Gemstone *nava-ratnamalas* must be made to order, but those of glass beads can be found in the bazaars near large temples such as the Minakshi Temple in Madurai. They are worn both by priests and the laity.

714. *Schematic arrangements of various forms of traditional jewelry using the nava-ratna gemstones. Vernacular terms in the diagram above are Hindi; those in the following list are Sanskrit unless otherwise indicated.*

Ring/Pendant
  Anguliya/Lambaka
Ring/Pendant
  Anguliya/Lambaka
Ring/Pendant
  Anguliya/Lambaka
Bangle
  Valaya

Garland-type Necklace
  Ratna mala
Armlet
  Bajubanda
Choker
  Graiveyaka
Flexible Bracelet
  H: Pahunchaband

715. Varanasi, Uttar Pradesh
Pair of gold nava-ratna armlets (nauratan bazuband)
Length 2¾ in. (7 cm); height and width 1⁹⁄₁₆ in. (4 cm)
Private Collection

Sometimes called *nauratan gir*, nine-planet gem-stone seizers, the *nava-ratna* gemstones appear here in a circular format, a variation of the classic square arrangement. Stones are set *kundan* style on a green enameled ground (*sabz zamin*) and interspersed with small turquoises.

716. Jaipur, Rajasthan
Pair of gold armbands (nauratan bazuband or bohalta) set with the nine nava-ratna gemstones in a linear arrangement. Enameled front and back
7¹⁄₁₆ x ¾ in. (18 x 2 cm)
Courtesy Sotheby's, New York

715

716

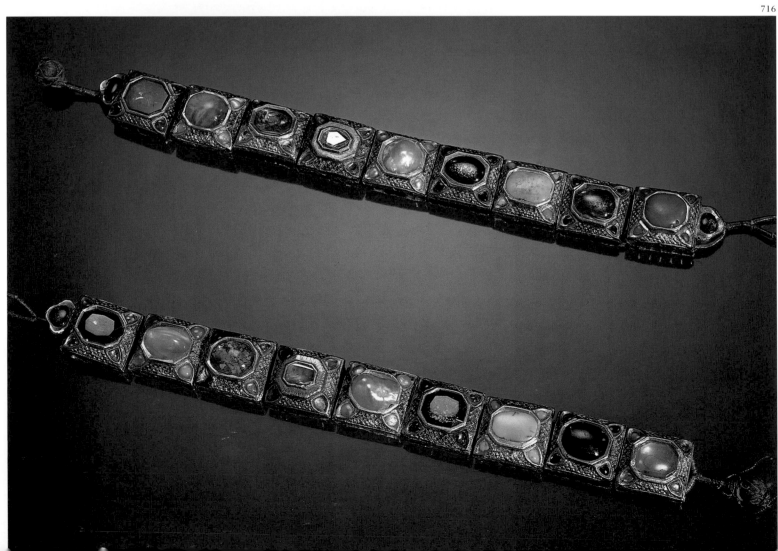

717

717 detail

718

717. Jaipur, Rajasthan. *Early 19th century*
*Gold necklace (patadi har or patri har) with pendant (jugni), the latter kundan set
with the nine nava-ratna gemstones and a pendant spinel.*
Length each side 10.5 in. (26.5 cm); pendant 3⅛ x 2 in. (8 x 5 cm)
Total weight 250 g
Collection Mis, Brussels. Courtesy Bernadette van Gelder, the Netherlands

*The necklace consists of two sets of nine parallel, hollow box units strung in five
strands, each unit separated by five pearls. All are polychrome enameled with corresponding mirror images depicting the nine nava-graha figures with their mounts.
A kundan-set diamond is at each corner. The unit reverses are polychrome enameled
with birds and floral themes on a white ground, safed chalwan style. The pendant
reverse (above right) bears a polychrome-enameled image of a seated Shiva, from
whose matted locks springs the Ganges River, flanked left by his shrine and right by
his emblems: a trident (trishula), and a pot (kamandulu), the latter used by mendicants to denote their ascetic life.*

718. Madurai, Tamil Nadu
*Two nine-gemstone bead rosaries (nava-graha jebamalai) in which each of the nine
Hindu planets is represented by its associated gemstone*
Left: Length 27½ in. (70 cm)
Collection the author, Porvoo
Right: Length 25³⁄₁₆ in. (64 cm)
Collection Maria-Liisa Saarenvirta, Porvoo

The Five *Maharatnani* Gemstones

719. Vadodara (Baroda), Gujarat. *c.* 1902
H. H. Maharaja Sayaji-Rav, Gaekwar, Sena Khaskhel, Shamsher Bahadur Farjand-i-Khas i-Daulat-i-Inglishia of Baroda
Collection India Office Library and Records, London

The Gaekwar is wearing his famous seven-row diamond necklace. He also wears a sarpech, turra, and a brooch (poshak zewar, garment ornament), all set with diamonds. In the late nineteenth and early twentieth centuries, virtually every Indian potentate commissioned state photographs of themselves wearing their most important regalia jewelry as a symbol of their power and position. These ornaments constitute an incomparable accumulation of precious gemstone jewelry existing in the world. More than 130 Indian princes, not to mention numerous wealthy landowners (zamindars) and officials, all possessed impressive collections of ancestral jewelry. Many of these personage portraits were done by Lala Deen Dayal (1844–1910), as is this one.

Diamonds

The word *diamond* immediately conjures up an image of cool, fiery glitter—and awesome wealth. In India, diamonds have always been a decisive symbol of power and impressive economic achievement. Historically, diamonds have been given to retain or regain a lover's or ruler's lost favor, as symbols of tribute, or as an expression of fidelity in exchange for concessions and protection. Mughal emperors used the diamond as a means of assuring their immortality by having their names and worldly titles inscribed upon them. Inscriptions on large gemstones originally from India, now in the Iranian National Treasure, include the name of the Emperor Akbar (eleven times); Jahangir (nineteen times); Shah Jahan (seven times); and Alamgir (Aurangzeb) (five times).

Indian history is replete with less happy connections with diamond possession. Many are the instances in which a diamond has played and continues to play a pivotal role in Indian social, political, economic, and religious events, as it often has done elsewhere. The drive to possess diamonds has resulted in more intrigue, scandal, treachery, violence, and prolonged or sudden death by ingenious means than any imaginative fiction writer could ever invent.

In Indian history, diamonds have been used to acquire military equipment, finance wars, foment revolutions, and tempt defections. They have contributed to the abdication or the decapitation of potentates. They have been used to murder a representative of the dominating power by lacing his food with crushed diamond.

Indian diamonds have been used as security to finance large loans needed to buttress politically or economically tottering regimes. Forced to flee to safer soils, diamond owners have appreciated the ease with which diamonds can be hidden and transported as a concentrated form of wealth. Victorious military heroes have been honored by rewards of diamonds. Diamonds have been used as ransom payment for release from imprisonment or abduction. Monarchs, the nobility, and the wealthy less willing to part with their diamonds endured torture, including maiming, eye branding or gouging, or slow death in an attempt to force them to reveal their diamond hiding place, at times swallowed or secreted elsewhere in the body.

At the conclusion of a war, royal treasuries have been looted for the diamonds they contained. Temples have been plundered and demolished because of their reputations as depositories of diamonds bequeathed to them by the pious. Entire cities and territories have been laid waste so that leaders might secure the impressive treasure gathered by forebears.

Through all these bizarre, sometimes horrifying events, the diamonds themselves remain coolly aloof. They are, in fact, blameless for their bewitching attraction. Guilt for the crimes of greed and zealotry in their pursuit rests solely with those who succumbed to their innocent seduction.

For more than two thousand years, India was the first and only source of diamonds known to the world. Until 1729, when diamonds were discovered in Brazil, the world's entire diamond supply came from India. This means that any diamond found in European or other jewelry created before that date is of Indian origin. The export of diamonds from India is believed to have begun as early as the fourth century B.C.

Diamonds figured importantly in the spiritual world of India, probably because its property as the world's hardest natural substance was recognized at an early date. Indra's magical weapon, the *vajra* (a metaphor for diamond that also means "hard") is described as being extremely hard and capable of generating lightning flashes, as is the polished diamond. In Sanskrit, diamond is *hira* or *hiraka*, which also means "a thunderbolt."

The idea of diamond hardness traveled to the Mediterranean area, where it was believed that diamond had an unconquerable power. From the Latin *adamantis*, or diamond (probably derived from the Persian *almas*), these concepts also entered the English language in the words *adamant*, referring to an imaginary stone of impenetrable hardness and formerly a name given to diamond, and *adamantine*, meaning made of or having the quality of adamant in hardness and luster, incapable of being broken, penetrated, or dissolved.

Diamonds were the subject of intense scrutiny in various ancient Indian writings. The *Arthasastra* of Kautilya (third century B.C.) is the main ancient source of information about diamonds and its trade. The best diamonds are described as being big, heavy, regular, light refractive and brilliant, and capable of scratching a (metal) vessel surface. The diamond is also discussed in the *Ratnapariksa* (c. fourth century A.D.), which reveals an early and extensive knowledge of diamonds and other gemstones and mentions the locations of its sources, the technical manuals *Ratnasastra* and *Brihalsamhita* (both c. sixth century A.D.).

720. *The Dresden Green diamond (large stone at bottom), a pendeloque of 40.7 metric carats, is the world's largest naturally green Golconda diamond. It is displayed, mounted in an epaulet, in the Green Vault in Dresden Castle.*
Courtesy De Beers Consolidated Mines Ltd., London

Golconda Diamonds: Fact and Fantasy

Among the earliest Western accounts of diamonds is that of Marco Polo, who in 1292 traveled through India on his return journey from China to Venice and recorded his findings. One of the places where he stopped was named Mutfili (identified as Telingana, later Golconda), "where diamonds are got." Although he had not seen the diamond mines himself, Polo gave a realistic account of alluvial diamonds and then repeated a fanciful narrative current throughout the civilized world concerning their origin.

First fact: "There are certain lofty mountains in these parts; and when the [heavy] winter rains fall … the waters come roaring down the mountains in great torrents. When the rains are over … they search the beds of the torrents and find plenty of [alluvial] diamonds."

Then fantasy: "In those mountains great serpents are rife … the most venomous in existence, … [and] anyone going to that region runs fearful peril…. Now among these mountains there are certain great and deep valleys … to which there is no access…. Men who go [there] in search of the diamonds take with them pieces of flesh … and cast them into the bottom of a valley. Now there are numbers of white eagles that haunt these mountains and feed upon the serpents. When the eagles see the meat thrown down they pounce upon it and carry it up to some rocky hill-top where they begin to rend it. But there are men on the watch, and as soon as they see that the eagles have settled they raise a loud shouting to drive them away … and the men recover the pieces of meat, and find them full of diamonds which have stuck to the meat … [diamonds *do* adhere to fatty substances]. For the abundance of diamonds down there in the depths of the valleys is astonishing, but nobody can get down; and if one could, it would be only to be incontinently devoured by the serpents which are so rife there." He also says that diamonds are found in the eagle's droppings and in their stomachs.

Marco Polo's fantastic account of the origin of diamonds is actually based on ancient Hindu mythology, which it closely follows. According to Hindu myth, the Nagas, or serpents, are the guardians of earthly treasures, including gemstones, which they hoard in their netherworld realm—equivalent to Polo's profound, unreachable valleys. Polo's account also specifically mentions the eagle (Garuda), who in Hindu mythology is the enemy of the Nagas, which they attack and devour. Garuda is often depicted with a serpent gripped in his beak. The eagle's access to the diamonds is an allegorical means of indicating its victory over the Nagas, with whom he constantly fought.

In returning to fact, Polo wrote: "No other country but this kingdom of Mutfili produces [diamonds], but there they are found both abundantly and of large size. Those that are brought to our part of the world [Europe] are only the refuse, as it were, of the finer and larger stones. For the flower of the diamonds and other large gems, as well as the larger pearls, are all carried to the Great Kaan and other Kings and Princes of those regions; in truth they possess all the great treasures of the world."

The diamond mines from which the great historic Indian diamonds came were distributed over a wide area on the eastern side of the Deccan plateau. Almost all sources were within the territory of the former kingdom of Golconda, although the term "Golconda mines" commonly found in diamond literature obscures the fact that the mines were scattered over a wide area.

The Golconda diamond industry was a large-scale, highly organized and controlled venture. Mine areas to be excavated were leased for one year with the agreement that all found

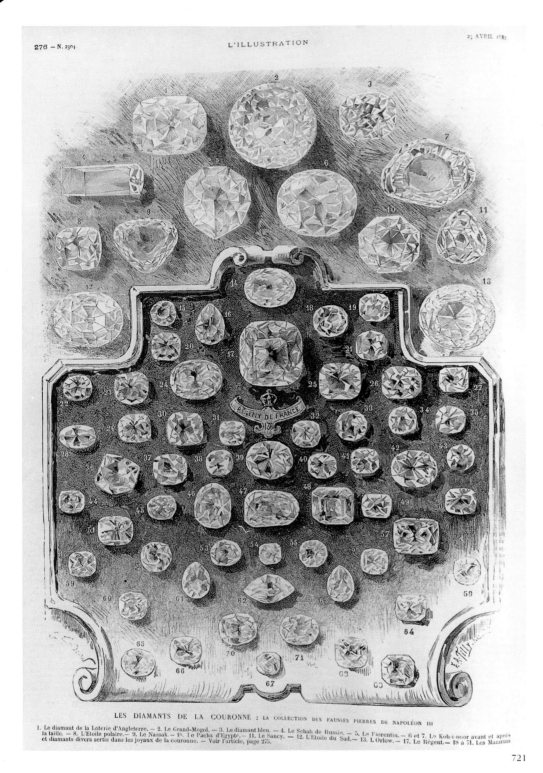

LES DIAMANTS DE LA COURONNE : LA COLLECTION DES FAUSSES PIERRES DE NAPOLÉON III

1. Le diamant de la Loterie d'Angleterre. — 2. Le Grand-Mogol. — 3. Le diamant bleu. — 4. Le Schah de Russie. — 5. Le Fiorentin. — 6 et 7. Le Koh-i-noor avant et après la taille. — 8. L'Étoile polaire. — 9. Le Nassak. — 10. Le Pacha d'Egypte. — 11. Le Sancy. — 12. L'Étoile du Sud. — 13. L'Orlow. — 17. Le Règent. — 18 à 71. Les Mazarins et diamants divers sertis dans les joyaux de la couronne. — Voir l'article, page 275.

721

721. This illustration by E. Godard, engraved by E. A. Tilly, from the French magazine L'Illustration, no. 2304 (April 2, 1887), 276, shows reproductions in crystal of the most important diamonds among the French Crown Jewels; the replicas were made for Emperor Napoléon III (ruled 1852–70). After the fall of the Second Empire, most of the Crown Jewels, which included many Indian diamonds, were disposed of at an auction that took place May 12–13, 1887. The Indian diamonds are (starting from the top, reading from left to right):

1. The Diamond of the Lottery of England (the Pigot); 2. The Great Mughal Diamond; 3. The Blue Diamond (of the Crown); 4. The Shah Diamond; 5. The Florentine; 6. and 7. The Koh-i-Nur (after and before cutting); 8. The Polar Star; 9. The Nassak; 10. The Pasha of Egypt; 11. The Sancy; 12. The Star of the South; 13. The Orlov; 14–16. (not given); 17. The Regent; 18–71. The Mazarins and various other lesser diamonds in the French Crown Jewels
Courtesy Catherine Arminjon and Cécile Tamalet, Paris

722. Persia. c. 1850 ➤
Miniature watercolor on paper of Nadir Shah (ruled 1736–47) by Abu 'l-Hasan Naqash Bashi
9 x 6½ in. (22.8 x 16.7 cm)
Courtesy Sotheby's, London

Nadir Shah, ruler of Persia, sacked Delhi in 1739 and plundered most of the enormous Mughal treasury, which included the Koh-i-Nur diamond set in an armlet (bazuband). In this painting, it is probably depicted as the central stone in the shah's right upper armlet, the same form and setting in which it eventually came to Queen Victoria. He also wears magnificent diamond-set ornaments and sits on a new "peacock" throne, made after his conquest and incorporating many Mughal gemstones. This throne still exists and is in a specially created vault in Tehran, Iran, designed to display the Iranian Crown Jewels, now the Iranian Treasure.

diamonds ten carats or over were the king's property; the rest belonged to the lease holder. Stones larger than ten carats were not unusual; when new Kollur mines were opened, diamonds in the ten-to-forty-carat category were common. Severe penalties were enforced should a worker be caught stealing any diamonds; nevertheless, ways were found to evade all precautionary measures. Even high officials were known to have sold large diamonds to the Portuguese, Dutch, English, and French. Diamonds not retained by the king were sold at official auctions, 25 percent of their price going to the government.

William Methwold, who served the English East India Company at Masulipatam, across

the Bay of Bengal from Burma, from 1618 to 1622 and was governor of Surat on India's west coast from 1633 to 1638, recorded the manner in which diamonds were mined. An enormous force of about thirty thousand men, women, and children—many tribal Gonds and Kols— were involved in various tasks. As these were alluvial mines, large open pits were dug to the diamond-bearing strata. Accumulated water and excavated earth were passed in buckets and baskets from one person to another, lined up from the pit bottom to the surface. Earth was dumped into a leveled, sloping area surrounded by a low mud wall with drainage openings. Wetted down, the earth was spread

out to a thickness of five inches (13 cm) to dry in the sun. The resulting clods were broken with a hand-held stone, pebbles removed, and the remainder sifted for diamonds.

Ultimately, Golconda's richest resource, its diamond mines, was also the cause of its downfall. Established as a Muslim sultanate in 1518 by the Qutb Shahi dynasty, Golconda became the object of covetous greed by the Mughal rulers of Hindustan to the north.

The great wealth of Golconda, initially the capital city of this kingdom of the same name, came principally from its intensive foreign trade in diamonds as well as the important *kalamkari* textile industry centered at Masulipatam, which was also the entrepot of the ruby trade from Burma. Once a flourishing city perched on top of a great hill and fortified by a crenellated wall of large granite blocks, with a multitude of gateways, Golconda now is a picturesque ruin of palaces, mosques, and other structures that suggest its former magnificence.

In 1631 Shah Jahan began an attempt to annex the Deccan sultanates of Bijapur and Golconda. In 1635, following a policy of ruth-

723. *The Koh-i-Nur Diamond, here replaced by a crystal reproduction, was originally set at the center of this gold armlet (bazuband). Given to Queen Victoria in 1850, the bazuband is now on view with the Crown Jewels in the Tower of London.*

less aggression, he succeeded in making Golconda a tributary state of the Mughal Empire. To indicate his submission, the Golconda ruler had to pay a regular, annual tribute, mainly in the form of diamonds.

In 1636, Shah Jahan appointed his son Aurangzeb viceroy of the Deccan, which he tried to annex totally. After Aurangzeb performed other tasks assigned to him, in 1653 Shah Jahan returned him for a second time to administer the Deccan, which he did from Daulatabad. Ambitious and aggressive, Aurangzeb determined to destroy the independence of Golconda and nearby Bijapur and gain possession of their immense treasure.

Aurangzeb was aided in his Golconda objective by Mir Jumla, commander of Golconda's troops and its virtual master as Prime Minister to Abdullah Qutb Shah. Before selling their precious gemstones, all merchants were required to first show them to Mir Jumla, a practice of which he made good use. When he fled to Delhi, after defecting to the Mughals, Mir Jumla carried with him an enormous personal treasure in diamonds.

Mughal Magnificence
Expressed in Gemstones

Of ... precious stones the Mogol [Aurangzeb] has a quantity inherited from ... his predecessors, also those obtained in the conquests of the Bijapur and Gulkandah kingdoms. In addition there are those he is daily buying. This takes no account of the fact that in these days he has become master of the diamond mines [in Golconda] and [as a result] there is no stint of stones, the largest and the best.

—Niccolao Manucci, *Storia do Mogor*

On his arrival at Delhi in 1656, Mir Jumla declared his allegiance to Shah Jahan and, to prove his fidelity, presented him with an enormous uncut diamond. The largest then in existence, weighing 787.5 carats, the famous Great Mughal Diamond came to symbolize the omnipotence of the Mughal dynasty. Obviously pleased, Shah Jahan returned the diamond to Mir Jumla to have it cut by a Venetian lapidary in residence named Hortensio Borgio.

Mir Jumla advised Shah Jahan, who had an insatiable desire to possess precious stones,

to send an army to Bijapur, Golconda, and Ceylon, where many such stones could be had, and Mir Jumla was ready to lead this mission. Niccolao Manucci, a European physician who served the Mughal court in India from 1656 to 1680, recorded the events in his *Storia do Mogor*: "Having spoken thus, he once more held forth his hand full of diamonds, already cut, of considerable size, though not as large as the first one."

Shah Jahan took this advice and sent a powerful army to the Deccan, as he was "extremely eager to possess the diamond mines." Aurangzeb led his forces and by treachery ravished Hyderabad City, which had become the new capital of Golconda. He then began a siege of the city of Golconda, determined to acquire all of its wealth, including its diamond treasures, and achieve control of the diamond mines. Finally the Golconda Shah agreed to pay an enormous indemnity, and Mir Jumla was again appointed Prime Minister of Golconda, this time responsible to the Mughal imperium.

In 1681 Aurangzeb, now Mughal emperor, determined to accomplish a final solution,

724. *The Imperial Crown of Queen Alexandra was the first British consort's crown to contain the Koh-i-Nur diamond (center, front). It was made for her in 1901 for her coronation in 1902 as Queen of Great Britain and Empress of India. After the coronation, its gemstones were replaced by replicas, and Alexandra gave the crown to the Museum of London, where it is now on view. The Museum of London, London (48.14/16)*

725. *The State Crown of Queen Mary was made by Garrard of London for the coronation in 1911 of the consort of George V. The Koh-i-Nur, removed from Queen Alexandra's crown, was placed before the cross-patée. Now called Queen Mary's Crown, it is exhibited (along with a crystal reproduction of the Koh-i-Nur) with the Crown Jewels in the Jewel House, Tower of London.*

726. *The State Crown of Queen Elizabeth was made for the coronation in 1937 of the consort of George VI (the present Queen Mother). The Koh-i-Nur was removed from Queen Mary's Crown and placed here, where it remains today. Now on view in the Jewel House, Tower of London, the crown is occasionally worn by the Queen Mother.*

went in person to attack Golconda in 1687. He bribed a treacherous Golconda officer to open a gate, and in October 1687 Golconda fell, thus ending the Qutb Shahi dynasty.

To a large extent, the reputation of the Mughal rulers as owners of inestimable wealth was based on their practice of concentrating their riches in the form of the major precious gemstones, such as diamonds, rubies, spinels, emeralds, sapphires, and pearls. Ostentatiously displayed in jewelry at public events, these ornaments were intended to awe and intimidate not only visiting dignitaries but also the rulers' own courtiers. Within the allowances of sumptuary laws, this practice was emulated by male members of the royal family, favored courtiers, and persons of high governmental rank, encouraged by the law in which all precious possessions of the upper classes upon their death became the ruler's property, excepting the jewelry owned by women, which they were permitted to retain. Although women were not seen in public, they too pursued avidly the accumulation of gemstones and jewelry.

A prime function of each dynastic ruler was to multiply his wealth by adding to the contents of the imperial treasury. Besides increasing the glory of the imperial dynasty, the accumulation of heirlooms to a great extent provided the empire with fiscal stability.

In biographies of the Mughal emperors, including those of Baber, Humayun, Akbar, Jahangir, Shah Jahan, and Aurangzeb, can be found innumerable references to the receiving or giving of gifts in the form of gemstones and gemstone-set jewelry and objects. Lists extracted from these volumes stagger the imagination, especially if one were able to total their value—which is often given. Further, the gifts mentioned were only those recorded. Not included were those that accrued by conquest of provincial Indian states or confiscations of wealth upon the death of a courtier.

Giving the emperor a gemstone of high value required a public ritual. The gift, marking the emperor's birthday or the New Year, was acknowledged as a symbol of subservience and loyalty. Accepted items were immediately evaluated and recorded. The ruler also publicly gave gemstones, and jewelry, to deserving family members or to military commanders after a successful campaign. The gift of a *saropa* (P: literally "from head [*sar*] to [*o*] foot [*pa*]") included jewelry, a turban, robe, sash, and possibly also a horse, elephant, or camel with trappings. This public gesture of generous omnipotence by the ruler was designed to encourage gratitude and loyalty.

After some time had passed, such gifts were often repaid with a countergift whose value was also immediately estimated and recorded by officials as if to keep a balance of accounts. The ruler was not, however, totally greedy, and many cases are mentioned in which several high-value gifts were spread before him, from which he made a selection of the best and returned the rest.

Tavernier: "Devoted to Diamond"

In India, as in Europe, it was the custom for rulers to deal personally with gemstone merchants. In some cases, rulers appointed agents to act for them when purchasing gemstones in places away from court or in foreign countries. Dealers commonly traveled to the ruler to sell stones, pieces of jewelry, or objects.

One such was Jean Baptiste Tavernier, Barone d'Aubonne of France (1605–1689), a great gemstone merchant. His unrelenting quest for diamonds, to which he was "devoted," made him the most renowned traveler in India during the apogee of the Mughal dynasty in the seventeenth century. Fortunately, he recorded and published a veracious record of his journeys in his book, *Travels in India*, published in France in 1676. To this invaluable work we owe the most accurate account of diamonds in India at the peak period of their discovery and supply to the world.

Tavernier made six voyages to the East: in 1631–33; 1638–42; 1643–49; 1651–55; 1657–62; and 1663–68. Of these, five took him to India, and four included trips to the diamond mines of Golconda. These eventful voyages, made at a time when world travel presented major difficulties, represent a major achievement.

Tavernier's intelligence and ability to adapt allowed him to learn quickly the manner of dealing with Indian gemstone merchants, coping with the labyrinthine paths of officialdom, the perils of power politics, and the psychological quirks of personalities, from emperors to governors to servants. No difficulty was insurmountable. He traded constantly, both en route to India and when returning, although he saved some of the best gemstones for France, several of which gained reputations among the world's most famous diamonds. In 1668 he sold a large number of diamonds and other gemstones to Louis XIV, who in gratitude granted him the title of baron.

In 1688 he was in Copenhagen where the only extant portrait of him, by Jacques d'Agar, was painted. On yet another journey to the East, armed with a Swedish passport, Tavernier entered Russia with the intention of continuing to Persia and probably India. In February 1689, at age eighty-four, death overtook him at Smolensk. Contrary to the claim of some writers, he was not devoured by Russian wolves chasing his sled.

Rose-Cut and Irregular Diamond Forms

The development of the flat-backed, domed, and faceted top that rises to a point called a rose-cut diamond is attributed to Indian lapidaries. It was invented to make best use of various irregular flat types of rough diamonds, available in quantity to Mughal jewelers, and too shallow to be treated otherwise. When placed in a closed, foil-backed mount, they were good

727. Jean Baptiste Tavernier, *painted by Jacques d'Agar*
Statens Museum for Kunst, Copenhagen (SP 705)

The only painted portrait of this eminent gemstone merchant, it was made in Copenhagen, probably in 1688, when he was eighty-three years old and the year after he set out on what would have been his seventh journey to Persia and India, which this time he never reached. The greater part of his trade was in large pearls and precious gemstones purchased mainly in India for resale to European royalty.

enough to create the aimed-for effect of glitter. The round or rounded Western rose-cut forms shown here all have a regular arrangement of facets, which are generally equilateral triangles and terminate in a point at the summit. In Mughal-style jewelry, many stones are similarly cut and basically are roses, but their forms may be irregular. The Western terminology for rough-diamond types is given below:

Macles Triangular-shaped, twinned diamond crystals used in the West for fashioning a *spread gem* or diamond with a flat, large table and a low crown or for *fancy cuts* such as triangle, keystone, kite, and half moon. All these cuts have their approximate Indian equivalents in the irregular diamond forms used in Mughal-style jewelry.

Flats A rough, flat diamond crystal, or *split*, which may or may not be a part of a macle.

Cleavages Slabs of cleaved diamond taken from large diamonds when dividing the rough prior to shaping; or broken crystals of usable thickness.

Lasques Flat, tabular diamonds, often cut from an inferior stone or a part of a diamond cleaved to remove a flaw.

Chip A small cleavage piece, weighing less than one carat, cut into an irregular shape and irregularly faceted or cut as a single rose.

The Mughal-Style Faceted Diamond

In recent Western diamond literature, the term *Mughal-style* cut diamond has come into use. This does not refer to a specific, regulated diamond-cut form but suggests a generic style of cutting used on major-size as well as smaller diamonds during the Mughal period. This style survives today for diamonds, generally of low value, used in the settings of contemporary jewelry created mostly in Jaipur, Rajasthan, where the traditional Mughal-Rajput style is followed.

The guiding principle of this diamond-cutting style was/is that regularity of form and cut is sacrificed in order to preserve as much as possible the maximum mass and weight of the original rough stone or of a cleavage piece from a large stone. Western diamond-cutting systems that developed from the fifteenth to the eighteenth century, to the contrary, attempted to maximize the refraction and dispersion qualities of a cut diamond, which give it the much admired unquenchable fire. These can only be revealed when the stone is properly proportioned in form and faceted in a perfectly symmetrical geometric cut, together termed good "make." However, a Western-cut diamond's dazzling brilliance normally is achieved at the expense of a loss of 50 percent or more of the stone's original volume, an idea that was anathema to Mughal objectives.

The Mughal preference for preservation of maximum diamond bulk prevented the early adoption by Indian lapidaries of Western faceted forms. This is why the supreme example of

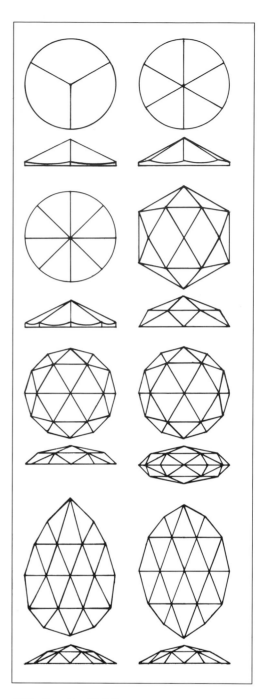

728. *Rose Cut (Polki)*

Designed to make optimum use of irregular stones, the Indian rose cut is believed to have been introduced to Europe by the Venetians. Probably inspired by the regular rose cut that appeared in common use in Europe about the first quarter of the seventeenth century, this form was especially popular through the end of the century, before the development of the brilliant cut. This diagram shows several types of rose-cut diamonds that frequently appear in Indian traditional jewelry, although not always so regularly cut: three-facet rose (top left); six-facet rose (top right); eight-facet rose (second left); half-Dutch rose (second right); full-Dutch rose (third left); double rose (third right); pear-shaped rose (bottom left); and a boat-shaped rose (bottom right).

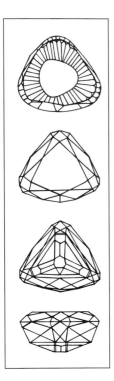

729. *The Nassak (Nashik) Diamond*

Originally cut Mughal style, this diamond went through two subsequent recuttings in the West to achieve a regular, symmetrical form

the result the appearance of an oversized rose cut. In the West, such a treatment is termed a *cap cut* or a *polished rough*.

The back of even large stones can be flat, as in the Orlov, or the pavilion-girdle perimeter can be treated in a manner similar to that of the crown, with generally irregular facets and a central counter table. It can also terminate in a faceted point. Irregular forms like these are not conducive to the creation of brilliance in a diamond and instead make them appear glassy and lumpy.

Mughal-Style Diamond Forms and Cuts

While, in the West, irregular forms are considered vastly inferior to the well-proportioned brilliant, what mattered in Indian stone-set jewelry was the preservation of maximum gemstone size and an impression of glitter and brilliance from a distance; intrinsic gemstone value was of relatively lesser importance. This practice made possible the use of all shapes and stone cuts in the same object. Strict symmetry was not considered essential, although

731. *The Shah Diamond*
Bar shaped, partially polished Golconda diamond, 88.77 carats

Inscribed with the names of three former owners: BOURHAN NIZAM SHAH II, 1000 (1591); SON OF JAHANGIR SHAH—SHAH JAHAN, 1051 (1641); and QAJAR FATH ALI SHAH, SULTAN. It was personally given by Khusrau Mirza, son of the Heir Apparent, Abbas Mirza, to Czar Nicholas I of Russia in compensation for the murder in Tehran on February 11, 1829, of the Russian Ambassador to Persia, Alexander Griboyedoff. It is now in the Russian Diamond Fund, The Kremlin, Moscow.

this concept, the brilliant cut, was not accepted in Mughal-style jewelry. Should a brilliant-cut stone be found in a "Mughal" piece of jewelry, it is probably either a replacement or recently made object.

The term *Mughal cut* actually refers to not one but several basic cut styles. Many such stones were set in jewelry with either side up, but for present purposes of discussion, the terms *upper, front, lower,* and *back* are used. The first of the following descriptions refers essentially to relatively large faceted stones. The Indian names for several other Mughal-style cuts of diamond, also commonly used then and now in Mughal-style jewelry, are given ahead.

Most commonly encountered in Mughal-cut diamonds is a stone with a flat upper table (the uppermost portion of a cut diamond, parallel to the girdle, which divides top from bottom, and the part seen when the stone is mounted). Large in proportion to the diamond size, it is usually irregular in outline, its shape following that of the stone's girdle perimeter, which can be roughly circular, oval, almond, or an irregular form.

The upper table is surrounded by one, two, or more registers of facets, inclined at angles and running parallel to the base. Their number and placement depend on the original form and size of the rough diamond.

Upper-diamond treatment varies. In some examples, the table is small but flat or is totally replaced by a small number of triangular facets cut at very shallow angles and meeting at a point, as at the apex of a rose-cut diamond. Examples of this treatment can be seen in very large stones such as the Great Mughal, the Koh-i-Nur in its original form, and the Orlov. Their upper high-domed surfaces are completely covered with small facets, which give

730. *The Daria-i-Nur (Sea of Light)*
Pink Golconda diamond
1⅝ x 1¼ in. (4.1 x 2.9 cm), estimated to weigh 175–95 carats

The Daria-i-Nur made up the major portion of the so-called Great Table Diamond (c. 250 cts); the rest is believed to be the Nur ul-Ain (60 cts) diamond. Tavernier was allowed to draw the Great Table Diamond, mined at Golconda, in 1665, when he examined the gemstone collection of the Mughal Emperor Aurangzeb. Now mounted in a gold setting as a hat ornament, it is on view in the National Iranian Treasure along with many other originally Indian Golconda diamonds, emeralds, rubies, and spinels.

it was aimed for and achieved as far as was possible with the stones available. The necessity of using many irregularly shaped stones in one ornament undoubtedly led to the evolution of the Indian *kundan* gemstone setting style, in which a pure 24-karat-gold fillet is forced between the stone and the depression surrounding it in its setting to form a bezel. The same technique is used in *kundan*-style enameled jewelry (see page 366) and when setting gemstones in a hardstone base (see page 118). The primary forms and cuts of Mughal-style diamonds are as follows:

Chakri A small, round stone with a flat top and bottom and faceted borders, often set in series, pavé style.

Karakht (P: unpolished, austere) An uncut diamond left as a rough as when found. In the West this is called a *naife* (from the word *naive*). Mughal rulers greatly prized such a stone when it was large. Occasionally they were considered more valuable than faceted stones. Some were octahedral in form, the primary natural form of a diamond crystal; others were an amorphic, irregular shape. At times a single face would be polished flat to permit the diamond to be inscribed with the name and date of its owner (see 731).

Manqvatdar A stone with a carved upper and, sometimes, lower surface, as the large emeralds often used in *bazubands* were treated; or one carved in the round, as in an emerald or ruby bead.

Muklassi A small stone faceted on both sides.

Parab (P: *para karna,* to cut in pieces; H: *parb,* a section, portion, division) A diamond section with a flat tabletop and bottom and irregularly faceted top and bottom. The flat table is usually set uppermost.

Polki Smaller than a *parab* stone, with one side flat and the other faceted to a taper or point, the *polki* is mounted either side up but often with the apex uppermost. When its facets are up, it resembles a rose cut. The term *parab-polki meenakar jewarat* (enameled jewelry made with *parab-* and *polki*-cut diamonds) is used in Jaipur to designate the Mughal-Rajput style of gold jewelry, decorated with such diamonds and enamel, made there.

Pota Cabochon-cut stone with a domed top and a flat, concave, or shallow convex bottom. This form is reserved for colored gemstones such as rubies, emeralds, and sapphires. In India, cabochon-cut stones are often referred to informally as "uncut," meaning they are not faceted. This is a misleading term as it does not describe the stone form but only the fact that it is not faceted.

Villandi or Bulandi (P: *buland*, high, elevated) A large stone whose upper pavilion is flat and from which slopes the part above the girdle, which is faceted in two or three registers. This part is mounted uppermost, and the area below the girdle is irregularly faceted to a vertex. It is this cut that is most often referred to as the *Mughal cut*. Generally such stones are made from a macle. Old *bulandi*-type stones of good quality are often removed from old settings and recut to Western brilliant forms, which greatly increases their value on the world market.

Two Indian terms for Western diamond cuts should also be mentioned here. One is the *tal-pain* (S: *tal*, from beneath, bottom, under; *pain*, channel, or water course), a series of rectangular or square calibré-cut stones set in a channel setting with no metal visible between them. They run together as a unit and were used occasionally in late Mughal jewelry, especially with rubies. The Sanskrit term *kanwal* (lotus) designates a diamond fully and regularly faceted in the European brilliant-cut manner. This is a relatively recent innovation in Indian diamond history, although of course today all the standard types of diamond cuts are used in Western-oriented Indian jewelry.

The European Diamond Trade with India

The Portuguese made their first voyage around Africa to India in 1498 and, a short time after, entered the gemstone trade between India and Ceylon and Europe. In 1510 the Portuguese established themselves in Goa, which became the most important center for Indian diamond export, a position it retained until the middle of the seventeenth century.

Early on, the Portuguese competed with the Venetians for control of the diamond business in Europe. Venetians preferred to deal in rough diamonds that were then cut in Venice because cut diamonds commanded a far greater

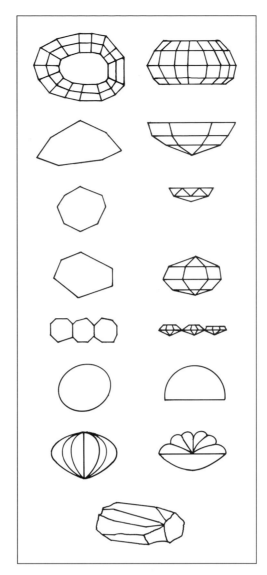

732. *Traditional Indian Diamond Cuts*

Top to bottom; top and side views: Parab; villandi; polki; muklassi; chakri; pota; manovatdar; karakht (*unpolished*)

profit than the sale of roughs. The Portuguese took rough and cut diamonds from India and re-sold them. The Dutch entered the raw-diamond trade in the first half of the seventeenth century, and Amsterdam became a center of diamond cutting.

To supply this growing industry, the Dutch bought large quantities of rough diamonds from Golconda, whose ruler regulated production and diamond prices in order to keep the supply low and thereby force a rise in prices. Despite this, the Dutch continued to buy. The Dutch and Portuguese battled for this market, but from 1642 onward the largest percentage of raw diamonds that left India were cut in Amsterdam. As the Dutch rose in their domination of the business, the Portuguese retreated and, by 1651, had practically abandoned the diamond business.

In 1654 the English and the Portuguese made a broad treaty of friendship, with the result that the English developed an interest in the diamond trade. By about 1670, the English

had taken over direct purchase of rough diamonds in India. The Dutch were no longer involved in its direct import but left the risks to the English. Meanwhile, the growth of commercial wealth among the European bourgeoisie brought about an increased demand for cut diamonds. London became the primary diamond market, but Amsterdam continued to be the primary diamond cutting and polishing center, establishing a monopoly by the eighteenth century.

The British diamond trade in the eighteenth and nineteenth centuries centered on the east coast of India at Madras. Up to about 1840, this trade was conducted mainly by English companies in residence. The diamonds exported were generally small, uncut stones that were sent to London in a packet called a *bulse* (from the Portuguese *bolsa*, a purse or bag used to carry diamonds, other stones, and gold dust). Messrs. de Fries of Madras was preeminent in the London market, and their packets of bulses were sold there by weight, without examination. Later the export trade fell into the hands of local diamond merchants, who pursued a tendency to speculate on prices, and, although prices rose, the trade changed as irregular practices multiplied.

Brazilian and African Diamonds

Just about the time when Indian diamond resources declined, diamonds were discovered and mined in Brazil in 1725. Suddenly, India no longer had a world monopoly on diamonds, and prices fell. Because they feared a sudden influx of diamonds on the market, which would cause a permanent drop in diamond values, Indian and European diamond merchants began a propaganda campaign that incorrectly claimed Brazilian diamonds were inferior to those from India and were difficult to cut and polish. Some Indian sources even stated that the new Brazilian stones were in fact inferior Indian stones sent to Brazil to be disposed of. Ironically, to get around resistance, Portuguese diamond merchants in Brazil did ship diamonds to the Portuguese Indian colony of Goa, where they were sold as Indian diamonds.

Until 1886, India and Brazil were the only known diamond sources. In that year diamonds were discovered in South Africa, where vast diamond-bearing deposits ultimately were uncovered. Later, diamonds were also found in other parts of Africa, and now South Africa holds third place in diamond production. Siberia is another important source.

The Contemporary Indian Diamond Industry

Although today the diamond mines there are almost depleted and India is insignificant in terms of world production of rough diamonds, it has rapidly become the world's leader in faceting imported diamonds in terms of total

733. Famous Golconda Diamonds
(not drawn to scale)

A. The Blue Diamond of the Crown
B. The Florentine
C. The Great Mughal
D. (top to bottom): Tavernier Blue,
    French Blue, Original Hope,
    Present Hope
E. The Hortensia
F. The Idol's Eye
G. The Koh-i-Nur before and after cutting
H. The Orlov
I. The Pigot
J. The Polar Star
K. The Regent
L. The Sancy
M. The Wittelsbach

Famous Golconda Diamonds

Diamond	Metric Carats	Color	Form/Style
Agra	31.50	pink	round/brilliant
Ahmedabad	94.78	colorless	pear/brilliant
Akbar Shah	71.70	colorless	pear/irregular
Arcot I	31.01	colorless	pear/brilliant
Arcot II	18.85	colorless	pear/brilliant
Arcot Brilliant	26.77	colorless	round/brilliant
Black Orlov	67.50	gun metal	cushion/brilliant
Blue Diamond of the Crown	67.00	sapphire blue	triangular/brilliant
Darya-i-Nur (Dakha)	150.00	colorless	almost square/Mughal cut
Darya-i-Nur (Iran) approx.	185.00	pale pink	rectangle/step tablet
De Guise	28.44	rose pink	cushion/brilliant
Dresden Green	41.00	apple green	almond/brilliant
Dresden White	49.71	blue white	oblong cushion/brilliant
Dresden Yellow I	38.00	yellow	round/brilliant
Dresden Yellow II	29.25	yellow	round/brilliant
Dresden Yellow III	23.10	yellow	round/brilliant
Dresden Yellow IV	13.48	yellow	round/brilliant
Empress Eugénie	51.00	colorless	oval/brilliant
Florentine	137.27	light green-yellow	double-rose pendeloque/mixed cut
Golconda d'Or	95.40	pale gold	emerald cut
Great Mughal	280.00	colorless	Indian high-rose cut
Great Table	250.00	pink	rectangular tablet/stepcut
Hope	45.52	sapphire blue	cushion/modified brilliant
Hortensia	20.00	peach pink	pentagonal pendeloque
Idol's Eye	70.21	aquamarine blue	antique triangle/modified brilliant
Indore Pear I	46.62	colorless	pear/brilliant
Indore Pear II	44.18	colorless	pear/brilliant
Iranian National	72.84	champagne	irregular pear/Mughal cut
	54.58	colorless	irregular oval/Mughal cut
	54.35	pale peach	cushion/brilliant
	47.31	colorless	rounded triangle/Mughal cut
Jahangir	83.00	colorless	pear/modified brilliant, hole
Koh-i-Nur	108.93	colorless	oval/brilliant
Le Grand Condé	50.00	pink	pear/brilliant
Mirror of Portugal	26.00	colorless	square/table cut
Moon of Baroda	24.95	canary yellow	drop/brilliant
Moon of the Mountains	123.20	colorless	cushion/brilliant
Nassak	43.38	colorless	emerald cut
Nepal	79.41	colorless	pear/brilliant
Nizam	277.00	colorless	irregular/Mughal cut
Nur-ul-'Ain	60.00	pink	oval with slight drop/brilliant
Orlov	189.62	pale blue-green	high rose/Mughal cut
Pigot	48.63	colorless	oval/brilliant
Polar Star (Yusupov)	41.285	trace of rose	oblong cushion/brilliant
Queen of Golconda	49.62	colorless	marquise/brilliant
Regent (Pitt)	140.50	colorless	cushion/brilliant
Sancy (Grand)	55.23	colorless	oval-pear/rose cut
Sancy (Beau)	34.50	colorless	pear/brilliant
Shah	88.70	yellowish	narrow oblong/partly polished
Shah of Persia	99.52	yellow	cushion/brilliant
Star of Este	26.16	blue-white	cushion/brilliant
Star of the East	94.78	colorless	pear/brilliant
Taj-i-Mah	115.06	colorless	irregular oval/Mughal cut
Wittelsbach	35.56	sapphire blue	oval/brilliant

carats of fashioned diamonds annually produced. Officially, faceted diamonds with a reported value of about 200 crores (1 crore equals 10 million rupees or 100 lacs) are exported annually from India, but the actual total is believed to be closer to 500 crores or more.

The gemstone industry in India is predominantly export oriented, and fashioned diamonds have become one of India's ten major export products. Diamonds constitute about 80 percent of the total value of exported precious stones, followed by colored gemstones, semiprecious stones, pearls, and fashioned synthetic stones. More than 90 percent of diamonds and other gemstones are exported through Bombay, the rest by Jaipur, Delhi, Madras, and Ahmadabad. Export is encouraged by government as revenues generated by this industry are an important means for the country to earn much-needed hard foreign currency.

The phenomenal rise of India as one of the world's three top producers of fashioned diamonds began after World War II, which disrupted the established diamond fashioning centers. India was quick to fill the void and now competes favorably with Antwerp, Belgium, and Tel Aviv, Israel, the world's two main centers in terms of the value of their output. The prevailing low cost of Indian labor gives India's products a price advantage. India's share in world fashioned-diamond production is 35 percent, but the total value represents only 10 percent. The main cause of this imbalance is that India has become a specialist in fashioning diamonds of under half a carat, mostly in the category called *makeables*, which do not require sawing before being faceted. Such diamonds can be profitably fashioned into gemstones only where costs are low. Because this area of diamond fashioning is proportionally lowest in earnings, it is not as readily entered into by competing centers, where the higher cost of cutting would exceed the value of such stones. India is also the world's largest producer of *briolette-cut* diamonds, generally fashioned in small sizes and pierced at the top for use as hanging pendants. This type of cutting concentrates in Jaipur, Rajasthan.

The picture, however, is changing. Indian diamond producers well realize the need for fashioning larger sized stones at higher profits. Efforts are being made constantly to acquire a greater share of the supply, but access is limited by tight international control of diamond distribution. As compensation, continuous growth in the international diamond consumer market has increased the world's consumption of small diamonds.

To assist in the growth and development of the Indian diamond world, an organization called the Gem and Jewellery Export Promotion Council was set up in 1966 under the auspices of the Ministry of Foreign Trade, Government of India. Its objectives are to improve and modernize the nation's lapidary industry and the quality of its products, collect

734. *Briolette Cut* (Tilkaridar)

This style of diamond cutting has become a modern Indian specialty and is a form of rose cut in-the-round. Variations include (clockwise from top left) triangular cut; step cut; and pampille cut. Briolettes are often top-drilled for suspension. Indian diamonds were drilled (H: kanudar; kanu, hole) long before the development of modern Western knowledge in the cutting and drilling of diamonds.

735. Bombay, Maharashtra

Contemporary Indian gouache rendering of a traditional three-strand necklace (tin lara har), set in platinum with diamonds, with a yoni-shaped central pendant
Courtesy Pesi F. Choksey, Bombay

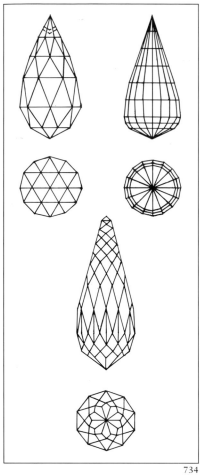

734

735

statistics and information, carry out research, act as a liaison between the industry and government agencies in matters concerning policy and regulations involving the Indian gemstone industries, and help increase export by propaganda means such as foreign publicity and publications.

Today more than four hundred thousand persons are involved in the numerous diamond-fashioning workshops, large and small, that sprang up rapidly after World War II and in associated aspects of the trade. This impressive total is greater than the combined sum of all other places.

Diamonds to be fashioned, and finished stones, are shuttled back and forth from place to place by bonded messengers (Guj: *angadia*). In an occupation requiring trustworthy people, many messengers are related to each other, and employment passes from father to son. On each trip, they carry diamonds worth huge sums under their clothing in bags strapped to their bodies (S: *ang*). Should accidents, losses, or robberies occur, the company that employs the *angadia* immediately reimburses the diamond owners. Prompt action maintains the industry's trust and the company's reputation of total reliability in its messenger service.

Bombay, the main port of diamond entry, remains the industry's main diamond exchange. The important diamond fashioning centers are at Bombay and, within a 180-mile (288-km) radius, Navsari, Surat, and Palanpur. As a whole, the diamond trade is dominated by about twenty Jain merchant families, such as the Shahs of Surat and the Jhaveris and Mehtas of Palanpur, who have established a highly regulated industrial structure following practices that resemble those of De Beers in London. Outsiders are excluded from this tightly controlled and integrated family network.

736. Delhi. *18th century*
One of a pair of gold bracelets (kara) whose diameter tapers toward the back. The entire outer surface is ornamented with 1,025 rubies, 7 diamonds, and 68 emeralds. The rubies and emeralds, bombé set in channel style, are cut to form the ground or convex-carved flower petals and leaves. The inner surface is polychrome enameled with a green ground (hara zamin).
Diameter 4⅝ in. (11.8 cm)
State Hermitage Museum, Oriental Collection, St. Petersburg (V3 720 and V3 721)

These were taken from the Mughal Treasury by Nadir Shah and in 1741 sent to Russia with other objects as gifts to proclaim his conquest of Delhi.

736

Rubies

The ruby (S: *manikya*; *kuruvinda*; H: *manak*; P: *la'l*; Tel: *kempu rai*; Tam: *manikkam*; *gembu kallu*; Burm: *kyouk-nis ballamya*; *mamawmaya*) has always maintained its important position in the Indian gemstone world because of its symbolic mythological connection with Surya, the sun god, the sun being the center of all phenomena in our solar system.

Termed an oriental ruby when it originates in an Eastern source, ruby is a form of corundum (S: *korund*) or aluminum oxide, colorless when pure but characterized as ruby when, due to the presence of an impurity in the form of the metallic oxide of chromium, iron, or both, its red color varies from transparent pink to rose to deep carmine. The most highly valued of these is a pure, deep red, often termed pigeon's blood. Ruby color varies with its place of origin, and in the trade this is used as one means of identifying its source, also determinable by the stone's internal structure and inclusions which also differ according to origin.

Corundum has a specific gravity of between 3.95 and 4.10 and a hardness of 9 on Mohs' scale, which among gemstones is inferior only to diamond. Some corundum, such as the dark, heavily flawed variety abundant in southern India, has no gemstone value but is crushed and used in India and elsewhere as an abrasive for carving and polishing softer gemstones.

Since prehistoric times, the chief source of gemstone rubies has been in Upper Burma, now called Myanmar. Most of the rubies found occur in the gem-bearing gravel of alluvial deposits. Over centuries they have been tumbled and worn to a rounded form. When polishing rubies, Indian and other eastern lapidaries have always aimed to preserve their maximum rounded size. This practice accounts for the character of south Indian traditional gold jewelry, which is dominated by the use of small cabochon-cut rubies. Their size is small because most rubies found average under a quarter of a carat. These were and still are readily available at a reasonable cost.

737. Madras, Tamil Nadu. *19th century*
Gold necklace (hangai pathakkam malai) set with diamonds, rubies, and emeralds; and pendant pearls
Length 15¾ in. (40 cm)
Private Collection

At the center are two pendants: the upper in the form of confronting peacocks flanking a large rosette; the lower an openwork, scrolling, foliated form. Suspended at the sides by three rows of floral units backed by three supporting, flat, braided wire bands, interrupted by rectangular spacer units and ending in an elaborate floral-form clasp flanked by two heart forms. Pendant reverses are engraved gold, not enameled as in the case of much north Indian gold jewelry. A dot-punched inscription on a pendant and the clasp records the name of the former owner.

738. Tamil Nadu
Rigid gold armlet (kappu or kadagam) set with rubies and diamonds, with a lower border of pearls
Height 2 in. (5 cm); diameter 3⅛ in. (8 cm)
Courtesy Gem Palace, Jaipur

The design consists of a central flowerhead addorsed by peacocks.

739. Jaipur, Rajasthan. *19th century*
(opposite page)
Gold necklace (kantha) set with rubies, diamonds, and pearls
Diameter approx. 8 in. (20 cm)
Courtesy Spink & Son, London

Thirteen main diamond-centered floral units, joined by three-lug hinges to ax-shaped, diamond-set units. All pendants are of a domed-lac composition that supports the overlapping layered tiers of rubies meant to simulate rose petals. In this construction, each ruby petal is pierced at the unseen, overlapped edge and threaded with a wire that is then twisted, its free end heated and embedded into the lac to hold the ruby in place. The reverse has an enameled floral pattern, the figure in gold, the ground in transparent green enamel, surrounded by an opaque white cartouche.

Large, minimally flawed stones of high quality are an extreme rarity and therefore command the highest price by carat weight among gemstones, including diamond. In the past, stones above five carats were considered the property of the local Burmese ruler. Despite the dire penalties imposed if caught, they were often smuggled out of the country, a practice that continues even today, although the ruby mines are presently owned by the Myanmar government.

Rubies are called Mogok, Kathé, and Kyatpyen after their main source villages in Myanmar. Mogok, in the past and still today, is the center to which most of the stones are brought and today also cut and sold to dealers in residence, who resell them mainly to Burmese, Thai, and Indian dealers. Once a small place, Mogok today is a bustling, frontier-type city with a population of about 100,000, which includes a complex growing network of miners, cutters, wholesalers, and retailers. The majority of the rubies and sapphires from all sources, including Myanmar, Thailand, and Sri Lanka, are cut in lapidary factories at Bangkok and Chanthaburi in Thailand and marketed there.

The origin of rubies here, and in Sri Lanka where they are also found, was known to European travelers since the end of the fifteenth century. According to the Englishman William Methwold, "The rubies and saphires [sic] … are found in the Kingdome of Ava … and [are] much esteemed in all parts of India." Rubies were exported from Burma at the seaport of Pegu, from which came "perfect rubies and saphires which are dispersed through the world." The six-month monsoon season regulated the pattern of trade. In September, ships with Indian pilots set sail from the Coromandel East Coast Indian port of Masulipatam and crossed the Bay of Bengal to Burma. The return journey took place in February or March, and the ships arrived at their place of departure in April.

Balas Ruby: Red Spinel

In the memoirs of the Mughal emperors, frequent mentions occur of the balas ruby (from A: *balakhsh*), which actually is not ruby but a pale rose to ruby red translucent spinel, in 1783 distinguished from ruby as a distinct magnesium aluminum oxide mineral, Mohs' scale 8 in hardness. Before then, garnet and red spinel were frequently regarded as kinds of ruby because their color can approximate ruby, and red spinel is often found in association with ruby and sapphire. Spinel also occurs in a variety of other colors, including purple, blue, dark green, and black, but the most desirable variety has always been the red that most closely resembes ruby.

Since antiquity, the most important red spinel source has been the alluvial deposits in the Badakchan Province of Balk, an area rough-ly corresponding to ancient Bactria, and now a district of northern Afghanistan on the banks of the Shignan River, a tributary of the Oxus. Spinels are also found in Mayanmar, Thailand, and Sri Lanka.

Because red spinel can be found in sizes up to 500 carats, they are comparatively less expensive than ruby. As one of the few large, transparent red stones, red spinel's impressive size was preserved simply by polishing its surface to bring out its true color. In that baroque form it was used in Indian jewelry and mounted on objects. Tavernier reported that he counted 108 large balas rubies mounted on the famous peacock throne of the Mughal emperors, all cabochon cut, the smallest weighing about 100 carats and some 200 carats or more. (These, and the 116 large emeralds he also counted on this throne, went to Persia in 1739, when Nadir Shah had the throne dismembered.) Most baroque red spinels were commonly drilled to make beads and used as pendant gemstones on necklaces, turban ornaments, and in earrings.

Sapphires

Sapphire (S: *nilamani, sanipriya*; H: *nilam*; Tam: *nilam*; Sing: *nil*) is associated in Indian mythology with Saturn (*sanipriya* translates literally as "favored by Saturn"), who represents darkness and is an enemy of light. Widely used in India, sapphire is a translucent, dark-blue variety of corundum, consisting of about 92 percent pure alumina plus about 3 percent iron oxide, titanium oxide, and possibly some cobalt oxide. Highest prices are paid for a stone with a medium-value blue color, clear—not milky—and one whose color after cutting is evenly distributed throughout the stone, which is often not the case when the crystal is found, but then only the blue portion is used.

The difference between sapphire and ruby lies in the coloring oxide they contain. Aside from red ruby and blue sapphire, sapphire is found in other colors, termed in the trade "fancy sapphires." This group includes oriental amethyst (purple), oriental emerald (green), oriental topaz (yellow), an orange-pink sapphire (Sinh: *padparadshah*) highly valued by the Mughals, adamantine spar (smoky brown), and white sapphire (colorless). The latter and colorless zircon are commonly used in contemporary Indian jewelry as a diamond substitute.

Sapphire, ruby, and topaz are abundant in India, but, although a stone of good quality is occasionally found, the majority lack translucency and are flawed. Unusable as gemstones, they are crushed and used for industrial grinding and polishing processes.

From about 1880 to 1920, very high quality sapphire was mined in Kashmir in Zaskar, at Kyaungdwin, a source now totally depleted. These were rightfully famous for their velvety deep cornflower-blue color, though they often

740. Paris, France. *1936*
*Platinum-mounted carved and faceted colored gemstone and diamond necklace, made by Cartier, Paris, with the
Cartier mark on the central drop and clasp, and the number 84598*
Collection Cartier, Paris

*Perhaps the most important and spectacular of the Cartier Euro-Indian designed necklaces created during the
Art Deco period, it incorporates the Rajput-Mughal concept of combining in one necklace four of the maharatnani
gemstones: diamond, emerald, ruby, and sapphire. The colored gemstones, mostly carved in the form of flower
heads, leaves, and as pierced beads, were purchased in India by Daisy Fellowes, who commissioned the necklace.
Combining all these colors in a single piece of jewelry, then new to European jewelry designers, became a fashion
there. The basic design consists of a graduated, articulated platinum chain encrusted with carved floral-pattern
colored gemstones and beads, many set with diamond studs to cover their holes. The thirteen faceted sapphire
drops and a clasp ornamented with two large carved sapphires dominate the design.*

741. Jaipur, Rajasthan. *19th century*
(opposite page)
*Gold choker (guluband) set with eighteen
large, octagonal (athphalu) emeralds, a
central unit with diamonds, and a pendant
(jugni)*
Length 8⅝ in. (22 cm)
Private Collection

*The emeralds retain their original cross-
sectional crystal forms. The reverse is
polychrome enameled in a white-ground
(safed chalwan) style.*

included rutile fragments. In general, however, sapphires have fewer inclusions than rubies or emeralds. Their high reputation continues, and sapphires incorrectly sold today as Kashmiri generally are from Myanmar.

The main sapphire source has long been Sri Lanka, known in antiquity to the West as Serendip (from S: *Simhala-dvipa,* island). From this comes the English word *serendipity,* the gift of unintentionally discovering valuable things. Sapphires of all colors and rubies are abundant in Sri Lanka, but from there also come alexandrites, aquamarine, cat's eye, chrysoberyl, moonstone, topaz, tourmaline, and zircon, all used in contemporary Indian jewelry. The most productive gemstone area in Sri Lanka is in the southeast part of the island, about 30 to 40 miles (48–64 km) from Ratnapura (whose name means "city of gemstones"), near Adam's Peak.

Thailand sapphires are found in the province of Battambong and at Chanthaburi, near Bangkok, where rubies are also found. Sapphires often occur in association with rubies and generally in greater numbers than ruby because the iron oxide that causes their color is more common in nature than chrome oxide, which gives ruby its color. Generally the sapphires are also larger than the rubies, but even so, because of ruby's greater rarity, sapphires generally are valued at one-third to one-half that of ruby.

Emeralds

Emerald (S: *vaidurya; marakata;* H: *panna;* P: *zammurud;* A: *samurod;* Tam: *pachchi-kallu*), a variety of beryl, is first mentioned in the *Rig Veda* (c. 1500–1000 B.C.), the sacred books upon which the Hindu religion is founded. Exactly when emerald was first used in India for personal adornment is unknown. No ancient jewelry set with emerald has been found, but many mentions of it occur in the extensive body of early Sanskrit literature, such as the *Mahabharata* (first–third century A.D.). In the *Agastimata,* the aforementioned treatise on gemstones, emerald is rated as one of the five *maharatnani.* In this work, the origins of gemstones are given, but India and Ceylon (Sri Lanka) are not named as emerald sources. It was not until 1943 that previously unknown and unworked emerald deposits were first discovered in India. In the past then, emeralds obviously came to India from elsewhere, and that place was Egypt.

Emeralds from Egypt were the earliest source available to the Mediterranean area and the East, including India. Egyptians of the Middle Kingdom (c. 2040–1633 B.C.) are believed to have been the first to know that emeralds existed in deposits in the eastern desert area, about one hundred miles north of Aswan on the slopes of Jebel Sikait and Jebel Zubara. (Unlike most diamonds, rubies, and sapphires, which are found free in alluvial

deposits, emeralds are usually embedded in layers of the host rock mica schist matrix.) The mines, a maze of scattered tunnels and chambers, were regularly worked by slave labor under appalling conditions. Alternately diligently exploited, then abandoned and lost for centuries, they produced emeralds as recently as the late nineteenth century.

In comparison with those found much later in Colombia, the Egyptian stones are small, light green in color, filled with flaws, and decidedly inferior in quality. Nevertheless, since antiquity, and especially during the late Ptolemaic period whose last Egyptian ruler was Cleopatra (51–30 B.C.), Egypt had a monopoly on their export, which was broken when Europeans first made contact with the "new world."

Colombian Emeralds: Obsession of Maharajas

In the early sixteenth century, through Spanish conquest the superior emeralds of Colombia became available to the rest of the world. Emeralds had been mined in Colombia since about A.D. 1000, and possibly earlier. The mines, systematically worked, supplied a vast New World export trade that extended to present-day Ecuador, Peru, Central America, and Mexico, where emeralds were highly valued among the Inka, Maya, Toltec, and Aztec peoples. By the time the Spanish appeared, the treasuries of these kingdoms were bulging with dynastic emerald collections that in effect became the earliest "emerald mines" for the Spanish before the Colombian mines, the source of them all, were located. From these treasuries came the first Colombian emeralds to appear in India.

We now know the strange and fascinating sequence of events by which many of these emeralds passed from the possession of New World *casiques* (chieftains) to their East Indian counterparts—Indian Mughal emperors and provincial maharajas. Among the emeralds now in Indian collections, and those in the Iranian National Treasure, are some of the very emeralds given to, or "collected" by, Hernando Cortés during his conquest of Mexico, which began in 1519.

From the contemporary account of this conquest by Bernal Diaz del Castillo, we know that when Cortés first approached the Aztec capital Tenochtitlán (now Mexico City), its ruler, Moctezuma II, dispatched six *casiques* to present him with gold and valuable emeralds, which certainly whetted the explorer's appetite for more. When Cortés and Moctezuma finally met, the latter presented him with more emeralds, "as a tribute for your Emperor and yourself." Under pressure from Cortés, Moctezuma became a vassal of the Spanish king, Charles I, who was also Holy Roman Emperor, Charles V. To signify his submission, Moctezuma sent Charles V a gift of emeralds. He was quoted as saying to Cortés, "I will give you some very valuable stones which you will send

to him in my name. They are *chalchihuites,* and are not to be given to anyone else but only to him your Great Prince."

In a short time, the Aztecs were conquered. With great energy, the Spanish gathered loot and treasure for remittance to Spain, such as the shipment of priceless emeralds sent to Charles V in 1525.

In 1532, thirteen years after Cortés began his Mexican campaign, Francisco Pizarro landed in Peru and began his conquest of the Inka Empire. From the Inka, he looted enormous quantities of Colombian emeralds. Colombia itself was conquered in 1537 by Gonzalo Jiminez de Queseda, who named it Nueva Granada. While on a consolidating expedition into the interior, he received emeralds as gifts from the local people. In that campaign alone he is said to have collected a booty of more than seven thousand emeralds. This assured him of the rumored proximity of their mine source, which he ultimately discovered at Chivor. About 1558, the Muzo emerald

mines were discovered approximately 80 miles (128 km) from Chivor.

The actively worked Muzo mines produced even larger emeralds of a richer green than the bluish-green ones from Chivor. The best of these were shipped annually to Spain so that, by the mid-sixteenth century, Spain was flooded with emeralds and anxious to dispose of the surplus, especially in exchange for gold or diamonds. Emeralds were sold to whoever could afford them, and in that category were the sovereigns and nobility of India, Persia, and Turkey.

In 1676, Tavernier reported that emeralds, "at present … are conveyed (from the New World) by the North Sea (Atlantic) to Spain." From there, the much-traveled emeralds continued their journey around the African Cape of Good Hope to the Portuguese trade enclaves of Goa and Diu, from where gemstone merchants dispersed them throughout India. Tavernier observed that, by 1660, emeralds were so abundant in India that they sold there at a price 20 percent less than in France.

742. Alwar, Rajasthan
His Highness Maharaja Swai Jai Singh Bahadur of Alwar, Knight Commander of the Star of India, Knight Commander of the Indian Empire, born 1882. Besides his traditional Indian ornaments, he wears for this formal portrait photograph the star insignia of the Indian orders granted to him, then considered part of the royal regalia. In Great Britain, the custom of granting honorary titles is long-standing. In colonial times, the British extended this practice to their Indian subjects, especially after the Indian Mutiny, to reward loyal Indian princes.

Many nineteenth- and early twentieth-century official portrait photographs of Indian princes were made for the great Indo-British durbars of 1877, 1903, and 1911. In them, along with their traditional Indian ornaments, they also proudly wear the collars and badges, and the official robes, of the British-Indian orders awarded to them. The Order of the Star of India and the Order of the Indian Empire were created by Queen Victoria in 1861 and 1877, respectively, and discontinued on August 14, 1947, with the transfer of British rule to India and Pakistan.

Indian sovereigns, most of whom were gemstone connoisseurs, and the privileged classes willingly expended large sums in gold to acquire these high-quality, deep green, unprecedentedly large emeralds. The avidity with which Indians accepted them contributed considerably to financing the transformation of Spain and Portugal into world powers.

In India, emeralds were used in turban ornaments, necklaces, armlets, rosaries, belt buckles, and other forms of traditional jewelry. Owners proudly displayed their emerald-set regalia on important occasions, such as annual state and high religious festivities and at weddings, both always occasions for ostentation.

In the nineteenth and early twentieth centuries, at events attended by several maharajas, a kind of competition grew among them as to whose jewelry made a more spectacular impression. Official photographs of the maharajas dressed in their most impressive jeweled regalia appeared in publications celebrating important Anglo-Indian imperial events, including the Great Delhi Durbars of 1877, 1903, and 1911. In the public imagination, the reputation of wealth enjoyed by Indian princes depended less on the extent of their invisible territories and more on the diamonds, emeralds, rubies, sapphires, and pearls they wore on such occasions.

Emerald Forms in Indian Jewelry

In traditional Indian jewelry, especially during Mughal times, standard forms for the use of emeralds developed. The greatest use of emeralds in traditional Indian jewelry is as beads. Most of these beads are irregular in form because they were made of smaller emerald crystals. This form was acceptable to Indian taste because it preserves maximum stone bulk. Stones of this kind were tumble polished by an old Indian method (see page 79). The resulting so-called baroque form was centrally drilled in its long axis to render it suitable for

743. Jaipur, Rajasthan. *19th century*
Gold necklace (guluband) set with nineteen large, foil-backed diamonds, from each of which is suspended a large baroque emerald bead; the reverse is polychrome enameled.
Length 13 in. (33 cm)
Private Collection

Necklaces such as this became a source of emerald beads used in various ways by European jewelers in the early twentieth century (see 853). In Europe, some were cut in half and fashioned into regular cabochons or European emerald-cut gemstones, whose value was thereby considerably increased.

744. Jaipur, Rajasthan. *19th century*
Gold necklace (guluband) set with diamonds on an enameled ground, with emeralds used as an inner border and lower fringe; the reverse is polychrome enameled.
12 x 2¼ in. (30.5 x 5.7 cm)
Private Collection

743

744

use as a bead or pendant. They often appear singly or in graduated sizes as a fringe on a crown (*mukut*), headdress (*sarpatti*), or turban ornament (*sarpech*). They are also strung in a necklace (*kantha* or *mala*), alone or in combination with pearls and rubies, the latter similarly treated. Necklaces of these kinds are frequently depicted in Mughal miniature portraits of both men and women.

Another popular bead form—the gadrooned or melon-shaped (*kharbuza*) bead—which inevitably meant a loss of original stone weight, was generally resorted to as a means of disguising emerald inner flaws. After the stone was shaped to a basic round or oval form and drilled (*nathna*), its surface was carved with a regular series of convex-curving flutes or parallel grooves that all terminate at the polar ends of the bead's drilled hole. When the stones used are of good quality, these melon-shaped beads are more valuable than the baroque. Gadrooned beads were generally used in long necklaces (*mala*), either in uniform or graduated sizes, sometimes combined with other gemstone beads and pearls. They often appear in European Art Deco jewelry (see 862).

Less frequently, emerald was cut into a regular circular or ellipsoidal cabochon form, a derivation of the polished lump. The resulting shallow-to-steep convex-top form is especially suited to strong-colored stones having less dispersion than the diamond, such as emerald, ruby, and sapphire. Unless the original raw stone approximates this form, however, cutting results in a considerable loss of bulk. The cabochon-cut form was reserved for relatively flawless rough emerald because, although its lenslike, convex form enhances the limpidity of the stone color, it also amplifies internal flaws. Also occasionally found and related to the cabochon cut are cushion-form emeralds with a square or rectangular contour and rounded upper surface, which sometimes appear in the belt buckles of maharajas.

Carved Emerald Amulets

Especially noteworthy among emerald forms are the large, six-sided (H: *chhakoni*) and eight-sided (H: *athkoni*) tablets or plaques, whose top and bottom have broad, parallel faces. The hexagonal form became typical in Mughal emeralds because it is physically possible to take a cross section, or basal-plane cleavage, from the hexagonal crystal in which emerald most commonly occurs. This naturally symmetrical six-sided form could be altered to an octagon with minimal loss simply by removing two opposite corners of the hexagon (see diagram). These two are the main, characteristic forms in which emerald was used as an amuletic armlet or as a necklace pendant. Their flat surfaces also lent themselves to carving in low relief and/or inscribing.

Emeralds carved and inscribed in low relief are probably among the most impressive achievements of Mughal lapidaries. They set a very high standard that has never been surpassed in India. As a result of this treatment, each of these emeralds has become a unique object that strongly evokes a sense of historic and cultural identity.

To begin with, it is prudent to define the terms used to describe this art for which Indian lapidaries were and are famous. In some gemstone literature, the words *carving* and *engraving* are used interchangeably to refer to the forming and surface ornamentation of hardstones such as emeralds and jade. These words embody entirely different technological concepts, and a clear distinction should be made between them.

Carving, when applied to stone, describes the shaping of hardstones by a *grinding* process in which rotating carving wheels are used in conjunction with an abrasive and a lubricant to shape and decorate the stone. Parts are

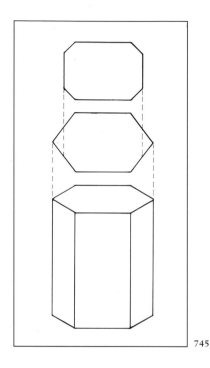

745

746

745. *Typical Indian Emerald Forms in Jewelry*

These cut-emerald (panna) forms are derived from the shape of the natural hexagonal emerald crystal from which cross sections are cut. The resulting hexagonal form is retained to conserve maximum gemstone size (see 741). An emerald crystal in hexagonal form incorporates two face types: six four-sided faces that make the prism and two six-sided faces at top and bottom that close the crystal. Bottom: The original hexagonal emerald crystal. Center: A cross-sectional slice from the hexagonal crystal to form a hexagonally shaped (shashpahlu or chhakona) gemstone having six angles and sides. Top: When two opposite corners of the above are removed, the result is an octagonal (athpahlu) gemstone with eight angles and eight sides (see 815). Other shapes come from irregularly formed crystals.

746. *The Taj Mahal Emerald*

A magnificent Mughal-cut Colombian gemstone in the hexagonal (shashpahlu) form, superbly carved, probably during Shah Jahan's reign (1628–58), with stylized poppies, lilies, and chrysanthemums amid foliage
1 9/16 x 2 in. (4 x 5.1 cm); weight 141.13 karats
Collection Benjamin Zucker, Precious Stones Company, New York

removed from the mass by abrasion, leaving a sludge residue. Forms can be created in the positive (relief), or the negative (intaglio).

Engraving is an inappropriate term to describe the shaping and decoration of stone; it correctly applies to a method of decorating metal, in which the metal is incised with a sharp pointed instrument called a graver or burin. No abrasive is used, and the tool literally gouges out slivers of metal.

Inscribing is an accepted generic term for referring to both stone and metal, but the tools employed for each material differ. Inscribing on stone is still a form of grinding or carving by which linear images, characters, or decorative patterns are imparted to it. Examples include the palindromic squares on jade, the inscriptions on hardstone seals, and the names inscribed on large gemstones by their owners.

To create such patterns or inscriptions and achieve quality results is a tedious, time-consuming process necessitating great caution and patience, especially when the material worked is a valuable hardstone and the scale of the work is small.

Although emerald is a hardstone (Mohs' scale 7.5–8), it is brittle. However, it lends itself to relief carving and inscribing primarily because, aside from basal plane cleavage, it is otherwise almost without cleavage planes (a condition in which a crystallized gemstone will readily split in specific plane directions parallel to a crystal face, leaving a more or less smooth surface). Because of the emeralds' relatively uniform structure, when it is carefully worked there is less danger of its breaking, and it can be carved and polished in any direction.

The ornamentation of emeralds by surface carving and inscribing was widely adopted by Mughal artisans for several reasons. First, large, well-formed crystals were available from which sizable cross-sectioned tablets could be produced. The characteristic internal irregularities of emerald color and structure could be obscured by carving and inscribing to break up and scatter surface light reflection, distracting attention from them. Emeralds' normally abundant inclusions (known by the French term for "garden," *jardin*) often tend to give the stone a semitranslucent appearance, increasing the visibility of the carved pattern, which is also enhanced by the emeralds' relatively deep color.

Second, in Mughal times, it was thought that emeralds' natural potency could be enhanced by carving it with a religious inscription, such as a quotation from the Qur'an, executed in Arabic letters in the Persian language that prevailed then at court. According to Islamic belief, religious inscriptions constitute a form of lawful, spiritual magic (A: *ar-ruhani*), permissible because it is practiced for a good purpose. Carved with such an inscription, an emerald was believed to prevent illness, ward off demons and devils, and counteract inadvertent or deliberate evil enchantment directed at the wearer. In some cases the owner composed a mystic phrase to be inscribed onto the stone.

A single emerald amulet was worn on the left upper arm as an armlet (*bazuband*) because it was nearer to the heart. Normally, the inscribed side of the stone was placed against the arm, and the visible side was decorated in low relief with a floral and vegetable pattern. When large emeralds were used for this purpose, their opposite ends frequently were drilled with a small depression sufficient for the insertion of a wire that like a claw secured it to its setting. (Drilling emerald is relatively easier than drilling ruby.) A large, single such ornamented stone might be worn alone or with two flanking stones as in the traditional *bazuband* format.

The Emerald Industry in India Today

Although knowledge of emeralds in India goes back to prehistoric times, emerald was not mined in India until 1943, when it was found at several locations in Rajasthan. The first green crystals identified as emerald by the Geological Survey of India were discovered near Kaliguman Village in southern Rajasthan. In 1944, the first emerald mining leases were granted and emerald mining was launched in India.

As the mica schist rock belt containing emerald extends in a more or less straight line over a distance of about 125 miles (200 km), other finds inevitably occurred. Places producing emeralds of commercial gemstone quality today include the aforementioned Kaliguman mine, the Rajgarh mines near Ajmer, the Tekhi mines near Deogarh, and the Bowani mines 70 miles (112 km) from Jaipur.

Like those formerly found in Egypt, most of the emeralds found in India contain numer-

747

748

747, 748. *Delhi*
Carved emerald (manovatdar panna) of 217.80 carats
2 x 1½ x ⅜ in. (5.1 x 3.8 x .08 cm)
Collection Allan Caplan, New York

Dated HIJRA 1107 (1695 A.D.), during the reign of the Mughal Emperor Aurangzeb. Emeralds of this form and size were commonly used in an armlet (bazuband) during Mughal times. Typically they were carved with a floral pattern on the obverse side (747), and had a Qur'anic inscription in intaglio on the side worn toward the skin (748). For mounting, it is drilled with small holes to a depth of about 2 mm in a direction parallel to the four sides.

In Mughal times, the potency of emerald was heightened by skilled calligraphic lapidaries who carved its reverse surface with mystic Persian inscriptions, often a quotation from the Qur'an. According to Muslim law (sharia't), such a magical (al- ruhani) inscription is permitted and lawful because it is used for a good purpose. An inscribed emerald worn on the body was therefore a powerful amulet that offered the wearer general protection but also specifically acted to prevent illness, ward off demons and devils, and counteract deliberate or unintentional evil enchantment directed at the wearer. The inscription here is a Shi'ah prayer invoking Ali, which indicates that this is a Nad-i-Ali Shi'ah amulet.

749. Lahore, Punjab, Pakistan. *1849*
Glass-reverse portrait of Maharaja Ranjit Singh (ruled 1780–1839) of the Punjab,
by Kehar Singh Sikh, Lahore
22⅞ x 16 in. (50.8 x 40.6 cm)
Victoria and Albert Museum, London (03530 IS)

In this realistic, unflattering depiction, the ruler's face is heavily pitted with smallpox
scars, and his blind left eye is clearly indicated. Once the owner of the Koh-i-Nur diamond,
he here wears a sarpech, sarpatti, pearl necklace, three armlets with huge emeralds and
diamonds, and bracelets, although he was reputed to be a man of simple tastes.

ous inclusions and flaws and are not considered to be worth much on the world gemstone
market. The best-quality emeralds, found in the
Rajgarh mines, are larger, better in color and
luster, and more transparent than those from
Kaliguman. Those of a deep bluish green compare favorably with Muzo Colombian emeralds
and are purchased by Jaipur lapidary merchants, whose skilled workers cut and tumble
polish them as baroques at a lower cost than is
possible in the West.

Jaipur, Rajasthan, is the main location in
India for the cutting and sale of emeralds.
Because of the many variables in emerald,
quality evaluation is made by individual, subjective judgment. In Jaipur, a top-quality emerald is termed, in Rajasthani, *ke Jaganath Seth
ki Khan,* literally meaning, "from the mine of
Jaganath Seth," referring to an early, much-
esteemed Jaipur gemstone and spice merchant.

When judging emerald quality, either
color (*rang,* meaning degree of greenness, *sabzi*)
or clarity (*saf,* translated as a lack of imperfec-

tions, or *nugs*) is believed to be primary. There
are two schools of thought: *Pani pradhan;
rangna sukshma* (Clarity supreme; color secondary), or *Ranga raja; pani pradhan* (Color is
Raja; clarity secondary). Imperfections or internal emerald flaws include sediments (*gadh*),
cloudiness (*badli*), opacity (*gilazat*), and spots
(*chitti*). Good emerald colors are described as
parrot green (*kirasi*), vegetable green (*sabuni*);
and verdigris green (*zangari*).

New emeralds (*raihani*) of good quality
are still mined in Colombia but are not as
numerous as formerly. As a result, gemstone
merchants in India and elsewhere turned to
recutting old emeralds sold by their owners,
especially during the early part of this century
and after Indian Independence in 1947. With
their loss in status, the rulers of former Indian
states and other landowners found themselves
in greatly reduced circumstances. To help
meet expenses, many were obliged to part with
some of their possessions, in particular loose
gemstones or ornaments set with gemstones.

This source for old emeralds reached a peak
during the 1960s.

At least half the old emeralds that came
onto the market this way were in the form of
baroque beads, a type very common in traditional Indian jewelry. Among them were superior emeralds (*zabari*) of good color and low in
inclusions. Because the Indian beads were
pierced, however, the possibilities of their use
was limited. European gemstone merchants
solved this problem by having some of the best
cut in half through the drilled hole, which resulted in two cabochons that could be reshaped
to a regular form more suited to Western usage.
Much of this reprocessing took place in Paris
and London on stones purchased in India by
European dealers. Those large enough and of
good quality were recut to emerald step-cut
forms. In either case, the results were of far
greater value than the original baroque emerald bead and were more easily sold. This practice has now nearly ended as the sources of
such emeralds is practically exhausted.

Ornaments of high quality, often including outstanding emeralds mounted in jewelry,
still appear from time to time at prestigious
auction house sales in Europe and America.
Those with large Mughal carved emeralds of
good quality now bring extremely high prices.

Pearls

In Indian mythology, pearls (S: *mukta*; H: *moti*;
Tam: *muththu*; P: *marwarid*; A: *durr*; Sing:
mutu) are associated with the moon, personified as the deity Chandra, an apt analogy since
both exhibit a softly radiant, satiny glow, in
pearl called *orient.* According to Hindu mythology, pearls are found not only in oysters, but
also in the temple of an elephant, the hood of
a cobra, the womb of a fish, and the head of a
hog. Pearls have been found at many archaeological sites in India, an indication that since
antiquity they have been admired and in use.
As one of the five great gemstones, pearls have
always appeared in traditional Indian jewelry.

Pearl, though not a mined mineral but an
organic product, is nevertheless included among
the traditional *maharatnanis.* Pearl is a growth
produced by certain varieties of shelled mol-
lusks, namely oysters and some fresh water
mussels, as a means of defense in isolating an
irritating substance that becomes wedged in
its mantle and cannot be expelled. Around this
intrusion the oyster deposits extremely thin,
concentric layers of a substance that consists
of calcium carbonate held together by arago-
nite, a nacreous material. The deposit continues during the oyster's lifetime, and in three to
seven years the result is a pearl, whose size and
color depends on the genus of oyster that
formed it, the time it has remained within the
oyster's mantle, and the properties of the water.
Pearls are especially appreciated in the jewelry
world because, unlike other precious stones,

750. Tamil Nadu

Bazaar oleograph of Hanuman, the monkey god, illustrating an episode that took place in the Ramayana, after the rescue of Rama's wife Sita, when all concerned returned to rule in Ayodhya. Sita rewarded Hanuman for his help with a gift of a magnificent pearl necklace (muththumalai), which he began to crush in his teeth. When the courtiers present ridiculed him, telling him he did not realize their value, he replied that he wanted to see if they contained Rama and Sita. Again they derided him, asking if he thought that Rama and Sita were everywhere, even in his own body? Tearing open his chest, he revealed to the astonished throng miniature images of Rama and Sita in the wound.

751. Patiala, Punjab

The Maharajadhiraja, His Highness Lieut. Col. Shri Sir Bhupendra Singh Mahindar Bahadur, G.C.I.E., G.B.E., born 1891

This photograph, taken about 1911, epitomizes the Western romantic image of what an Indian maharaja should look like. On his head he wears a magnificent sarpech of diamonds and pendant emeralds executed by Cartier, Paris. Additionally, his turban (pagri) is ornamented with an egret crest (kalgi), a pearl-tasseled turra, and side strands of alternating pearls and emeralds with diamond pendants. Around his neck is a necklace of fourteen strands of natural matched pearls, the lowest hung with thirty-nine pendant emeralds, and a central, large diamond, possibly the Sancy, which he is reputed to have owned. He also wears medals and three badges of British-Indian orders granted to him; emerald-set armlets; and a five-strand pearl "sacred thread."

they can be used as found and only need to be drilled or pierced.

The most important sources of natural pearls, which until 1908 were the only kind in use, were the oyster shoals on sandbanks off the island of Bahrein in the Persian Gulf, where the best-quality large pearls were found, called Basara pearls, and the waters of the Gulf of Manaar between India and Sri Lanka's west coast, where the pearls, according to Tavernier, were "most beautiful but rarely exceeding 3 or 4 carats in weight," and are called Kahil pearls. All natural pearls that came from Asian waters were termed *oriental* pearls in the West.

Pearls from both these sources were long sought by the potentates and the wealthy of India. Marco Polo relates that the King of Maabar (Thanjavur) "controlled the pearl trade in the area, and … nobody is permitted to take [large pearls] out of his kingdom … unless he manages to do it secretly … because the king desires to reserve all such to himself; and so … the quality he has is something almost incredible." The same can be said of the Indian maharajas closer to our time, as the many photographs of them taken during the nineteenth and early twentieth centuries clearly show. The natural pearls of the Maharaja of Patiala are believed to be among the world's finest.

752. Bombay, Maharashtra
Designed by Ambaji Shinde, made by Nanubhai Jewellers, Bombay, before 1960
Modern pearl necklace (moti mala) with diamonds set in platinum and at the pearl holes
Length 15⅜ in. (39 cm)

The Pearl-Fishing Industry

Sri Lankan pearl-fishing, now less active than before the development of the cultured pearl, is described here as it was in its heyday. The trade was under government control and followed an annual seasonal pattern divided into two periods, each inaugurated by religious ceremonies. One began in March and lasted through April or mid-May, and the second, in August, continued through September. The reason for this division was the changing of wind patterns during the northeast and southwest monsoons. Between the two comes a suitable period during which the small pearl fishing boats could safely be used; otherwise, the waters were too rough for them. A fleet of from 150 to 250 dhowlike sailboats, manned by ten rowers, a steersman, and ten pearl divers (Tam: *salapangkulippon*), left port in groups of 50 to 60 in the middle of the night, when the wind direction prevailed from land to sea, so they could arrive at the shallow pearl-fishing banks about sunrise. By the time of their return around noon, the wind would have reversed direction to blow toward land. The area fished was six to eight miles northwest of Manaar Island, in the Gulf of Manaar near the coast of the Goajira Peninsula. Once there, the pearlers transferred to small boats anchored at buoy- and flag-marked locations.

Each fleet brought with them a shark charmer (H: *hai banda*; Tam: *kadal-katti*; Sing: *pillal karras*) who loudly recited charms to prevent dreaded shark attacks on the divers. Marco Polo said, "Their charm holds good for that day only, for at night they dissolve the charm so that the fishes can work mischief at their will."

Divers ranged from teenage boys to men of seventy, who, like the gemstone miners of India, were grossly underpaid. When a signal gun was fired, the almost naked divers descended from their boats in groups of five, while the other five who alternated with them worked ropes from the boats.

Each boat had a side landing platform from which the diver descended standing on a 40-pound (18 kg) flat granite stone with an attached rope; another rope circled the diver's body under his arms. The diver took a deep breath (some placed clamps on their noses) and descended to a depth of between twenty and sixty feet (6–18 m). The released stone was then pulled up for the next diver's use.

Pearl diving required stamina and speed. Most divers could stay underwater for fifty to sixty seconds, a few as long as ninety seconds. Wearing leather gloves to protect the hands, in each dive they collected from twelve to a hundred oysters with irregular shell surfaces—an indication they might contain pearls. Shell size also indicates age. The oldest, about seven years, contain the largest pearls. The shells were placed in a net from which another rope passed to the boat above. When a diver reached his endurance limit, he jerked his body rope to signal the helper to bring him up quickly. The oyster net was then pulled up to the boat. Each diver made between forty and fifty descents daily. In a normal season, the fleet could collect as many as 45 million oysters. The workday ended at about noon with a fired signal gun. The fleet returned in daylight in order to discourage thieving.

Oysters were piled up on mats laid out within a beach enclosure (*kottu*) and divided into four equal heaps. One quarter went to the divers, who could take away or sell their share, and the rest was government property to be sold by a government agent that day at auction. The bidders gambled on how many pearls the shells might contain and their quality. In general, the yield was low.

Oysters were left exposed to the sun so that their shells opened and they died and putrefied, which facilitated pearl extraction but produced an abominable stench and swarms of flies. Once the pearls were removed, the debris was washed to recover any small pearls overlooked. Occasionally a worker might try to steal the best pearls he found by swallowing them. Anyone suspected of having done so was incarcerated and given a strong emetic to induce vomiting.

Pearls are classed by size by passing them through brass sieves from small to large, then sorted for color, and finally valued. Size, relative roundness, iridescence, color, and freedom from blemishes are all considered. Natural pearls possessing all these qualities are rare and obtain high prices. Gathering enough of them in matching sizes, color, and quality takes a long time, which explains why matched strands of natural or cultured pearls are extremely expensive.

Indian pearl merchants (*tasavi*) classify natural pearls into three basic grades; *gasandi*, the best quality; *golava*, first quality; and *gola-va*, second quality. Tavernier said all qualities were acceptable in India because "the Indians are not as particular as we are,... [and] ba-

◄ 753. Lucknow, Uttar Pradesh
Gold necklace (tikdi har) with pearls
Courtesy Shanti Vijay and Sons, New Delhi

754. Tamil Nadu
Four-strand pearl necklace (muthumalai) with crescent-shaped (valarugira-kadukkan)
central pendant of gold, set with rubies and diamonds, with a pearl fringe
Length 15¾ in. (40 cm)
Private Collection

The pendant is supported by four strands of 132 beads, each made of a cluster of
seed pearls and separated by small green enameled beads, each of five to six units
kept apart by gold spacers. At the back are four elongated gold, green enameled beads.

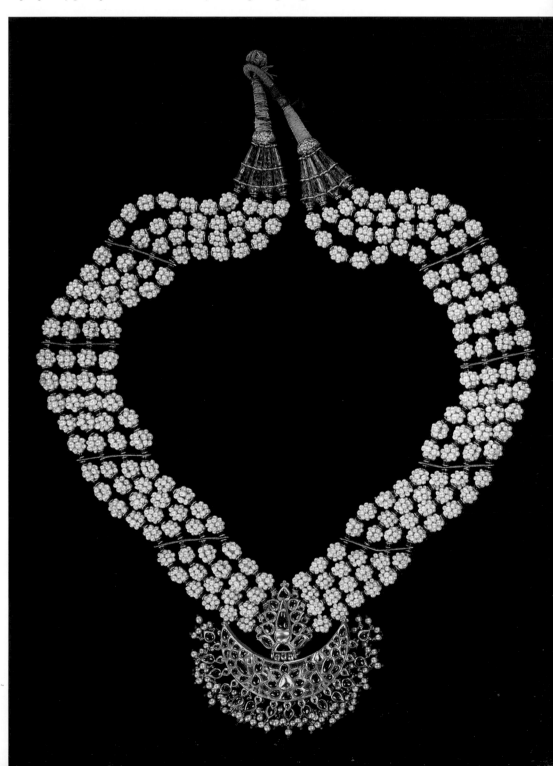

roques as well as the round" all found a purchaser. He also said that in his time the Portuguese at Goa operated the largest Asian
trade in pearls and gemstones. Merchants preferred to go there to sell their best pearls and
gemstones because "they had there full liberty
to sell [at any price agreed upon], whereas, in
their own country, if they showed anything to
the Kings or Princes, they were compelled to
sell at whatever price [the purchasers] pleased
to fix." Goa continued as an active pearl market,
until it was absorbed into present-day India after
1947. Today, pearl trading centers at Bombay.

Most of the pearls used in traditional
Indian jewelry are pierced and strung as beads.
Pearl drilling requires care and patience
because the hole must be very small (by international agreement today 0.3 mm), straight,
and centered or the pearl will hang off-balance
and make the strand appear to be irregular,
thus reducing its value. Indian pearl boring
was a hereditary occupation in the past, and
Bombay borers were and still are famous for
their ability to drill even very small seed pearls,
which even today are strung in networks used
in India for head ornaments, necklaces, and
bracelets. Some pearls were drilled halfway
through and mounted in ornaments by
cementing them onto a wire post joined to the
main body of the object. Large and small pearls
were and are commonly used as pendants.

Today cultured pearls are used extensively in Indian jewelry. They came into mass production after 1908, when Mikimoto of Japan
received a patent for producing round pearls
with a preformed oyster-shell nucleus inserted
in the mantle of a live oyster.

▲ 755. Bikaner, Rajasthan
Women celebrating the Govardhana festival puja, which commemorates the incident in Hindu mythology in which Krishna, by one uplifted hand, raised up the Govardhana mountain in Vrindavana to provide shelter for people and cattle against a vengeful rainstorm instigated by Indra. All wear a seed-pearl head ornament (moti-jala), here used by upper-class married women. They are creating a floor pattern (mandana) in colored powder pigments, at whose center they have modeled a mud image of Krishna.

756. Bikaner, Rajasthan
Baniya woman wearing gold bracelets covered with a network of pearls (moti-jali) and other pearl ornaments

757. Bikaner, Rajasthan
Pair of pearl and gold bracelets of eight half-cylindrical, hinged sections, with screw clasp
Outer diameter 3⅛ in. (8.2 cm); inner diameter 2½ in. (6.3 cm)
Courtesy Chhote Bharany, New Delhi

Their exterior is completely covered with a closely strung pearl network (moti-jali) of square-woven, uniform-diameter seed pearls that cover and are attached to the gold units, whose interiors and top and bottom edges are all polychrome enameled.

 756
757

Synthetic Gemstones

Because gemstones in India are traditionally thought to be far more than simple decorative objects but also to have complex mystic meaning, one is inclined to wonder what ancient gemologists would say about whether man-created synthetic gemstones (*thodarpana mani*) function in a manner similar to the natural which they essentially approximate. Do they also act as a medium for planetal influences, and do they have magical properties and prophylactic qualities?

Judging from the existence of an extensive industry in the manufacture and cutting of synthetic gemstones for use in Indian jewelry, centered in and around Tiruchchirappalli, Tamil Nadu, South India, it would appear that a large segment of the contemporary gemstone-using public think those questions irrelevant. Not concerned with metaphysics, they appreciate the more affordable cost of synthetic gemstones as compared with that of the originals. To a layman, synthetic, cabochon, or faceted gemstones are indistinguishable from those made of natural substances. Using synthetic imitations therefore gives the object the appearance of greater value than its actual worth and is just as effective in heightening the wearer's social prestige.

The gemstone-synthesizing process initially was invented to duplicate the ruby. The first commercially viable process for creating synthetic gemstone occurred in France, where in 1904 Auguste Victor Louis Verneuil finally published his method, one of several later in use, but still the most common and economical process in practice. Once known, the industrial production of synthetic gemstones rapidly expanded in Europe and America. In 1911 Verneuil added the synthesis of blue sapphire to his repertoire, and soon afterward came colorless zircon, spinel, and other stones.

The chemical composition of these gemstones are reconstituted in the laboratory, and the conditions of high pressure and temperature under which they were created in nature are duplicated by a specially designed apparatus. The result, after about four hours, is a single, solid, cone-shaped, 200–500-carat crystal called a *boule* (*dalam*), whose composition, color (or the lack of it), and properties such as hard-

758. Tiruchchirappalli, Tamil Nadu

Lapidary (ratthinaviyapari) preparing synthetic ruby gemstones (thodarpana manikkam) for hand faceting by mounting them on a dop stick covered on one end with a lac compound that holds them in place.

ness and optical characteristics are identical with those of the natural gemstone it duplicates.

Cutting and polishing synthetic gemstones began in India around 1918, and the boules used then were imported from Europe. By 1946, the volume had grown considerably, and today this essentially hand-manufacturing industry involves about 25,000 artisans engaged in the various stages of production. In 1956, boule manufacture began in India, when the joint-venture Indo-Swiss Synthetic Gem Manufacturing Co. Ltd. was established at Mettuppalaiyam in Tamil Nadu. This source now supplies the ever-growing demand for synthetic ruby, sapphire, and zircon gemstone boules processed by lapidaries into the synthetic gemstones ubiquitous today in Indian jewelry.

Entrepreneurs purchase the boules and sell them to about sixty-five small workshops in this area, where about three hundred workers, in the only mechanically powered process in this industry, after cleaving the boules longitudinally in half to relieve internal stresses, saw them into cubes of required sizes. To a lesser extent, cleaved boules are also divided manually with hammer and chisel. These results are then passed to outworkers in Tiruchchirappalli and nearby agricultural villages, where part-time workers, in home workshops, process them into faceted stones on a hand-powered bow lathe. In this case, the large abrasive wheel impregnated with either diamond borte or corundum is fixed vertically, and against this the dop-mounted stones are pressed. The process of faceting (*vandigai*) and polishing (*merugu*) is carried out at various locations that specialize in different stone sizes and girdle outlines, including cabochon cut (*paymaravattu pattai*); faceted, round, and brilliant cut (*kamalam pattai*); square cut (*sathukam pattai*); oval cut (*andakaram pattai*); and triangular cut (*mukkonam pattai*).

In southern India, various colorless synthetic stones are used to simulate diamond (*vairam*), such as (in order of popularity) zircon (*tursava*) or white sapphire (*vellai nilamani*); red or ruby stones (*sivappu*); blue or sapphire stones (*nilam*); and green or emerald stones (*pachchaikkal*). Faceted stones are used in contemporary Westernized styles of jewelry. Cabochon-cut synthetic rubies are especially popular in contemporary traditional styles of ornaments in southern India.

Because emeralds are high in price or often unavailable, green hardstones have been and still are used in Indian jewelry. Green hardstones used this way include chalcedony stained green with chromic acid, green garnet, green sapphire (oriental emerald), green zircon, plasma, and phrase. In some cases, clear

rock crystal backed with a green-colored foil was used. In old jewelry where this was done, the substrate green pigment has sometimes disintegrated and the subterfuge is apparent.

Green-glass imitations to simulate emerald (and red glass for ruby) started in India soon after the correct metallic oxide necessary to produce glass of the proper color was known. Green glass simulating emerald baroque beads are made either with a mold or by the wound-glass bead-making method. Some are even carved in the same way as actual emerald. From a distance, Indian emerald and ruby glass simulations are convincing because the refractive index of glass encompasses that of emerald and ruby. Techniques were even invented to simulate natural emerald inclusions, so that glass imitations, called *paste* in the West, often display a remarkable casual similarity to the actual stone, until closely or scientifically examined.

759. Tiruchchirappalli, Tamil Nadu
After the lac is heated to soften it, the stone is pressed into it and the compound is allowed to cool and harden. Putting this "handle" on a gemstone permits it to be easily manipulated during shaping operations on a skeif or lapidary's gemstone shaping and faceting wheel.

760. Mathura, Uttar Pradesh ➤
Detail of a zari (metallic-yarn) embroidered horse's saddlecloth (jhul) employing imitation pearls in profusion, couched gold zari wire of many kinds, and spangles. Articles like this one, designed for a wedding procession, as well as theatrical costumes and crowns, often employ imitation pearls and synthetic gemstones. They are a specialty of Mathura zardozi embroiderers, almost all of whom are men.

Gemstone Color Symbolism and Gem Therapy

Color symbolism pervades the spiritual thinking of all Indian cultures, and to a great extent springs from an elemental logic that connects nature with human thought and behavior. Indians imbue all gemstones, particularly those with distinct, pure colors, with symbolic significance. As exemplified by the *nava-ratna*, gemstones are mythologically connected with the planets, which generally are believed to exert an influence on all aspects of human life.

Gemstones in India are used, both internally and externally, by some people to eliminate illness. In the latter case, a powder (*bhasma*) is made by crushing and burning the stones and ingesting the result. The patient is said to benefit from the stones' active principle, which is the specific cosmic ray color, connected with their associated planet, which they emanate. Gemstones are said to restore the equilibrium in the human spiritual force field, which is centered in the body's seven spinal yogic *chakras,* each of which is associated with an endocrine gland whose secretions pass directly into the blood or lymph system.

In the commercial world of colored gemstones, their colors are not scientifically, rationally standardized, though this *has* been done for diamonds. What exists is an intangible, subjective appraisal of color guided by a gemologist's or dealer's abstract image of what, over the centuries, they have decided is the most desirable color for a specific colored (or "colorless") gemstone. Only a limited number of gemstones achieve this most desirable color; the rest are merely variants of the ideal. Closeness to the desired color considerably heightens its value.

Red, the color of ruby, among Hindus is a warm, aggressive color associated by its intensity with the sun, blood, and sensual emotion, all essential to human and animal life. In gem therapy, ruby is used to treat blood diseases such as anemia, heart diseases, and conditions of the circulatory system, as well as to eliminate fevers and prolong life.

Sapphire blue is a cool, passive color identified with spirituality by most religions. It is connected with concepts of space because blue is the color of the all-pervading sky beyond which lies the infinite universe. According to gem therapy, the sapphire induces tranquillity and concentration and is used to cure rheumatic pain, ulcers, and to treat eye afflictions.

Green of the emerald, which combines blue (water) and yellow (sun) is an intermediate color between warm and cool colors. Since the inception of Islam, emerald has been adopted as a symbolic analogue of that religion as green is believed to have been favored by the Prophet Muhammad. Perhaps one explanation for this lies in green's connection with plant life, whose reproduction depends on water and sunlight. In gem therapy, emerald is used for curing high blood pressure, headache, neuralgia, to increase appetite, as an aid in digestion, and as an antidote to poison.

White, like the diamond, actually has no color and is the universal symbol of primal creation and unblemished purity. White light has long been known to embody the seven principal colors of the spectrum, which can be seen when light is refracted by the dispersion of a faceted white diamond. White, the essence of light, is diametrically opposed to black or darkness and its negative connotation of death. Diamond in gem therapy is used for sexual disorders, infections, and in the treatment of cancer.

Pearls as Medicine

Natural pearls of no commercial value (*thool*) were washed in lime juice, then crushed into a powder, in rose water, and eaten with betel as a refined kind of lime. Pearl powder was also used in liquids for medicinal purposes as prescribed in the Indian Ayurvedic and Unani systems of medicine. Ranjit Singh, ruler of the Punjab from 1799 to 1839, is reported to have been a heavy drinker who liked to arrange special drinking parties with the object of inebriating all present. On such occasions, he drank a special raisin wine mixed with a quantity of pearls ground to a powder, which he offered to favored guests.

When such a powder was prepared, the pearls were purified by boiling them in water with herbs and flowers, then placed in a covered crucible and calcined to a powder called pearl ash (S: *mukta bhasma;* Tam: *muththuchchunnam*). The *Indian Materia Medica* recommends pearl ash for the treatment of urinary diseases, for checking a feeling of irritation during urination, in treating gonorrhea, low fevers resulting in burning sensations of the eye, palm, or sole, and as an aphrodisiac.

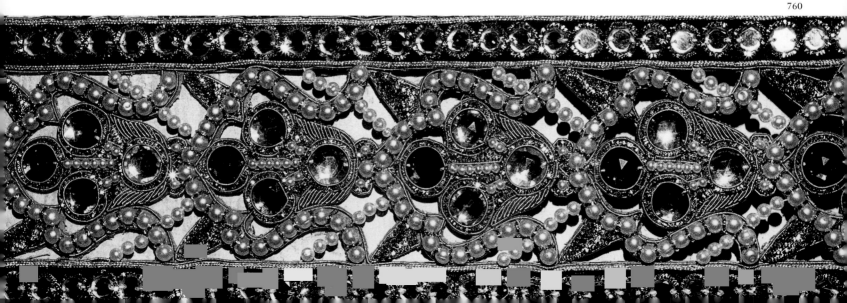

6 THE MUGHAL JEWELRY TRADITION

One of the richest periods in the development of traditional jewelry in India occurred during the Mughal dynasty, from the sixteenth to nineteenth century. Its most important rulers were Babur (ruled 1526–30); Humayun (ruled 1530–40, then 1555–56); Akbar (ruled 1556–1605); Jahangir (ruled 1605–27); Shah Jahan (ruled 1628–58); and Aurangzeb (ruled 1658–1707). Their reigns covered a period of 181 years, after which the dynasty struggled on until 1858, when the last Mughal emperor was deposed by the British after the Sepoy Mutiny and banished to Rangoon, Burma. In this short time, the Mughal design style dominated all fields of artistic production and its influence spread throughout the entire Indian subcontinent. Its energy, compelling logic, and endlessly inventive forms are so vital they survived the Mughal's political demise. Mughal design concepts have become ingrained in the Indian jewelry idiom to the extent that they will probably always influence future Indian design developments.

In the past, the evolution of the arts in India derived its impetus essentially from imperial will, sponsorship, and the concentration of wealth and power at the ruler's disposal. The ruler, through patronage, created a material royal lifestyle that was emulated by courtiers. Mughal culture owes much to the artisans' unhindered opportunity to fully realize their creative capacities.

The Mughal legacy exists today in structures such as mosques, forts, and palaces but relatively few extant decorative objects. To animate this environment, we must turn to the miniature paintings that depict the *dramatis personae* who give this era of cultural history a human dimension. Many of these portraits have historic value as relatively faithful depictions of their subjects. Of greater importance here is their finely detailed representations of the jewelry the subjects wore. When we come to the late nineteenth century Mughal style, their designs illustrate the height of Mughal jewelry decadence or, alternatively, goldsmith work of the highest technical achievement, depending on one's point of view. Their splendor provided the subject with the requisite appearance of oriental opulence that so appeals to Westerners and Indians who romanticize the glories of the Mughal past.

Mughal Ceremony and Jewelry in Miniature Paintings

761

Considering their minute scale, this representation of jewelry is a technical feat. Its execution called for a style of painting developed just for this purpose, known as "fine work" (H: *mahin kari*), or "the painting of pearls" (H: *moti mahavar*). *Mahavar* is carmine, a red organic dye contained in lac, used to color a pigment employed as a ground color when depicting gold jewelry. Over this base was painted pure gold pigment made by finely grinding gold leaf in a dish with honey, washing away the honey, then adding some gum as a binder. When dry, the painted gold was burnished with an agate burnisher to brighten its appearance, then at times stamped with a miniature pattern punch to create a design or texture on its surface. Silver prepared in the same way was painted over a white ground. (In old miniatures, silver has turned dark due to oxidation, unlike pure gold, which resists it.) Colored stones were represented by painting a transparent color, most often red for rubies and green for emeralds, over a burnished gold or silver ground, respectively.

Pearls are represented in profusion in most portraits of both Mughal women and men. They were painted with a special, very fine, round-ended brush (P: *danaki kalam,* seed or dot painting brush). The white pigment was laid down and often left in relief as a small, round dot that cast its own tiny shadow, heightening the illusion of dimension.

Mughal rulers commissioned miniature paintings of court events to allow them to savor the pleasure of the occasion in the future. In characteristic detail, these paintings illustrate the hieratic pageantry of court life in which the ruler was glorified as a semidivine being. Courtiers publicly demonstrated their fidelity at ceremonial state occasions in a ritual that followed strictly enforced decorum and sumptuary rules. On such occasions the emperor wore elaborate ornaments in a lavish display of wealth that confirmed his authority. As the sovereign he was beyond any petty criticism that might be leveled against him for indulging in ostentatious display—it was his birthright.

In any tradition-oriented society, concepts of personal relationships are vital. Rank among members of the court became particularly obvious in Mughal court rituals. Procedures and ceremonies followed a carefully orchestrated sequence in which the roles of each individual present could be identified by the clothing and ornaments worn. Such traditions not only helped to establish the idea that dress and ornament symbolized more than worldliness but also had political and spiritual implications.

In general, except at the highest levels of society in Indian culture, personal appearance is more important than the appearance of the environment in which one lives, and a proportionately larger percentage of financial resources goes to personal dress than to home embellishment. In Mughal society in particular, a noble was expected to maintain a standard of dress and ornamentation for himself, his family, and his servants that reflected his social and political standing.

Particularly telling were the dimensions of the gemstones used in the court ornaments, the most important power symbols that could only be afforded by the wealthy. Certain taboos on the use of materials prevailed, such as the prohibition against the use of gold for foot ornaments by all excepting the ruler or those granted royal permission to do so. Waiving this prohibition became a form of political reward envied by others.

761. Jaipur, Rajasthan. *c. 1775* (opposite page)
Mughal window-appearance (jharoka) style miniature portrait of Maharaja Sawai Madho Singh (ruled 1760–78)
9¾ x 6⅞ (24.8 x 17.5 cm)
Courtesy Sotheby's, New York

Typical Mughal-style ornaments shown here include, on the head: a gold band (sarpatti) with integral aigrette (sarpech), set with emeralds and emerald bead pendants; a feather plume (kalghi) weighted with emerald beads; a tassel (turra-i-Marwarid) possibly of diamonds (silver paint, now tarnished); two oval head ornaments (kut-biladar) (also tarnished silver paint); and a gold-wire ear hoop strung with a central ruby flanked by two pearls (bala). On his neck is a tight pearl neckband (galapatti) and a four-strand (char lara) pearl necklace (motimala) with spaced emerald beads, each strand with a central gold pendant (jugni) set with emeralds.

◄ **762. Jaipur Rajasthan.** *c. 1790*
Miniature painting of a woman combing her hair
Victoria and Albert Museum, London (IS 142)

She wears necklaces, earrings, armlets, and bracelets with pearls, all in the style of the Mughal-Rajput tradition. One of the shorter strands of twenty-seven pearls (nakshatra mala), according to astrology, alludes to the twenty-seven asterisms or lunar mansions in the moon's path.

763. Jaipur, Rajasthan
Gold necklace (baleora) of seven chains ornamented with seven clasp units (five of them floral roundels) decorated with gemstones. The back clasp closes by a screw. A foliate, gemstone-set pendant (dhukdhuki or jugni) is attached to the central unit.
Courtesy Sotheby's, London

This form was worn until the early twentieth century by male Brahmans and Jain merchants.

764. Delhi. 19th century
Gold necklace (baleora) with pendant (nam) set with rubies, emeralds, and diamonds
Length 7½ in. (19 cm); weight 133 g
Courtesy Sotheby's, London

The articulated band design has thirteen flower-head units that interlock to form a continuous band. Another form of this design was established in Mughal times (see 763).

The Emperor's Weighing Festival

Before leaving India on his last voyage there, in late October 1665, the gemstone merchant Jean Baptiste Tavernier took his leave of Emperor Aurangzeb, who invited him to stay long enough to witness the six-to-nine-day Festival of Weighing the Emperor (P: tuladan), traditionally carried out annually in celebration of the emperor's birthday. The emperor was weighed against gold, silver, textiles, and other valuables taken from the treasury, all given away afterward to charity. Aurangzeb promised that once the festivities were over, as a special favor never before granted to any other "Frank," he would give the order for Tavernier to be allowed to see his best gemstones, objects of pride to Aurangzeb despite his often expressed disinterest. Greatly honored, Tavernier accepted.

After the weighing ceremony, a long retinue of gift-bearing family members, nobility, provincial governors, and high officials filed past. Each presented a gift, which was either accepted, selected from several offered, or returned. Those accepted were immediately evaluated, and scribes recorded them. Tavernier reported, "On this day Aurangzeb receives diamonds, rubies, emeralds, pearls, gold, silver … carpets, brocades, elephants, camels, and horses worth more than [then] £ 2,250,000." The total value of these gifts without doubt surpassed that of what Aurangzeb gave away in his weighing ceremony.

On November 2, 1665, Tavernier was taken to see Aurangzeb. Akil Khan, chief of the Jewel Treasury (toshakana), ordered four eunuchs to bring in the gemstones and jewels, which arrived on two lacquered and gilded wooden trays. The objects were counted three times, then a list of them was prepared by three scribes also present. Tavernier weighed some of the gemstones shown to him and made drawings of them, which were published in his book. By so doing he performed a service of great historic importance to the world of gemstones.

Akil Khan placed in Tavernier's hands the Grand Mughal Diamond presented to Shah Jahan by Mir Jumla. Tavernier described it as a round rose-cut stone, higher on one side, with a small notch at the basal margin and a little flaw inside. Its water (transparency) was "beautiful," and it weighed 319.5 rattis, equal to 280 carats, the ratti being equal to seven-eighths of our carat. The diamond in its rough state had weighed 900 ratis, equivalent to 787.5 carats, and had several flaws but was nevertheless extremely rare.

Tavernier observed that "if this stone had been in Europe it would have been treated differently … some good pieces would have been (cleaved) from it, and (the final result) would have weighed more than it does." Instead, the stone was ground down by …"Sieur Hortensio Borgio, a Venetian who … was reproached for having spoilt the stone, which ought to have retained a greater weight … the King fined him 10,000 rupees, and would have taken more if he had possessed it."

Mughal miniature painters were noted for their ability to observe, and particulars such as personal ornaments did not escape their attention. These paintings give a fairly accurate account of many of the styles of ornament in use, especially those executed in the seventeenth and eighteenth centuries, although their extremely small scale does not permit highly detailed representation and, in this respect, they cannot match the glowing descriptions of contemporary foreign observers.

The basic types of men's ornaments given here with their Mughal names are typical of Mughal times. Within each category, a wide variety of forms, materials, and decoration techniques were used. Some have persisted to the present, perhaps more so in rural but also urban areas, especially in northern India on an occasion such as a wedding, when the groom often becomes a Mughal "prince" for the duration of the event. Although men's ornaments are not as numerous as the forms worn by women, it was common practice on special occasions, particularly in late Mughal times, for a man to wear his own or a borrowed ornament that might also be worn by a woman, such as a necklace.

765. Bikaner, Rajasthan
Maharaja Colonel Raj Rasheshwar Narendra Sri Sir Ganga Singh Bahadur, G.C.I.E., K.C.S.I., of Bikaner (born 1880; ruled 1887–1943), installed on a scale for a tuladan ceremony in the Lallgarh Palace, Bikaner. To celebrate his fiftieth (Golden Jubilee) year of rule, 1937, he was weighed against gold ingots. He weighed 14 stones and 8 pounds, and the ingots had an equivalent value of Rs 3,021,915. Its cash equivalent was given to the Golden Jubilee Fund and distributed as charity.

أعظم نمودند نام ردر منزل بازه گم خجری دنوشمالی که رست و آثر پشتناه اوسندیده است

766. Delhi; or Agra, Uttar Pradesh. *Attributed to Manohar. 17th century*
Mughal miniature painting of the Emperor Jahangir (ruled 1604–27), from the Tuzuk-i-Jahangiri *(Memoirs of Jahangir) manuscript*
11⅛ x 5 in. (28.4 x 12.8 cm)
The British Museum, London. Bequest of P. C. Manuk, Esq. and Miss G. M. Coles, through the N.A.C.F. (1948.10-9069)

In the ceremony (tuladan) depicted, Prince Khurram, Jahangir's son, the future Emperor Shah Jahan, is being weighed on his sixteenth lunar birthday in 1607. The same ceremony was performed on the sovereign's birthday. This custom spread all over India, even to Hindu courts. In Travancore (Kerala), the raja wore ceremonial jewelry, and special gold coins (tulabhara kasu) were struck for the occasion (tulapurushadanam). In some of the trays below is an assortment of jewelry, intended either as presents for the occasion or to be used as counterweights, then distributed to charity.

Mughal Men's Ornaments

Head

Bali: A circlet earring in the form of a gold wire hoop, strung with two pearls separated by a ruby or emerald

Kalghi: Black heron's plumes with a pearl suspended at its tip, its stem bound with gold or silver wire, worn projecting backward in the turban, normally behind the sarpech

Mukut: A multipeaked crown in precious metal, frequently ornamented with gemstones and enamel. Although seldom in actual use during early Mughal times, the *mukut* was often depicted in miniature paintings symbolically hovering over the head of a ruler. In the late Mughal period, *mukuts* achieved a state of great elaboration and were worn by both the Mughal emperor and provincial rulers.

Sarpech: A spray of gemstones worn at the front or side of a turban, called *jiqa* in Persian (see page 380)

Turra: Turban ornament, often in the form of a bird from whose beak is suspended a multiple-strand pearl tassel, each ending with an emerald and a small gold tinsel tassel

Neck

Latkan: A precious-metal, gemstone-set pendant of various forms, worn singly near the neck or placed in the center of a *mala* necklace

Mala: A long single or double strand of pearls, alone or interspersed with ruby and/or emerald beads. Several in graduated lengths were often worn together. Strings of pearls and gemstone beads were also worn around the head over the turban.

Ta'wiz: Amulet of precious metal, without or with gemstones, usually bearing a religious inscription. A special type, called *haldili* (see page 116), made of jade, is often inlaid with gemstones *kundan* style.

Arms

Bazuband: A one- or three-part hinged armlet ornament, often with a central inscribed gemstone amulet, tied to the upper arm with cords. In late Mughal times, it might also be worn at the front of the turban.

Kara: Penannular wrist bracelet with animal-head terminals. Other types of wrist bracelets were also worn, some set with gemstones.

Fingers

Anguthi: Precious-metal ring set with a gemstone or gemstones

Bagh Nakh: Weapon ring in bar shape, with end holes for two or four fingers, and attached with four curving steel claws. Worn concealed in the palm of the hand, it was used like an animal's claws to surprise attack an enemy in hand-to-hand combat.

Muhr: Seal ring inscribed with the owner's

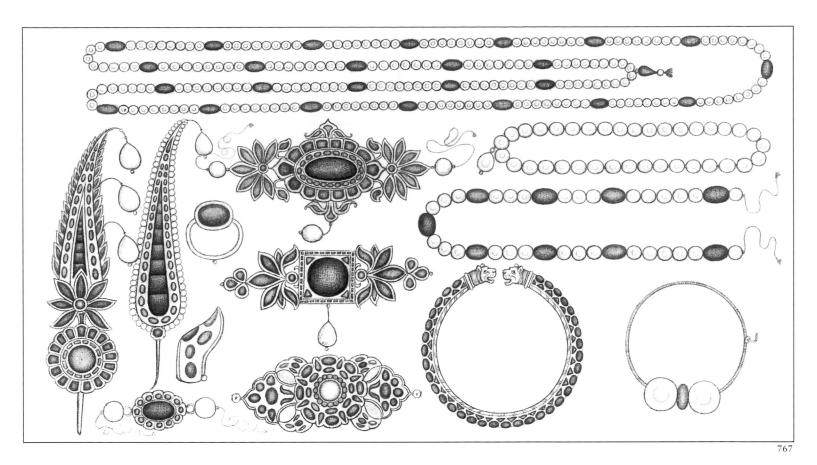

767

name, or a religious text, applied to attest to the authenticity of a document (see page 259)

Subha: Hand-held rosary of 33, 66, or 99 beads used for counting prayers, made of pearls, precious or semiprecious stones, coral, wood, and a variety of other materials (see page 72)

Zihgir; shast: Archer's thumb ring used in the Mongolian system of arrow release, made of jade, gold often set with gemstones, agate, ivory, or coral (see page 267)

Torso

Baldric: Broad gold brocaded belt with enameled or gemstone-set buckle, worn diagonally on the chest over the left shoulder as an ornament but also to support a sword

DAGGERS

Sheath-type daggers were worn thrust into the girdle or under a belt, and those with highly decorated hilts and scabbards can be considered as a form of ornament. They were frequently given as royal gifts at state levees or formal receptions (*durbars*), to honor a guest or a deserving courtier. Hilts frequently took the shape of a pistol grip or an animal head, such as that of a horse, lion, tiger, or antelope. Some of the more common dagger types are the following:

Bank: Curved blade and a hilt with a knuckle guard

Bich'hwa: Doubly curved, double-edged blade, resembling a scorpion's tail (hence the name) and a strong central rib

Jambiya: Curved, double-edged blade with a central rib and a straight, pistol-grip or animal-head hilt

Jamdhar: Straight, broad blade, with two handles

Jamdhar dolikaneh: Straight-bladed, with two points

Jamdhar sehlikaneh: Straight-bladed, three points

Katara: Wide, straight, triangular blade

Khanjar: Curved, double-edged blade

Peshkabz: Straight, single-edged, T-shaped sectioned blade and slender point, meant to penetrate armor

Kamarband: Belt of precious metals. Some, set with gemstones, are represented in miniature paintings. These could be worn with summer dress or over a sash (*patka*) worn over a robe.

Yakbandi: Sword belt with mountings and a sling with hooks used to support a sword hanging at the left side

Ankles

Paizeb: Ankle bracelet, usually of chain construction, in precious metal, with or without gemstones

767–69. Faizabad, Oudh (Avadh), now Uttar Pradesh. 1774
Watercolor paintings (possibly by Nevasi Lal, Mohan Singh, or another local Indian artist) from the Gentil Album showing Mughal ornaments for men (767; see also 761) and women (768, 769) Each page 14½ x 21 in. (37 x 53.5 cm) Victoria and Albert Museum, London (IS 25-1980, folios 33, 48, 49)

French adventurer and collector Jean Baptiste Gentil was employed from 1763 to 1775 by Shuja 'ud-Daula at his court in Faizabad, a flourishing, strongly Muslim cultural center. In 1774, Gentil supervised the compilation of a fifty-eight-page album of Company paintings that record faithfully the traditional styles of Mughal jewelry, most of which were developed during the earlier apogee of Mughal art and culture. Many examples illustrated here closely resemble current jewelry types, underscoring the vitality of this tradition.

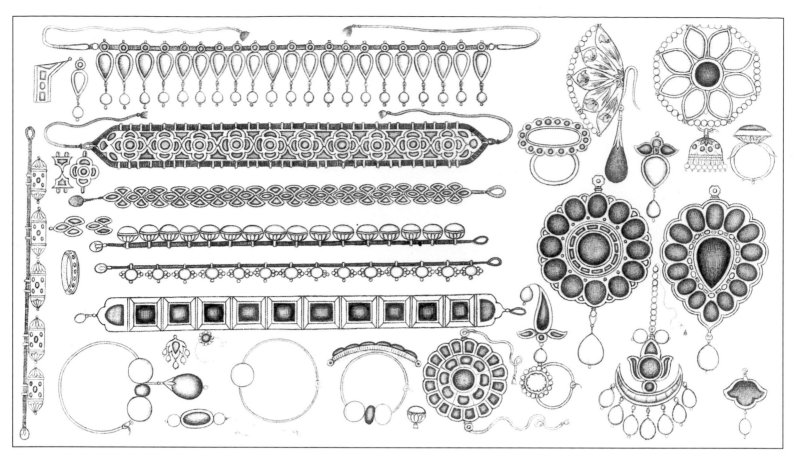

768, 769. Faizabad, Oudh (Avadh), now Uttar Pradesh.
Mughal women's ornaments from the Gentil Album, 1774

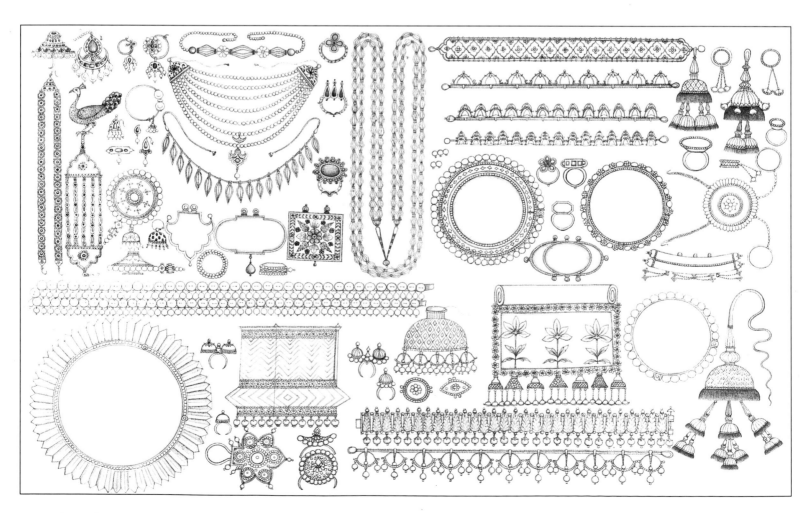

Mughal Women's Ornaments

Head

Binduli: Smaller than a gold *mohur* coin, worn on the forehead

Kotbiladar: Consists of five bands and a long center drop, worn on the forehead

Mang: Chain or string of pearls worn over the hair part

Sekra: Seven or more strings of pearls linked to studs and hung from the forehead to conceal the face. Worn at marriages and birth celebrations

Sisphul: Head ornament resembling a marigold

Nose

Besar: Circular, broad gold wire hoop strung with pearls, hung from a nostril

Laung: Stud in the shape of a clove, placed in a nostril

Nath: Gold circlet strung with a ruby between two pearls, or other gemstones, suspended from a nostril

Phuli: Shaped like a bud, the stalk of which is passed through a nostril

Ears

Bali: Circlet with a pearl

Karnphul: Ear ornament or stud shaped like the magrela flower (*Nigella sativa*)

Mor-bhanwar: Peacock-shaped ear pendant

Pipal-patti (pipal leaf): Crescent shape with leaf pendant, eight or nine worn in each ear

Neck

Guluband: Five or seven rose-shaped gold units strung on silk thread, worn tightly around the neck

Hans: Torque necklace

Har: Long necklace of strings of pearls interspaced with gold units

Arms

Bazuband: Armlet of various kinds

Chur: Bracelet worn above the wrist. A smaller variation was called *bahu*.

Churin: Bangles thinner than the *chur*, seven worn together

Gajrah: Bracelet of gold and pearls

Jawe: Five gold barleycorns (*jau*) strung on silk, a pair worn one on each wrist

Kangan: Rigid, hollow bracelet

Tad: Hollow tube shape, worn on the upper arm

Fingers

Anguthi: Finger rings of various kinds

Waist

Chhudr-khantika: Gold bells strung on a gold wire placed around the waist

Kati-mekla: Decorative gold belt

Feet

Anwat: Ring for the great toe

Bhank: Worn on the instep, triangular or square

Bichhwah: Worn on the instep, shaped like half a bell

Ghunghru: Small gold bells, six on each ankle, strung on silk, worn between the *jehar* and *pail*

Jehar: Three gold anklets worn together in descending order: the *chura*, two-part hollow tubes joined as a ring; *dundhani*, like the former but engraved with a design; and *masuchi*, like the second but differently engraved

Pail: Anklet (called *khalkhal* in Arabic)

Women's Jewelry in Aurangzeb's Court

Mughal court goldsmiths, as described by Niccolao Manucci, were almost continuously busy with the making of ornaments:

The best and the most costly of their productions are for the king's person, the queens, and the princesses. The latter make it one of their diversions to examine and show to others their jewellery. But they have their reasons for this; for I have noticed several times myself when introduced into the rooms of these ladies, they have asserted that they had some (ostensibly medical) reason for consulting me, that they often cause their ornaments and jewels to be brought, solely as an opening for a conversation. The things are brought on great trays of gold. They would inquire of me their virtues and properties, and make other similar remarks. During this time I had sufficient leisure to examine them, and I may say I have seen every sort of stone, some of an extraordinary size, and strings of pearls very equal in size....

These ladies keep their rubies in ... [irregular form] condition in order not to diminish their size and weight, for they know quite well that no one but themselves would be able to wear them, and, on the other hand, they have no need to sell them. Thus they do not mind their being pierced.... Usually they have ... three to five rows of pearls hanging from their neck, coming down as far as the lower part of the stomach. Upon the middle of the head is a bunch of pearls which hangs down as far as the centre of the forehead, with a valuable ornament of costly stones formed into the shape of the sun, or moon, or some star, or at times imitating different flowers. This suits them exceedingly well. On the right side [of the nose] they have a little round ornament, in which is a small ruby inserted between two pearls. In their ears are valuable stones....

They wear on their arms, above the elbow, rich armlets two inches wide, enriched on the surface with stones, and having small bunches of pearls depending from them. At their wrists are very rich bracelets, or bands of pearls, which usually go round nine or twelve times. In this way they often have the place for feeling the pulse so covered up that I found it difficult to put my hand upon it. On their fingers are rich rings, and on the right thumb there is always a ring, where, in place of a stone, there is mounted a little round mirror, having pearls around it. This mirror they use to look at themselves, an act of which they are very fond, at any and every moment. In addition they are girdled with a sort of waistbelt of gold two fingers wide, covered all over with great stones. At the ends of the strings which tie up their drawers there are bunches of pearls made up of fifteen strings five fingers in length. Round the bottom of their legs are valuable metal rings or strings of costly pearls.

All these princesses own six to eight sets of jewels, in addition to some other sets of which I do not speak, worn according to their fancy.... When these ladies want to dispose of their jewels, it is almost impossible for them to do so.... Some of these princesses wear turbans by the king's permission. On the turban is a valuable aigrette, surrounded by pearls and precious stones. This is extremely becoming and makes them look very graceful. During entertainments, such as balls and such-like, there are dancing women who have the same privilege.

They live in this way, with no cares or anxieties, occupying themselves with nothing beyond displaying great show and magnificence ... and pleasing the king.... [Should they die] ... the king seizes all the wealth of the defunct.

770

770. Jaipur, Rajasthan. 19th century
Rigid gold necklace (hansuli or kantha) with hinged back, mounted with diamonds, rubies, and emeralds and edged with pearls. From the bottom edge fall twenty crescent-shaped, gem-set pendants, to which a final fringe of emeralds, pearls, and enamel beads are fixed. The reverse is elaborately enameled in polychrome.
Courtesy Georgia Chrischilles, Brussels

771. Bikaner, Rajasthan. 19th century
Gold necklace (arya), set with diamonds kundan style, with pearl borders and fringe, polychrome enameled at the back
Courtesy Naulakha, New Delhi

Among the most complex of constructions in Indian traditional jewelry, this necklace is a masterpiece of the Indian goldsmith's achievement (see 3).

772. Bikaner, Rajasthan.
Marwari woman wearing a 22-karat gold choker (galapatia or galsari) and a gold necklace (arya or ad). Visible parts are pavé set with diamonds and ornamented with pearls; the reverse (not seen) is polychrome enameled. Her gold top-of-head ornament (rakri) and earrings (jhumka) are set with diamonds and pearls.

Jean Baptiste Tavernier relates an instance of confiscating the valuable possessions of deceased nobility: "As soon as Aurangzeb had news [of the death of his father, Shah Jahan, whom he had imprisoned at Agra Fort], he came to Agra to seize all the jewels of the late King … which he had not touched during his life. Begum Sahib [Shah Jahan's daughter Jahanara Begum] also had a quantity of precious stones which he had not taken from her when he placed her in the [Agra] fortress [where she tended to her father]." When Aurangzeb entered the Agra Seraglio, Begum Sahib presented him with a large golden basin full of jewels. She was removed to Jahan-abad and, a short time later, died there, it was believed by poison.

The private women's quarters (zenana) of a palace or home was a guarded, sequestered place to which access was possible only by the husband and trusted servants, such as older women and eunuchs. Royal zenanas were in fact elegant prisons. To help them pass the time, women were provided with a monthly allowance to purchase clothing and ornaments. When they wanted something and it was within their allowance, they applied to whoever controlled cash outlay, and the item was secured for them. Dress and appearance played an important role in gaining the favor of their husband or master, who when pleased bestowed upon them further gifts of jewelry as a conspicuous sign of his approval. The desire and competition to own orna-ments was great, and their possession often created jealousy among the wives and concubines inhabiting the zenana.

On special occasions that took place once a month, or to celebrate the new year, a large zenana bazaar called khushroz (the joyful day), was organized. Merchants sent their best wares,

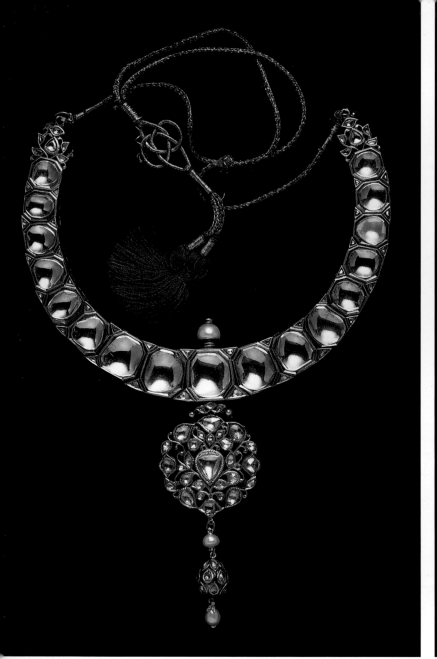

773. Delhi. 19th century
Gold necklace (articulated hansuli) of seventeen closed setting, foil-backed, large, Mughal-cut diamonds, each mounted on a separate gold unit that interlocks with the others, forming an articulated series
Courtesy Fred Leighton, New York

From the above hangs a central pendant (jugni) similarly ornamented, with an additional smaller gemstone-set pendant and pearls.

774. Reverse side of the necklace, polychrome enameled in the red-ground (lal zamin) style

and all the zenana women attended. The wives and daughters of well-placed nobles were also invited to come and buy. The emperor would be present and delighted in haggling over prices with the women who acted as sales persons. Great sums were spent, and marriage affiliations were often arranged on this occasion. The following day, a similar bazaar would be set up for the men of the court.

The A'in-i-Akbari, the third volume of the Akbar-nama, written by Shaykh Abu'l-Fazl 'Allami, Akbar's minister, about A.D. 1590 as a memorial to the emperor, gives a uniquely detailed and accurate account of the Emperor Akbar's government in all its departments. In volume 3 of the orientalist H. Blochmann's translation, under Jewels, is listed the typical Mughal (and Hindu) jewelry forms in current use. A selection of their names and brief descriptions given on pages 344–47 tell us that many of the traditional forms of ornaments in use today were already established in that time, four hundred years ago, and earlier. He comments, "All these are plain or studded with jewels, and are of many styles. What words can express the exquisite workmanship of the [goldsmith's] trade?"

775. Madras, Tamil Nadu. Late 19th century ➤
Gold necklace (maharakantimalai) set with foil-backed diamonds, rubies, and emeralds, with pearl and ruby cluster drops
Length 15 in. (38 cm)
Private Collection

The basic form of the Mughal-style long necklace (patadi har) has been elaborately ornamented here to simulate a flower garland. The central double pendant is flanked by gem-set peacocks (mayil), and the clasp is flanked by double peacocks. The pendant reverses are ornamented with twisted wirework.

Regal and Rural Jewelry:
Polarity and Hybrid Developments

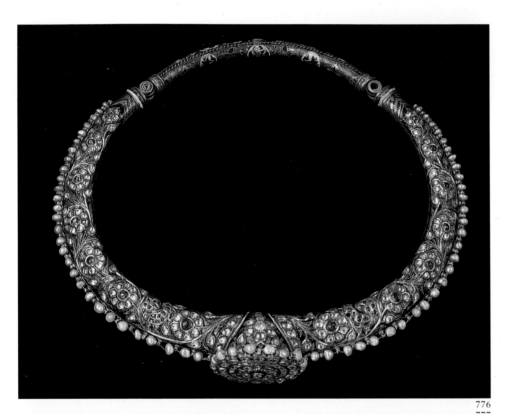

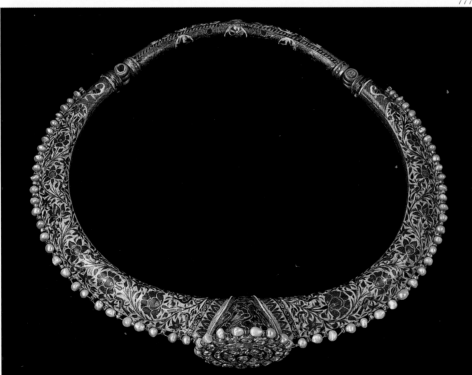

776
777

Mughal court craftsmen set a standard aspired to by the craftsmen who worked for the non-aristocratic classes of society, who inevitably were influenced by and emulated ideas and usages originating at court. As far as possible, goldsmiths and silversmiths working outside the confines of the royal workshops provided their clientele with jewelry inspired by those in court use, interpreted and modified according to their ability. The result was a hybrid class of ornaments, in which we encounter basic jewelry forms used by rural people that undoubtedly originated in ancient rural jewelry concepts but were executed with an unprecedented degree of refinement and ornamented in a manner meant to disguise their origin and suggest a connection with upper-class usage.

For example, the rigid, solid-silver torque (*hasli*), universally used among rural people, might be executed in hollow-form sheet-metal gold, its visible surface covered with gemstones, and its reverse surface intricately enameled in the manner of court jewelry. This kind of ornament might be worn by the wife of a wealthy landowner (*zamindarin*) or an affluent merchant's wife (*baniyin*). Such people, by caste connections more closely related to the middle and lower strata of society than to the aristocracy, wore these ornaments as a display of affluence and a material indication of social superiority to those of lesser economic means. It is significant, however, that in so doing they did not abandon basic design forms of ornaments that identified their origins.

776. Bikaner, Rajasthan
Rigid gold torque (minaraki jarai ka has), *the obverse decorated with diamonds and rubies on a blue ground* (nil zamin) *and an outer perimeter of strung pearls*
Diameter 8½ in. (21.5 cm); approximate weight 255 g
Private Collection, Brussels

777. *The reverse side is polychrome enameled, with a white ground* (safed chalwan).

Jaipur Jewelry Forms: Plain or Enameled

Rajasthan, formerly a complex of independent Indian principalities, is a place where conservative traditions in ornaments have in general been preserved from outside influences. Listed below are common traditional forms of jewelry made in Jaipur that are also common throughout northern India. In their simplest state, they can be of silver and in gold, without enamel, but often they employ enamel on the reverse and sometimes also on the obverse side.

Gold enameled jewelry for women is frequently sold today in sets meant to be worn together, most usually as a part of a woman's dowry. In Jaipur, a complete set, or *parure* (*pura* "set"), includes a necklace, hanging earrings or tops worn on the earlobe, a pair of bangles, and a ring. A half-set (*adha* "set") includes all but the bangles.

Head

Bor; borla; mang: Ornament worn at the center of the forehead at the start of the central hair parting (*mang*). Usually it is of a precious metal, has a round, convex, visible face set with gemstones, and tapers in a cone shape to the back, where it ends with a loop by which it is attached to the hair with a cord. In Rajasthan, this is one of the ornaments that indicates the woman wearing it is married. *Mang bhari* is the mark of red-lead powder commonly placed at the same position as a sign of marriage. This ornament may be worn alone or with two attached chain-like ornaments called *chir patti* (split strip), or *mang patti.*

Chand: Forehead ornament in crescent-moon shape, with hanging pearls

Chotla: Compound ornament worn to cover the entire surface of the hair braid at the back of the head. Usually it starts at the top with a separate or attached large ornament and continues downward with an articulated form whose units graduate in diminishing sizes to a bottom point, where a tassel (*paranda*) may be attached. This ornament is comparable to the *jadanagam* used by southern Indian *bharata natyam* dancers.

Dauni: Two elaborate, chainlike strips worn joined at the forehead, where a *tikka* may be attached, then down the sides of the face, often ending in attached earrings.

Mor patti (peacock strip): Long, narrow chain-like ornament, worn on both sides of the head, that starts with a hook for attachment to the hair, followed by a half-moon and flower unit (*kanoti*), from which descend four rows of strung pearls or chains interrupted halfway by a unit in the form of a peacock, followed by more pearls or chains and a tasselated end ornament that hangs over the ears. The pair may be worn alone or with a central forehead ornament (*tikka*) to which they are attached. *Jhala* is a similar ornament that has more metal units, shorter pearl or chain strands between units, and no bottom fringe. In some cases, *karanphul jhumka* earrings are attached to its lower ends and fixed in the earlobe.

Rakdhi; sisphul: Round ornament worn on the hair at the back of the head. *Sisphul* also means "husband" or "lord."

Ears

Bali: Hoop earrings with a *flat* frontal surface, the obverse side decorated with gemstones, the reverse often enameled

Kan-jhumka: Ear ornament that follows the ear shape, covering the entire helix, and has a *jhumka* suspended at the bottom, without which it is simply *kan.*

Kan ki bala chand sath machhli: Large earrings in the shape of an upward-pointing crescent moon (*bala chand*), from which hangs one large or several smaller fish-shaped (*machhli*) pendants, symbols of fertility. Small leaf-shaped pendants (*panri*) may also hang below. Worn in a pair, their weight is often supported by two converging strings of seed pearls attached by cords to the hair. This style of ear ornament has long been popular for use by a Muslim bride.

Kan phul; karanphul: Round disc, flower-head-shaped

Karanphul jhumka: Ear ornament (*karan,* ear) that consists of two main parts: a disc in flower-head form (*phul*) at the earlobe; from which hangs a semicircular dome form (*jhumka,* a bunch of flowers) whose edge is generally ornamented with a pendant fringe that hangs down (*jhumna*). This classical Mughal form is worn in pairs (*jora*) all over India, interpreted in a variety of styles.

Kundal: Large, circular earring, the front surface set with gemstones, the back often enameled, worn by placing the back cylindrical stud through a large earlobe hole.

Mor ka karanphul: Peacock-shaped (*mor*) earring

Neck

Ariya (H: *ariyal,* very wealthy): An extremely rich necklace consisting of a broadly curved, long oval form that surrounds the front half of the neck, from which is suspended a complicated chain-mail network of joined small units, from which in turn another series of triangular small units are suspended. At the bottom center is often found a good-luck amulet (*jugni* when small; *jugnun* when large).

Champakali (S: *champa; Michelia champaca,* a tree; *kali,* an unblown flower or bud): The *champa* tree bears a fragrant yellow flower whose bud form is rendered in precious metal and strung in series on a long necklace.

Galapattia; guluband (P: *neck band*): Choker-type necklace made of many identical units assembled in straight series (*patti,* strip), their total length not completely encompassing the neck (*gala*). Strung on cord, they often have a lower fringe of hanging elements, such as baroque emeralds or pearls.

Har (H: *hara,* a garland): A generic term for any long necklace suggesting a garland, of which there are several basic types:

Ath pahlu har: Necklace of separate octagonally shaped (*ath pahlu*) units, sometimes mounted at the back with Partabgarh *thewa* plaques (see page 300) instead of enamel

Lara har (H: *lar,* a series, as in string, cord, or row): Long necklace that hangs on the chest, consisting of an odd-numbered, graduated series of strands of pearls, beads, or chains, each with a small, central pendant (*latkan*). All strands are suspended from a pair of triangular end-spacer units. *Tin lara har* has three strings; *panch lara har* has five strings; *sat lara har* has seven strings; *nau lara har* has nine strings.

Patri har (H: *patri,* narrow strip): Long necklace of two matching side strips usually of four pearl strands regularly interrupted by metal units and coming together at the bottom, where a central pendant (*bich ka latkan*) joins them. The pendant (H: *latakta;* P: *awekta*) can take several forms, such as a single or double crescent shape, in which case the necklace is called a moon garland (*chandan har*); or a fan shape (*phanki ka har*).

Attached to the pendant on either side is a triangular metal unit (*chevara*), followed usually by four short strands of pearls (*moti ka lara*), then a square or rectangular metal unit (*chip*) and several alternations of the same, their number depending on the necklace length; the strip finishes with another triangular *chevara*. To each end are attached cords (*sarafa*) and a length-regulating, sliding yarn ball (*gundhi*) from which the two cords emerge, ending with tassels (*phundna*).

Rupaya har (H: *rupaya,* rupee coin): Necklace made of a series of rupee coins, or round forms simulating coins, with a central pendant

Has; hasli; hansli: Rigid torquelike neckpiece, usually wide at the front and tapering toward the back. Some are round-sectioned, tapered cone forms, some flat, and others are square in section at the front. The *hansli* (collar bone, so called because the front rests on the collar bone), is a common rural woman's ornament, usually made of a solid bar of ornamented silver. A variant, of gold set with gemstones and enameled (*minakari jarai ka has*), is hollow.

Kantha (S: *kanth,* throat): Close-fitting necklace, usually of flower-form units at center and sides, interspaced with interlocking stylized foliage units

Katsari: Neck-hugging necklace that rests on

the upper chest and consists of a series of units, usually of the same form, strung on cord.

Tamania (A: *tamaniyat,* happiness; H: *tinmania,* three gemstones): Necklace with a frontal unit consisting of an upper tube form incorporating three spaced, round, beadlike forms (*mani*), to which a rectangular plaque is attached below, its surface profusely decorated. It is worn suspended by side bunches of glass seed beads or pearls. It is called *panchmania* when there are five (*panch*) large bead forms.

Pendants

The Mughal period was an especially rich era in the development of new pendant forms, which still persist. Some examples are given here. Among the essentially two-dimensional forms are the following:

Boli patti: Pointed, seed-shaped pendant

Chand: Crescent-moon-shaped pendant, single or double, at times incorporated into the upper part of a *niyam* form

Niyam: Flower-shaped pendant with cabochon-cut gemstones (or glass) on the front and enamel on the back

Pankhi: Fan-shaped pendant

Sri Nathji Kavach: Hindu amulet in arrowhead shape bearing an image of the footprints of Sri Nathji, a deity especially worshiped at Nathadwara, Rajasthan, as a form of Krishna; his name appears at the back. *Ram novami ka kantha* is essentially the same as the one described but bears the name of Ram, or Shri Ramji.

Three-dimensional pendant forms include:

Harad (A: making a sound): Barrel-shaped pendant, possibly containing pellets that create a sound

778

Kairi (a small, unripe mango): Small mango-shaped pendants are commonly found in Indian jewelry. To Hindus, the mango connotes auspiciousness. The same shape may also be used by Muslims in a locket (*kibla namah*) that contains a small compass to indicate to the wearer the direction to Mecca, toward which a Muslim must face five times daily when saying prayers (A: *salawat;* P: *namazha*).

Tar ke mina moti (wire with enamel bead): A typically Indian system of jewelry decoration, used with many enameled jewelry forms, that employs a fringe of small hanging ornaments at the bottom. One type is made of a length of gold wire whose end when melted automatically forms a gold granule (*rawa*). Another treatment uses enamel in a unique way. The end of a clean gold wire is dipped into a gum solution and then thrust into finely ground, dry enamel of a color meant to suggest either a ruby, emerald, sapphire, or turquoise. The enamel adheres to the wire end. The wire, held enameled-end down, is heated with a torch to form an end enamel ball. The result is threaded with a small seed pearl (*moti*) or a gemstone bead (*poth*), which rests on the gold or enameled ball end. The opposite free wire end is passed through an integral loop at the bottom of the unit, then spiraled around the wire to hold the pendant in place.

Shoulders

The shoulder epaulette (*khunda ki jawahar,* or *khag*) is an example of a cross-cultural ornament, as it seems to be derived from Western military uniform decoration, though its boat shape is unique. Convex-ribbed lengthwise to accommodate its position on the shoulder, it was frequently decorated lavishly with gemstones, enameled on the reverse, and fringed with hanging chains and pendants of pearls and emeralds. The original was used to hold a shoulder belt in place; worn by all ranks, it was abolished in the British Army in 1855 but continued in this form in Rajasthan throughout the nineteenth and early twentieth century as an ornament worn by maharajas.

Arms

Bangri gokru: Bangri is a general term for an annular bracelet, of which there are many types. This is a bangle with a series of pointed projecting parts.

Bazuband (P: *bazu,* arm; *band,* a fastening): A very common type of Indian and Persian upper arm ornament, the *bazuband* generally consists of one or three parts hinged together and tied to the arm. Another type consists of many side-by-side or interlocking units, which, in its most highly developed form, could be set with gemstones on the obverse side and enameled on the reverse. Elaborate armlets were a sign of royalty.

Bazu-ta'wiz: Armlet incorporating an amulet, sometimes in box form containing a written charm or a miniature copy of the Qur'an

Chura: Wide bangle or a wrist ornament simulating a series of bangles joined together by hinges (*kulti-bhirti chura,* open-close bracelet)

Churi: Rigid, thin annular bangle

Kara: Penannular tube (*nali*) or solid (*thos*) bracelet with animal-head terminals: either crocodile or mythic acquatic animal (*makara; magar*); parrot (*toti*); lion (*singha*); or tiger (*nahar ka kara*)

Fingers

Anguthi: Ring usually set with a gemstone on the front and possibly counterenameled on the reverse

Arsi: Ring set with a small round or heart-shaped mirror, possibly counterenameled

Hathphul (*hath,* hand; *phul,* flower) or *ratan chur:* Compound ornament consisting of a wrist chain to which is attached by chains an ornament resting at the back of the palm above the fingers, connected with chains to attached rings for all five fingers, or only the index and small fingers

Waist

Kamarband; kangati: Belt of many units joined by links, possibly counterenameled

Feet

Kara: Tubular penannular anklet

Paizeb: Several chainlike or other shaped units linked together, edged with a fringe of bells.

Sankra: Chain-type anklet

778. Jaipur, Rajasthan. *Late 18th century Enameled gold cuff (chura), the form simulating a series of joined bangles, all set kundan style, with rubies and emeralds. The bands are enameled externally and internally.*
Height 3⁹⁄₁₆ in. (9 cm); top diameter 2¾ in. (7 cm); bottom diameter 2³⁄₁₆ in. (5.5 cm); weight 250 g
Collection Ivory, New York

A matching cuff that makes a pair with this one is in the Wernher Collection at Luton Hoo, Bedfordshire, England.

779. Kangra, Himachal Pradesh ➤
Mercury-and-gold-amalgam-gilded (garm mulamma) silver end-of-hair-braid ornament (chhoti or jutti), enameled blue and green in the local champlevé style. During heating, the mercury volitilizes, leaving a dull gold surface, which is then polished by rubbing with an agate or steel burnisher (muhari or badi).
Upper unit 5⅜ x ¾ in. (13.7 x 1.8 cm); lower pendant length 9⅛ in. (23.2 cm); weight 194 g
Collection the author, Porvoo

780. Nurpur or Jagat Sukh, Kangra District, Himachal Pradesh ➤
Silver necklace (chaunki) with five blue-and-green enameled units, each depicting a central, four-armed, crowned Vishnu
Total length 26⅜ in. (67 cm); large unit 4³⁄₁₆ x 3½ in. (10.7 x 9.9 cm); small unit 2¹¹⁄₁₆ x 2⁷⁄₁₆ in. (6.8 x 6.2 cm); weight 422 g
Collection the author, Porvoo

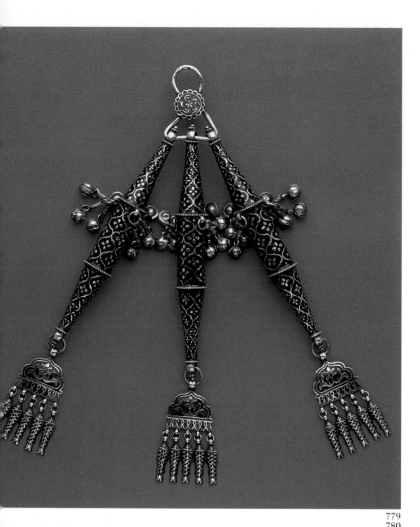

781. Nurpur or Jagat Sukh, Kangra District, Himachal Pradesh
Rigid silver upper armlets (bazu-chura) with blue and green enamel typical of enameled objects made here
Outer diameter 4 in. (10.1 cm); inner diameter 3½ in. (8.8 cm);
weight of pair 501 g
Collection the author, Porvoo

782. Nurpur or Jagat Sukh, Kangra District, Himachal Pradesh.
19th century
Gilded silver anklet (paizeb) of thirty-two units enameled blue and green, with flower-bud pendants
Outer diameter 5⁹⁄₁₆ in. (14.2 cm); width 1¹¹⁄₁₆ in. (4.3 cm); weight 206 g
Victoria and Albert Museum, London (IS 25256)

779
780

781
782

784

◄ **783. Nurpur or Jagat Sukh, Kangra District, Himachal Pradesh.** *19th century*
Silver necklace (chandraseni har), enameled blue and green
Total length 38 in. (96.5 cm); width 2¹⁵⁄₁₆ in. (7.5 cm); pendant 4 x 4⁵⁄₁₆ in. (10 x 11 cm); weight 718 g
Collection the author, Porvoo

784. Kullu, Himachal Pradesh
Silver necklace (chandraseni har) worn by a local woman attending the Dussera festival at Kullu. Its heavy weight is supported by a central hook to the garment. She also wears three-ball earrings (gokru), many small ear loops (bali), a tight-flower-bud necklace (tupchi), and bracelets (toké).

Mughal-Style Enameling: An Aggregate of Skills

Enameled jewelry ranks high among the great achievements of Indian jewelers. Creating it requires the combined skills of a working team of several specialist craftsmen. Of all the techniques employed in Indian-jewelry fabrication, the number of specialists required for enameled jewelry is probably the greatest. They include the designer (*naqash; chitera*), the goldsmith (*sonar swarnakar*), the engraver (*qalamkar; khodnakar; gharaiwala*), the enamelist (*minakar*), the polisher (*ghotnawala; chiknanawala*), the stone setter (*jadia; murasakkar; kundansaz*), and the stringer (*patu'a*).

In this group effort, each artisan has a clear understanding of what is required and works toward realizing the commonly shared image of the finished work. Because the object makes use of traditional design concepts and forms, executed in specific techniques, it takes on a predictable stylistic character that identifies its origin and exhibits a high degree of technical excellence. We follow the fabrication of an enameled gold and stone set piece of traditional jewelry as generally carried out in Jaipur, Rajasthan, where the best enameled gold jewelry was made in the past and is still in production today.

Designing

In each location where enameling is practiced in India, the design style takes on a unique identity through its use of particular motifs, color combinations and arrangement, and the particular metal used. Traditional designs are not static but evolve slowly. Those typifying Jaipur enamel work have been in use at least since the seventeenth century and express the local Rajput aesthetic, influenced by design styles established during the Mughal period, when the patronage of all the sumptuary arts was at its apogee. Favorite Jaipur enameling subjects in jewelry are birds, flowers, creepers, and foliage. Less often seen are figural motifs. In all of these, the enamel colors are flat and there is no attempt at shading or chiaroscuro. Many traditional designs are so familiar to the designer they can be drawn directly on the metal without the need for preliminary sketches. Others must first be carefully worked out on paper, then transferred to metal.

In Jaipur and elsewhere, it is a common practice for the designer to keep a book of old as well as new designs. Many of these are black rubbings of finished work made after the engraving has been completed. These books can be shown to a client or to a goldsmith-merchant, who then places an order for the manufacture of a specific design.

The basic precious-metal form is created by the goldsmith from such a drawing. The result is passed back to the designer, who draws on its surface the outlines of the pattern to be enameled using a sharply pointed steel stylus (*salai*). The surface is rubbed with an agate burnisher (*mashkala*) to brighten it and make the design lines more visible. The object is then passed to the engraver.

Goldsmithing

The gold alloy used for enameled jewelry and objects in India is generally 22 karat, which is 91.67 percent gold. Pure gold, 24 karats, is not suitable for use in jewelry because it is too soft. An object made of it would not retain its shape in use and would wear rapidly, thus diminishing its volume. In India this is a critical issue as the price of gold there is almost twice its quotation on the international market. The addition of a small percentage (8.33 percent) of an alloying metal or metals, usually copper alone, or half copper and half silver, renders a material more rigid and hard.

Enameling 22-karat gold presents no technical difficulties. Indian gold enamelists often claim that they use a high-quality gold alloy because gold less than 22 karats will not hold the enamel. Yet 18-karat, 14-karat, and even lower karat gold alloys are used extensively in the West as an enameling substrate. Success in enameling lower karat gold alloys depends not upon their gold content but on the component metals of the alloy.

Objects prepared for enameling fall into two basic categories: flat (*hamwar*) or three-dimensional, fabricated hollow (*khukhla; pola*) units. This flat or hollow condition is important to the enamelist as well as the gemstone setter, whose work begins once enameling is completed.

Hollow parts must be assembled with solder. When ordering hollow work of the highest quality, the merchant specifies the use of a special gold solder (*ravatti*), which has a high melting point, above that required for fusing the enamel later placed upon the object, so the form will not come apart under heat. Its color matches 22-karat gold and does not affect the color of the transparent enamels that are so characteristic of Jaipur enamel work.

Engraving

The engraver receives the object with the design outlined upon it. Within these lines he carves out the metal in those areas that will be replaced by enamel. As the design scale is always small, this operation requires great skill. Some enamelists are able to draw and engrave their own designs, but employing a specialist engraver for this work is a more common practice. The best gold engravers in Jaipur are Hindus, formerly of the Khati, or carpenter's caste, who took to engraving.

Small, flat objects such as the units commonly used in Indian enameled jewelry are prepared for engraving by fixing them on a

785

786

787. Jaipur, Rajasthan (opposite page)
Gold necklace (mina ka kanthal or kathla) of nine units, enameled in a rare figural-subject style, strung on cord
Courtesy Chhote Bharany, New Delhi

788. Jaipur, Rajasthan. *Probably 18th century (opposite page)*
Enameled 22k-gold armlet (bazuband) in three-hinged, interfitting curved units
1½ x 3¹⁵⁄₁₆ in. (3.2 x 10 cm)
Courtesy Spink and Son Ltd., London

Seated on a throne within the cartouche of the central unit are Sita and Rama, with Hanuman on the left and Lakshmana on the right. In the side units beyond the cartouche are two lady attendants and birds. The reverse is enameled with flowers and foliage on an exposed gold ground (bund tila–style enameling). This is an outstanding example of rarely produced Jaipuri figural subjects in enamel.

785. Jaipur, Rajasthan
Gold choker necklace (guluband) made of twenty-five identical units set with diamonds and rubies, the reverse polychrome enameled, with a fringe of seed pearls strung on gold wire, each with an enamel ball end
Length 11 in. (28 cm); unit 1⅛ x ⅜ in. (2.5 x 1 cm); weight 234 g
Collection the author, Porvoo

786. Jaipur, Rajasthan. *18th century* ➤
Gold champlevé-enameled amulet pendant (jantr), reverse
Approximately 1¹⁵⁄₁₆ x 1⅞ in. (4.9 x 4.8 cm)
Otis Norcross Fund
Courtesy, Museum of Fine Arts, Boston (39.764)

Figural subjects include (center) blue Krishna reciting the Bhagavadgita to Arjuna before the great battle in the Mahabharata; (top, left) lion-headed Narasimha faced by a worshiper; Hanuman worshiping Rama, Sita, and Lakshmana; and the Jagannath Triad; and (from upper left to upper right) Vishnu's ten incarnations (avatara).

shellac stick (*hundi*), a flat, circular wooden disc with an attached handle below. The working surface is spread with a shellac composition, heated to make it plastic, into which the object is pressed. Upon cooling, the hardened shellac holds the object firmly in place. The same tool is used by gemstone setters to hold work while stones are set in place (see page 802).

Engraving for Champlevé Enameling

Almost all enameling done in India is in the champlevé method practiced in Jaipur, Lucknow, Hyderabad, Kangra, Kachchh, and Kashmir. In this technique, the design areas to receive enamel must first be excavated below the original metal surface; the enamel that replaces it restores the finished surface to its original level. In Varanasi some enameled areas may be left higher than the original surface, but not in Jaipur.

Of all enameling techniques, the champlevé method presents the fewest technical difficulties. No solder is present on the surface where the enamel will be placed, an important fact. Should solder be present (as in cloisonné work, where it is used to fix to the substrate the cloisons that separate the colors), when the enamel is heated for fusing, the solder *can* melt and seep through into the areas holding enamel, and this can result in color irregularities. Also, the different rates of contraction between enamel, solder, and base metal during cooling can cause the enamel to crack or fly off the metal. These problems are avoided in champlevé enameling, in which each color is separated by a border of exposed substrate metal that surrounds each figure in the design.

Various end-shaped engraving tools, called burins (Jaipur: *salai*; Varanasi: *bulli*) are used depending on the shapes of the figures to be

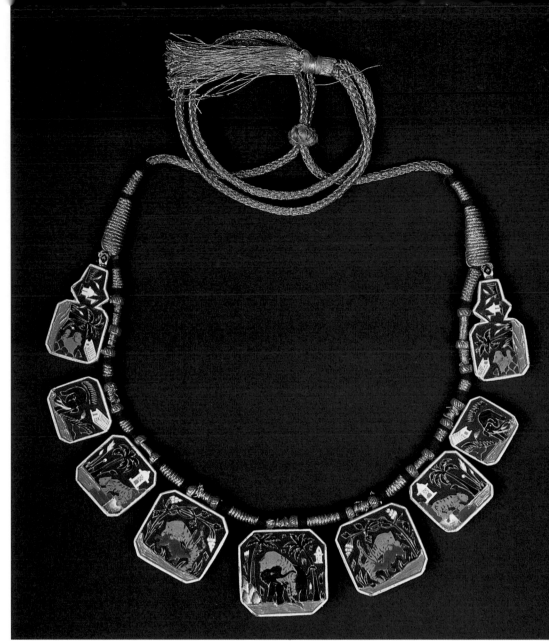

excavated. Some cutting ends are flat, others are round bottomed, or V-shaped.

The entire space within the first engraved outline of a subject is hatched with a series of parallel lines, usually with a V-shaped burin. There are two reasons for this. First, during fusion, the enamel will bond better to the metal substrate by becoming keyed to it, thus reducing the chance of its later chipping away from the metal. Second, the hatchings diffuse and reflect light back through transparent enamel, heightening its color brilliance and intensity, especially in the case of transparent red, the color on which rests much of the fame of Jaipur enameling.

Enameling

Enamel (*mina*) is composed of chemicals similar to those contained in clear glass, plus a small percentage of metallic oxide used as a colorant. The proportion of an enamel's components is calculated to achieve elasticity, a low degree of viscosity, low surface tension, and a coefficient of thermal expansion and contraction compatible with that of the metal substrate upon which it is fused.

The types of enamel used in India are Indian (*desi mina; desi,* own country), foreign (*vilayati mina; vilayati,* foreign, alien), soft (*mulaim mina*), hard (*sakht mina*), transparent (*khula mina,* "open" enamel), and opaque (*bandh mina,* "closed" enamel). Enamel colorants, in the form of metallic oxides, include cobalt oxide for blues; copper oxide for greens; manganese, iron, and cobalt oxides for black; and gold chloride for red. The percentage of oxide to the other ingredients determines the color produced. To make an enamel opaque, an opacifier such as tin oxide is added to the melt.

The aforementioned transparent ruby-red enamel found in most Jaipur enamels is famous for its brilliance and clarity. The colorant is a form of metallic gold, gold chloride, in a concentration of about 0.003 percent of the total ingredients. This small amount of gold does not justify the claim made by some Jaipur enamelists and merchants that this red is very expensive to use. Its cost is somewhat higher than other colors, but in the small amounts in which it is used on a piece of jewelry, this difference is negligible. What *is* important is the skill required in firing this color, as described ahead.

Transparent red appears at its best seen over a high-karat gold ground, characteristically bright yellow in color, resulting in a brilliant red. Should the *same* red enamel be applied over a white, silver ground, it would appear *orange,* not red.

Formerly, the best Indian enamels were manufactured in Lahore by Muslim families of the Miyan group, who also made glass for bangles. Some descendants of these families who worked in Haveli Miyan in Lahore still keep to their traditional occupation, but, after

Jaipur, Rajasthan

ENAMELING PROCESS (*MINAKARI KAM*)

789. *Pieces of enamel (mina) are cleaned in a dilute acid solution. The amount needed is knocked off the solid mass with an iron pestle (mugdar) and placed in a mortar (karchi). The pieces are ground until the enamel attains a small particle size.*

In the late eighteenth–nineteenth century, enamels came mainly from foreign sources. Today, these stocks, carefully hoarded, are declining. An important enamel manufacturer in India is Sticks Company, Amritsar, the first modern-day Indian enamel manufacturer, established in 1935.

The enamel is washed four times with water to remove impurities. This is especially important in order to achieve maximum transparency and color brilliance with transparent enamels. The ground enamel is free of impurities when, after stirring and settling the enamel, the water poured off is no longer cloudy.

790. *Enamel is placed in a color palette (rang rakhene ka patra) and just enough water added to form a paste. With a pointed spatula applicator (takua), the enamel is applied, champlevé style, to the engraved depressions on the object. After use, enamels are stored in shallow, interfitting porcelain cups.*

791. *The dried object (here a bangle) is placed on an iron trivet, whose points hold it suspended in air, and introduced to the charcoal-fueled, preheated kiln (bhatti) with tongs (chimta). After heating the object to redness (one to five minutes or more, depending on object size), the enamel fuses. The red-hot object is quickly removed from the kiln and allowed to cool. Exposed metal is cleaned with dilute citric acid, and the surface is ground level with a corundum stick (sohan). A second application and firing of enamel usually follows; it is always necessary in the case of the famous Jaipur color red in order to develop it fully to clarity and brightness.*

792. *All exposed gold is brightened with a burnisher (badia). The finished interior (when hollow) is filled with surma lac, a compound of lac mixed with antimony, to prevent the gold from denting. To accomplish this, lac is heated to viscosity and dribbled through one of the openings made in the object for the setting of a gemstone. Finally, a gemstone setter (murassakar) sets the gemstones kundan style (see page 367).*

789

790

791
792

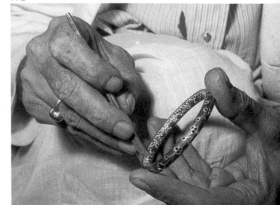

partition in 1947, many left this work for different occupations.

Enamelists in India tend to be reluctant about parting with information concerning sources of supplies and materials or their techniques. Many claim that the enamels they use were manufactured in Lahore, now in Pakistan, and always they say these are superior in quality. Some of the enamels they use undoubtedly were of foreign origin, probably French or Swiss. Today in India enamels are manufactured in Jaipur and Calcutta.

Enamel Preparation: The Melt

It is usual to prepare and place the enamel constituents in a crucible. When fused, the crucible is lifted out of the furnace with tongs and the viscous enamel is poured out onto a clean, thick steel or marble flat surface. The hot mass spreads out and forms a smooth, flat, circular slab called *kanch* (glass), which can be stored when cool.

Enamel in this form can be kept indefinitely without deteriorating. For this reason Jaipur enamelists still have stocks of old enamels purchased by their ancestors or themselves many years ago, which they keep wrapped up in old rags without any labels. This is surprising, but perhaps the need for labels is not so necessary when so few colors are used in this work as compared with the number used by Western enamelists.

Enamel Color-Firing Sequence

Because the various enamels used are of different degrees of hardness, they are fired in a specific sequence, from hardest to softest. Hard enamels require a higher fusing temperature, and, once fired, will not be affected by the lower temperature used subsequently to fire softer enamels. The firing order used in Jaipur is: white firing (*safed ki anch dena,* from *anch,* heat, *dena,* to give or apply); blue firing (*nila ki anch dena*); green firing (*hara* or *sabz ki anch dena*); turquoise firing (*firozi ki anch dena*); black firing (*kala ki anch dena*); yellow firing (*pila ki anch dena*); and red firing (*lal ki anch dena*).

More than one color can be fired at the same time provided they are not too close to each other in the design. Blue and green are often fired together. An object with several colors may go through as many as four, five, or more firings. Most critical is the treatment of red, which must be fired twice, the second time at a lower temperature, to develop fully its color and transparency. The accuracy of the temperature in both firings is very important.

Jaipur Enameling Types

In Jaipur jewelry, the enameling treatment can be categorized as follows:

Recto enamel (*ek posta,* one side; *agari ko mina,* from *agari,* front): Enamel only on one side or only the *front* side of the object, sometimes around set stones. In Delhi the term for this

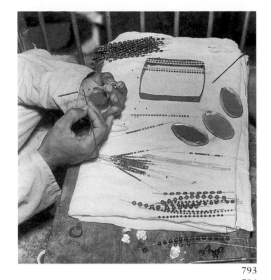

793
794

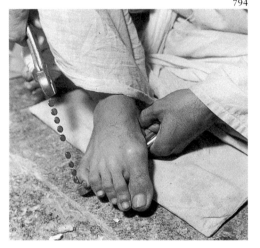

Nathadwara, Rajasthan

MAKING ENAMEL BEADS

793. *In this enameling center, besides a large production of enameled silver jewelry and small objects, a specialty exists in the manufacture of beads made entirely of enamel* (mina ka moti)*. In this process, a soft iron wire* (loha tar) *is coated with a liquid kaolin slush and dried. Pure silver foil* (chandi ka warak) *is wrapped around the wire at spaced intervals where the bead will be formed. Either a transparent or an opaque enamel paste including gum* (gond) *is applied over the foil with a spatula. The wire with prepared beads is placed horizontally on an iron supporting rack, allowed to dry, and is fired. When fired, enamel shrinks in volume. To increase the bead to the desired size, additional enamel is added in the same way over the fired bead and refired. Beads of a single color are often decorated with dots, stripes, and ridges in transparent or opaque colors that contrast with the base color.*

794. *To remove the fired enamel beads from the supporting wire, each end is grasped with pliers. A foot holds one end down. With the other hand, the opposite wire end is pulled. Under the tension created, the soft iron wire stretches just enough to allow the beads to be slipped off. Each bead now has an internal, supporting silver foil core to which the enamel adhered. When the enamel is transparent, the foil reflects light through it and intensifies the color.*

style is *kanta aur partaj,* or *chantwan.* It is done mainly in green or blue but sometimes includes red.

Verso enamel (*pharfura mina; pichhari ko mina,* from *pichhari,* back): Enamel on the *reverse* side only of an object, often the case when the front side is only set with gemstones

Recto-verso enamel (*do posta,* two sides): Enamel on both sides of a hollow constructed jewelry unit, one side of which has one or several openings where stones will be set. Typically the front is somewhat convex, the sides square, and the back flat.

Edge enamel (*pahulpar ko mina,* enamel on the sides): Done on the straight sides of three-dimensional, hollow jewelry units

Three-dimensional enamel (*sab jagah ko mina,* from *sab jagah,* everywhere): Enamel on an object in the round. Examples include turban ornaments (*turra*), decorative bird figures (*chirya*), and chess men (*shatranj*).

Recto-enamel ground colors are generally chosen to contrast with the color of the gemstones used on the same surface. Diamonds or colorless stones are used with a blue (*nil zamin*) and/or green (*sabz zamin,* from *zamin,* ground) background. Rubies are used with a green and/or blue ground. Emeralds can be used with a blue or red ground (*lal zamin*), although the latter is rarely done.

Verso-enamel ground colors can be of any combination because generally, but not always, only enamel and no stones are used on the verso side. Verso-enamel ground colors are almost always chosen to contrast with those (if any) used on the recto side. The colors used often depend on the subject of the design. Birds are done in green, blue, turquoise, white, or red; flowers are red, white, or blue; and foliage is green. Geometric patterns may use any combination of colors. Flowers and other subjects are often placed within a cartouche of round, oval, or other shape. The ground color within the cartouche is different from the ground color outside it. Opaque ground colors surrounding a figure are used to contrast with the transparent enamel color used for the design subject. All colors are flat, without gradation or chiaroscuro within the areas where they are used.

JAIPUR STYLES OF ENAMEL WORK:

Jaipur enamelists designate their styles of work by the style of the engraved pattern that backs a transparent color; the ground color used and whether it is transparent or opaque; the number of colors used; and whether the background or the figure is exposed in gold. The most common engraved-pattern ground style is *pardazi,* a figural area engraved with hatched lines to reflect light, then covered with a transparent enamel. With *ab-e-lahr* (*ab,* water; *lahr,* wave), the ground is engraved with lines representing conventionalized waves, then covered with a transparent enamel. The latter is commonly used in the background around an opaque enamel figure.

When a single transparent colored enamel is used to fill the ground around an opaque figure, the color of the ground is chosen to contrast with and set off that of the subject. Examples include *lal zamin,* transparent red ground; *sabz zamin,* transparent green ground; *nil zamin,* transparent blue ground. A special type is *ek rang khula mina,* in which a single-color transparent enamel fills all engraved areas, leaving gold outlines exposed around figural details.

In an opaque enamel ground (*bandh mina ke zamin*), a single opaque color is placed around the figure, which is of a transparent color or colors. The particular color used determines the identifying name. Examples are *firozi zamin,* opaque turquoise ground; *bandh sabz zamin,* opaque green ground; and *safed zamin,* white ground. In *ek rang bandh mina* (one-color opaque enamel), the entire ground around an engraved subject is filled with one opaque color, allowing only plain gold outlines around figure and details.

Opaque cartouche, or outline (*bandh mina khaka*), is a technique in which the figure in transparent color is surrounded by an opaque enamel cartouche. For example, in *safed chalwan,* an opaque white outline cartouche surrounding a figure is fired and leveled. The design subject—flowers, birds, or leaves—is engraved within the outline, then filled with a contrasting color (*khilaf rang*) and fired. A thin gold outline remains between the surrounding white cartouche and the figural subject.

A special multicolored style of enameling is termed *pachrangi mina* (five-color enamel). The five colors used are opaque white (*safed*); opaque light blue (*fakhtai,* from *fakhta,* a dove); transparent dark blue (*khula nila*); transparent green (*khula sabz*); and transparent red (*khula lal*).

Unusual Enameling Techniques:
Teh zamin: One transparent color completely covers the entire engraved metal design, usually at the flat back, rarely at the front. This can be compared to the Western style called *basse taille.*
Chitai ke mina: Transparent enamel completely covers a three-dimensional but frontal design executed in repoussage and chasing.
Pardarshak mina (*pardarshak,* transparent): A European style of open-backed enamel work where the enameled areas have no supporting metal behind them, called *plique à jour* in the West. This is rarely done in India.
Bund tila ka mina (*bund,* drop or spot; *tila,* gold: "color spots on gold"). This style of work has colored enameled areas isolated on a plain gold ground. It originated in eighteenth-century Qajar Persia. Rarely practiced in Jaipur, it was once in greater use in Varanasi and Hyderabad, where it is still done occasionally. The figure in transparent and opaque enamels appears within a cartouche or other shape, and the ground beyond it is left plain polished gold.

The Paradox of Reverse-Side Enameling:

Perhaps the most salient characteristic of Jaipur traditional jewelry is its use of the unseen reverse side for elaborate enameling of technically demanding, intricate designs. The visible front usually displays gemstones. The unrivaled reputation Jaipur enamelists enjoy in general is based on this reverse-side enamel decoration that is never intended to be seen. Its "secret" presence would seem to imply a modest concealment of virtuosic skill.

It may rightfully be asked—why put all this effort into invisible places? One explanation relates to the Indian convention of ornamenting unseen areas on objects. In so doing, the artisan gives full vent to his skill and enjoys the satisfaction of this knowledge. Another is the appreciation of that skill by the purchaser. *She* is the sole person who, when the object such as a necklace is worn, has sure knowledge of the presence of this decoration, though its presence may be surmised by those familiar with this style of work.

Technical reasons also contribute to the use of reverse-side enamel. In India the high-karat gold of this jewelry is valued far more than the enamel work, which has little intrinsic value, despite its high level of artistic achievement. Covering the reverse side with enamel protects the gold against the abrasion that occurs with normal use, a concept important to Indians, all of whom wish to conserve the object's original gold volume. At the same time, the presence of enamel acts to stiffen the gold and gives the object the rigidity necessary to retain its form.

Some claim that enamel is used on the reverse side of jewelry to prevent the allergic reaction some wearers experience on contact with metals. In the case of gold of such high quality, the chance of such a reaction is very small, and accommodating the minuscule number of persons who might be so affected would hardly account for the practice.

Multan Enameled Jewelry

Enameled jewelry from Multan, Punjab, which became part of Pakistan in the partition of 1947, frequently comes to the Indian market and is mistakenly identified as of present-day Indian manufacture. Multan production flourished in the nineteenth century but virtually ended after partition, when the Hindu enamelists emigrated to India. It is discussed here to clarify its origin and because the style of this work resembles that of Kangra and Hoshiarpur in the Indian Punjab.

The opaque enamels used in this work owe their existence to the longtime presence in Multan of ceramic manufacture in which colored, vitrified glazes were used for ceramic objects and architectural tile decoration. Both those ceramic glazes and enamels for enameling were manufactured by the people who supplied the larger requirements of the ceramic industry. The most characteristic colors are a deep lapis-lazuli blue and a lighter blue, but others, such as black, green, red, pink, yellow, and white, were also used to a lesser extent when enameling an object with an elaborate pattern.

The Multan enameling style as in the case of Jaipur is also a type of champlevé. In older work, the pattern was created by hand engraving, but, as noted in 1909 by Percy Brown, "modern" demand required a quicker technique, and, "within recent years most of the patterns have been stamped from a die … this modern practice having supplanted the older and more artistic method of engraving." He continued: "The strange part about Multan enameling is that the engraving [and stamping] of the metal is done at Bahawalpur, [capital of] a neighboring State [about 60 miles, or 100 km, south of Multan], the metal parts being afterwards brought to Multan for the enamel to be applied by the Multan workers."

The use of stamping dies to create the depressions into which the enamel was placed gives this work its character and accounts for the overall design uniformity encountered in the style; many similar versions of the same subjects are found on the market. Generally the design appears in line in the base metal, and the ground is a one-color enamel. In some cases, such as where figural or geometrized floral patterns are made, the image may be filled with enamels whose colors differ from the ground color.

The metal used was an alloy of silver and copper; some sources say the proportion was half and half, used because the enamelists claimed that this alloy was better able to withstand the heat of fusing the enamel to the metal. Firing was done in a primitive muffle-chamber kiln made of a wire cage covered with pottery shards, the whole placed over a charcoal fire. After the first enamel firing, the enamel was ground level with the metal pattern. It was then refired to restore its gloss.

The enameled jewelry made in Multan included rings for fingers and toes, a very popular large, *arsi* thumb ring installed with a round mirror, necklaces, bracelets, and belts made of linked or strung units; belt buckles, buttons, brooches, and pendants. Small objects made include bowls, covered cups and glasses, plates, and several kinds of small boxes or containers for eye liner and red forehead-dot cosmetic.

Varanasi Pink Enamel

The rich history of Varanasi (Anglicized formerly to Benares), India's oldest continually occupied city, reaches back more than five thousand years. Considered by Hindus to be preeminent among all holy sites, it is full of temples and shrines. Sited on the left bank of a bend in the Ganges River, Varanasi is accessible by flights of stairs (*ghats*) lining the shores. Masses of pilgrims descend them at dawn to greet the sunrise and the sun god Surya and immerse themselves in the river to

795. Multan, Pakistan. *19th century*
Silver plaque (patrian), *enameled opaque blue*
2¾ x 3 in. (7 x 7.6 cm)
Collection Ghysels, Brussels

wash away their sins. A daily event, this is one of the "sights" of India.

Because it constantly attracted a floating pilgrim population, many of whom purchased a souvenir to commemorate this significant journey, Varanasi has always been a center of handcraft production. Among its several specialties in wood, metal, stone, and fibers are the famous Varanasi handwoven gold brocades and a style of painted enamel work (*rangne minakam*) produced only there at least since the eighteenth century.

Pink enamel (gulabi mina; *from* gulab, rose) is the term that has popularly become associated with this traditional enameling style because it includes areas of painted enamel, generally flowers, executed in translucent pink on an opaque white ground, although it is not uncommon to find blue used in the same way. All *other* enameled areas on the object are created in the champlevé style, which makes this a mixed style of enameling.

Considered typical of Varanasi, this painted enamel style was established there by emigrant Persian enamelists in India as early as the seventeenth century, when the Mughal Court was at its apogee. Typical of enameling done at the Persian court at Isfahan, the technique reached a peak of perfection there during the Qajar dynasty (1795–1924). Many examples of Qajar enameled objects now in the Iranian State Treasure clearly illustrate

this technical (although not stylistic) relationship. The Persians in turn derived their inspiration from contemporary European overglaze painting on porcelain, and the Swiss painted-enamel watch cases of the seventeenth and eighteenth centuries, both very popular in Persia.

In some Varanasi work, the entire object, such as a pendant, is covered with this technique, and in others, as mentioned, it is combined with champlevé. The polychromed result, as seen, for example, on a typical pair of *kara* bangles with three-dimensional *makara,* elephant, lion, or bird head terminals, additionally decorated with diamonds, rubies, and emeralds, as they often were, is a dazzlingly opulent object that embodies a galaxy of goldsmith arts.

Present-day Varanasi enamelists interviewed claim that as recently as ninety years ago approximately one hundred enamelists practiced this art. Today their numbers have been reduced to only ten who enamel on gold and about twenty-five who enamel on silver. Of these about twenty make enameled jewelry and five produce enameled objects. A revival of enameling seems to be in progress in Varanasi, however, because several of those who formerly worked only in gold have shifted to using silver as a base metal. This happened as a result of the sudden rise in the international gold price in the late 1970s, which acted to suppress both the Indian and the foreign market for enamel-on-gold objects and increase the

796. Varanasi, Uttar Pradesh. *19th century*
Left: *Rigid gold bangle* (bangri) *set with repeated nine-planet gemstones* (nava-ratna kara)
Outer diameter 4 in. (10 cm)
Right: *Gold bracelet* (kara), *set with diamonds, enameled with a blue ground* (nil zamin); *opens for placement on the wrist*
Outer diameter 3⅜ in. (8.4 cm)
Private Collection

Both are enameled in the Varanasi pink-enamel style.

use of silver as a substrate metal. At that time, several enamelists abandoned their hereditary work for other crafts, such as weaving, and in some cases became machinists or dealers in sandalwood.

Varanasi enamelists produce objects for two distinct markets, the ongoing Indian traditional jewelry purchasers and the tourist trade. At least five outstanding enamelists, who depend for their livelihood mainly on sales to foreigners, now make enameled silver objects of impressive quality. Their works appear in the stock of the best urban goldsmith shops and in boutiques in hotel arcades in the major Indian cities. At first glance, this new work recalls old Lucknow enameling, which was also done on silver. However, its Varanasi origin is identified by the inclusion of areas of painted enamel on an opaque white ground, a technique never practiced in Lucknow, but carried over from Varanasi work on gold. Because the Varanasi technique is so unique in India, it is described here.

The process is carried out on jewelry and objects, now made mainly of 99 percent fine silver (sil chandi), some very large in size. Except for their distinctive painted areas, the enamel is applied in the champlevé style and the tools used are essentially the same as in Jaipur, and, although some terminology differs, the first processes need not be repeated here. We start the description from the point where, after engraving the design for those areas done in the champlevé style and hatching all areas to receive enamel, the application of enamel on the object begins.

The creation of a "pink enamel" object requires at least five separate enamel applications. Each application is followed by a firing to fuse the enamel to the base metal. Some Varanasi enamelists still use charcoal-fired kilns, but the younger generation of enamelists use an electrically heated kiln (kashih bijli ka bhatti).

In the first filling (pahle bharna) of enamel, transparent colors (khula mina), generally blue, and sometimes green—the two most common colors used—are applied (mina pakna), followed by the first firing (pahle anch). After this and every subsequent firing, the exposed metal of the object is cleaned to remove surface oxidation (as is also done in Jaipur enameling), and the areas meant for the next transparent enamel application are burnished to brighten them and maximize their ability to reflect light through the transparent enamel. These refinishing and preparatory steps will not be mentioned ahead but are to be understood.

In the second filling (dusri bharna), transparent enamel is added to top off the first application and bring the enamel there to the metal level. Additional colors are applied for the first time (not possible previously because of their proximity to another unfired color). The second firing (dusri anch) follows.

The third filling (tisra bharna) is for opaque colors (bandha mina), which may be white (safed), yellow (pila), turquoise (firozi), or pistachio green (pistai). These are applied in a greater thickness than transparents because in this case transparency is not a concern. The third firing (tisra anch) follows.

All enamels fired up to this point are ground down to make them level with the metal. Stone grinding (sang pisna) is accomplished with an appropriately shaped carborundum stick (kurand ka sang), which renders the whole surface smooth but leaves the enamel matte. The object is washed in water and dried.

In the fourth filling (chautna bharna), a second application of opaque white is placed only in those areas where the enamel painting will be done over white. Repairs to other colors, where needed, can now also be done. At the subsequent fourth firing (chautha anch), the surface of the transparent and opaque enamels that were ground down becomes smooth and shining; at the same time, the second white coating is fused. Because this second coat of white is not subsequently ground down to the metal level, these white areas that will be painted are somewhat raised above the metal surface and appear slightly convex. The second coat of white is necessary to assure a pure white ground upon which the translucent pink (or blue) will be painted.

Painting the pink enamel on the white area (gulabi likhai) requires a specialist. A small hair brush (mu qalam) of hair from a young squirrel's tail is used to apply the pink enamel, which in truth is not pink but a transparent red enamel finely ground to a consistency devoid of any visible or palpable particles (karda). To make a paste (lehi) that is suitable for painting, the enamel is mixed with a small amount of sandalwood oil (chandan ka tel), which acts as a binder and color extender.

The process begins by painting the flower, usually a rose (gulab) or a lotus (padma), in a relatively heavy outline (bhari rekha). With the same brush, these lines are feathered or drawn out (rangna barhana, to draw out color), which shades each petal from dark to pale pink to white. The color remains darkest near the original line and lightens as the brush draws it farther away. No attempt is made to shade the color realistically as if light were coming from a single source. The effect therefore remains relatively flat.

The fifth or final firing (taiyari anch; from taiyar, finished) is also called the "pink firing" (gulabi ki anch dena). Fusing the pink to the white ground requires a fast, hot fire of short duration.

Finally the object is passed to the polisher and cleaned. Any exposed metal is burnished to a bright shine by the use of hand burnishers. Mechanical polishing methods are not used.

Gemstone Setting: *Kundan* Style

In his *A'in-i Akbari* (1590), Abul-Fazl 'Allami was probably the first Indian to describe the indigenous process of setting gemstones by the use of pure, soft gold strips (kundan). He wrote, "In other countries the [gemstones] are secured in the sockets [bezels] made for them … but in Hindustan, it is effected with kundan which is gold made pure and ductile." He then gives a description of how the gold is prepared for this use.

The typically Indian kundan process of ornamenting and setting a gemstone in jade has been described on pages 117–18. Although similar, this technique when used in the setting of a gemstone in gold jewelry, such as that made in Delhi and Jaipur in the Rajput-Mughal traditional style, is distinctive because the process of setting a gemstone in metal requires additional presetting and postsetting processes. Because of the importance of its continued contemporary use it is described here in detail.

The great advantage of the kundan setting system in metal is that it eliminates the need for fabricating a bezel or gemstone-setting frame to hold each gemstone used, a time-consuming and difficult process, especially since a great number of gemstones, often of individual, irregular shape, are used in this style of jewelry. By its nature, this process allows stones of any shape or size to be used and their settings created, *without the need of heat,* around the stone when in situ. This also means that a stone does not have to be cut to a regular shape, a condition that satisfied the constant Indian aim of preserving maximum original stone size. These reasons may account for the Indian lack of interest, until the nineteenth century when foreign influence seriously intruded into the jewelry field, in the use of symmetrically cut gemstones such as diamonds, which in the West had long been set in open, claw settings. In this traditional Indian style of jewelry, stone quality and regularity of cut, though not totally ignored, were of lesser importance than the general effect of glitter and opulence created.

Unlike a jade haldili amulet, the gold jewelry unit made to receive a gemstone is generally of hollow (do-posta) construction, the parts joined by solder (jor). Before engraving the design and applying the enamel, an opening that matches the shape of the gemstones to be used is made in the upper part at a position designed to receive it or them, allowing a little extra space around the perimeter for the insertion of the kundan foil.

After the enameling and polishing processes are completed and before a stone can be set, the entire hollow space within the unit must be filled with a composition prepared for this purpose. Besides providing a bed upon which the gemstone rests, this method, in use for centuries, has the practical function of

Varanasi, Uttar Pradesh

MAKING METAL LEAF

798. *Making gold and silver leaf (H: sone aur chandi ka warak; Tam: thangkarekku, gold leaf; vellithazhai, silver-leaf beating; daftri kut; P: daftar, book; H: kutkar, cutting and hammering) involves the placement of pieces (diwali) of precious-metal leaf (panna or warak) between pages of a gold leaf–beating book (daftar) containing three hundred pages of sheep's scarf skin (jilli), which lies just below the wool. The skin is treated with a variety of herbs, then dried and cut into pages. Thin skins are used for gold-beating books, thick ones for silver. Bound in book form, each page is rubbed with plaster of Paris (chuna). Leaf pieces are placed between all pages; the book is slipped into a leather case, tied up, and is ready for beating.*

799. *The book is placed on a flat stone slab sunk into the workshop floor and hammered with a heavy hammer (mogra) for three to four days; about 150,000 blows are required to expand the highly malleable gold or silver into thin leaf form. The results are used to ornament wood and lac ornaments worn by dancer-actors and to decorate sweets and desserts.*

supporting the metal against possible injury and collapse due to accidental impact.

The ingredients of the compound used for this purpose vary at different localities. In Jaipur a typical composition used especially for this function, *surmai ki lakh* or *lakh surma satheni,* contains one part powdered black antimony sulfate (*surma*) to three parts sealing wax (*chapra*) of good quality. Some jewelers use a 50-50 composition, which is said to adhere well to the metal, is very long lasting, and, due to the antimony property of expanding upon cooling and solidifying, fills the hollow well. Once the heated mixture has become viscous, "threads" lifted up from the mass with a metal tool are dribbled in a thin, stringlike stream into a gemstone opening in the unit. When full, the unit is heated to be certain that the compound completely fills it and air pockets are eliminated. It is then allowed to cool and solidify.

A similar compound is also placed in the hollow parts of jewelry undergoing decorative processes that involve tool pressure, such as repoussage, chasing, other kinds of punchwork, and piercing, which in traditional jewelry is not done with a jeweler's sawblade but with small, sharp chisels that push the resulting sharp edges inward out of harm's way.

The use of polished gold or silver foil to back a transparent or translucent gemstone is standard practice in traditional Indian jewelry. The foil back improves the gemstone's appearance by providing a polished metal surface from which light passing through the stone is reflected. Because *all* settings in the *kundan* style completely enclose the lower portion of the stone, light is only accessible to it from above, as opposed to a Western, open-backed claw setting in which light enters the stone from all directions. Because the *kundan* set-

ting is closed, the presence of a foil backing is invisible.

The metal foil (H: *dak; dank; panni*) used for *kundan* setting is heavier and stiffer than metal leaf (H: *panna; pakhrauta*; A: *waraq*; H: *sone ka patti,* gold leaf; *chandi ka patti,* silver leaf) used to ornament theatrical jewelry and decorate certain foods. First, the cleaned foil is polished to brightness by rubbing it with an agate or hematite burnisher (A: *misqal*; H: *mashkala*; P: *saiqal*). Silver foil is used under colorless stones such as diamond, zircon, and white sapphire, all found in this type of jewelry. It is also used for emeralds and sapphires of good color. When it is hermetically sealed in the *kundan* setting, the foil will not darken; however, should air and moisture gain access

to the foil over time, they will cause it to darken by oxidation, which will make colorless stones appear gray.

Colored stones are often backed with foil that has been coated with a thin layer of an appropriately colored, transparent lac. In Jaipur the use of colored foil under gemstones to create color uniformity in an ornament with a multistoned *kundan* setting is called *joban kundan* (S: *joban,* beauty). Red foil is used for ruby (*lal joban*), green foil for emerald (*hari joban*), and blue foil for sapphire (*nil joban*).

The use of colored foils to improve gemstone color is not considered fraudulent in India as it was in sixteenth-century Europe, because in India the practice is generally known and accepted. Its presence can be detected in some cases by looking through the stone from the side and comparing the color seen there to its appearance when looking at the stone perpendicularly from above. Occasionally, in old jewelry, one discovers that colorless rock crystal has been made to look like a ruby or emerald by the use of a color-tinted foil backing. In some old jewelry, the color pigment on the foil has disintegrated, which makes this obvious.

Contemporary with Mughal times, and even earlier in Europe, the practice of using foil to back a gemstone mounted in a closed setting continued well into the nineteenth century. It was also common Indian practice to use foil backing for cabochon-cut (*pota*) transparent glass stones, especially in rural silver jewelry, where genuine gemstones were rarely used. Another development in the use of gold, silver, and colored foils occurred in the Punjab and Delhi. Foils were fixed in an upstanding, three-dimensional arrangement within a space provided in a hollow, open-fronted ornament, and the space containing them was then covered with a protecting glass sheet (see 227). Various three-dimensional patterns were made in this manner, the result resembling a glittering, many-petaled flower.

The *Kundan* Process

Today, *kundan* can be purchased ready-made from gold suppliers in Surat, Gujarat, a center for mechanical gold and silver manufacture in many forms. The traditional method of preparing *kundan* for use as described here is carried out at Varanasi, but the process is essentially the same wherever it is done. Its purpose is to remove all alloying metal from the gold and leave it pure (*khalis sona*, free of mixture) and malleable (*mulaim*).

Gold wire initially of the highest possible purity is drawn out with a drawplate and tongs. Lengths of it are beaten to make a flat strip (*patti*). A preparation is made of 10 percent ashes (*rakhi*) of cowdung cakes (*gobar ka tikiya*), two parts mustard oil (*sarson tel*), and one part salt (*namak*). The gold is immersed in this solution placed in a lidded pot. The pot lid is covered with cowdung cakes, which are burned for six hours. The result is allowed to cool, and the wire is washed and dried by drawing a cloth down its length. This sequence is repeated ten times. The resulting wire is wrapped around a flat iron strip or bar (*tili*) about four inches (10 cm) long and one inch (2.5 cm) wide, and beaten until each wire overlaps and joins the other. The result, a pure gold foil, is annealed and ready for use after it is folded several times to form a strip (*sona ka patti*), the form best suited to its placement around the stone.

In the Jaipur *kundan* gem-setting process (*kundan jarao kam*), the setter heats the unit by holding it over a metal bowl containing burning charcoal (*ag rakhne ka piyala*) for a time sufficient to soften the surface of the filler composition it contains. A suitably shaped piece of backing foil is placed over the opening in the unit where the stone is to be set and pressed into the filler. Over this the gemstone is placed and pressed down (*dabana*) into the filler, which forces it and the foil to take on the shape of the gemstone bottom. Displaced filler that may rise around the gemstone is allowed to cool and harden and is then scraped away. In cases where the gemstone bottom is flat, it was sometime the practice to preform the foil by pressing it into a metal mold to give it the appearance of being faceted, the pattern seen through a transparent gemstone after setting.

When surrounding a gemstone with *kundan*, the unit is fixed in the top flat disc of the handled shellac stick (*hundi; bini*) whose surface has been spread with a layer of shellac or resin softened over a charcoal fire, into which the warmed unit is pressed. Upon cooling, it solidifies and holds the unit firmly in place for working. The tool handle (*ghoti*) can either be held in one hand and the work accomplished with the other, or it can be placed in a hole made in a low worktable (*tipai ka khana*), before which the worker sits on the floor, leaving the two hands free for work.

The folded *kundan* strip (*kundan pattli*), cut to the required length with a scissors (*kainchi*), is led around the stone with a stylus (*salai*), which also is used to press it into the space between the unit metal surrounding the stone. Because the gold is pure, it has the unique ability to be welded simply by pressure, without heat. This makes it possible, without heat, to form the gold into any shape wanted around the stone, usually leaving a ridge that grips the stone at its base and acts as a bezel. In this process, loose pieces of *kundan* that fall into a metal tray (*tazli*) below are stored in a box (*kundan ka dibbi*) to be reclaimed. Finished work is pried loose from the shellac stick.

800. Delhi
Silver ear studs (karanphul) set with clear-glass, kundan-set, cabochon-shaped "stones" backed with foil; with black studs. Through the small integral loop on the stud, a chain with an end hook is attached and hooked to the hair to prevent loss.
Above: Diameter 1¾ in. (4.6 cm); weight (one) 19 g
Below: Diameter 1½ in. (3.9 cm); weight (one) 26 g
Collection the author, Porvoo

Kundan surrounding a stone may be left plain, which is the most usual treatment. An optional process is to decorate the exposed, visible edge (*bar; jah*) of the *kundan* with ornamental patterns that impart to the stone an illusion of brilliance by heightening its ability to receive, reflect, and disperse light. In all cases, they are created by impressing an appropriately patterned, design-ended punch into the soft gold. Many patterns are possible, and a few examples are listed below:

Bargola chhilai (*bar*, edge; *gol*, round; *chhilai*, from *chhil jana*, to be rubbed off): A series of small, round depressions

Bharak chhilai (*bharak*, splendor, blaze): Lines radiating outward from the stone and completely surrounding it in a sunburst effect

Laharia chhilai (*laharia*, waves): A series of zigzag or chevron lines

Sada chhilai (*sada*, blank, without ornament): Plain *kundan* without surface ornament

Delhi

GEMSTONE SETTING, KUNDAN STYLE

802. *The gemstone setter (H: kundansaz) folds the nearly pure (23k or higher) gold foil into a strip (sona patti) and cuts it in pieces. The object has been fixed on a shellac stick.*

803. *The foil is picked up with tweezers (H: chimti), placed around the gemstone, and pressed with a stylus (H: salai) into the space in the setting allowed around the gemstone perimeter.*

801. Delhi. *1902* ➤
Drawing by John Lockwood Kipling (Rudyard's father), of a Delhi gemstone setter (kundansaz or murassakar) at work
Victoria and Albert Museum, London (IS 0929)

He squats on the floor before a low workbench. All his tools are visible: a charcoal fire in ceramic bowl (right) to heat the lac; scissors to cut the foil into strips; tweezers to handle the foil; stylus to apply pressure on the foil; shallow bowl to hold fallen gold pieces; a box to store surplus gold foil for reclaiming; and magnifying spectacles held on his nose by a string attached to his turban.

Patu'a Work: Yarn Craft in Jewelry

(Terms used in this section are Hindi unless otherwise designated.)

The word *patu'a* designates a craftsman who makes objects from thread, yarn, and cord and who is a Hindu, usually of the Patvegar caste. The *patu'a*'s Muslim counterpart is the *'ilaqa-band* (from P: *'ilaqa*, connection), who generally produces articles that require greater refinement and are more expensive.

The *patu'a* and *'ilaqa-band* manipulate yarns primarily by twisting (*batwa'i; ainthna*), braiding or plaiting (*gundhnai*), wrapping (*ghernai*), knotting (*ganth banana*), netting (*jal banana*), and tassel-making (*phundna banana*). With these methods, they make a variety of yarn objects, such as pajama cords (P: *izarband*), waist belts (P: *kamarband*), loops and round yarn buttons (*ghundi*) used for clothing, and a variety of animal ornaments and decorations. We concentrate here on the work connected with jewelry and body ornaments.

Yarn objects in this category can have both religious and secular use. In the first group are the magic ornaments, such as knotted strings for the neck, upper arm, wrist, and torso. Of a quasi-religious nature are the *rakhi* (see page 42) and *sehra* (see 297, 299). Special types of garlands made in Thanjavur with yarn and tinsel also belong to this category. In the secular division are the stringing of beads and metal units used in necklaces, pendants, belts, wrist and ankle bracelets, braid ornaments, tassels, and pompons.

In India it is common for necklaces and other ornaments made of gold or silver to consist of several large or many small units, or a combination of these. These units are most often strung on cord. A supple, braided wire is used instead in some places (see 495). Frequently the units are separated from each other by a yarn ball, sometimes by precious-metal beads. The use of yarn for such purposes appreciably reduces the cost of the jewelry, but the cord mounting and yarn balls do not last long when a piece is in frequent use and must be replaced from time to time.

On a neckpiece, the two cord ends are brought together at the back and threaded through a yarn ball, which slides on them and permits adjustment of the neckpiece length. At their joined ends is a tassel (*jhabba*), which hangs down the wearer's back. Today ready-made replacement cords equipped with attached size-adjustment ball and tassel are available in jewelry bazaars for those who wish to renew worn cord ends.

Patu'a Yarns

The *patu'a* uses a wide range of yarns. Sizes range from cord (*dora; rassi; taga*) to fine string (*dori; sut*), depending on the need.

804. Murshidabad, West Bengal. *c. 1780–90*
Miniature painting of Nawab Muhammad Reza Khan of Kasimbazaar, Murshidabad
11¼ x 9⅛ in. (8.5 x 23.2 cm)
Collection Alderman-Zebrowski, London

He wears a silk cord belt (azarband) around his waist ending in an elaborate patu'a-work tassel (phundna), an excellent example of a contemporary patu'a's skill.

805. Calcutta, West Bengal ➤
Patu'a working at a client's home

Cotton (*rui*) is the most common yarn material used. When threading a necklace, the required length is approximated. That length is doubled, folded in half, and twisted to make a ply (P: *tah*). As many of these are combined as deemed necessary, the limit often depending on the size of the opening in the units or beads through which the cord must pass. The plying process (*tah karna; shikan karna*) is followed by twisting all the combined cords. Through one looped end of the result a fine wire is passed, folded in half, and twisted to form a flexible threading "needle." A rigid needle is not used because in many cases it will not pass through the often irregularly drilled or formed holes in the unit or bead threaded.

Wool (*un*) yarn is often used on silver necklaces of heavy units with large threading openings, such as those worn by rural people who lead more physically active lives than urban people. Silk (*pat; resham*) yarn is generally reserved for use with gold ornaments. It is purchased already twisted in skeins that must be reeled onto spools. Another type, which might be termed "bulk silk," comes from the unwoven warp ends of a silk cloth, such as a *sari*, which remain after the finished cloth is cut from the loom. The *patu'a* purchases this colored waste silk (*kattan,* cut off) by bulk weight from hand weavers of silk. It is used for making tassels by combing it out until the strands are parallel, attaching this to the end of the stringing yarn, tying it up, then trimming away uneven ends.

Rayon, a glossy cellulose fiber, commonly called "art silk" in India, is popular as an inexpensive silk substitute because of its shine. Synthetic materials such as nylon and Dacron are coming into wider use because of their strength and long life.

Metallic gold or silver yarns (*zari*) can be incorporated with silk or synthetic yarns to create a more elegant effect. In former days, *patu'a* work done for wealthy clients used genuine precious-metal yarn, but this is rare today, and substitutes such as gold- or silver-plated copper, or even anodized aluminum yarns, are used. Metallic yarns are manufactured mainly in Surat, Gujarat, and Varanasi, Uttar Pradesh.

Metallic yarn, called *zari* (P: *zar,* gold; *zar-i-sufed,* silver), is made in two basic types: flat or spiral. The collective name for all flat wire yarn is *badla* (from H: *badalna,* to be altered or assume another form), so called because ordinarily it is not used in plain form but is processed by spiraling it around a supporting silk, rayon, or cotton core yarn to make the forms mentioned ahead.

The collective name for spiraled or coiled *zari* wire forms is the Persian word *salma.* One ounce of precious metal makes six thousand yards of *salma.* Spiral wire is made in several types. All are produced by winding the flat *badla* around a steel spindle to make it assume a spiral form. Spindles can be round, triangular, square, or pentagonal and of various diameters. Each results in a different faceted type of *salma,* and all catch the light and glitter.

When the *patu'a* uses spiral *salma,* it must be supported by inserting a length of silk or cotton thread through the spiral before it is used, otherwise the spiral would stretch uncontrollably. The primary *salma* types used by the *patu'a* are as follows:

Chopal: Before winding the wire on the spindle, it is regularly beaten to make small, flat sections. When wound, it appears to be faceted, which heightens its reflectivity.

Dapkahua: Similar to *kora* but finer and highly polished

Ghizai: A coarse, relatively large spiral is made of a broad *badla,* first drawn through an eyelet shaped to give it a half-round form, then wrapped around the spindle

Kora: A spiral of smaller diameter than *ghizai,* with a dull surface

Motiya: Finely spiraled wire, spiraled again around a larger spindle

Naqsh: A square-sectioned, shining spiral

Tikorna: Created when the wire is spiraled around a three-sided spindle to give it a faceted effect

Any of the above can be combined to produce various effects, and many of the results are extremely elegant. Normally, flat types are contrasted with spiral types.

Imitation metallic-wires or tinsel are used on inexpensive objects. They do not retain their luster for long (as compared to gold-plated wire), but become tarnished from exposure to air or alcohol in cosmetics or perfumes.

Patu'a Tools and Techniques

Patu'a work is carried out in any jewelry bazaar, where several *patu'as* can always be found seated on a cloth spread out on the sidewalk or in a small open sidewalk stall. Nearby, also always available, is a metal-ornament cleaner and a gold plater, whose jobs are to clean and, if necessary, gold-plate jewelry units before they are restrung. The client often waits and watches the undertaken work until it is done.

The *patu'a's* tools are few and simple, each well designed for manipulating yarn and finishing the work. Because the tools are all portable, a *patu'a* is frequently called upon to work at the home of a client, where work can be carried out in privacy under the client's supervision.

The *patu'a* begins with the *natai,* a drum on which skein-wound yarn is placed to be unwound onto a small, long-handled wooden reel (*charkhi; batani; tili*), from which yarn is released during work. The tool and thread are manipulated by first anchoring the yarn end, then rotating the reel by its long handle to carry the thread in a spiral motion around the necessary places over the foundation cord.

The ornament is worked on by hooking one end of the supporting cords to an upright pillar or post (*thannu* or *thunnu*) of stout wood about eighteen inches (46 cm) high, anchored in a heavy, weighted base, often a large stone with a central hole to accommodate the shaft, which has an iron hook (*ankra; ankora*) attached to its top. The threads being worked must be held under tension.

The same name and function apply to a loose iron hook with a large attached loop. This could be termed the *patu'a's* "traveling hook," because it is used when he works away from his usual location and does not bring the *thannu* and its heavy base with him. The hook's large eye is slipped over the large toe of his right foot, half-extended before him at the

805

necessary length while he sits on the floor. The distance depends on the length of the cord needed to thread the units. The hook end points toward him. Around this the stringing cords are looped. During work he places tension on the string simply by extending his foot. In this position, with the cord held taut, he can best judge the spacing of the units.

Indian craftsmen often use bare feet and toes to perform many tasks. This practice is astonishing to Western craftsmen, whose feet are immobilized in shoes. J. L. Kipling, Rudyard Kipling's father, who lived and worked in India, remarked that this "quadrumanous facility (found in all primates except man, but highly developed among Indian craftsmen) is of the greatest use in silk-winding, braiding, and gilt-cord making in which the great toe is constantly used to hold the work (and tool)."

Other *patu'a* tools include scissors (*katarni*; P: *qainchi*; *miqraz*), used to cut thread; a knife (*chhuri*) whose edge is used in cutting, and whose side is sometimes used as a surface against which yarn balls are smoothed; and a large needle (*salai*) used for smoothing and compacting thread wound around other thread in various systems.

A flat, smooth, ivory spatula (*mathar*, from *mathna,* to squeeze) is used to squeeze wound yarns tightly by rotating the part against it with the thumb and for purposes similar to those of the *salai* on occasions when that tool is not suitable. A large darning needle (*sua*) is used to bring yarn ends between other tight threads in the work to anchor and finish them off. A small, fine needle (*sui*) is used for similar purposes but on a smaller scale.

The *Paranda:* A Popular *Patu'a* Product

This woman's hair-braid ornament variously called *paranda, phundri, chotia,* or *balchoti* is used all over India. It consists of a loose hank of normally black silk, rayon, cotton, or synthetic yarn, about twelve inches (30 cm) long, or longer, divided into three loose groups that are braided with the hair into a queue (*choti*) that hangs at the back, with this fancy yarn tassel or a metal ornament attached to its end. Adding this yarn to the natural hair in the braid increases its bulk, which is desirable among Indians because voluminous hair is a mark of feminine beauty. Its additional weight tends to keep the braid in place at the wearer's back, which is why it is used by professional dancers. The Persian term *parand,* from which *paranda* comes, meaning "winged creature or bird," refers to the braid's flying motion in response to the wearer's movements.

The best *parandas* are elaborate inventions that exploit all the *patu'a's* tricks of the trade. Ornate, expensive *parandas* are often used by a bride at her wedding and by others at special occasions. A skillful *patu'a* can make about three intricate *parandas* in a day.

806

807

◄ 806. Thanjavur, Tamil Nadu
*Garland maker (malaikkarar) preparing
a presentation garland (oppuvikkaimalai)
using gold tinsel (kakkayppon), press-
molded beads scented with civet cat
musk (punugupunai), strung aromatic
spices (sugantharavasthu), including
cloves (kirambu) and cardamum (elam)*

*This style of garland is a specialty of the
Venugopalam family in Thanjavur, famed
for their manufacture of elaborately constructed garlands of natural materials
combined with metallic tinsel in ingenious, inventive ways. These carefully
constructed structures, unique in India,
embody great elegance in refinement
of form and proportion. The care taken
in their design details gives them the
appearance of south Indian oversized
jeweled malai-type necklaces (iraththina-
malai). A style of garland started by this
family, its production began in 1955
when the local collector asked the maker
to create a new kind of garland, "which
would be creditable to the artistic tradition of Tanjore."*

◄ 807. Ajmer, Rajasthan
*Woman's hair-braid ornament (paranda
or balchoti) of red wool with gold-yarn
(zari) ornamentation
Tassel length 7 in. (17.8 cm)
Collection the author, Porvoo*

*Braided into an Indian woman's hair,
which is often arranged in a three-lock
plait at the back, this ornament is symbolic of the mystic union of three sacred
Indian rivers: the Ganges, Jamuna, and
Saraswati, the latter a venerated river
said to have gone underground. Their
confluence (triveni) occurs at Allahabad,
an auspicious site. Paranda, "a winged
creature," is the Malayalam name for the
sacred Brahmany kite (Halliastur indus),
associated with Garuda. It is held in
great veneration by women, who apply
its name to this "flying" end of braid
ornament.*

808. Jodhpur, Rajasthan
*Gold-tinsel turban ornament (turra) worn
throughout Rajasthan by bridegrooms
and sometimes used to ornament a horse
Height 15¾ in. (40 cm)
Collection the author, Porvoo*

*In about ten shops in the Kapra Bazaar,
Jodhpur, patu'as work in the purest
Rajput style. This ornament was made
by Duli Chand Jain Turewala.*

7 EURO-INDIAN AND INDO-EUROPEAN JEWELRY: A CROSS-CULTURAL EXCHANGE

Western interest in Eastern design traditions has a long history in the development of its arts. For more than three hundred years, British-Indian colonials were exposed to Indian jewelry and the persistent cultural obsession of Indians with precious metal jewelry and gemstones. The Portuguese, French, and Dutch who were also there availed themselves of India's jewelry resources, especially the diamonds, garnets, agates, and other stones that fed the European gemstone market. Each of these countries played a part in the dissemination to Europe of Indian design concepts in jewelry and especially textiles.

The flow of technical and stylistic resources between India and the West constituted a creative melting pot. For convenience in discussing this complex interchange, designs originating in India that came to Europe can be termed Indo-European; those that emigrated from Europe to India, Euro-Indian. Among the latter are the introduction of the cameo, and a form of miniature portrait painting used in jewelry, both discussed ahead. In the nineteenth century especially, European technical innovations were introduced, such as the use of claw settings for gemstones and mechanical polishing, both alien to traditional Indian jewelry manufacture and not discussed here.

809, 810. *Queen Alexandra of Great Britain as she appeared in costume for a fancy dress ball at Devonshire House, given on July 2, 1897 to celebrate Queen Victoria's Diamond Jubilee. Alexandra represented Marguerite de Valois and wore many pieces from the suite of traditional Indian jewelry (810) given to her by Queen Victoria in 1863 at the time of her marriage to Edward, Prince of Wales, later Edward VII. (Valuable Indian jewelry was presented to Queen Victoria by the East India Company in 1851, at the closing of the Great Exhibition, and these items may have been among them.) Among the items visible in the photograph are a seven-strand pearl necklace (sat lara har) with emerald pendants, two diamond-set armlets (bazuband) edged with pearls, a long pearl necklace with gemstones placed at intervals (vijayamala), and a necklace with a diamond and emerald pendant (kantha), here placed at her waist. The bazubands seem to be fixed to the sides of her bodice. Over her white kid gloves are a pair of jeweled Indian bracelets (kara). Queen Alexandra apparently considered these Indian pieces to be "costume" jewelry, only suited for use on such a light-hearted occasion. The Hulton-Deutch Collection, London*

809

810

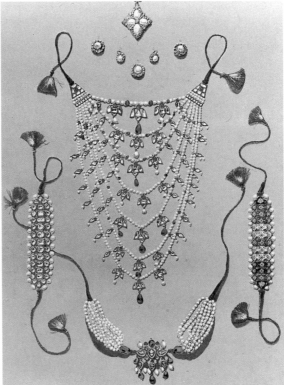

811. Punjab. *c. 1902 (opposite)*
King Edward VII and his consort, Queen Alexandra, depicted as the King-Emperor and Queen-Empress of India
Miniature painting in gouache on paper
9¹⁵/₁₆ x 7¾ in. (25 x 19.5 cm)
National Gallery of Modern Art, New Delhi (2336)

This royal icon of the imperial rulers, interpreted by an Indian artist, is an amusing cultural blend of East and West. It was probably painted in 1902, when the subjects were enthroned as rulers of Great Britain and emperor and empress of India, the latter title inherited from Queen Victoria. Their faces are depicted with exquisite verisimilitude, but their attire and ornaments, though appropriate to their high status in India, are totally fanciful.

The emperor's turban (pagri) is heavily ornamented with a sarpech, a frontal ornament in the form of a crown, topped by the three feathers, his symbol as Prince of Wales. Around his neck is a six-strand pearl choker, a necklace with pendant emeralds, a long necklace with large rubies, and a collar and badge of an imaginary order. In his right hand he holds a gemstone-ornamented sword (talwar), a symbol of manhood and authority. All these ornaments have their counterparts in contemporary photographs of Indian maharajas (see 719, 742).

Empress Alexandra is depicted as a jewel-bedecked maharani. Among her ornaments are an Indian septum ring (bulaq), a thumb ring with mirror (arsi), and ankle bracelets (paizeb) on her bare feet, whose toes unaccountably lack rings, which, as a married woman, she should have worn. The only concession to reality here is her miniature diamond-studded crown, which she inherited from Queen Victoria in 1901.

812. Bombay, Maharashtra. *19th century*
Silver necklace (kantha) made for a European client
Total length 15 in. (38.2 cm); chain width ⅞ in.
(2.2 cm); center height 6½ in. (16.2 cm);
weight 248 g
Victoria and Albert Museum, London (IM 1-1942)

The design incorporates Indian construction concepts
as are found in chain anklets (paizeb). The crescent
motif, here ornamented with miniature torsos of an
unidentifiable crowned deity with upraised arms lacks
that accuracy in iconography that is always present in
swami-style work. Ornamented with hanging bells
(ghungrus).

813. Northern India ➤
Necklace of seven strands (sat lara har) of pearls
regularly interspersed with ruby and emerald beads;
each strand has a central gemstone-set pendant
(tikri) (see 863).
Length 10¼ to 17⁵⁄₁₆ in. (26–44 cm)
Courtesy Gem Palace, Jaipur

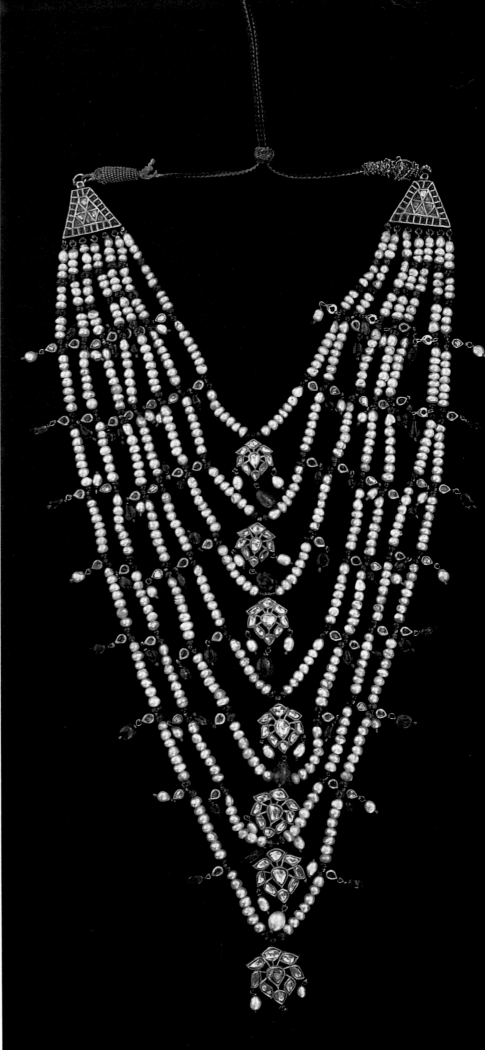

Early Exchanges

Mughal Cameo Carving: A European Glyptic Transplant

The carving of precious or semiprecious hardstones to create small figural intaglios and cameos in relief had no ancient precedence in India, nor was it one of the established traditional accomplishments of Mughal court lapidaries. This is remarkable when one considers the high level of Mughal achievement in the use of hardstones for the manufacture of flat objects such as seals, amulets, and mirror backs, and three-dimensional archer's rings, dagger handles, wine cups, ink pots, and bowls.

Cameos became well known to the Mughal court from European examples brought to India by merchants and European royal emissaries. When Francisco Pelsaert, head of the Dutch East India Company factory at Agra from 1624 to 1627, compiled a suggested list of objects to be sent from the Netherlands as gift offerings to the Emperor Jahangir to solicit his support, he mentioned Italian agate portrait cameos such as those already brought to India overland from Venice, which had been given by others as presents and favorably received. Existing miniature paintings depicting Jahangir show him and other court members wearing cameos, and it is known that cameos and miniature portraits bearing his image were given as presents of favor to princes and court members who proudly wore them on their turbans.

Considering this background, it is surprising that the art of cameo carving apparently did not find lasting patronage. The few that remain, from the reign of Shah Jahan, are now in the collections of Western museums. Additional examples may yet appear as hardstones are durable, and the low intrinsic value of the hardstone used for a cameo precludes its conversion to other uses.

In the West, royal courts in Italy and France, during a time span that includes the High Mughal period, became centers for the manufacture of particularly noteworthy carved hardstone objects and cameo portraits. The main Italian centers were Milan and Florence, and later on manufacture returned to Rome,

814. Delhi; or Agra, Uttar Pradesh.
c. 1630–40
Sardonyx cameo (khodi patthar taswir) depicting Shah Jahan at about age forty-five
1 15/16 x 3/4 in. (2.3 x 2 cm)
Victoria and Albert Museum, London (IS 14-1974)

This cameo was believed to have been made by a resident European lapidary, who modeled it after a painted miniature portrait (shast) of the shah. It was given by him as a reward for services rendered to a relative, envoy, or a courtier, who wore it on his turban as a sign of the shah's favor, a practice most common during the reign of Jahangir, father of Shah Jahan.

815. Maharaja Dhulip Singh of the Punjab *(1837–1893), painted by J. A. Goldingham. Besides his splendid Indian ornaments, he wears a diamond framed miniature portrait of Queen Victoria and a cameo ring with her effigy, both given to his father, Ranjit Singh, by Lord Auckland, as well as the collar and badge of the Most Exalted Order of the Star of India (see 742).*

At the conclusion of the Second Sikh War in 1849, the British annexed the Punjab, and this son of Ranjit Singh, and the last Punjabi ruler, was at age twelve placed in the charge of Dr. John Login, his British tutor-guardian. In 1854 he chose to become a Christian and move to England, where he led the life of a wealthy country gentleman. A favorite of Queen Victoria, he was often invited to royal dinner parties and made many court visits, where he appeared, as here, in Indian costume suited to a Maharaja and wore fabulous jewelry he still possessed.

Years later, Dhulip became resentful of his settlement treatment. He returned to the Punjab, where he reembraced the Sikh religion and began a life of intrigue. The disapproving British government ordered his return to England, but he went to Russia and France, where he unsuccessfully sought support for his claim to the objects in the Lahore Treasury, which had been sold at auction in 1850–51 as state property. As a result of his activities, his pension was discontinued, but when he repented, the queen pardoned him and it was restored. He returned to England but thereafter led a restless life of travel in Europe.

where the art had originated. The extremely subtle relief carving in these miniature cameos, among the best this genre ever produced, suggests the influence of contemporary Renaissance low relief alabaster and marble sculpture. An Indian example of this genre is illustration 816.

Unlike the Shah Jahan cameos reproduced here, few of the early Italian and French cameos were signed. Signatures became more common in the second half of the sixteenth century, when the craft grew in popularity and cameo production in Italy became an organized, mass-production enterprise carried out in large workshops.

It is known that French and Italian jewelers and lapidaries worked at the Mughal court, and portraits and figural cameos done there obviously embody the technical principles that long governed European glyptics. It is the lack of any precedence for this particular genre in India that has suggested to some historians that these cameos were probably created by Europeans working for the Mughal court. The high skill evident in them could conceivably be explained by the sudden appearance there of a European artisan already possessing mature skill in this demanding technology.

Yet only circumstantial conjecture of this kind supports this claim, and their authorship must be left uncertain. On the other hand we must take into account the amply recorded ability of many Indian craftsmen to imitate exactly any exotic model in any medium.

Signatures such as that which appears in Persian on the portrait cameo of Shah Jahan shed no light on this question. It is not a European name but an honorific one awarded to the maker. In Mughal times, this was often done, even when the artisan was a foreigner. Its presence, however, implies that the maker must have earned this title not simply by this single achievement but by the fabrication of others, of which at present no trace exists.

A Shah Jahan Cameo: Prince Khurram Attacks a Lion

This unique Mughal sardonyx cameo is now one of the Islamic treasures in the Cabinet des Médailles of the Bibliothèque Nationale in Paris. It is mounted in a seventeenth-century enameled gold frame with a suspension loop, typical of others used with contemporary European cameos. Its sunburst design of pointed and trilobic projecting elements suitably symbolizes the Hindu and Muslim convention of radiance (S: *prabha*) emanating from its exalted main subject, Prince Khurram.

The hieratic theme of a king attacking or killing a lion to symbolize a ruler's power was a frequent subject in ancient stone carvings from Mesopotamia and Iran. This cameo, however, commemorates an actual event that took place in December 1610, as described by Emperor Jahangir, prince Khurram's father, in his memoirs, the *Tuzuk-i-Jahangiri*. The same incident is the subject of an earlier miniature painting, probably commissioned by Jahangir, in the *Badshah Nama*, a collection of miniature paintings now in The Royal Collection, The Royal Library, Windsor Castle.

816. Delhi; or Agra, Uttar Pradesh
Polychromed alabaster bas-relief portrait of Shah Jahan at about age forty-five, shown at an oriel window (jharokha) on the face of a palace wall, a practice that indicated to the watching public that he was still alive
4½ x 3⁵⁄₁₆ in. (11.5 x 8.4 cm)
Rijksmuseum, Amsterdam (AK-NM-12249)

The only known alabaster life portrait of the shah, it may have been executed by a resident foreign carver. The emperor wears a sarpech with black heron plumes on a red and gold turban draped with pearls, an arrowhead-shaped amulet, and two necklaces, one of pearls, the other of pearls and larger precious gemstone beads (mala).

817. Delhi; or Agra, Uttar Pradesh ➤
17th century
Sardonyx cameo of Prince Khurram fighting a lion who had attacked Anup Ray, a courtier. Set in an enameled gold frame
2⅝ x 2¹³⁄₁₆ in. (6.7 x 7.2 cm)
Bibliothèque National, Paris (B 88782)

The cameo bears two separate Persian inscriptions. At the top left, just behind the prince's back is carved *shabih-i sahib-i qiran-i sani shah jahan padshah-i ghazi* (LIKENESS OF THE SECOND LORD OF THE [AUSPICIOUS] CONJUNCTION, SHAH JAHAN, THE KING, WARRIOR OF THE FAITH). Since Prince Khurram, the main character depicted, had already become Emperor Shah Jahan, as evidenced from this title on the cameo, it must have been made *after* his accession to the throne in 1628, a time lapse of at least eighteen years from the date of the incident. The cameo was probably executed at someone's suggestion to please Shah Jahan after he became emperor or by order of the emperor himself to commemorate the event.

The second inscription just below the prince's feet reads *amal-i kan atamm* (WORK OF KAN ATTAM, SUPREME ENGRAVER). If it is correct to assume that the unknown maker was a European employed by the court, this was his honorific title, granted by the shah in recognition of his excellence. Presumably done by the cameo maker, both inscriptions are extremely small and well executed, attesting to the carver's skill.

The incident depicted began with Prince Khurram accompanying his father, Jahangir, on a hunting expedition. Beaters reported a tiger on the scene (in the cameo it has become a lion, possibly due to an error in etymology). Although it was late in the day, Jahangir decided to pursue the animal and ordered someone to so inform Prince Khurram, who rushed on horseback to where the others had gathered. The roaring animal charged Jahangir, who fired his rifle. Although hit, the lion continued its attack, and, in their haste to escape its rage,

nearby servants trampled Jahangir. The lion charged at an attendant, Anup Ray, who bravely faced it and "struck it twice on the head with a baton (*kutaka*) which he held with both hands." The animal seized and bit both of Anup Ray's arms with such force that its teeth passed through them, but "the baton and the *bracelets* on his arms were helpful, and did not allow his arms to be destroyed." (An unexpected commentary on the prudence of wearing jewelry when hunting.)

Prince Khurram and an assistant came to Ray's rescue but could not kill the beast. Anup Ray "with force dragged his arms from the lion's mouth, but they were partly torn." The lion and Ray stood up, then "rolled over each other, holding on like two wrestlers." Finally the lion retreated, but Anup Ray, unbested by all that had happened, vengefully followed him and struck a blow to its brow that caused the skin to fall over both its eyes. At this terrible denouement, others finished off the suffering beast.

Jahangir tells us that Anup Ray, the *real* hero of the incident, recovered from his wounds. For the service of having protected Jahangir's life, he was given the title *Anira'i Singh-dalan* (Leader of an Army, Lion Slayer), presented with one of Jahangir's swords, and awarded an increase in his official station (*mansab*).

In this excellent quality sardonyx cameo, the lion and Anup Ray's head are carved in the uppermost dark brown stratum of the stone. Most of the rest of Anup Ray and the lion's rear legs are in a beige stratum, which carries over into Prince Khurram's turban (*pagri*), armlet (*bazuband*), sash (*patka*), and dagger (*khattam*). Prince Khurram and his sword are formed

completely in the next, white stratum, appearing as if in a spotlight. The background is in a bluish-brown stratum, and a surrounding intaglio cartouche, and the inscriptions are in a final, lowest, light blue stratum. This makes a total of at least five color strata, a tour de force achievement that gives the whole the appearance of a grisaille painting.

Mughal Miniature Portraits: Ivory Icons as Jewelry Insets

Before the advent of the Mughals, the realistic representation of individuals did not exist in Indian miniature painting. Representations depicting such persons abounded but were influenced by Persian miniature idealized painting styles and cannot reliably be considered realistic.

The trend toward realism in Mughal miniature portraiture in the sixteenth and seventeenth centuries can be attributed in part to the influence of European styles of painting, which became available to court miniature painters through increased contact with Westerners by trade and the arrival of resident missionaries, such as the Jesuits. European prints, portrait miniatures, and paintings, often with religious subjects, were given as gifts to Mughal rulers and courtiers in attempts to proselytize them. Many extant miniature paintings, obviously based on such European subjects, were reproduced by Indians who carefully emulated the European three-dimensional, chiaroscuro style. Further inspired by foreign portrait miniatures that expressed the personality of the subject, Indian miniature painters produced innovative portraits representing actual features of specific individuals, even when the result might be unflattering. The novelty of the paintings attracted the rulers, who ordered miniatures incorporating this new approach.

The idea of the miniature portrait (*chhoti taswir*) as a head and shoulders composition in a round, square, or, after 1570, oval format typical of contemporary European miniature portraits, and the concept of mounting them in jewelry did not exist in India until after contact with the British.

British miniature portraits of the late sixteenth century were particularly skillful. They were painted on vellum or parchment glued to card, a stiff pasteboard that often served as the ground support. When such portraits started in India, the ground was paper, but sometime in the mid-seventeenth century, an indigenous material—ivory—eminently suited to this purpose was introduced. The use of an ivory slab (H: *hathi dant ke takhti*) as a ground seems to be the Indian contribution to this genre, and miniature portraits on ivory (H: *shabih par hathi dant*) in opaque watercolors later became the specialty of some British and Continental miniaturists, beginning with the reign of James II (1685–88).

In India, artists were ordered to attend important court functions to record events with sketches from life, then create a painting in the royal ateliers (H: *taswir khana*). It was not unusual for the miniature portraits in figural compositions to be the work of a portrait specialist. Likeness was most important and was often commented upon in marginal inscriptions written by the subject or a relative.

In Great Britain, sovereigns gave miniature portraits of themselves as gifts to express favor or to reward the receiver, and courtiers presented theirs to the ruler to signify fidelity. British rulers also commissioned them for use in international trade negotiations and diplomacy. This we know from the writings of Sir Thomas Roe, who served as the first British Ambassador to India from 1615 to 1619 in an attempt to establish "quiet Trade and Commerce without any kind of hindrance or molestation."

Roe presented a portrait of James I to the Mughal Emperor Jahangir, who considered himself to be a connoisseur of painting. He thought highly of his court miniature painters, as evidenced by Roe's description of his reaction to what may have been his first exposure to British miniature portraits. In his journal entry of July 13, 1616, Roe wrote, "I had a picture [miniature portrait] of a friend of mine that I esteemed very much, . . . which I wanted to give to His Majesty as a present, seeing as how he is so much affected by that art… [and] assuring myself that he never saw any equal to it." He showed it to Prince Asaf Khan, Jahangir's brother-in-law, through whom Roe

819

820

819, 820. Delhi.
c. 1660–70
Album page (with detail at right) painted by Bichitr, a master court painter to the Emperor Jahangir
10 x 7⅛ in. (25.3 x 18.1 cm)
Courtesy of the Freer Gallery of Art, Smithsonian Institution, Washington, D.C. (42.15A)

In this allegorical composition, Jahangir is enthroned on an hourglass. He is attended by King James I of England among others. The portrait of James I (820) seems to be a faithful copy of one believed to have been made by Isaac Oliver and presented by Sir Thomas Roe, the first English ambassador to India, as an official gift to Jahangir. He wears the famous gemstone-set "feather" aigrette on his hat.

dealt with the emperor, who "assured me it would be the most welcome gift I ever presented … and Asaf Kahn … presented it to the King," who "took extreme content, and showed it to every man near him," then sent for his chief painter and asked his opinion of it. "The foole answered he could make as goode." Jahangir said to Roe, "My man says he can do as well as this, what do you say to that?" Roe replied, "I know the contrary." "But if he does, said the King, what do you say?" Roe replied he would give him 10,000 rupees, "for I know none in Europe but the same master [Isaac Oliver] could do so." Jahangir then ordered his four best painters to try.

Twenty-four days later, the miniatures were completed. Again the emperor asked Roe what he would give if he could not recognize his original painting. They jestingly discussed a reward to the painter. Roe was invited to return that night, and by candlelight Jahangir showed him six pictures, five painted by the chief court painters. Roe "was troubled to discern which was which." He praised the emperor's painters and Jahangir was loud with pleasure. Roe agreed: "I saw His Majesty needed no picture from our country." Roe showed Jahangir a miniature of James I, and Jahangir offered to send one of himself to James. Roe accepted the offer and asked for one for himself, "to keep and leave to my posterity as a sign of His Majesty's favor." Jahangir agreed and ordered them to be made.

It became the custom at the Mughal court to emulate British prototypes. Portraits made of the emperor were a form of imperial propaganda, symbolic rewards to deserving members of the royal family and vassals as a sign of high royal favor. A number have survived, and some are depicted in miniature paintings being worn as personal adornments on a turban or suspended from a necklace.

Nineteenth-Century Indian Portrait Miniatures

The first quarter of the nineteenth century witnessed a proliferation in Delhi of popular miniature portraits on ivory made in the British oval format. The subjects, historic figures from the Mughal past, were personalities who evoked the drama, mystery, and former splendor of life at the Mughal court. The most sought after subjects were Nur Jahan, the clever, talented, manipulating wife of Jahangir; Mumtaz Mahal, the ideal, much-loved wife of Shah Jahan, for whom he built the faultless Taj Mahal; Jahanara, faithful daughter of Shah Jahan; and the great Mughal emperors Akbar, Jahangir, and Shah Jahan. These were the main themes used for portraits on ivory used in jewelry.

As in Europe, repetitions of these subjects led to standardized face masks that were accepted by the anonymous Delhi miniaturists who produced them. Cult images of men, though also stylized, came closer to verisimili-

tude since their prototypes were paintings made during the subject's lifetime. Those of the court women, on the other hand, are imaginary because these women lived secluded lives almost entirely confined to harem quarters, and were never seen by outside men. Different in style from miniature portraits at their prime in the seventeenth and eighteenth centuries, these tirelessly repeated nineteenth-century formula portraits still follow traditional representational conventions: full face (P: *sanmukh,* front face; also called *do chashm,* two eyes); three-quarter face (*paunedo chashm,* three-quarters); one side plus one fourth (*sawa chashm,* one and a quarter more: from temple to chin); right profile (*dahini ek chashm*); and left profile (*bai ek chashm*).

After 1845, ivory miniature portraits of Mughal luminaries found new patronage. British residents in India and intrepid travelers in search of the picturesque purchased them as worthwhile souvenirs. Foreigners seem to have responded to the white-skinned, almond-eyed beauties who could pass as Victorian ladies in masquerade-ball dress. They, and their illustrious partners painted on ivory, were mounted in jewelry covered with a protecting crystal.

Mounted portraits were set in gold frames by Indian jewelers who sought European patronage by imitating fashionable European contemporary forms of jewelry. Frames were usually executed in the Indian equivalent of the European cannetille gold-filigree style (so called after a European type of embroidery popular there in the first half of the nineteenth century and continuing in India throughout the century). Miniatures were framed in filigree brooches or placed in lockets. Especially popular was a bracelet composed of five or more subject units, their frames linked by loops or hinges in the basic format of popular contemporary European bracelets set with a series of cameos based on portraits from Roman antiquity or Swiss enameled portraits of ladies in Cantonese costumes.

821. Delhi. *c. 1890*
Miniature portraits, in gouache on ivory, of Mughal court ladies, presumed to be Nur Jahan (left), and Mumtaz Mahal (right)
Approximate height 2³⁄₁₆ in. (5.5 cm)
Victoria and Albert Museum. London (IS 531-1959)

822. Delhi. *c. 1615–30*
Mughal miniature portrait, in gouache on paper, of a European lady, probably copied by an Indian artist from a European original
Fondation Custodia (Collection F. Lught), Institut Néerlandais, Paris (1986-T37)

Such a portrait in an oval format is the type painted by Isaac Oliver of the wife of Sir Thomas Roe, which Roe gave to the Emperor Shah Jahangir to be copied for the amusement of his wives. Gold and silver pigment was used to delineate the jewelry.

823

824

823. Delhi. *19th century*
Gold bracelet (taswir par hathidant pahunchi) with five miniature portraits on ivory
7⅛ x 1½ in. (18.2 x 3.8 cm)

Left: An unidentified man, possibly the heir apparent; center: the Emperor Dost Muhammad
Khan Bahadur Shah II, the last Mughal emperor (died 1862); and three Mughal court ladies
(Begams), possibly his wives and daughters. In 1883, the leading Delhi miniature portrait on ivory
painters were Zulficar Khan; Kutb-u-Din; Mohamad Husain; and their workshop.

824. Delhi. *Mid-19th century*
*Gold bracelet (taswir ka pahunchi) of five hinged units, the three central ones a framework for
miniature portraits on ivory depicting Mughal nobility*
Height 2⅜ in. (6 cm); weight 97.8 g
Courtesy Christie's, London

Represented here is Nur Jahan, wife of Emperor Jahangir, painted by a Delhi portrait miniaturist,
probably a Muslim. The bracelet is fabricated in repoussage with wirework and shot applications
(a style called cannetile in contemporary Europe) and set with rubies, emeralds, and pearls. Such
portraits were also set in earrings, brooches, pendants, and necklaces, and their backs sometimes
ornamented with Partabgarh thewa work units (see 708).

380 · A Cross-Cultural Exchange

Eventually supplanted by photography, miniature portraits on ivory of the same subjects continue to be made by specialists in Old Delhi, although not nearly to their former extent, and they are no longer mounted in jewelry, but are fixed on objects or framed. Nineteenth-century "originals" occasionally appear in antique shops in Calcutta, New Delhi, or Bombay, but they are more likely to be found in jewelry shops in London, where the descendants of relatives who acquired them in India now dispose of them.

Indian *Sarpeches* and European *Aigrettes*: Turban-Ornament Interchange

An ideal illustration of the design interchange that took place in the Indian and European jewelry encounter occurred in the case of the Indian *sarpech* and the European *aigrette*, the former traditionally worn on the turban (S: *chira; sirastraka;* H: *sarband; dastar; pagri;* P: *dulband;* Turk: *dulbend; turbant; tulipant*), a head covering widespread in India and also formerly worn in Persia and Turkey. Turban form, and the jewelry used in its decoration, were stylistically related in these places but ultimately distinctive in each.

Although turbans have been in use in India since antiquity, they were especially prominent during Mughal times. Formerly turbans were worn by men of all social strata, from ruler to peasant. Today it is found largely to the provincial areas of Rajasthan and Gujarat, where it is used as a head cover by shepherds and farmers mainly as protection against exposure to the hot Indian sun. Military personnel in India formerly wore turbans to cushion a sword blow to the head, but only a few special troops do so now for ornamental or religious reasons, as among Sikh soldiers. Most Indian men, particularly in cities, have adopted Western dress, but, because of the turban's symbolic significance, it is commonly worn on special occasions such as a wedding. A groom often wears traditional festive dress, which includes a turban with an attached *sarpech* ornament, as if, in so doing, for this occasion his status is elevated to that of the nobility.

Various turban-tying styles distinguish groups by religion, region, or indicate the wearer's social position or occupation. Additional information about the wearer can be communicated by a turban's shape, color, and the jewelry used in its ornamentation.

According to Indian thought, the turban is a sexual symbol representing manhood and personal dignity. Related symbolic attributes include virtue, honor, reverence, respect, and brotherhood.

A man's turban is his sacrosanct property, and custom forbids another to touch or forcibly remove the turban worn by a Hindu or Muslim. A turban could, however, be removed *willingly* by a wearer according to a Mughal custom in which two men of equal rank *exchange* turbans as a symbol of an everlasting bond of brotherhood. The term to describe this act is "turban-exchanged brother" (*pagri badal bhai*) and was thereafter applied to their honor-bound relationship. Two men might resort to this custom as a means of confirming an agreement, on which they staked their honor and veracity.

825. Kamadeva

The Hindu god of love is depicted in this popular bazaar painting as a handsome young man wearing a full lexicon of turban ornaments in use in the nineteenth century and many other ornaments.

Should a person be in distress, when appealing to an official for clemency, he would remove his turban and touch his head to the ground before him. A defaulter or accused placed his turban at the feet of the person to whom he was indebted or those of his accuser. By this servile act, punishment might be avoided or at least mitigated. If a suppliant removed and threw a *jeweled* turban at the feet of the person appealed to, this act, considered to be one of *desperate* humility, often effected sympathetic results.

That a turban consists of many layers of wrapped cloth suggested its use as a safe hiding place for small, extremely precious objects, such as a gemstone, which is safest upon its owner's person. This practice, in conjunction with the aforementioned Mughal custom of "honorary turban exchange," was the impetus for the famous event by which, in 1739, the Koh-i-Nur diamond passed from its owner, the Mughal Emperor Muhammad Shah, emperor of Delhi from 1719 to 1748, to Nadir Shah, the rapacious conquerer from Persia.

Chief among several kinds of ornaments used to decorate a turban are the *sarpech,* the *kalgi,* the *sarpatti,* and the *turra.* According to Mughal sumptuary laws, these ornaments could only be worn by royalty, blood relatives of a chief, and honored individuals, the latter generally being nobility or high officials. They acquired special importance as symbols of hierarchical power.

Turban Feathers:
Kalgi, the Indian *Aigrette*

The concept of giving the gold turban ornament a featherlike form combined with an actual cluster of handsome feathers, an *aigrette,* was inspired by the plumes that project from the heads of some birds and grow on the backs, wings, and tails of others. Long plumes that protrude rearward from the back of a bird's head are called occipital crests because they emerge near the occipital bone, part of the posterior compound bone of a bird's skull.

Using plumes with the Indian turban ornament is associated with the Mughal court, but the practice originated in Turkestan and came to India from there with the invasion of the Mughals in the thirteenth century. The most distinguished Mughal variety consisted of three black occipital heron feathers (*kalgi*), whose use was reserved by Mughal royalty as a symbol of high status.

Several heron species are indigenous to India, but only a few bear black occipital head plumes, and their relative rarity contributed to the high value placed upon them. The main source of them is the male gray heron (*Ardea cinerea*). Persons using such feathers as crests appear in the portraits (*tasawir*) of rulers and the nobility in Mughal miniature paintings. In these representations, the feathers do not stand upright but, corresponding to those on the bird,

extend backward, their ends drooping. To exaggerate this admired downward curve, pearls, large or small, were attached as weights to the feather ends.

The concept of attaching pearls to the ends of actual *kalgi* plumes was transferred to gold gemstone-set turban *sarpech* ornaments stylistically designed as curving precious-metal "feathers." At their terminal points was suspended either a pearl, a smooth-surfaced emerald, ruby, or spinel drop, or a briolette-faceted diamond.

Another feather commonly associated with the *aigrette* (and from which the term is derived) and still in use as a crest is the long, white feather that during the mating season grows as nuptial plumage on the lower back of certain species of both male and female white egrets, who inhabit wetland areas. As a prelude to mating, the male uses them to attract the female by erecting and agitating them. After mating, they are molted and next year grow again.

True egrets belong to the genus *Egretta,* family *Areidae.* In India three species of white egrets are common: large (*Egretta alba*), medium (*Egretta intermedia*), and small (*Egretta garzetta*). The cattle egret (*Bululcus ibis*), often seen feeding on insects while standing on the backs of herbiverous grazing cattle, has orange-buff mating feathers that are not used for this purpose.

826. Jaipur, Rajasthan

A bridegroom (dulha) in traditional dress for the occasion, as a Rajput maharaja, wearing an aigrette (sarpech) with a black heron feather crest (kalgi), and a gemstone-set necklace, probably borrowed from relatives

827

Until recently, monal or impeyan pheasant (*Lophophorus impejanus*) iridescent neck feathers were used in Himachal Pradesh as a crest (*kalgi*), placed at the side of the upturned velvet band of a man's woolen hat. This bird, which inhabits the Himalayan hill range, is now a protected species (see 57).

The *Sarpech*

The word *sarpech* literally means "head, front, or forepart" (*sar*) and "screw" (*pech*). In Persia where it was also worn, it was called *jikka* or *jiqa,* which means "crest" or "tuft," and in Turkey it is *sorguch,* a corruption of the Persian *sarpush,* from which came the Indian Urdu term *sarpech.* In India a distinction is made between the ornament (*sarpech*) and the feather tuft (*kalgi*). Together, turban ornament and ornamental plume (*sarpech-sant-kalgi*) formed part of the insignia of rank of both Muslim and Hindu princes.

In India, the design of the *sarpech* underwent several stages of development. Those of the sixteenth to seventeenth centuries took the form of a single, formalized, vertically rising plume (*par*) that, like many feathers, was bent (*khami*) at its end toward the left (*bayani khamdar*) because it was generally worn on the right side of the turban, although it could also be placed at the center and be upright (*diyanatdar*). Its attached gold stem was equivalent to a feather's natural, hollow, barrel or calamus (*par-nali*), commonly called the quill. The gold version was flattened to better suit its function of preventing rotational movement.

The *sarpech* was not provided with any attached findings, such as a pinstem by which

827. Murshidabad, West Bengal. *c. 1757*
Gold sarpech and armlet (bazuband). The sarpech (obverse) is an openwork floral unit set with a large sapphire surrounded by diamond and ruby petals, from which the tapering plume (kalgi) rises, its spine of emeralds, and the barbules of diamonds and rubies, the apex ending in a pendant emerald (reverse) polychrome enameled bund tila (drop-in gold) style in which the subject can be colored enamel and the ground left gold, or the opposite. The accompanying three-part, hinged bazuband could also be used as a turban ornament (called a sarpatti). It is set with a central emerald flanked by rubies and diamonds.
Sarpech 6⅝ x 2⅜ in. (16.9 x 6.1 cm); Bazuband length 4³⁄₁₆ in. (10.6 cm); height 1⅜ in. (3.6 cm)
Victoria and Albert Museum, London. (Sarpech) (IS 3-1982); (Bazuband) (IS 3a-1982)

The importance of these two ornaments is mainly their datability and provenance, both rare in the case of traditional Indian jewelry. On July 26, 1757, after the Battle of Plassey, they were presented by the Nawab of Murshidabad, Mir Ja'far Ali Khan to Admiral Charles Watson, who had commanded the fleet. In a contemporary portrait of Watson and his son, the latter is dressed in Indian costume and wears them in his turban.

828. Delhi. *17th century* ➤
Aigrette with three plumes (tin kalangi sarpech) of hololithic white nephrite, carved in deep relief and set kundan style with 29 diamonds, 47 rubies, 39 emeralds, 1 garnet, and 3 rock crystals. The reverse is also carved in relief and mounted with small rubies.
6¾ x 2 in. (17.1 x 5 cm)
The State Hermitage, Special Treasury, Oriental Department, St. Petersburg (V3 443)

Formerly hung with pearls or gemstone pendants, the aigrette was sent by Nadir Shah of Persia in 1741 through his Ambassador to Russia as a gift to Johan Antonovich.

829, 830. Delhi. *Early 18th century* ➤
Gold, reversible, two-faced (do rukh), symmetrically designed Mughal or Rajput sarpech
6⅝ x 2¼ in. (16.8 x 5.8 cm)
Victoria and Albert Museum, London (IM 240-1923)

Believed to have been given to a Jaipur noble by the Mughal ruler, the ornament's design is inspired by the symmetrical (or asymmetrical) floral unit (buta) commonly found in Indian textiles and used in other media during Mughal times and thereafter. It is set with foiled diamonds, rubies, and pale beryls on both sides, but in different arrangements. Obverse: diamond flowers with ruby centers. Reverse: ruby flowers with beryl centers. The stem has traces of green enamel.

831. Jaipur, Rajasthan. *19th century* ➤
Five-part, hinged aigrette (ek-kalangi sarpech), gold openwork set with foiled diamonds, kundan style, and eight drilled pendant emeralds. The reverse is polychrome enameled.
4⅛ x 7⅞ in. (10.5 x 20 cm)
Private Collection

Smaller versions worn by a woman, when permitted, were called titah.

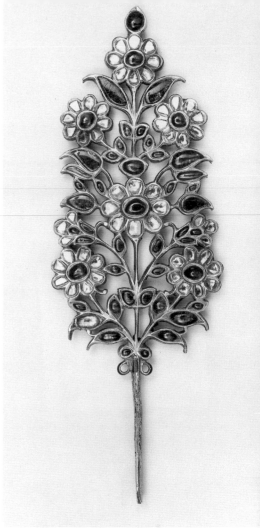

828

829

830

831

it could be fixed upon a turban to hold it in place: its stem was simply pushed into the turban folds. In some cases, the quills of the feather crest placed behind it could be forced into a ring (*halqa*) or tubular sleeve (*phonphi*) joined at the *sarpech* back for this purpose. Lacking these, both ornament and crest could be temporarily sewn to the turban.

The basic structure of a gold Indian *sarpech* is generally flat (*hamwar*). Fabricated of sheet metal, when gemstone set it would probably be of hollow construction. Designs were usually symmetrical (*ba-qarina*), although later forms generally favored assymmetry (*nahin ba-qarina*). Gemstones were normally set (*jarau*) only on the front face (*rukh*), but some were set with gemstones on both sides (*do-rukha*) to render it usable on either side. The back could be gold, plain or pattern chased, or enameled (*minawari*), either with a single color or in polychrome. The back enameled side, often elaborately executed, remained hidden from the viewer.

The original sixteenth-to-seventeenth-century *sarpech* unit was one piece (*ek tukra*) of rigid (*kara*) construction. From the eighteenth century onward, two additional side units were often added to the main, upstanding central unit, which increased the object's width, and the central unit's lower stem disappeared as other means were substituted to secure the ornament. To allow this wider ornament to fit around the curved turban form, the two added side units were hinged (*gabza lagana*) to the central unit. With the nineteenth-century tendency toward jewelry elaboration, the additional units could multiply to four or six, resulting in a five- or seven-unit *sarpech*, all parts hinge-joined. A *sarpech* of this length would extend halfway around a turban's circumference. To hold three-part and multihinged *sarpech* types on the turban, each extreme end was provided with an integral loop to which a *patu'a* attached cords ending in small tassels, and by this it was tied at the turban back.

Normally the *sarpech* had only one central, upward-projecting unit (*ek kalangi*). By the late eighteenth to early nineteenth century, each hinged unit could have its own, smaller projection, the total always in odd numbers. *Sarpeches* with three projections (*tin-kalangi*) and five projections (*panch kalangi*) exist.

During Mughal times, it was common for trained designers to prepare designs for more than one medium. As a result, similar generic floral motifs appear in all the decorative arts, including jewelry, textiles, carpets, bookbinding, and works in metal, stone, wood, and ivory. This interaction may account for the introduction, in the late seventeenth to early eighteenth century, of floral *sarpech* designs, which seem to have been inspired by contemporary textile patterns.

In textiles these designs were independent elements not physically connected to adjacent patterns which simplified their extraction and utilization in metal. Floral realism in *sarpech* and *bazuband* (armlet) jewelry could be heightened by the use of gemstones carved in petal and leaf forms (see 739), an idea that relates to the use of three-dimensional floral motifs in Mughal-Muslim architecture, such as the floral dadoes surrounding the base of the Taj Mahal.

In textiles, the floral unit underwent a progressive stylistic change that was paralleled by its use in *sarpech* designs. Early sixteenth- and seventeenth-century flower units on woven or printed textiles were arranged in a seminatural, open (*jalidar*) manner, often rising from a stem or vase, a type called *shamdas*. By the early eighteenth century, the floral unit was more compact, and the flowers multiplied and became more diverse. By the mid-eighteenth century, their shape assumed the unit design called a *buta*, used in corners and in repeats at textile garment ends. This style continues today. The consolidated silhouette often resembled other subjects whose names were used to describe it. Among them are the almond (*badam*), mango (*am* or *khairi*), cypress tree (*saro*), and the pan leaf (*pan patta*).

The *Sarpatti*

The late eighteenth century marked the development of a turban ornament, called the *sarpatti* (*sar,* head; *patti,* strip), that combined elements of the *sarpech* and the *bazuband,* or armlet. This form was suggested by the initially unconventional but later common use of the *bazuband* as a front-of-turban ornament, either alone or in combination with a *sarpech.* The practice is seen in mid- to late nineteenth-century photographs. As a synthesis of the two forms, the *sarpatti* consisted basically of the three, five, or seven hinged units of the *bazuband,* to which was added an upstanding small or large *kalgi* fixed to the top edge of the central unit. Often a single central gemstone pendant hung below this, or several were attached as a fringe to the bottom of each of the main

units. Because it covered the broader area of the turban front and was visible in its entirety, *sarpatti* designs often reached a degree of elaboration beyond that of the *bazuband,* which only encircled a smaller part of the upper arm.

The European *Aigrette*

The Indian turban ornament, the *sarpech*, is a prime example of how an Eastern form of jewelry came to influence the development of related forms in the West, and conversely, how Western design concepts in turn were eventually accepted in India and affected its formal development there. We know that actual examples of Eastern *sarpeches* found their way to Europe with Portuguese, English, French, Dutch, and Danish ships because *sarpeches* are frequently represented in contemporary European portraits, where they were depicted with exquisite accuracy because rarity made their ownership prestigious. Close examination of these early illustrated *sarpeches*, whose design is generally in a feather or *buta* form, and a comparison of them with those depicted in oriental portraits and extant contemporary examples from India, Persia, and Turkey confirms that they were fabricated in the East.

Many of these portraits in Great Britain commemorated an event such as a marriage. Some depict noblewomen whose families had a connection with Indian trade or the East India Company, which probably accounts for the *sarpech* they wear. These paintings illustrate the often unconventional manner in which this man's ornament was put to use mainly by women in the West. With their aid, we are also able to trace changes in the formal development of the *sarpech*.

One jeweler among the many who adapted the Indian *sarpech* design was Arnold Lulls. Born in Antwerp, he lived in London, where he was active from 1585 to 1621. As a court jeweler, he executed commissions for King James I of England and his consort, Anne of Denmark. Several portraits of James show him wearing an *aigrette* in his hat, among them the famous "feather," a British interpretation of the *sarpech*. Anne is believed to have popularized the use of the *aigrette* in a woman's hair.

Some of Lulls's work, thought to have been made around 1610, was recorded in an album of drawings presumably by him and now in the archives of the Victoria and Albert Museum, London. Of particular interest here are the six pages with representations of *sarpech-aigrettes*. All are distinctly Indian in format and closely comparable to those in contemporary Indian use. These drawings are important because they illustrate concretely the link between Indian and later European *sarpech-aigrette* design concepts. Inspired by such prototypes, European jewelers, beginning early in the seventeenth century, designed and fabricated *aigrettes* that became a fashionable jewelry item among Europe's wealthy.

833
834

833. England. c. 1615
Detail of a portrait by Robert Peake the Elder (1551–1619) of Elizabeth, wife of Edward, Lord Montagu of Boughton
Overall 30 x 23¼ in. (76.2 x 59 cm)
Yale Center for British Art. Paul Mellon Collection (B1974.3.31)

Elizabeth wears a gemstone (probably diamond)-set char kalangi sarpech-aigrette in her piled, bouffant hair, whose styling resembles a turban. The sarpech feather spray has migrated to the back of her head. As depicted, the sarpech is incorrectly worn on the left side so that the terminal, free-hanging pendants on the kalangi ends fall back on the rest instead of moving freely in air, which they would do when worn correctly, on the right side of the head.

834. England. c. 1620
Detail of a portrait by Daniel Mytens of Martha Cranfield, daughter of the first Earl of Middlesex, and wife of Henry Carey, Earl of Monmouth (1601–1667)
Collection Knole, the Leicester Gallery, Sevenoaks, Kent (no. 198)

In her hair she wears an Indian tin kalangi sarpech-aigrette of gold, set with rubies and emeralds, with an egret feather spray. Her father was a merchant and probably had a connection with the then-important East India Company trade.

835

835. Spain. 1830
Detail of a portrait by Lopez y Portana of Queen Maria Christina of Spain (1806–1878)
Collection Real Patronato del Museo del Prado, Madrid

Her aigrette, worn at the top of her head, is the ultimate in size and extravagance. Set only with diamonds, probably in silver backed by gold, as was then common, its form consists of a large, central flower from which rise a floral spray, a stalk of wheat, a large feather, and a leafy vine. The separate, huge male bird of paradise tail-feather spray frames her entire head.

836

836. London, England
Three record or design drawings in pencil, pen and ink, colored wash, and gold from the workbook of Arnold Lulls
Volume 8⅝ x 6⅛ in. (22 x 15.5 cm)
Victoria and Albert Museum, London
Two at left, page 37 (V 1281); one at right, page 45 (V 1285)

Represented in this book are six gold sarpech-aigrettes, three of which (two asymmetrical, one symmetrical) are shown here, created c. 1604–5. Their form includes the functional, integral lower stem (P: tana), which in India was inserted into the tight turban folds to secure the sarpech in an upright position. In the 18th century, the stem was eliminated in India in favor of hinge-joined side units with end loops that held attached strings, which were tied around the head to hold the sarpech in place. Here the original, basic format includes a lower main unit, all of which incorporate an Islamic upward-pointing crescent-moon (A: halal qamar) form, set with large gemstones, including diamonds, rubies, emeralds, and sapphires. From this rise stylized "feathers," set with smaller gemstones.

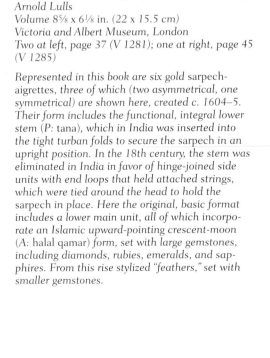

837. Punjab ➤

Maharaja Dhulip Singh of Lahore, commissioned by Lord Dalhousie in 1852
Portrait in oils by George Beechy, painter to the Nawab of Avadh
36 x 29⅛ in. (91.5 x 74 cm)
Private Collection

Dhulip Singh, then age fifteen, was living at Fattegarh, Uttar Pradesh, before he was taken to England. He is wearing an aigrette with three plumes (tin kalangi sarpech) received from the Punjab Treasury on his eleventh birthday. He wears the same one in the Goldingham (see 815) and Winterhalter portraits.

838. Paris, France. c. 1930

Diamond- and emerald-set platinum sarpech-aigrette, made for an Indian client in an unidentified European workshop
4³⁄₁₆ x 4¹⁵⁄₁₆ in. (10.7 x 12.5 cm)
Private Collection

Its design is strongly influenced by Art Deco forms. Its European manufacture is indicated by the use of calibrated baguette diamonds set in channel settings, and the presence of old European mine-cut diamonds. The central carved emerald and emerald drop are of Indian origin.

All the Lulls *aigrettes* have the plain, flat, bottom stem that in Indian *sarpeches* was inserted between a turban's folds to secure the ornament. That this purely functional projection was included in these designs when turbans were not in ordinary European use indicates that Lulls had direct reference to and followed the basic format of actual Indian examples. Later European *aigrettes* used a pin-stem and catch at the back to permit it, like a brooch, to be fixed to a garment or to the hair, and the flat stem disappeared.

Lulls's *aigrettes* also follow the Indian design concept of conventionalized, curving feather forms ornamented with gemstones. In two of them, below the main, central unit is the distinctly Mughal-Muslim motif of a gem-set, upward-pointing crescent moon, representing the increasing moon in its first quarter, a design element also commonly used in later eighteenth-century European *aigrettes*.

Some Indian and European *sarpech-aigrettes* from this time survive in royal collections, state treasuries, museums, and private collections. Good European examples are in the Waddeston Bequest in the British Museum, London, and the Schatzkammer der Residenz in Munich.

Not only did European *aigrettes* frequently incorporate stylized feather forms in their design, they also were worn with actual feathers. The conceptual connection between the ornament and the feather is indicated by their designations in different countries. Some names used for this object refer specifically to the ornament alone, others use separate terms for the ornament and the plume, and in some cases the terms for both are interchangeable. The English, for example, called the ornament a *feather* and the plume a *crest*; the French used *aigrette* for both, but the plume alone was often referred to as a *panache*; and so on.

Seventeenth-century European men wore *aigrettes* on a hat, often one with a broad brim. European women placed them in the bouffant coiffures then in fashion, in which the hair was piled high on the head and its bulk increased by the addition of extra hair switches and hidden pads; or in wigs, which were in use especially during the seventeenth and eighteenth centuries before the French Revolution. Hairstyles such as these could be considered to be analogous in form to a turban; the parallel was even more apparent when the hair or wig was powdered white with rice or wheat flour. An *aigrette* in the hair or in a woman's turban-formed hat most closely approximates its original Eastern (albeit male) use. Portraits tell us that the *sarpech-aigrette* was also worn as a central bodice brooch, and a portrait of Queen Elizabeth I of England shows her wearing a *sarpech* on her sleeve.

Once European jewelers took up the *sarpech-aigrette*, its form underwent transformations in ways that expressed the European designer's inventive talents. Although it was

Egret Feathers and European Fashion

Egret feathers have always been and still are used with the sarpech *in India. In Europe, during the nineteenth and into the early twentieth century, the* aigrette *was customarily worn with an egret-feather plume, which was also used on women's hats and in men's military headgear. To satisfy an extensive demand, the egret was avidly hunted in India by a network of birdcatchers who sold their harvest to feather exporters. Egret feather gathering was easily accomplished because, during their mating season, these gregarious birds gather by the thousands in rookeries, where they nest on trees and the ground. Plumers invaded their nesting places and slaughtered adults, stripping them of their white, back feathers and leaving the young to starve. The egret was soon on the verge of extinction.*

In the early 1900s, the American Audubon Society sponsored worldwide passage of stringent protective legislation banning egret-feather trade, a regulation adopted by most Western countries. The international embargo that followed saved the menaced birds, who made a remarkable comeback and are no longer an endangered species.

Other feathers used with an aigrette *include the tail feathers of adult male birds of paradise of New Guinea, the slender, drooping feathers with greatly developed aftershafts of the Australian emu, the long upper-tail covert feathers of the Central American male quetzal, the curling tail feathers of an Egyptian adult male ibis, and the white wing and tail feathers of the African ostrich.*

used alone in the hair, to a great extent its fashionability was coupled with Western women's adoption of the turban as headgear. Whenever the turban came into vogue in one form or another, the *aigrette*, with or without a plume, became indispensable. Some of these innovations ultimately reached India and in turn influenced its design there.

In the eighteenth century, the dominant gemstone in use for the *aigrette* and other jewelry was the diamond, which was usually set in silver, a white metal thought to augment its brilliance, while the back normally was of gold. As in India, gemstone settings were at first closed at the back, but by the mid-eighteenth century in Europe, open-backed settings became more common, eventually replacing closed-back settings completely. Indian traditional jewelry, however, retained the closed-back setting. *Aigrettes* were used as an accessory for evening wear only since they were considered to be too showy for daytime display.

The use of a feather in the design of a woman's *aigrette* was never abandoned. Many other subjects, however, were developed, among them the naturalistic flower sprig or bouquet, some inhabited by butterflies and other insects; birds with upward-extending tails; a sheaf of wheat stalks; a fountain; a spray with a crescent, stars, or arrows; and purely geometric designs. For men, the *aigrette* in the form of a military trophy appeared early in the seventeenth century and continued through the nineteenth. This motif consisted of crossed arms, a subject taken from an ancient Greek custom in which a defeated enemy's arms were fixed to an oak tree as a symbol of victory.

In the early nineteenth century, the Empire or Neoclassical style in women's dress often included a turban, to which was pinned an *aigrette*. Another peak in the *aigrette*'s popular-

ity began about 1860 and continued into the 1890s, when it became the most favored of all European women's head ornaments. Again, they were worn on a woman's turban or in a piled coiffure.

The *aigrette* also became prominent during the Edwardian era, prior to World War I. Influential Parisian fashion designers such as Charles Frederick Worth, who was succeeded by his sons; Paul Poiret; and Paul Iribe designed formal dresses inspired by oriental styles, especially after the enormous success of Les Ballets Russes in 1909–10, several of whose productions were based upon oriental themes. Turbans became smaller and tighter as the 1920s approached.

An *aigrette* was also mounted on a tiara, which was often worn on a festive occasion or at a costume ball. In the 1920s the tiara became a bandeau that could be compared to the *sarpatti*, often mounted with a feathered *aigrette*. As in the past, the *aigrette* could also be worn in the hair or fixed to the side of a small, helmetlike cloche hat.

The Platinum Indo-European *Sarpech-Aigrettes*

What appears to be the final incarnation of the *sarpech-aigrette* took place after 1900, when the European *aigrette* achieved its epitome in elegance and refined form. This became possible because of the relatively recent introduction of platinum in European jewelry-making. A precious, nonoxidizing white metal, its strength allowed the fabrication of lightweight, almost invisible settings, generally for diamonds, held in delicate claws so that they dominated.

Indian clients of European jewelry made at this time, among them the maharajas and their families, enthusiastically accepted the new look made possible by platinum. Many commissioned the great jewelry houses of Paris and London to make platinum *sarpech-aigrettes* and other jewelry. These results constitute a new category of Euro-Indian *sarpech-aigrettes,* which combine the formal aspects of Indian design with the technological innovations of Europe.

Swami Jewelry: A Euro-Indian Phenomenon

Little attention has been paid to an Anglo-Indian hybrid style of jewelry that flourished during the peak period of the British Raj in India. This jewelry was created mainly by P. Orr and Sons of Madras, Tamil Nadu, established in 1849 to manufacture gold and silver objects and continuing in operation into the early twentieth century. Orr's catalogue from 1876 claimed that it was "the pioneer manufacturing firm in India," a reference to its use of a highly regulated European system of jewelry and object manufacture, albeit mainly by hand technology. George Watt reported that Orr employed more than six hundred Indian artisans, who worked under European supervision, and that it was "the largest and best appointed establishment of this kind in India."

Of special interest here was the jewelry described in the catalogue as "gold and silver embossed *swami* jewellery." The local vernacular term *swami*, meaning "god or goddess," referred to the ornamentation of these pieces with one or more images of "heathen deities or *'Swamies'* of the Hindu Pantheon." All were created by very skillful hand-chasing in the *alto-relievo,* or high relief technique. Orr kept a large stock of such items on hand, but special orders could also be commissioned.

In addition to *swami* jewelry, Orr manufactured conventional European styles of jewelry fashionable at the time. Another department executed tea sets, trays, dessert services, goblets, spoons, sporting trophies, presentation pieces, address caskets, and boxes. Like the jewelry, these objects either faithfully followed European stylistic prototypes or were designed in a uniquely hybrid style of European-inspired forms elaborately decorated with Indian motifs. All were essentially oriented toward Westerners.

Helping to establish their acceptance was the wide Victorian interest in relief cameos with mythological and classical allegorical subject references. But perhaps of greatest importance in the popularity of *swami* jewelry in Great Britain was the official visit of Edward, Prince of Wales, to India in 1875–76. During that visit, the prince was presented with official gifts whenever he appeared, and many were for his wife, Alexandra, Princess of Wales, who did not accompany him. Among these gifts were an elaborate Orr-produced *swami*-decorated tea and dessert service from the Maharaja of Baroda and suites of *swami*

839. Madras, Tamil Nadu. *19th century*
Tapered cone form bracelet (kadakam) *in six hinged, box-constructed panels of repoussé-work silver, swami style*
Unit width at top $1\frac{3}{8}$ in. (3.4 cm); width at bottom $1\frac{1}{4}$ in. (3.1 cm); top inner diameter $2\frac{5}{8}$ x $2\frac{1}{8}$ in. (6.6 x 5.5 cm); bottom inner diameter $2\frac{3}{8}$ x $1\frac{15}{16}$ in. (5.9 x 4.9 cm); total length $9\frac{1}{8}$ in. (23.3 cm); weight 83 g
Collection the author, Porvoo

Each panel depicts a different Hindu deity and its animal vehicle. At the center is the bull, Nandin, Shiva's mount.

◄ **840. Madras, Tamil Nadu.** *19th century*
Two-part belt buckle (kachchupputtu) *of sheet silver ornamented swami style in repoussage with figures of Garuda* (left) *and Hanuman* (right), *crowned and garlanded, standing on lotuses*
$4\frac{3}{16}$ x $3\frac{1}{8}$ in. (10.6 x 7.8 cm); weight 87 g
Collection the author, Porvoo

jewelry in gold intended for the princess. Upon the prince's return to England in 1876, the gifts were displayed at the Indian Museum in South Kensington, and crowds thronged there daily to see them. The press urged the public to see the Orr pieces especially, as they formed "a conspicuous feature of the exhibition." The London *Court Circular* of April 22, 1876, observed that, because the Princess of Wales had "received specimens of this jewelry ... it is evident that it will become popular during the coming season ... and will be eminently fashionable."

The popularity of *swami* jewelry was further enhanced when in 1876 Messrs. P. Orr and Sons "received from the Prince of Wales the appointment of Jewellers and Silversmiths to His Royal Highness." To meet the inevitable demand for the jewelry in Great Britain, Orr appointed Messrs. Halling, Pearce, and Stone, Waterloo House, Pall Mall, East London, as their agents for its sale.

An important source of inspiration for this type of jewelry was the highly influential line-engraved illustrations in Edward Moor's book *The Hindu Pantheon,* which first appeared in 1810 and in great detail describes and illustrates Hindu deities for the enlightenment of Western readers. The original edition contained 105 plates that included nearly two thousand subjects. For this pioneering work, Moor, a lieutenant in the British East Indian Army, spent years collecting representations of Indian Hindu deities, which he had faithfully and accurately copied and engraved for use in the book. The edition most easily available today is that of 1864, in which some of the original illustrations were replaced by other examples. A separate volume of the original plates from the 1810 edition, published in London in 1861 by Williams and Norgate, was probably used by Orr as a reference. There is a marked similarity in the style of those engravings and that of the subjects on *swami* jewelry. Thanks to Moor, therefore, all the deities depicted on objects in the *swami* style produced by Orr, and also by European and Indian competitors in India, are always iconographically correct. No Hindu would have any difficulty in identifying them.

Another source of inspiration is referred to obliquely in the Orr catalogue in a reference to "Trichinopoly Jewellery," an Anglicized spelling of Tiruchchirappalli, "city of the three-headed Demon," about 187 miles (300 km) southwest of Madras. It is famous for its enormous Dravidian-style temples, some on the two huge dominating rocky outcroppings within city limits and others nearby, including Sri Rangam (dedicated to Vishnu) and the Jambukeswar (Shiva) temple. All are profusely ornamented with myriad Hindu deities in the southern Indian style of sculpture in stone and plaster. As in the case of all important places of pilgrimage in India, many goldsmiths are established there. Some produced work that characteristically includes miniature repoussé-worked and chased depictions of Hindu deities on gold marriage ornaments (*thali*) and necklaces such as those made for the wealthy Chettiar community (see 306). This traditional southern Indian Hindu genre is probably what suggested the style adopted by Orr and his followers for *swami* jewelry. For their execution in the miniature relief process, Orr drew on existing artisanal skills.

The quintessential difference between traditional Tiruchchirappalli jewelry and that of Orr is that, although they share a comparable use of *swami* imagery, the completely Indian forms of jewelry produced by the former were meant solely for Indian use, and the latter, which employed contemporary, fashionable European forms of jewelry, were created for Westerners.

Included in the Orr production were necklaces of several kinds; a favored design, illustrated at right, was derived from the eighteenth-century European garland style. Bracelets were made in the wide, two-part,

N.º 21.

841. Madras, Tamil Nadu. *Late 19th century Drawing by C. Paczensy in the catalogue of P. Orr and Sons Ltd., Madras, of a swami-style necklace Victoria and Albert Museum, London (Library)*

842. Madras, Tamil Nadu. *19th century Repoussé-work silver swami-style necklace (ani-vadam), manufactured by P. Orr and Sons Ltd., Madras*
Length 17⅞ in. (45.4 cm); largest swami unit 1⁵/₁₆ x 1¹/₁₆ in. (3.3 x 2.7 cm); weight 108 g Victoria and Albert Museum, London (IS 1985-1-231)

This basically European design concept in necklaces made from 1800 to 1820 features eleven pierced-work medallions, each with a mythological subject joined with three chains, the lowest falling in catenary curves.

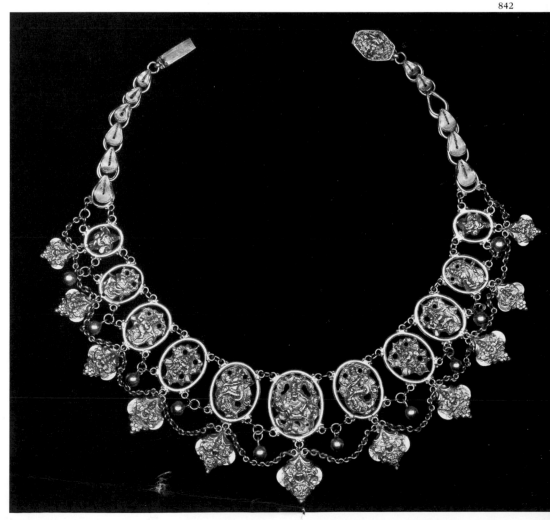

843. Madras, Tamil Nadu. *19th century*
Repoussé-work silver swami-style locket (thukkanampetti) with suspension link
2½ x 1¾ in. (6.4 x 4.5 cm); weight 45 g
Collection the author, Porvoo

The locket subject represents Subrahmanya or Karttikeya, god of war, on his peacock vehicle.

844. Madras, Tamil Nadu. *19th century*
Repoussé-work silver swami-style locket (manikkadaipputtu) with suspension ring
2 x 1¾ in. (5.1 x 4.3 cm); weight 29 g
Collection the author, Porvoo

Maya, Buddha's mother, is shown giving birth to Buddha in a standing position while holding on to a branch of an ashoka tree (Saraca indica). Buddha emerged from her right side.

845. Madras, Tamil Nadu. *19th century*
Repoussé-work gilded silver swami-style locket (manikkadaipputtu) with suspension loop
2 x 1¾ in. (5.1 x 4.4 cm); weight 35 g
Collection the author, Porvoo

Karttikeya rides his peacock vehicle flanked by two attendants holding yak tail whisks (thudaippam), each enshrined in an arch on a temple chariot (ratham), as indicated by the two wheels below, drawn by devotees at temple festivals. On the suspension loop is the goddess Devi.

846. Madras, Tamil Nadu. *19th century* (opposite) ➤
Seven-part hinged belt buckle (kachchupputtu) of cast silver, swami style
Height 2⅞ to 3⅝ in. (7.2–9.3 cm); central unit width 2⅛ in. (5.5 cm); total length 13¼ in.
(34.7 cm); weight 250 g
Collection the author, Porvoo

Probably the most extravagant of all belt buckles in this style, each unit was cast and chased to refine forms and create details. The central image is a Raja-Naga mounted on cobras, flanked by units with a central shield, the others with worshipers, hands placed in the honor-bestowing gesture (angali mudra).

843

844

845

single-hinged form called "deep gauntlets" in the Orr catalogue and known as *manchettes* (French for "cuff") in Europe, where they were popular in the 1850s; in narrower, rigid, two-part, single-hinged forms that copied the broad, so-called "bangle" being mass produced in Birmingham and elsewhere; and, especially popular according to Orr was the six-part, hinged, flexible bracelet, each unit bearing a different deity image. Among the most elaborate was a bracelet of ten panel units hinged together, each of which depicted one of the ten incarnations (*dasavataras*) of Vishnu. Orr also made brooches, belt buckles, earrings, and finger rings for women and cuff links (called "sleeve links"), studs, and cravat pins for men. The small pieces were especially admired because of the minute scale of their *swami* subjects.

Probably the most popular item of all was the locket, which might contain two *carte de visite* photographs of loved ones trimmed down to the locket shape and placed under thin glass, thus catering to Victorian sentimentality. Like their counterparts made in Europe, which were ornamented on front with floral or geometric engraving, and sometimes gold appliqués, lockets could be worn separately on a cord or ribbon or attached to a flexible, broad, fancy-link chain or collar. Indian lockets, also made in oval, square, or lozenge forms, were ornamented on one or both sides. The latter, depicting different deities, was reversible. Plain backs could be engraved with monograms or commemorative inscriptions.

As Orr's catalogue states, "Special care is paid … [to faithfully rendering] representations of the particular deities [so that] even those unacquainted with the country [and culture] cannot fail to [have] a tolerably correct idea of the originals." Generally, however,

Western purchasers understood little of the identity, character, significance, or histories of the subjects, many of which, had they been known, undoubtedly would have offended, or even shocked Victorian sensibilities.

The deities used constituted Hinduism's most common iconographic images. They might be depicted mounted on their animal or bird vehicle (*vahana*): Vishnu on the man-bird, Garuda; Karttikeya or Subramanya, the god of war, on his peacock; Ganesha on his giant rat; Brahma, with three of his four heads seen, on his goose; and Sarasvati riding a peacock. Baby Krishna is shown stealing butter from a pot; Kali or Durga riding a lion while slaying the buffalo demon, or just astride her lion; and Shiva simply stands before Nandin, his bull vehicle. Other subjects include Rama flanked by Sita and Hanuman; Lakshmi purified by poured oblations from addorsed elephants; Vishnu sleeping on the serpent Shesha; Shiva Nataraja creating the Universe in a cosmic dance; and Krishna as Venu-Gopala standing cross-legged in front of a cow while playing on his flute.

No incongruity was found in the "application of Native ornamentation to European forms." Despite its exotic subject matter, this jewelry, "rich and massive in character [and] elegant though bizarre in design," was "not at all outré, extravagant, or overdone" to most Victorian eyes. A segment of society, however, presumably high-principled Christians, did consider it morally unacceptable to depict *swami* "heathen deities" in jewelry meant to be worn by European women. In deference to that point of view, and to "meet the religious prejudices of those who object to the native '*swamies*' as a subject for personal ornamentation," Orr produced an alternative. The same

basic jewelry forms were available with subjects in high relief that suggest an origin in the well-known "Company pictures" commonly ordered from Indian artists by the British who served in India. The original paintings, as did those of this genre on Orr jewelry, often depicted persons of low Indian castes pursuing common occupations—such as the washerman, barber, water bearer, toddy drawer, snake charmer, vegetable seller, lapidary, horsekeeper, grass cutter, roadmaker, scavengers or sweepers, and the universal Indian woman with a water pot on her head (*panihari*)—all familiar to British residents in India. Today the idea of British Victorian ladies consenting to wear jewelry ornamented with subjects of low or untouchable castes, whose contact Hindus would consider to be polluting, seems ludicrous and indicates their dearth of knowledge about Hindu culture and social hierarchy.

All ornaments were available in 22-karat gold (stamped ORR 22), but by far the greater number were produced in silver of a quality close to sterling. Because no system of hallmarking was practiced in India, none of these pieces bear local hallmarks, even those produced by European-owned companies such as Orr's. Occasionally one finds British hallmarks on imported *swami* jewelry.

That demand for these pieces must have been considerable is evidenced by Orr's proud catalogue announcement that they were available for purchase not only in British Indian cities but also in Europe, Australia, and the United States. In addition, they could be purchased by mail order at the phenomenally low cost of "one shilling per pound." A considerable number were acquired by foreigners in residence and by visitors who found them "quaint mementoes" of an Indian sojourn. Those

that made their way to Great Britain now frequently appear in antique shops and street markets.

As is often the case, the success of Orr's *swami* jewelry resulted in many imitators in Madras and Tiruchchirappalli. This type of decoration also appeared on jewelry and tea sets produced in Great Britain—a curious once-removed imitation of an Indian style that in turn imitated European forms. However, the deity images depicted on British-made objects were usually completely fanciful. One way their origin can be identified is that, when of precious metal, they have British hallmarks.

847. Madras, Tamil Nadu. *19th century*
Repoussé-work silver swami style bracelets (kadakam)

Above: Seven hinged units depicting alternating subjects: Krishna Murlidar with cow, and Durga on a lion
Each unit 1 x 1 in. (2.6 x 2.6 cm); length 8⅝ in. (22 cm); weight 75 g
Below: Ten hinged units depicting the ten incarnations (avataras) of Vishnu
Each unit 1¼ x ¾ in. (3.1 x 2 cm); length 7⅝ in. (19.4 cm); weight 71 g
Collection the author, Porvoo

848. Madras, Tamil Nadu. *19th century*
Illustration of bracelets in the swami style from the catalogue of P. Orr and Sons, Madras
Victoria and Albert Museum, London

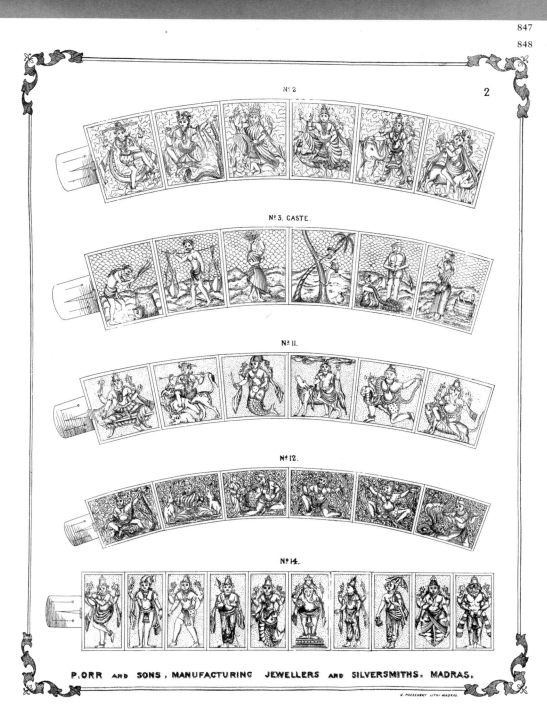

Western Oriental-Design Imperialism

The question arises, To what can be attributed the frequent Western return to Eastern design as an inspirational source? Part of the answer may be that Westerners believed they, to some extent, could penetrate the elusive mystique of the Eastern mentality through the adoption of its designs. Another explanation involves long-standing Western attitudes toward the East. Indian design concepts, for example, are perceived in the West to be imbued with a vital, fertile energy as well as exuding an element of seduction. Thus the words "Mughal" or "oriental," when used in Western advertising to identify an Indian design source, evoke a stereotypical image of sensual pleasure.

Western designers who exploit the exotic appeal of Eastern forms could rightfully be called oriental-design imperialists. In nineteenth-century Europe, design imperialism was a manifestation of colonialism and was encouraged to a great extent by the series of international exhibitions in Great Britain and Continental Europe, in which India as a colony of the British Empire participated (see page 394). The Indian jewelry displayed at these exhibitions attracted considerable popular attention. Before long, evidence of the aesthetic impact of Indian design concepts appeared in the works of several well-known European jewelers who turned to various exotic Eastern cultures for inspiration.

Many Indian-influenced European examples of jewelry from around 1850 to the present have survived from a far greater body of work created in this genre. Considered as an entity, they support the premise that a Euro-Indian jewelry-design style did evolve, to which too little attention has been paid in Western historic jewelry literature.

The influence of India on Western jewelry was not continuous. Like other Western fashion themes, it has occurred in waves—cresting, falling, and reemerging as a "novelty." In Western fashion, interest in a particular design source often is short-lived, and revivals recur regularly.

Hindu and Islamic, "Indian" and "Persian"

Especially during the last half of the nineteenth century and into the early twentieth, Indian Hindu and Islamic design concepts became increasingly evident in Western jewelry. In the West, a distinction between these two sources generally is not made. Of the two, the Indo-Islamic aesthetic is more familiar to Westerners and is usually termed "Mughal" or "Persian," labels often capriciously applied to a design that may be purely Hindu. Each of these religions developed its own design idiom whose motifs and forms were generated by religious and ethnic folk beliefs. To be able to distinguish between the two requires familiarity with the symbolic design vocabulary of each religion and the life-style of its adherents.

Another confusion that persists among Western designers and the general public involves a distinction between things Indian and Persian. It is true that during the Mughal period in India, an active cross-cultural exchange existed between both places. Yet, even long-standing, typically Indian motifs, such as the lotus, peacock, and elephant, may be termed "Persian" when adopted by Western designers. Unaccountably, in the vocabulary of the Western fashion world the designation "Persian" has acquired greater *éclat* than that of "Indian."

Applied to the field of jewelry, this terminological confusion is particularly inappropriate. No parallel can be drawn between the considerable contribution made by Indian jewelry design to Western jewelry and the elusive, or even nonexistent, impact of Persian jewelry. Western jewelry makers today often perversely continue to evade acknowledgment of Indian jewelry design concepts they use. The time has come to rectify this oversight and give the Indian contribution its due.

Differentiating Indian and European Jewelry

Indian and Indo-European jewelry share basic concepts: both employ precious metal and gemstones, and both are completely hand made. Differences due to cultural nuances can, however, be identified. Indian jewelry always manifests an acceptable irregularity, which typifies hand work there. In contrast, Western interpretations of Indian jewelry strive for an impersonal, faultless regularity whose ideal is near-mechanical perfection.

For example, the finish of traditional Indian jewelry normally shows some evidence of the tools and processes brought to bear upon the work. In Euro-Indian jewelry, all such signs have been meticulously expunged. The ultimate refinement in early twentieth-century Indo-European jewelry was the use of platinum as a substitute for the high-karat gold of traditional Indian jewelry. Because platinum is stronger than gold, the amount of metal needed to support the gemstones is appreciably reduced, and it becomes almost invisible in the finished piece. Thus, in Indo-European jewelry, the interaction between the gold and gemstones found in traditional Indian jewelry is abandoned.

Another difference can be seen in the character of the gemstones used. In traditional Indian jewelry, gemstone quality is irregular. The stones used in one piece are varied in outline, color, and style of faceting. Western jewelers generally reject flawed gemstones and often use calibrated gemstones with regularly cut, proportioned forms designed to achieve maximum refractive brilliance. To further increase their fire, they are normally placed in open-backed, light-admitting (*à jour*) claw settings, which are never used in traditional Indian jewelry. Due to these differences, even when Western adaptations closely follow the design of Indian originals, they acquire a sanitized, Westernized appearance that easily identifies them.

Western Jewelers and Indo-European Jewelry

Carlo and Arthur Giuliano

In the second half of the nineteenth century, when eclecticism dominated European arts, Carlo Giuliano (1831–1895) and his son, Arthur Alphonse (1864–1914), who succeeded him, were foremost among the several jewelers who were influenced by Indian traditional jewelry designs and formal concepts. Originally from Naples, Carlo Giuliano is believed to have trained in the Roman workshop of Fortunato Pio Castellani, whose production never showed any evidence of interest in Indian-inspired jewelry concepts. Giuliano moved to London about 1860, became a naturalized British subject, and registered his hallmark in 1863. After working in his workshop for several years, he opened a retail shop in 1874.

In his book *Castellani and Giuliano*, Geoffrey C. Munn calls the Indian influence in Giuliano's works "quite pronounced." Perhaps Giuliano's interest in Indian design can be attributed to a desire to assert a "claim" to a historic or cultural design style that could be associated with his production. Although such "titles" were not watertight, one could say that Castellani and Mellilo relied heavily on classical Greek, Etruscan, and Roman models; William Burgess on the Gothic; John Brogden on Egypt and Assyria; and others, including Giuliano at times, turned to the Renaissance. These results today are termed "the school of historicism."

Public European exposure to Indian jewelry came first with London's Crystal Palace Great Exhibition of 1851 (further examples came to Britain as a result of looting during the Indian Mutiny of 1857–59). This was followed by the International Exhibition, London, 1862; L'Exposition Universelle, Paris, 1867; a series of Annual International Exhibitions, South Kensington, London, in 1871, 1872, 1873, 1874, 1878, and 1879; the Exhibition of Indian Gifts to the Prince of Wales at the South Kensington Museum, London, 1877; L'Exposition Universelle, Paris, 1878; the Colonial and Indian Exhibition, 1886; the Glasgow International Exhibition, 1888; and L'Exposition Universelle, Paris, 1889.

It is reasonable to suppose that the Giulianos could have studied examples of Indian jewelry displayed at these international exposi-

849. London, England. *c.1890*
Gold necklace by Carlo Giuliano, with pearls, two diamonds, and black enamel
Schmuckmuseum, Pforzheim (1977/8)

Based on the traditional Indian patadi har, this necklace has only one division separator on the pearl strands, which are supported by an additional gold chain.

tions, which were so popular in the late nineteenth century. In any case, the influence of Indian jewelry design concepts on the Giulianos is evident in a group of multistrand seed-pearl necklaces that, though reduced in scale, follow the traditional format of the *patadi har*. In them, several side-by-side strands of pearls end at top and bottom with triangular, enameled-gold terminals that join at the front and support a central pendant with a baroque pearl drop (*jugni* or *nam* type). Another Indian design detail used by the Giulianos, commonly seen in the Mughal-Rajput style of Jaipur gold necklaces, consists of many identical units, each terminating in a small bunch of gold-wire-strung pearls or beads that form a fringe. They also made use of multicolored gemstones in conjunction with polychrome enamel, which relates to both Renaissance and Indian practice, as does the also-used idea of enameling the obverse and reverse sides of the units composing a necklace. The Giulianos directly utilized another Indian design in a gilded silver necklace with three large trapezoid forms, which they made for the painter Edward Poynter to be worn by his model for his well-known painting, *Helen of Troy* (1887). The unit of this ethnic-style necklace is a nearly exact copy of a traditional Gujarati necklace. They also commissioned pseudo-Muslim enameled gold amulets in traditional Indian forms such as the oval cartouche, the pentagon, hexagon, and the arrowhead shape, their surfaces bearing Arabic inscriptions.

Robert Phillips

In the jewelry collection of the Victoria and Albert Museum, London, is a striking gold necklace made by Robert Phillips (1810–1881) of Phillips Brothers and Son, London. A pastiche of an Indian prototype, it utilizes the common Indian necklace-design concept of identical unit repeats. Here the unit form is the traditional Indian arrowhead amulet, polychrome enameled in contrasting ground colors on both sides, another Indian concept. This necklace was shown at the L'Exposition Universelle, Paris, 1867, where it was purchased by the museum. It is known that Giuliano as an outworker supplied Phillips and others with his creations, which they sold.

India and Arts and Crafts Jewelry

The jewelers of the British Arts and Crafts movement of the latter quarter of the nineteenth century were devoted to the cause of a new art that rejected a mechanical, industrially manufactured appearance. They also showed considerable interest in the jewelry of India.

Rejecting the aforementioned prevailing reliance on European historic styles for inspiration, they turned their attention to the special qualities of handcrafted work. The concept of bringing man closer to nature as a moral obligation dominated their philosophy. This they felt could be achieved by embracing the humanizing aspects of hand craftsmanship—the basic nature of Indian jewelry. They occasionally adopted its specific forms but, more important, its spirit, as well as certain symbolic subjects, such as the lotus and the peacock, the latter shown entirely or represented by a single feather.

It is known that several members of the Arts and Crafts movement, including William Morris and Dante Gabriel Rossetti, were interested in ethnic jewelry because they felt it was in keeping with their involvement with handmade objects. As with Indian jewelry, the jewelry of the Arts and Crafts movement de-emphasized the intrinsic value of the materials used and instead stressed artistic concerns. The use of both semiprecious, cabochon-cut gemstones—

850. London, England. *c.1867*
Gold necklace of twenty-four arrowhead-shaped pendants, enameled on both sides in the Jaipur-Mughal-Rajput style, with pendant pearls, by Robert Phillips of Phillips Brothers of Cockspur Street, London
Victoria and Albert Museum, London (549-1868)

The inspiration of Indian jewelry design concepts is obvious in the forms and the style of decoration. Acquired at the Paris Exposition Universelle, 1876.

less ostentatious than faceted gemstones—and colored enamels relates to the Indian polychrome style of jewelry.

Contemporary commercial enterprises also encouraged an interest in things Indian. Foremost among them was Liberty and Company in London, founded by Arthur Lasenby Liberty. In 1875 he opened East India House, an "oriental" warehouse and retail shop on Regent Street. Liberty and Company regularly imported oriental art and artifacts, such as Indian jewelry and handwoven silk, and the latter became a Liberty specialty. Extremely influential in establishing a taste for handmade Indian objects, Liberty was patronized by leading artists and their followers as well as a wide public sympathetic to the ideas of the Arts and Crafts movement. Today Liberty continues to import good-quality Indian jewelry.

Louis Comfort Tiffany

On the other side of the Atlantic Ocean, in New York City, designer Louis Comfort Tiffany was collecting a vast number of examples of archaeological and ethnic jewelry (including traditional Indian jewelry) and artifacts from the Near East, where he had traveled in his youth, and from the Far East, particularly Japan. This collection, to which he continually added, eventually became an available reference resource for his staff designers and artisans in the various enterprises he established. His greater awareness of Indian jewelry may have come about through his association with his then partner, Lockwood de Forest, a painter who admired Indian wood carving, textiles, and jewelry and who traveled and worked in India, where he established a wood-carving, furniture, and architectural-ornament project in Gujarat. In 1915 de Forest compiled a collection of Indian jewelry for the Metropolitan Museum of Art in New York, with which Tiffany was certainly familiar.

In 1881, Louis Tiffany was invited by his father, Charles Lewis Tiffany, a great lover and manufacturer of jewelry of a more traditional kind, to join the board of directors of Tiffany and Co. Louis's independent operation was the Tiffany Glass and Decorating Company, which he established in 1892 (renamed Tiffany Studios about 1900 and in existence until 1938).

◄ **851. Paris, France.** *1950*
Flexible yellow-gold necklace and matching bracelet, both set with rose-cut diamonds, produced by René Boivin, Paris
Courtesy René Boivin

Called a "Hindu" parure, its basic, articulated design concept successfully interprets the traditional Rajasthani armlet (bazuband, see 564–67). In this case, a loop-in-loop gold chain, which emulates the heavy black cord of its Indian counterpart, passes through the upper and lower loops on each unit and terminals, and continues to form the closing.
René Boivin introduced several "Hindu"-inspired jewelry pieces in Paris in 1926. The flexible design concept, used here as part of a passementerie group, appeared in 1950 in necklaces, bracelets, rings, and earrings. Variations of this popular design continue to be created.

852. New York, New York. *c. 1900*
Gold handpiece by Tiffany and Co., probably designed by Louis Comfort Tiffany
Courtesy Tiffany and Co. Archives, New York

Obviously inspired by the traditional Indian hand ornament (hathphul or ratanchur, see also 621, 627), this piece is set with a variety of colored gemstones including rubies, amethysts, aquamarines, topazes, and turquoises. The incorporation of so many gemstones may have been influenced by the Indian use of the planetary gemstones (nava-ratna) in one object.

In 1893 this company was divided into the Stourbridge Glass Co. (reorganized into Tiffany Furnaces in 1902) and the Allied Arts Company, which dealt with all other media, though Louis designed jewelry that was produced at Tiffany Furnaces. It was during the 1890s that he created his internationally famous favrile glass and enamel-on-metal objects.

Although Louis Tiffany initially designed jewelry as early as 1893, it was not until 1902, when his father died, that he could without compunction follow his own artistic inclinations in this area. In his jewelry, characteristically, each piece was one-of-a-kind, with a deliberately cultivated "hand wrought" appearance, qualities that echoed the philosophy of the British Arts and Crafts Movement, whose leaders he had met in Europe, as well as Indian principles and practices. Several of his designs from 1902 onward were substantially inspired by Indian traditional jewelry forms and style of decoration, which suited his lifelong preoccupation with surface decoration and sumptuous color, both common in Indian jewelry.

Specifically, these works embodied such stylistic Indian concepts as the use of gold decorated with polychrome enamel on one or both sides and the incorporation of mainly cabochon-cut precious and semiprecious colored gemstones selected more for their enrichment of the design than their intrinsic value. As in much Indian traditional jewelry, Tiffany's design themes relied heavily on nature, flowers in particular. Although he had strong ideas about this genre, he also referred to published examples from his voluminous private library. For instance, he is known to have possessed copies of the influential *Journal of Indian Art* (published in London from 1880 to 1917), which often featured lavish, and for this time, well-illustrated articles on Indian traditional jewelry as well as other Indian crafts.

After his participation in the Louisiana Purchase Exposition of 1904, where he exhibited some early jewelry produced at Tiffany Furnaces, Tiffany's jewelry designs became increasingly inspired by "Islamic," especially Indian, design concepts sympathetic to his design outlook. Among the traditional Indian jewelry forms he synthesized were the straight, elaborately gemstone-set choker (*guluband*) with pearl fringe, which ended in a pair of gold chains that emulated the common Indian use of thick cords for this purpose, and the exotic hand ornament with five attached chains ending with rings for each finger (*hathphul* or *ratan chur*).

Janet Zapata states that Tiffany's most important extant piece of jewelry is a "peacock necklace" created around 1905 and now in the Charles Hosmer Museum of American Art, Winter Park, Florida. Its basic format resembles an Indian *dauni,* or headpiece. Its design is dominated by one of Tiffany's often reiterated themes, the peacock, also popular in Art Nouveau design. Like traditional Indian jewelry, this piece utilizes cabochon-cut gemstones on the obverse side, and the reverse is elaborately polychrome enameled, though in cloisonné, not the champlevé style typically used in India. In most of his jewelry, Tiffany showed a decided preference for placing cabochon-cut colored gemstones in closed collet settings, completely encircling the stone, comparable in essence to the Indian *kundan*-style closed setting and contrary to the prevailing Western use of open-backed, claw settings, which includes the famous (Charles) Tiffany six-prong platinum setting for a diamond.

In 1907 Louis Tiffany sold the jewelry and enameling departments at Tiffany Furnaces to Tiffany and Co. A special, new department for the manufacture of art jewelry was established in an upper floor of the Tiffany and Co. building, then on Fifth Avenue and 37th Street, under the artistic leadership of Louis Tiffany, who had become the artistic director of the company. A special art-jewelry sales section was established in the store. Much of the jewelry produced there essentially followed Louis Tiffany's previous designs inspired by "exotic Eastern sources" as well as the currently popular historical styles that made use of the considerable collection of faceted gemstones gathered by his father. Tiffany continued to design jewelry until his retirement in 1918. Tiffany and Co.'s jewelry workshop continued until 1933, the year of Tiffany's death.

Maharajas and the *Grands Joailliers*

The latter half of the nineteenth century in India saw a period of comparative political calm and prosperity. After years of interaction with foreign thought and values, many Indians of the upper and growing middle classes looked toward the Western life-style of their British rulers as a model for their own. Seduced by Western technology, they came to believe that Indian products and culture were somehow inferior. This thinking not only encouraged the acceptance of Western industry but also affected cultural realms—including that of jewelry.

From about 1880 to 1940, many Indians who could afford it made journeys abroad, primarily to England but also to the European continent, America, and elsewhere. On such journeys, maharajas and their retinues were feted and lionized by Western royalty and high society, to whom they were exotic *rara avises*. As was expected of them, they appeared at such events splendidly ornamented with their finest ancestral jewelry. Trying their best not to be outdone, hostesses and other guests emulated this opulent oriental style by displaying the not inconsiderable contents of their own jewel caskets.

As jewelry connoisseurs, the maharajas quickly became familiar with fashionable European jewelry styles as well as the *grands joailliers,* the undisputed leaders in Western jewelry design. Foremost among them was Cartier, who probably had the longest and most productive association with Indian clients, closely followed by Boucheron, Chaumet, Van Cleef and Arpels, and others. No European expedition was complete without a ritual visit to these temples of wealth and beauty, whose high priests, realizing the purchasing potential of this new class of clients, eagerly sought to satisfy their every whim. Indian maharajas patronized French firms in Paris and their London branches, a practice that continued even 'during the Great Depression of the 1930s. Indian patronage of the *grands joailliers* undoubtedly contributed to their prosperity during those hard times.

Wealthy Indian families already possessed a quantity of accumulated ancestral gemstones and traditional jewelry. It became common practice when traveling to Europe to bring along old jewelry and unmounted gemstones, some of which had been languishing in dusty treasuries and bank vaults. Ready access to a supply of gemstones considerably reduced the cost of creating new ornaments. In this process scores of Indian diamonds, rubies, emeralds, and sapphires underwent transformation in Europe, emerging in refaceted European forms that greatly increased their market value. In this way also, jeweled Indian masterworks of decided cultural importance were sacrificed.

At this time more than ever, India became for Western jewelers a major source of important secondary or reused gemstones. Loose stones and expendable ornaments containing them were purchased for European jewelers by agents stationed in India. European jewelry establishments regularly sent representatives to India or owners went themselves. Important Indian gemstones, particularly diamonds and emeralds, also appeared—and continue to do so—at the auctions held by the great auction houses, such as Sotheby's and Christies in London and their American and other branches.

Historic coincidence also contributed to the enrichment of Euro-Indian jewelry. After the Russian Revolution in 1917, the maharajas of India replaced the Russian aristocracy as the paramount purchasers of expensive gemstones and jewelry made by Europe's great jewelry houses. Displaced Russian nobility, who managed to take with them remnants of their wealth in the form of jewelry and gemstones, sold them piecemeal to stay alive. When many important Russian-owned gemstones (often with an Indian provenance) came to market, Indian maharajas vied with European royalty and the wealthy to acquire them. Many such gemstones were used by the maharajas in an unprecedented number of notable jewelry commissions, called *commandes speciales*, placed with the great jewelers.

Crown Jewels
designed and Mounted
for
H.H. The Maharaja Dhiraj
of Patiala
by
Cartier

Cartier
PARIS
NEW-YORK
LONDON.

853. Paris, France
Advertisement by Cartier, Paris, including two necklaces designed for the Maharaja of Patiala (see 751). The upper one follows the format of an Indian choker (guluband), the lower a two-strand necklace (do lara har), both tied in the Indian manner with flexible, tassel-ending chains that follow the concept of patu'a-style cords.
Archives Cartier, Courtesy Cartier, Paris

Due to the understandably confidential nature of a client's private jewelry commissions, knowledge of the actual projects jewelers completed for maharajas is limited. Several makers, however, publicly exhibited executed commissions, presumably with the approval of their ultimate owners, and advertised such displays. Some additional information is given in a series of recent books (see the bibliography at the back of this book) relating the history of the great French jewelry houses. The full extent of the patronage of the maharajas will probably never be revealed, but what is already known is impressive enough.

France has long enjoyed the reputation of being the European fountainhead of the decorative and fashion arts, and this domination made inevitable the emulation of Franco-Indian designs by all others. Exercising their aptitude for brilliant interpretation, Indian-inspired French jewelry concepts, even now, are more than distinguished imitations of their Indian counterparts.

Cartier

Louis-François Cartier (1819–1904) established the firm that bears his name in 1847. His son Louis-François Alfred Cartier (1841–1925) had three sons, Louis (1875–1942), Pierre (1878–1965), and Jacques (1884–1942), all of whom entered the business. Although in his later years the elder Cartier became proficient in oriental languages, it was his grandson Louis who showed the greatest interest in Eastern and Islamic art. It was through his efforts that Indian design concepts were later integrated into Cartier's Art Deco design production. Jacques Cartier also developed extensive social contacts with Indian maharajas as potential clients.

To attract the wealthy, Cartier, like all other important European jewelers, had to maintain a respectable gemstone stock. For this purpose, repeated direct contact with India was essential. In May 1909, Cartier sent Jules Glaenzer and René Prieur on one such journey to India, where they visited scores of small gemstone merchants in the labyrinthine jewelry bazaars of Calcutta, Delhi, Agra, and Madras. In general, they were disappointed by the quality of what was offered to them and horrified by the inflated prices asked for inferior merchandise. Many exceptional stones, however, could be purchased from maharajas and wealthy Indian families who wished to dispose of their surplus. One such opportunity presented itself after the death of Queen Victoria on January 22, 1901, at the subsequent coronation of Edward VII. This event brought numerous Indian maharajas to London, and in 1902 Cartier opened a London branch.

A few months after Queen Victoria's death, Queen Alexandra summoned Pierre Cartier to London and commissioned him to create an Indo-European necklace using gemstones taken from various Indian ornaments in the royal collection. (Queen Alexandra wore hardly any of the large collection of Indian jewelry owned by the Royal House of Windsor. She felt they were made mainly for men and considered them "stiff and heavy.") The result was an elegant Indo-European necklace set with ninety-four cabochon emeralds, twelve cabochon rubies, and seventy-one pearls. Conceived to be worn with three Indian-made gowns sent to her by Mary, wife of Lord Curzon, then Viceroy of India, the necklace pleased Queen Alexandra and she wore it frequently. For Cartier this was the first direct contact with outstanding Indian jewelry.

Another famous Cartier commission for Queen Alexandra followed. It was a *collier résille* (hair net), created in 1904 in the French eighteenth-century garland style popularized

855

◄ **854. Paris, France.** *c. 1925*
Rendering by Charles Jacqueau of Cartier, Paris, for a headdress ornament (parure de tête) for a turban (pagri), a project suggested to the Francophile Maharaja of Kapurthala
Archives Cartier, Courtesy Cartier, Paris

The sarpech, sarpatti, and turra have become integrated into one continuous ornament, and the Indian turban has been transformed into a stylish French cloche hat, a form introduced by Paul Poiret after the success of the Ballets Russes in Paris in 1911. An extravagant, theatrical creation based on Indian prototypes as interpreted by a European, it is better suited to the stage than reality and was not executed.

855. Paris, France. *c. 1911*
Platinum forehead ornament (chand mang-tika), made by Cartier, Paris, for the Maharani Darkati II of Patiala, Punjab
Diameter 2 in. (5 cm)
Archives Cartier; Courtesy Cartier, Paris

This cross-cultural design, derived from the Indian mang tikka form, incorporates four concentric new crescent moons (H: naya chand; A: halil) mounted with diamonds and pearls. It includes a central painted enamel-on-gold miniature portrait of the Maharaja of Patiala wearing his famous pearls, copied from a photograph. The attached pearl cord follows the hair part (mang) and is used to secure the ornament to the hair.

856

857

by Cartier in the 1890s and in favor until the beginning of World War I. (The style was also admired by many Indian maharajas, who ordered necklaces in this mode for themselves and their wives.) It contained 1,027 brilliants weighing an impressive 141.4 carats, all culled from dismantled Indian necklaces presented to her and Edward VII on various occasions.

Among Cartier's influential designers (who, like their Indian counterparts, were for the most part anonymous during their working lives) was Charles Jacqueau (1885–1968) who was hired by Cartier in 1909 and was Director of Design in Paris from 1911 to 1935. His career coincided with the kaleidoscopic explosion of orientalism initiated by the popularity of the Ballets Russes, whose productions greatly influenced him. His stylistic innovations were initiated with his design collection of 1913, which emphasized Indian, Persian, and Tibetan motifs adapted to Western use. These were among the earliest distinguished manifestations of jewelry in the Indo-European Art Deco idiom that he was influential in popularizing.

Jeanne Toussaint (1887–1978) was another important Cartier designer, who worked there from 1910 into the 1970s. She also often took her design inspirations from Indian jewelry. For instance, in the 1930s she popularized the traditional Indian use of high-karat yellow gold in combination with colored gemstones. Also in the Indo-European style, she initiated designs utilizing many multicolored, carved gemstones in a single object, often additionally enameled in the polychrome Jaipur manner.

Other Important *Grands Joailliers*

The jewelry firm Boucheron was established in Paris in 1858 by Frédéric Boucheron (1830–1902), who was succeeded by his son Louis (1874–1959), his grandson Gérard, and his great-grandson Alain. In 1893 this establishment moved to the Place Vendôme, where today several of the most prestigious jewelry firms in Paris are housed almost side by side around that beautiful square. A London branch was established in 1907. Like others, Boucheron created many outstanding special commissions for Indian potentates and their families.

Chaumet, founded in 1780 by Etienne Nitot as a jeweler to European royalty, acquired its present name in 1889, when Joseph Chaumet (1854–1928) became its director. Its main showroom is also located at Place Vendôme, and a branch was established in London in 1875. Chaumet also executed many commissions for the Indian aristocracy.

Charles Van Cleef was a Dutch diamond cutter. His son, Alfred Van Cleef (1873–1938),

856. Paris, France. *c. end of 19th century* Rendering by a Chaumet staff designer, of a proposed ensemble of ornaments for the uniform of a maharaja, with diamonds, emeralds, and pearls Courtesy Hélène Chaumet, Relations Presse, Chaumet, Paris

Another design for the theater, it includes a necklace en risaille, a shoulder écharpe with attached pendant and swag, a belt, and cuff ornaments.

857. Paris, France. *c. end of 19th century* Rendering for an écharpe designed by Chaumet, Paris, for a maharani Courtesy Hélène Chaumet, Relations Presse, Chaumet, Paris

Around 1910 the epaulet or écharpe (shoulder sash) appeared as a new type of shoulder ornament that had been used in the eighteenth century but had since fallen out of fashion. In this, the major unit, sometimes called a knot, was fastened to one shoulder. From it hung one or two gemstone ornamented strands and parallel swags draped in a series of articulated strands that met at an ornament fastened to the breast. The concept, extravagantly interpreted here, well suits the Indian woman's manner of wearing a sari, which always covers one shoulder and leaves the other exposed. Chaumet did several such ornaments for Indian clients, as did Cartier. This one is probably the most sumptuous of them all.

became a jeweler and in 1898 married his cousin Estelle Arpels, daughter of Léon Arpels, a precious-stone merchant. In 1867 a partnership was formed between Van Cleef and Léon's brothers Charles (1880–1951) and Julien (1884–1964), and the Paris firm titled Van Cleef and Arpels was born. Louis Arpels (1886–1976), a younger brother, joined the firm after World War I, and the establishment has continued into the next generations. This company was very active in creating commissions for the wealthy of India. To gather suitable gemstones, Julien Arpels, who was responsible for their acquisition, repeatedly visited India and other Eastern sources.

Maubusson came to the Place Vendôme in 1945, and Cardeihac in 1906. They also had their share of commissions for Indians.

Indo-European Art Deco Jewelry

A decided Indian influence on European jewelry occurred with the introduction of the Art Deco style that prevailed during the first three decades of the twentieth century. Officially launched at the Paris Exposition Internationale des Arts Décoratifs et Industriels Modernes in 1925, Art Deco jewelry, as it is now called, incorporated contemporary European art trends, such as Cubism and Abstraction, both of which emphasized geometric forms. European jewelry designers culled additional ideas from the plethora of Indian formal and design components compatible with this direction to create an amalgam of Art Deco–style jewelry in the Indo-European mode.

Turra Tassels: Precious *Passementerie*

Tassels (H: *jhabba; phunda*) consisting of short strings of pearls of equal length, gemstones, and hardstones and combinations of these, are commonly found in traditional Indian jewelry and were used to an unprecedented extent in Art Deco jewelry. The adoption of tassels as an important design element in European jewelry occurred almost overnight with the performance on June 4, 1910, of the Paris Opéra production by Les Ballets Russes of *Shéhérazade*. Its costumes and scenery, designed by Léon Bakst, were a phenomenal success. A master at creating mood through color and pattern, Bakst's work often reflected his ongoing interest in ethnic cultural models, in this case, Indian and Persian concepts. The result was a riotous fantasy of sumptuous "orientalist" sensuality, to a large extent well researched and relatively authentic.

Bakst's Indian costume and jewelry designs came instantly into vogue. Fashion arbiters such as Iribe, Paquin, Poiret, and Worth took up the theme, and the designers of the great jewelry houses were quick to follow.

858. New York, New York. 1965 (opposite page)
Gold Indo-European necklace created by Van Cleef and Arpels, New York (V.C.A. N.Y. 35376)
Private Collection

This spectacular necklace, a Western interpretation of an Indian traditional kantha design style (see 770) using four maharatnani gemstones, illustrates a successful cross-cultural fusion. The collar consists of four concentric rows of pearls and claw-set emeralds, diamonds, and rubies. At its lower edge are nineteen flower heads whose centers alternate with diamonds and emeralds. Fifteen pear-shaped cabochon-emerald pendants fall from these and the central, detachable pendant in the form of an oval cluster of seven similar flower heads and a pear-shaped central emerald.

859. Jaipur, Rajasthan
Enameled gold side-of-turban ornament (turra) with diamonds
Length 5½ in. (14 cm)
Courtesy Deeva, London

A parrot (toti)—from whose beak is suspended a jhumka and a tassel (jhabba) of pearls and emerald beads—is surmounted by a diamond-set flower. When in use, the tail is forced into the turban folds and the tassel hangs freely in air. This type of ornament inspired the European vogue for pearl and other gemstone tassels commonly found in Art Deco jewelry.

859

860. Paris, France. *c.1955*
Gold, two-part, hinged bangle-bracelet (kara),
made by Cartier, Paris
Approximate diameter 3⅛ in. (8 cm)
Collection Ralph Esmerian, New York

The concept of a bracelet with protome terminals
in the form of animal heads originated in the
Middle East and has been in use in India since the
3rd century A.D. The Indian bangle-bracelet (kara)
with two facing makara head terminals inspired
this design (see 581, 796). Introduced by Cartier
in the 1920s, it became one of the most typical
designs of the Art Deco style. Instead of using an
unknown Indian term like makara, Cartier adopted
the chic-sounding chimera bracelet designation,
after a Greek mythological she-monster with a
lion's head, killed by Bellerophon. In the 1950s,
the Cartier designer Jeanne Toussaint revived the
design, and this is probably one of hers. Typically,
the heads are carved in salmon-red coral, and
the bracelet is ornamented with diamonds, cabochon rubies, and—like its Indian prototype—
polychrome enamel.

861. Paris, France. *c.1938*
Emerald, diamond, and platinum necklace made
by Cartier, Paris
Approximate length 18 in. (45.7 cm)
Courtesy Christie's, London

The twenty-nine Indian, tumble-polished, baroque
emeralds (H: adi banki panna) represent a common
form of this gemstone in Indian ornaments. Jewelry
using Indian emeralds (originally from Colombia)
were created by the grands joailliers of Paris and
elsewhere. Here they are mounted with platinum
additions such as the pavé-set diamond studded
loop and cap for each emerald and the roundel
spacers. Typically Art Deco in style, this necklace
was purchased by the actress Merle Oberon.

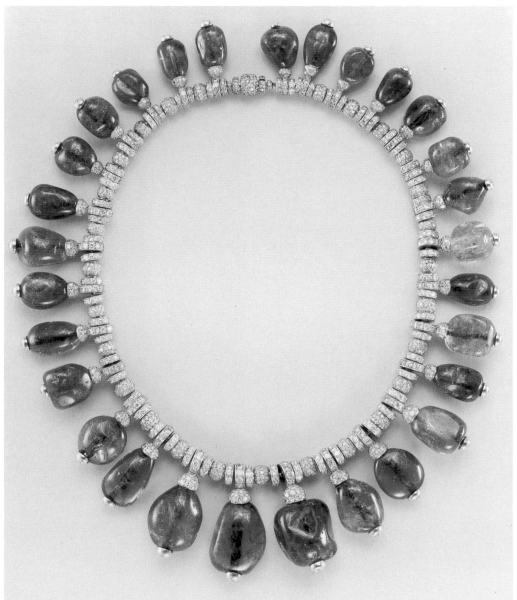

Popular traditional Indian jewelry forms that inspired European interpretations included the tight, straight choker (*guluband*); the multistoned collar type necklace with drops (*kantha*); the bangle (*churi*) with "chimera" (*makara*) terminals; the wide cuff bracelet (*chur*); and the flat, straight armlet (*bazuband*), which inspired the Art Deco articulated-diamond-studded bracelet of many interlocking units (see 851). Outsized women's hats, formerly fashionable, became outmoded and were replaced by the turban or the tight-fitting cloche hat, more often than not decorated in the Indian manner with either an *aigrette* or a tassel.

These two elements most closely identified with Art Deco jewelry—the *aigrette* and the tassel—the first soaring upward, the other drooping, were borrowed from two of the traditional turban ornaments used in India during Mughal times, normally as men's ornaments, but sometimes in smaller sizes also used by women. The *sarpech-aigrette* has been discussed. The other is the *turra* (P: crest worn on the head; a forelock or curl), which could take the form of a stemmed rosette or a stylized enameled-gold parrot with an S-shaped body and tail. From the rosette or the parrot's beak fell a pendicle cluster of short, free-hanging strings of pearls, emeralds, or another gemstone, each strand often ending with a contrasting gemstone bead and gold-yarn-tassel terminal. The *turra* was fixed to the turban by forcing the rosette stem or the parrot's S-curving tail into one side of its tight folds. Its outward curvature allowed the tassel to fall freely.

In Art Deco jewelry, the Indian tassel could be enlarged, miniaturized, elongated, or moved to other places. It became a central ornament on a long, single-strand *sautoir*, or a garlandlike necklace of several strands of plaited seed pearls, both related to the Indian *mala*. The latter design was introduced by Cartier, who called it a *bayadère*, French for an Indian *nautch* dancer, a character who appeared in the Ballets Russes production of *Le Dieu Bleu* (Krishna), performed in 1912. Its costumes and ornaments, also designed by Bakst, included copies of authentic traditional Indian jewelry.

Besides their use in necklaces, tassels could be applied to earrings. They also dangled from armlets and bracelets in the Indian manner, hung from belts or a vanity case, and were even fixed to the tapering apex of a train on a lady's evening gown.

Indian Emeralds in Art Deco Jewelry

The manner by which quantities of Colombian emeralds came to India during the sixteenth to eighteenth centuries has been described (see page 328). In twentieth-century Europe, emeralds of the size and quality in Indian collections could no longer be matched. Thus, they were eagerly sought after, and, from time to time, but especially in the 1920s and 1930s, some Indian owners parted with portions of the emerald hoards accumulated by their ancestors. Several such sales were made to finance new European jewelry commissions. Because the availability of these emeralds coincided with the flourishing of the Art Deco jewelry style, they became a distinctive element of this design idiom.

Mughal Indian jewelry featured emeralds in hexagonal, octagonal, and cabochon forms, and as baroque and melon-shaped beads. In Europe, stones purchased in these forms were generally used intact, although some of particularly fine quality underwent recutting. European jewelry designers used great ingenuity to meet the challenge of how to best use them in their unaltered state. Large, carved emeralds from Indian *bazubands* became the central gemstone of an imposing neckpiece or a pendant on a long *sautoir* necklace. Melon-shaped beads (P: *kharbuza;* H: *tarbuz*) and baroque cabochon beads or pendants were reused as pendants or strung in necklaces, often in combination with platinum spacer units set with diamonds. Small emerald beads were used for tassels in a variety of ways. Others were placed in tiaras, *aigrettes,* earrings, brooches, and other forms of European jewelry.

Multicolored Carved Stones in Art Deco Jewelry

One of the distinctive characteristics of traditional Mughal jewelry is the use of several differently colored, often carved gemstones in a single ornament, a style that continues in India. In Indo-European jewelry of the late 1920s, the concept was introduced and became common, and it appeared again in the 1960s, when the Art Deco style experienced a revival.

To Western eyes, this polychromatic gemstone style provides Indian jewelry with a quality of exotic richness. The effect of exuberant luxury was achieved in the Indo-European version by means somewhat different from that of the Indian model. The irregularly colored and shaped gemstones used in Indian jewelry were replaced in Western versions with carved gemstones of good quality that were naturally uniform in color and often in matching, calibrated sizes. The idea of using existing carved emeralds, rubies, and sapphires in Art Deco jewelry probably suggested the practice of carving other gemstones and hardstones, such as black onyx, coral, lapis lazuli, turquoise, and crystal, whose use became another characteristic of Art Deco jewelry.

Pearls in the Art Deco Style

Pearls have long been the mainstay of European jewelry merchants. Before the production of cultured pearls in Japan (1915) and their commercial introduction in London (1921), natural pearls of good quality and size sold for enormous prices. In the pearl trade that developed, Bombay on the Arabian Sea became a primary natural pearl market. Most of the annual natural pearl harvest from Bahrain and Ceylon was brought there to be sorted for size, color, shape, and quality. Pearl piercing became a process for which Indian lapidaries were and still are famous, especially in the case of minute seed pearls. European dealers and the agents of most major jewelers still maintain contact with Indian dealers and pay regular visits to Bombay to buy natural pearls and gemstones.

The most characteristic pearl ornament of the Art Deco style is the long, single strand pearl *sautoir,* often interspaced with gemstone beads. Its origin is seen in Mughal miniature paintings, where it was commonly worn by emperors and the nobility (see 1, 761).

Art Deco Platinum Settings

After 1910, in Europe the use of platinum took precedence over gold for settings. Indian clients of Art Deco jewelry accepted the Western preference for platinum to mount and display brilliant-cut diamonds and cabochon rubies, emeralds, and sapphires, which these light, strong settings emphasized. As platinum was then not yet used in India, the result was a reduction in the patronage of native Indian jewelers and an increase in major commissions and purchases of jewelry from Western jewelers.

Epilogue

Skillfully handcrafted, traditional 22-karat gold (and silver) jewelry continues to exude a strong vitality in India. While designs are still fundamentally based on the forms illustrated in this book, the present development of gold jewelry can be characterized as showing ever greater refinement and elaboration, whereas silver jewelry tends toward simplification. Whether produced for urban or rural consumption, this jewelry's continued use is founded on the endurance of the dowry system throughout India and the ingrained Indian dependence on gold and silver as a means of investment and security against adversity.

This dependence is dramatically illustrated by statistics on annual global gold consumption, which clearly indicate India's preeminence. In 1993 India consumed 424 metric tons of gold. By comparison, the United States consumed 279 metric tons; Saudi Arabia, 239; China, 223; Japan, 221; Italy, 113; Germany, 87; France, 48; and the United Kingdom, 33 metric tons. In 1994 India diverted 349 metric tons of its gold, most of it imported, to jewelry fabrication. Each year, jewelry production continues to expand, an indication that India's gold consumption will also continue to rise.

Transforming the precious metals into jewelry are an estimated one hundred thousand domestic jewelry manufacturers made up of from three to ten workers. Additionally, about one hundred factories exist that each are staffed by several hundred goldsmiths, whose nationwide total is now close to two million. No country in the world can match these consumption, employment, and production figures.

A relatively small but growing number of manufactures in India produce jewelry designed to please an international export market. The gold they use is 18, 14, and sometimes 9 karats, standards acceptable in many Western markets. Their results offer no competition to the high-end indigenous market.

In the West, *grand-joaillier* establishments still intermittently appropriate traditional Indian jewelry design concepts, a tribute to their enduring relevance and worldwide consumer appeal. Generally unrecognized is the considerable Indian export of nonprecious metal and hardstone costume jewelry (the former not discussed in this book), which may also be inspired by traditional forms. Thus, the evidence is clear that, whatever the type, or the reason for its use, traditional Indian jewelry will continue to delight not only Indian jewelry lovers, but also jewelry makers and wearers around the world.

862. Paris, France.
c.1925
Art Deco emerald
necklace with platinum
mounted diamonds, based
on the Indian mala, a long,
gemstone-bead necklace
Collection Ralph Esmer-
ian, New York

The emerald beads in
melon form (kharbuza)
probably came from a
Mughal Indian necklace
of emerald beads (panna
moti ka mala). Such neck-
laces also used ruby and
pearl beads in various
combinations. Many were
sold to European jewelers,
who then used the beads
in new arrangements. This
is a particularly successful
example.

863. Paris, France.
c.1925
An Art Deco interpreta-
tion of the seven stranded
traditional Indian neck-
lace (sat lara har)
Length 16½ in. (42 cm)
Private Collection

The platinum triangular,
openwork terminal spacers
and the center-of-strand
pendants with pearl drops
have all been geometrized
in European Art Deco
fashion and set with brilliants and calibré emeralds.
The pearl strands incorporate emerald beads, and
the traditional patu'a style
of tying-on cord has been
retained.

Traditional Indian Jewelers' Tools and Materials: Vernacular Terms

The transliteration system used in this table is a "simplified" one for readers unfamiliar with Indian languages.

ENGLISH	HINDI	BENGALI	TAMIL
Basic Terms:			
workshop	jauhari karkhana	sonar dokan	aparanattorirsalai
workbench	kam kimez	tebil (table)	paddarai mesai
bench pin	kili	jibi / kili	mesainakku
bench vise	hathkal	angel / "bench" sarashi	pidicchiravi
leather apron	chamra ka tukra	chamrar chadar	tolulla munthanki
light source	batti	obati (table light)	velicchattukkuriya minjaram
electricity	bijli	bijli	minsaram
goldsmith's scale	kanti	nikti	taddan tarasu
weights	tolne ke bat	batkhara	padikkal
crab's eye seed	ratti	kunchbichi	kundumani
touchstone	kasauti	kastipathor	uraikal
ruler	mistar / salaka	fut kati	chaddappalakai
scriber	bal / salai	dagmara	chuchikiru
compass	parkar	"compass"	kavarakkol
ingot	kandla	bat	palakatti
ingot mold	rezi	dhala	kattikal
crucible	gutli / ghariya	muchi / gharia	musai
crucible tongs:			
small	chimta	choto chimti	musaikkuradu
large	kamu / jamuri	boro chimti	parumaiyulla musaikaradu
tongs	chimti / chimta	chimta / sandasi	ilaikkurathu
furnace	bhatthi	bhatti	sulai/ulaikkalam
hand fan	pankha	pakha	visiri
hand bellows	khal / dhaunkni	hapur	ulai
Metals:			
gold	sona	sona	pon / tangam
silver	chandi	rupo / chandi	velli
copper	tamba	tama	tambiram / sembu
brass	pital	pitol	pittalai
bronze	kansa	kansa	vengalam
tin	kalai	ranga / tin	takaram
lead	sisa	sis	iyam
zinc	jasta	dasta	tuttangam
Forms of Metal:			
sheet	patra	pat	takadu
tubing	nali	chungi / nal	kural
wire	tar	tar	kambi
gold foil or leaf	sone ka varaq	sona pata	melis pon takudu / ponrekku
silver foil or leaf	chandika varaq	rupo pata	melis velli takudu
solid	thos	niret / thons	uruthiyana
hollow	pola	phanpa / phonk	chilgai
cast	dhalna	dhalai kora	kaddimuttu
stamped	thappe ka kam	thokai kaj	kambattam
stamping die	thappa	thosa / chane	mathiri acchu
rolling mill	lurakne ki "machine"	dalai "machine"	thagadakkumyanthiram
rolling sheet	patriki "machine"	patir "machine"	thagaduyanthiram
rolling wire	tar ki "machine"	tare "machine"	kambiyanthiram
drawplate	jantri	janturi / janta	kambicchaddam / kambi acchu
wire-drawing tongs	jamur	sarasi / siari	pattikuradu
lubricating oil	sarsan ka tel	sorse tel	azhuththvenneyenney

Tools:

scissors	kaimchi	kainchi	kattarikkol
shears	katira	kainchi	kattiri
jeweler's sawframe	ari	dal	val
jeweler's handle	muth	dal hatal	valppidi
jeweler's sawframe screw	aripech	dal pech	valttirukani
jeweler's sawblade	fanar	karat	valkkambi
lubricating wax	mom	mom	mezhugu
chisel	chheni	chheni	veddirumbu / uli
scraper	khurchan / chhilni	tripat	sivuli
engraver's burin	kalam / salai / ulchaiya	buli / salai	chethukkili
tool-sharpening stone	jilla kisan	jilla san / san pathar	chanaikkal
wooden mallet	lakrika hathaura	kathir hatudi	maracchukkiyam
hammer (small)	hathauri	choto hatudi	chuttiyal / chammaddi
hammer (large)	hathaura	bairo hatudi	sammatti
anvil	nihai	nehi	adaikal
design block	sadavia thappa	thosa	chalangai acchu
dapping block	makal / pansa	kansuli	kambattamulai
round-ended punch	tona	togna / goba	kurikaru
other punches	chita ka chheni / tukilna	tokna / kalam	karu
circle cutter	tikkikatne ka sumba	golok kanci	vaddam kuttukaru
file	reti	uko / sohana	aram
round file	gol reti	gol uko	vaddamana aram
half-round file	nimgol reti	mekun uko	araivaddamana aram
square file	chauras reti	chouko uko	chaturamana aram
triangular file	tikonireti	tinkona uko	mukkonamana aram
flat file	chapta reti	chatta uko	taddaiyana aram
knife-shape file	chhurireti	chhuri uko	kattiyaram
pump drill	dhagevalla verma	pamp turpun	tamarpidi
drill bit	phal / sui	chuch	cholti
borer or gimlet	barma	kshudro turpun	turappanam

Joining:

solder (hard)	tanka	pan	vilakkuppodi pattu
soft solder	halka tanka	norom pan	miruthuvana pattu
gold solder	sone ka tanka	shona pan	tangappodi
silver solder	chandika tanka / nargi	rupo pan	vellippodi
solder/snippets	rai	chutto pan	podi narukku
snips (small)	katira	choto katuri	kattarikkol
snips (large)	kaet	bodo katuri	periya kattarikkol
boral flux	sohaga / tinkal	suhaga	velikkaram / vengaram
iron binding wire	lohe kitar	lohar tar	irumbukkambi
soldering lamp	diva	prodip	vilakku
lamp wick	ruika dhaga	sutuli	vilakkuththiri
fuel	tel ka diva	indhon tel	vilakku enney
mouth blowpipe (small)	banknal	chunga nali	uthukural
mouth blowpipe (large)	phunkni	bagnol damba phunkni	periya kural
charcoal	lakrika koila	kath koila	marakkari
coke	patthar ka koila	pathor koila	nilakkari
asbestos board	gata	"asbesta"	kalnarppalamai
clay	mitti	matti	kaliman
red ocher	lal mitti / geru	girimati	karkkavi
yellow ocher	pilimitti	girimati	pittaman
nitric acid	shore ka tezab	shora omlo	vediyupputtiravakam
sulfuric acid	gandak ka tezab	gondhok omlo	kanthakappulippu
acid container	byam	chatu	puli adakkuvathu
lathe	kharad / charakh	korad	kadacham / kadaicchal paddadai
screw	pech	pench	thirigani
screw plate	pech patti	"escruplate"	maracchaddam
screwdriver	pech kash	penne debar jontro	thirupuli

Finishing:

soapnut	ritha	ritea phol	pungakottai
soapnut brass-wire brush	ritha kikuchi	ritea "burus"	pittalaikkucchu
burnisher:			
steel	mashkala / saiqal	moskola / ispater	merukkukaru
agate	hakika / mohari	gomeder shan	vaiduriyam thulangkachcheyvon
chalk	chun	karimatti	chunnambu
spit	thuk	thuk	tuppal
gold plating	mulamma	sonar jol	pottakadu
silver plating	chandika pani	rupo jol	vellittakadu
enameling	minakam	minakam	azhuththamakkugai
mica sheet	abrak patra	aubhro pat / meghnala	appirakam takadu
shellac	lakh	gala / lakha	arakku
shellac stick (stone setting)	hundi	lakh hundi	umicham

Bibliography

The bibliography is divided into broad categories, beginning with general references on jewelry, which are divided among books, government monographs, census reports, museum catalogues and guidebooks, and journals and periodicals. This section is further broken out into specialized subject categories such as amulets, beads, and gemstones. These are followed by general references on Indian culture: history, trade, and travel; society; religion; tribal culture; arts; crafts; dance and drama; and ancient literature.

1. Jewelry and Related Subjects

Books

Ahmad, Khwaja Muhammad. *Western Chalukyan Ornaments*. Hyderabad: Hyderabad Museum, 1949.

Air India Art Studio Illustrated Calendar: Traditional Jewellery of India. Text by Shakunthala Jagannathan; photographs by Ajit Patel. Bombay, 1980.

Air India Art Studio Illustrated Calendar: Brides of India. Text by Nirmal Seshadri; photographs by C. V. Kamar. Bombay, 1982.

Ali, Salim, and Laeeq Futehally. *Common Birds*. India—The Land and People Series. New Delhi: National Book Trust, 1967.

Auboyer, Jeannine. *The Art of Afghanistan*. Feltham, Middlesex: Paul Hamlyn, 1968.

Aziz, Abdul. *The Imperial Treasury of the Mughals*. Lahore: Published by the author, 1942.

_____. *Arms and Jewellery of the Indian Mughals*. Lahore: Published by the author, 1947.

Balfour, Edward G. *The Cyclopaedia of India, and of Eastern and Southern Asia: Commercial, Industrial, and Scientific*. 3 vols. London: Bernard Quaritch, 1885.

Bhan, R. K. *Economic Survey Report of Silverware in Kashmir*, no. 3. Srinagar, 1938.

Bhardwaj, H. C. *Aspects of Ancient Indian Technology*. New Delhi: Motilal Banarsidass, 1979.

Borel, France. *The Splendor of Ethnic Jewelry: The Colette and Jean-Pierre Ghysels Collection*. Photographs by John Bigelow Taylor. New York: Harry N. Abrams, Inc., 1994.

Boyer, Martha. *Mongol Jewellery*. Nationalmuseets skrifter, Etnografisk rœkke, 5. Copenhagen: Gyldendalske Boghandel, Nordisk Forlag, 1952. Reissued by Ida Nicolaisen, editor-in-chief, The Carlsberg Foundation's Nomad Research Project. London: Thames and Hudson Ltd, 1995.

Brijbhushan, Jamila. *Indian Jewellery, Ornaments and Decorative Designs*. Bombay: D. B. Taraporevala Sons and Co., 1964.

Brosh, Na'ama, ed. *Jewellery and Goldsmithing in the Islamic World*. Papers from the First International Symposium on Islamic Jewellery. Jerusalem: Israel Museum, 1991.

Brunel, Francis. *Jewellery of India*. New Delhi: National Book Trust, 1972.

Butor, Michel. *Adornment: The Jean-Paul and Monique Barbier-Mueller Collection*. Photographs by Pierre-Alain Ferrazzini. London: Thames and Hudson Ltd., 1994.

Casanowicz, Immanuel M. *The Collection of Rosaries in the United States National Museum*. Proceedings of the National Museum, vol. 36. Washington D.C.: Government Printing Office, 1909. Reprint, Albany, Calif.: The Northern California Bead Society, 1980.

Chandra, Rai Govind. *Studies in the Development of Ornaments and Jewellery in Proto-Historic India*. Chowkhamba Sanskrit Series Studies, vol. 41. Varanasi: The Chowkhamba Sanskrit Series Office, 1964.

_____. *Indo-Greek Jewellery*. New Delhi: Abhinav Publications, 1979.

Daniell, Clarmont John. *The Gold Treasure of India*. London: Kegan Paul, Trench and Co., 1884.

Dikshit, Moreshwar G. *History of Indian Glass*. Pandit Bhagwahlal Indraji Endowment Lectures, 1967. Bombay: University of Bombay, 1969.

Dongerkery, Kamala S. *Jewellery and Personal Adornment in India*. New Delhi: Indian Council for Cultural Relations, Vikas Publications, 1971.

Field, Leslie. *The Queen's Jewels: The Personal Collection of Elizabeth II*. New York: Harry N. Abrams, Inc., 1987.

Filliozat, J., and P. Z. Pattabiramin. *Parures divines du sud de l'Inde*. Pondichery: Institut français d'indologie, 1966.

Gail, Adalbert J. *Handwerker/Künstler in Indien und Nepal*. Graz, Austria: Akademische Druck- und Verlagsanstalt, n.d.

Glover, P. M. *Lac Cultivation in India*. Nakum, Ranchi, Bihar: Indian Lac Research Institute, 1937.

Haque, Zulekha. *Gahana: Jewellery of Bangladesh*. Dhaka: Bangladesh Small and Cottage Industries Corporation, 1984.

Hendley, Thomas Holbein. "The Influence of Politics and Geography on Jewellery in Rajputana." Paper read before the Victoria Institute, London, 1905.

_____. *Indian Jewellery*. London: William Griggs and Sons, 1909.

_____. "Indian Jewellery." In *Reprints of Journal of Indian Art*. 2 vols. New Delhi: Cultural Publishing House, 1989.

Hendley, Thomas Holbein, and Swinton S. Jacob. *Jeypore Enamels*. London: William Griggs and Sons, 1886.

"Indian Jewellery." *Marg* 17, no. 4 (1964): entire issue.

Jacobson, Doranne. "Women and Jewellery in Rural India." In *Main Currents in Indian Sociology*. Vol. 2, *Family and Social Change in India*, edited by Giri Raj Gupta, 135–83. New Delhi: Vikas Publishing House, 1976.

Jain, Jyotindra, and Mallika Sarabhai. "Ornaments." In *Crafts of Gujarat*, 43–64. New York: Mapin International, 1985.

Janata, Alfred. *Schmuck in Afganistan*. Graz, Austria: Akademische Druck- und Verlagsanstalt, 1981.

Kipling, John Lockwood. *Beast and Man in India*. London: Macmillan and Co., 1891.

Krishnadasa, Rai. "The Pink Enamelling of Banaras." In *Chhavi: Golden Jubilee Volume*. Vol. 1, edited by Anand Krishna, 321–34. Varanasi: Banaras Hindu University, 1971.

Kuppuram, G. *Ancient Indian Metallurgy and Metal Industries*. 2 vols. New Delhi: Sundeep Prakashan, 1989.

Loth, Anne-Marie. "Les Bijoux." In *La Vie publique et privée dans l'Inde ancienne*. Fascicle 9.1 Publications du Musée Guimet, vol. 6. Paris: Presses universitaires de France, 1972.

Maxwell-Hyslop, K. R. *Western Asiatic Jewellery, c. 3000–612 B.C.* London: Methuen and Co., 1971.

Menkes, Suzy. *The Royal Jewels*. London: Grafton Books, 1985.

Mukherjee, Meera. *Metalcraftsmen of India*. Calcutta: Anthropological Survey of India, Government of India, 1978.

Nadelhoffer, Hans. *Cartier: Jewelers Extraordinary*. New York: Harry N. Abrams, Inc., 1984.

Nandagopal, Choodamani. "The Traditional Jewellery of Karnataka." In *Decorative Arts of India*, edited by M. L. Nigam, 195–202. Hyderabad: Salar Jung Museum, 1987.

Pakistan International Airlines Calendar: Folk Jewellery of Pakistan. 1963.

Pant, G. N. *Indian Arms and Armour*. 3 vols. New Delhi: S. Attar Singh, Army Educational Stores, 1978, 1980, 1983.

Postel, Michel. *Ear Ornaments of Ancient India*. Project for Indian Cultural Studies, publication no. 2. Bombay: Franco-Indian Pharmaceuticals, Ltd., 1989.

Pressmar, Emma. *Indische Ringe*. Frankfurt am Main: Insel Verlag, 1982.

_____. *Indian Rings*. Ahmadabad: New Order Book Co., 1986.

Raulet, Sylvie. *Van Cleef and Arpels*. New York: Rizzoli, 1987.

Ray, P. C. *A History of Hindu Chemistry*. 2d ed. 2 vols. Calcutta: Chuckervertty, Chatterjee and Co., 1907, 1909.

Sah, Oved. *Book of Necklaces*. London: Barker, 1953.

Sen, H. K., and S. Ranganathan. *Uses of Lac*. Nakum, Ranchi, Bihar: Indian Lac Research Institute, 1939.

Sen, Jyoti, and Pranar Kumar Dasgupta. *Ornaments in India: A Study in Culture Trait Distribution*. Anthropological Survey of India, memoir no. 22, 1968. New Delhi: Government of India, 1973.

Silver Filigree Craft of Cuttack (Orissa). All-India Handicrafts Board Survey Report, no. 53. New Delhi: Government of India, Ministry of Industry, 1964.

Singer, Jane Casey. *Gold Jewelry from Tibet and Nepal*. London: Thames and Hudson Ltd., 1996.

Tewari, S. P. *Nupura: The Anklet in Indian Literature and Art*. New Delhi: Agam Kala Prakashan, 1982.

Tushingham, A. D. "Persian Enamels." In *The Memorial Volume of the 5th International Congress of Iranian Art and Archaeology*, vol. 2: 211–22. Teheran, 1972.

Untracht, Oppi. *Enameling on Metal*. New York: Greenberg; Philadelphia: Chilton Book Company, 1957.

_____. *Jewelry Concepts and Technology*. Garden City, New York: Doubleday and Co.; London: Robert Hale Ltd., 1982.

_____. "[Jewellery of] India," and "Materials and Techniques [of Jewellery Making]." In *Ethnic Jewellery*, 65–93, 173–99. London: British Museum Publications; New York: Harry N. Abrams, Inc., 1988.

Watt, George, ed. *A Dictionary of the Economic Products of India*. 10 vols. Calcutta: Office of the Superintendent, Government Printing, 1889–93.

_____. *Commercial Products of India*. 1 vol. Abridged edition of *A Dictionary of the Economic Products of India*. London: John Murray, 1908.

The Wealth of India: A Dictionary of Indian Raw Materials and Industrial Projects. New Delhi: Publications and Information Director, CSIR, 1964.

Weihreter, Hans. *Schmuck aus dem Himalaya*. Graz, Austria: Akademische Druck- und Verlangsanstalt, 1988.

Jayakar, Pupul, and John Irwin. *Textiles and Ornaments of India*. Edited by Monroe Wheeler. New York: The Museum of Modern Art, Simon and Schuster, 1956.

Wilkinson, Wynyard R. T. *Indian Colonial Silver: European Silversmiths in India (1790–1860) and Their Marks*. London: Argent Press, 1973.

Windisch-Graetz, Stephanie, and Ghislaine Windisch-Graetz. *Juwelen des Himalaja*. Luzern: Reich Verlag, 1981.

Wulff, Hans E. *The Traditional Crafts of Persia*. Cambridge, Mass.: MIT Press, 1966.

Younghusband, G., and C. Davenport. *The Crown Jewels of England*. London: Cassell and Co., 1919.

Zapata, Janet. *The Jewelry and Enamels of Louis Comfort Tiffany*. New York: Harry N. Abrams, Inc., 1993.

British–Indian Government Handicraft Monographs

"The government of India annually prescribes the subject on which each Local Government is required to submit a monograph, the object being to prepare, in a series of years, a fairly complete survey of the existing [craft] industries of India." (Nissim, *Wire and Tinsel*, Bombay, 1909: 1). Today, these monographs provide a wealth of information on jewelry and include lists of regional jewelry. Entries are arranged by author.

Burns, Cecil L. *A Monograph on Gold and Silver Work in the Bombay Presidency*. Bombay: Government Central Press, 1904.

Charles, A. F. *A Monograph on Gold and Silver Ware Produced in the United Provinces*. Allahabad: Government Central Press, 1905.

Henniker, Frederick C. Hanclos. *A Monograph on the Gold and Silver Wares of Assam*. Shillong: Assam Secretariat Printing Office, Agra, 1905.

Maclagan, Edward Douglas. *Monograph on the Gold and Silver Works of the Punjab, 1888–89*. Lahore: The Civil and Military Gazette Press, 1890.

Mookerji, D. N. *A Monograph on Gold and Silver Work in the Bengal Presidency*. Calcutta: The Bengal Secretariat Book Depot, 1905.

Nunn, H. *Industrial Monograph on Gold and Silverware of the Central Provinces*. Allahabad: The Pioneer Press, 1904.

Census of India

Census reports for the years 1881, 1891, 1901, 1911, 1921, 1931, 1941, 1951, 1961, 1971, 1981—published by the Office of the Registrar General, Ministry of Home Affairs in New Delhi—were valuable sources for information connected with Indian crafts. For the Census of 1961, Ashok Mitra was Registrar General. Under his extraordinary guidance, many volumes dealing with individual crafts were published. Those of special interest are listed below.

Chadra, Sekhar A. "Filigree Industry of Karimnagar." In *Census of India, 1961*. Vol. 2, *Andhra Pradesh*, part 7A1, *Selected Crafts of Andhra Pradesh*: 1–14. 1965.

Chadra, Suman. "Bibliography of Indian Arts and Crafts." In *Census of India, 1961*. Vol. 1, part 11 (2). 1967.

"Glass Bangles at Tarapur, District Thana." In *Census of India, 1961*. Vol. 10, *Maharashtra*, part 7A1, *Handicrafts in Maharashtra*. 1964.

Gowd, K. V. N. "Studded Bangles of Hyderabad City." In *Census of India, 1961*. Vol. 2, *Andhra Pradesh*, part 7A1, *Selected Crafts of Andhra Pradesh*: 115. 1965.

Green, L. B. "Bangle Industry." In *Census of India, 1931*. Vol. 14, *Madras*, part 1, *Report*, appendix 2: 242.

Pal, M. K., comp. "Jewellery and Ornaments of India: A Historical Outline." In *Census of India, 1971*. Series no. 1, paper no. 1. 1971.

Patra, Atul Chandra. "The Laws Governing Craftsmen and Their Crafts from Ancient Days until Today in India." In *Census of India, 1961*. Vol. 1, Monograph Series, part 7A, Monograph no. 2. 1966.

Ray, Sudhansu Kumar. "The Sankhakaras." In *Census of India, 1961*. Vol. 16, *West Bengal and Sikkim*, part 7A1, *The Artisan Castes of West Bengal and Their Craft*: 340–41. 1963.

Sen, Dipanhar. "Conch Shell Products." In *Census of India, 1961*. Vol. 16, *West Bengal and Sikkim*, part 7A1, *Handicrafts Survey Monograph*: 132. 1965.

Sharma, Lakshmi Chand. "Gold and Silver Ornaments." In *Census of India, 1961*. Vol. 7, *Himachal Pradesh*, part 7A1, *Rural Craft Survey*. 1965.

Sharma, R. C. "Lapidary Work of Jaipur." In *Census of India, 1961*. Vol. 14, *Rajasthan*, part 7A1, *Survey of Selected Crafts*: 71. 1966.

"Silver Ornaments at Hupari, District Kolhapur." *Census of India, 1961*. Vol. 10, *Maharashtra*, part 7A1, *Handicrafts in Maharashtra*. 1964.

"Silversmithy of Tarbha." In *Census of India, 1961*. Vol. 12, *Orissa*, part 7A1, *Survey of Traditional Crafts, Orissa*, book 3: 143–201. 1967.

Sinha, Sukumar. "Lac Ornaments: Jhalda." In *Census of India, 1961*. Vol. 16, *West Bengal and Sikkim*, part 7A2, *Handicrafts Survey Monograph*. 1967.

Trivedi, R. K. "Agate Industry of Cambay." In *Census of India, 1961*. Vol. 5, *Gujarat*, part 7A1, *Selected Crafts of Gujarat*. 1964.

Museum Catalogues and Handbooks

Allan, J. *Catalogue of Ancient Indian Coins in the British Museum*. London: British Museum Publications, 1936.

Baden-Powell, B. H. *Handbook of the Manufactures and Arts of the Punjab*. Handbook of the Economic Products of the Punjab, vol. 2. Lahore: Punjab Printing Company, 1872.

Barbier, Jean-Paul. *Art du Nagaland*. Exhibition catalogue. Geneva: Musée Barbier-Mueller, 1982.

Birdwood, George Christopher Molesworth. *Paris Universal Exhibition of 1878*. Handbook to the British-Indian Section. London: Offices of the Royal Commission, 1878.

_____. *The Industrial Arts of India*. South Kensington Museum Art Handbooks. London: Chapman and Hall, 1880.

_____. *The Arts of India: A Handbook to the Collection of His Royal Highness the Prince of Wales, Compiled for the Yorkshire Fine Art and Industrial Institution, York*. London: R. Clay, Sons, and Taylor, 1881.

_____. *Indian Art in Marlborough House: A Catalogue of the Collection of Indian Arms and Objects of Art Presented by the Princes and Nobles of India to H. R. H. the Prince of Wales on the Occasion of His Visit to India in 1875–1876*. London: W. Griggs, 1891–92.

Brown, Percy. *A Descriptive Guide to the Department of Industrial Art [of the Lahore Museum, Punjab]*. Calcutta: Messrs Thacker Spink and Co., 1909.

Cole, H. H. *Catalogue of the Objects of Indian Art Exhibited in the South Kensington Museum, London [Science and Art Department]*. London, 1874.

Colonial and Indian Exhibition, 1886. Official Catalogue. London: William Clowes and Sons, 1886.

Coronation Durbar, Delhi, 1903. Photographs by Bourne and Shepherd, Official Photographers to the Durbar. London: Eyre and Spottiswoode, 1903.

Czuma, Stanislaus J. *Kushan Sculpture: Images from Early India*. Exhibition catalogue. Cleveland: Cleveland Museum of Art, 1985.

Desai, V. *Life at Court: Art for India's Rulers, 16th–19th Century*. Exhibition catalogue. Boston: Museum of Fine Arts, 1985.

Egerton, Wilbraham. *Handbook of Indian Arms: A Classified and Descriptive Catalogue of the Arms Exhibited at the India Museum*. London: William H. Allen and Co. and William Griggs, 1880.

Fern, Ernest R. *Catalogue of the Industrial Section, Victoria and Albert Museum, Bombay*. Bombay: Times Press, 1926.

Gamble, J. S. *A Manual of Indian Timbers*. London: Sampson Low, Marston and Co., 1922.

Grierson, George A. *Bihar Peasant Life: Being a Discursive Catalogue of the Surroundings and the People of That Province*. 2d ed. Patna: Government Printing, Bihar and Orissa, 1926.

Griffiths, John, ed. "Gold and Silver Work, Bombay Presidency." In *Calcutta International Exhibition, 1883–84*. Exhibition catalogue. Bombay: The Superintendent of Government Printing, 1884.

Guy, John, and Deborah Swallow, eds. *Arts of India: 1550–1900*. Exhibition catalogue. London: Victoria and Albert Museum, 1990.

Harris, H. T. *The Madras Industrial Arts Exhibition 1903: Official Catalogue*. Madras, 1905.

Hasson, Rachel. *Early Islamic Jewellery*. Exhibition catalogue. Jerusalem: L. A. Mayer Memorial Institute for Islamic Art, 1987.

_____. *Later Islamic Jewellery*. Exhibition catalogue. Jerusalem: L. A. Mayer Memorial Institute for Islamic Art, 1987.

Hendley, Thomas Holbein. *Memorials of the Jeypore Exhibition [1883]*. 4 vols. London: William Griggs and Sons, 1884.

_____. *London Indo-Colonial Exhibition of 1886: Handbook of Jeypore Courts*. Calcutta: Calcutta Central Press Co., 1886.

_____. *Handbook to the Jeypore Museum*. Calcutta: Calcutta Central Press Co., 1895.

_____. *Jeypore Guide*. Jaipur: His Highness the Maharaja's Printing Department, 1876.

Höpfner, Gerd, and Gesine Hasse. *Metallschmuck aus Indien*. Exhibition catalogue. West Berlin: Museum für Völkerkunde, 1978.

Ivanov, A. A., Lukonin, V. G., and L. S. Smesova. *Oriental Jewellery from the Collection of the Special Treasury, the State Hermitage, Oriental Department*. Exhibition catalogue. Moscow: Iskusstvo, 1984.

Jain, Jyotindra. *Folk Art and Culture of Gujarat*. Guide to the Collection of the Shreyas Museum of Gujarat. Ahmadabad: Shreyas Prakashan, 1980.

Jain, Jyotindra, and Aarti Aggarwala. *National Handicrafts and Handlooms Museum: New Delhi*. Museums of India Series. Ahmadabad: Mapin Publishing, 1989.

Jenkins, Marilyn, ed. *The al-Sabah Collection: Islamic Art in the Kuwait National Museum*. Exhibition catalogue. London: Sotheby's, 1983.

Jenkins, Marilyn, and Manuel Keene. *Islamic Jewelry in The Metropolitan Museum of Art*. Exhibition catalogue. New York: The Metropolitan Museum of Art, 1982.

Kalter, J. *Orientalischer Volksschmuck*. Exhibition catalogue. Stuttgart: Linden Museum, 1979.

Kalus, Ludvik. *Cachets, Bules et Talismans Islamiques*. Exhibition catalogue. Paris: Bibliothèque Nationale, 1981.

_____. *Islamic Seals and Talismans*. Exhibition catalogue. Oxford: Claredon Press, Ashmolean Museum, 1986.

Komleva, Galina. *Jewellery*. Exhibition catalogue. Leningrad: Aurora Art Publishers, State Museum of the Ethnography of the Peoples of the USSR, 1988.

Latif, Momin, Jeanine, Jean-Pierre Schotsmans, and Zdzislaw Zamoyski. *Mughal Jewels*. Exhibition catalogue. Exhibition organized by the Société Générale de Banque, Brussels, January 21–March 31, 1982.

Latif, Momin, et al. *Joyaux et saris de l'Inde du 17ième au 19ième siècle*. Exhibition catalogue. Paris: Printemps Haussmann, 1983.

Lerner, Martin. "Pair of Royal Earrings" [The Kronos Earrings]. In *Far Eastern Art; Indian and Southeast Asian Art: Notable Acquisitions, 1981–1982*. Selected by Philippe de Montebello, 69–70. New York: The Metropolitan Museum of Art, 1982.

_____. *The Flame and the Lotus: Indian and Southeast Asian Art from the Kronos Collections*. New York: The Metropolitan Museum of Art, 1984.

Lynch, Brendan. "The Near East, India." In *Ivory: A History and Collector's Guide*, 200–25. London: Thames and Hudson Ltd., 1987.

Madras Exhibition of Arts and Industries, 1915–1916. Official Guide and Descriptive Catalogue. Madras: Higginbothams, 1915.

Magnificent Jewels: An Important Collection of Moghul Jewellery. Exhibition catalogue. Geneva: Christie's, 1991.

Mallebrein, Cornelia. *Die Anderen Götter: Volks- und Stammesbronzen aus Indien*. Katalog zu einer Ausstellung des Rautenstrauch-Joest-Museums für Völkerkunde der Stadt Köln. Cologne: Edition Braus, 1993.

Markevitch, Elizabeth, ed. *Indian Jewellery*. Exhibition catalogue. Geneva: Sotheby's, 1987.

Mukharji, T. N. *Art Manufactures of India*. [Specially compiled for the Glasgow International Exhibition, 1888.] Calcutta: Superintendent of Government Printing, 1883.

Museums and Art Galleries [in India]. New Delhi: Government of India, Ministry of Information and Broadcasting, 1957.

Olson, Eleanor, ed. *Catalogue of the Tibetan Collection and Other Lamaist Articles*. Vol. 4. Newark, New Jersey: The Newark Museum, 1961.

Orr, P., and Sons. *Embossed "Swami" or Trichinopoly Jewellery and Silver Plate*. Exhibition catalogue. Madras, 1880.

Pal, Pratapaditya, Janice Leoshko, Joseph Dye III, and Stephen Markel. *Romance of the Taj Mahal*. Exhibition catalogue. Los Angeles: Los Angeles County Museum of Art, 1989.

Rivett-Carnac, Mrs. "Peasant and Savage Jewelry." In *Indian Department Annual International Exhibition*. Exhibition catalogue. London, 1872.

Rogers, J. M., and Cangiz Köseoglu. *The Tokapi Saray Museum: The Treasury*. Boston: Little, Brown and Co., 1987.

Rose, Benjamin J. *Paris Universal Exhibition, 1900*. Report on the Indian Section. London: Eyre and Spottiswoode, 1901.

Scerrato, Umberto, and Maurizio Taddei. *Mostra di monili dell' Asia dal Caspio all' Himalaya*. Exhibition catalogue. Rome: Istituto Italiano per il Medio e Estremo Oriente, 1963.

Scheurleer, Pauline. "Court Gems from India." *Aziatische Kunst: [Rijksmuseum] Bulletin of the Society of Friends of Asiatic Arts* 21, no. 3 (September 1991).

Shangraw, Clarence F., et al. *Beauty, Wealth and Power*. Exhibition catalogue. Seattle: University of Washington Press, Asian Art Museum of San Francisco, 1992.

Singh, Duleep, Maharajah. *Two Sales Catalogues of Jewels and Other Confiscated Property*. London: Privately published, 1885.

Skelton, Robert A., et al. *The Indian Heritage: Court Life and Arts under Mughal Rule*. Exhibition catalogue. London: Victoria and Albert Museum, 1982.

Smart, Ellen S., and Daniel S. Walker. *Pride of Princes: Indian Art of the Mughal Era in the Cincinnati Art Museum*. Exhibition catalogue. Cincinnati: Cincinnati Art Museum, 1985.

Spink, Michael, ed. *Islamic Jewellery*. Exhibition catalogue. London: Spink and Son Ltd., 1986.

_____, ed. *Islamic and Hindu Jewellery*. Exhibition catalogue, with essay by Oppi Untracht, "The Nava-ratna," 17–30. London: Spink and Son Ltd., 1988.

_____, ed. *Islamic Jewellery*. Exhibition catalogue. London: Spink and Son Ltd., 1996.

Spranzi, Francesca, ed. *Gioielli dall'India*. Exhibition catalogue. Milan: La Rinascente, Galleria Ottavo Piano, 1996.

Stronge, Susan, Nima Smith, and J. C. Harle. *A Golden Treasury: Jewellery from the Indian Subcontinent*. Exhibition catalogue. London: Victoria and Albert Museum, Mapin Publishing, 1988.

Traditional Ornaments of Kerala. The Kerala State Handicrafts Apex Cooperative Society, no. H231. Ernakulam, Kerala: Department of Industries and Commerce, Kerala State, n.d. [1970s].

Untracht, Oppi. "The Ornaments of India, Nepal, and Tibet." In *The Art of Personal Adornment*, 6–9. Exhibition catalogue. New York: Museum of Contemporary Crafts, 1963.

_____. "Indian Silver." In *Mughal Silver Magnificence*, edited by Christine Terlinden, 27–50. Exhibition catalogue. Brussels: Antalga, 1987.

Watt, George. *Indian Art at Delhi, 1903*. Official Catalogue of the Delhi Art Exhibition, 1902–3. Illustrated by Percy Brown. Calcutta: Superintendent of Government Printing, 1903.

Welch, Stuart Cary. *India: Art and Culture 1300–1900*. Exhibition catalogue. New York: The Metropolitan Museum of Art; Holt, Rinehart, and Winston, 1985.

Journals and Periodicals

Auboyer, Jeannine. "La vie privée dans l'Inde ancienne d'après les ivoires de Begram." In *Mémoires de la délégation française en Afganistan*, 61–82. Paris: Musée Guimet, 1939–40.

Bere, Brigadier Ivan de la. "The Orders of the Indian Empire." *Apollo* (June 1950).

Birdwood, George Christopher Molesworth. "Art of the Jeweller." *Journal of the Society of Arts, London* (March 22, 1889).

_____. "Artistic Treatment of Jewel and Address Caskets." *Journal of the Society of Arts, London* (March 4, 1892).

_____. "Goldsmiths' Work." *Journal of the Society of Arts, London* (March 9, 1894).

Brownrigg, Henry. "The Place of Gold in Indian Society." *Optima* 31, no. 1 (1982): 18–29.

Cammann, Schuyler V. R. "The Story of Hornbill Ivory." *University Museum Bulletin, University of Pennsylvania* 15A (1950): 19–47.

Carter, H. J. "On the Natural History of the Lac Insect." *Journal of the Agricultural and Horticultural Society of India* 11, part 2 (1859–60): 37–45.

Chandra, Moti. "Design in Traditional Jewellery in the Punjab." *Marg* 6, no. 1 (1952): 61–65.

Chatterjee, K. N. "The Use of Nose Ornaments in India." *Journal and Proceedings of the Asiatic Society of Bengal* 23 (1927): 287–96.

Clarke, C. Purdon. "The Process Employed in Casting Brass Chains in Rajputana." *Journal of the Iron and Steel Institute* 11 (1886).

Dales, George F., and Jonathan Mark Kenoyer. "Shell Working at Ancient Balakot, Pakistan." *Expedition* (University Museum, Berkeley, Winter 1977): 13–19.

Dasgupta, N. N. "Nose Ornaments in India." *Calcutta Review* (May 1937): 142–44.

Dhamija, Jasleen. "Jewellery." *Marg* 23, no. 2 (Himachal Pradesh Issue, 1970): 42–46.

Diwatia, N. B. "The Nose Ring." *Journal of the Asiatic Society of Bengal* 19 (1923): 67.

Fabri, Charles L. "Two Notes on Indian Head-Dress." *Journal of the Royal Asiatic Society of Great Britain and Ireland* (1931): 597–601.

Fischer, Ludwig Hans. "Indischer Volksschmuck und die Art ihn zu Tragen." *Annalen des Naturhist. Holmuseums* (Vienna, 1890): 287–315.

Francis, Peter, Jr. "Early Human Adornment in India. Part I: The Upper Paleolithic." *Bulletin of the Deccan College Research Institute* (Poona) 40 (1981).

Gabriel, Hannelore. "Shell Jewellery of Himalayan and Sub-Himalayan Areas." *Ornament* 8, no. 4 (1985): 51–55.

_____. "Shell Jewelry of the Nagas." *Ornament* 9, no. 1 (1985): 37–41.

Ganguli, Kalyan Kumar. "A Note on the Nose Ornament in Mohenjodaro." *Indian Culture* 5 (1939): 342–43.

_____. "The Harappa Hoard of Jewellery." *Indian Culture* 6 (1939–40): 415–20.

_____. "Symbolism in Early Indian Jewellery." *Indian Historical Quarterly* 16 (1940): 506–10.

_____. "Jewellery in Ancient India." *Journal of the Indian Society of Oriental Art* 10 (1942): 140–59.

_____. "Early Indian Jewellery." *Indian Historical Quarterly* 17–18 (1942): 46–59, 110–27.

_____. "Jewellery in Indian Art." *Art in Industry* 2, no. 2 (1952): 7–13.

Ghosh, Manoranjan. "Use of Glass in Ancient India." *Journal of the Bihar and Orissa Research Society* 10, no. 3 (1924): 194–201.

Gode, P. K. "The Antiquity of the Hindoo Nose Ornaments Called 'Nath.'" *Annals of the Bhandarkar Oriental Research Institute* 19, part 4 (1938): 313–22.

_____. "Notes on the History of Glass Vessels and Glass Bangles in India, South Arabia, and Central Asia." *Journal of Oriental Studies* 1 (1949): 11–16.

Hora, S. L. "Lac and the Lac-Insect in the Atharva-Veda." *Journal of the Asiatic Society* 18, no. 1 (series 3, Letters, 1952): 13–16.

Hornell, James. "The Chank Bangle Industry: Its Antiquity and Present Condition." *Memoirs of the Asiatic Society of Bengal* 3, no. 7 (1913): 407–48.

Ishwaran, K. "Goldsmiths in a Mysore Village." *Journal of Asian and African Studies* 1 (1966): 50–62.

Johnston, E. H. "A Terracotta Figure at Oxford." *Journal of the Indian Society of Oriental Art* 10 (1942): 94–102.

The Journal of Indian Art (JIA). See the entries given at the end of this section.

Man, E. H. "On the Andamanese and Nicobarese Objects." *Journal of the Royal Anthropological Institute of Great Britain and Ireland* 12 (1883): 69–116, 117–75, 327–434.

Manson, C. F. "Note on the Lac Industry in the Santal Parganas." *The Indian Forester* 7 (1882): 247–79.

Marg. Indian art periodical first published in Bombay in 1946. Many issues contain articles on jewelry.

Marshall, John L. "Jewellery Collection from the Trans-Indus Country." *Archaeological Report* (1902–3).

Mehta, Kusum. "Tribal Jewelry of Andaman and Nicobar Islands. *Lapidary Journal* (San Diego, November 1982): 13–26.

Puri, Shital. "Mughal Jewellery." In *An Age of Splendour: Islamic Art in India*, 84–87. Bombay: Marg, 1983.

Rauber-Schweizer, Hanna. "Der Schmied und sein Handwerk im traditionellen Tibet." *Opuscula Tibetana* 6 (1976).

Rupam (Calcutta). Edited by O. C. Gangoly. 10 vols. (1920–30). An illustrated quarterly journal of Asian art, chiefly Indian.

Sankalia, H. D. "The Antiquity of Glass Bangles in India." *Bulletin of the Deccan College Research Institute* 8, nos. 3–4: 252–59.

Speel, Erika. "Enamel Portrait Miniatures: 17th Century." *Glass on Metal* 6, no. 5 (1987): 84–87.

_____. "Enamel Portrait Miniatures: 18th Century." *Glass on Metal* 6, no. 6 (1987): 113–19.

_____. "Enamel Portrait Miniatures: Mid 19th-Century to the Present." *Glass on Metal* 7, no. 2 (April 1988): 36–39, 43.

Stronge, Susan. "Mughal Jewellery." *Jewellery Studies* (London) 1 (1983–84): 49–53.

_____. "Indian Jewellery and the West: Stylistic Exchanges 1750–1930." *South Asian Studies* (London) 6 (1990).

_____. "Jewels for the Mughal Court." In *Victoria and Albert Museum Album* (London) 5 (1986): 309–17.

Untracht, Oppi. "The Body Encrusted: Traditional Jewelry from India." *American Craft* (August/September 1980): 42–49.

_____. "*Swami* Jewellery: Cross-Cultural Ornaments." In *Marg: The Jewels of India*, edited by Susan Stronge, 117–32. Bombay: Marg, 1995.

"Uses of Seeds for Ornamental Purposes." *Royal Botanic Gardens [Kew] Bulletin* 7 (1906).

Vinson, Julien. "Les Bijoux indiens du pays Tamoul." *Journal Asiatique* (Pondichery) 3, no. 10 (1904): 239–57.

Watt, George. "Lac and Lac Industries." *Agricultural Ledger* 9 (1901).

The Journal of Indian Art (JIA) was established as a quarterly in August 1883. 17 vols. London: William Griggs and Sons, 1884–1916. From vol. 6 onward, the name sometimes appears as *The Journal of Indian Art and Industry*. Particularly useful articles are listed below, arranged alphabetically by author.

Bidie, G. "Art Industries of Madras." *JIA* 3, no. 29 (1890): 25–32.

Havell, Ernest Binfield. "The Art Industries of the Madras Presidency: Jewellery." *JIA* 4, 5, 6, nos. 34, 40, 48 (1892, 1894, 1895): 7–8, 29–34, 69–70.

Hendley, Thomas Holbein. "Enameling and Other Industrial Arts of Rajputana, Central India, and Adjacent Provinces." *JIA* 1, no. 2 (1884): 1–5.

_____. "Industrial Arts of Rajputana: Garnets." *JIA* 1, no. 2 (1884): 11–12.

_____. "Art Industries: Jeypore, Rajasthan." *JIA* 1, no. 12 (1885): 1–4.

_____. "The Arts and Manufactures of Ajmere-Merwarra." *JIA* 3, nos. 25, 26 (1889): 1–4, 5–8.

_____. "Indian Jewellery." *JIA* 12, nos. 95–107 (1909). Part 1, "Jewellery of Delhi and the United Provinces of Agra and Oudh," 1–16; parts 2–3, "Jewellery of Rajputana and Malwa or Central India," 17–42; parts 4–5, "Jewellery of the Punjab, Kashmir, Afganistan, &c," 43–67; part 6, "Jewellery of the Bombay Presidency, Including Aden," 69–86; part 7, "Jewellery of Bombay [cont.]: The Central Provinces, and Miscellaneous Observations," 87–98; part 8, "Jewellery of the Madras Presidency," 99–114; part 9, "Jewellery of Bengal," 115–27; part 10, "Jewellery of Eastern Bengal and Tibet," 129–39; part 11, "Jewellery of Eastern Bengal [cont.], Burma, Nepal, and Adjacent Countries," 140–56; part 12, "Antique Jewellery and Ornaments, General Conclusions," 157–89.

_____. "Sectarian Seals and Other Religious Objects." *JIA* 17, no. 129 (1915): 3–4.

Kipling, John Lockwood. "Art Industries of the Punjab." *JIA* 1, no. 10 (1886): 1–8.

_____. "The Industries of the Punjab: Babul Work." *JIA* 2, no. 20 (1888): 26.

_____. "The Industries of the Punjab: Miniature Painting on Ivory: Delhi." *JIA* 2, no. 23 (1888): 32–33.

_____. "The Industries of the Punjab: Seal Engraving." *JIA* 2, no. 23 (1888): 59.

_____. "The Industries of the Punjab: Multan Enamels." *JIA* 2, no. 24 (1888): 67–68.

Rivett-Carnac, J. H., Mrs. [Marion]. "Ancient Indian Beads." *JIA* 9, no. 71 (1900): 5–12.

_____. "Notes on a Collection of Brooches Worn in India." *JIA* 10, no. 123 (1913): 9–16.

Amulets

Andrews, W. S. *Magic Squares and Cubes*. Chicago, 1917. Reprint, New York: Dover Publications, 1960.

Budge, E. A. Wallis. *Amulets and Superstitions*. 1930. Reprint, New York: Dover Publications, Inc., 1978.

Cammann, Schuyler V. R. "Islamic and Indian Magic Squares." Parts 1–2, *History of Religions* 8, nos. 3, 4 (1969): 181–209, 271–99.

Dikshit, Moreshwar G. "Notes on Some Indian Amulets." *Bulletin of the Prince of Wales Museum Bombay* 2 (1951–52): 86.

Douglas, Nik. *Tibetan Tantric Charms and Amulets*. New York: Dover Publications, 1978.

Gifford, Edward. *The Evil Eye: Studies in the Folklore of Vision*. New York: Macmillan and Co., 1958.

Gupta, Beni. *Magical Beliefs and Superstitions*. New Delhi: Sundeep Prakashan, 1979.

Maloney, Clarence, ed. *The Evil Eye*. New York: Columbia University Press, 1976.

Moberly, A. N. "Amulets as Agents in the Prevention of Diseases in Bengal." In *Memoirs of the Asiatic Society of Bengal*, vol. 1. Calcutta, 1905–7.

Pavitt, William, and Kate Pavitt. *The Book of Talismans, Amulets, and Zodiacal Gems*. Philadelphia: D. McKay, 1914. Reprint, North Hollywood, Calif.: Wilshire Book Co., 1970.

Schienerl, Peter W. "Major Trends in the Historical Development of Amulets." *Ornament* (Winter 1985): 19–25.

_____. "A Historical Survey of Tubular Charm-Cases Up to the 7th Century A.D." *Ornament* 4, no. 4 (1980): 10–14.

Shah, Haku. "Indian Amulets." *Graphis* (Switzerland) 136 (1972): 454–57, 464–65.

Beads: India and Neighbors

Allen, Jamey D. "Amber and Its Substitutes." Part 1, "Historical Artefacts"; part 2, "Mineral Analysis." *The Bead Journal* 2, nos. 3, 4 (1976): 15–19, 11–22.

Arkell, A. J. "Cambay and the Bead Trade." *Antiquity* 10, no. 39 (1936): 292–305.

Beck, Horace C. "Classification and Nomenclature of Beads and Pendants." *Archeologia* 77 (1928): 1–76.

_____. *The Beads from Taxila*. Memoirs of the Archeological Survey of India, no. 65. New Delhi, 1931.

_____. "Etched Carnelian Beads." *The Antiquaries Journal* 13 (1933): 384–98.

_____. "The Magical Properties of Beads." *The Bead Journal* 2, no. 4 (1976): 32–39.

Codrington, Kenneth de Burgh. "Tibetan Etched Agate Beads." *Man* 32, no. 156 (1932):128.

Deo, S. B. *Etched Beads in India*. Monograph Series 4. Poona: Deccan College, 1949.

Dikshit, Moreshwar G. "Beads from Ahichchhatra." *Ancient India* 8 (1952): 33–63.

Dubin, Lois Sherr. *The History of Beads*. New York: Harry N. Abrams, Inc., 1987.

During Caspers, E. C. L. "Etched Carnelian Beads." *London University Institute of Archeology Bulletin* 10 (1971–72): 83–98.

Ebbinghouse, David and Michael Winsten. "Tibetan dZi Beads." Parts 1, 2. *Ornament* 5, nos. 3, 4 (1982): 19–25, 36–39.

Ebbinghouse, David. "Additional Unreported Patterns of dZi Beads." *Ornament* 6, no. 1 (1982): 61.

Eisen, Gustavus. "Characteristics of Eye Beads from the Earliest Times to the Present." *American Journal of Archeology*. Second series 20 (1916): 1–27.

Francis, Peter, Jr. *Third World Beadmakers*. The World of Beads Monograph Series 3. Lake Placid, N. Y., 1980.

———. "The Earliest Beads in India." Part 1. *Ornament* 5, no. 4 (1982): 18–19.

———. "The Earliest Beads in India." Part 2. *Ornament* 6, no. 1 (1982): 14–15, 60.

———. "When India was Beadmaker to the World." *Ornament* 6, no. 2 (1982): 33–34, 56–57.

———. "Tibetan *dZi* Beads." *Ornament* 6, no. 2 (1982): 55–56.

———. "Minor Indian Beadmakers." *Ornament* 6, no. 3 (1983): 18–21.

———. "Bangles and Beads." *Ornament* 6, no. 4 (1983): 36–37, 57.

———. "The Asian Bead Study Tour 4; A Little Tube of Glass." *Ornament* 10, no. 1 (1986): 54–56, 74–76, 78.

———. *Bead Emporium: A Guide to the Beads from Arikamedu in the Pondichery Museum*. Museum Publication, no. 2. Pondichery, 1987.

———. "The Greatest Trade Bead of All Time." *Ornament* 13, no. 3 (1990): 78–82.

Handler, Jerome S., Frederick W. Lange, and Charles E. Orser. "Carnelian Beads in Necklaces from a Slave Cemetery in Barbados, West Indies." *Ornament* 4, no. 2 (1979): 15–18.

Janaki, V. A. *The Commerce of Cambay from the Earliest Period to the Nineteenth Century*. Baroda: M. S. University of Baroda, Department of Geography, 1980.

Kenoyer, Jonathan Mark. "The Indus Bead Industry: Contribution to Bead Technology." *Ornament* 10, no. 1 (1986): 18–23.

Liu, Robert K. "Identification: *Tsi* Beads." *Ornament* 4, no. 4 (1980): 36, 56–60.

———. "*DZi* Beads: Follow-up." *Ornament* 8, no. 3 (1984): 29.

———. *Collectible Beads: A Universal Aesthetic*. Vista, Calif.: Ornament, Inc., 1995.

Mackay, Ernest J. H. "Bead Making in Ancient Sind." *Journal of the American Oriental Society* 57 (1937): 1–15.

Nebsky-Wojkowitz, R. "Prehistoric Beads from Tibet." *Man* 52, no. 183 (1952): 131–32.

Ogden, Jack M. "Materials and Techniques. Lives of the Cambay Bead Makers." *Society of Jewellery Historians Newsletter* (London) 9 (1992): 7, 11.

Piddington, H. "Deo-Monnees or Sacred Beads of Assam." *Journal of the Bengal Asiatic Society* 16: 713.

Possehl, Gregory L. "Cambay Beadmaking. An Ancient Craft in Modern India." *Expedition. The University Museum Magazine of Archeology/Anthropology. University of Pennsylvania* 23, no. 4 (1981): 39–47.

Reade, Julian. *Early Etched Beads and the Indus-Mesopotamian Trade*. British Museum Occasional Papers, no. 2. London, 1979.

Sahni, M. R. "Agates and Other Forms of Chalcedonic Silica; Their Origin, Distribution, and Economic Possibilities with Particular Reference to Rajpipla State." *Geological Survey of India* 2, no. 4 (1948).

Sleen, W. G. N. van der. "Ancient Glass Beads of East and Central Africa and the Indian Ocean." *J. Roy Anthropological Institute* 88, part 2 (1958): 203–16.

———. *A Handbook on Beads*. York, Penn.: Liberty Cap Books, 1973.

Vidale, Massimo. *Produzione Artigianale Protostorica*. Parte Terza, Ricerche e Idee, *Lavoratori dell'agata, Gujarat (India)*, 1989–90, 197–227. Saltuarie dal laboratorio del Piovego 4. Dipar-timento di Scienze dell'Antichità, Università degli Studi di Padova, 1992.

Wheeler, R. E. Mortimer, A Ghosh, and Krishna Deva. "Arikamedu: An Indo-Roman Trading Station on the East Coast of India." *Ancient India* 2 (1946): 17–124.

Wilson, W. J. *Report on Beads Imported to India*. Calcutta: Government of India, Department of Revenue and Agriculture, 1883.

Precious and Semiprecious Gemstones

Ariyaratna, D. H. *Gems of Sri Lanka*. Colombo: Privately printed, 1977.

Balfour, Ian. *Famous Diamonds*. London: William Collins Sons and Co., 1987.

Ball, S. H. "Some Facts about Famous Emeralds." *Jeweler's Circular Keystone* 88, no. 10 (1924).

Ball, Valentine. "The True History of the Koh-i-Nur." *The English Illustrated Magazine* 8 (1891): 538–42.

Bhat, M. Ramakrishna, trans. and ed. *Varahamihira's Brhat Samhita*. With English translation, exhaustive notes, and literary comments. 2 parts. New Delhi: Motilal Banarsidass, 1982.

Bhattacharyya, Benoytosh. *Gem Therapy*. Calcutta: Firma K. L. Mukhopadhyaya, 1958. Revised and enlarged edition, 1976.

Birdwood, George Christopher Molesworth. "Ruby Mines of Burma." *Journal of the Society of Arts, London* (February 22, 1889).

Brown, J. C. "Emeralds in India." *The Gemmologist* 22 (1953): 133–36, 165–68.

Buddhabhata. *Ratna Pariksha* [Test of Precious Stones, 5th–6th century A.D.] Edited by Louis Finot. In *Les lapidaires indiens*, 1–58. Paris: Bibliothèque de L'Ecole des hautes études sciences, philologiques et historiques, 1896.

Caplan, Allan. "An Important Carved Emerald from the Mogul Period of India." *Lapidary Journal* (San Diego) 21 (1968): 1336–39.

Chabouillet, P. M. A. *Catalogue genéral et raisonné des camées et pierres gravées de la Bibliothèque Impériale*. Paris: Cabinet des médailles, 1858.

Crookshank, H. "Emerald in Mewar." In *Geological Survey of India: Indian Minerals*. Vol. 1, 28–30. 1947.

De Smet, K. *The Great Blue Diamond*. Antwerp: Standard-Boekhandel, 1963.

Finot, Louis. *Les lapidaires indiens*. Paris: Bibliothèque de L'Ecole des hautes études sciences, philologiques et historiques, 1896.

Gaal, Robert A. P., ed. *The Diamond Dictionary*. 2d ed. Santa Monica, Calif.: Gemological Institute of America, 1977.

Garbe, R. von. "Die indischen Mineralien, ihre Namen und die ihren zugeschriebener Kräfte." In Naharari's *Rajanighantu*, varga 13. Leipzig: Verlag von S. Hirzel, 1882.

Geological Survey of India. "Investigations for Emeralds in Udaipur." *Indian Minerals* (Calcutta) 5 (1951): 148–50.

Grodzinski, Paul. "The History of Diamond Polishing." In *Industrial Diamond Review*, special supplement no. 1 (1953).

Gübelin, E. J. "Some Additional Data on Indian Emeralds." *Gems and Gemology* 7 (1951): 13–22.

Herdman, W. A. "The Pearl Fisheries of Ceylon." *Annual Report, Smithsonian Institution* (1905): 485–93.

Howarth, Stephen. *The Koh-I-Noor Diamond: The History and the Legend*. London: Quartet Books, 1980.

Khalik, M. I. A. "Nava-ratna Ring." *The Astrological Magazine* 61, no. 7 (1972).

Krenkow, F. "The Chapter on Pearls in the Book on Precious Stones of al-Beruni." Part I. *Islamic Culture* 15 (1941): 399–421.

Krishna, Vijay. "Gemmology in Ancient India." *The Gemmologist* 16, no. 194 (1947): 251–54.

Kunz, George Frederick. *The Curious Lore of Precious Stones*. Philadelphia: Lippincott Company, 1913. Reprint, New York: Dover Publications, Inc., 1971.

La Touche, T. H. D. "The Sapphire Mines of Kashmir." *Records of the Geological Survey of India* 23, part 2 (1890).

Lenzen, Godehard. *The History of Diamond Production and of the Diamond Trade*. London: Barrie and Jenkins, 1970.

Markel, Stephen. "Carved Jades of the Mughal Period." *Arts of Asia* 17, no. 6 (1987): 123–30.

———. "Jades, Jewels, and Objets d'Art." *Romance of the Taj Mahal*, chapter 4: 128–69. New Delhi: Time Books International, 1989.

Mawe, John. *A Treatise on Diamonds and Precious Stones, Including Their History, Natural and Commercial*. 2d ed. London: Longman, Hurst, Rees, Orme and Brown, 1823. Reprint, London: The Industrial Diamond Information Bureau, 1950.

Meen, V. B., and A. D. Tushingham. *Crown Jewels of Iran*. Toronto: University of Toronto Press, 1968.

Meen, V. B., A. D. Tushingham, and G. G. White. "The 'Darya-i Nur' Diamond and the Tavernier 'Great Table.'" *Lapidary Journal* (San Diego) 21, no. 8 (1967).

Middlemiss, C. S. *Precious and Semi-Precious Gemstones of Jammu and Kashmir*. Jammu and Kashmir Mineral Survey Reports. Jammu, 1931.

Morel, Bernard. *The French Crown Jewels*. Antwerp: Fonds Mercator, 1988.

Patch, Susanne Steinem. *Blue Mystery: The Story of the Hope Diamond*. Washington, D.C.: Smithsonian Institution Press, 1976.

Roy, B. C. "Emerald Deposits in Mewar and Ajmer Merwara." *Records of the Geological Survey of India* 86 (1955): 377–401.

Saha, N. N. *Stellar Healing: Cure and Control of Diseases through Gems*. New Delhi: Sagar Publications, 1976. Reprint, 1982.

Sen, N. B. *Glorious History of the Koh-i-Noor Diamond*. New Delhi: New Book Society of India, 1970.

Sen, Ram Das. *Ratnarahasya* [Treatise on diamonds and precious stones, in Sanskrit]. Calcutta, 1884.

Shipley, Robert M. *Famous Diamonds of the World*. 6th ed. Los Angeles: Gemological Institute of America, 1955.

Streeter, Edwin W. *The Great Diamonds of the World*. 6th ed. Edited and annotated by Joseph Hatton and A. H. Keane. London: George Bell and Sons, 1898.

Taburiaux, Jean. *Pearls, Their Origin, Treatment, and Identification*. Ipswich, Suffolk: NAG Press, 1985.

Tagore, Sir Surendra Mohan. *Mani Mala, or A Treatise on Gems*. 2 vols. Calcutta: Stanhope Press, J. C. Bose and Co., 1879, 1881.

Tank, Raj Roop. *Indian Gemmology*. Jaipur: Dulichand Kirtichand Tank, 1968.

Tavernier, Jean Baptiste. *The Six Voyages of Jean Baptiste Tavernier, and The Description of the Seraglio*. Translated by J. Phillips. London 1678.

———. *Travels in India by Jean Baptiste Tavernier, Baron of Aubonne*. Translated from the French edition of 1676 by Valentine Ball. 2 vols. London: Macmillan and Co., 1889.

Tillander, Herbert. "Six Centuries of Diamond Design." *The Journal of Gemmology* (London) 9, no. 11 (1965).

_____. *The 'Hope' Diamond and Its Lineage: A Challenge for Further Research.* Paper presented at the 15th International Gemmological Conference held in the Smithsonian Institution, Washington, D.C., October 1975.

_____. *The History of Diamond Cuts.* London: Art Books International, 1993.

Tolansky, S. *The History and Use of the Diamond.* London: Methuen and Co., 1962.

_____. "The Great Table Diamond of Tavernier." *Journal of Gemmology* 3, no. 5 (1962).

Wojtilla, Gy. "Indian Precious Stones in the Ancient East and West." *Acta Orientalia* (Budapest) 27, fasc. 2 (1973): 211–24.

2. Indian Culture

History, Trade, and Travel

Alexander, Michael, and Sushila Anand. *Queen Victoria's Maharajah, Duleep Singh 1838–93.* New Delhi: Vikas Publishing House, 1979.

'Allami, Abu'l-Fazl. *The Ain-i Akbari.* Vol. 1, translated by H. Blockmann, 1873; revised and edited by D. C. Phillott, 1939. Vols. 2–3, translated by H. S. Jarrett, 1894; revised and edited by Jadunath Sarkar, 1949, 1948. Reprint, New Delhi: Oriental Books Reprint Corporation, 1977.

Babur. *Babur-Nama or Tuzuk-i-Babari.* Translated by Annette Susannah Beveridge from the original Turki text of Zahiru'd-din Muhammad Babur Padshah Ghazl. 2 vols. 1922. Reprint, New Delhi: Oriental Books Reprint Corporation, 1979.

Bedi, Ramesh. *Ladakh, The Trans-Himalayan Kingdom.* Photographs by Rajesh Bedi. New Delhi: Roli Books International, 1981.

Bernier, François. *Travels in the Mogul Empire, A.D. 1656–1668.* A revised and improved edition based upon Irving Brock's translation by Archibald Constable. Westminister: Archibald Constable and Co., 1911.

Buchanan, Francis. *An Account of the Districts of Bihar and Patna in 1811–1812.* Vol 2, books 3–4: 620–21. Patna: Bihar and Orissa Research Society, n.d.

_____. *A Journey from Madras through the Countries of Mysore, Canaras, and Malabar.* 3 vols. Madras, 1807.

Carré, Abbé. *The Travels of Abbé Carré in India and the Near East, 1672–74.* Edited by Charles Fawcett and R. Burn; translated by Lady Fawcett. 2 vols. London: The Hakluyt Society, 1947–48.

Dalboquerque, Alfonso. *The Commentaries of the Great Alfonso Dalboquerque, the Second Viceroy of India.* Edited and translated by Walter de Gray Birch. 4 vols. London: The Hakluyt Society, 1875, 1875, 1880, 1883.

Fortescue, John. *Narrative of the Visit to India of Their Majesties King George V and Queen Mary and of the Coronation Durbar Held at Delhi 12th December, 1911.* London: Macmillan and Co., 1912.

Gul-Badan, Begam (Princess 'Rose-body'). *The History of Humayun [Humayun-Nama].* Translated by Annette S. Beveridge. New Delhi: Idarah-i Adabiyat-i Delli, 1972.

Hendley, Thomas Holbein. *The Rulers of India and Chiefs of Rajputana, 1550–1897.* London: William Griggs and Sons, 1897.

Historical Record of the Imperial Visit to India. Publisher n.a., 1911.

The Imperial Coronation Durbar, Delhi, 1911. Vol. 1. Lahore: The Imperial Publishing Co. (Khosla Brothers), 1911.

Jehangir, Sorab. *Princes and Chiefs of India: A Collection of Biographies with Portraits and Brief Historical Surveys of Their Territories.* 3 vols. London: Waterlow and Sons, 1903.

Jouher. *Tezkereh al Vakiat (Private Memoirs of the Mughal Emperor Humayun).* Translated by Major Charles Stewart. Santiago de Compostela: Susil Gupta, n.d. Reprint, 1932.

Khan, 'Inayat. *Shah Jahan Nama.* Translated by A. R. Fuller, 1851; edited by W. E. Begley and Z. A. Desai. New Delhi: Oxford University Press, 1990.

Khan, Mu'tamid. *Iqbal Nama.* Jahangir's stopped recording his memoirs after the seventeenth year of his reign. At the nineteenth year, Kahn picked up the narration in his own name until Jahangir's death. Publication information n.a.

Khan, Saqi Must'ad. *Maasir-i'Alamgiri: A History of the Emperor Aurangzeb-'Alamgir.* Translated by J. N. Sarkar. Calcutta: Bibliotheca Indica. 1947.

Lockhart, L. *Nadir Shah: A Critical Study Based Mainly on Contemporary Sources.* London, 1938.

Login, Lena, Lady. *Sir John Login and Duleep Singh.* London, 1889. Reprint, Patiala: Languages Department, Punjab, 1970.

Manucci, Niccolas. *Storia do Mogor, 1653–1708.* Translated by William Irvine. 4 vols. London: John Murray for Government of India, 1906–8. Reprint, New Delhi: Oriental Books Reprint Corporation, 1981.

Marshall, John, Sir. *Mohenjo Daro and the Indus Civilization.* 3 vols. London: Arthur Probsthain, 1931.

_____. *Taxila.* 3 vols. Cambridge: Cambridge University Press, 1951.

Mawjee, Purhotam Vishram. *The Imperial Durbar Album of the Indian Princes, Chiefs and Zamindars.* Vol. 1. Bombay: Lakshmi Art Printing Works, 1911.

McCrindle, J. Watson, trans. *The Indica of Arrian.* Bombay: Educational Society's Press, 1876.

_____. *Ancient India as Described by Megasthenes and Arrian.* Calcutta, 1877.

_____. *The Commerce and Navigation of the Erythraean Sea; Being a Translation of the Periplus maris Erythraei, by an Anonymous Writer, and of Arrian's Account of the Voyage of Nearchus.* Calcutta, 1879. Reprint, Oxford: Oxford University Press, Oxford in Asia Historical Reprints, 1979.

Moorcroft, William, and Trebeck, George. *Travels in the Himalayan Province of Hindustan and the Punjab from 1819 to 1825.* Vol. 1, Ladakh. Oxford: Oxford University Press, Oxford in Asia Historical Reprints, 1979.

Moreland, W. H., ed. *Relations of Golconda in the Early Seventeenth Century: As It Appeared to Dutch and English Merchants.* London: The Hakluyt Society, 1930.

Muthiah, S., ed., et al. *An Atlas of India.* New Delhi: Oxford University Press, 1990.

Pelsaert, Francisco. *The Remonstrantie of Francisco Pelsaert.* Translated by W. H. Moreland and P. Geyl. Cambridge, 1925.

Polo, Marco. *The Book of Sir Marco Polo, the Venetian, Concerning the Kingdoms and Marvels of the East.* Translated and edited by Henry Yule. 3d ed., revised by H. Cordier. 2 vols. London: John Murray, 1875.

Roe, Sir Thomas. *The Embassy of Sir Thomas Roe to the Court of the Great Mogul, 1615–1619.* Edited from contemporary records by William Foster. 2 vols. London: The Hakluyt Society, 1899. Reprint, Nendel, Liechtenstein: Kraus Reprint, 1967.

Rogers, Alexander, trans. and Henry Beveridge, ed. *Memoirs of Jahangir (Tuzuk-i-Jahangiri).* Oriental Translation Fund, New Series 19, 22. 2 vols. London: Royal Asiatic Society, 1909, 1914. Reprint, Munshiram Manoharlal, 1968.

Rousselett, Louis. *L'Inde des rajas: Voyage dans l'Inde centrale.* Paris: Librairie Hachette et Cie, 1875.

Russell, William Howard. *The Prince of Wales's Tour: A Diary in India.* 2d ed. London: Sampson Low, Marston, Searle, and Rivington, 1877.

Singh, Khushwant. "Kashmir and the Koh-i-Noor." Chapter 10 in *Ranjit Singh, Maharajah of the Punjab, 1780–1839.* London: George Allen and Unwin, 1962.

Tod, James. *Annals and Antiquities of Rajast'han.* 2 vols. London: George Routledge and Sons, 1914.

Valle, Pietro della. *The Travels of Pietro della Valle in India.* Edited by Edward Grey from the English translation of 1664 by G. Havers. 2 vols. London: The Hakluyt Society, 1891.

Warmington, E. H. *Commerce between the Roman Empire and India.* Cambridge, 1928.

Wheeler, Stephen. *History of the Delhi Coronation Durbar.* Held on the first of January, 1903, to celebrate the coronation of His Majesty King Edward VII, Emperor of India. London: John Murray, 1904.

Society

Barton, William. *The Princes of India.* London: Nisbet and Co., 1934.

Dunbar, Janet. *Golden Interlude: The Edens in India, 1836–1842.* London: John Murray, 1955.

Eden, Emily. *Up the Country.* 2 vols, 1866. Reprints (2 vols. in 1), Oxford: Oxford University Press, 1970; London: Curzon Press, 1978.

Elson, Vickie C. *Dowries from Kutch.* Los Angeles: Museum of Cultural History, University of California, 1979.

Ghurye, G. S. *Caste and Class in India.* Bombay: Popular Book Depot, 1957.

Kautilya. *The Arthasastra of Kautilya.* Translated by R. Shamasastry. 8th ed. Mysore: Mysore Printing and Publishing House, 1967.

Lal, S. K. *The Mughal Harem.* New Delhi: Aditya Prakashan, 1988.

Mandelbaum, David G. *Women's Seclusion and Men's Honor: Sex Roles in North India, Bangladesh, and Pakistan.* Tucson: The University of Arizona Press, 1988.

Singh, St. Nihal. *The King's Indian Allies: The Rajas and Their India.* London: Sampson Low, Martson and Co., 1916.

Religion

Ayyar, P. V. Jagadisa. *South Indian Festivities.* New Delhi: Asian Educational Services, 1920. Reprint, 1985.

Dhanjal, Beryl. *Sikhism.* Dictionaries of World Religions. London: B. T. Batsford, 1987.

Dubois, Abbé J. A. *Hindu Manners, Customs, and Ceremonies.* Translated and edited by Henry K. Beauchamp. 3d ed. Oxford: Clarendon Press, 1906. Reprint, 1953.

Fergusson, James. *Tree and Serpent Worship.* London: William Griggs and Sons, 1873. Reprint, New Delhi: Oriental Publishers, 1971.

Gupte, Ramesh Shankar. "Study of the Jewellery Portrayed." In *The Iconography of the Buddhist Sculptures of Ellora,* 133–43. Aurangabad, 1964.

Hartsuiker, Dolf. *Sadhus: Holy Men of India.* London: Thames and Hudson Ltd., 1996.

Hopkins, Edward W., ed. *The Ordinances of Manu: Manava-Dharma-Sastra.* London: Trubner and Co., 1884.

Hughes, Thomas Patrick. *Dictionary of Islam.* 1885. Reprint, Calcutta: Rupa and Co., 1988.

James, E. O. *The Cult of the Mother Goddess.* London: Thames and Hudson Ltd., 1959.

Jayakar, Pupul. *The Earthen Drum.* New Delhi: The National Museum of India, 1980.

Jouveau-Dubrevil. *Iconography of Southern India.* Original French edition, 1915. Translated by A. C. Martin. Paris: Libraire Orientaliste Paul Geuthner, 1937.

Martin, Rev. E. Osborn, *The Gods of India.* London: J. M. Dent and Sons, Ltd., 1914.

Moor, Edward. *The Hindu Pantheon.* 1864. Reprint, Varanasi: Indological Book House, 1968.

Nadkarni, K. M. *The Indian Materia Medica.* Bombay: Published by the author, 1927.

Nandagopal, Choodamani. "Jewellery." In *Dance and Music in the Temple Architecture,* 129–40. New Delhi: Agam Kala Prakashan, 1990.

Sompura, Padmashri Prabhashankar O. *Album of Hindu Iconography.* Ahmadabad: Sompura and Brothers, 1976.

Stutley, Margaret, and James Stutley. *A Dictionary of Hinduism.* London: Routledge and Kegan Paul, 1977.

Thomas, P. *Hindu Religion, Customs, and Manners.* Bombay: D. B. Taraporevala Sons and Co., 1956.

_____. *Festivals and Holidays of India.* Bombay: D. B. Taraporevala Sons and Co., 1971.

Edgar Thurston. *Omens and Superstitions of Southern India.* New York: McBride, Nast and Company, 1912.

Waddell, L. Austine. *The Buddhism of Tibet, or Lamaism.* Reprint, Cambridge: W. Heffer and Sons, 1959.

Tribal Culture

Baruah, Tapan Kumar. *The Idu Mishmis.* Shillong: Advisor to the Governor of Assam, 1960.

Basu, P. C. "Headdress of the Hill Tribes of Assam." *Journal of the Royal Asiatic Society of Bengal* 25 (1929): 103–14.

Biswas, P. C. *Santals of the Santal Parganas.* New Delhi: Bharatiya Adimjati Sevak Sangh, 1956.

Cipriani, Lidio. *The Andaman Islanders.* London: Weidenfeld and Nicolson, 1966.

Crooke, William. *The Tribes and Castes of the North-Western Provinces and Oudh.* 4 vols. Calcutta: Office of the Superintendent of Government Printing, 1896. Reprint, New Delhi: Cosmo Publications.

Dalton, Edward Tuite. *Descriptive Ethnology of Bengal.* Calcutta: Office of the Superintendent of Government Printing, 1872. Reprint, Calcutta: Firma K. L. Mukhopadhyaya, 1960.

Dave, P. C. *The Grasias.* New Delhi: Bharatiya Adimjati Sevak Sangh, 1960.

Elwin, Verrier. *The Baiga.* London: John Murray, 1939.

_____. *The Agaria.* London: Oxford University Press, 1942.

_____. *The Muria and Their Ghotul.* London: Oxford University Press, 1947.

_____. *Bondo Highlander.* London: Oxford University Press, 1950.

_____. *The Tribal Art of Middle India.* London: Oxford University Press, 1951.

_____. *The Art of the North East Frontier.* Shillong: North-East Frontier Agency, 1959.

_____. *Nagaland.* Shillong: North-East Frontier Agency, 1961.

Endle, Sidney. *The Kacharis.* London: Macmillan and Co., 1911.

Enthoven, R. E. *The Tribes and Castes of Bombay.* 3 vols. Bombay, 1920. Reprint, New Delhi: Cosmo Publications, 1975.

Fürer-Haimendorf, Christoph, von. *The Naked Nagas.* Madras: Thacker, Spink and Co., 1946.

_____. *The Apa Tanis and Their Neighbours.* London: Routledge and Kegan Paul, 1962.

_____. *The Konyak Nagas: An Indian Frontier Tribe.* New York: Holt, Rinehart, and Winston, 1969.

_____. *The Gonds of Andhra Pradesh.* New Delhi: Vikas Publishing House, 1979.

Grigson, Wilfred. *The Maria Gonds of Bastar.* London: Oxford University Press, 1938.

Gurdon, P. R. T. *The Khasis.* London: Macmillan and Co., 1914.

Handbook of Castes and Tribes Employed on the Tea Estates in North East India. Calcutta: Tea District Labour Association, 1924.

Hartwig, W. *Wirtschaft und Gesellschaftsstruktur der Naga in der zweiten Hälfte des 19. und zu Beginn des 20. Jahrhunderts.* Veroffentlichungen des Museums für Volkerkunde zu Leipzig, Heft 20. Berlin, 1970.

Herle, Anita. "Naga Body Decoration: Continuity and Change." *Ornament* 12, no. 1 (1988): 28–33, 81.

Hodgson, T. C. *The Meitheis.* London: David Nutt, 1908.

_____. *The Naga Tribes of Manipur.* London: Macmillan and Co., 1911.

Hutton, J. H. *The Sema Nagas.* London: Macmillan and Co., 1921.

_____. *The Angami Nagas.* London: Macmillan and Co., 1921. Reprint, London: Oxford University Press, 1969.

_____. "Naga Chank Ornaments and South Indian Affinities." *Man* 30, no. 65 (1930).

Ibbetson, Denzil. *Punjab Castes.* 1916. Reprint, New Delhi: Cosmo Publications, 1981.

Iyer, L. K. A. *Cochin Tribes and Castes.* 3 vols. Madras, 1909–12.

Jacobs, Julian, Alan MacFarlane, Sara Harison, and Anita Herle. *The Nagas.* Stuttgart: Hansjörg Mayer; London: Thames and Hudson Ltd., 1990.

Logan, W. *Malabar.* 3 vols. Madras: Government Press, 1887–91.

Luiz, A. A. D. *Tribes of Kerala.* New Delhi: Bharatiya Adimjati Sevak Sangh, 1962.

Mathur, P. R. G. *The Khasi of Meghalaya.* Reprint, New Delhi: Cosmo Publications, 1979.

Mills, J. P. *The Ao Nagas.* London: Macmillan and Co., 1921.

_____. *The Lohta Nagas.* London: Macmillan and Co., 1922.

_____. *The Rengma Nagas.* London: Macmillan and Co., 1937.

Nanjundayya, H. V., Bahadur Rao, and L. K. Ananthalkrishna Iyer. *The Mysore Tribes and Castes.* Mysore: The Mysore University, 1931.

Nath, Y. V. S. *Bhils of Ratanmal.* Baroda: The Maharaja Sayajirao University, 1960.

Parry, N. E. *The Lakhers.* London: Macmillan and Co., 1932.

Risley, H. *The Tribes and Castes of Bengal.* 4 vols. Calcutta, 1891.

Rivers, W. H. R. *The Todas.* London: Macmillan and Co., 1906. Reprint, 1967.

Roy, E. C., and R. C. Roy. *The Kharias.* 2 vols. Ranchi, 1937.

Roy, Sachin. "Dress Ornaments and Decoration of the Adis of the North-East Frontier Agency." *Vanyajati* 6 (1958): 4.

_____. *Aspects of Padam-Minyong Culture.* Shillong: North-East Frontier Agency, 1960.

Roy, Sarat Chandra. *The Mundas and Their Country.* Calcutta: Kuntaline Press, 1912.

_____. *The Oraons of Chota Nagpur.* Ranchi: The Brahmo Mission Press, 1915.

Russell, R. V., and Rai Bahadur Hira Lal. *Tribes and Castes of the Central Provinces of India.* 4 vols. London: Macmillan and Co., 1916.

Shah, P. G. *Dublas of Gujarat.* New Delhi: Bharatiya Adimjati Sevak Sangh, 1958.

Shakespear, J. *The Lushei Kuki Clans.* London: Macmillan and Co., 1912.

Sharma, R. R. P. *The Sherdukpens.* Shillong: Research Department, Adviser's Secretariat, 1961.

Sher, Singh. *The Sikligars of Punjab.* New Delhi: Sterling Publishers, 1966.

Sherring, M. A. *Hindu Tribes and Castes as Represented at Benares.* 3 vols. Calcutta, 1872–81. Reprint, Cosmo Publications.

_____. *The Tribes and Castes of Rajasthan: Together with Description of the Sacred and Celebrated Places of Historical Value in Rajasthan.* 1881. Reprint, Cosmo Publications.

_____. *The Tribes and Castes of the Madras Presidency: Together with an Account of the Tribes and Castes of Mysore, Nilgiri, Travancore, etc.* 1909. Reprint, Cosmo Publications.

Shukla, Brahma Kumar. *The Daflas of the Subansiri Region.* Shillong: North-East Frontier Agency, 1959.

Sinha, Raghuvir. *The Akas.* Shillong: Research Department, Adviser's Secretariat, 1962.

Smith, William Carlson. *The Ao Naga Tribe of Assam: A Study in Ethnology and Sociology.* London: Macmillan and Co., 1924.

Srinivas, M. N. *Religion and Society among the Coorgs of South India.* Oxford: Clarendon Press, 1952.

Srivastava, N. P. *The People of Nefa: The Gallongs.* Shillong: Research Department, Adviser's Secretariat, 1962.

Srivastava, S. K. *The Tharus: A Study in Culture Dynamics.* Agra: Agra University Press, 1958.

Stack, Edward. *The Mikirs.* London: David Nutt, 1908.

Stonor, C. R. "Ancestral Ornaments of the Lhota Nagas." *Man* 28 (1948): 172–73.

Thurston, Edgar. *Castes and Tribes of Southern India.* 7 vols. Madras: Government Press, 1909.

Arts

Archer, Mildred. "British Painters of the Indian Scene." *Journal of the Royal Society of Arts* 115, no. 5135 (1967).

_____. *India and British Portraiture, 1770–1825.* London, 1979.

_____. *India Observed: India as Viewed by British Artists, 1760–1860.* London, 1982.

"The Conch Shell Industry." In *Arts of Bengal and Eastern India,* 21. Booklet published on the occasion of the exhibition at the Commonwealth Institute, London, May 1982. London: Crafts Council of West Bengal.

Desmond, R. *Victorian India in Focus.* London, 1980.

_____. "Photography in Victorian India." *Journal of the Royal Society of Arts* 134 (1985).

Gray, Basil, ed. *The Arts of India.* London: The Phaidon Press, 1981.

Kramrisch, Stella. *The Art of India.* London: The Phaidon Press, 1954.

Pal, P., and V. Dehejia. *From Merchants to Emperors: British Artists and India, 1757–1930.* Ithaca, 1986.

Postel, Michel, A. Neven, and K. Mankodi. *Antiquities of Himachal.* Project for Indian Cultural Studies, publication 1. Bombay: Franco-Indian Pharmaceuticals, Ltd., 1985.

Sivaramamurti, Calambur. *The Art of India*. New York: Harry N. Abrams, Inc., 1977.

Civilian Costume and Ornament
Alkazi, Roshen. *Ancient Indian Costume*. New Delhi: Art Heritage Books, 1983.

Altekar, A. S. "Dresses and Ornaments of Hindu Women." *Journal of the Benares Hindu University* 2 (1938).

Chandra, Moti. "Indian Costumes from Earliest times to the 1st Century B.C." *Journal of the Bharatiya Vidya Bhawan* (Bombay) 1, part 1 (1939): 28–36.

_____. "A History of Indian Costume from the First Century A.D. to the Beginning of the Fourth Century A.D." *Journal of the Indian Society of Oriental Art* (Calcutta) 8 (1940): 185–224.

_____. "A History of Indian Costumes from the 3rd Century A.D. to the End of the 7th Century A.D." *Journal of the Indian Society of Oriental Art* (Calcutta) 12 (1944): 1–97.

_____. "Costumes and Ornaments." Chapter 4 in *Jain Miniature Paintings from Western India*. Ahmadabad, 1949.

_____. "Costumes and Coiffure in Ancient India." *Journal of Indian Textile History* (Ahmadabad) 6 (1961).

Chopra, P. N. "Dress, Toilet, and Ornaments during the Moghul Period." *Proceedings of the Indian History Congress, 15th Session* (Calcutta, 1954): 210–28.

Doshi, Saryu. "Attire and Ornaments." In *Shivaji and Facets of Maratha Culture*, edited by Saryu Doshi, 166–72. Bombay: Marg Publications, 1982.

Fabri, Charles. *A History of Indian Dress*. Calcutta: Orient Longmans, 1960.

Majumdar, G. P. "Man's Indebtness to Plants: Dress and Other Personal Requisites in Ancient India." *Indian Culture* 1, no. 2 (1934): 191–208.

Purohit, Veena. *Indian Hair Styles*. Bombay: Published by the author, 1962.

Solvyns, Baltazard F. *The Costume of Hindustan 1798–99*. London: Edward Orme, 1807.

Williamson, Thomas. *The Costumes and Customs of Modern India*. London: Edward Orme, 1813.

Crafts
Chattopadhyaya, Kamaladevi. *Indian Handicrafts*. New Delhi: Indian Council for Cultural Relationships, Allied Publishers, 1963.

Codrington, Kenneth de Burgh. "The Minor Arts of India." In *Indian Art*, edited by Sir Richard Winstedt. New York: October House, 1967.

_____. "Birdwood and the Study of the Arts of India." *Journal of the Royal Society of Arts* 98, no. 5163 (1970): 135–41.

Coomaraswamy, Ananda K. *The Indian Craftsmen*. London: Probsthain and Co., 1909.

_____. *Arts and Crafts of India and Ceylon*. London: T. N. Foulis, 1916.

_____. *Mediaeval Sinhalese Art*. 2d ed. New York: Pantheon Books, 1956.

Dahiya, Neelima. *Arts and Crafts in Northern India: From the Earliest Times to c. 200 B.C.* New Delhi: B.R. Publishing Corporation, 1986.

Dhamija, Jasleen. *Indian Folk Arts and Crafts*. New Delhi: National Book Trust, 1970.

_____, ed. *Crafts of Gujarat: Living Traditions of India*. New York: Mapin International, 1985.

Fisher, Nora, ed. *Mud, Mirror, and Thread: Folk Traditions of Rural India*. Ahmadabad: Mapin Publishing; Santa Fe: Museum of New Mexico Press, 1993.

Frater, Judy. *Threads of Identity*. Ahmadabad: Mapin Publishing, 1995.

Jaitly, Jaya, ed. *Crafts of Kashmir, Jammu, and Ladakh*. Photographs by Kamal Sahai. New York: Abbeville Press; Ahmadabad: Mapin Publishing, 1990.

Kale, B. D. *A Survey of Handicrafts in South Mysore*. Institute of Economic Research, Dharwar, publication no. 1. Bombay: Bhatkal Books International, 1963.

Kalter, Johannes. *The Arts and Crafts of the Swat Valley*. London: Thames and Hudson Ltd., 1991.

Krishna, Nanditha. *Arts and Crafts of Tamil Nadu*. Ahmadabad: Mapin Publishing, 1992.

Nath, Aman. *Jaipur: The Last Destination*. Bombay: India Book House Ltd., 1993.

_____, and Francis Wacziarg, eds. *Arts and Crafts of Rajasthan*. Ahmadabad: Mapin Publishing, 1989.

Reeves, Ruth. *Cire Perdue Casting in India*. New Delhi: Crafts Museum, 1962.

Riazuddin, Akhtar. *History of Handicrafts: Pakistan-India*. Islamabad: National Hizra Council, 1988.

Saraf, D. N. *Indian Crafts: Development and Potential*. New Delhi: Vikas Publishing House, 1982.

Sen, Prabhas. *Crafts of West Bengal*. Ahmadabad: Mapin Publishing, 1992.

Dance and Drama
Ashton, Martha Bush. "A Structural Analysis of Costume [Jewelry] and Makeup in Yaksagana Badagitittu Bayalata." In *Structural Approaches to South Indian Studies*, edited by Harry M. Buck and Glenn E. Yocum. Chambersburg, Pa.: Wilson Books, 1974.

Bolland, David. *A Guide to Kathakali*. New Delhi: National Book Trust, 1980.

Devassy, M. K. "Costumes and Accessories in Kathakali." In *Census of India, 1961*. Vol. 7, *Kerala*, part 7A1, *Selected Crafts of Kerala*: 26–74. 1964.

Devi, Rangini. *Dance Dialects of India*. New Delhi: Motilal Banarsidass, 1972.

Ilango-Adigal. *Silappadikaram* [*The Ankle Bracelet*, epic drama in Tamil]. Translated by V. R. Ramachandra Dikshitar. Madras: Oxford University Press, 1939.

Lal, P., trans. *Great Sanskrit Plays: Shakuntala, The Toy Cart, The Signet Ring of Rakshasa, The Dream of Vasavadatta, The Later Story of Rama, Ratnavali*. Norfolk, Connecticut: New Direction Books, 1964.

Lightfoot, Louise. *Dance-Rituals of Manipur, India*. Hong Kong: The Standard Press, 1958.

Sarabhai, Mrinalini, and Mohan Khokar, eds. *The Performing Arts of Kerala*. Ahmadabad: Mapin Publishing, 1990.

Vatsyayan, Kapila. *Indian Classical Dance*. New Delhi: Government of India, Ministry of Information and Broadcasting, 1974.

Wilson, H. H., et al. *The Theatre of the Hindus*. Calcutta: Susil Gupta, 1955.

Ancient Literature
Agastimata, or *Agastiya*. Believed to have been written in the sixth century A.D., in the Deccan, edited by Parab in the *Kavya-Mala*. This, and the *Ratnapariksa* of Buddhabhatta are the most important known *sastras*, or ancient treatises on precious stones. More recent than the *Ratnapariksa*, it is believed to be an adaptation of an older *sastra*.

Agastiya Ratnapariksa, attributed to Agasti. A traditional treatise on gemstones, it contains about 100 *slokas* (stanzas).

Brhatsamhita of Varahamihira. Lists and discusses twenty-two stones. This and the *Ratnapariksa* of Buddhabhatta seem to be abridgements of an earlier *Ratnasastra* that no longer exists.

Narayana. *Nava-ratna-pariksha* [a *sastra* written after A.D. 1256]. Edited by Louis Finot. Reprinted in *Les lapidaires indiens*, 141–78. Paris: Bibliothèque de L'Ecole des hautes études sciences, philologiques, et historiques, 1896.

Navaratnapariksa. An abridged, ancient revision, in 126 *slokas*, of a yet more ancient text, intended as a definitive text on the subject.

Puranas. Post-Vedic writings classified into major (*Mahapuranas*) and minor (*Upapuranas*), each with eighteen works relating to Brahma, Vishnu, and Shiva. Some deal with the astral deities as well as astrology and astronomy.

Ratnapariksa. The term literally means "appreciation of gems"; *pariksaka* means "expert" in Sanskrit. This *sastra*, written before the sixth century A.D., is a manual of jeweler's usages and a guide to gemstones for royalty, who historically enjoyed the art of judging precious-stone qualities as a form of self-glorification. Those with the ability to judge precious-stone quality were revered and offered garlands, perfumes, and seats of honor. Several versions of the *Ratnapariksa* are known.

Rayana Parikkha. This Prakit version of the *Ratnapariksa* is the only Prakrit text on this subject, all others being in Sanskrit. Seeramula Rajeswara Sarma's translation was reprinted in the *Aligarh Journal of Oriental Studies* 1, no. 1 (Spring 1984):1–84.

Ratnapariksa of Buddhabhatta. This treatise, written by a Buddhist *acarya*, consists of 252 *slokas*. It is an abridgement of the *Brhatsamhita* of Varahamihira.

Ratnapariksa of Thakkura Pheru. Pheru, born c. A.D. 1270, wrote this *sastra* in A.D. 1315 for his son, Hemapala, "during the reign of Alaudin . . . after having seen [in Delhi] with my own eyes the vast collection of gems in Alaudin's treasury." As he was probably an Assay Master at the Delhi Mint, the text also deals with assaying techniques and coin exchange rates. Reprinted in *Journal of Oriental Studies* 1, no. 1 (Aligarh, 1961) and as part of the Rajasthan Oriental Series, Jodhpur, 1961.

Index

Place names as they relate to Indian jewelry are in **boldface** type. Vernacular terms are in *italic* type. Numbers refer to page numbers. Numbers for pages on which illustrations appear are in *italic* type. The spelling of names of similar objects may vary among regional vernacular terms (see also page 20).

sutya, 227
svayambara marriage garland, 33
Svayambhu, the "Self-Originated," 75
swami jewelry, 93, 96, 237, 246, 374, 388, 388–92, 389, 390
symbolic values, 15, 19
syngkha, 257

T

taboos, 55, 341
tad, 347
tada, 249, 250
Tahmid, The, 72
Taj Mahal Emerald, The, 330
Takbir, The, 72
takhti, 115, 116
tali. See thali
Tallur-Muttai, 263
Talukdars of Oudh, 211
talukku, 218
Talwar, Mahendra Singh, 116
tamania, 354
Tamburatti, Cheria, 201
Tam-din, the Red Tiger-Devil, 73
Tamerlane. See Timur Lenk
Tamil Nadu, 32, 35, 39, 50, 51, 71, 75, 90, 93, 96, 102, 122, 123, 132, 156, 168, 168, 169, 176, 196, 205, 208, 215, 218, 221, 225, 237, 245, 247, 251, 266, 309, 324, 333, 335
    Ambasamudram, 232
    Ambedkar District
      Vellore, 70, 245
    Ayodhya, 333
    Coimbatore, 253, 286, 293
    Madras, 51, 93, 122, 209, 218, 234, 241, 246, 247, 252, 254, 255, 319, 321, 323, 351, 388, 388, 389, 390, 391, 392, 392, 399
      Arcot, 284
    Madurai, 18, 24, 192, 194, 195, 202, 221, 237, 309
    Mettuppalaiyam, 338
    Nilgiri Hills
      Ootocamund. See **Udagamandalam**
      Udagamandalam, 227
      Yepparshkood, 227
    North Anantapur, 279
    Palni, 32
    Pudukkottai, 158, 159
    Rirunelveli, 220
    Saidapet, 203
    Thanjavur, 185, 207, 285, 368, 370
    Tiruchchirappalli, 169, 337, 337, 338, 389, 392
      Shri Rangam, 25
    Tirunelveli, 220
    Tirupati, 192
    Trichinopoly. See **Tiruchchirappalli**
tandatti, 221
Tandava dance, 39
taouli, 167
tarkashi kam, 296–99
tar ke mina moti, 354
tarkulia, 223
Tasbih, 72
tassels, 72
taswir ka pahunchi, 380
taswir par hathidant pahunchi, 380
tattooing, 28, 28, 57, 121, 188, 225. See also mehndi
Tavernier, Jean Baptiste, 316–17, 317, 318, 328, 334–35, 343, 349
    Travels in India, 316
Tavernier Blue Diamond, The, 320
tawati, 212
ta'wiz, 110, 111, 113, 127, 129, 212, 344
ta'wiz-janzir, 239
ta'zim, 275

teen lara necklaces, 46
teeth, 59
teh zamin enameling, 362
Tejaji, 100
temple jewelry, 193–95
temple ornamentation, 82, 192–95
temple treasury, 192–93
Thailand, 324, 327
    Bangkok, 324
    Battambong province, 327
    Chanthaburi, 324, 327
Thakor, Shri Kesarisingh Mavinh, 65
Thakur, 275
thalaikkachchu, 215
thalaisaman, 215
thali (also tali), 156, 158, 159, 167, 168, 169, 192, 233
thali malai, 224
Thalkar community, 243, 255
thallukku, 218
thandatti, 221
thandotti, 220
thanduvetti, 218
Thani, Bani, of **Kishengarh**, 10
Thapar, Romila, 260
thattu, 218
thayittu, 158
theatrical ornamentation, 196–201
theliya, 294
thewa ka mala, 301
thewa work, 300–303
    background of, 300
    versus enameling, 300
    process of, 302, 302–3, 303
thihna, 82
thirumangaliam, 220
thodu, 215, 218
thongattam, 218
thorn work, 295
thrang-nga, 141, 149
thukkanampetti, 390
Tibet, 72, 81, 83, 124, 137–38, 143, 145, 146, 148, 149, 151, 155
    Kham, 73
    Lhasa, 141, 142, 145, 147
Tibetan ga'u, 140–47
Tibetan Nyingma-pa School of Buddhism, 145
Tibetan ornaments, 137–52
    Ladakhi, 149–52
Tiffany, Charles Lewis, 397–98
Tiffany, Louis Comfort, 397, 397–98
Tiffany and Co., New York, 397, 398
tigers, 58, 91–94, 95. See also amulets, tiger-claw
tikdi har, 335
tikka, 24, 156, 165, 166, 231, 289, 353
tikorna salma, 369
tikra, 244
tikri, 374
tilak, 163, 214
tilaka, 25, 70
Tilly, E. A., 314
timani, 163
timaniya, 231
Timur Lenk, 268
tin kalangi sarpech, 383, 385, 386
tin lara, 119
tin lara har, 235, 322
tin mania, 231
Tirthankara, 100
Tiruchendur Murugan, 32
tiruchurnam, 25
tiryakpundra, 25
Tod, 43
todo, 273
toké, 82, 357
tola, 285
tomara, 212

tomukch, 138, 139
tongue ornamentation, 24
tools, 176, 179, 183, 282, 283, 285, 299, 299, 359–60, 366, 369–70
topi, 163, 164, 212
top-of-ear ornaments, 219
top-of-head ornaments, 212, 213
torques
    cast-brass, 64
    rigid, 227, 228
torso ornaments, 239, 345
    Mughal men's, 345
totemism, 59
touchstone, 75, 281
Toussaint, Jeanne, 401, 404
Tower of London, 315, 316
Tract, Chief Somra, 54
trailing technique, 184
Tree of Life, 90, 98, 100, 103, 106, 116–17, 117, 143
tree worship, 41, 291
tre-kho, 73
tribal ornament tradition, 18
Tripura
    Dumbur, 124, 219
tri-ratna, 289, 290, 291
tri-ratna mala, 289, 291
trishula, 24, 24
trophy jewelry, 95
tsaru, 152
tsa-tsas, 144
tsoga-mini, 68
tubular suspension systems
    of amulets, 126
tulasimanittavadam, 25
tumpio, 123
tunglak, 152, 176
tupchi, 357
"turban-exchanged brother," 381
turban ornaments
    feather, 381–82, 387
    interchange of, 380–92
Turewala, Duli Chand Jain, 371
Turkey, 268, 380
turquoise, 144–45, 149, 150, 151
turra, 207, 207, 210, 211, 312, 333, 340, 344, 371, 381, 403
    tassels for, 403–5
tusks, 59
Tuzuk-i-Jahangiri (Jahangir), 104, 119, 210, 344
Tvastr, 283
twisting technique, two-ply, 183
typology, 17, 211

U

ultik, 154
umlakh, 166
Unani medicine, 339
Union Territory of Andaman and Nicobar. See **Andaman and Nicobar Islands**
United States
    California, 278
    Nevada, 278
    New York, 11, 11, 281, 397, 397–98, 402
un ka dora, 82
upanayana ceremony, 42, 88
uru, 232
urukkumani, 218
ustana, 269
utrasam tree, 71
Uttar Pradesh, 26, 90, 107, 113, 137, 138, 156, 179, 211, 235, 258, 275, 277, 283
    Agra District, 210, 268, 344, 349, 375, 375, 376, 377, 399
      Firozabad, 182–83, 183–84, 185, 186, 302
    Allahabad, 370
    Bahraich, 231

Photograph Credits

The author and publisher wish to thank the museums, galleries, and private collectors, named in the illustration captions, who supplied photographs for reproductions. Additional photograph credits are listed below. Abbreviated citations are given for those images reprinted from book sources; please see the bibliography for complete reference information. Numbers refer to illustration numbers, unless otherwise indicated.

Maurice Aeschimann, Geneva: 37, 71, 156, 442
Sangeet Natak Akademi, New Delhi: 52, 379
William L. Allen, Washington, D.C.: 79, 120, 231,
   519, 589
American Institute of Indian Studies, Centre for
   Art and Archaeology, Varanasi: 113, 179, 229,
   533, 582, 692
Archaeological Survey of India, Government of
   India, New Delhi: 312

Archaeology Department, Government of Tamil
   Nadu, Madras: 372
Courtesy Jean-Paul Barbier, Geneva: 283
Michael Berger (drawings), from Dr. Emma Pressmar, *Indische Ringe*: 24, 27
By Courtesy of the Board of Trustees of the British
   Museum, London: 80, 84
Tommy Caraway, New York: pages 2–3, illustration
   nos. 86, 284, 473